# CRITERIA QUESTIC

Throughout THE WRITER'S WORK you will find ten different tan-colored Criteria Questions boxes. These boxes will serve as quick reminders of the questions about **Purpose, Audience, Code, Experience,** and **Self** that you should be asking yourself as you plan, draft, and revise your writing.

# The Writer's Work

## A Guide to Effective Composition

THIRD EDITION

**Frank O'Hare**

*The Ohio State University*

**Dean Memering**

*Central Michigan University*

**PRENTICE HALL, Englewood Cliffs, NJ 07632**

Library of Congress Cataloging-in-Publication Data
O'Hare, Frank.
The writer's work : a guide to effective composition / Frank O'Hare, Dean Memering.—3rd ed.
p. cm.
ISBN 0-13-969635-0
1. English language—Rhetoric. I. Memering, Dean, date. II. Title.
PE1408.0374 1990
808'.042—dc20 89-16398
CIP

Development editor: Kate Morgan
Editorial/production supervision: Jan Stephan
Interior design: Anne T. Bonanno
Cover art: Design Photographers International
Cover design: Bruce Kenselaar
Manufacturing buyers: Ray Keating and MaryAnn Gloriande
Page layout: Karen Noferi
Photo research: Tobi Zausner

Part Opener Art Credits
Part One: Steve Krongard/The Image Bank. Part Two: Michel Tcherevkoff/The Image Bank. Part Three: David Parker/Science Photo Library, Photo Researchers. Part Four: Hans Peter Danke/The Image Bank. Part Five: Linda D. Bohm



Printed in the United States of America
10 9 8 7 6 5 4 3 2 1

ISBN 0-13-969635-0

Prentice-Hall International (UK) Limited, *London*
Prentice-Hall of Australia Pty. Limited, *Sydney*
Prentice-Hall Canada Inc., *Toronto*
Prentice-Hall Hispanoamericana, S.A., *Mexico*
Prentice-Hall of India Private Limited, *New Delhi*
Prentice-Hall of Japan, Inc., *Tokyo*
Simon & Schuster Asia Pte. Ltd., *Singapore*
Editora Prentice-Hall do Brasil, Ltda., *Rio de Janeiro*

Acknowledgments appear on pages 606 and 607, which constitute a continuation of the copyright page.

# Contents

## *PART THREE: WRITING FOR SPECIAL PURPOSES*

### CHAPTER NINE: WRITING WITH SOURCES *308*

## PART FOUR: COMPOSING AND REVISING PARAGRAPHS AND SENTENCES

### CHAPTER TWELVE: EFFECTIVE PARAGRAPHS 436

## CHAPTER THIRTEEN: REVISION USING SENTENCE COMBINING *468*



## CHAPTER FOURTEEN: EFFECTIVE SENTENCES *502*

# *PART FIVE: HANDBOOK OF THE WRITER'S CONVENTIONS*

## CHAPTER FIFTEEN: EFFECTIVE DICTION *520*



## CHAPTER SIXTEEN: USAGE *540*

# Preface

In the past twenty five years, there has been a virtual explosion in research on how people learn to write. Many of the research findings have strongly suggested that revision is central to the composing process and that the writer's work involves a heavy emphasis on planning, drafting, and revising. In the past, traditional textbooks assumed that adhering to a prescribed form was the most important skill for writers and that to become a competent writer all a student had to do was master the "five-paragraph theme," with its introduction, body, and conclusion. As writers, students said what they were going to say, then said it, then said what they had said. There was an underlying assumption that once they had organized everything in a formal outline, the paper would write itself. In this scheme, revision was restricted to cleaning up the surface features of the paper by searching for and eliminating any errors that were found. Common sense and the experience of professional writers, as well as recent research findings, have led our profession to reject this rigid, linear, error-oriented approach to writing and to substitute a more dynamic, recursive model of the composing process, one that focuses on the multitude of choices facing writers as they plan, draft, and revise their work. It is this new model that is reflected in the third edition of *The Writer's Work*.

## INNOVATIVE FEATURES IN THE THIRD EDITION

The Third Edition departs from the second in that it features concepts and techniques that can deepen both the student's and the teacher's exploration of the writing process. The Writer's Mind at Work case studies, PACES, model student drafts, and strategies of development and thinking are all effective in helping students manage the writing process, yet they retain the idea that the process is filled with possibilities.

### ► The Writer's Mind

Most modern "process" textbooks (including the second edition of *The Writer's Work*) virtually ignore an important aspect of the writing process: how writers actually **think** while they write. These texts **talk about** invention, drafting and revision, but they fail to **show** illustrations of the writer's mind at work, of the **thinking** writers actually do when engaged in a writing task. In its third edition, *The Writer's Work* provides dozens of examples of such thinking in sections called "The Writer's Mind at Work" and "The Writer's Mind." These examples of the writer's mind help to demystify the writing process by presenting the thinking processes of a variety of individual writers as they plan, draft, and revise.

### Student Examples of Multiple Drafting

Although many modern textbooks talk about multiple drafting and the importance of revising, they usually only provide their readers with one brief chapter that displays a few examples of invention notes, a rough draft, and a final draft. The third edition of *The Writer's Work* enthusiastically embraces the concept of invention and multiple drafting and presents students with abundant, detailed examples of planning, drafting, and revising for every major aim of writing.

### PACES: Purpose, Audience, Code, Experience, Self

In order to integrate the concepts of the writer's mind and the composing process, the third edition of *The Writer's Work* introduces an innovative, nonlinear conceptual framework, **PACES** (purpose, audience, code, experience, self). Designed to help writers manage the complex, essentially recursive process of planning, drafting and revising their work, the conceptual framework of PACES is used with every major type of essay assigned throughout the text. In the pilot-testing of this conceptual framework, students found the sets of PACES criteria questions especially useful in both generating and analyzing drafts of their papers at every stage of the writing process. As one writer said, "Using PACES gives me confidence because it helps me to **control** my process as I move from draft to draft." Another writer remarked, "Whenever I begin to lose control of my writing because things are getting too complicated, I switch back to the five basics—PACES. They put me back in charge."

### Strategies of Development and Thinking

Comparing and contrasting, defining, classifying, and so on have traditionally been treated as essay types or as modes of discourse. In the third edition of *The Writer's Work,* they are treated as **thinking** skills and introduced as means to an end, not as ends in themselves. Their usefulness as strategies of thinking about and developing a writer's ideas is stressed. Writers compare, contrast, classify and define to achieve an overall purpose in their writing; to illustrate this point, we analyze short examples from longer pieces that demonstrate how experienced writers use these strategies of thinking and development.

## CHAPTER BY CHAPTER CHANGES

### Part One: The Composing Process

A dramatic addition to the third edition of *The Writer's Work*, Part One consists of four new chapters that together form a cohesive whole by providing an overview of the composing process.

Chapter One, "The Writer's Mind At Work," introduces the key concepts that inform the remainder of the text, and it offers a conceptual framework that writers can use to analyze, understand, and control the multitude of choices they are faced with in almost every writing task. The writer's choices consist of five interrelated components: purpose, audience, code, experience, and self, which we refer to as PACES. The chapter then sketches the stages of the composing process: planning, drafting, and revising, and suggests that time spent on the planning stage will reap rich rewards.

Chapter Two's title, "Planning and Discovery, Discovery and Planning," suggests that writers often generate subject matter and plan their writing simultaneously. The chapter begins by stressing the importance of planning and then describes in detail invention techniques that can be used at every stage of the writing process. Chapter Two then deals with how to select and narrow a topic by showing several writers' minds at work as they use some of the invention techniques just introduced. The assumption is that if inexperienced writers are exposed to a number of these scripts of writers' minds at work, they will realize that there is no single way to select or narrow a topic or discover and develop a plan for a paper. Much depends on the individual writer's background and the unique constraints of the topic and audience.

Chapter Three, "Drafting and Revising," extends the discussion of preliminary planning, moves on to explain the scratch outline and the exploratory draft, and then deals with the thesis idea and the thesis statement before exploring the use and the misuse of the formal outline. These principles are illustrated for the most part with examples from the work of student writers introduced in Chapter Two. Chapter Three also uses the PACES framework to show students how all the elements of good writing work together in both their own writing and that of others.

Part One concludes with Chapter Four, "Strategies of Development, Strategies of Thinking." This chapter encourages writers to take advantage of the thinking skills of comparing, contrasting, defining, analyzing, and classifying that they use every day of their lives and to examine how experienced writers use these same skills to think about and develop their ideas. Because it is rare to encounter an essay that is an extended example of pure comparison and contrast, definition, classification, and so on, most of the examples used in this chapter are short pieces culled from longer texts.

## ▶ Part Two: The Aims of Writing

The conceptual framework developed and illustrated in Part One provides the skeletal frame for each of the chapters in Part Two. In Chapters Five through Eight, student writers are shown how to plan, draft and revise a variety of different types of essays by analyzing and discussing exploratory, working, and final drafts of each type of paper. These chapters also provide numerous examples of the writer's mind at work and scripts of the writers mind, as well as other invention and planning strategies, to encourage writers to commit themselves to the demanding but rewarding process of multiple drafting described in Part One.

Each chapter focuses on an important purpose or aim of writing, one that should prove useful to writers as they pursue their college careers. Chapter Five, "Expressive Writing," focuses on the self, on the writer's reactions to people, places, and events. Student writers are encouraged to keep a detailed journal of their experiences and are provided with extensive training in journal writing. After covering voice and dialog, Chapter Five introduces its major focus, the Personal Experience Narrative, and then moves on to a related type of personal experience writing, description: how to describe a person or place. The chapter also includes sets of PACES criteria questions to help students revise the various drafts of these narrative and descriptive essays.

To anyone familiar with the chapter on informative writing in the second edition, it will quickly become evident that Chapter Six, "Informative Writing," has been completely reconceived in the third edition. The first and most common of all the types of writing students will encounter in college and in the world of commerce and industry is the "What It Is" paper. Students are shown examples of essay assignments and exam questions that ask for this kind of informative response, and, with criteria questions provided, are asked to respond to the working draft of a student paper that had been developed through the exploratory draft stage in Chapters Two and Three. (This deliberate connecting of a paper from Part One with Part Two is an attempt to dramatize the important connections between the conceptual framework described in Part One and the aims of writing described, analyzed, and exemplified in the different chapters in Part Two.) Several interesting "What It Is" papers are offered for analysis using PACES criteria questions, and then a case study with planning notes, writer's mind materials, multiple drafts and peer responses is presented. The second half of the chapter deals with two kinds of process papers: How It Works and How To Do It. The characteristics of each of these papers are explained in detail, and students are asked to analyze examples of each.

In the second edition, evaluative writing was a fairly small part of a chapter called "Evaluative and Persuasive Writing." In this edition, evaluative writing merits a chapter of its own, Chapter Seven. "Evaluative Writing" introduces students to the objective summary and the critical summary and gives them practice in analyzing and generating these two kinds of summaries. Students are then presented with an explanation of the evaluative paper, in which writers examine a subject in detail, judge its worth, and then report their evaluation to readers. After being given advice about planning their own arguments, students are shown a case study of a writer planning, drafting, and revising an evaluative paper. The chapter concludes by asking students to analyze several evaluative papers by using PACES criteria questions.

Chapter Eight, "Persuasion," presents a much more comprehensive treatment of persuasion than was provided previously. Focussing on the needs of the writer's audience, the chapter begins with a discussion of the three principles of persuasion: respect your readers, be fair, accept compromise. Following a full treatment of logic, including syllogistic reasoning and the common fallacies, the chapter uses the PACES conceptual framework to explain in detail the characteristics of the persuasion paper. Then appear detailed case studies of writer's minds at work and a comprehensive set of PACES criteria questions that students can use to analyze examples of persuasion papers and to produce their own persuasion essays.

## ► Part Three: Writing for Special Purposes

Part Three presents an extensive treatment of the most common specialized writing assignments encountered in college: the research paper and the essay examination. Comprehensive coverage of how to write a research paper is presented in two full chapters: Chapter Nine, "Writing with Sources," and Chapter Ten, "Documenting Sources." Chapter Nine presents the innovative Search Strategy, a systematic procedure for selecting and refining an interesting, relevant research question and for accumulating information to answer that question. The chapter also includes an introduction to the library and detailed advice on how to evaluate sources, record information, and avoid plagiarism. An interesting new feature of this chapter is a section dealing with sources outside the library. It includes information on how to correspond with and interview people, and how to conduct field observations and surveys. The chapter concludes with advice on organizing the research paper.

Chapter Ten continues the coverage of the research paper by explaining how to choose a documentation format and handle documentation notes. It provides a thorough explanation of what information should be documented and detailed treatment of MLA and APA documentation formats. Following a case study of a writer's mind at work drafting and revising a sample research paper, the chapter concludes with a list of possible research topics.

Chapter Eleven, "Writing Responses to Essay Exam Questions," is a new chapter designed to help students understand the nature of the essay exam, especially the problem of writing under pressures of time. It gives advice on how to study for exams and on how to gather and review information in preparation for writing exams. Especially useful are the strategies offered for interpreting the exam question and the advice on how to plan, draft, and revise a written response in a restricted time frame.

## ► Part Four: Composing and Revising Paragraphs and Sentences

Part Four gives students practice in composing and revising sentences and paragraphs not as discrete skills, but as options to be exercised depending on the rhetorical situation. It includes principles of paragraph development, sentence combining, and revising for sentence effectiveness.

Chapter Twelve, "Effective Paragraphs," deals with the composition, arrangement and revision of paragraphs. It discusses the usefulness of the topic sentence, methods of paragraph development, and the principle of coherence. The chapter introduces a number of approaches to paragraph structure, including Frances Christensen's generative rhetoric of the paragraph. Finally, the chapter presents about a dozen methods of producing both introductory and concluding paragraphs.

Chapter Thirteen, "Revising Using Sentence Combining," contains exercises based on the signal system developed by Frank O'Hare in his NCTE research monograph "Sentence Combining: Improving Student Writing Without Formal Grammar Instruction." These exercises cue students to revise at the sentence level by adding, deleting, embedding, transforming, and punctuating. The chapter also deals with a new concept, chunks—units of discourse longer than a sentence, shorter than a paragraph—to give students practice in handling the sentence boundary, the most common source of error (run-on sentences and fragments) in student writing. These sentence-combining exercises will aid students in achieving the syntactic fluency characteristic of a mature writer and make them much more efficient when revising the style of their essays.

Chapter Fourteen, "Effective Sentences," is a natural offshoot of Chapter Thirteen in that it treats the rhetorical and stylistic considerations of effectiveness in sentence structure based on principles of clarity, economy, emphasis, and variety. The chapter demonstrates flaws to be avoided or revised, as well as the many options available to writers as they revise their work.

### ► Part Five: Handbook of the Writer's Conventions

Part Five concerns itself with the surface features of the language, those matters of grammar, punctuation, and usage that become vitally important at the final-draft and proofreading stages of the composing process. (The handbook appears in the hardcover edition only; *The Writer's Work* is also available in a paperback version without the handbook.)

Chapter Fifteen, "Effective Diction," highlights the vocabulary choices writers make, as well as those they avoid, based on the overall purpose and stance of individual writers. This chapter contains a dictionary section that discusses entries and connotative and denotative definitions.

Chapter Sixteen, "Usage," describes grammatical choices and problems. Because the writer cannot ignore the usage expectations of readers, usage choices become the means for fulfilling those expectations.

Chapter Seventeen, "Mechanics," provides a reference guide to punctuation, spelling, and capitalization. Rules and principles of mechanics are explained and illustrated, as are significant options and variations. The spelling section contains a guide to trouble spots.

## ACKNOWLEDGMENTS

As in previous editions, many instructors offered generous suggestions and helpful criticism. Special thanks to the following: Katherine H. Adams, University of Tennessee; Mary M. Blackburn, University of South Alabama; Bonnie

Braendlin, Florida State University; Joyce Compton Brown, Gardner-Webb College; Nancy A. Cox, California State University—Long Beach; Carol David, Iowa State University; Mark DeFoe, West Virginia Wesleyan College; Charles B. Dodson, University of North Carolina at Wilmington; George Hammerbacher, Kings College; Frank Hodgins, University of Illinois; John Hollow, Ohio University; George Otte, Baruch College; James E. Porter, Indiana University; Morton D. Rich, Montclair State College; Lawrence Schwartz, Montclair State College; Nancy L. Walker, Southwest Missouri State University; Irwin Weiser, Purdue University; Holly M. Wescott, Florence-Darlington Technical College.

Colleagues at Ohio State University—Randy Davis, Sherry Finkle, Kevin Griffith, Sue V. Lape, Joe Lehmann, R. Gerald Nelms, Dennis Quon, Tom VonGunden, Eric Walborn, and Gretel Young—contributed in important ways to many aspects of this third edition. I also wish to recognize the significant contribution of W. Dean Memering to the quality and success of the first two editions of *The Writer's Work*. Many of his insights continue to enhance the pages of this third edition.

The people at Prentice Hall provided invaluable assistance with this project. Editor in Chief Phil Miller gave strong support to the dramatic changes included in the third edition, especially its innovative commitment to "The Writer's Mind" and PACES as a conceptual framework. An ideal Development Editor, Kate Morgan not only helped in the development of the manuscript, she contributed in creative ways to translating its innovative theoretical concepts into manageable classroom practice. Kate's knowledge, experience, and boundless enthusiasm make her an ideal Development Editor. Production Editor Jan Stephan's patience and considerable skills were also appreciated.

## TO THE STUDENT

*The Writer's Work* is based on the assumption that most people can learn to write with confidence and competence. Writing is not some complex, mysterious act requiring a special gift, but a process that can be learned. Part One of this book gives you an innovative and practical way to build both your skills and your confidence by presenting you with an overview of the composing process (planning, drafting, and revising) and a framework for understanding and controlling the choices you will be making as you write (PACES: Purpose, Audience, Code, Experience, Self). In addition, you will be introduced to the concept of "The Writer's Mind at Work," which is based on the idea that analyzing examples of writers' thought processes as they write is a powerful way to improve one's own writing. The four chapters of Part One are, therefore, designed to encourage you to develop your own unique approach to writing by examining the thinking and drafting processes of other writers.

Part Two starts with expressive writing such as freewriting and journal writing which will help you gain confidence and fluency in writing. It then moves on to the increasingly formal aims of writing, from informative through evaluative to persuasive.

Part Three covers the special contexts of research writing and preparing for and taking essay exams. Research writing can be rewarding if you follow the advice in Chapters 9 and 10 and reach beyond mere footnoting to the real challenges of learning how to come up with a worthwhile research question and, by means of a research strategy, how to locate data, evaluate evidence, and share the results of your investigations with your readers. How you approach the numerous essay exams you will encounter in college can often mean the difference between success and failure, so Chapter 11 offers advice on this important area of writing.

Parts Four and Five present skills and conventions of language that students, and even very experienced writers, often find confusing. Some researchers claim that these skills can only be acquired. While we recognize the enormous importance of acquisition, especially from extensive reading and writing experiences, *The Writer's Work* is built on the assumption that you can also benefit from limited, periodic reviews of the skills that are giving you problems with your own papers. If, for example, you are searching for an interesting introduction or conclusion for an essay, the examples in Chapter 12 should help you. Chapters 13 and 14 will help you improve the effectiveness of your style. The reference handbook in Chapters 15 through 17 should prove useful when you are proofreading your final drafts, especially if you are discussing your work with others.

The very title of our book, *The Writer's Work*, confirms what all good writers know—writing *is* work; it is a demanding activity in which you will have to call upon your inner resources. In *The Writer's Work*, you will see numerous examples of writers like yourself working through the entire process of writing—from conception of a topic to the final draft. Though the process can be a struggle, we have presented it as a struggle rich with possibilities. You may even be surprised where your writing takes you. And it is the surprise and spontaneity of the writing process that motivates writers to produce high-quality, memorable prose. As Hemingway once said, "No surprise for the writer, no surprise for the reader." The writers who produced the examples you will be studying in this text often talked about how demanding, yet richly rewarding and enjoyable, they found the writer's work to be. We trust you will too.

Frank O'Hare
Columbus, Ohio

# *The Writer's Work*

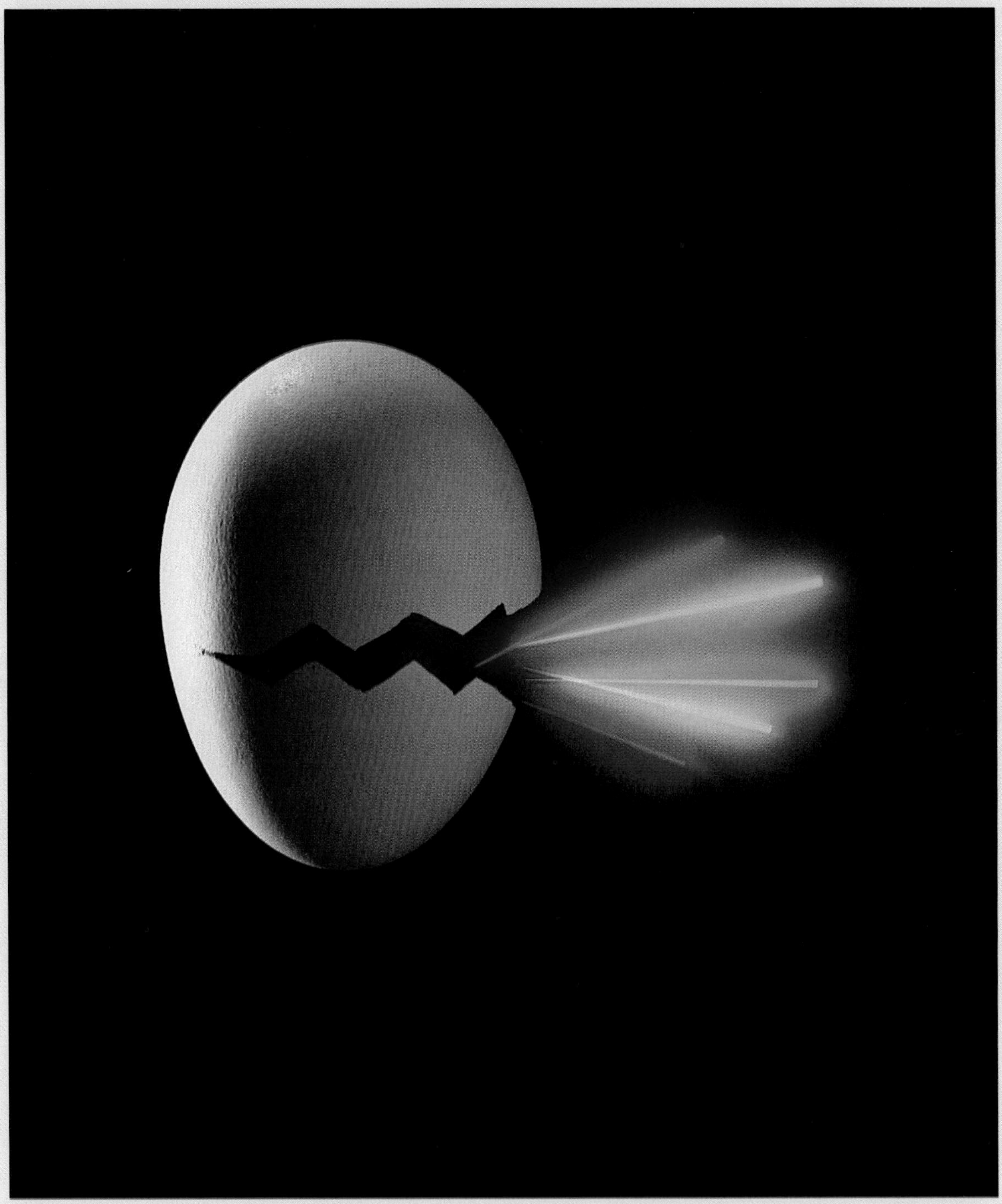

# PART ▲ ONE

# *The Composing Process*

1 The Writer's Mind at Work
2 Planning and Discovery, Discovery and Planning
3 Drafting and Revising
4 Strategies of Development, Strategies of Thinking

# CHAPTER ▲ ONE

# *The Writer's Mind at Work*

**"How do I know what I think until I see what I said?"**

**E. M. FORSTER**

You may have encountered people who explained away the fact that they hadn't written anything for months or years by claiming that they lacked inspiration, that their muse had abandoned them. In *The Writer's Work*, we will be taking a different position: Writing is not some mysterious gift, but a craft that can be learned by reasonably intelligent college students, such as you. Inexperienced writers are often convinced that to write well they have to be exceptionally gifted with language, that writers are born, not made. This is simply not true. To write competently, you don't have to be unusually gifted. Although writing is challenging and sometimes difficult, you are equal to the challenge. For example read the following paragraph:

> As he sat tightly strapped to the chair, the young man listened while the warden read the execution order and then asked the condemned man if he had anything to say. The riflemen who were to be his executioners were hidden from the man, behind a dark-colored curtain, and he gazed for a long moment at the ceiling and then back at the warden, uttering a brief sentence. There was a loud explosion, and the five bullets that tore through Gary Gilmore's heart ended not only his life, but also the uneasy moratorium on the death penalty that had begun nearly ten years before.
>
> MICHAEL C. KNAPP

This is good writing by any standard, and it was written by a student in college.

The British statesman Winston Churchill once said, "Writing is an adventure." Novelist Henry Miller claimed that "Writing is a voyage of discovery." Voyages of discovery often prove challenging to the voyager. If *The Writer's Work* is to succeed in helping you on your journey to successful writing, you need to have trust, commitment, and a willingness to take chances and make mistakes.

First, you must learn to trust yourself and be willing to explore your own life honestly and in detail. We are convinced that you and every other college student have lived interesting lives and that in your experiences you will discover something to say that others will want to hear. You must also trust the language skills you have acquired from your previous reading and writing as well as from all the forms of human speech you have encountered. A sense of commitment, of caring, is another essential if you are to write well. Writing is often plain hard work, but hard work can be enjoyable, especially when you are wrestling with problems that matter to you. Commitment to your subject will make you sensitive to your readers' needs and willing to search for the best arguments to support your position.

Finally, you must be prepared to take chances, to risk failure, to admit that you may not always know exactly where you are going. A willingness to risk failure is really an act of faith—in your own potential inventiveness and in the composing process itself. In *The Writer's Work*, planning, drafting, and revising are viewed not as a predictable, linear progression, but as a recursive, essentially unpredictable process. This process is different every time for every writer. Sometimes the writer's work goes smoothly and the piece writes itself. At other times—and much more frequently—the writer's work is a messy, complex, seemingly endless series of choices, rejections, and additional choices as the writer moves through three or four drafts of a paper in order to get it right for his or her readers. Not surprisingly, most writers throw away much of what they write.

As a writer, you should not only accept but welcome error as a powerful means of improving your writing skills. Think of how you learn any new skill, like snow skiing, for instance. By falling. How do children achieve the most amazing and complex of all human skills: speech? By practicing. By receiving informed feedback on their errors and trying again. In a *Saturday Evening Post* article (October 1976), scientist Lewis Thomas explained it this way:

> Mistakes are at the very base of human thought, embedded there, feeding the structure like root nodules. If we were not provided with the knack of being wrong, we could never get anything useful done. We think our way along by choosing between right and wrong alternatives, and the wrong choices have to be made as frequently as the right ones. We get along in life this way. We are built to make mistakes, coded for error.

Error then is a necessary, not an accidental, step to writing improvement.

At an international conference on writing in Ottawa, Canada, Professor Donald Murray, winner of a Pulitzer Prize for journalism, said, "Writing is re-re-re-rewriting." During a reception later that evening, Murray was asked if he had intended to use five "*res*" in his speech.

"Yes," said Murray.

"Are you going to add another "*re*" in your next speech?"

"Of course!" the grinning Murray said.

The writer's work, then, consists of planning, drafting, and, especially, revising.

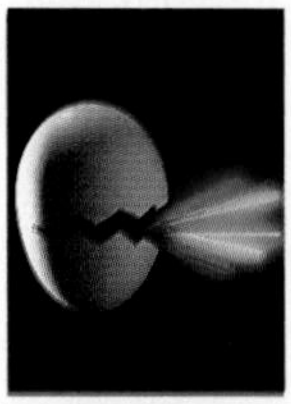

## THE WRITER'S MIND

In *The Writer's Work* we will try to help you help yourself become a better writer by having you learn to think as writers think, by having you develop your own writer's mind. We'll accomplish this by showing how people like yourself work on their writing. We'll examine scripts of writers' minds as they think and talk to themselves while planning, drafting, and revising their writing.

Of course, writing does not always involve a complex process of multiple drafting. Notes, short letters, brief memoranda, and the like are, quite appropriately, dashed off in five to ten minutes with little need for trust, commitment, or risk taking. Indeed, Chapter 11, "Responses to Exam Essay Questions," describes a writing process that does not—and cannot—accommodate multiple drafting, because the typical exam question asks students to regurgitate facts and ideas from a textbook or a professor's lecture notes. But most of the writing tasks you will experience as you use *The Writer's Work* involve serious and extensive planning, drafting, and revising and therefore demand trust, commitment and risk taking. Even for what seems a straightforward writing task, such as the informative paper, you will learn how to make the subject matter truly your own and to arouse your readers' interest. You'll examine the work of student writers who, committed to their subjects and audiences, offer a fresh perspective on their topics.

## THE WRITER'S CHOICES

Central to the writing process and to the writer's mind is the act of choosing. Writing involves an almost endless series of choices, rejections, and additional choices, whose sequence a writer cannot predict. Writing is not simply a linear process. You cannot say, "First, I should always do $x$, then $y$, and then $z$." There is really no "always" in writing. Every writer's process is unique for every paper.

One way of bringing order and control to the writing process is to view it as consisting of five interrelated components that we will refer to (according to their initial letters) as PACES: *p*urpose, *a*udience, *c*ode, *e*xperience, and *s*elf. Think of what happens when you write. Sometimes your *purpose* is to entertain, sometimes to discover what you think. Your *audience* is just as variable; on one occasion it may be your closest friend, on another a group of nameless, faceless strangers. Indeed, your readers may even be hostile to your views. Writers also have to select the appropriate *code* to communicate their ideas. Code is a combination of the language, structures, and strategies writers use to arrange and express their ideas. You will also have to select from your *experience* the facts, ideas, and evidence you use in a paper and the persona or *self* you wish to project to achieve your overall purpose.

A productive way to grasp how the five elements of PACES interrelate during the composing process is to visualize in your mind's eye a three-dimensional figure around which flow considerations of purpose, audience, code, experience, and self (See diagram on page 8). As each element flows in various directions around this three-dimensional figure, it encounters the other elements, influencing and being influenced by them in nonlinear and unpredictable ways. It is important to realize that the figure displayed here is not a scientific diagram designed to represent any physical reality, but a visual, cognitive *metaphor* to help you understand and appreciate the dynamic and complex nature of the

**A Three-Dimensional Diagram of the Writer's Choices**

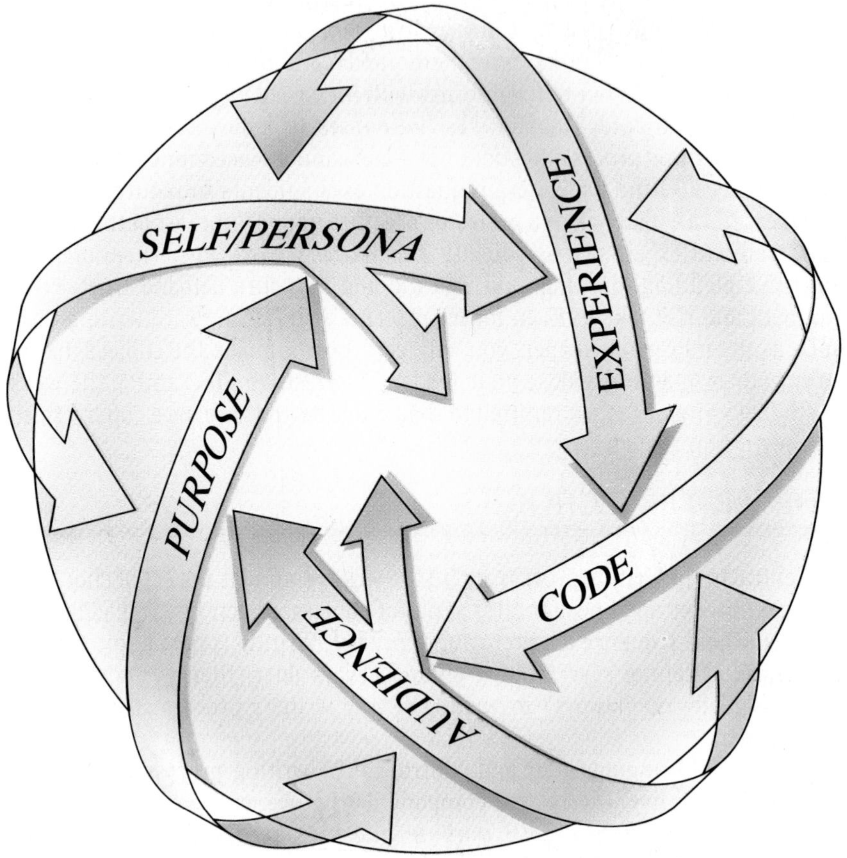


Notice that each of the arrows representing an element in the composing process is a different color. These colors will be repeated throughout the book wherever PACES is referred to in order to help you remember the various elements of the composing process.

---

writer's mind at work. Using the PACES metaphor as a conceptual framework will also enable you to *manage* your writing process. No matter how complex a writing task becomes, you can always regain control by returning to the simplicity of the five basic elements: purpose, audience, code, experience, and self. The creative delight of the writer's work, the challenge to the writer's mind, is to orchestrate these elements into a coherent whole. The three-dimensional PACES metaphor will give you a sense of control over your own writing process. When a piece of writing fails, usually the writer's mind has failed to synthesize the five elements of PACES. Just as notes, rhythm, pace, and lyrics must blend together to make a real song, the writer's mind must achieve balance among the elements of PACES. A closer look at each component will explain how this balancing of interrelated choices may be achieved.

## ▶ The Writer's Purpose [P]

The term *purpose* means *the writer's intention, why the writer is writing*. It is also the unifying principle of any written work: not only what the writer is attempting, but what the composition is attempting.

If the question is, What prompts you to write? You may answer "to entertain, inform, persuade, impress, evaluate, or express myself." There may be many possibilities. Sometimes you may not have a clear notion of why you are writing when you start. And it often happens that you have more than one motive.

If you ask yourself, What is my purpose? you will realize that you need to think about all the components of the writing process before you can answer. Experienced writers are never satisfied with a superficial analysis of their motives. Therefore, you should always ask yourself, *What are my* true *motives*? Also, if you discover your purpose, it must be aimed at the reader. And if you are selecting elements from your experience to write about, you must be aware that your selection is not random. Analysis of your experiences, your audience, and your view of self are all involved in this selection. Even the code—the language or development strategies you use—depends on its interaction with the other four PACES components.

To summarize: Purpose is the overall controlling set of decisions you make in a piece of writing. It includes your view of self and your motives; your attitudes toward and decisions about your experiences; your decisions about and attitudes toward your audience or projected audience; and your decisions about the code you will use to convey your ideas to the reader. These factors influence and are influenced by each other as they flow together in your writer's mind (see page 8). Their harmony or pattern becomes the unifying principle of the written work.

## ▶ The Writer's Audience [A]

Writing directed at no one in particular usually fails. A keen sense of audience helps you refine your purpose, choose an appropriate self, and select from your experience. You will discover that whom you write to powerfully influences what and how you write. What do you know about your audience? What do they know about you? Is your audience the instructor? What does he or she expect? Are you your own audience (as in a diary)? Is your audience the "general reader"? What does your audience know about the subject of your paper? How do they feel about this topic? Will they react favorably to your point of view? Will emotion more than cold fact persuade them? Should you adapt yourself to the audience? Or can you make them accept you as you are?

Answering such questions creates a sense of audience in your writer's mind.

You can assess whether you should define your terms for this audience, make a particular comparison, or quote other people to be believable. In short, what you decide about your readers influences the writing strategies you choose.

For most college writing, it is useful to imagine a composite general audience, such as the people in your writing class. You can assume that such a group will probably understand and appreciate many of the things you know and enjoy. And if you're ever in doubt about their opinions on a particular subject, you can always ask them.

## ► The Writer's Code [C]

Having interesting ideas is only a beginning; writers must be able to present them clearly and efficiently. Knowing what to say is not enough; you must also know *how*. This *how* skill—the kinds of language and the different strategies used by writers—is what we call *code*. Code includes the words writers select from their lexicon, the store of words at each writer's disposal. It also refers to writers' syntax, the sentence structures they have at their disposal. Code functions at the macro as well as the micro level. It is not restricted to an essay's lexicon and syntax but includes its overall structure as well as the coherence among its linguistic elements. Code is the writer's language and how that language is arranged; it is the fusion, the mixture of words, structure, and strategy. A writer may compare, contrast, classify, define, and develop an analogy, in a phrase, sentence, paragraph, or throughout an entire book. Code also includes style and is clearly related to tone and voice. It is the language and form writers select for their work. Decisions about the code you choose to express your ideas depend, of course, on your essay's overall purpose. In the best writing, purpose, audience, and code form a seamless whole.

### ► WRITING ACTIVITY ◄

Recall or imagine a brief incident in your life: a car accident, an argument with your boss, an upsetting encounter in school or on a trip, the time when you came home in bad shape, and so on. Write about it in different styles: formal language, street slang, childlike simplicity, newspaper style, telegram style, *Time* magazine style, and so on. How do the changes in code affect the meaning of your message?

## ► The Writer's Experience [E]

In our view of the composing process, *experience* means every instant of your life: everything you have known, done, remembered, read, seen, thought, experienced or dreamed—the sum total of your existence.

You may feel that your experience is limited at this stage in your life. Let us emphatically assure you that it is *not*. Every undergraduate has lived a unique and interesting life. There is no one else in the world exactly like you. Many people have had similar experiences, but they have never had them in exactly the same sequence or location, nor were they surrounded by the same family members, school friends, or acquaintances. To write well, you must reflect on the entire range of your experience. All your opinions, loves, hates, prejudices, joys, tears, and triumphs are possible resources for your writing.

How can you gain access to your experience? Here are some possibilities.

*Memory* Look back over past experiences; search through your life for incidents, events, people, places, and things to write about. Your memory is a vast repository of data concerning all your experiences. You can search this repository, forcing yourself to remember and bring back, in surprising detail, your past life.

*Observation* Examine the world around you; analyze the events and issues of your daily life. To observe your world, watch television and films and read books, magazines, and newspapers. Modern communication systems provide everyone with a wealth of material to observe, think about, and write about.

*Participation* Your daily experiences, talking with friends, going on dates, participating in sports, may not be extraordinary (few are), but the writer can draw on all of them. Vicarious experiences, such as an intense involvement with great literature and films, also are good resources for the writer. In fact, the entire inner world of subjective responses—emotions, sensations, feelings—can become the source of your writing.

*Imagination* Project yourself into situations and into other bodies. This is the major technique of the fiction writer, but the nonfiction writer too may speculate and hypothesize. You may invent (speculate on) a confrontation between China and Russia along the Sino-Soviet border in order to imagine or hypothesize what action the United States might take in such an event. You can also use your imagination to describe an object. For example, you can project yourself into the object you're describing and imagine how the object must appear to someone unfamiliar with it.

*Research* Conduct experiments, interview knowledgeable people, use the library to search for data that will help you solve your writing problems. Especially for academic writing, skillful and energetic use of a well thought out library search strategy can make you familiar with practically any topic.

In Chapter Two and throughout the book, we will show you many different ways of exploring your experience to generate subject matter for your writing. If you invest enough energy in the search, you will be surprised and delighted by the richness of your experience.

## ► The Writer's Self [S]

A writer's attitude toward self and outlook on life are fundamental components of his or her motives. Therefore, every writer must try to *find* his or her self. Only when you have developed a sense of self can you begin to communicate with your audience. People are complex, multifaceted, and many layered. Are you an optimist or a pessimist, a mystic or a realist, a believer or a nonbeliever? Your view of self is part of your point of view.

In considering your attitude toward your self and your subject, you must make an important decision: How do you want to appear to your reader? What persona do you want your reader to see? Suppose that you have been assigned a serious paper for an academic audience. You are genuinely interested in the topic but realize that your writing style—as in letters to friends—is informal and sprinkled with slang. You also tend to use biting, sometimes offensive, humor. Realizing that lack of control, informality, inappropriate language, and insensitivity will alienate your audience and, consequently, defeat your purpose, you decide to project a more serious self, one that is genuinely fascinated by the topic. A fairly formal style and tone should help convince your readers of the reasonableness of your position.

Each person is made up of many different selves; therefore, you should examine your many selves, carefully selecting one that will reinforce the overall purpose of your paper.

### ► WRITING ACTIVITY ◄

Write a paragraph or two in which you project a character trying to persuade a particular audience to act or think in a certain way. Try to project a self whom the audience will view sympathetically. Then, in a paragraph or two, project a second persona, whose purpose is the same, but whose writing personality will almost certainly alienate the audience.

What effect did the change in self have on the piece of writing? How did you show the two different selves? Describe each persona in a sentence or two.

# THE WRITER'S CHOICES: IN THE MIND AND ON PAPER

Do writers first decide their purpose, then determine their audiences, then select a self, then choose an experience, and finally use an appropriate code to express themselves? For many writers, the writing process—especially the initial stages—is confusing, disorderly, even chaotic. How are the choices we have been talking about really made? Here is what can happen when you are assigned to write a typical college paper.

Suppose that you have just heard a lecture given by a renowned scientist on the future of organ and limb transplants. You decide that this topic might make an interesting paper for assignments you have in both your biology class and your composition class. You begin jotting down informal notes from past experiences—what you know about people who have lost limbs and about organ donors and recipients—from books, magazines, newspapers, scientific journals, films, and radio and television programs. Next, you skim several articles from *Time*, *Redbook*, and *Harper's*; two or three from scientific journals recommended by your biology instructor; and the relevant sections of Alvin Toffler's *Future Shock*. You take detailed notes, especially from the scientific journals, because they cover unfamiliar territory. A quick look at all your notes reveals that they're sketchy and unorganized, and that there are striking differences in their level of formality. Some summarize scientific concepts in complex language; others, like the ones about your grade-school classmate who had a kidney disease, are short anecdotes.

At this point, perhaps, you decide to write the paper for your composition course, partly because your paper is due soon in that class and partly because you are more interested in the human than the scientific aspects of your topic. You select the composition class as your audience and decide that your purpose will be not only to inform but to entertain them. You may even impress them with your scientific knowledge. A too formal tone will be forbidding and dull, so you decide to try for a relaxed, reasonable tone somewhere between the familiar and the formal.

You begin making careful notes, expanding on the jottings you have about your classmate. You quickly write out a page and a half describing how difficult it was for her to keep up in school when she spent so much time in the hospital undergoing dialysis treatment. As you reread these pages, you realize that focusing on your classmate's school problems has turned out to be depressing, not entertaining. What you've written sounds too personal and emotional when you had intended to sound relaxed and informative. And with this emphasis, you haven't a way to include any of the ideas you heard at the lecture that initially aroused your interest in the subject.

As you review your notes, you become convinced that a better approach is to use a historical perspective. You decide to compare and contrast today's techniques for kidney transplants, which you've become fairly knowledgeable about from your reading, with past treatments for kidney disease. You'll illustrate the situation in the past by using two or three anecdotes about your classmate's experience with dialysis. You'll then connect these perspectives with your sense of the way kidney disease will be treated in the future, as described by the lecturer. You sketch out a rough outline to keep your ideas straight and then begin the process of producing an exploratory draft.

The concept of choice is at the heart of the composing process, but just as

**Chart: A Linear Representation of the Writer's Options and Choices for the Paper on Organ and Limb Transplants.**

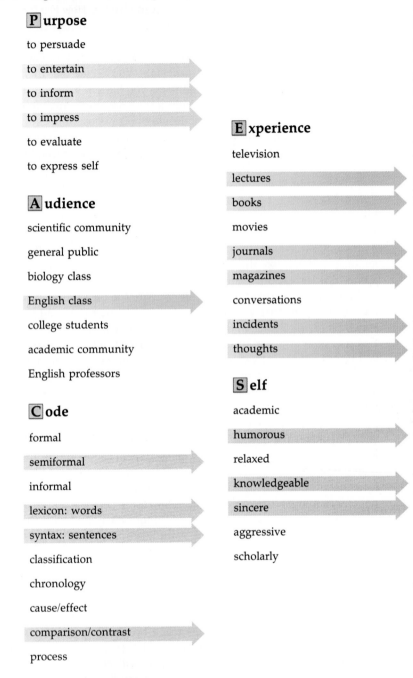

### Purpose

to persuade

to entertain

to inform

to impress

to evaluate

to express self

### Audience

scientific community

general public

biology class

English class

college students

academic community

English professors

### Code

formal

semiformal

informal

lexicon: words

syntax: sentences

classification

chronology

cause/effect

comparison/contrast

process

### Experience

television

lectures

books

movies

journals

magazines

conversations

incidents

thoughts

### Self

academic

humorous

relaxed

knowledgeable

sincere

aggressive

scholarly

Notice that each of the choices the writer has made for this paper have been shaded in the color representing that element of the PACES composing model. See page 8 for a general color-coded model of the PACES composing process.

important are the choices writers consider and then decide *against*. Composing involves an almost endless series of choices, rejections and additional choices. It should prove illuminating to chart the actual options considered and then chosen or rejected during the planning of the paper on organ and limb transplants (see chart on page 14). In the chart, each of the PACES components displays, one under the other, the many options that were considered. To highlight the choices that were *actually made*, we have covered each of them with appropriately colored arrows.

The diagram on page 8 and the chart on page 14 complement each other and are designed to suggest both the complexity and the essential simplicity of the *writer's choices* in action. The process can be extremely complex and sophisticated, but at any stage, you, the writer, can stop, step back, and focus on the simplicity of the three-dimensional PACES diagram. As suggested previously, overemphasis on any one of the components of the writer's choices will unbalance your paper. We have created PACES to remind you that the composing process involves not one, but five elements. PACES is easy to remember—purpose, audience, code, experience, self—and monitoring each component should help you to control the process. Whenever you feel lost while working on an important paper, return to the safety, simplicity, and control of PACES, a major ally of the writer's mind. PACES is never too simple or too narrow and never so complex that you can't control your writer's choices.

By now, you probably understand that we are not describing a sequential process like baking a cake, in which each step follows in prescribed order and, once completed, need never be thought about again. In writing, disorder is *normal*. Multiple purposes, audiences, codes, experiences, and selves have to be sifted, weighed, evaluated, reconsidered, and reworked. Like painting or sculpting or composing music, writing evolves from a complex series of decisions that must mesh and contribute harmoniously to an outcome you may not have foreseen at the start. The sculpture that so delights its viewers may have started simply as an exploration in clay, its outcome ultimately determined by an ongoing process of choices, decisions, reconsiderations, and changes. The same may be said of the compositions you write.

## ▶ WRITING ACTIVITY ◀

Select a real or imagined event—a news report, a family incident, a sports report, a fashion show—and relate it in a paragraph or two to a particular audience. Your purpose should be to present the event in a favorable light. Then, using the same incident, write a paragraph or two in which your purpose is to present the same incident in an unfavorable light. Compare the results. What happens when you change purpose?

## AN OVERVIEW OF THE STAGES IN THE COMPOSING PROCESS

There is no single right way to write well, no magic step-by-step formula or procedure that guarantees success. Sometimes writing is very difficult. Many modern writers have complained that the process can be agonizing and painstaking. William Styron said, "Let's face it, writing is hell" and went on to describe the struggle he had getting his ideas on paper. Sometimes writing can come easily too. A celebrated example of a work flowing onto the page is that of "Kubla Khan" by the British poet Coleridge, who vividly described how the poem wrote itself. A number of writers have remarked on the same phenomenon. Sometimes their writing flows with surprising ease. Usually when this happens, it is a sign that the writer has done a great deal of preliminary planning and drafting in his or her head.

Less experienced writers, however, need a systematic approach to the task of writing. Therefore, we have divided the writing process into several stages: planning, drafting, and revising.

### ► Planning

We define *planning* as all the mental and physical activities writers engage in before they produce an exploratory draft. Recent research on writing suggests that the planning stage of the process, when you thoroughly explore the topic by using a variety of invention techniques and then sketch a preliminary plan, is even more important than had been previously thought. Yet planning is often neglected by inexperienced writers who want to arrive at a sophisticated draft as soon as possible. Most writers find getting started difficult because the initial stage of writing is disorderly, even chaotic. It is a time of intense creativity as the mind searches, discovers, sifts, sorts, and rearranges the various components of writing.

At this stage, you should exercise "energized" patience. Do not settle for the first thoughts you have about a prospective topic. Dig into the topic, approaching it from every angle. As your mind wrestles with it, put everything down on paper. Take notes, formal ones as well as scribbles and jottings. Although you may not be consciously aware of it, during this planning stage you will be making decisions about the five components of *PACES*. Don't rely on your memory. Remind yourself on paper about the problems you're having and the preliminary decisions you're making. Above all, be patient. The time you spend on discovery and planning, especially as you energetically probe your experience, usually pays rich dividends. Indeed, it is almost impossible to spend too much effort on discovery and planning. Eventually things will begin to come together, and you will know that it is time to begin drafting your paper.

## ▶ Drafting and Revising

*The exploratory draft* This draft is often referred to by professional writers as the "zero draft." It's something you have to get out, something to start with, not agonize over. This draft should be written fairly quickly, without letting concerns about correctness slow you down. Don't write and edit simultaneously. Laboring over every word and sentence, checking spelling, crossing out and rewriting, then making the additional changes are discouraging and laborious, especially as you are still exploring your topic. The crumpled-paper syndrome is evidence of an author who is stuck. It is better to skip over any sticking point and to force yourself to complete the draft, realizing that you will probably delete sections later. Why waste time crafting and polishing during your preliminary planning when you might delete the entire paragraph later? Resist rewriting until you get to the end of your exploratory draft; otherwise, you may not reach the end.

After you have completed the exploratory draft, let it cool for at least a day. Then you can approach it more objectively. The British novelist E. M. Forster once said, "How do I know what I think until I see what I said?" The exploratory draft lets you see what you know and think about your topic. It also reveals what you do not know. Your next task as a writer is to examine this draft to see if you are saying what you intend to say. Then the real challenge can begin—that of rewriting, or reenvisioning.

*The working drafts*

> Rewriting is when playwriting really gets to be fun. . . . In baseball, you only get three swings and you're out. In rewriting, you get almost as many swings as you want and you know, sooner or later, you'll hit the ball.
>
> NEIL SIMON

Quite often an exploratory draft doesn't reflect your planning. Don't be discouraged; instead view this phase of the process as an opportunity to produce a better draft. Exploratory drafts tend to be written from the writer's viewpoint. Working drafts concern themselves more with the reader. The more critically and thoroughly you analyze your exploratory draft, the more likely you are to achieve your purpose in a working draft.

*The final draft* You may compose several working drafts before you come up with one that satisfies you. Again, we recommend that you let any draft cool off for a day or two in order to see more clearly what it conveys. As you work on the final draft, keep in mind that two very important sections of the composition are worth all the effort you can put into them: the beginning and the ending. Furthermore, the body of your essay will benefit from a highly critical examination and revision. Would the composition improve if you rearranged the paragraphs? Added to them? Subtracted from them? Substituted for them?

One of the chief problems with many papers by beginning writers is that they lack sufficient evidence; they don't have enough information. Give the final draft a reading in which you concentrate on the evidence only; imagine yourself as a reader who doesn't know the topic as well as you do. Will that reader need additional data, examples, and reasons, more or different illustrations and details?

In the final draft you also need to think of a critical reader who will respond not only to the information in your paper but to your style of writing as well. This is the place to cut excess verbiage, prune clichés and jargon, and in general clean up your English. In the final draft you need to look at your sentences and paragraphs the way a critic would. Can they be made more accurate? Can they be made more readable? By combining some and deleting others, you will probably improve the style and tone and efficiency of your writing.

> I believe a story can be wrecked by a faulty rhythm in a sentence—especially if it occurs toward the end—or a mistake in paragraphing, even punctuation. Henry James is the maestro of the semicolon. Hemingway is a first-rate paragrapher. From the point of view of ear, Virginia Woolf never wrote a bad sentence. I don't mean to imply that I successfully practice what I preach. I try, that's all.
>
> TRUMAN CAPOTE, *Writers at Work*, Malcolm Cowley, ed.

It is in the final draft that you must use the real skill of an artisan. This means seeing that a word you've used is not exactly right. It means seeing that changing the punctuation of a sentence changes the emphasis and gives new meaning to the sentence. Far from merely finishing work, most writers say this final draft is the one that counts, and the one you should give your maximum effort to.

> I rewrote the ending to *Farewell to Arms*, the last page of it, thirty-nine times before I was satisfied [. . . .] Getting the words right.
>
> ERNEST HEMINGWAY, *Writers at Work*, George Plimpton, ed.

As your final draft nears completion, you'll find it useful to review the five components of the writing process—purpose, audience, code, experience, self—and the decisions you made as these components interacted in your writer's mind and on paper. This review should help you to make last-minute improvements in your final draft.

*Proofreading* After rewriting, reenvisioning, it is time to move to proofreading—finding slips of the eye and hand in your final draft. The purpose of proofreading is to make sure that the composition says what you think it says. Check spelling, punctuation, grammar, and other mechanics. Proofreading means examining the finished copy to find and fix errors. Errors may be neatly painted out with correction fluid and the correction carefully penned in. You may cross out neatly with a pen and write the corrections above the errors, provided there aren't too many of them. (Of course, if you use a word processor, corrections are even easier.) About sixty percent of the errors in final drafts are caused not by ignorance of the conventions of the written language but by carelessness. A careful rereading of the paper a day after you think it is completed often reveals enough errors to negatively influence a reader's evaluation.

# CHAPTER ▲ TWO

# *Planning and Discovery, Discovery and Planning*

**"If I had eight hours to chop down a tree, I'd spend six sharpening my axe."**

**ABRAHAM LINCOLN**

Choosing a subject that will interest you and your potential readers, generating enough material to support your position, organizing your ideas into a coherent whole—all of these constitute an exciting challenge. The discovery and planning stage of the writing process is vitally important, and yet our experience and research suggest that most young writers spend only a few minutes on this aspect of their writing. In contrast, Donald Murray, a Pulitzer Prize–winning journalist, examined his own writing process and was surprised to discover that he spent as much as eighty percent of his time on planning and discovery. The process of planning and discovering will be the central concern of this chapter. First, we will describe invention techniques to help you generate and select interesting topics. Then we'll show you how to use these techniques to narrow the focus of your paper and to discover ideas, opinions, and information you'll need to plan and develop your topic. In this chapter, we will also focus on the thinking processes of several writers, that is, on their *writer's minds*. We will share with you what they were thinking as they worked with their topics. Seeing how other writers think while engaged in the planning process should help you to expand your repertoire of planning strategies and develop a confident, successful writer's mind of your own.

The secret of successful planning is to resist premature closure. Let ideas percolate through your consciousness. Learn to think about your topic as you take a shower, drive on the highway, or stroll by the river. Try for a systematic flexibility in your thinking while avoiding rigidity in your planning. Welcome the inevitable tension that will occur as you constantly think and rethink in order to discover order in the sometimes chaotic jumble of your writer's mind. Above all, be patient. If you invest enough time in planning and discovering, your writer's mind will usually achieve success.

## INVENTION

Gaining access to the ideas, opinions, facts, details, examples, and reasons they need to convince their readers is a critical initial step for writers. Although there is no simple formula that enables you to generate the material you need, there are several invention techniques that can help. Invention—derived from the Latin word *invenire*, "to find" or "to come upon"—involves searching to find the material you need and the strategies to organize and present it.

Experiment with each of the invention techniques described in this chapter, from free-association *brainstorming* and *free writing* to *clustering*, which is designed to tap the neglected resources of the right hemisphere of your brain, to the more structured *journalistic formula* and *pentad*. One of them may seem intuitively right immediately; make sure, however, to give the others a fair trial. In our experience, at least two or three of these techniques, often used in combination, become comfortable and productive "invention" friends to writers who are willing to practice using them.

## ► Freewriting

When confronted with a writing task, many beginning writers say, "I just can't write. My mind goes blank. I can't think of anything to say." They are surprised to hear that this feeling of hopelessness is common among experienced writers too. But experienced writers know this fear is a writer's hang-up, not a sign that they can't write. Getting started is often the hardest part of writing, and experienced writers have discovered that one solution to the problem is to force themselves to begin writing immediately.

If you allow your mind to go blank each time you sit down to write, you may develop a kind of writer's paralysis, in which you are permanently conditioned to freeze up when you have to write. To overcome this fear of the blank page, practice *freewriting*—sitting down and writing anything at all, without interruption. Free writing is "free" in the sense that there are no rules to follow. Spelling, punctuation, and grammar are ignored; you don't even need an idea or plan. The only thing that *is* important is not stopping. Let the words pour forth spontaneously, from your mind onto the paper.

Freewriting is designed to sharpen your ability to think on paper. You may believe that professional writers think out in detail what they are going to say, make an outline, and then dash off the finished work. Very few writers can do that. Most say that their writing begins to take shape *after* they have struggled with their ideas *on paper*. Writing itself is an act of discovery. Instead of first thinking and then writing, you need to learn to think and write simultaneously.

Here is the freewriting of a writer whose mind is blocked. He is convinced that he has nothing to say until he forgets that he is writing and begins to think on paper.

**Carl Winslow**

Nothing, nothing, nothing, nothing, nothing, nothing, nothing, nothing, nothing. I have nothing to say, nothing, blah, blah sounds like a duck blah blah, quack quak what is this anyhow? What a rut nothing I thought this was suppose to be college? Free writing, free writing FREE WRITING. How can I write if I din't have nothing to say. Let your hand do the writing the man says—let your fingers do the walking just like in the yellow pages, everybody is doing it, write, write, write. The guy next to me is drawing doodles—like this ~~~~ wonderful. I paid a fortune for this? or my dad did anyway. Why? This is how I get to be an engineer, sitting here trying to unfreeze my mind. My mind's set in cement, maybe that's the point too much mind cement, a mind set. Don't let the ink dry. Isn't ten minutes up yet, forgot my watch. Something, something, something.

## ► WRITING ACTIVITY ◄

Try a ten-minute freewriting. Start writing as fast as you can. Instead of thinking about what you are saying, let your hand copy whatever is going on in your head—words, pictures, emotions, physical sensations, anything at all. Don't censor your mind: Let it range freely. If your mind truly is blank, just write "nothing" or "blank" over and over. Remember, don't stop; don't let the ink dry before you write the next word. Keep practicing freewriting until you have proved to yourself that you have conquered your fear of the blank page.

## ► Focused Freewriting

When you are confident that you can write freely, you'll discover that there is little difference between thinking and writing. When you reach the point where your hand automatically records what your mind is thinking, you can set your mind in any direction you like and produce freewriting on specific subjects. In the three examples of freewriting that follow, the writers aren't controlling their minds consciously; they are focusing on specific topics but allowing their thoughts to flow freely.

**Tim Meekins**

Squirrels--gray, usually. Sometimes reddish-brown. Most of the squirrels I see are large fat ones of the gray variety. They always sit around eating nuts--getting fatter and fatter. It's really amazing how much these squirrels can eat. Ever watch one of them eat? Sometimes they will sit in the crotch of a tree or they'll hang on the side of a tree with their rear legs while holding nuts with their front feet. How can they possibly hold on with just those back legs. I wish I could do this sometimes. Heck, I wish I could just climb a tree. Squirrels can also be the most notorious around a bird feeder. We have one and almost everyday he eats every sunflower seed we put in it. How can he eat so much? I've tried everything to keep him out--I built a sheet metal guard but he can jump all the way around it. There's a second squirrel that can jump from the ground all the way to the feeder--almost five feet off the ground. I didn't believe my own eyes watching him do this. Have you ever seen such a thing? These little "innocent" criminals are absolutely the most incredible jumpers and leapers. I've watched them many times climb to the top of a tree and jump from tree to tree. I live in the middle of the woods and I've watched squirrels cross the entire woods by tree-hopping. Without ever touching the ground.

**Carol Brown**

*If I had my life to live over again, I'd live it as an Irish Setter. What beautiful, total, blissful freedom. Not really bright enough to perceive the fence that limits her freedom, the Irish Setter races across the yard, chasing a bird, an insect, a dream. The goal is not important. The chase is. The wind blows just enough to enhance her full feathering, her coat glistening red in the sunlight. No responsibility for this animal, she knows joy. Joy is catching a ball, romping in the grass, wading along the river's edge, being told she's loved. Sometimes, just for a moment, I'd like to exist in that unthinking world of hers.*

**Jerry Nelms**

Sunny day outside. What to write, to write. Write write. write. Fatherhood. Dad's visit. My son and my father. I'm in middle. Before my son's birth, my dad and I were not close. Divorce. Mom and Dad. Now mom's dead and here we are. Survivors. Well, sort of. Dad just had heart surgery and almost died 2 years ago. Got me remembering. Funny how I always associate my father with a story of Pearl Harbor. It's kind of like a little myth I have--my father telling me that story. I can't remember if he really told it to me or if someone else did or if I dreamed it or what--same with little story about Dad's teaching me not to be afraid of the dark. All on Dellwood Place, that idyllic surburban place that I remember as nothing but good. How close families were, always cooking out together. That's how it is in my mind: a summer's night, a cookout at our house. My father teaches me not to be afraid of the dark and tells me (and other kids?) of bombing of Pearl Harbor--how he came running up on deck, thinking it was trash men banging cans the way they did, not remembering it was Sunday morning and then,

```
seeing the smoke, the planes, the bombs. He es-
caped. And every year he takes Dec. 7th off. He
just stays home and sleeps in his easy chair or
fiddles with his cars or something mechanical
like it was a Saturday or any other day. This
bit of reality is my myth--it brings me back to
the real world. But did it ever really happen?
Could be this is all myth? Could it become an
essay--my dream father--is that how my son will
remember me--is that what memories are--dreams
or nightmares?
```

## ► WRITING ACTIVITY ◄

Try a focused freewriting. Set your mind to thinking about some subject that interests you. Write about the stars, your goals, someone you saw on the bus, a problem you're having—anything at all. If you begin to daydream or wander from the subject, let it happen. If your mind doesn't want to stick to the subject you have chosen, discover what it does want to think about, and write about that.

## ► Keeping a Journal

Many writers keep a collection of their thoughts and perceptions by writing in a journal. To keep a journal, you must first have some place to store your writing: a folder that can hold loose-leaf pages, a notebook, or even a word processor if you prefer writing with one. Then, write often and regularly in your journal, perhaps a page a day. Journal writing is very similar to freewriting in that the goal is not to compose perfectly coherent, error-free prose, but writing that could lead to other writing. In your journal you can write on anything. Record your reactions to your experiences: what you do, what you see, what you read. Write about your own writing. The journal is a good place to work out problems with your writing because it allows you to generate and test ideas in an open, non-threatening environment. Since journal writing can be such a fruitful invention technique, you shouldn't allow your journal to become a diary that merely lists daily events. Remember, the writing in your journal could be of use to you later, especially when tackling a paper assignment. (For a more in-depth treatment of journals, see Chapter Five, "Expressive Writing.")

As you read the student journal entry below, think of the potential paper topics it could generate. Where could the writer go from here? Is the journal the beginning of a draft?

**Kevin**

I don't know. What to write about today. Let's see. What happened last weekend. Went to the mall... oh yeah — saw Mississippi Burning at the matinee. Admission was half-priced, but I would have gladly paid the $5.00 to see it anyway. What an intense film. Right from beginning they've got you worked up because these three civil rights workers are chased down by the police and shot at point-blank range. That first scene just burns itself into your mind, and you have little trouble understanding why Gene Hackman's character uses such extreme measures on the townspeople during the F.B.I.'s investigation of the murders. Some critics have argued that the film is too violent, but I think the violence serves a point — like in Platoon. Just hinting at all the atrocities that occurred during this tense period in the South is not enough to really shake people up and drive a point home. You can talk all you want about the cruelty and injustice, but graphically illustrating it is a different story. Besides, since Alan Parker directed it (he also directed Pink Floyd's The Wall) you would have to expect some violence I just wish more people would go see it. Some people charge that the movie's not historically accurate, but all of the things shown in the movie did occur in the South at the time, whether they occurred in that particular town or not. Maybe if more people were aware of the things this film has to teach us, we wouldn't be electing a former KKK Wizard to an important position in the government. But that's a topic for another journal entry.

Kevin's journal entry certainly doesn't consist of the organized, flowing prose found in an essay. He's also opinionated, almost reactionary at times, but that's the point—a journal entry should be a soapbox, as well as a storehouse for ideas of all sorts. Kevin has plenty of potential paper topics, too. An obvious essay stemming from the entry would be an evaluative paper on *Mississippi Burning*. But there are other possibilities, such as an informative or persuasive paper on violence in the movies, an informative paper on the directing style of Alan Parker, or a persuasive paper urging people to see these kinds of thought-provoking films rather than the standard mindless action or comedy films. Perhaps nothing will come of the entry, but it is always there in the journal if the writer needs it.

## ► WRITING ACTIVITY ◄

Keep a journal for at least two weeks, writing approximately one page a day. Write on anything you like, but keep in mind that the journal is not a diary listing daily events. Refer back to your journal when you're searching for a topic or a way of developing a topic further.

## ► Clustering

Clustering is another invention technique to stimulate you to fill that blank page staring up from the desk at you. Developed by Gabrielle Rico, clustering taps the right hemisphere of the brain, the hemisphere that perceives patterns and general forms from experience, that makes connections and sees associations among and between ideas.

To do clustering, set aside ten minutes of uninterrupted silence. Write a word or your "topic" in the middle of a sheet of paper and circle it. Then begin to playfully free-associate, allowing your creative mind to make connections, writing down ideas as they come to you, circling each one and connecting it by a line or arrow from a response word to the word that triggered it. If you find you've run out of associations along one line of thought, begin again, from a different spot on the topic circled in the center. Don't try to make sense of these chains of words. Don't try to make them connect logically. Simply let your creative energy flow onto the paper. After you have clustered for five to seven minutes, stop, allow your mind to wander over your cluster, and then start writing. We call the writing you produce from your cluster a vignette. Do not feel bound to include in your vignette all the material and insights mapped by your cluster.

At the end of this process of creating a cluster and its vignette (the total process usually takes about twelve to fifteen minutes), you may find it useful to read your vignette aloud to yourself.

Examine the following example of clustering.

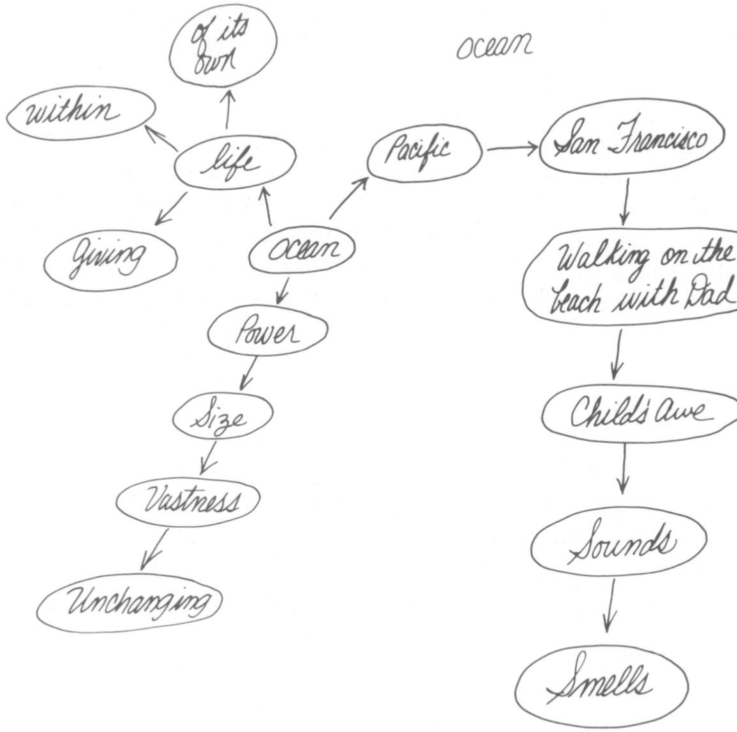


When I was younger, my family would take short trips to San Francisco, usually to see how many relatives we could visit within a three day span. I don't remember the visits too well, but on every trip, without fail, my father would drive me to the beach to see the ocean. I never forgot that. We didn't go to swim, or sun, or collect seashells, but only to stand, or maybe to walk, and always to look, feel, and smell. The ocean moved and roared, and spread itself like nothing I had ever imagined, and I was absolutly in awe of its greatness. Its power frightened and thrilled me and I stood in wonder at the life that swirled above and within its waters. Nothing, however, could tame or change its constant motion or its vastness, and it seemed to defy limitations, as I knew them. I would stand on the beach, letting the waves break in front of me, and my father would stand back a little, and sometimes we would just smile and never say a word.

When we analyze Theresa's cluster and vignette, we see that her writing includes all of the ideas mentioned in her clustering. The vignette, typically short, takes on a poetic life of its own as Theresa grapples with her ideas and memories.

In the section on focused freewriting (pages 25 to 26), we saw Jerry's early attempt to work through the experience he discussed in "Sunny day outside." With his cluster and vignette, he focuses on his father and works toward an exploratory draft, probing his feelings about their relationship. Notice the characteristics of his clustering and the sophistication of his vignette. Also notice that Jerry's vignette uses only part of his cluster; this is typical. But he has discovered a subject that matters to him and is on his way to the first draft of his paper.

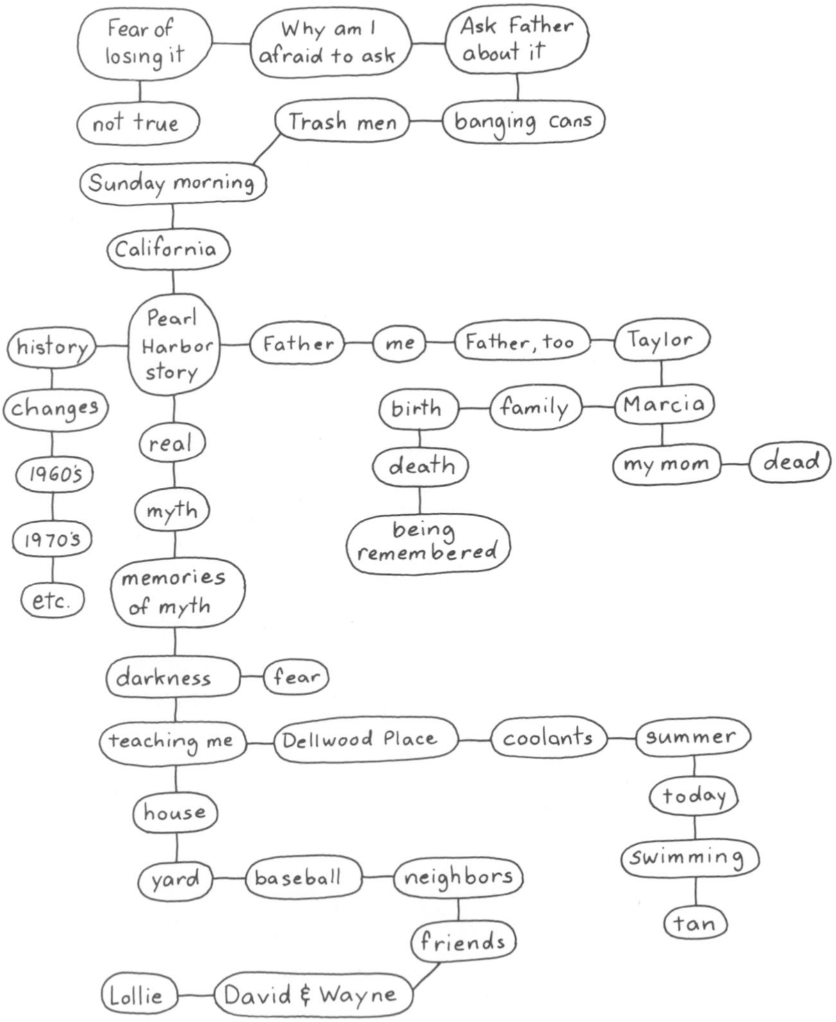

My father and I have never been close. When I was a child, he was always out of town on work, and when he was home, we rarely spent much time together. By the time I went to high school, our interests were as different as could be. He loved things mechanical. I loved things artistic. With the birth of my son, we have found the one important thing of our mutual interest.

In fact, I remember only one time that my father ever really talked to me about anything more important than mowing the lawn. Surely, there were other times, but I remember only one. That in itself is meaningful, I guess.

I don't remember how old--or young--I was, but I was young enough to still be scared of the dark. It was during a neighborhood cookout on Dellwood Place, where I grew up, in Decatur, Georgia. My father took me away from the lights and the people to the other side of the house, where there were no lights, where you could barely make out the silhouette of the pine trees against the stars. Uncharacteristically, he took the time to show me how our eyes adjust to darkness, and how nothing really changes in the dark. The trees remain trees, the grass does not turn into sea nor shadows into bears. There was nothing to be afraid of in the dark, he said. This was in the time before children were stolen, before drugs and fanaticism demonized the land. This was in a time when the suburbs of Atlanta seemed safe.

On this same extraordinary evening--at

least, in my memory--my father also told me the story of his experience at Pearl Harbor. He was stationed on the California. It was 7:30 A.M., Sunday, December 7, 1941. My father slept. He was awakened by a loud banging. During the week and on Saturdays, the native Hawaiian garbage collectors took great joy in waking up sailors on ships in port by pounding the metal cans as they passed. Still drowsy, my father, then a naval chief, climbed out on deck in his shorts to curse them. He saw the first bombs hit. In only his pants, he was able to escape the California after she was first struck. Many of his friends and mates were not so lucky.

How true the story is I don't know. How much such truth matters I tend to suspect more and more as I grow older. But I do know that as a child the story mesmerized me. Even today in our jaded world, to witness such events places one in league with heroes and gods. And for my father's generation, the generation I still glorified in my boyhood, before Woodstock and the shootings at Kent State, the bombing of Pearl Harbor was the event of the century. My father had almost died in the early daylight, ten years before my own birth. It explains a lot, I suspect.

For one thing, it explains why he would not fear darkness and why, even today, he does not fear it, while his son, now with a son of his own to feel protective about, fears it perhaps even more than he did as a boy.

Ever since, my father, committed much more than I to the work ethic, without exception, always took December 7th off from his job. A symbolic act, you might say, designed to forever keep the memory of the event alive. But, those days were never spent in contemplation, as I would have spent them perhaps. Instead, my father worked on our car, or fixed our television, or worked on some other mechanism. The day was always spent productively.

More puzzling than that: my father never spoke of it again. I never heard the story again. And more puzzling even than that: I never asked about it. It was too great a risk to ask. I might find out the truth and lose the memory.

## ► WRITING ACTIVITY ◄

Try clustering with any topic you like. Allow the strings of associations to develop freely, no matter how strange or "unconnected" they may seem. When you feel the cluster is finished, begin writing your vignette. Don't worry if your vignette doesn't contain everything from your cluster; the important thing is that you allow the writing to flow freely from the cluster. Let the writing happen. You may be surprised where your cluster will take you.

## ► Brainstorming

As we have seen, Jerry was able to combine freewriting and clustering to generate a subject. The other techniques of invention we will cover in this chapter—brainstorming, the journalistic formula and the Pentad—can also be combined. Let's see how they can help you produce interesting material on a general topic, such as the tobacco industry.

Brainstorming, or free association, is a popular and easy-to-use invention technique; many professional writers claim it is the only method they employ to generate and organize subject matter. In reality, they probably have unconsciously assimilated more formal strategies of finding and shaping what they want to say, and call them brainstorming. In our view, it is an excellent way to begin to explore a subject.

Assume that, having just seen a cigarette ad or read an article on the tobacco industry, you decide that this might be an interesting topic. To begin brainstorming, write down everything that comes into your mind that is related in any way to the tobacco industry and smoking. Approach the subject from every angle and write every thought in your mind. Write down each fact, opinion, statistic, or idea in a single word, phrase, or complete sentence. As you work at your subject, one of two things will happen. First, you may realize that this topic is not for you; it may seem boring or you may not know enough about it, nor care to find out. (This rarely happens.) Second, and more likely, your mind will begin to spill out a flood of information about it. Facts, opinions, and counterarguments will appear seemingly without order on the page. Your mind will probably run ahead of your hand. Don't sift and analyze at this stage. Keep writing. Even if you suspect a fact or idea isn't relevant, put it down; you can delete it later. Surprisingly, many seemingly irrelevant facts turn out to be useful as you develop your paper. Examine the following example, which shows a page of brainstorming that you might come up with on the general subject, the tobacco industry.

Even names of cigarette brands sound cool.

The Tobacco Industry

huge multinational corporations
lots of people work in this industry. The U.S. is a BIG tobacco producer. There are lots of ads in magazines and on T.V. These ads make smokers look really COOL. Advertisers must spend a lot of money making smoking advertisements. There's obviously a lot of money in this industry. Smoking is an expensive & habit.

Money involved in all parts of industry.

But is smoking cool? It's a health hazard. There are warnings on the packages. It can cause heart attacks, lung cancer, poor circulation, and emphysema. Eventually it causes death. Smoking is a dangerous addiction.

Smoke irritates a lot of people. Some people are allergic to it.

But we die anyway. Lots of people enjoy smoking.

Is smoking a habit worth breaking? Smokers feel calmer, more comfortable with cigarettes in their hands. Smoking also keeps weight under control. They even have cigarettes called "slims." It's tough to imagine stopping. A lot of people (George Burns) smoke all their lives. How much you smoke seems to make a difference. Occasional smokers don't seem to be taking such huge risks.

Can smokers control their habit? Is smoking a crutch a lot of smokers feel they must have to function? This sounds like Linus's blanket. He never wanted to give it up. His blanket didn't cause him health problems though. Smoking is more dangerous than a blanket. What alternative is there? Chewing tobacco is pretty disgusting. Pipes are just as dangerous. My grandfather died of throat cancer. He was also really old though.

There's still peer pressure to smoke too.

People who get irritated by smoke seem to want the whole nation to be smoke free.

Smoking is more than just a health hazard. Fires have been caused by people who smoke in bed.

## ► WRITING ACTIVITY ◄

Try to brainstorm over a period of two or three days, perhaps a half hour at a time, to allow your unconscious mind to work over the topic, to incubate ideas and associations. You will discover that your best ideas frequently appear when you allow evidence to simmer for a while in your subconscious. Previously unconnected ideas will suddenly fit together, providing you with new insights and attitudes toward your subject. New angles will develop as your mind wrestles with the topic. You will begin to see the problem you are trying to solve in an entirely new or different light. Counterarguments will suddenly spring up, and the simple solution you had originally may become more problematic. The other side may not be totally wrong; some of your arguments may be less effective than you thought. You'll probably need to take a more balanced, more judicious approach than you first planned. You may also need more evidence to support your position.

As you examine the brainstorming sheet on page 34, you can see that your experience has yielded a rich harvest. You have a great deal to say on this subject. Don't worry about whether it all looks confusing and disorganized. You will have the opportunity later in the process to organize your ideas.

## ► Focused Brainstorming

It is now time to focus, to zero in on your topic, to discover if you have a workable idea to develop. As you think about the ideas you've accumulated, you realize that the subject is too broad. What really interests you is the effects of smoking, a subject you have fairly strong feelings about.

The next step is to do a focused brainstorm on your new, more focused subject, the effects of cigarette smoking. Your brainstorming sheet clearly shows that most of your data favor or attack cigarette smoking, so you decide to compile two lists in no special order. (You'll find, though, that like things will tend to drift together. The mind instinctively tries to organize experience.) The figure shows the lists, one headed *Against Smoking* and the other *For Smoking*.

AGAINST SMOKING

Causes lung cancer
Should ban smoking
Ban smoking in public
Ruins teeth
Causes emphysema
Poor circulation
Heart trouble

FOR SMOKING

Constitutional right – smoke if you want to
Economic disaster
Kids get started smoking to be cool
Settles your nerves
Stops hunger pangs (temporarily)

Causes early death (males and females)
Nonsmokers nauseated by fumes
Cancer of lips and throat
Economic benefits - fewer days missed from work

A way to communicate socially
A habit not worth the effort of breaking
Can't stop
Life boring if we banned everything bad for us (saccharin, fast foods, beer). We die anyway.

## ▶ WRITING ACTIVITY ◀

Try a focused brainstorm on an intriguing aspect of your topic that came up during the more general, exploratory brainstorm. See if you can get an angle, a perspective, on the more focused topic and use the brainstorm to compile data you may have to include as you pursue the topic further.

## ▶ The Journalistic Formula and the Pentad

This new list may make you a little uneasy. Moving from the more general subject of the tobacco industry to the more focused subject of the effects of cigarette smoking caused you to discard many facts and ideas. You have a more manageable topic, but have you exhausted all its possibilities? Are there areas within this focused topic that you have not explored or discovered? At this stage in the process of invention, it's useful to examine the facts and ideas of your more focused subject more systematically by using two complementary invention devices: the journalistic formula and rhetorician Kenneth Burke's *pentad*.

The journalistic formula consists of asking Who? What? When? Where? Why? How? News reporters are trained to use these six questions as they learn to produce news copy. If you employ them creatively, you will discover many aspects of your subject that did not occur to you during the initial brainstorming. The *pentad* restates the journalistic formula in a more revealing way by stressing the possibilities for interaction between its different elements:

*Action*: What is happening?

*Agent*: Who is causing it to happen?

*Agency*: How is it being done?

*Scene*: Where and when is it being done?

*Purpose*: Why is it happening?

Although not all these questions will produce useful information for every paper, they are designed to cover most of the possibilities, especially if you use the basic questions in a variety of ways. Instead of simply asking the *Who*? or the *Agent* question—"Who smokes?"—you can ask "Who does not smoke?" One possible answer: people who suffer eye and throat irritation or infections. Isn't most of the statistical evidence that is cited to support a ban on cigarettes based on data from people who smoked cigarettes with a high tar and nicotine content? What if they had smoked cigarettes with low tar and nicotine content? A question like "Who has a stake in the cigarette industry?" might provoke economic arguments against banning cigarettes. "Why do people smoke?" might produce a number of productive responses. What effect would a ban on cigarette smoking have on individuals? Would it result in diet problems or in nervous disorders? Why *do* people smoke? As you ask these questions while examining your *For* and *Against* lists (see below), you might generate new notes like the following:

*Irritates eyes and throats of others*

*Cigarettes expensive – an unnecessary luxury*

*Psychological crutch*

*** NEED STATISTICS ON HEALTH HAZARD — CHECK MAGAZINES

*But smokers seem unrelaxed especially when they're dying for a cigarette*

*Nail biting*

*Economic disaster for huge tobacco industry – thousands would be out of work*

*Psychological crutches may be necessary – like Linus's blanket*

*Social acceptance, especially teen in groups*

*Helps you relax (say smokers)*

The *pentad* is especially useful when you begin investigating your topic in magazines and journals. If, for example, you are examining an article that is pro-tobacco industry (*Action*), it would be sensible to ask who wrote the article and check on the author's background (*Agent*). Why does the writer favor the tobacco industry (*Purpose*)? You might be swayed by the statistics used in the article only to discover they were supplied by the cigarette industry, which even solicited the article.

The journalistic formula and the pentad have almost limitless possibilities for generating information, especially when you go beyond the simple "Who did it?" or "When did he or she do it?" to ask more complex questions. For example, the *Who*? or *Agent* question can also be "Who could have . . . ? Who should have . . . ? Who will have . . . ? Who must have been . . . ? Who has . . . ? Who is . . . ? Who might have . . . ? Who will have been . . . ? This approach to generating information can also be expanded by combining different *kinds* of questions. For example, if you combine questions about agent and purpose, you might ask "Who objects to cigarette smoking and why?" or "Who is defending cigarette smoking and why?" Don't be discouraged if some of your questions produce information you cannot use. Learning to recognize and reject irrelevant data is as important a skill as selecting arguments and facts to support your thesis.

### ► WRITING ACTIVITY ◄

Use the journalistic formula or Pentad to explore a topic further. Consider all the possibilities as you answer questions in each scheme. Though some elements of the journalistic formula and pentad will yield obvious information, others may not. And what seems obvious at first may become problematic as you consider it further.

As you examine the latest version of your brainstorming sheet, you will have more questions. Articles must be read, statistics checked. But you will also be fairly confident. You feel strongly about your topic—banning cigarette smoking—and have facts and details to back this assertion. You are now ready to begin working on an exploratory draft of your paper.

In the next section of this chapter, we will discuss how to select a suitable topic, using the invention techniques we have described. In varying degrees, they are *systematic* approaches to creating subject matter. Yet, though they differ, a common thread binds them—each attempts to get your writer's mind generating and creating. We also want you to rely on the unsystematic, the intuitive. Writers often refer to intuition as something mystical. They struggle with a section of their writing, abandon it in frustration, and, later, inspiration strikes—a solution to the problem appears, seemingly from nowhere. We want you to combine the intuitive and the systematic as you work on selecting and developing topics for your papers.

## SELECTING AND NARROWING A TOPIC

The discovery techniques we have described can be used at every stage of the writing process—from selecting a topic to creating ideas about it through planning to drafting and revising.

Selecting a suitable topic is of crucial importance to writers. Many writers fail because they are dealing with subjects about which they know or care little. A good rule for selecting a topic is to *write only as an expert*. Of course, we don't mean that you should be formally certified in that area of your topic (you don't need a Ph.D. in it), but we urge you to pick topics about which you feel confident and knowledgeable and about which you care.

Writers also fail because they write for themselves, ignoring their readers' needs and experiences. The formation of volcanoes on the ocean floor is a potentially interesting topic for people who know little about this subject, but you would be courting disaster if you were to write it for the local geological society, whose members have probably forgotten more than you know about undersea volcanic activity. The most crucial principle, then, for selecting a suitable topic is to pick one that will engage both you and your readers.

As you search for a topic suitable for a college writing assignment, you may be tempted to select one that is far too broad in scope—"What Is Wrong with the Human Race?" "War Since the Cave Dwellers," "The Meaning of Life," "The History of Democracy." Although such topics may be potentially stimulating to you and your readers, they probably could not be dealt with satisfactorily in less than a book-length manuscript. Make sure you have a manageable topic, one that you can cover in a 500- to-700-word paper. Focusing on a specific area of your topic will help you avoid writing a series of sweeping generalizations that may suggest to your readers that you have only a vague notion of your subject. Readers usually prefer the concrete, the specific. They are more persuaded by facts and details than vague generalities. They prefer writers who *show* rather than *tell*.

Don't assume that every topic you select will demand that you narrow your focus. Most experienced writers assigned a 500-word writing task instinctively limit the focus because they have a keen sense of their audience's interest. For example, professional writers might initially let their minds range over the possibilities of an essay on health and fitness, but experience would almost immediately guide them to select not simply a more focused topic, but one appealing to readers who have read dozens of such articles. Inexperienced writers would tend to write about topics like "Exercise is Good for You." In contrast, experienced writers sensitive to their audience would move to a more focused topic likely to catch attention, such as "Weightlifting for Women" or "Exercises for the Television Couch Potato."

Many inexperienced writers faced with selecting a suitable topic and devising a plan for its development frequently choose something safe and easily organized. Let's imagine a writer, Tom, who after selecting the general topic of child abuse, decides to write on the more focused subject "We Ought Not to Kill Defenseless Two-Year-Old Babies." Because his topic is so noncontroversial, Tom can immediately come up with an overall plan for his paper.

> I could begin by introducing the topic of killing people in general, suggest that, in the last half of the twentieth century, humans ought to have devised ways to eliminate murder, and conclude this introductory paragraph with my thesis statement that we ought not to allow the killing of innocent, helpless, defenseless two-year-old babies. In the second paragraph, I could give graphic examples of how upset neighbors and other civic-minded people get when people abuse little babies. In the third paragraph, I could use

specific examples of close friends and relatives reacting to the mutilation of babies. I'll focus especially on the reactions and feelings of members of the immediate families—brothers, sisters, fathers, mothers. Then, using specific examples of beatings, torture and murder, illustrate how babies themselves react with strenuous negativeness to this treatment. In the concluding paragraph, I'll restate my thesis. . . .

Let's allow Tom to drift off as we, his audience, are no doubt nodding off too. This paper, although it has a clear thesis, many specific details to support its generalizations, and a well-defined plan of organization, *ought never to have been written*. It fails topic selection's most important test: *So What*? It is obvious that his readers would wonder why an intelligent individual like Tom would produce such a trite, obvious, boring paper. Learn to ask the *So What*? question of yourself. Each of you has dozens of ideas that would fascinate your readers. If you respect your readers and yourself, you will be able to select subjects that will satisfy you both. Instead of a perfunctory "So What?" your readers will say, "Extraordinary . . . glad I read this."

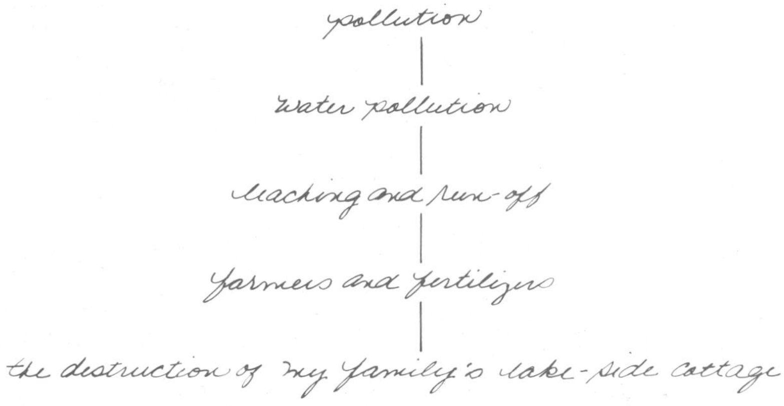


In the above outline, we see a student in the process of narrowing her topic from a broad and general consideration of "Pollution" to a more specific analysis of one type of "Water Pollution." Realizing that her topic is still too broad to be handled adequately in a five-to-seven-page paper, she narrows the "Water Pollution" focus to a consideration of the leaching of the soil and runoff caused by defoliation. Yet this topic is still too general. So she decides to limit her focus to a discussion of water pollution resulting from the farmer's use of fertilizers on lands rutted by runoff. Still not content, she recalls how the beauty and peacefulness of her parents' cottage were destroyed when the lake it overlooked was slowly choked by agricultural runoff, its waters bloated with algae, its fish killed. Now this is a topic she can commit herself to in detail in five to seven pages.

Examine the following two examples which show two other students exploring their initial paper ideas and then discovering various, more focused topics.

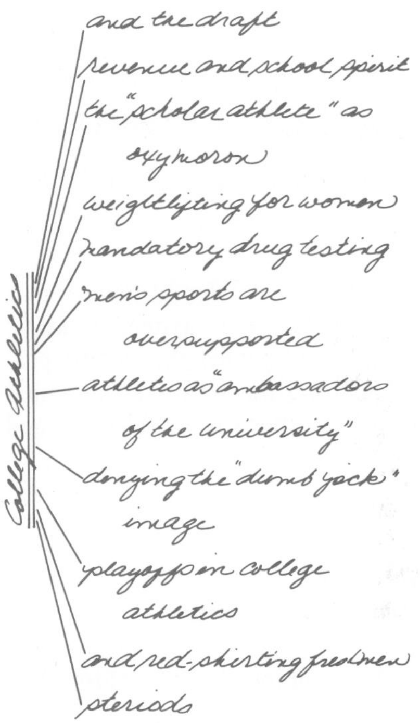


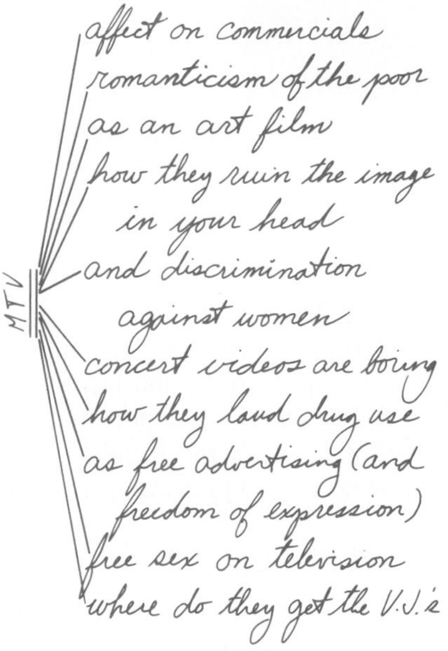


Although we have been stressing the importance of discovering a topic that is sufficiently narrow, it is possible to make it too narrow. If you find yourself with a topic about which very little can be said, return to the invention strategies illustrated earlier in this chapter and repeat several of them with it. You may discover that you have more to say than you initially had imagined. Not every topic will work for everyone, however, so learn to trust yourself as a writer, relying on your own judgment as well as on the advice and suggestions of others. Example A showed a writer discovering a topic that is personal and analytical—the cottage was a place in this young woman's experience; the emotions and feelings were her own.

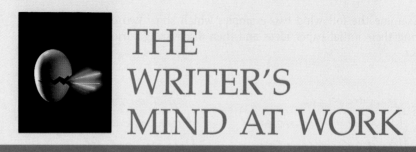

# THE WRITER'S MIND AT WORK

## CONSIDERING THE TOPIC

Let's follow Susan as she explores the possibilities of different topics she is considering for her paper. We will show you scripts of her "writer's mind" as she uses various invention techniques to weigh and ponder the writing possibilities in each of her potential topics. Analyzing the scripts of her mind should give you some insights into how writers move from selecting and narrowing a topic to devising a preliminary plan.

### PLANNING STRATEGY:
### Brainstorming "Weightlifting for Women"

Initially attracted to the subject of "Weightlifting for Women," Susan then created the following brainstorm.

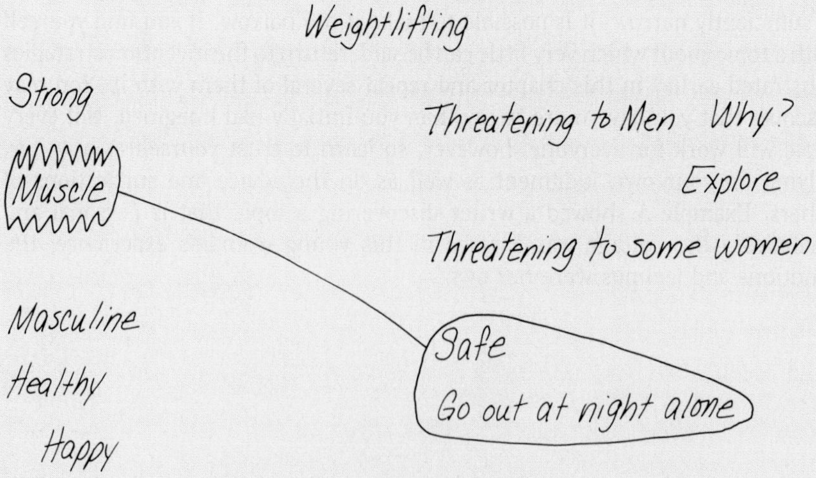

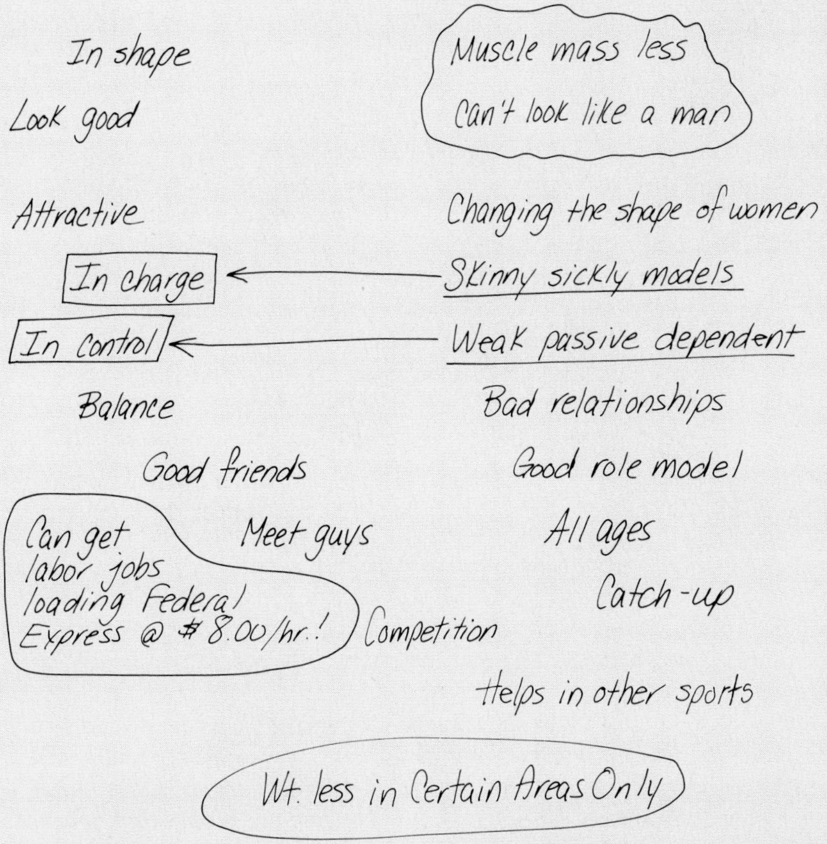


Susan's brainstorm is first rate. You can almost see her mind flashing from one aspect of weightlifting to the other. The arrows she draws indicate that she is already making connections. "In charge" "In control" and "Threatening to men" and "Threatening to some women" come together provocatively, eliciting a real writer's response: "Why?"—"Explore." What follows is a script of Susan's writer's mind as she mulls over weightlifting and two other possible topics.

### THE WRITER'S MIND: Considering Several Topics

*I have three possible topics—"Weightlifting For Women," "Secondhand Clothes," and "Non-Credit Courses For Credit." I like the first one best . . . it's personal. I've done it. I* do *it. Also I came up with some interesting ideas in my brainstorm. But the audience probably will be limited to women. Most of the things I discovered in my brainstorm appeal mostly to women. Stuff like not looking like a sweetweakling, passive and dependent, but being in charge and in control of your life when you feel good and strong about yourself.*

*And somehow I get the feeling that what I really want to write about is not just weightlifting, but something about changing the feminine profile . . . you know, from brittle-breaky model-thin to strong. A pretty complicated subject. I think I should wait on this topic. Maybe I can use it later after I have a better idea of what it is I really want to say.*

*Okay. So that leaves "Non-Credit Courses" and "Secondhand Clothes." I really like the idea of the non-credit/credit thing because the audience would be both men and women, students . . . and maybe administrators? See, I know that there are courses I'd like to take, but never do because they "don't count in my major." Stuff like "Chinese Calligraphy" or "Beginning Ballet." I think it would do me* good *to get out of my rut, I mean to learn about another culture or to try my toes on point. I think it would be great for somebody, say in Engineering, to take a pottery course or for an Art major to take a course in automechanics. Really open up your perspective. But the thing of it is I have to do so much research for this, or not research, but I at least have to know something about general university requirements, etc. That part doesn't appeal to me a whole lot. Besides, I don't have a lot of time, and anyway, is what I write even going to have any effect? I'm not so sure. And I like to think that what I write is going to affect* somebody, *even one little person. No, this topic is too vague, sort of "fictional." I need a topic that'll stand on its own without too much propping. Like the second-hand clothes idea.*

*Okay. Secondhand Clothes. I know this topic, too. I've bought and sold in secondhand stores. But what's my investment? I mean do I really care if anyone buys second-hand clothes? Do I? I don't know. I mean I guess I think— well I* know *I think people spend too much $ on clothes. I mean that somebody would pay 60 bucks for a* yard *of cloth! (about what it takes to make a skirt for me). Ridiculous!!!!! So I guess I do have an "ethical investment" in this topic. Better than that, though, is the fact that I have* facts. *That newspaper article in last Sunday's paper which for once in my life I had the brains to save just in case . . . it's* full *of details. Add to that my own personal experience and, yes, my "ethical investment." And what do you get? Sum-Total? A paper topic! A good paper topic I think.*

As you can see from an examination of Susan's writer's mind at work, there are no fixed rules for selecting a topic. Much depends on the individual writer's background and interests. Her fellow students thought that Susan's brainstorm on "Weightlifting For Women" was interesting, full of useful details and insights. They expected her to select weightlifting. But Susan, a person who knows her own mind, rejected this topic. (She does mention, however, that she may return to it later.)

Susan is clearly leaning toward secondhand clothes as the topic to focus on, but before she does, she decides to further explore its possibilities by doing a focused freewrite. Examine her focused freewrite, which follows, noting especially the thoughts she has afterwards. Do you agree with Susan that she now has an idea worth developing?

## PLANNING STRATEGY: Focused Freewrite for "Secondhand Clothes"

Talking about secondhand clothing stores--places where you can get quality clothes for less. Most cities have several (Columbus has about 9). Some of these places are non-profit like the stores run for Children's Hospital, etc . . . others are for profit, business, people in it to make money! Every kind of clothing--for women, men, kids, yuppies, hippies, groupies, whateveries. There are specialty shops, too, like "Re-runs for Wee-Ones" (YUK!), also vintage shops that deal in 1930's, Art-Deco, turn-of-the-century stuff, etc. I gotta emphasize the quality of the clothing--that the clothing in these stores is not old, moldy, frayed and faded, although faded can be ok. for levis, etc., but that you can find good stuff in these places. In fact, these stores are similar to regular stores--both carry name brands . . . the real difference is the price you pay for the name. Important point to make. Name some popular brands. Compare with price of regular purchase in retail store . . . retail, is that what it's called. Yes, different from wholesale. Show savings. But, what about stores like Discount Stores? Are the bargains the same in Secondhand stores . . . less??? Gotta think too about the audience . . . so many kinds of clothes, etc. So--this paper would appeal to who? Maybe students who don't have much money. Yeah. You can look great but not pay a lot of $ for it. So--would guys go for this? The store owners say most of their customers are women, but I don't think that's necessarily so around campus. There is that vintage store . . . what is it . . . Atlantis, I think, near campus. I've seen lots of guys there . . . and lots of clothing for men which, of course, women can wear too, though I doubt guys would buy women's clothing . . . well some might . . . this is getting off the subject. The point is I don't want to limit my audi-

OK. Some of the clothing is actually NEW! Bought for a gift—person didn't like it, wrong size, etc.

Evan Picone shirt reg. $100, only $35 in 2nd handshop. Ralph Lauren for $60/45. But I need brands Students would get into—Levis, Guess, etc.

ence to just women--that was the trouble with the other paper. I tell you one thing. Smart people would shop at a second-hand clothing store and that's going to be one hel-lavan appeal. In fact, I think I should profile a "typical customer" . . . that would give me a good fix on my audience. I like to have a "person" to write to when I write even if that person really represents a lot of others in the audience. I wonder if I could even interview some shoppers???? "Why do you shop here, etc?"

My own experience, too!

Oh, I have an idea. I should talk about the history of secondhand stores and I think maybe that will help explain the difference between these stores and discount stores. See these stores, secondhand stores, originally I think, came about to provide a means for generating $ for charity. Somebody probably said, "Hey, these stores make money for charity so why not for me?" Sounds a little selfish, but wait. There is nothing wrong with recycling clothes. It's good! Waste not want not, etc. I should check this out but I know I'm right. Egomania. You could call a store "Egomania." Hey, I could go into business for myself! Shut up. Write. Get started on the paper. Get rich later.

This might be another appeal to "environmentally aware" students.

Susan continues to try to convince herself that "secondhand clothes" is the subject she should write about. Examine her writer's mind as it focuses on what she calls her "Audience Profile." Although Susan makes some very provocative, perhaps wrong-headed, comments about her audience, what do you think of this "Audience Profile"? Is the confidence she has gained justifiable?

## THE WRITER'S MIND: Audience Profile For "Secondhand Clothes"

*Okay. So my audience is students, but what kind of students? Well, students not necessarily defined by age because they can be all ages. The thing they have in common is lack of money. So, my reader isn't poor but has to watch dollars and cents. And, my audience is SMART because it's a student audience, right? And even if my audience wasn't all brilliant, I'm going to treat it that way because that's a great appeal . . . "Flattery will get you anywhere," etc. Anyway, my audience is made up of smart students, male and female, who have great taste but not much money to indulge their stylish desires. And the thing that's really good about this whole thing is that I'm a student too! I don't have much money either, but I like to look good. So I have a connection already with the reader, what's it called . . . oh, yeah . . . Credibility. I have credibility with the reader. I like the topic I've selected.*

Having decided on the topic she'll pursue, Susan is now ready to move to the preliminary planning stage of her paper. Let's wish her luck.

## DISCOVERING A PLAN

It has often been said that the purpose of a university education is not merely to assimilate as many facts as you can—a great deal of which will quickly become outdated—but to develop the ability to both think for yourself and to plan and communicate these thoughts with clarity, style and force. Selecting an interesting, workable topic and putting together a sound plan for presenting that topic to your audience often necessitates trying several different invention techniques. Just as importantly, however, it requires you to think carefully and critically about the strengths and weaknesses of the different ideas you have generated through these invention strategies, and to make the sound judgments and choices that will result in a topic that is appealing to both you and your audience.

In the last section of this chapter, we will accompany a student writer, Todd, as he works on discovering and developing a plan for his paper. We will watch him as he explores several possible options for paper topics by employing some of the invention techniques described at the beginning of this chapter. We will then follow his progress as he goes through the process of trying to select a suitable topic, much as Susan did with her paper on secondhand clothes. Our primary focus, however, will be in observing the thought processes of Todd's "writer's mind" as he first attempts and then critically thinks about different techniques for his planning process. Pay close attention to the "Writer's Mind" sections, where Todd's critical thought processes are presented. By observing him at work, you should gain insight into both the different options for planning and for the equally critical phase of analyzing the plans that are generated by working through these invention techniques. Eventually you will develop confidence in your own ability to plan, analyze, and organize your writing. The scripts of Todd's writer's mind will demonstrate that the creative process is often nonlinear and unpredictable, and that the planning process depends heavily on the writer's personality, experiences and thought processes as well as on the unique demands of the subject matter. There are no fixed rules for developing a plan for a piece of writing; there is no ideal plan of attack for a writer. Experienced writers often claim that discovering a plan can take on a life of its own, with a piece of writing sometimes heading in a direction that is surprising even to the person who is writing it. Remember that the process of thinking carefully and critically about your ideas and your writing is a skill that must be developed and practiced just as diligently as you practice the writing itself. Todd's writer's mind at work should serve as a flexible model for the kinds of thinking you need to practice to discover and develop attractive and effective plans for your own writing.

# THE WRITER'S MIND AT WORK

## DISCOVERING AND DEVELOPING A PLAN

A sports enthusiast, Todd decided to write on the general subject of sports. He was aware that he knew a great deal about this topic and, therefore, he decided to begin with a brainstorm to generate material. He hoped that the brainstorm would help him focus his general topic down to a workable paper topic.

**PLANNING STRATEGY:**
**Brainstorm on Sports**

Sports

Everybody grew up doing sports.
Sports are part of our culture. Lots of famous athletes.
I like a lot of different sports. Athletes do commercials.

They endorse a lot of products
They are respected

Health benefits of sports
discipline coordination
practice muscle control
relaxing aerobic benefits
emotional control

raquetball, swimming, "triathaloning", cross-country skiing, basketball, tennis, table tennis, downhill skiing, cycling, hiking, baseball, football, soccer, running, speed-walking, frisby, wrestling, discus, archery

Do people know the difference between downhill and cross-country skiing? Cross-country skis are not as firmly attached to feet. You need to move more. You can ski this way in more places

"loner" sport compete against self.
calming

There are competitive sports, but some sports you can do alone. Some people just compete against themselves. Lots of effort put into sports. Money invested too.

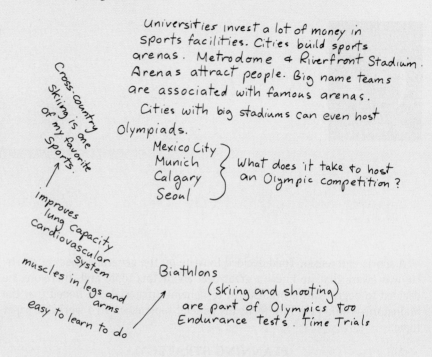

Universities invest a lot of money in sports facilities. Cities build sports arenas. Metrodome & Riverfront Stadium. Arenas attract people. Big name teams are associated with famous arenas.

Cities with big stadiums can even host Olympiads.

Mexico City
Munich
Calgary
Seoul
} What does it take to host an Olympic competition?

Cross-country skiing is one of my favorite sports.

↑

improves lung capacity
cardiovascular system
muscles in legs and arms
easy to learn to do

→ Biathlons (skiing and shooting) are part of Olympics too
Endurance tests. Time Trials

After brainstorming the topic of sports, Todd chose skiing as a more manageable and, since he was an avid skier himself, interesting topic for his paper. Todd tried Burke's pentad as a way to develop this topic and hoped that the multiple perspectives of the pentad would prove useful.

## PLANNING STRATEGY:
## Pentad on Skiing

Act: What is happening, What happens

Well, basically you slide along the snow with a couple of slats stuck to your feet. You stand at the top of a hill, your feet firmly buckled into boots and boots rigidly attached to skis and you simply let her go. Well actually it isn't quite that simple. After all, you have to steer yourself--in fact that's the whole art of skiing--controlling that slide down the hill. Anyone can put on a pair of skis and fall down and break their neck--the real skill is in schussing down a mountain, real fast, without hurting yourself--and I don't mean snow plows--in fact skiing is even jumping--ski jumps in which the skier comes off that jump and flies through the air--that takes skill--and what about X-country skiing--there you have to propel yourself--you have to cause the action (Well that's not entirely true, because on most X-country trails you do have some downhill.)

Agent: Who causes it to happen

Obviously the skier is causing the skiing to happen, he's causing the act--he has to slide down that hill and get back up--actually he usually has help getting back up--you have lifts--chairlifts, t-bars, rope tows (I hate those!), gondolas--and you have to have an operator, and you have to wait in long lift lines, and you have to stop each time some jerk falls off a t-bar--and if you rent skis you have to deal with more lines, more hassle, more pushy clerks who don't really care if your boot fits or not. (Well some clerks are nice but I guess I've just had some bad experiences). Of course in X-country skiing you don't have all that hassle--no lift lines, no clerks to deal with--but of course you can't go as fast--but still you are the primary--the only agent. (Of course if you rent equipment you still might run into some hassle.)

Agency: How it is being done

Well, it depends on the type of skiing--obviously downhill skiing will be very different from ski jumping, which will be very different from X-country skiing--the movement itself is different--you control the skis differently--in ski jumping, the skis are wide and heavy--and you need to position your body just right when you come off that ski jump--lean forward, arms at the side--you need that jump to get a lift and the exact shape of the jump and shape of the hill will influence the jump itself--but body positioning is important as well.

In downhill skiing of course you have poles--you need that slope as well--can't ski without a slope--the skis are a little narrower so you can control the lateral movement--need lifts--need <u>money</u>--boy does it cost a bundle to spend a day on the ski slopes--and all that crowd--all those "ants" filling the slopes. You can't even go fast--in X-country skiing at least you're not so dependent on the ski resort--you don't have to worry about lift lines and all that hassle--<u>you</u> just go--you control the game.

<u>Scene: Where and when it is being done</u>

I can't think of a more seasonal sport than skiing. You have to have snow. And you have to have enough snow so your skis aren't scuffed up. It has to be cold enough so the snow won't melt--some ski areas can make their own snow but if it's 50 degrees and sunny the snow won't stay. So you can only ski in certain parts of the country--mostly the north and northwest--and you need a mountain for downhill skiing, a jump for ski jumping and some kind of a track for X-country skiing. Actually skiing is a <u>privilege</u>--it's not like walking--you have to be at the right place at the right time. Most of the time ski jumping is done in a meet or in practice--in a spread time. Downhill skiing is a little flexible but you still need to go to a slope and pay a lot of bucks--you need a track in X-country skiing--actually there are tracks made by special machines usually at ski slopes but I don't like them--usually the tracks are crowded, and they're over flat areas--I like X-country skiing in the woods--usually you can find some snow mobile tracks snaking through the woods and follow these--you need some kind of track--trying to plow through unpacked powder with skis stuck to your feet is worse than trying to run through water. But on a crisp day, with a cold, clear sky, with the sun beaming, lighting the forest but not really warming the air, with the sound of wind through the pines, and squirrels chattering, and water running under ice, boy what a difference from that lift line with the fashion-conscious fools in their stylish but impractical ski suits!

Purpose: Why it happens

It's fun--pure and simple. Sure, there are contests for different kinds of skiing--competitions in high school, college--even the Winter Olympics has all these sports. Every once in a while you can check out Wide World of Sports and watch ski jumping or racing--Jean Claude Kily and all that. (I wonder how much money these guys make?)--But still--most amateurs ski because it's fun--zipping down a hill, feeling the wind race past your ears--man, you feel like you're flying! I suppose some people go to ski slopes because it's fashionable, like tennis or golf, but those types you see plopped on sofas in the ski lodge, swilling booze and eyeing each other--maybe occasionally you'll see them "hopping" down the bunny slope.

But skiing can be exciting and you feel a thrill zooming down that mountain, knowing that there are many more thrills that might be coming. (Maybe a broken neck!!!) It's also great exercise--especially X-country skiing--it's like jogging except you don't have that pounding of the feet--great aerobic exercise--gets the heart muscle pumping--and that can be relaxing--especially if you're going through a quiet woods--get exercise and get relaxation at the same time--what else can you ask for?

An examination of the material he had generated using the pentad convinced Todd that he wanted to think and talk about cross-country skiing specifically, rather than skiing in general. Much of the material he had written was relevant to cross-country skiing, so he hadn't wasted his time. Todd immediately began a cluster-vignette on his narrower, more focused topic "Cross-Country Skiing."

## PLANNING STRATEGY: Cluster on Cross-Country Skiing

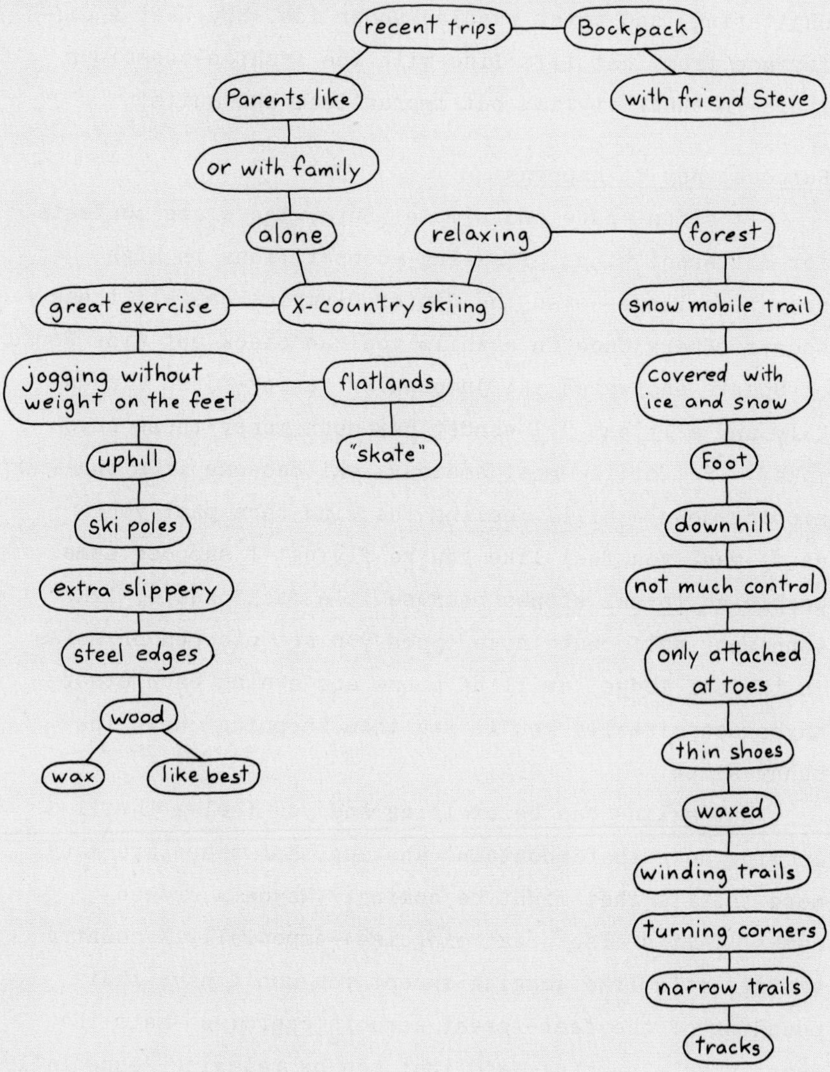


## PLANNING STRATEGY: Vignette on Cross-Country Skiing

Gliding across the snow on a crisp winters morning, through the woods, smelling the pines--falling into a rhythm, kick off with one foot, push off with the ski pole and glide, kick off with the other foot, push ski pole and glide, stride--rhythm--your feet seem to float off the ground as you slide forward--into the groove--you almost feel a part of the trail, a part of the snow--it offers no resistance, even the hills--the hills you duck walk, side slip off, maneuvering your skis to the extension of your feet--light skis--only attached to your feet at the toe of your boot--you barely feel the weight as you shush down the hill--feeling the wind whip your face, the snow offering no resistance--and then the jump--the snow in the snow mobile trail--for a second you feel as if you're flying, part of the air--but the landing assures you you're not--as you lie in the snow your body still vibrates from the energy of the rhythm you've established, you've slid into--you get up--dazed and dizzy, slide off again, push off with the pole, kick off with the foot and the rhythm takes over.

Todd's vignette focuses almost exclusively on the process of cross-country skiing, especially the physicality of his pleasure while gliding across the countryside. The details are rich and informative, at times almost poetic. After completing it, he decided to try a more contrastive, analytic approach, so he reread the material he had generated using the pentad and then produced the following focused freewrite.

## PLANNING STRATEGY:
## Focused Freewrite on "Cross-Country Skiing"

Cross-country skiing is similar to downhill skiing--you have poles--you slide across snow--zip down hills--danger of falling.

But it is really dissimilar--the skis are much lighter and thinner, the foot is attached only at the toe--the boot doesn't cover the whole of the ankles. You have much more control over the forward movement because you can move both your knees and flex your ankles, whereas in downhill you can't easily move yourself forward but you can more easily control the lateral movement because your feet are more firmly attached to the skis.

Downhill skiing requires slopes and you have to have rides up the slopes--you need machinery to take you up the mountain. X-country skiing requires snow, a trail, skis, poles and that's it--you don't need a well-groomed trail, you don't need lifts up the mountain--you can enjoy skiing without a large group of people.

There's variety in X-country--you can go on snowmobile trails, tracks, golf courses, snowed-over ponds, and woods.

You can race, be a nature enthusiast, get terrific exercise--aerobics and all that. You can get the best relaxation, floating over the land, seeing the woods, peace of mind--and that's important in this hectic world.

After reading all the work he had done, Todd thought about his emerging plan.

### THE WRITER'S MIND: Planning for "Cross-Country Skiing"

*I want to show the difference between downhill skiing and cross-country skiing. I think I need to do this because when somebody says skiing, most people (I think) think of downhill skiing only. The media certainly covers downhill skiing to a greater degree than cross-country skiing. But I think cross-country skiing has many more things going for it.*

*Like—no crowds*
*no lifts—no waiting*
*good exercise, etc.*

*Of course, the equipment is very different for the two—different boots, skis, poles—this makes the whole movement different—in downhill skiing you're more interested in moving side to side—in X-country in moving forward—the rhythm is different.*

*(I don't want to make too much of this—be careful not to make the descriptions too long and make sure they're clear.)*

*Is the difference between the equipment used in X-country skiing and that used in downhill skiing common knowledge? I don't think so, though I don't want to play up the differences too much. Is this even important to the paper? See what happens.*

*I need to describe the whole feeling of cross-country skiing, to capture its allure. I need to maybe get a little poetic here but I don't want to go overboard—the rhythm: Kick with one foot, push with the pole, glide, kick with the other foot, push with the other pole, glide (I guess I do need to describe the way the boot is attached to the ski because this is important in the rhythm the skier establishes.)*

*What about the dangers of X-country skiing? Of falling? Should I work this in? The UPSET of the rhythm? This might take away from the allure of X-country skiing, after all it's not too much fun falling down. But it is an important part of skiing. I'll play around with this.*

*What else? Does this do it? I'll end with a contrast of cross-country skiing to downhill skiing to reemphasize the joys of cross-country skiing.*

Having completed the preliminary planning for his paper, Todd is now ready to move to the drafting stage, which we will see him begin in Chapter Three.

You may find these criteria questions useful as you complete the "Writing Activity" that follows.

## CRITERIA QUESTIONS: EVALUATING A PRELIMINARY PLAN

**P urpose.**

1. Is my topic sufficiently significant to suggest a strong purpose for my paper?

**A udience:**

2. Will the audience selected for the potential paper want to read it?
3. Will the selected audience want to see a developed version of this plan? Am I paying enough attention to the needs of my readers?
4. Have I presented enough background evidence for my readers?

**C ode:**

5. Is this interesting topic treated in an uninteresting way?
6. Is the preliminary plan focused enough? Is it manageable? Does it cover too much territory? Which areas of my plan need further development?

**E xperience:**

7. Are there enough facts, ideas, details to support my tentative thesis?
8. Do I know enough about this topic? Will I need to increase my own knowledge by doing outside reading? To develop this paper, will I need to quote outside sources?

**S elf:**

8. Is it too soon to decide on the voice I'll project in this paper?
9. Is there a persona present in my preliminary plan?

## ► WRITING ACTIVITY ◄

Go through the process Todd has just completed by

1. listing at least three or four potentially interesting topics,
2. selecting the topic that best suits you,

3. narrowing the topic to manageable proportions,
4. generating material for your topic,
5. producing writer's mind scripts for *every one* of these planning stages.

# CHAPTER ▲ THREE

# *Drafting and Revising*

**"Writing and rewriting are a constant search for what one is saying"**

**JOHN UPDIKE**

The central focus of Chapter Two was discovery: finding an appropriate topic, a topic rich and stimulating enough to be of real interest to potential readers. Selecting a suitable topic, of course, involved you in some serious thinking about a preliminary focus or plan for your paper. Preliminary planning and topic selection were complementary acts, mutually interdependent decisions. You will discover in this chapter that, in similar fashion, planning and discovery are an integral part of the process of drafting and revising.

Chapter Three will extend our discussion of preliminary planning or sketching and move to the scratch outline and exploratory draft. It will then deal with the thesis statement and the more formal outline as revision strategies for the production of a working draft. Next will come a discussion of strategies for revising working drafts into a final proofread draft. (To get a brief overview of the general stages in the composing process, see Chapter One, pages 16 to 19.) To demonstrate these stages of the composing process in action, we will resume our examination of Todd's writer's mind as he continues to plan, draft, and revise his paper on skiing.

The stages in the composing process just described should not be viewed as a recipe for composing: "First you do this, then you do that, and so on. . . ." Some experienced writers claim that much of their planning and drafting is done, sometimes subconsciously, in their heads. Others speak of a piece writing itself. Still others, however, assert that our description is not complicated enough, that composing is often of necessity a messy, recursive process involving dozens of revisions over a period of months and even years. We agree with all of these statements. There is no easy way to predict how a piece of writing will develop, how an individual writer's mind will work on a given writing task. But for most of the writing tasks you will face in college and in the world beyond college, the planning, drafting, and revising strategies described here should prove useful often enough to warrant your careful attention.

## PLANNING AND SKETCHING THE EXPLORATORY DRAFT

After you have examined your topic from as many viewpoints as possible and generated as much information as you can, let your ideas incubate for at least a day before you begin to write your exploratory draft. At this initial draft stage of composing, don't even think of formulating a final, complete, detailed plan for your paper. The emphasis should be on the tentative nature of this exploration. What you are after is a preliminary sketch of where your paper might go—not where it must go.

At this stage you might find it useful to think of how creative people have viewed the search for form in their material. Think of Michelangelo planning his statue of the young King David: After contemplating for days on end a magnificent piece of marble that, unfortunately, had a large crack in it, Michelangelo was asked what he was thinking. His reply: "I'm trying to free David from the stone." Similarly, the artist George Biddle claimed that "drawing is the architectonic, . . . the living skeleton of painting." Both of these creative people are emphasizing the tentative and exploratory nature of designing a plan.

An even more illuminating analogy can be found in the work of an architect. Imagine yourself an architect with a specialty in regional planning who has been hired to draw up plans for a very large tract of land recently purchased by a company interested in creating the ideal new town for a population of some 45,000 new residents. How would you go about planning this community? It is obvious that, initially, you would not prepare detailed blueprints for every structure and street in the development. Instead, after a careful examination of the geographical layout, you would determine the overall constraints of the project: the type of community desired, the financial constraints involved, and the kinds of industries and businesses contemplated. Dozens of specific constraints would have to be juggled, each influencing and being influenced by the others. Countless questions would have to be answered and countless new problems solved. At this stage, you would be wise to attempt a preliminary sketch of the area, an exloratory draft to ascertain whether the competing priorities can be satisfied. If the hospital is situated here and the airport there, won't the result be planes flying a few hundred feet above the hospital? And so on. Back to the drawing board. Another sketch, in all likelihood, a more sophisticated one, would appear.

Working on an exploratory draft for a paper is obviously a similar kind of task. After you have generated a substantial amount of information, established a tentative focus for your paper, and considered your audience's needs and the possible strategies you might use to develop your ideas, it is time to design a preliminary, tentative sketch for your exploratory draft.

## ► The Scratch Outline

To produce a preliminary sketch of how the initial draft will be developed, writers often use a scratch outline. Again, think of yourself as the architect planning the community. As the architect, you would roughly, tentatively sketch onto a map of the area the major structures and streets and how they would fit. The scratch outline serves the same purpose for a writer, providing you with a rough, general sketch of where your paper is headed. At this stage, there is no point in creating a detailed blueprint of your paper. The emphasis is on the word "scratch." Writers rapidly scratch down on paper a rough sketch that they can readily alter. The point is to produce a "living skeleton" of their exploratory draft. See page 67 for an example of the scratch outline.

### ► The Exploratory Draft

The exploratory draft should usually be written at one sitting. The items in your scratch outline are mere signposts to guide you on your way; they are more suggestion than command. If, as you are writing the exploratory draft, you discover a better way to develop a particular idea, follow your instincts. Also, if you are developing an idea that you thought had promise and it turns out to be a failure, don't hesitate to abandon it at this stage. You can always return to it later and give it a more thorough examination.

The exploratory draft has a dual function: It will tell you not just what to do, but what not to do and what to avoid. It is often only after you have produced a preliminary draft of your ideas that you can get a real sense of the strengths and weaknesses in your concepts. An idea that sparkled in your mind sometimes looks rather dull when you commit it to paper. Indeed, professional writers often refer to the exploratory draft as the "zero draft." Once written, it doesn't count at all. They describe it as a way to unload the clutter from their minds. Many experienced writers have also claimed that the actual writing of the exploratory draft will uncover additional supportive details or ideas and that the language itself often leads to a more effective design for the paper. The exploratory draft is usually written for the writer; it tends to be, as rhetorician Linda Flower says, "writer-based" rather than "reader-based." The scratch outline and the exploratory draft, then, should be viewed not as final commitment to your readers but as tentative, private, writer-based exploration.

## REVISING

When writers have produced their exploratory draft, they can then begin revising. The process of revision serves two purposes: to further clarify and amend the writer's ideas and to shape and recast these ideas so that they will be clearer to the reader in a working draft.

Consider for a moment the constituents of the word *revision*. *Re*-again and *vision*-seeing. It means more than merely "seeing again." For a writer, *revising* means reenvisioning, reconceptualizing; its purpose is to create anew. When writers revise, they talk of recasting, reshaping, "remaking." Each time you begin revising a draft, approach the task with the attitude that you are, in effect, creating a new paper, not just tinkering with an existing one. Of course, you will probably retain many of the ideas, much of the organization, actual paragraphs of your previous draft, but the new draft represents a fresh approach to your topic.

Revision does not, as most inexperienced writers believe, involve merely polishing the rough edges of a draft, checking for spelling problems and errors in mechanics and usage, and changing the wording in a sentence or two. Revision involves much more than cosmetic changes to the surface features of your exploratory draft's code. The process of revision will concern itself not only with these relatively minor aspects of code, but also with the other four components of the composing process: purpose, audience, experience, and self. Indeed the next draft you produce—the working draft—will demand that you focus most of your energy on purpose, ideas, and organization. It is only when you are proofreading your final draft that the surface features of the language you use in your paper will become the primary focus of your attention.

## ► Revising for Yourself and Others

Few writers work in total isolation. Writers usually benefit from the responses of editors, friends, colleagues, and classmates to their drafts. We encourage you to do likewise. As author Tim Foote put it, "Every writer needs an editor." But writers must also develop the ability to read critically and respond to their own drafts, to become their own editors. They need to develop what we call the "objective third eye," a critical consciousness that can examine a draft after a day or two and see it as an objective editor might see it. Experienced writers often talk about this critical consciousness, this objective third eye, as the ability to see not what they intended to say, but what they actually said.

To revise an exploratory, writer-based draft to a more reader-based working draft, you must learn to put yourself in your readers' shoes, to read and respond as your audience would, to become, as writing teacher Kenneth Burke put it, "consubstantial" with your readers. It is, of course, impossible to identify completely with your audience and experience your draft as another reader would, but if you want to communicate your message to others, you need to make a conscious effort to switch your perspective from that of a writer to that of a reader. If you pretend for a short time that the paper's ideas are new to you, that its sentences are unfamiliar and that its attitude and message belong to some other writer, you will find it easier to detect problems in the text. Writers often use terms that have special significance to them, meanings that a reader cannot possibly share. For example, you may have written that visiting the dentist is "as bad as having to go home for Thanksgiving dinner." For you, the writer, this analogy carries negative connotations that would escape any reader unfamiliar with your life. You may have had a car wreck, an illness in the family, an argument with a close friend or a terrible turkey dinner the last time you went home for Thanksgiving. Much of your responsibility in revising consists of anticipating where your readers will have problems and adjusting your text to clarify your ideas for them.

The main goal of the exploratory draft is to establish a focus, a sense of direction for the working draft. Inexperienced writers often forget this principle and become prisoners of their exploratory drafts, treating them as though they were carved in stone. The inevitable result is superficial revision and a text that leaves its readers befuddled. Skillful revising demands from the writer patience, energy, commitment, and above all, a creative flexibility.

## Revision: From Exploratory Draft to Working Draft

Although an initial draft can sometimes serve as a final draft, our experience tells us that this occurs so rarely that we can safely ignore such an eventuality. For most writers, experienced and inexperienced alike, a series of drafts is not only useful but inevitable. How should writers go about revising their exploratory drafts?

Writers often talk about their instinctive gut feelings informing the revision of their work. Inexperienced writers don't have that instinctive urge to fall back on. We suspect, however, that effective writing depends very little on instinct. Our hypothesis is that experienced writers, through wide reading and abundant practice with writing and revising, have unconsciously established a set of criteria that they use when engaged in the process of revising their drafts. To assist you in formulating a useful set of principles to use in revising your drafts, we suggest you ask yourself the following questions:

### CRITERIA QUESTIONS: EVALUATING AN EXPLORATORY DRAFT

**[P]urpose:**

1. Is the topic significant enough to suggest a strong purpose for this paper?
2. Is the thesis appropriate for the purpose of the paper?

**[A]udience:**

3. Have you addressed specific readers in this exploratory draft? Who are they and what do they know and feel?
4. Does the draft handle the audience with skill and sensitivity?

**[C]ode:**

5. Is the draft fairly well organized? Is it still too chaotic?
6. What strategies of development could you use to elaborate on your ideas?
7. Are the paragraphs purposeful and well constructed?
8. Do you have an introduction? Is it effective enough?
9. Do you have a conclusion? Can you think of a more effective one?

**[E]xperience:**

10. Do you have an interesting topic, one worth writing about?
11. Is there enough evidence—facts, details, reasons—to support your position?

**12.** Have you used all the resources of your experience? Does your draft reflect a thorough exploration of this experience?

**[S]elf:**

**13.** Have you projected an appropriate writing personality or self?

**14.** Are the style and tone appropriate?

You no doubt noticed that these questions for revising exploratory drafts focus on the purpose or purposes of your paper, its central focus or thesis, the characteristics of your intended audience, and the specific details, examples, and reasons you used to support your ideas. At this exploratory stage, little or no attention is being paid to the surface features of your text, such as mechanics, usage, spelling, punctuation, and capitalization. Indeed, the only aspect of the writer's code being emphasized is the strategies of development: comparison, contrast, definition, classification, and so on (for a detailed treatment of these strategies of thinking and development, see Chapter Four).

Let's examine a scratch outline and its accompanying exploratory draft to get a more specific idea of their form and function. The scratch outline was sketched by Susan, whose freewriting and writer's mind scripts were displayed in Chapter Two. You might find it illuminating to read her planning notes in Chapter Two before you examine Susan's scratch outline and exploratory draft for her paper, "Second-Hand Clothes."

# THE WRITER'S MIND AT WORK

## THE SCRATCH OUTLINE AND EXPLORATORY DRAFT

### SCRATCH OUTLINE:
### "Second-Hand Clothes"

- fun fashion aspect
- that they're really good clothes, not duds
- saving money
- where the clothes come from
- expressing myself by what I wear

### EXPLORATORY DRAFT:
### "Second-Hand Clothes"

Most large cities have what is called "second-hand clothing" stores. When most people hear the word "second-hand," they immediately think of "second-best," the kind of clothes that are a little on the crummy side. But clothing found in resale stores is of a different quality. The clothing in these stores has been carefully selected to appeal to customers who are looking for quality at a cheaper price. The people who sell clothes to these kinds of stores are not down-and-out; they might be quite well off. But if they have paid $200 for a cocktail dress that they are never going to wear again, they might like the opportunity to get a little money back on their investment. So they turn the dress over to a resale store. If and when the dress sells to someone else, someone who is maybe in the market for a nice cocktail dress but they don't want to pay big bucks for it, well the original owner will get a percentage of the sale.

Resale stores also get clothing that has been outgrown, usually children's clothes, but also if someone has gone on a diet and has lost a lot of weight, that person might like to unload an entire wardrobe on a resale store. There is also the fact that salesmen's samples are often bought by resale stores (Dispatch article). These clothes would actually be new clothes, but they would be for sale at less than the original price.

Students can do really well at resale stores, too. Of course a student can sell clothes there, but also if you're a student and don't have a lot of money, as is the case for most students, you can get some nice buys on clothes at a resale store. You can get brand names at resale stores like Izod and Polo. Maybe you would like to show off in an Izod shirt, but can't afford it. Go to a resale store and maybe you can afford it.

If clothes make the individual, then everybody ought to try to dress like who they really are. Of course this takes money and most students don't have money. But if you take the time to look in a resale store, I am sure you can find just the item you need to express yourself.

Since a discussion of Susan's exploratory draft will be included in the sections following on the thesis statement and the more formal outline, let's proceed at once to the concept of the thesis statement.

## ► The Thesis Statement

The primary function of the exploratory draft is to determine whether you have a topic worth pursuing and a significant viewpoint on that topic. The thesis idea is the bedrock, the basic idea, upon which you will build your paper. The thesis statement, usually a one-sentence assertion of your main idea, provides the central focus for the paper. The thesis statement signals to your readers the focus, the approach you are going to take to the topic. It serves as a statement of commitment and a forecast of how you will develop your paper. The thesis statement is useful for both writers and their readers. It serves to sharpen the focus of the writer's ideas by committing the writer to a certain line of action. Also, it helps writers determine whether a particular fact, detail, or idea will strengthen their position. The thesis statement orients the readers by suggesting to them the writer's aims. An effective thesis statement arouses its readers' interest and prepares them for the main ideas the writer will be presenting.

In Chapter Two, we discussed in considerable detail the importance of narrowing your focus so that you are not detailing with a topic that is too broad. You should adhere to the same principle when you are shaping your thesis statement. Although it is difficult to generalize about thesis statements because of the bewildering variety of writing situations in which they appear, their most common fault is a lack of precision: They tend to be too vague and general.

### ► DISCUSSION ACTIVITY ◄

Examine the following attempts at thesis statements and decide whether they are effective.

**1.** The City of San Francisco is unique in many ways.

**2.** People's personalities are reflected in the clothes they wear.

**3.** The main idea that I'll develop in this essay is campus parking.

**4.** Private radar detectors should be outlawed because they set up an adversarial relationship between the police and private citizens and thus encourage contempt for the law in general.

**5.** The role of blacks and women in our society has undergone dramatic changes in the last 100 years.

**6.** Although mud wrestling has many things wrong with it, it also has many good attributes too.

**7.** If I had a choice of living in town or in the country, I'd pick the country, and I think you should too.

The major problem with thesis number 1 is that the writer has selected a topic that is far too broad to be covered in a short paper. Tourist guidebooks, ranging from 50 to 250 pages, address this same subject. The writer needs to narrow the topic and focus the thesis, perhaps to one unique aspect of San Francisco, perhaps the architecture, the aura, or the food.

The major problem with thesis number 2 is the potential for making the illustrations too generalized, drawing on popular, often-clichéd stereotypes.

The major problem with thesis number 3 is its mechanical nature. No angle or slant on the topic is presented. As we remember, a thesis should indicate the writer's topic and stance on that topic. We find here an illustration of the typical "This-is-what-I'm-going-to-say-this-is-what-I'm-saying-and-this-is-what-I've-said" formula.

Thesis number 4, complete with a clear sense of topic and focus, is a good statement to the reader of the writer's approach to the paper that will follow.

There are two major problems of focus with thesis number 5. The first concerns time span. One hundred years of sociological history is far too long a period to discuss in four to six pages. Perhaps a decade might be manageable, but even this time span might be too broad to be analyzed in a short space. The second problem is the focus on blacks *and* women in the proposed thesis. In a short paper, it would probably be better to focus on just one of these groups. A discussion of the role of black women would result in a more focused analysis.

The major problem with thesis number 6 is that it seems to indicate a general discussion of mud wrestling, a topic that may still be too broad for a short paper. In addition, the "although-there-are-good-things-about-x-there-are-also-bad-things-about-it" formula may be too mechanical to interest a reader.

The potential problem with thesis number 7 is that the writer may be unable to generalize beyond purely personal-experience examples and illustrations in what promises to be a persuasive essay. In persuasive writing, as we will discuss in greater detail in Chapter Eight, the audience component of PACES (purpose, audience, code, experience, and self) becomes very important as the writer tries to influence a reader's thoughts or actions through her writing.

The discussion we have almost completed on the thesis statement was brief by design. The best way to learn about the thesis statement is to struggle to compose and shape an effective one as you plan, draft, and revise your papers. However, since there is a fair amount of controversy about the ideal placement of the thesis statement in a four-to-six-page paper, we thought it might be useful to give you some idea of the various arguments on this topic.

In our view, the shakiest position is that some successful essays never explictly state their thesis, but imply it by the author's judicious use of argument and detail. In our experience, the only type of essay where the thesis statement is usually absent is the narrative. The most common opinion is that the thesis statement should be placed at or very close to the end of the introductory paragraph. Others claim that it can be placed at the beginning of the introduction; still others claim the middle. A minority assert that the thesis statement is best postponed until the conclusion. Introduce your topic in general terms, they say, then lead your readers through the evidence, explaining your position as you go. By the time you reach the conclusion, the logic of your position will have overwhelmed them. Your readers will have "earned" your thesis statement. Why, they ask, should you give away your thesis at the beginning? By so doing, you have lost any sense of suspense, with the result that your readers will doze off in the middle of your essay.

Our solution to this problem is initially a cautious one: because the vast majority favor placing the thesis statement at the end of the introductory paragraph, we recommend that you seriously consider that position. But since so many of the enlightened minority favor the other positions we have just described, it would obviously be wise to consider their arguments with some care, too. However, the best solution, in our opinion, is the simplest: *It all depends*. It all depends on the rhetorical context, on the unique constraints of your paper, and on the complex interaction of PACES (purpose, audience, code, experience, and self).

## ► The Formal Outline

There is as much controversy about outlining as there is about the thesis statement. If you write a paper that is poorly organized, and if you also have not prepared a detailed formal outline, then many people will be convinced that it was the absence of the formal outline that caused the confusion. The formal outlining format uses numbers (Roman and Arabic) and letters (upper and lowercase) to label the headings and subheadings in an essay. People who don't believe in formal outlines would counter by saying that successful, well-organized essays never attract people's attention to their outlines, that we only notice the *absence* of an outline. No one checks a well-organized essay to see if it had a formal outline or if the author actually followed the outline.

Formal outlines are useful and important devices for some writers and more trouble than they're worth for others. But every writer needs a plan to develop an interesting, well-organized paper.

Fairly detailed outlines are useful to inexperienced writers, especially after they have produced an exploratory draft. A careful analysis of the exploratory draft will help you build an outline for your working draft by exposing the strengths and weakness in the exploratory design. An effective outline will help you achieve order, balance, and unity among the various sections of your essay, allowing you to relate the parts to each other and to the whole. When you are mired in the sometimes chaotic process of planning and drafting, it's as if you are slogging on foot across densely wooded terrain with little sense of where you are going. The outline functions like a helicopter that lifts you above the dense forest and permits you to see where you have been and where you must head. It helps you form a frame, a flexible plan of order for your essay. It gives you a sense of proportion, of emphasis and of direction. Above all, it gives you a sense of control.

## The Sentence Outline

Using the invention notes in Chapter 2, page 34, a student writer, Peter Grantz, developed the following brief outline for a paper on smoking.

*Outlaw Smoking*

I. *Smoking is harmful.*

II. *Smokers suffer coronaries and lung cancer.*

III. *Nonsmokers suffer from passive smoking.*

IV. *Everyone will benefit from a smoking ban.*

Since this outline is in sentence form, its series of assertions gives us a clear idea of what Peter has in mind for the paper he is planning. It resembles the scratch outline we discussed earlier. For Peter, each sentence after the initial thesis idea "outlaw smoking" probably served as a reminder to him of what he had already decided would be the main ideas of his paper. We, his readers, can only speculate at this stage about the facts, details, and evidence that have informed his beliefs. Each sentence in Roman numerals, then, has served as a signpost for Peter but would probably mystify any reader. This is of no concern to Peter, since his sentence outline was by design writer based.

## The More Formal Outline

Imagine now that Peter has produced an exploratory or "zero" draft of the paper on outlawing smoking and has decided, after examining it carefully, to throw it away, lest he become a prisoner of this exploratory sketch. With his readers' needs foremost in his mind, he prepares to write his working draft by constructing a fairly detailed, rather formal outline, like this:

```
OUTLAW SMOKING
   I. Introduction
      A. Personal connection with topic
      B. Thesis statement: outlaw smoking
  II. Why smoke
      A. For pleasure and status
      B. Ignore dangers
 III. Dangers real for smokers
      A. Medical evidence
         1. Coronaries
         2. Lung cancer
```

```
    B. Smokers' acknowledgment of danger
       1. Men
       2. Women
IV. Danger to nonsmokers
    A. Passive smoking
    B. Carbon-monoxide poisoning
 V. No escape for smokers or nonsmokers
    A. Need for nonsmoking areas
    B. Total ban most effective solution
```

Peter has carefully followed the accepted rules for outlining. He has a Roman numeral for each of his major points. He has both an *A* and a *B* for each of his secondary points, and for illustrative subcategories, Arabic numerals. When Peter earlier used a sentence outline, he made sure that each assertion was a full sentence. In constructing this more formal topic outline, he has consistently avoided full sentences. This more detailed outline should serve Peter well as he works on the next draft of his paper. Many students make an outline *after* they have completed their papers only because they are required to hand one in. An outline constructed after the fact will often highlight weaknesses in organization and suggest where additional information may be needed. We, however, recommend that you construct a detailed outline as a "living skeleton" of your next draft, before you start writing it.

## FROM EXPLORATORY DRAFT TO WORKING DRAFT

In this section, we describe and illustrate a variety of revision strategies to facilitate the production of the working draft. The scratch outline, the exploratory draft and its criteria questions, the thesis statement and the formal outline—all are interdependent functions of your overall planning. If they work well together, your working draft will benefit.

### ► WRITING ACTIVITY ◄

Go back and reexamine Susan's exploratory draft on second-hand clothes, using the criteria questions for evaluating an exploratory draft on pages 65 to 66 and the knowledge and skills you have acquired from your study of the thesis statement and outlining. Then write Susan a one-page letter of advice on how she might plan and execute her working draft. Specifically what should she include in a detailed outline of her paper? You might even add a second sheet showing your version of an outline for her working draft.

We thought you might find it interesting, after you had completed your letters to Susan, to see the actual outline she produced for her working draft.

Susan used a very formal method of outlining, with precise and elaborate subheadings.

```
SECOND-HAND CLOTHES
    I. Where the clothes come from
       A. who sells the used clothes to the store
          1. rich people
          2. students
          3. salesmen
       B. why people sell their clothes to the store
          1. want return on investment
             a. cocktail dress
             b. wool coat
          2. lost weight
          3. want fast cash
             a. Spring break
             b. money for books
          4. want to trade own clothes
   II. Why students should shop at second-hand clothes
       store
       A. save money
       B. fashion finds
          1. brand names
          2. unique
  III. Clothes express who you are
       A. social status
       B. age
       C. personality
          1. define interesting
          2. define character
```

## FROM WORKING DRAFT TO FINAL DRAFT

The outline is your tentative commitment to yourself about the direction of your working draft. It is important to view the working draft as a stage in a fluid process, as means rather than end. There is a sense of adventure in writing a working draft because, although the outline is suggesting quite specifically and in some detail the direction your paper should take, there is no telling where your language will lead you. Experienced writers often talk about their language compelling them to follow an unplanned lead. Sometimes they are delighted by the discoveries they make; just as often, a glimmer of an idea that appeared to have real potential for illuminating a paper will fade in the harsh glare of the working text in progress.

The working draft is your attempt to explore all the possibilities embedded in the outline. It is the place where you can see your concept laid out before you, where you can discover its strengths and weakness. The working draft is an invitation to you to revise, recast, reconceptualize. You may need more than one draft at this stage in the writing process to work out your concept so that you can say, "Yes, I'm getting close to where I want to be."

To decide what changes you'll need to make to arrive at the final draft, you need to enter into a dialogue with yourself in your writer's mind. You need to use the objective third eye you have been training, the eye that examines your paper as an intelligent, committed, concerned reader would.

Although we have used PACES as the organizing principle of the criteria questions that follow, it is important to remember that none of the five components is more important than any of the others and that it is the *interaction* of these components, how they influence and are influenced by each other, that is at the heart of successful drafting and revising.

Before you actually use the set of detailed criteria questions below, it is important to approach the task of revising a working draft into a final draft with a set of carefully ordered *priorities*. Most inexperienced writers view the final draft as a sanitized version of the "rough" draft. They are convinced that if you clean up errors in mechanics and usage, spelling and punctuation, change a few words, rewrite a sentence or two, the final draft will be complete. Moving from working to final draft should entail much more than these fairly minor operations within the writer's code. Your revision of the working draft should concern itself with the large, global matters that encompass all of PACES.

Feel free to use these questions in any order you please. The constraints of the paper you are working on will no doubt suggest to you an appropriate sequencing of these criteria questions.

## CRITERIA QUESTIONS: REVISING A WORKING DRAFT INTO A FINAL DRAFT

### [P]urpose

1. What is your overall purpose in this paper?
2. What is the unifying principle of your paper?
3. What main idea or dominant impression are you trying to establish?

4. What are your *true* motives? What other motives might also be influencing you in positive and negative ways? Do you want to entertain your readers or to impress them?
5. What specific changes should you make in this working draft in order to produce a final draft that will achieve your overall purpose?

**Audience**

1. Is your audience the general reader found in a college setting? Are they undergraduates like you? Are you your own exclusive audience?
2. If the audience consists of other people, what do you know about them as individuals or as members of a group? What do they know about you?
3. Will your audience be influenced more by emotion than by cold fact?
4. What do they know about your topic and how do they feel about it? Will they agree with your point of view?
5. Should you adapt yourself to the audience or have them accept you as you are?
6. Does this working draft handle the audience with skill and sensitivity?

**Code**

1. Since code deals with form and language and strategies of development, what elements of code are you focusing on to revise your working draft? Which elements are you postponing dealing with until the proofreading stage of the final draft?
2. How is your draft organized? Can the organization be improved?
3. What strategies of development (comparison, contrast, analogy, simile, metaphor, definition, classification, description, and so on) have you used to elaborate on the points you want to make? Do any of your ideas lend themselves to being developed by these strategies? (See Chapter Four for a detailed treatment of some of these strategies of thinking and development.)
4. Are the paragraphs well constructed and coherent? Which of them should be rewritten? Redesigned?
5. Does each paragraph support your overall purpose? Should any of the paragraphs be deleted? Expanded?
6. What kind of introduction have you used? Will the introduction of the draft work for your readers? What other methods of intro-

ducing your draft have you considered? (For detailed suggestions about and examples of introductory paragraphs, see Chapter 12.)

7. Can you think of a more effective conclusion? (For detailed suggestions about and samples of concluding paragraphs, see Chapter 12.)
8. Is your style appropriate to the aims of your paper? Have you captured the appropriate tone? Is your language too informal? Too formal?
9. Does each sentence clearly convey what you have to say? Will your sentences maintain your reader's interest?
10. Should any of your sentences be deleted? Rearranged? Substituted for? Expanded?
11. What words in your draft lack precision? Can you make them more effective?

**E xperience**

1. Have you used all the resources of your experience? Does your draft reflect a thorough enough exploration of this experience—every instant of your life? Have you energetically used your powers of memory, observation, and imagination?
2. Have you researched your subject, where appropriate, in the community and in the library?
3. Does your draft have enough facts, details, and reasons to convince your readers of the truth of your position?
4. What other evidence or support might prove useful?
5. Is your topic worth writing about? Reading about?
6. Are your ideas clear?

**S elf**

1. From among the many selves that make up your personality, have you chosen an appropriate persona, one that reinforces the overall purpose of your paper?
2. Where in your draft, if anywhere, have you failed to project the writing personality you desire? How can you adjust this draft to produce an appropriate self?
3. Is your writing personality lively enough? Serious enough? Too stiff and formal? Confident? Arrogant?
4. What specific adjustments, usually at the level of sentence and phrase, will make readers more sympathetic to the self you are projecting?

## Proofreading the Final Draft

When you have satisfactorily dealt with the important components of your final draft, then, and only then, should you proofread your paper with great care. If your paper is an accurate reflection of you and your view of the world, only you could have planned, drafted, and revised it as you did. Proofreading, we like to say, can be done by strangers. But since it is difficult to locate people who know enough about edited written English and care enough to revise with sufficient care any errors you may have made in your papers, we recommend that, after letting the final draft cool for at least a day or so, you spend at least fifteen to twenty minutes searching for and correcting your own errors. Readers will appreciate your presenting them with your best proofread effort.

At the end of Chapter Two our case study subject, Todd, had just completed his planning notes and focused freewrite for the prospective paper on cross-country skiing. We strongly recommend that you turn back to Chapter Two and reread pages 49 to 57 to remind yourself of Todd's experiences as he worked on the process of discovery and preliminary planning for his paper. We now examine how Todd proceeds with his paper from exploratory through final draft. A careful examination of Todd's writer's mind at work should help you develop your own approach to the composing process.

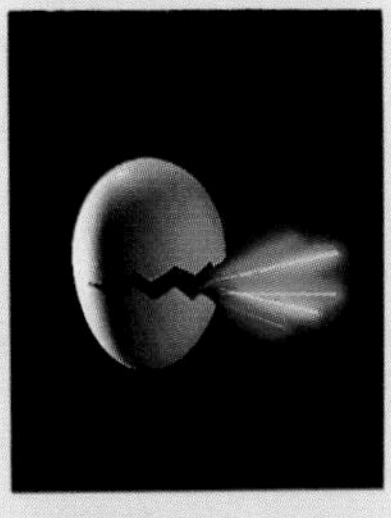

# THE WRITER'S MIND AT WORK

## FROM EXPLORATORY TO FINAL DRAFT

In his planning notes (Chapter Two, pages 49 to 57) for his paper on cross-country skiing, Todd had done much toward finding his own angle into his general topic. Yet before he actually took the step of drafting, Todd decided to think more carefully about just what he wanted to accomplish in his paper. He wanted to articulate for himself a concrete thesis that would bind into a coherent whole all the ideas in his paper. Todd waited for a day after he wrote his planning notes, then returned to these notes with a fresh attitude. Todd decided to think in terms of PACES to help him formulate an effective thesis statement.

### THE WRITER'S MIND: Asking Criteria Questions

Purpose: *What do I want to do in this paper? Well, I want to introduce more people to the joys of cross-country skiing, at least as well as I can on paper. I think many people think x-country skiing is boring because when they think of skiing they think of glamorous downhill skiing. I want to dispel these possible prejudices people might have against x-country skiing.*

Audience: *Who am I writing to? Well, I guess I'm writing for those people who are not very familiar with cross-country skiing. I'm guessing that the notion of downhill skiing will get in their way of imagining cross-country skiing so I'll have to take this into account. I'll rely on their knowledge of downhill skiing.*

Code: *Well, I want to be, like I said in my planning notes, a little poetical when I describe x-country skiing itself. I'm afraid I'll have to use some technical terminology when I describe some of the differences between the equipment of downhill skiing and x-country skiing. As far as the actual organization of the paper, maybe I'll try a quick scratch outline, describe how downhill skiing is not as good as x-country skiing, then maybe show the technical differences between equipment, then describe the joys of cross-country skiing (hopefully I'll have gotten downhill skiing out of the way), the dangers of cross-country skiing (after all, you* can *get hurt if you're not careful), then I might end up with restating the joys of x-country skiing (I don't want to scare people off).*

Experience: *Well, I guess I'm pretty much of an "expert"—I'll rely on my own personal experience of both downhill and cross-country skiing—both the outfitting and the practice. I'll also count on the audience's knowledge of downhill skiing, perhaps through their own practice, certainly through television and advertisements.*

Self: *I like both sports but I'm more partial to x-country skiing—I just like the wonderful feeling of relaxation you can get floating over the snow—I don't like the hassles involved in downhill skiing. I'm hoping that through describing my own attitude toward cross-country skiing, I'll be able to get some of my readers to feel the same way I do.*

Thesis Statement: *Well, I guess it's pretty clear. "Despite popular opinion, cross-country skiing is more fulfilling than downhill skiing." It really is!*

By using PACES, Todd was able to get a clearer sense of what he wanted to do in his paper. He was able to articulate a concrete thesis statement, which will help to guide him steadily as he develops the exploratory draft of his paper on cross-country skiing. By considering such things as purpose, audience, code, experience, and self, Todd was able to get a more vivid sense of how he might construct this exploratory draft. His scratch outline is enough to give Todd a sense of where to begin his paper and how to proceed, but it is not so rigid or prescriptive that it will prevent him from discovering new, possibly more effective, ways of organizing his material *as* he writes the exploratory draft.

After generating material and planning how that material might be organized in a draft, and after articulating a concrete thesis and considering the subject in terms of PACES, Todd was eager to produce an actual draft, to create a work for another reader. Todd found a comfortable, quiet spot to work in, read over all his notes carefully, and produced the following exploratory draft.

## EXPLORATORY DRAFT: Cross-Country Skiing

When most people think of skiing, they probably imagine somebody zooming down the side of a mountain, holding two pointed sticks, with his feet stuck to two fiberglass slats, surrounded by a sea of other people doing the same. They may recall a popular media image of the daredevil racer whizzing around flagged sticks stuck in the snow, his mouth set in a confident sneer of exhilaration. Skiing is associated by many with the glamorous notion of gliding down a hill. Yet there are other aspects of downhill skiing which are not so glamorous: long lines of people waiting to be ferried back up the mountain, overcrowded slopes on which the skier must concentrate always on avoiding collision with others. There is, however, another way of enjoying the feeling of floating over the snow, a way which gets around all the hassles of downhill skiing. For me, cross-country skiing is the only way.

Some people believe that cross-country skiing is dull and boring, that you can't go very fast shuffling yourself over the snow. This would be true if you used downhill skis to travel cross-country. Although both downhill skiing and cross-country skiing require skis, boots, and poles, there are a number of basic differences between this equipment. Downhill ski boots cover the entire foot and ankle and are attached to the ski at both the heel and toe, allowing the skier more easily to control the lateral movement of the skis but not allowing him to push himself very far forward on a flat surface. Cross-country ski boots, on the other hand, usually extend only to the top of the ankle and are attached to the ski only at the toe. This arrangement allows the cross-country skier to lift his heel entirely from the ski as he moves along. The cross-country skier can easily propel himself forward by kicking his heel off the ski and leaning forward. Any loss of lateral control compared to the downhill skier is more than compensated by the cross-country skier's increased ability to thrust himself forward. Also, cross-country skis are narrower and lighter than downhill skis, making it that much easier for the cross-country skier to ski up small hills. Even though cross-country skiers can't travel as fast as downhill skiers, still the nature of their equipment allows them to outdistance easily even the fastest of joggers.

Cross-country skiing can be an especially relaxing sport. Away from all the crowds and all the waiting in long lift lines, all you need to cross-country ski is skis, poles, boots, a snow filled trail . . . and you're off. You start out on an old logging road which creeps into the woods, the snow packed into a firm track by the snow-mobiles which have thoughtfully broken trail for you. You fall into a rhythm: kick off with one foot, push off with the pole, glide . . . kick off with the other foot, push off with the other pole, glide. It's like a cross between skating and jogging, only your toes never leave your skis and your skis never leave the snow. Once you've established your rhythm, you can easily glide over small hills without any great effort. The continuing rhythm--kick, push, glide-kick, push, glide--soothes the mind while it offers great aerobic exercise for your body. As you freely slide your waxed skis over the snow, you soon begin to feel as if your skis are a part of your feet and your poles a part of your arms; your body begins to operate as one fluid mechanism, alternately propelling itself forward, and then passively gliding along.

Steep inclines and declines, of course, offer somewhat of a problem to all but the most experienced of cross-country skiers. Short inclines a skier can usually side step up--larger ones may require the skier actually to take off his skis and carry them up. Declines are tricky for cross-country skiers in a way they aren't for downhill skiers. Since cross-country ski boots are attached to the ski only at the toe, it's very difficult for a cross-country skier to quickly and sharply move from side to side--it's much easier for a cross-country skier to go straight. So unless the cross-country skier has excellent balance and unless there is an amply flat and long "runway" at the bottom of the hill, the cross-country skier often ends up walking down steep hills as well as up them. Yet as you become more and more at ease with cross-country skiing, even going up and down steep hills can become a natural part of your overall rhythm.

All in all, cross-country skiing is the best way to float over the snow. The rhythm of cross-country skiing allows a concentration and a relaxation that you just can't get with downhill skiing, with its crowded slopes and its jammed lift lines. With cross-country skiing you don't have to be concerned about being carted around; you do all the carting yourself. Cross-country is the only way to ski.

After writing the exploratory draft and then reading it back to himself, Todd was fairly pleased with his work. He knew he had to make some changes, perhaps even some major changes, before he would be fully satisfied with the paper, but on his first rereading, Todd felt that his draft fairly successfully captured much of what he wanted to communicate about cross-country skiing.

After reading his exploratory draft with the "Criteria Questions for Revising the Exploratory Draft" in mind, Todd felt good about some parts of his draft but a little uneasy about others. He had an interesting subject and quite a few strong specific details about this subject. But he was concerned about the focus of the draft. He had wanted to write essentially about cross-country skiing, yet, in the first draft, he had devoted quite a bit of attention to downhill skiing. In his planning notes, Todd had felt that he needed to spend time in his paper distinguishing between downhill and cross-country skiing, but as he reread the first draft of his paper, he was less confident about this decision. He decided to collect some other reactions to this first draft.

Although it is not absolutely necessary to do so, we encourage you to get other readers' reactions to your drafts. Reading their reactions will introduce you to different perspectives on a piece of writing. Try to get your readers to be honest with you. Insincere flattery may delude you into thinking your paper is stronger than it actually is. Especially at the beginning of a writing course, encourage your readers to provide you with a 50–50 balance of positive and negative comments. Knowing what is working in a draft is at least as important as knowing what is not working. For various reasons, readers will misread your paper and give you advice that is either wrongheaded or not very useful. Your job as author is to spot poor advisers and find those who are energetic and committed. Rejecting a reader's advice often proves constructive, since the rejection itself forces you to justify your decision.

Todd gave copies of his exploratory draft to two friends, Alfred and Margaret, who made the following comments:

## EXPLORATORY DRAFT WITH PEER COMMENTS: Cross-Country Skiing

When most people think of skiing, they probably imagine somebody zooming down the side of a mountain, holding
a. two pointed sticks, with his feet stuck to two fiberglass slats, surrounded by a sea of other people doing the same. They may recall a popular media image of the daredevil racer whizzing around flagged sticks stuck in the snow, 1.
his mouth set in a confident sneer of exhilaration. Skiing is associated by many with the glamorous notion of gliding down a hill. Yet there are other aspects of downhill skiing which are not so glamorous: long lines of people waiting to be ferried back up the mountain, overcrowded slopes on which the skier must concentrate always on avoiding collision with others. There is, however, another way of enjoying the feeling of floating over the snow, a way
B. which gets around all the hassles of downhill skiing. For me, cross-country skiing is the only way.

Some people believe that cross-country skiing is dull and boring, that you can't go very fast shuffling yourself over the snow. This would be true if you used downhill skis to travel cross-country. Although both downhill skiing and cross-country skiing require skis, boots, and poles, there are a number of basic differences between
C. this equipment. Downhill ski boots cover the entire foot 2.
and ankle and are attached to the ski at both the heel and toe, allowing the skier more easily to control the lateral movement of the skis but not allowing him to push himself very far forward on a flat surface. Cross-country ski boots, on the other hand, usually extend only to the top of the ankle and are attached to the ski only at the toe. This arrangement allows the cross-country skier to lift his heel entirely from the ski as he moves along. The cross-country skier can easily propel himself forward by

**Reader:** *Alfred*
**Author:** *Todd*
**Date:** *October 10*
**Paper:** *"Cross-country Skiing"*

A. Nice opening image.

B. I think you should define Cross-Country skiing here. Just what is it?

C. Your focus on equipment becomes somewhat boring here. Equipment isn't the most exciting aspect of skiing. I'd like to hear more about skiing itself.

D. Good description of feelings as you ski. You might add even more sensory details. Where are you? What do you see? What do you hear?

E. Again great details. But what are you feeling here? I think you focus too much here just on the abstract process of cross-country skiing.

**Reader:** *Margaret*
**Author:** *Todd*
**Date:** *October 10*
**Paper:** *"Cross-country Skiing"*

1. I'm not sure about comparing downhill to cross-country skiing. To me they are very different sports with different purposes and participants.
2. I'm not sure that such a detailed description of equipment is so effective here. This technical stuff isn't very interesting compared to your description on the next page.
3. I like your description of cross-country skiing here! I can really visualize you doing all this.
4. I'm still not sure what your purpose is in this paper. What do you want to tell us about cross-country skiing?

kicking his heel off the ski and leaning forward. Any loss of lateral control compared to the downhill skier is more than compensated by the cross-country skier's increased ability to thrust himself forward. Also, cross-country skis are narrower and lighter than downhill skis, making it that much easier for the cross-country skier to ski up small hills. Even though cross-country skiers can't travel as fast as downhill skiers, still the nature of their equipment allows them to outdistance easily even the fastest of joggers.

Cross-country skiing can be an especially relaxing sport. Away from all the crowds and all the waiting in long lift lines, all you need to cross country ski is skis, poles, boots, a snow filled trail . . . and you're off. You start out on an old logging road which creeps into the woods, the snow packed inside a firm track by the snow-mobiles which have thoughtfully broken trail for you. You fall into a rhythm: kick off with one foot, push off with the pole, glide . . . kick off with the other foot, push off with the other pole, glide. It's like a cross between skating and jogging, only your toes never leave your skis and your skis never leave the snow. Once you've established your rhythm, you can easily glide over small hills without any great effort. The continuing rhythm-kick, push, glide--kick, push, glide-soothes the mind while it offers great aerobic exercise for your body. As you freely slide your waxed skis over the snow, you soon begin to feel as if your skis are a part of your feet and your poles a part of your arms; your body begins to operate as one fluid mechanism, alternately propelling itself forward, and then passively gliding along.

Steep inclines and declines, of course, offer somewhat of a problem to all but the most experienced of cross country skiers. Short inclines a skier can usually side step up--larger ones may require the skier actually to

take off his skis and carry them up. Declines are tricky for cross-country skiers in a way they aren't for downhill skiers. Since cross country ski boots are attached to the ski only at the toe, it's very difficult for a cross country skier to quickly and sharply move from side to side--it's much easier for a cross country skier to go straight.
E. So unless the cross-country skier has excellent balance and unless there is an amply flat and long "runway" at the bottom of the hill, the cross country skier often ends up walking down steep hills as well as up them. Yet as you become more and more at ease with cross-country skiing, even going up and down step hills can become a natural part of your overall rhythm.

All in all, cross country skiing is the best way to float over the snow. The rhythm of cross country skiing allows a concentration and a relaxation that you just 4.
can't get with downhill skiing, with its crowded slopes and its jammed lift lines. With cross country skiing you don't have to be concerned about being carted around; you do all the carting yourself. Cross country is the only way to ski.

After considering Alfred and Margaret's comments on his exploratory draft and carefully rereading this draft, Todd decided to make some major changes. To help him more clearly decide and articulate what he might keep and what he might change from the first draft, Todd jotted down the following.

### THE WRITER'S MIND: Replanning "Cross-Country Skiing"

*I think maybe I'm making too much of the differences between downhill skiing and cross-country skiing. After all, so what about the differences between the two sports? Big deal—what I really want to do is to show the unique pleasures of cross-country skiing. I think in my first draft I get way too bogged down in my comparison and contrast. I definitely spend too much time contrasting the equipment. I mean who really cares about bindings and boots and all that? That stuff may be important, but I don't want to make it the main focus of my paper.*

*The description in the third paragraph of the first draft is more what I think I'm really after—I don't need to totally eliminate the contrasts between downhill skiing and X-country skiing, but I don't want to make that the focal point of my paper.*

*I think I'll begin with a description of a cross-country skier in the woods and describe the scene around him—the smell of the pines, the crunch of the densely packed snow, the chattering of the birds, the sound of the water in the stream moving under the ice—that's what I need—that's what makes cross-country skiing enjoyable—THEN I can maybe move into the actual process of X-country skiing—the rhythm—how the rhythm (kick with the foot, push with the pole, glide—yeah, that's it)—the rhythm is what's special about cross-country skiing.*

*THEN describe the equipment—the special bindings and boots (maybe here throw in a SHORT contrast with downhill skiing—but keep it short!)*

*How about the business about the inclines and declines? That's important because it's not just the skier's movement alone that makes cross-country skiing. It's also the type of track you're skiing on. This is important in x-country skiing but I don't like the way I've handled it in the first draft—there I just talk about up and down. But there's more to the terrain than that.*

*Such as—wide trails through fields*
*foot bridges over streams*
*narrow, winding trails through the woods*

*It's not merely up and down. I need to spend more time on this part—to describe how the skier adapts to his terrain.*

*Also I want to emphasize the peace of mind that comes with X-country skiing—the relaxing feeling when you put your body on "auto pilot" and let the rhythm take over. THAT'S what cross-country skiing is all about. That great feeling of release.*

Todd realized that the new emphasis of his paper required a modification of his thesis. He needed to refocus his attention more exclusively on cross-country skiing itself. Instead of saying "Despite popular opinion, cross-country skiing is more fulfilling than downhill skiing," Todd modified his thesis statement to read "Cross-country skiing is the most rewarding activity you can do." This restatement of his thesis helped Todd decide what to keep and what to change in working on the next draft. Ready to recast his paper, Todd again found a quiet, comfortable place, read through his first draft and his replanning notes, and produced the following draft:

**WORKING DRAFT:**
**Cross-Country Skiing**

The skier quietly skis deeper and deeper into the woods. The crisp morning air whips against his face, bringing a dark red to his cheeks, but the heat his moving body generates keeps him comfortably warm even though he is not clothed very warmly. He puts his poles into the white powder. He moves his arms back and forth, and pushes his skis over the trail the snowmobiles have left behind. A quiet pervades the forest. The quiet seems even more intense because of the occasional chirping of birds. The skier's skis make a crunching sound as they move over the hard snow of the track. Away from the noise and bustle of the city, the cross-country skier enjoys a feeling to be found in no other activity. Cross-country skiing over a forest trail is undoubtedly one of the most rewarding of sports. It not only exercises the body, but it also relaxes the mind.

The rhythm of the skier makes cross-country skiing truly unique among sports. Many other sports involve jerky or sporadic movements. Cross-country skiing, however, depends on one fluid movement. You kick off with one foot, push off with the pole . . . and glide. Kick off with the other foot, push off with the other pole . . . and glide. The movement is like a cross between skating and jogging, only your toes never leave your skis and your skis never leave the snow. Unlike downhill skis, which are attached to both the boot's heel and toe, cross-country skis are attached only to the toe of the ski boot. This lets the skier easily move his foot and lift his heel entirely off of the ski. The cross-country skier can therefore thrust himself forward by kicking the back of his foot from off the ski, just as a jogger pushes his foot from the ground.

Unlike the jogger, however, the cross-country skier gets to relax and enjoy each kick forward. For kicking and pushing are only a part of the rhythm--after the vigorous thrust forward comes the easy glide. The slide of course depends on the force of the thrust forward. Thus the more the skier exerts himself, the more he can relax. Once the skier has established a smooth rhythm and a brisk pace, he becomes both the horse drawing the sleigh and the sleigh rider.

The terrain is another important factor in the rhythm of the cross-country skier. The skier usually has a perfectly flat surface for only a part of the trail—other parts are not so flat. The frequent ups and downs of the trail he usually encounters forces the cross country skier continually to adjust his rhythm. He has to be very careful in zipping down hills. He has to go a lot slower when he comes across trees. He has to watch out when he accelerates across flat fields. Yet these adjustments to the terrain may become an almost purely physical matter for the skier once he has gotten into his rhythm. His skis become a part of his feet. For the rhythm of the experienced cross country skier may seldom ever be broken. The kicking, pushing, and gliding may differ with the surface feature of the trail. However, the basic rhythm itself remains the same.

Curiously the physical senses become heightened, not dulled, as the skier builds up and falls into his rhythm. The eye picks up everything: the squirrel perched on the highest limb of the bare oak tree, the white-furred rabbit barely distinguishable from the snow. Over the sound of the movement of the skis, the ear is able to hear pine boughs rustling in the breeze, snow sliding off them as the sun climbs higher in the sky, and the muffled rumbling of water flowing under the frozen-over stream. The cross-country skier is able to experience much more than his own body moving through the woods. The rhythm of the cross-country skier allows him to get great aerobic exercise without focusing exclusively on his own physical movement. On the contrary, once the skier falls into his rhythm, he is able to feel himself as almost a part of the scenery, to let his mind range over whatever he wishes. Away from the crowd, the cross-country skier can relax his mind while he gives his body a great workout.

After completing the working draft of the cross-country skiing paper, Todd felt much better about his accomplishment. He felt that this draft much more successfully captured what he felt are the joys of cross-country skiing. Yet Todd realized that the paper might still be improved. To decide what he might do to improve this new draft, Todd examined the list of criteria for the working draft of a paper on pages 75 to 77 and then produced the following final draft:

**FINAL DRAFT:**
**"Floating Over the Snow"**

Floating peacefully over the snow, the skier quietly delves deeper and deeper into the woods. The crisp morning air whips against his face, turning his cheeks a dark red, but the heat his moving body generates keeps him comfortably warm despite his light clothing. He digs his poles into the white powder, arms pumping back and forth, and lightly shuffles his skis over the densely packed trail left by the snowmobiles. The scent of pine needles fills the air. A solemn quiet pervades the forest, a quiet intensified by the occasional chattering of a blue-jay or a "chick-a-dee-dee-dee," and constantly underscored by the smooth crunch of skis gliding across the crystallized snow of the track. Away from the noise and bustle of the city, alone in the serene setting of the woods in winter, the cross-country skier enjoys a feeling to be found in no other activity. Cross-country skiing over a forest trail is undoubtedly one of the most rewarding of sports, one which not only exercises the body but also relaxes the mind.

The skier's rhythm makes cross-country skiing truly unique among sports. Many other sports involve jerky or sporadic movements, constant starting and stopping, jumping up and down, shuffling back and forth. Cross-country skiing, however, involves one fluid, continuing pattern of movement. You kick off with one foot, push off with the pole . . . and glide. Kick off with the other foot, push off with the other pole . . . and glide. The movement is like a combination of skating and jogging, only your toes never leave your skis and your skis never leave the snow. Unlike downhill skis, which are attached to both the ski boot's heel and toe, cross-country skis are attached only to the toe of the ski boot, allowing the skier easily to flex his foot and to lift his heel entirely from the ski. The cross-country skier can therefore thrust himself forward by kicking the back of his foot from off the ski, just as a jogger pushes his foot from the ground.

Unlike the jogger, however, the cross-country skier for a long moment gets to relax and enjoy the force of each kick forward. For kicking and pushing are only half of the skier's rhythm--after the vigorous thrust forward comes the easy glide. The harder the skier kicks his foot and pushes his pole, the longer and faster is each glide forward. Thus the more the skier exerts himself, propelling himself forward, the more he can relax and glide, experiencing the wonderful sensation of floating over the snow. Once the skier has established a smooth rhythm and a brisk pace, he becomes both the horse drawing the sleigh and the sleigh rider--both creating and enjoying the energy moving him over the snow.

There is one other important factor determining the rhythm of the cross-country skier: the terrain. Very seldom does the cross-country skier encounter nothing but flat surface; often a woods trail will lead up and down hills, over footbridges, through fields, across frozen-over ponds and bogs. The frequent inclines and declines and narrow windings of the trail he usually encounters force the cross-country skier continually to adjust his rhythm, causing him to increase his thrust up slopes, to exercise great caution in zipping down hills, to slow down as he engages sharp curves around trees, to accelerate across flat fields. Yet for the experienced skier these adjustments to the terrain may become an almost purely physical, mechanical concern once he has gotten into his rhythm; as his body begins to operate as one fluid mechanism, he doesn't need to concentrate consciously on the features of the terrain before him. His skis become an almost integral part of his feet, virtually adjusting themselves to the terrain of their own accord. For the rhythm of the experienced cross-country skier may seldom ever be broken. The relative proportion of kick, push, glide may differ with the surface feature of the trail, but the basic rhythm itself, the essence of cross-country skiing, remains the same.

Curiously the physical senses become heightened, not dulled, as the skier builds up and falls into the rhythm. The eye picks up everything: the squirrel perched on the highest limb of the bare oak tree, the white-furred rabbit barely distinguishable from the white powder in the fields, the thin blades of dried up grass jutting here and there through the two foot deep blanket of snow. Over the "shush-shush" of the skis sliding over the snow, the ear is able to detect pine boughs rustling in the breeze, snow sliding off them as the sun climbs higher in the sky, and the muffled rumbling of water flowing under the frozen over stream. The cross-country skier is able to experience much more than his own body moving through the woods. The rhythm of the cross-country skier allows him to get great aerobic exercise without focusing exclusively on his own physical movement. On the contrary, once the skier falls into his rhythm, he is able to feel himself as almost a part of the scenery, to let his mind range over whatever he wishes. Away from the crowd, dependent only upon himself for the enjoyment of his sport, the cross-country skier can relax his mind while he gives his body a great workout, floating over the snow.

The overall structure of the final draft is very similar to that of the working draft; both drafts of Todd's paper have nearly identical content and focus. Yet the prose style, the actual development and articulation of sentences and paragraphs, Todd's handling of the writer's code, is in many respects quite different. The style of the final draft is considerably more refined and eloquent than that of the working draft. We can point to several kinds of stylistic revisions Todd incorporated into the final draft:

*Verbs*: Todd relies fairly heavily on general verbs such as "moves" and "pushes" in his second draft. In his third draft, Todd uses more descriptive and colorful verbs. For instance, "he moves his arms back and forth" in the second draft becomes "arms pumping back and forth" in the third draft; "pushes his skis" is revised as "lightly shuffles his skis." The more concrete verbs of the third draft help provide the reader with a more vivid portrait of the cross-country skier in action.

*Details and Examples*: In the third draft, Todd gives the reader more concrete details supporting images he wants to create and points he wishes to make. For instance, whereas in the first draft Todd tells us that other sports "involve jerky or sporadic movements," in the third draft Todd explains just what kinds of movements he means by providing examples ("constant starting and stopping, jumping up and down, shuffling back and forth"). Whereas in the second draft Todd tells us that the skier will encounter more than flat surfaces, in the third draft Todd *shows* us exactly what other kinds of terrain the skier may expect to encounter (e.g., woods, trails, footbridges, frozen ponds). The additional graphic details in the third draft give the reader a fuller sense of cross-country skiing.

*General fluency*: Several of Todd's sentences in his second draft are a bit awkward. For instance, in his second draft, Todd writes, "A quiet pervades the forest. The quiet seems even more intense because of the occasional chirping of birds. The skier's skis make a crunching sound as they move over the hard snow." In the third draft, Todd conveys the same essential information in a smoother, more fluent manner: "A solemn quiet pervades the forest, a quiet intensified by the occasional chattering of a blue jay or a 'chick-a-dee-dee-dee,' and constantly underscored by the smooth crunch of skis gliding across the crystallized snow of the track."

What other examples of stylistic revision can you point to in Todd's third draft?

In the next chapter, "Strategies of Thinking, Strategies of Development," you will examine many different examples of the various strategies writers use to elaborate their ideas. Before we move to this challenging area of the writing process, we would like to remind you of the anecdote we related in Chapter One about Donald Murray, a Pulitzer Prize–winning author, who suggested that writing is an almost endless series of revisions—"Writing is re-re-re-rewriting." Gustave Flaubert, one of the greatest writers of all time, obviously believed in this dictum, too: He took ten years to plan, write, and revise his novel *Madame Bovary*. We are not suggesting, however, that you should spend inordinately large chunks of time working on your paper. Indeed, you will have to commit a great deal of time to most papers, but it is the quality of your effort, not the quantity, that will determine your success as a writer. If you commit yourself to the process of discovery, planning, drafting, and revising we have covered in Chapters Two and Three, we are confident that you and your audience will usually enjoy reading what you have to say. Todd succeeded because he trusted himself and the writing process. We urge you to do so, too.

## ► WRITING ACTIVITY ◄

You'll remember that at the end of Chapter Two you selected a topic and began planning for an exploratory draft. Now go through the process Todd has just completed by

1. composing an exploratory draft on a topic you developed at the end of Chapter Two.
2. revising the exploratory draft by asking yourself the PACES questions on pages 65 to 66
3. developing a thesis statement
4. sketching an outline that will lead to a working draft
5. composing a working draft
6. revising your working draft into a final draft by checking the PACES questions on pages 75 to 77
7. proofreading your final draft

Remember that during the process of writing your drafts you'll want to

8. produce scripts of your writer's mind for your planning of each draft
9. have your peers respond to at least one of your drafts

# CHAPTER ▲ FOUR

# *Strategies of Development, Strategies of Thinking*

**"How can we know the dancer from the dance?"**

**WILLIAM BUTLER YEATS**

In this chapter we will examine, in some detail, the more important strategies of development used by experienced writers. We will see how they *compare, contrast, define, analyze* and *classify* at a variety of levels of discourse from the sentence, to the paragraph, to the entire essay. For the writer, the strategies of development function simultaneously as strategies of thinking. Writers use these strategies to discover and create their ideas for themselves as well as to develop them for their readers. These thinking strategies are not, of course, the exclusive preserve of writers: Thinking is as natural to humans as breathing, and even very young children can use their cognitive skills with facility and great skill.

We want you to take advantage of the wide experience you have had with comparison, contrast, definition, analysis, and classification in your everyday life. This chapter is designed to help you to refine, polish, and adapt these cognitive skills to the special demands of writing. Ideally, these developmental and cognitive strategies will eventually merge to enrich your writer's mind by furnishing it with a repertoire of practical choices as you work on your papers in every classroom across the curriculum and in the world you'll inhabit after you leave college.

## THINKING AND DEVELOPING: USING COMPARISON AND CONTRAST

The ability to compare and contrast one thing to another is a basic strategy in writing because it is a fundamentally important thinking skill. Reflecting upon similarities and dissimilarities between two or more objects, events, or ideas may lead a writer to significant discovery. Confronted with just one object, a writer can learn much through analysis: If you study the anatomy of a moth, you may discover something about how an insect flies. But if you compare and contrast the anatomy of a moth with that of a bird, you may note how dissimilar species of animals are equipped in startlingly different ways to perform essentially the same activity. In this case, comparison and contrast may lead to a fuller, more sophisticated understanding of what it means to "fly."

The strategy of comparison and contrast may also help you to consider a specific "fact" or observation from a useful, meaningful perspective. Discovering that someone fails to achieve a certain goal 60 percent of the time might lead us to conclude that this person is unsuccessful. If a student fails to pass his or her exams 60 percent of the time, he or she would be performing unsatisfactorily. Yet in major league baseball, a player who fails to get a hit *only* 60 percent of the time at bat is a phenomenal success; a .400 batting average is a great achievement. A player with such an average could command a high salary and would be a definite candidate for the baseball Hall of Fame. In fact, this achievement is so rare that the last player to bat over .400 was Ted Williams back in the 1940s. Even Hall of Famer Hank Aaron, who hit more home runs than any other player in major league history, was never able even to approach such a batting average. By contrasting a .400 batting average with the batting average of other major league players (whose collective average is well under .300) we can better appreciate just how successful is a 60 percent failure rate.

A writer may use comparison and contrast to create a context necessary to achieve a desired response from a reader. For instance, if in your writing, you wished to emphasize the enormity of one million American citizens, you might compare this number with the population of a fairly small U.S. city: "one million people—four times the population of Mobile, Alabama." Conversely, if you wished to make this *same* number of people seem relatively small, you might compare it with the number of people in the entire United States: "one million people—less than a quarter of a percent of the total U.S. population . . . ." Assertions such as "big," "small," "complex," "simple," "fast," and "slow," often become truly meaningful only when a writer constructs a contrastive context for them, one that clarifies their particular quality in a given situation by answering such questions as "How big?" or "How small?"

## ► READING ACTIVITY ◄

In his essay "The Two Faces of Vermont," Noel Perrin discusses an identity crisis within the state. Perrin argues that there are, in effect, two separate Vermonts. In the following passage, Perrin highlights one particular aspect of Vermont's confusion of identity. How does he dramatize this identity crisis?

> On the one hand, it's to the interest of everyone in the tourist trade to keep Vermont (their motels, ski resorts, chambers of commerce, etc., excepted) as old-fashioned as possible. After all, it's weathered red barns with shingle roofs the tourists want to photograph, not concrete-block barns with sheet aluminum on top. Ideally, from the tourist point of view, there should be a man and two boys inside, milking by hand, not a lot of milking machinery pumping directly into a bulk tank. Out back, someone should be turning a grindstone to sharpen an ax—making a last stand, so to speak, against the chainsaw.
>
> On the other hand, the average farmer can hardly wait to modernize. He wants a bulk tank, a couple of arc lights, an automated silo, and a new aluminum roof. Or in a sense he wants these things. Actually, he may like last-stand farming as well as any tourist does, but he can't make a living at it. In my town it's often said that a generation ago a man

could raise and educate three children on fifteen cows and still put a little money in the bank. Now his son can just barely keep going with 40 cows. With fifteen cows, hand-milking was possible, and conceivably even economic; with 40 you need all the machinery you can get. But the tourists don't want to hear it clank.

Perrin uses the strategy of comparison and contrast to illustrate the disparity between the two faces of Vermont, showing the differences between the native's and the tourist's perception of the state. Concentrating on the dairyfarmer's barn, Perrin, in the first paragraph, uses such colorful, vivid details as a shingled roof, a man and two boys milking cows by hand, and a person hand grinding an ax in order to evoke the tourist's view of Vermont as a quaint, old-fashioned place where custom is preserved. Using the same focal point of the barn, Perrin proceeds in the second paragraph to dramatize the conflict between the tourist's and the native's point of view, noting that the native dairy farmer wants to modernize the farm by adding an aluminum roof and pointing out that milking by hand is virtually inconceivable for a barn full of forty cows. Perrin places several particular elements of the tourist's and the native's view of Vermont side by side, graphically demonstrating how differently the same place is perceived by different groups of people. In two brief paragraphs, Perrin has effectively illustrated the dilemma in Vermont's identity by using the strategy of comparison and contrast.

## ► READING ACTIVITY ◄

In the following passage, Larry Bedesky, a student writer, shows the decline of one of the greatest boxers in sports history: Muhammad Ali. How does Bedesky use comparison and contrast to achieve this purpose?

### ALI THEN—AND NOW
**Larry Bedesky**

"That's it. It's over," trainer Angelo Dundee screamed to referee Richard Green as Muhammad Ali slumped on his stool in the corner of the boxing ring. Ali tried to lift his head to protest but was too weak to do so. Instead, he sat motionless, with horrible welts under both his half-shut eyes, a steady trickle of blood coming from his puffy nose, and every ounce of energy drained from his thirty-eight-year-old body. Ali, who had been heavyweight champion of the world three times, had just foolishly attempted to acquire the championship an unprecedented fourth time by taking on the thirty-one-year-old, 211-pound, and superbly conditioned current champion, Larry Holmes. The fight against Holmes was the final crack in the erosion of Muhammad Ali's career. Ali had been fighting an uphill battle to retain his skills ever since his third fight with Joe Frazier, appropriately called "the thrilla' in Manila," in October of

> 1975. The Frazier fight seemed to sap the last bit of greatness from Ali, and he was never the same awesome fighter afterwards.
>
> In his prime—from 1965 to 1967—and up until his third fight with Frazier, Ali needed motivation to produce greatness. When Ali seemed to be missing his punches or was less than expected, it was because of boredom and complacency. Ali claimed that he had trouble with lesser opponents like Rudi Lubbers, George Chuvalo, and Doug Jones because he had lacked the motivation, desire, and pressure to produce what he called "the real Muhammad Ali."
>
> But since the Frazier fight, Ali had experienced a steady decline. Today it is years—not boredom—which have taken away Muhammad Ali's skills. Ali trained vigorously for the Holmes fight, losing over thirty pounds, quite possibly too much weight loss, in preparing for the fight. Just months before the fight, Ali was a blubbery 256 pounds. His flabby arms and legs, a portly gut which protruded inches out and which sagged to below his waist, and graying hair gave Ali the appearance of an unemployed, Schlitz-loving, middle-aged man.

Bedesky illustrates the deterioration of Ali's boxing skills not by describing Ali's career in straightforward chronological order (a common technique used to indicate change over time), but by beginning with an extended, detailed description of the end of Ali's career. Bedesky first describes the beaten Ali, and then contrasts this with an image of Ali in his prime, the unbeatable young boxer of the 1960s. In the second and third paragraphs, Bedesky examines one way in which Ali in his prime differed from Ali at the end of his career. In his prime, when Ali was "less than expected," it was because he lacked motivation; his opponents did not provide him with a great enough challenge. At the conclusion of his career, however, Ali's aging physique fully explains his unimpressive performance. Bedesky alternates his focus between the young and the aging Ali; this immediate contrast gives his reader a more vivid sense of the deterioration of Ali's skills as a boxer.

## ► READING ACTIVITY ◄

The following is a passage from Laurence Shames's essay entitled "Champs," in which the author uses the examples of two different squash players to illustrate his conception of sportsmanship. How does the strategy Shames employs help him to achieve this goal?

> On an old squash team of mine, there were two guys—we'll call them Mutt and Jeff—who, while they were not dissimilar characters off the court, exhibited wildly contrasting behavior on the court and who, though they were roughly equal in ability, competed with strikingly different degrees of success.

> Mutt usually won—sometimes against opponents who looked like better athletes and who seemed far more intent on winning than Mutt was. Mutt played as hard as anybody, yet there was always at the heart of his effort a sort of amused relaxation, a casualness that tended to disconcert his do-or-die rivals. Watching Mutt smilingly dispatch opponents, applauding their good shots and ceding them all close calls, one came to a new understanding of the expression "killing with kindness."
>
> Jeff was another story. A sweetheart till you put a racket in his hand, Jeff would become—to put it bluntly—a bit of a jerk when the score was being kept. He'd become downright paranoid about the rules; in tough situations he actually seemed to be suffering out there. It didn't help that he usually lost—sometimes to players with less talent and who seemed to have far less at stake.

Shames uses comparison and contrast here to illustrate his view of sportsmanship. Shames shows us the great differences between the two players Mutt and Jeff: He first describes Mutt's behavior in one paragraph, giving us a brief but vivid profile of Mutt's good-natured attitude on the court, and he then proceeds to describe Jeff's poor sportsmanship in the next paragraph. By contrasting the behavior of the two different squash players, Shames is able to dramatize colorfully and effectively that the essence of the sport is to be found not necessarily in success on the court but in the attitude of the individual player. Indeed, Shames's examples even suggest that your attitude toward playing may actually contribute to your success in squash.

Note that Shames not only describes Mutt and Jeff in some detail, but he also explains to us the purpose of these descriptions. When you use comparison and contrast, detailed and graphic descriptions are necessary to show similarities or differences between two or more objects, events, or ideas. Your reader must also understand the point of your comparison or contrast.

In some comparison and contrast pieces, the author divides the events compared into discrete parts and compares each of them separately; in the Shames passage, the author employs a relatively extended description of one whole example followed by a similarly extended description of the other. However, in most long pieces that employ comparison and contrast, writers usually employ both of these patterns of development, approaching the objects, ideas, or events as complete wholes and as discrete parts. This pattern of development involves fairly sophisticated planning by the writer. And yet comparison of parts and wholes often is the most productive pattern of development because it allows you to discover insights about your subject at all levels.

Comparison and contrast should be employed only to develop a specific purpose the writer wishes to communicate. Your writer's mind should consider this strategy of development as a useful means to convey a point. Each of the writers we have briefly examined uses comparison and contrast to develop intriguing material. But more importantly, each writer uses comparison and contrast for a specific purpose.

## THINKING AND DEVELOPING: USING ANALOGY

One special type of comparison writers frequently use is the analogy: the imaginative substitution of one thing for another to make a particular point. We frequently use analogies as we communicate with one another. In fact, many of our most common idioms are based on analogies. Someone who is striving to excel in a competitive career is often said to be "climbing the ladder of success." Climbing a ladder obviously requires more effort than does walking; thus the image of the ladder suggests the great effort often required to succeed in a difficult career. The effectiveness of an analogy depends on the relationship between the image and what that image is meant to represent. Does it make sense to describe, for instance, a certain person's burst of anger as a "bomb exploding"? The writer's analogy will work only if the reader can perceive some meaningful connection between the image and the idea it symbolizes. An excessive use of time-worn clichés may, of course, signal to a reader that you have nothing new to say. But a truly creative, imaginative analogy may help to provide your reader with a more vivid, potent sense of the idea you wish to communicate.

### ► READING ACTIVITY ◄

The following is the concluding passage of Margaret Walker's essay "On Being Female, Black, and Free." What is Walker's point, and how does she use the strategy of analogy to communicate it?

> I am a black woman living in a male-oriented and male-dominated white world. Moreover, I live in an American Empire where the financial tentacles of the American Octopus in the business-banking world extend around the globe, with the multinationals and international conglomerates encircling everybody and impinging on the lives of every single soul. What then are my problems? They are the pressures of a sexist, racist, violent, and most materialistic society. In such a society life is cheap and expendable; honor is a rag to be scorned; and justice is violated. Vice and money control business, the judicial system, government, sports, entertainment, publishing, education, and the church. Every other arm of this hydra-headed monster must render lip service and yeoman support to extend, uphold, and perpetuate the syndicated world-system. The entire world of the press, whether broadcast or print journalism, must acquiesce and render service or be eliminated. And what have I to do with this? How do I operate? How long can I live under fear before I too am blown to bits and must crumble into anonymous dust and nonentity?

Walker perceives society as motivated primarily by material gain; she believes that the desire for money predominates over every other motive. Walker sees this abstract but pervasive power as a dehumaninizing influence in society. Her analogy of the octopus with its "financial tentacles . . . encircling everybody and impinging on the lives of every single soul" conveys a sharp sense of this materialism. The image of the "hydra-headed monster" seems designed to elicit disgust from her readers, a response that the more abstract phrase "materialistic society" cannot achieve by itself. Walker uses analogy here not only to provide her readers with a clearer intellecutal sense of the society she wishes to criticize, but also to bring about a particular emotional reaction, one that strongly supports her overall purpose.

## ► WRITING ACTIVITY ◄

Write a brief piece in which you use the strategy of comparison and contrast to achieve some purpose. Concentrate on the points of comparison or contrast of the two or more things you chose for your subject as well as on the purpose of your comparison or contrast. You might also use an appropriate analogy to emphasize a particular point you are comparing or contrasting.

## THINKING AND DEVELOPING: USING CLASSIFICATION

Classification is the means by which the mind groups experiences into types. The mind cannot handle very many unrelated ideas, objects, or events. It is necessary to find some pattern, some common property, in order to catalog many separate things into a smaller number of *types*. For example, we can discuss singers because we can classify singers as sopranos, tenors, basses, and so forth, and also as classical, rock, country, and a number of other things. Thus, classification is really a basic skill of analysis. This may seem perfectly obvious as long as you are talking about familiar subjects (like singers), but suppose you were talking about nonhuman singers. The high-pitched squeals, whistles, grunts, and clicks of the humpback whale are called songs. If you were faced with the job of analyzing whale singers you would see immediately how important it is to be able to group, sort, divide, and catalog these apparently random noises:

> When you go out to listen to a humpback sing, you may hear a whale soloist, or you may hear seeming duets, trios, or even choruses of dozens of interweaving voices. Each of these whales is singing the same song, yet none is actually in unison with the others—each is marching to its own drummer, so to speak.
>
> ROGER PAYNE, "Humpbacks: Their Mysterious Songs," *National Geographic*

There is nothing very obvious about the number of whales making noises, and it is no simple analysis to discover that each whale is singing the same song out of synchronization with the others. And there is nothing mechanical about the act of classifying. Classification is a creative analytical procedure. The close analysis of a group of distinct items may produce a concept that can govern them. A writer may be able to arrange these items into a meaningfully coherent set of categories by perceiving previously unseen similarities and dissimilarities between these items. The principle of classification a writer discovers (or "invents") is equivalent to an *idea* about the items. This strategy may be useful both in discovering and in developing an idea.

## ► READING ACTIVITY ◄

The following is a complete essay by student writer Patti Dewitt, entitled "Who Is an Alcoholic?" In what ways has Dewitt used classification to achieve her purpose in this essay?

### WHO IS AN ALCOHOLIC?
**Patti Dewitt**

Alcoholism isn't a very pretty subject to talk about. It makes some people uncomfortable and others angry. College students act like alcoholism is something that happens only to old people; some students refuse to talk about it. But some people want to know what the symptoms of alcoholism are or when do you "become" an alcoholic. There doesn't seem to be just one answer to this question; alcoholism seems to be very individualistic. From my work in the Crisis Center and from what I've observed with friends and relatives, I think there are too many individual variations to give a complete list, but if people can recognize the main types, they will be more able to tell whether a roommate or friend or relative is—or probably is—an alcoholic.

States thesis that there are many types of alcoholics, and understanding these types will help a person recognize if someone is an alcoholic.

The first type is simply the heavy drinker. Most people agree that two or three drinks of any kind should be the limit at a party: two or three glasses of wine, two or three mixed drinks, two or three glasses or cans of beer are the maximum for most people. And even then we are talking about occasional drinkers who drink once or twice a week. The heavy drinker usually has much more than two or three drinks and is likely to have them several times a week.

First type—the heavy drinker (examples).

There are basically two kinds of heavy drinkers: those who get very drunk and those who don't. We all know someone who can seemingly drink all night without becoming rowdy or unsteady or falling asleep. Sometimes these heavy drinkers appear sober even after they have enough to drink everybody else "under the table." Usually people admire this kind of alcoholic; they say things like "So-and-so can really hold his liquor." But So-and-so is usually the type who looks sober enough to drive, and he will fight anyone

Two kinds of heavy drinkers (examples).

who tries to stop him. I would say that many college students are this type. The other type of heavy drinker is easy to recognize; he or she is the one who gets noisy and may even fall down or pass out. People usually say, "There goes So-and-so, drunk again." While the heavy drinker obviously drinks more than the light drinker, he or she resents any suggestion of alcoholism. And since they may not drink "too much" every time, many people will say those drinkers are not alcoholics but just "heavy drinkers," people who "really like their liquor." At a college bar, these drinkers are usually the ones who make fools of themselves or start fights.

Second type—the binge drinker (examples).

A different kind of drinker is the "binge" drinker. This is someone who does not drink at all or who seems to be just a normal (light) drinker most of the time. But every now and then the binge drinker will "fall off the wagon" and drink very heavily for a night or a weekend or several days. Since binge drinkers can sometimes go for quite a while without a drink they are frequently thought to be nondrinkers. Or they may be thought to be not alcoholics because they can "stop" drinking. Sometimes the binge drinker can go on for surprisingly long periods without a drink, but sooner or later this kind of drinker goes off on a binge and usually drinks until he passes out. Often these drinkers are not thought of as having a drinking problem; instead they are said to be people who "shouldn't" drink because liquor "affects" them so badly. Often this kind of drinker is tolerated, depending on how often and how bad the binges are. "So-and-so is on a binge again" means the binge is a laughable thing because it will soon pass and then old So-and-so will be himself again. If the binges get very bad, the drinker may find himself in a crisis center or an alcoholic hospital. But since the binges wear themselves out, this kind of drinker is quickly "cured" and released. One thing that is common among binge drinkers is unexplained bumps and bruises. Drinkers who seem to have more than their share of black eyes and split lips may be binge drinkers, who usually do not stop drinking until they pass out. Almost all binge drinkers deny they are alcoholics and become very angry at the suggestion, because they only drink "now and then" and because "having a little too much to drink," they say, is something that can happen to anyone. Many binge drinkers, to avoid the charge of alcoholism, drink "only" beer and wine because they believe beer and wine are harmless social drinks and that "everybody" drinks beer and wine.

Third type—the habitual drinker (examples).

The most common type of alcoholic is the habitual drinker, someone who drinks every day. Some of these drinkers may be heavy drinkers; if more than two or three drinks is "heavy," then most of them are heavy drinkers. But they usually don't think of themselves as heavy drinkers, and they may not be seen as heavy drinkers by their friends (who are likely to be the same type of drinker). People who have a beer or cocktail for lunch and/or a couple of before-dinner drinks and/or wine with dinner and/or one or two after-dinner drinks will usually "explain" that the alcohol is "absorbed" or "diluted" by food, and so they insist that their drinks are not the same as an equal number of drinks served without food. Or they will explain that two drinks before dinner and two drinks after dinner don't add up to four drinks because they are "separated" by food. The exact number of drinks isn't as important as the fact that drinking has become habitual. A person who has "only" two martinis for lunch and two before dinner several hours later, but *every* day, is an alcoholic, even though not very much alcohol is involved. Such drinkers will usually get upset if they have to miss one of their drinks. They will select restaurants, motels, and even their friends, based on whether or not they can get drinks. (I have a friend who won't go to a restaurant if it doesn't serve drinks.) Many drinkers of this type begin thinking about "happy hour" before it arrives, and as the drinking hour gets closer they become more and more "thirsty." Since many drinkers fall into this category, few people are concerned about this kind of alcoholic. But at the Crisis Center many alcoholics say the habit grows and gets worse. The drinking hour comes earlier and earlier, the drinking "hours" increase (morning eye-openers, mid-day pick-me-ups, after-dinner drinks, nightcaps). Potentially, the habitual drinker faces as severe a drinking problem as any other kind of alcoholic.

Fourth type—the all-day drinker (examples).

Finally there is the all-day drinker. There is sometimes a line between the habitual drinker who is drinking frequently during the day and the all-day drinker; at least, many habitual drinkers like to think so. If there is a line, it is crossed when there are no longer any periods between drinks. The all-day drinker is the one most people think about when you say "alcoholic." They are the ones shown in movies: housewives at home drinking all day, businessmen and laborers either secretly or openly drinking on the job, and skid-row bums drinking out of paper bags. The all-day drinker starts drinking when he or she wakes up. The same way many people need several cups of coffee to start the day, these drinkers need several drinks. After this the drinks continue in about the same way that some people drink water or coffee all day. The all-day drinker is likely to be "tipsy" or "stoned" all day. A semisober state becomes their natural condition. People who don't know such drinkers are "high" get the impression that they are "strange" or "a little off balance." Oddly enough, these all-day drinkers can become so used to their alcoholic state that they are able to live and function for years in a semistupor without being very unusual looking to others. Of course, many of them end the day passing out in bed and many others end by ruining their lives. Even many of these obvious alcoholics will deny they are alcoholics since, according to them, their drinking doesn't interfere with their lives. Most parents would be shocked to find out how many college students are all-day drinkers. Every dormitory has at least one.

Concludes that alcoholics' drinking habits will likely fall into one of those four categories.

These four basic types—the heavy drinker, the binge drinker, the habitual drinker, and the all-day drinker—pretty well cover the alcoholics. Surprisingly few of them end up on skid row. Some of them don't even get "drunk" in the movie and television sense. We might conclude from this that practically anybody who drinks is an alcoholic, but this is not true. Those who are defensive about their drinking like to pretend that all nondrinkers or light drinkers are little old ladies who think anyone who has "a few beers"

> is an alcoholic. By this they mean it's natural and even "macho" or "sexy" to drink. But this classification of alcoholics doesn't mean everyone who drinks is an alcoholic. It only means those who regularly drink are alcoholics, those whose drinking falls into a recognizable pattern. One basic difference I have observed about the way alcoholics drink is how hard it is for them to change the pattern of their drinking. Heavy drinkers can't easily become light drinkers. Binge drinkers can't stop forever or break the routine of their binges. Habitual drinkers find it very hard to become occasional drinkers. If there is anything to be concluded from this classification it is probably just that once drinking becomes a habit, the habit takes over and becomes very difficult to change.

Many of us have some general understanding of what alcoholism is but probably haven't distinguished between different kinds or degrees of alcoholism with any real sophistication. Dewitt offers one way of dealing with this vast concept. After analyzing her work experience at a Crisis Center, Dewitt has discerned several distinct types of alcoholics, which she arranges into several categories. It is clear that Dewitt's paper is not just an exercise in organization. On the contrary, her classification serves a definite, worthwhile purpose. Dewitt's examination of the different types of alcoholism allows her to draw the conclusion that alcoholics are not only people whose drinking is out of control, but those whose drinking falls into a pattern they cannot easily change. Dewitt's paper offers a fairly sophisticated characterization of the general concept of alcoholism. You may disagree with her; there may be more or fewer groups according to your analysis. But it is clear that, by using the strategy of classification, Dewitt has come up with some thought-provoking insights on a very serious subject.

## ► READING ACTIVITY ◄

In his essay, "The Four Kinds of Reading," the poet Donald Hall speculates on reading—an act important to us all. Though radio and television have become increasingly influential over the last few decades, the printed word remains a singularly powerful means of communication. The basic ability to read well is a prerequisite for active, responsible participation in society throughout most of the world. Yet as Hall discovers in his essay, reading is more than a "basic ability"; it involves much more than merely decoding printed symbols scattered across a page. Through analyzing this fundamental activity, Hall creates several categories of reading. What overall purpose does Hall's strategy of classification serve? Why does Hall divide reading into the categories he does?

> It seems to me possible to name four kinds of reading, each with a characteristic manner and purpose. The first is reading for information—reading to learn about a trade, or politics, or how to accomplish something. We read a newspaper this way, or most textbooks, or directions on how to assemble a bicycle. With most of this sort of material, the

Thesis—reading can be classified into four types.

First type—reading for information (examples).

reader can learn to scan the page quickly, coming up with what he needs and ignoring what is irrelevant to him, like the rhythm of the sentence, or the play of metaphor. Courses in speed reading can help us read for this purpose, training the eye to jump quickly across the page. If we read *The New York Times* with the attention we should give a novel or a poem, we will have time for nothing else, and our mind will be cluttered with clichés and dead metaphor. Quick eye-reading is a necessity to anyone who wants to keep up with what's happening, or learn much of what has happened in the past. The amount of reflection, which interrupts and slows down the reading, depends on the material.

Second type—reading literature (examples).

But it is not the same activity as reading literature. There ought to be another word. If we read a work of literature properly, we read slowly, and we hear all the words. If our lips do not actually move, it's only laziness. The muscles in our throats move, and come together when we see the word "squeeze." We hear the sounds so accurately that if a syllable is missing in a line of poetry we hear the lack, though we may not know what we are lacking. In prose we accept the rhythms, and hear the adjacent sounds. We also register a track of feeling through the metaphors and associations of words. Careless writing prevents this sort of attention, and becomes offensive. But the great writers reward this attention. Only by the full exercise of our powers to receive language can we absorb their intelligence and their imagination. This kind of reading goes through the ear—though the eye takes in the print, and decodes it into sound—to the throat and the understanding, and it can never be quick. It is slow and sensual, a deep pleasure that begins with touch and ends with the sort of comprehension that we associate with dream.

Compares reading literature to third type—intellectual reading (examples).

Too many intellectuals read in order to reduce images to abstractions. With a philosopher one reads slowly, as if it were literature, but much time must be spent with the eyes turned away from the pages, reflecting on the text. To read literature this way is to turn it into something it is not—to concepts clothed in character, or philosophy sugar-coated. I think that most literary intellectuals read this way, including the brighter Professors of English, with the result that they miss literature completely, and concern themselves with a minor discipline called the history of ideas. I remember a course in Chaucer at my University in which the final exam largely required the identification of a hundred or more fragments of Chaucer, none as long as a line. If you liked poetry, and read Chaucer through a couple of times slowly, you found yourself knowing them all. If you were a literary intellectual, well-informed about the great chain of being, chances are you had a difficult time. To read literature is to be intimately involved with the words on the page, and never to think of them as the embodiments of ideas which can be expressed in other terms. On the other hand, intellectual writing—closer to mathematics on a continuum that has at its opposite pole lyric poetry—requires intellectual reading, which is slow because it is reflective and because the reader must pause to evaluate concepts.

But most of the reading which is praised for itself is neither literary nor intellectual. It is narcotic. Novels, stories and biographies—historical sagas, monthly regurgitations of book clubs, four- and five-thousand word daydreams of the magazines—these are the opium of the suburbs. The drug is not harmful except to the addict himself, and is no more injurious to him than Johnny Carson or a bridge club, but it is nothing to be proud of. This reading is the automated daydream, the mild trip of the housewife and the tired businessman, interested not in experience and feeling but in turning off the possibilities of experience and feeling. Great literature, if we read it well, opens us up to the world, and makes us more sensitive to it, as if we acquired eyes that could see through things and ears that could hear smaller sounds. But by narcotic reading, one can reduce great literature to the level of *The Valley of the Dolls.* One can read *Anna Karenina* passively and inattentively, and float down the river of lethargy as if one were reading a confession magazine: "I Spurned My Husband for a Count."

Fourth type—narcotic reading (gives examples).

In this four-paragraph excerpt, Hall suggests that the particular nature of a piece of writing often strongly influences how someone will read it. For instance, we read a newspaper quite differently than we do a poem; we read a *Time* magazine article differently than we do a work like *Moby-Dick*. Yet Hall suggests that there is something more significant than the nature of the printed material itself that allows us to categorize several different kinds of reading. For Hall, the expectations of the individual reader most strongly characterize the different classes of reading. Hall identifies four essential "aims" in reading: (1) reading for information, (2) reading to enjoy and appreciate the use of language, (3) reading for abstract ideas and images, and (4) reading for the pure enjoyment of the act itself.

Hall's purpose in making these distinctions is not, however, merely to analyze isolable acts and arrange them in some hierarchy of value. Instead he suggests that responsible reading often includes a combination of the different kinds of reading he describes. We may read the same work with several aims. For example, we can read an essay for enjoyment of the language, for abstract ideas, and for enjoyment of the act of reading, all at the same time. Hall's classification of the four different kinds of reading is not meant merely to help us describe and define different ways that people read. Instead, Hall's classifications bring our attention to the different aims of reading so that we may read with a richer, fuller experience. Hall believes that a more conscious understanding of the complexities of reading may provide us greater control over our own reading.

It is important to remember that Hall's classification system is his own invention and reflects his own individual perception of reading. We may or may not choose to accept the whole of Hall's classification as useful or even accurate. What other ways might you classify the different kinds of reading? What other principles of classification might you use to categorize reading?

The strategy of classification is often used to sift through masses of information and discover ways to present this information in a useful, manageable form. The *power* of classification to reduce extraordinary amounts of data to manageable categories is illustrated by a space-age event in 1977:

> . . . two extraordinary spacecraft called Voyager were launched to the stars. After what promises to be a detailed and thoroughly dramatic exploration of the outer solar system from Jupiter to Uranus between 1979 and 1986, these space vehicles will slowly leave the solar system—emissaries of Earth to the realm of the stars. Affixed to each Voyager craft is a gold-coated copper phonograph record as a message to possible extraterrestrial civilizations that might encounter spacecraft in some distant space and time. Each record contains 118 photographs of our planet, ourselves, and our civilization; almost 90 minutes of the world's greatest music, an evolutionary audio-essay on "The Sounds of Earth"; and greetings in almost sixty human languages (and one whale language). . . .
>
> CARL SAGAN et al., "Preface," *Murmurs of Earth*

The extraordinary *Voyager* recording will doubtless outlast the earth and all its civilization. Long before any alien race is likely to find the recording, earth will have been gone for eons. The message is just a fraction of the possible messages we might send out to the stars, just a few photographs out of all the archives of the world, a few fragments of music out of all that has ever been recorded. The selection of the pieces to be included—and excluded—was a monumental job of analysis and decision making. If the task were yours, which pictures would you send, what music? Indeed, which languages would you select from the approximately 3,000 now known to exist? To answer this question, Carl Sagan and the others on the project had to derive some principles for selection, some system for classifying the great numbers of items they had to select from. For the full story of how the project was completed, you should read the book *Murmurs of Earth*; all we can say here is that in the end, the *Voyager* record contained what was hoped would be a representative sampling of earth pictures and music and languages.

However, the *Voyager* project illustrates the primary function of classification: the analysis and sorting of large numbers of items into groups and types. It is by sorting into groups that we reduce large numbers to smaller and more readily manipulable sets. At any university, for example, there are likely to be too many students to allow us to make meaningful statements about "students." Fortunately, we have a number of classifications we can take advantage of to reduce this large group of smaller subgroups: men and women students for example, or freshmen, sophomores, juniors, and seniors; or science, art, business, and education majors. The more discriminating our categories can become, the more accurate we can make our statements about them.

Which classification system we adopt depends on our purpose and, in the case of composition, on PACES: purpose-audience-code-experience-self. Obviously we could invent trivial classifications: students with freckles, students with younger brothers, students with expensive cars . . . but it would take an unusual writing situation to justify such classifications. If you were asked to describe the types of students who could benefit from a course in modern poetry, the writing situation would have built-in constraints that would suggest the classes or types you should use. If you found yourself in a job that involved large numbers of items, which you had to sort by some criteria, the purpose of classifying would be built into the situation. For example, two scientists were once faced with the difficult problem of determining the population of elephants in an area of Africa, because in large numbers elephants will damage whole forests. The problem was how to keep track of elephant births and deaths. The solution depended on being able to recognize elephants (who all tend to look very much alike, even to scientists):

> Learning to remember an individual became like a geography lesson, in which the shape of a country's borders had to be memorized. Often an ear would be almost smooth, with only one or two small nicks, but the shape of the nick, whether it had straight or curved sides, its depth and position on the ear, provided useful material. Some nicks looked as if they had resulted from the ear catching on a thorn, others as if they had been deftly cut by a tailor's scissors in neat straight lines. Certain elephants had ears with as many holes along the edge as a Dutch coast line plastered with bomb craters along its dykes. The cause of these holes I never discovered, but I suppose it must be due to some internal physiological process, the result of which gave the ears a decaying appearance.
>
> IAN AND ORIA DOUGLAS-HAMILTON, *Among the Elephants*

The Douglas-Hamiltons solved their problem in part by learning to classify elephants by the configuration of ears. The scientists in this instance had a ready-made problem with its built-in purpose. They needed a classification system by which they could identify elephants. Analysis for classification will provide you new insight into subjects, even those you already know well. In short, classification is not simply an exercise you are asked to undertake to see whether you can do it. All the strategies of development are functions of the human mind, and all normal human beings can and do use them whenever the need arises.

It is important to remember that it is people who set up classification systems. No matter how logical or obvious our categories seem, the act of creating the categories is specifically an act of the human mind. There is no normal, natural, or necessary way to classify anything, and there should be nothing mechanical about the way you arrive at your categories of classification. A famous composer has illustrated this point:

> We all listen to music according to our separate capacities. But, for the sake of analysis, the whole listening process may become clearer if we break

> it up into its component parts, so to speak. In a certain sense we all listen to music on three separate planes. For lack of a better terminology, one might name these: (1) the sensuous plane, (2) the expressive plane, (3) the sheerly musical plane. The only advantage to be gained from mechanically splitting up the listening process into these hypothetical planes is a clearer view to be had of the way in which we listen.
>
> AARON COPELAND, *What to Listen for in Music*

What Copland achieves with this classification is not just a "clearer view" of listening but the conclusion, as he says later at the end of the section, that the reader should strive for "a more *active* kind of listening . . . not just listening, but . . . listening *for* something." Thus his classification has a point; it serves a purpose. It was probably not obvious to you or to many others before Copland explained them that there *were* such planes of listening to music. They are his categories, invented to suit his purpose—to help the reader understand music better. The real question to ask is not "What classification can I make?" but "What *point* can I make that classification will help establish?"

### ► WRITING ACTIVITY ◄

Write a piece in which you use the strategy of classification to achieve a specific purpose. Focus upon clearly distinguishing the categories you discover or invent. Make sure you can clearly explain the purpose of your classification.

## THINKING AND DEVELOPING: USING DEFINITION

As speakers and writers, we sometimes use words or refer to concepts of which we or our listener-readers have only an imprecise, cloudy understanding. Some people do not bother themselves about the definitions of things; their concepts are unexamined. As a writer, you cannot afford to operate with unexamined or naive concepts. Your writer's mind must carefully analyze the terms you use and by doing so reexplore and redefine your perception of reality. The dictionary is not always helpful for the purpose. Dictionary definitions are invented by dictionary makers, who must give in the least possible space, with the fewest possible words, the most general, overall definition. The dictionary is a good place to start if you are trying to define a word, but as a writer you then go on from this general definition to say what the word means in a given context.

### ► READING ACTIVITY ◄

In her 1977 book *The Plug-In Drug*, Marie Winn discusses the effects of television in America, arguing that many Americans are "addicted" to "the tube." In the following passage from her book, Winn carefully defines her concept of what exactly constitutes an "addiction." What are the essential elements of Winn's definition; what purpose(s) might Winn have in defining this term in the way she does?

> When we think about addiction to drugs or alcohol, we frequently focus on negative aspects, ignoring the pleasures that accompany drinking or drug-taking. And yet the essence of any serious addiction is a pursuit of pleasure, a search for a "high" that normal life does not supply. It is only the inability to function without the addictive substance that is dismaying, the dependence of the organism upon a certain experience and an increasing inability to function normally without it. Thus a person will take two or three drinks at the end of the day not merely for the pleasure drinking provides, but also because he "doesn't feel normal" without them.
>
> An addict does not merely pursue a pleasurable experience and need to experience it in order to function normally. He needs to *repeat* it again and again. Something about that particular experience makes life without it less than complete. Other potentially pleasurable experiences are no longer possible, for under the spell of the addictive experience, his life is peculiarly distorted. The addict craves an experience and yet he is never really satisfied. The organism may be temporarily sated, but soon it begins to crave again.

Winn uses a common technique in her definition: She begins with the popular connotations of "addiction" and contrasts these with her own definition. Since the concept of addiction is so crucial to Winn's argument, she wisely begins by ensuring that both she and her audience are working with the same understanding of the word. Winn anticipates that many of her readers might automatically associate an "addiction" with a physically harmful substance, a drug, or alcohol, for instance. She downplays this common connotation—instead, she emphasizes the addict's constant need to repeat an activity, a need that preempts the regular pattern of the addict's life. For Winn, the fact that the addict is "never really satisfied" is crucial—she needs to establish this important aspect of her definition in order meaningfully to discuss Americans' addiction to television.

## ► READING ACTIVITY ◄

In the following passage, David Elliott Kidd, a student writer, describes his conception of swimming. How has Kidd used the strategy of definition to achieve this purpose?

> Swimming. What is it? Side-stroke. Back-stroke. Breast-stroke. Crawl. Dog Paddle. Dead Man's Float. I believe that swimming is greatly misunderstood. A vast majority of the earth's surface is covered in water and yet most people believe that swimming is something you do in a sunken

> box filled with a mixture of chlorine, water and urine. This is false. The Romans knew, this is a *bath*. Swimming in such a place is like watching church on television; it shows a serious lack of commitment. Swimming is a sacred ritual, and the greater the lengths to which you go in order to participate, the stronger your faith.
>
> Coming from a predominantly Calvinist background, I believe that swimming can only occur in one place: a long deep lake in the Adirondack mountains. Swimming in my family is the total immersion of one's self in icy dark water. The colder the water, the better.

Kidd begins by listing common elements many people associate with swimming, noting that most people think of swimming as something done in a pool. His description of the typical pool ("a sunken box filled with a mixture of chlorine, water, and urine") prepares us for his description of the ideal swim, one which takes place in "a long deep lake in the Adirondacks." By illustrating the drawbacks of swimming in an artificially constructed pool, where he anticipates that most of his readers usually swim, Kidd is better able to dramatize what is, for him, the superiority of lake swimming.

Definition is a crucially important strategy. Writers are constantly defining and redefining ideas, terms, objects, situations and so on, not out of curiosity or as an intellectual exercise, but because they are aware that we react to reality according to the way we define it. Throughout the 1960s there was a great deal of discussion about the threat of communism, especially in Southeast Asia. Terms like *democracy*, *socialism*, *communism*, *fascism*, *social democracy*, *the domino theory*, and *national socialism* were used in ill-defined or undefined ways to mean anything . . . and came to mean nothing. *Social democracy* and *socialism* meant *communism*. A fascist state was one you disliked. People argued for the domino theory without understanding what it meant and with no knowledge of the history of Southeast Asia. To avoid such confusion, you should carefully and clearly define important words or phrases which your audience may either not fully comprehend or interpret differently than you intend. In many instances, unnecessary and false disputes can be avoided by a wise application of the strategy of definition.

One particularly effective way to define a word or concept is through examples or illustrations. Many words function at a level of abstraction that may not be useful in some contexts. For instance, to say "Mr. Johnson looked displeased" gives us a general idea of Mr. Johnson's disposition, but *displeased* by itself is an abstract, highly judgmental term that could be clarified. Just what does the writer mean by *displeased?* Behavior or appearance which one person may interpret as displeasure may not appear the same to another person. We might make this statement stronger and more meaningful by giving examples of Mr. Johnson's displeasure. For instance, "Mr. Johnson looked displeased, brow furrowed, face red, lips tightly pursed, shoulders trembling with tension." These specific signs of displeasure give us a more vivid sense of Mr. Johnson's attitude.

## ► READING ACTIVITY ◄

In his essay "The 'Miracle' of Technofix," the political writer Kirkpatrick Sale critically examines what he perceives as the unbounded faith many people have that high technology can solve all our problems. How does Sale use the strategy of definition to argue his point?

> Somehow this nation has become caught in what I call the mire of "technofix": the belief, reinforced in us by the highest corporate and political forces, that all our current crises can be solved, or at least significantly eased, by the application of modern high technology. In the words of former Atomic Energy Commission chairman Glenn Seaborg: "We must pursue the idea that it is more science, better science, more wisely applied that is going to free us from [our] predicaments."
>
> Energy crisis? Try synfuels. Never mind that they will require billions—eventually trillions—of dollars transferred out of the public coffers into the energy companies' pockets, or that nobody has yet fully explored, much less solved, the problems of environmental damage, pollution, hazardous-waste disposal and occupational dangers their production will create. Never mind—it's technofix.
>
> Food for the hungry world? Try the "Green Revolution." Never mind that such farming is far more energy- and chemical-intensive than any other method known, and therefore generally too expensive for the poor countries that are supposed to benefit from it, or that its principle of monoculture over crop diversity places whole regions, even whole countries, at the risk of a single breed of disease or pest. Never mind—it's scientific.
>
> Diseases? Try wonder drugs. Never mind that few of the thousands of drugs introduced every year have ever been fully tested for long-range effects, or that they are vastly overprescribed and overused, or that nearly half of them prove to be totally ineffective in treating the ailments they are administered for and half of the rest produce unintended side effects. Never mind—it's progress.

Sale criticizes the belief that high technology is the answer to all of society's problems by focusing on what he calls "technofix." The specific examples of "technofix" give us a clear understanding of this term. But even more, Sale's examples support his skepticism concerning the overly optimistic belief that high technology can "save the world." For instance, the drawbacks of many "wonder drugs" Sales highlights in the last paragraph not only enhance Sale's definition of "technofix," but also demonstrate the shortsightedness of a blind faith in medical technololgy.

## ► WRITING ACTITIVY ◄

Write an extended definition of some important term, idea, or object. Concentrate on giving your reader a vivid sense of what you are defining; do not simply restate the dictionary. Most importantly, think about what purpose your definition serves.

## THINKING AND DEVELOPING: USING CAUSAL ANALYSIS

Detective stories have traditionally been one of the most popular kinds of writing. Over the years, sales of Agatha Christie's mystery novels have surpassed those of all other books except the Bible. Much of the enjoyment people get from reading detective fiction comes from tracing all the clues the writer provides, trying to discover some meaningful, revealing connection between seemingly unrelated facts.

People have always been interested in understanding the causes of situations and events in the world; we are constantly asked the question "Why?" What causes inflation? Why has terrorism become such a common mode of protest in the contemporary world? Writers frequently employ the strategy of causal analysis to help us better understand the nature of important situations and events that affect many of us.

If we understand why a particular event occurred or how a particular situation came about, we will often be in a better position to control similar situations. For instance, economists study closely the possible causes of inflation and depression to help us better control the fluctuations of the economy. Psychologists study the possible causes of certain emotional disorders to help ensure their patients' mental health.

When using causal analysis, try to keep several things in mind. First you should recognize that many events and situations cannot be attributed to one single cause. Often causal forces work in conjunction with (or even in opposition to) other forces in such a complex way that they may not be easily discerned or characterized. For example, the relative worldwide frequency of terrorism as a means of political protest cannot be fully explained by any single factor. A variety of factors helps determine any individual act of political terrorism. One factor may be that the press can spread the news of any terrorist act throughout almost the entire world in a matter of minutes. Terrorists realize that their activity will probably be reported to millions of people worldwide. Another factor is that it has perhaps become easier for small groups to obtain powerful, sophisticated weapons. The third possible factor is that the world has come more and more under the influence of the "superpowers," making it increasingly difficult for smaller political groups to exert any significant influence through legitimate and accepted means of political dialogue. These and perhaps many other different factors have contributed to the disturbing growth of political terrorism in the last few decades. When writers hypothesize about one possible causal factor of an event or situation, they should recognize that there may be other significant causal factors as well—to concentrate on one factor is not to rule out the possible influence of others.

As writers you should also keep in mind that even a successful investigation into the causes of a situation does not necessarily assure our ability to control that situation or event. Though economists may be able to identify some of the major causes of inflation and recession, that does not mean that we can easily control the value of the dollar. Knowledge does not always bring power; understanding a cause may not always help us to control its effects. Yet despite our limitations, one thing is certain: Willful ignorance will never allow us to better control our condition.

Causal analysis begins every time we inquire into what happens around us. We often begin with a situation or event about which we are curious, something that bothers or disturbs or perhaps pleases us, and speculate upon it.

## ► READING ACTITIVY ◄

In the following passage, Daniel Greenberg claims that everyday life in the modern world requires little real brainwork. How does Greenberg account for this decline in necessary intelligence?

> Tomes of research are not needed to conclude that the necessity for brainwork in ordinary day-to-day matters has substantially diminished in recent years, pretty much in step with the declining test scores. For both customer and clerk, the simple exercise of calculating change has been eliminated widely by the electronic cash register. Hand-held calculators make it possible to do household arithmetic with scarcely any investment of brainpower, or even much attention. Kids witness that and eventually take part in it themselves. Soaring sales of even smarter electronic devices are hailed widely by the computer trade as the beginning of a new age of grander, intellectual horizons for ordinary folks. For many, it may turn out that way. But for many more, the new gadgets will mean a decline in the need to think hard, just as the revolution in mechanical machinery produced a decline in the need to work hard.
>
> The removal of mind from living has been immensely accelerated by electronics, but it's also to be found in other manifestations of high-tech society. So-called convenience foods, for example, which are booming despite their higher costs, enable the consumer to buy the manufacturer's skills, rather than go through the mental process of acquiring and employing those skills. Time is saved, but, again, at the cost of thinking how to get something done.
>
> Similarly, manual transmissions, the one-time standard that's become unstandard in the automobile industry, require some thought to operate—at least until their use becomes second nature—and working them provides some insight into the tradeoff between power and speed. But

> for millions of young people, driving involves no more than shifting to "drive" and taking off.

In his essay "Electronic Gizmos Make Us Stupid," Daniel Greenberg is disturbed by what he perceives as "the removal of mind from living." In the passage above, Greenberg develops and supports the hypothesis that the decline in intelligence may be partially attributed to an increased dependence on technology, that while technology may open "greater intellectual horizons for many," it may also close some avenues of the mind for many others. To illustrate just what he means, Greenberg offers specific examples of "manifestations of high technology." Convenience foods keep people from seriously thinking about finding means of sustenance. Hand-held calculators allow people to perform "household arithmetic with scarcely any brainpower." Can you think of other examples of technology that might support Greenberg's hyopothesis? Or can you offer arguments or examples that might refute Greenberg's position on this issue? Remember, causal analysis is a strategy of development that often involves theorizing or guesswork. We shouldn't expect either to agree or disagree wholeheartedly with any causal hypothesis we encounter.

## ► READING ACTIVITY ◄

Thomas Maugh is impressed by the great success of Rick Barry's foul-shooting and consequently inquires just why Barry's underhand shot was so effective. In the following passage from "The Physics of Basketball," he offers physicist Peter J. Branacazio's explanation of why Barry was able to make 93.5 percent of his attempted free throws in his last season in the NBA. How does the writer Maugh develop his analysis of Barry's shot?

> Take the case of Barry, for example. Brancazio has shown that a ball spinning backwards loses more energy when it hits the rim of the basket or the ground than does a ball spinning forward, or one with no spin at all. The greater the amount of backspin, the more energy the ball loses. Therefore when a ball with a high backspin hits the rim, it doesn't bounce off wildly but "dies" there, with a much greater chance of falling through the hoop.
>
> Barry's two-handed technique of swinging the ball between the legs puts a great deal of backspin on it. Spectators have often noted, in fact, that when his shots hit the inside of the rim, they generally fall through. "I found a quote reading through some coaching books," Brancazio says, "where Red Auerbach [general manager of the Boston Celtics] says 'Backspin helps the shot to be lucky and fall in.' Well, it's not luck. There really is a physical reason why that happens.

Maugh goes beyond the uninquisitive, dumbfounded awe of the fan who is captivated by the uniqueness of Barry's underhand foul shot. Instead, the admiring Maugh attempts to discover why Barry's shot was so successful. He concentrates on the distinguishing feature of Barry's shot—the great amount of backspin the underhand release gives to the basketball. Following Brancazio's observations that a backward-spinning ball loses energy when it hits a stationary object (in basketball, the rim or the backboard), Maugh is able to offer a hypothesis as to why Barry's particular method of foul shooting is so accurate. By analyzing the peculiar aspects of Barry's shot, aspects which most strongly distinguish his shot from that of others in the NBA, Maugh is able to offer a reasonable explanation for Barry's uncommonly high free-throw percentage.

In addition to generating their own causal hypotheses, writers frequently speculate on the adequacy of previously advanced hypotheses. We are continually dispelling theories of causes we find to be ill founded or prejudicial. The once-popular belief that all individual behavior was the result of personality has been questioned by many modern psychologists, who now suggest that environmental and situational factors, not merely personality, affect individual behavior. The particular selection of aspects of a situation or event we emphasize in determining the cause of that situation or event is crucial. Selection (the excluding of certain details and the highlighting of certain others) is inevitable; our minds cannot possibly synthesize every aspect of a given event or situation. We must choose only those we believe are significant. Two different observers of an event may focus on two different sets of "facts" and consequently arrive at two different explanations of the same event.

## ► READING ACTIVITY ◄

In the following passage, student Jeff Simek speculates as to why public education has been so criticized by many people. How does Simek develop his response?

> The major fault of critics of our public schools lies in their misconception of the purpose of public education. They fail to understand that our schools must be institutions of learning, and that our classrooms cannot be, and should not be used as a panacea for all of this society's ills. Already our schools have been used as a testing ground for coping with America's inability to solve its racial problems. Busing and forced integration, while noble in theory, have too often caused our schools to become societal battlefields. Similarly, roles previously performed by parents and family have been assigned to the schools, such as the areas of sex education, driver training, and drug and alcohol awareness. Schools have been given drastically increased responsibilities with unfair expectations. Our society has not competently dealt with these problems, so it has simply passed these duties on to the schools. Too many Americans have withdrawn their involvement and support, but then have complained when the results have not met their lofty expectations. This approach is neither fair nor effective.

Simek first suggests that most critics of public education claim that schools have failed to perform their function of reforming society. After identifying the nature of this criticism, Simek then argues that these critics have unfair and unrealistic expectations of what public education is designed, and should be expected, to do. By analyzing the cause of criticism of public education, Simek shows why he feels this criticism is largely unfounded. How would you respond to the critics of public education Simek mentions and to Simek's reaction to these critics?

The examples we've read attempt to discover the possible causes of existing events or situations. Yet principles of causal analysis may also help a writer to speculate about future events or situations. That is, a writer may theorize on the possible future outcomes of what he perceives as current trends. First the writer gathers information and intuitions about current patterns of events and then projects this perceived pattern into the future. This is a common method of anticipating events in the world around us. Population scientists study patterns of migration within the United States in order both to discover possible causes for these patterns (national shifts in employment opportunities, etc.) and, in conjunction with the latest census figures, to predict the future population growth of certain areas of the country.

### ► WRITING ACTIVITY ◄

Write a brief piece in which you either suggest a possible cause for a current event or situation, analyze an already advanced causal hypothesis, or theorize about a future result that a current situation or trend may bring about. Choose a topic that is significant but which you can handle fairly fully in a paragraph or two.

## THINKING AND DEVELOPING: USING COMBINED STRATEGIES

The strategies discussed in the preceding pages are useful as means; they may assist a writer in the presentation and development of important concepts or ideas. It is important to remember that there are no set rules for the use of the strategies of development. Their use depends entirely on the writer's particular needs, on the specific purpose the strategy is meant to fulfill. Writers seldom set out to write a comparison and contrast or a classification essay; instead, they usually begin with some purpose which they discover may be usefully developed by means of comparison and contrast or classification. Purpose determines the use of a strategy; not the other way around.

Because they are flexible tools, strategies of development are easily adapted and altered to writers' specific needs. Writers frequently combine strategies, often using two or more to suit a particular end. Indeed, it is rare to find an essay that uses a single strategy. Combining strategies of development can be a powerful, effective way to approach an idea. In fact, in almost any piece of professional expository prose, a number of strategies of development might be identified.

## ▶ READING ACTIVITY ◀

In the following passage, scientist James Jeans explains why the sky is blue. What strategies does James use to serve his purpose?

> Imagine that we stand on an ordinary seaside pier, and watch the waves rolling in and striking against the iron columns of the pier. Large waves pay very little attention to the columns—they divide right and left and reunite after passing each column, much as a regiment of soldiers would if a tree stood in their road; it is almost as though the columns had not been there. But the short waves and ripples find the columns of the pier a much more formidable obstacle. When the short waves impinge on the columns, they are reflected back and spread as new ripples in all directions. To use the technical term, they are "scattered." The obstacle provided by the iron columns hardly affects the long waves at all, but scatters the short ripples.
>
> We have been watching a sort of working model of the way in which sunlight struggles through the earth's atmosphere. Between us on earth and outer space the atmosphere interposes innumerable obstacles in the form of molecules of air, tiny droplets of water, and small particles of dust. These are represented by the columns of the pier.
>
> The waves of the sea represent the sunlight. We know that sunlight is a blend of many colors—as we can prove for ourselves by passing it through a prism, or even through a jug of water, or as nature demonstrates to us when she passes it through the raindrops of a summer shower and produces a rainbow. We also know that light consists of waves, and that the different colors of light are produced by waves of different lengths, red light by long waves and blue light by short waves. The mixture of waves which constitutes sunlight has to struggle past the columns of the pier. And these obstacles treat the light waves much as the columns of the pier treat the sea-waves. The long waves which constitute red light are hardly affected but the short waves which constitute blue light are scattered in all directions.

Jeans explains why the sky is blue first by establishing the analogy between sunlight (which is difficult to imagine as a discrete object) and ocean waves (which are fairly easy to visualize), and second by investigating the causes and effects of sunlight moving through the earth's atmosphere. Jeans' combined use of analogy and causal analysis finally results in an imaginative, easily understood explanation of why the sky looks blue. Can you identify any other strategy of development James uses in this passage?

## ► DISCUSSION ACTIVITY ◄

Read the following essays and discuss which combination of strategies each writer uses. What particular purpose does each strategy achieve? How does each strategy serve the main purpose of the essay?

### THE GREAT AMERICAN COOLING MACHINE

**Frank Trippett**

1 "The greatest contribution to civilization in this century may well be air conditioning—and America leads the way." So wrote British Scholar-Politician S. F. Markham 32 years ago when a modern cooling system was still an exotic luxury. In a century that has yielded such treasures as the electric knife, spray-on deodorant and disposable diapers, anybody might question whether air conditioning is the supreme gift. There is not a whiff of doubt, however, that America is far out front in its use. As a matter of lopsided fact, the U.S. today, with a mere 5 percent of the population, consumes as much man-made coolness as the whole rest of the world put together.

2 Just as amazing is the speed with which this situation came to be. Air conditioning began to spread in industries as a production aid during World War II. Yet only a generation ago a chilled sanctuary during summer's stewing heat was a happy frill that ordinary people sampled only in movie houses. Today most Americans tend to take air conditioning for granted in homes, offices, factories, stores, theaters, shops, studios, schools, hotels and restaurants. They travel in chilled buses, trains, planes and private cars. Sporting events once associated with open sky and fresh air are increasingly boxed in and air cooled. Skiing still takes place outdoors, but such attractions as tennis, rodeos, football and, alas, even baseball are now often staged in synthetic climates like those of Houston's Astrodome and New Orleans' Superdome. A great many of the country's farming tractors are now, yup, air-conditioned.

3 It is thus no exaggeration to say that Americans have taken to mechanical cooling avidly and greedily. Many have become all but addicted, refusing to go places that are not air-conditioned. In Atlanta, shoppers in Lenox Square so resented having to endure natural heat while walking outdoors from chilled store to chilled store that the mall management enclosed and air-conditioned the whole sprawling shebang. The widespread whining about Washington's raising of thermostats to a mandatory 78°F suggests that people no longer think of interior coolness as an amenity but consider it a necessity, almost a birthright, like suffrage. The existence of such a view was proved last month when a number of federal judges, sitting too high and mighty to suffer 78°, defied and denounced the Government's energy-saving order to cut back on cooling.

Significantly, there was no popular outrage at this judicial insolence; many citizens probably wished that they could be so highhanded.

4 Everybody by now is aware that the cost of the American way is enormous, that air conditioning is an energy glutton. It uses some 9% of all electricity produced. Such an extravagance merely to provide comfort is peculiarly American and strikingly at odds with all the recent rhetoric about national sacrifice in a period of menacing energy shortages. Other modern industrial nations such as Japan, Germany and France have managed all along to thrive with mere fractions of the man-made coolness used in the U.S., and precious little of that in private dwellings. Here, so profligate has its use become that the air conditioner is almost as glaring a symptom as the automobile of the national tendency to overindulge in every technical possibility, to use every convenience to such excess that the country looks downright coddled.

5 But not everybody is aware that high cost and easy comfort are merely two of the effects of the vast cooling of America. In fact, air conditioning has substantially altered the country's character and folkways. With the dog days at hand and the thermostats ostensibly up, it is a good time to begin taking stock of what air conditioning has done besides lower the indoor temperature.

6 Many of its byproducts are so conspicuous that they are scarcely noticed. To begin with, air conditioning transformed the face of urban America by making possible those glassy, boxy, sealed-in skyscrapers on which the once humane geometrics of places like San Francisco, Boston and Manhattan have been impaled. It has been indispensable, no less, to the functioning of sensitive advanced computers, whose high operating temperatures require that they be constantly cooled. Thus, in a very real way, air conditioning has made possible the ascendancy of computerized civilization. Its cooling protection has given rise not only to moon landings, space shuttles and Skylabs but to the depersonalized punch-cardification of society that regularly gets people hot under the collar even in swelter-proof environments. It has also reshaped the national economy and redistributed political power simply by encouraging the burgeoning of the sultry southerly swatch of the country, profoundly influencing major migration trends of people and industry. Sunbelt cities like Phoenix, Atlanta, Dallas and Houston (where shivering indoor frigidity became a mark of status) could never have mushroomed so prosperously without air conditioning; some communities—Las Vegas in the Nevada desert and Lake Havasu City on the Arizona-California border—would shrivel and die overnight if it were turned off.

7 It has, as well, seduced families into retreating into houses with closed doors and shut windows, reducing the commonalty of neighborhood life and all but obsoleting the front-porch society whose open casual folkways were an appealing hallmark of a sweatier America. Is it really

surprising that the public's often noted withdrawal into self-pursuit and privatism has coincided with the epic spread of air conditioning? Though science has little studied how habitual air conditioning affects mind or body, some medical experts suggest that, like other technical avoidance of natural swings in climate, air conditioning may take a toll on the human capacity to adapt to stress. If so, air conditioning is only like many other greatly useful technical developments that liberate man from nature by increasing his productivity and power in some ways—while subtly weakening him in others.

8 Neither scholars nor pop sociologists have really got around to charting and diagnosing all the changes brought about by air conditioning. Professional observers have for years been preoccupied with the social implications of the automobile and television. Mere glancing analysis suggests that the car and TV, in their most decisive influences on American habits, have been powerfully aided and abetted by air conditioning. The car may have created all those shopping centers in the boondocks, but only air conditioning has made them attractive to mass clienteles. Similarly, the artificial cooling of the living room undoubtedly helped turn the typical American into a year-round TV addict. Without air conditioning, how many viewers would endure reruns (or even Johnny Carson) on one of those pestilential summer nights that used to send people out to collapse on the lawn or to sleep on the roof?

9 Many of the side effects of air conditioning are far from being fully pinned down. It is a reasonable suspicion, though, that controlled climate, by inducing Congress to stay in Washington longer than it used to during the swelter season, thus presumably passing more laws, has contributed to bloated Government. One can only speculate that the advent of the supercooled bedroom may be linked to the carnal adventurism associated with the mid-century sexual revolution. Surely it is a fact—if restaurant complaints about raised thermostats are to be believed—that air conditioning induces at least expense-account diners to eat and drink more; if so, it must be credited with adding to the national fat problem.

10 Perhaps only a sophist might be tempted to tie the spread of air conditioning to the coincidentally rising divorce rate, but every attentive realist must have noticed that even a little window unit can instigate domestic tension and chronic bickering between couples composed of one who likes it on all the time and another who does not. In fact, perhaps surprisingly, not everybody likes air conditioning. The necessarily sealed rooms or buildings make some feel claustrophobic, cut off from the real world. The rush, whir and clatter of cooling units annoys others. There are even a few eccentrics who object to man-made cool simply because they like hot weather. Still, the overwhelming majority of Americans have taken to air conditioning like hogs to a wet wallow.

11 It might be tempting, and even fair, to chastise that vast majority for being spoiled rotten in their cool ascendancy. It would be more just,

however, to observe that their great cooling machine carries with it a perpetual price tag that is going to provide continued and increasing chastisement during the energy crisis. Ultimately, the air conditioner, and the hermetic buildings it requires, may turn out to be a more pertinent technical symbol of the American personality than the car. While the car has been a fine sign of the American impulse to dart hither and yon about the world, the mechanical cooler more neatly suggests the maturing national compulsion to flee the natural world in favor of a technological cocoon.

12 Already architectural designers are toiling to find ways out of the technical trap represented by sealed buildings with immovable glass, ways that might let in some of the naturally cool air outside. Some have lately come up with a remarkable discovery: the openable window. Presumably, that represents progress.

**1.** Why is Trippet concerned so early in his essay (paragraph 2) with describing how wide ranging the implementation of air-conditioning has become? How is this related to his purpose?

**2.** How does Trippet categorize the various effects of air conditioning? Is this strategy the most effective for illustrating all of the possible effects of air conditioning?

**3.** Is Trippet suggesting that air conditioning should be completely eliminated? Does this suggestion underlie the cause and effect structure of the essay?

## FROM *PORNOGRAPHY AND OBSCENITY*

**D. H. Lawrence**

1 What is pornography to one man is the laughter of genius to another.

2 The word itself, we are told, means "pertaining to harlots"—the graph of the harlot. But nowadays, what is a harlot? If she was a woman who took money from a man in return for going to bed with him—really, most wives sold themselves, in the past, and plenty of harlots gave themselves, when they felt like it, for nothing. If a woman hasn't got a tiny streak of harlot in her, she's a dry stick as a rule. And probably most harlots had somewhere a streak of womanly generosity. Why be so cut and dried? The law is a dreary thing, and its judgments have nothing to do with life. . . .

3 One essay on pornography, I remember, comes to the conclusion that pornography in art is that which is calculated to arouse sexual desire, or sexual excitement. And stress is laid on the fact, whether the author or artist *intended* to arouse sexual feelings. It is the old vexed question of intention, become so dull today, when we know how strong and influential our unconscious intentions are. And why a man should be

held guilty of his conscious intentions, and innocent of his unconscious intentions, I don't know, since every man is more made up of unconscious intentions than of conscious ones. I am what I am, not merely what I think I am.

4 However! We take it, I assume, that *pornography* is something base, something unpleasant. In short, we don't like it. And why don't we like it? Because it arouses sexual feelings?

5 I think not. No matter how hard we may pretend otherwise, most of us rather like a moderate rousing of our sex. It warms us, stimulates us like sunshine on a grey day. After a century or two of Puritanism, this is still true of most people. Only the mob-habit of condemning any form of sex is too strong to let us admit it naturally. And there are, of course, many people who are genuinely repelled by the simplest and most natural stirrings of sexual feeling. But these people are perverts who have fallen into hatred of their fellowmen; thwarted, disappointed, unfulfilled people, of whom, alas, our civilisation contains so many. And they nearly always enjoy some unsimple and unnatural form of sex excitement, secretly.

6 Even quite advanced art critics would try to make us believe that any picture or book which had "sex appeal" was *ipso facto* a bad book or picture. This is just canting hypocrisy. Half the great poems, pictures, music, stories, of the whole world are great by virtue of the beauty of their sex appeal. Titian or Renoir, the Song of Solomon or *Jane Eyre*, Mozart or "Annie Laurie," the loveliness is all interwoven with sex appeal, sex stimulus, call it what you will. Even Michelangelo, who rather hated sex, can't help filling the Cornucopia with phallic acorns. Sex is a very powerful, beneficial and necessary stimulus in human life, and we are all grateful when we feel its warm, natural flow through us, like a form of sunshine. . . .

7 Then what is pornography, after all this? It isn't sex appeal or sex stimulus in art. It isn't even a deliberate intention on the part of the artist to arouse or excite sexual feelings. There's nothing wrong with sexual feelings in themselves, so long as they are straightforward and not sneaking or sly. The right sort of sex stimulus is invaluable to human daily life. Without it the world grows grey. I would give everybody the gay Renaissance stories to read; they would help to shake off a lot of grey self-importance, which is our modern civilised disease.

8 But even I would censor genuine pornography, rigorously. It would not be very difficult. In the first place, genuine pornography is almost always underworld, it doesn't come into the open. In the second, you can recognise it by the insult it offers, invariably, to sex and to the human spirit.

9 Pornography is the attempt to insult sex, to do dirt on it. This is unpardonable. Take the very lowest instance, the picture postcard sold underhand, by the underworld, in most cities. What I have seen of them has been of an ugliness to make you cry. The insult to the human body,

the insult to a vital human relationship! Ugly and cheap they make the human nudity, ugly and degraded they make the sexual act, trivial and cheap and nasty.

10 It is the same with the books they sell in the underworld. They are either so ugly they make you ill, or so fatuous you can't imagine anybody but a cretin or a moron reading them, or writing them.

11 It is the same with the dirty limericks that people tell after dinner, or the dirty stories one hears commercial travellers telling each other in a smoke-room. Occasionally there is a really funny one, that redeems a great deal. But usually they are just ugly and repellant, and the so-called "humour" is just a trick of doing dirt on sex.

12 Now the human nudity of a great many modern people is just ugly and degraded, and the sexual act between modern people is just the same, merely ugly and degrading. But this is nothing to be proud of. It is the catastrophe of our civilisation. I am sure no other civilisation, not even the Roman, has showed such a vast proportion of ignominious and degraded nudity, and ugly, squalid dirty sex. Because no other civilisation has driven sex into the underworld, and nudity to the w.c.

13 The intelligent young, thank heaven, seem determined to alter in these two respects. They are rescuing their young nudity from the stuffy, pornographical hole-and-corner underworld of their elders, and they refuse to sneak about the sexual relation. This is a change the elderly grey ones of course deplore, but it is in fact a very great change for the better, and a real revolution.

14 But it is amazing how strong is the will in ordinary, vulgar people, to do dirt on sex. It was one of my fond illusions, when I was young, that the ordinary healthy-seeming sort of men in railway carriages, or the smoke-room of an hotel or a pullman, were healthy in their feelings and had a wholesome rough devil-may-care attitude towards sex. All wrong! All wrong! Experience teaches that common individuals of this sort have a disgusting attitude towards sex, a disgusting contempt of it, a disgusting desire to insult it. If such fellows have intercourse with a woman, they triumphantly feel that they have done her dirt, and now she is lower, cheaper, more contemptible than she was before.

15 It is individuals of this sort that tell dirty stories, carry indecent picture postcards, and know the indecent books. This is the great pornographical class—the really common men-in-the-street and women-in-the-street. They have as great a hate and contempt of sex as the greyest Puritan, and when an appeal is made to them, they are always on the side of the angels. They insist that a film-heroine shall be a neuter, a sexless thing of washed-out purity. They insist that real sex-feeling shall only be shown by the villain or villainess, low lust. They find a Titian or a Renoir really indecent, and they don't want their wives and daughters to see it.

16 Why? Because they have the grey disease of sex-hatred, coupled with

the yellow disease of dirt-lust. The sex functions and the excrementory functions in the human body work so close together, yet they are, so to speak, utterly different in direction. Sex is a creative flow, the excrementory flow is towards dissolution, decreation, if we may use such a word. In the really healthy human being the distinction between the two is instant, our profoundest instincts are perhaps our instincts of opposition between the two flows.

17 But in the degraded human being the deep instincts have gone dead, and then the two flows become identical. *This* is the secret of really vulgar and of pornographical people: the sex flow and the excrement flow is the same to them. It happens when the psyche deteriorates, and the profound controlling instincts collapse. Then sex is dirt and dirt is sex, and sexual excitement becomes a playing with dirt, and any sign of sex in a woman becomes a show of her dirt. This is the condition of the common, vulgar human being whose name is legion, and who lifts his voice and it is the *Vox populi, vox Dei*. And this is the source of all pornography.

**1.** Why is Lawrence concerned with defending feelings of sexual arousal? Why does Lawrence establish what pornography is *not* in the first part of his essay?

**2.** What are the various types of "genuine" pornography? How does Lawrence's use of classification help to define genuine pornograpohy?

**3.** How is Lawrence able to arrive at his assertion that pornography is hatred of sex?

## ► WRITING ACTIVITY ◄

Review the pieces you have written for the strategies of development discussed in this chapter. Identify where you have combined strategies. What other strategies are included in your comparison and contrast, classification, definition, and causal analysis? Strategies of development are seldom used in isolation from one another; it is natural to discover several strategies at work even in a short piece of writing.

It is important to keep in mind when using these and other strategies of development how much your audience needs to know. For instance, when you use the strategy of comparison and contrast, you probably do not need to compare and contrast *every* aspect that you can possibly think of about the two or more subjects. Lawrence Shames did not contrast "Mutt" and Jeff's favorite movie. Similarly, in her use of the strategy of definition, Marie Winn did not enumerate every popular connotation of "addiction". These writers knew when enough was enough; they knew just how much to explain to their readers. These writers chose the strategies they did to achieve specific purposes, and these purposes determined just how each of the strategies was used. As you read each of the following chapters, notice how specific purpose governs how each writer uses the strategies of development discussed in this chapter.

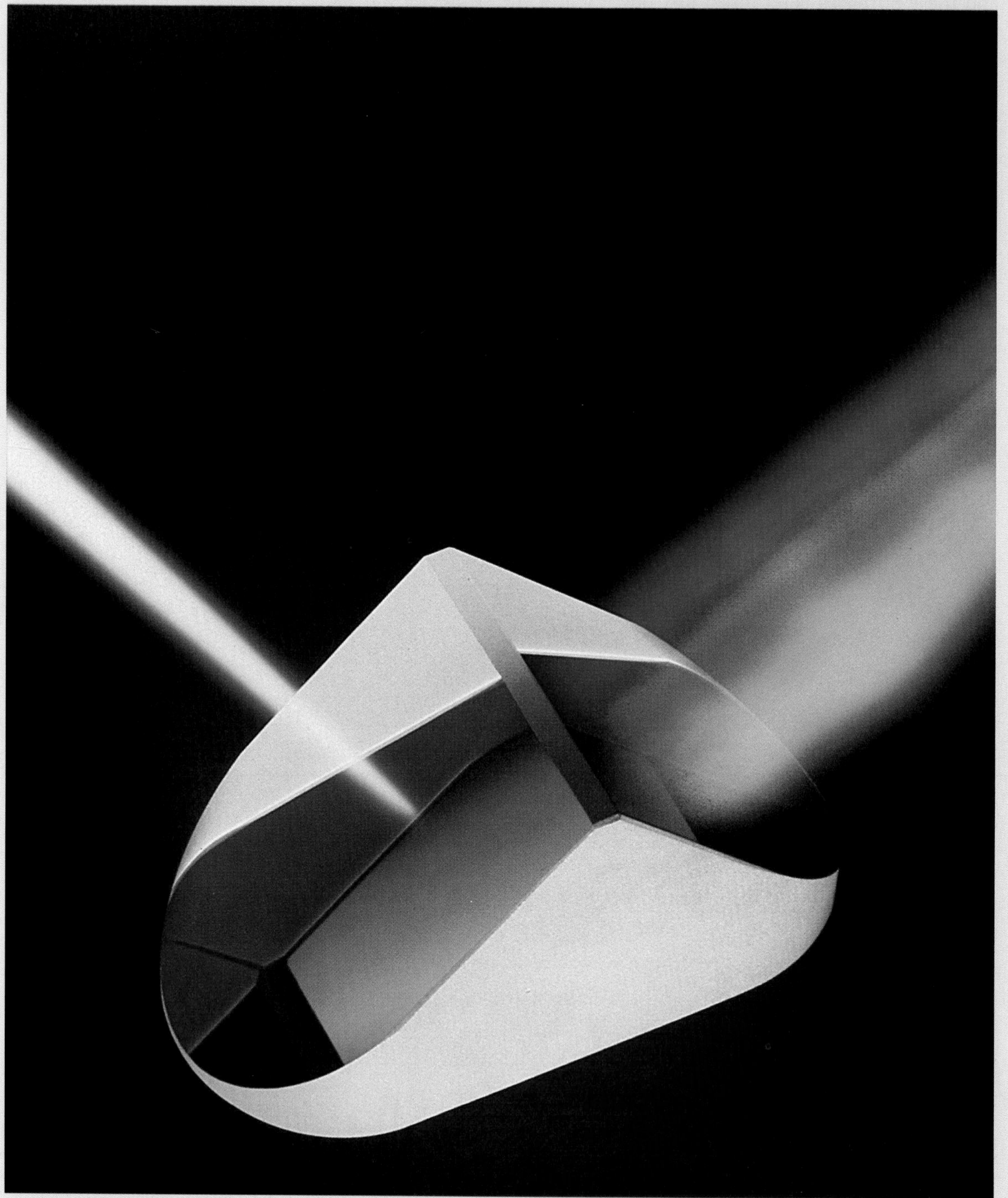

# PART ▲ TWO

# *The Aims of Writing*

# CHAPTER ▲ FIVE

# *Expressive Writing*

**"It is enough if I please myself with writing; I am sure then of an audience."**

HENRY D. THOREAU: *Journal*

## THE WRITER'S VIEW OF REALITY

Personal writing emphasizes *self*. How do *I* see the world? What does *my* life mean? Some of this expressive writing can be private, such as a diary; but most of it is written to share personal views with others. The familiar essay, the memoir, the personal experience story, sometimes even fiction can be seen as an author's personal view of reality.

Expressive writing is concerned with the details of everyday life and usually includes the author's reactions to people, places, and events. The common theme of such writing is that the life of a single individual counts for something. Instead of focusing on extraordinary people and unusual events, it reveals the significance of common events, the strength, humor, sorrow, and vitality of human life. For example:

**Kevin Stotts**

He was *my* dog.

He came to the house one warm, late, summer afternoon.

I thought at first he was a pup. But when he finally let me get close to him, I could see the gray hairs and cracked, calloused pads.

His tan and white short hair, barrel-round body, too short legs, and desperate stare made me love him.

Dad said I couldn't keep him. ("Don't feed him or he'll stay.") Mom helped me sneak him food.

I called him Brownie.

He followed me on my bike rides.

I remember once he carried off a little stale cookie and buried it. He always buried a part of his food. He must have done it because he was never sure that food would be there the next day.

My cousin, Miles, still teases me about the time I watched Brownie run back home from his house, down the tar-bubbly gravel road and said, "Brownie's going home. I'll have to go, too."

And when I needed somebody just to listen to me, Brownie was always there. He never laughed at the wrong time or yawned from boredom. Instead, his cinnamon eyes gazed at mine, almost as a lover's do.

He was my dog and everybody knew it.

My best friend in high school was Mike Barnes. When juniors, Mike and I and our new Argentinian friend, Jorge, spent a hot, wet, laughter-filled day at Cedar Point. I got home at about midnight—exhausted, dirty, and still thoroughly excited about that day. Mom was still up. That struck me as a little unusual, since she had always "trusted me" and staying up for me was not something she did.

She was very quiet. Solemn. I knew something was wrong. That awful feeling grabbed me. My neck went stiff, my ears buzzed, my breath quickened, and a fine film of perspiration burst over my entire body.

"Brownie's dead," she said.

The word hung there in the air—above and in front of my face. An invisible barrier was keeping those words from actually passing by my ears into my head. But the words had been spoken and they had sunk into my brain. I guess I was only pretending I hadn't heard them and was only acting like I could keep from hearing them.

I didn't say anything . . . but Mom knew that I wanted to know how it happened. And God, I wish she had lied. My dad and brother, Randall, were cutting the grass in my uncle's orchard with a tractor and side-arm mower. They hadn't seen Brownie running beside them. The scissorlike blades had caught Brownie's front legs and nearly severed them. Dad and Randall stopped their work immediately and tried to save him, Mom said, but he was hurt too badly. Dad put him out of his misery with one shot from his .22.

Mom found out how it happened, she said, when she came home from the grocery store and found Dad and Randall crying. She thought that while working together, they had gotten into their usual fight.

She told me more than just about Brownie's death. She told me that Dad and Randall felt so bad about what they had done, that I was not to say anything to them. But damn it, he was my dog and I didn't want to pretend that the whole thing hadn't happened. I was angry and in shock and her request made my chest hurt even worse. But I agreed not to say anything and shrank into bed—the one I still shared with my older brother—and lay there, awake.

The next morning I avoided my father's and Randall's eyes. After two weeks or so we could talk to each other almost normally. And now, fourteen years later, I still haven't talked to them about it. I love them—they are, after all, my father and my brother. But a little part of me hates them.

They killed my dog.

Personal writing succeeds to the degree that we identify with the author. We may not have actually experienced the same thing before, but if the author has written convincingly we can share in the experience through the words on the page; to a degree we can step into the author's shoes. The writer has extended a bridge to us; for a moment we can share in the life of another human being.

## JOURNALS

If you decided to become a ballet dancer, an artist, a pianist, a tennis or racquetball player, you would spend a great deal of time—some enjoyable, some tedious—practicing these skills. You could not become proficient by practicing only once a week. Like any other worthwhile skill, writing also takes practice.

To get regular practice in writing, keep a journal for at least two weeks. You'll remember that in Chapter Two we discussed keeping a journal as an invention technique. Keeping a journal is not only a good way to get daily practice in writing, it also gives you the opportunity to practice specific writing skills. The journal allows you to describe objects, people, and events from different perspectives, to zero in on a subject, to practice noting details, to *focus*. The journal is a place where you can discover what you really think of some issue or person. Sitting down to write in your journal can give you a break from your daily responsibilities and problems; it can help you slow down and focus on your life. The journal can also be a notebook of your ideas, a source for essays and stories you might want to write later, even a soapbox where you can expound on life, art, the latest fashions, politics. See, for example, what these journal writers have done:

**Cathy Cordell**

I sit alone in my room—the night life on High Street rushes by—people never sleep. I wish my neighbors would get off their roof and stop drinking and turn down that stereo. In my own haven, comfortable but not satisfied, I look out my window again. People—what they do they do until all hours of the morning—you can only drink so much. What do people think about and do—they eat, man do people eat when they're drunk—buffalo wings, gyros, popcorn, or ice cream.

Friends having fun, people walking hand in hand, dogs barking at each other. The nightlife never ceases. The cars and the cabs, the bikers, the joggers, the street people. The music makers and the singers. It's truly hard to describe this scene to anyone not sitting here next to me. How can you say this place is so tacky—you'd absolutely adore it. It's a kaleidoscope of colors and people and different scenes all the time. If I had written this last fall I would have totally been negative about it all. Now I wouldn't trade this scene in for the Eiffel Tower.

**Anne Moody**

I worked for Linda Jean throughout my seventh grade year. But that spring and summer Raymond tried farming again, and I was only able to help her on weekends. When I entered eighth grade the following fall we were poorer than ever. Raymond had worse luck with the farm than the year before, so we weren't able to buy any new clothes. I had added so much meat to my bones that I could squeeze into only two of my old school dresses. They were so tight I was embarrassed to put them on. I had gotten new jeans for the field that summer, so I started wearing them to school two and three days a week. But I continued to fill out so fast that even my jeans got too tight. I got so many wolf whistles from the boys in class that the faster girls started wearing jeans that were even tighter than mine. When the high school boys started talking about how fine those eighth grade girls were, the high school girls started wearing tight jeans too. I had started a blue jeans fad.

**Henry David Thoreau**

April 16, 1852
His tail was also brown, though not very dark, rat-tail like, with loose hairs standing out on all sides like a caterpillar brush. He had a rather mild look. I spoke to him kindly. I reached checkerberry leaves to his mouth. I stretched my hands over him, though he turned up his head and still gritted a little. I laid my hand on him, but immediately took it off again, instinct not being wholly overcome. If I had had a few fresh bean leaves, thus in advance of the season, I am sure I should have tamed him completely. It was a frizzly tail. His is a humble, terrestrial color like the partridge's, well concealed where dead wiry grass rises above darker brown or chestnut dead leaves—a modest color. If I had had some food, I should have ended with stroking him at my leisure. Could easily have wrapped him in my handkerchief. He was not fat nor particularly lean. I finally had to leave him without seeing him move from the place. A large, clumsy, burrowing squirrel. *Arctomys*, bear-mouse. I respect him as one of the natives. He lies there, by his color and habits so naturalized amid the dry leaves, withered grass, and the bushes. A sound nap, too, he has enjoyed in his native fields, the past winter. I think I might learn some wisdom of him. His ancestors have lived here longer than mine, he is more thoroughly acclimated and naturalized than I. Bean leaves the red man raised for him, but he can do without them.

## ► How to Write a Journal

How you handle your journal is your decision, but the following hints may help you get started:

**1.** Write every day. Regular, specified periods of writing are better than fewer and longer sessions. Don't try to cram a week's worth of writing into one night; you'd get the same effect as if you tried to cram a week's worth of jogging into a single session.

**2.** Discover the time and place best for you to write, and then don't let anything interfere with your schedule.

**3.** Write at least a page a day, even on the days when you'd rather not. (Especially then.)

**4.** Write anything you want, any way you want, but remember that a journal is *not* a diary or a private, intimate document for your eyes alone. A journal is a record of your thoughts that others should be able to read. Your instructor may want to check your journal to see your growth as a writer.

**5.** Do not treat your journal as if it were merely a record of your activities:

> Got up early. Studied for test. Went bowling in the afternoon. Nothing much happened today.

Entries like this are a waste of time because the writer is *avoiding* his thoughts and recording only actions. Instead, the writer might have written about why he studied for the test. Was he worried about failing? Is he chasing grades? If so, why? Did he enjoy the bowling? What is the significance of "Nothing much happened today"? Is he bored? Disappointed? A journal should be a record of what your *mind* is doing.

## ► WRITING ACTIVITY ◄

Keep a journal for at least two weeks. Write in it at least once a day. If you can find the time, write in it more than once a day. On days when you can't think of anything to write, try one of the following:

**1.** Speculate. Why do you spend so much time in a certain place? Why do you like a certain kind of movie or TV show?

**2.** Record your observations about a song, film, TV show, live concert, or other media event.

**3.** Try to recapture on paper an incident or moment of terror from your past. Were you afraid of the dark as a child? Did you have a special routine before going to bed at night, such as looking behind the door or in the closet? What particular things frightened you as a child? How did you overcome your fear? Or did you?

**4.** Invent a new word—perhaps a *sniglet*. Carefully define this word and explain why it should be officially added to the language. Write several sentences using this new word. Demonstrate why only your new word could work in these sentences.

**5.** Observe a stranger performing a task or just sitting and thinking. Make up an imaginary life for this person. What is his or her name? What is he or she thinking about at this moment?

**6.** Listen to a piece of music you've never heard before. A symphony. The overture to an opera. Music from a Broadway musical. Describe your reaction. Why would this music attract some people?

**7.** Go someplace you've never been before. A preschool. A retirement home. An ethnic food store. A junk store. An antique store. Describe what you see. Try to capture the atmosphere of the place.

**8.** Without opening your closet door, describe the contents of your closet in as detailed and organized a manner as you can.

**9.** Write a complaint letter. Or a letter telling someone off.

**10.** Now put yourself on the other side of the mailbox. Write a response to your letter.

## VOICE IN PERSONAL WRITING

Journal writing helps you learn to think on paper; it builds your confidence as a writer. When you become completely at ease with your writing, the *voice* on the paper will begin to "sound" like you. Voice is the writer's personality or attitude as expressed in the text. If you look back at the examples in this chapter, you will see that each one sounds different; each has a different voice. Of course, we can never be sure whether the voice in a paper is really the writer's own or an imaginative creation. Fiction writers often create stories whose narrators have totally different personalities and attitudes—different selves—from the writers'. Such literary selves, or *personas*, are masks the writers put on for their narrative purposes. But in nonfiction writing, most readers assume that the voice they hear represents the writer's true self.

Composition textbooks often warn against trying to sound too academic or phony, advising writers to "try to sound natural; sound like yourself." This is good advice, but there is a snag to it. As we pointed out in Chapter One, the self is very complex; you have many selves and, therefore, many voices. When you talk to your family, you use your family voice. And you have more than one of those too, depending on whom you are talking to and why: there's the voice you use when you want the family car or some other favor, the voice you use when you are explaining why you didn't take out the garbage or something else you should or shouldn't have done, and several others. Then there is the voice you use with friends—different voices for different friends and different situations. And there is the voice you use with strangers and unfamiliar situations: the one for the judge in traffic court, the one for a personnel director during a job interview, and so on.

The problem in college composition is, which voice should you use when you write? Your writing will have a voice even if you are trying to sound bland, objective, and toneless. Which of your many voices is appropriate for college writing? The voice you have been developing in your freewriting and journal entries comes close to it. In college, you can write more formally in this natural, "journal" voice simply by avoiding anything that will distract readers who expect a certain degree of formality. The end product should still sound like you, minus some of the informalities (slang, abbreviations, nonstandard spelling or punctuation) you would allow in your journal writing. In short, the writing voice you select should be your natural voice modified by your purpose and audience.

## ▶ READING ACTIVITY ◀

You may think your college writing should sound very learned and formal. That assumption usually leads to difficult writing and forces the reader to pay more attention to *how* you are writing than to *what* you are saying. For example, here is a paragraph about a student's first impressions of college. The writer has made some assumptions about what the composition teacher expects, and these cause some problems. Why is the student writing this way? Is this an effective way to write? What would you tell this student to do to improve her writing?

> Being that I am a freshman at this university, which I just enrolled at, I feel I have some authority for the assertions which I am about to elucidate. This institution is one of higher learning, and one could suppose that its intentions were of the highest academic merit. But this is not the case in actuality. In fact the conditions are such that just exactly the reverse is true. The average freshmen here, of which I count myself as one, soon discovers that instead of serious contemplation of scholastic matters, a rather casual attitude is prevalent concerning the acquisition of progressive knowledge. The real function of this university is as to promote the social development of the individual, which is essentially a high-school orientation of education.

The student has used a dollar's worth of language to convey a dime's worth of information: She is unhappy because she finds college too much like high school. Because she is criticizing the college, she feels that she must adopt the very formal voice of someone intelligent and well educated. The student assumes her subject is very important, and she assumes the professor will enjoy a display of big words. The true motive behind such writing is to impress the reader with the writer's intelligence. But the outcome sounds unnatural and pretentious, and most readers come away with a negative reaction to both the writing and the writer.

Translate this student's language into a more natural student voice by, first of all, deciding what the student wants to say and then saying it as clearly as possible. Examine one student's attempt:

> Since I'm a freshman at this University, I believe I'm qualified to say a few things about the education system here. While we are supposed to be here to learn new ideas, new skills, and new information which we may need later in life, we are really just learning how to get along with each other. It's the same casual attitude I found in high school. Nobody cares about what you learned or what you know. Everybody cares about how you behave.

The message, although not novel, is clear, the writer's voice, natural and relaxed.

## ► Dialog

Dialogs enliven writing by making it more immediate and, therefore, more realistic. They invite readers to participate as spectators of the actual scene, to experience not what happened, but what is happening. Dialogs are not simply audiotaped recordings of everything said. An effective dialog is an edited version of a conversation and retains only those details that allow the writer to paint a "sound" picture of the participant's moods, attitudes, or personalities.

### ► READING ACTIVITY ◄

How effective is the dialog in the following episode? Has the writer created a convincing picture in sound for his readers?

**Dan Nielsen**

"Stop that bike and hop your fanny off 'afore I pull it off, boy!" the police officer hollered brazenly through the open window of his police cruiser.

"Whaa?" I turned my head and sure enough, my ears hadn't failed. I was staring eyeball to eyeball with one of the thickest-skinned rhinos on the force.

After wrestling my bike over to the loose gravel shoulder and calming down a certain female passenger who was alternately screaming and scolding me for the minor confusion I'd created, I climbed off, immediately putting on my give-me-a-break face. I actually didn't even know what I had done.

"Do you know you're riding that bike with an out-of-date license?" the cop hollered while climbing out of his vehicle.

I managed to glance at the man before reaching for my wallet. He would have made a good-sized refrigerator freezer. I pulled out my driver's license and gave him probably one of the most confused looks he has ever gotten.

"It says here it's good until 1991."

"No, you smart-assed kid, not driver's license, license tags, boy, the metal things you get from the state every year to put on the back of your bike."

I felt like a real dummy as I walked around to the back of the bike and looked at the muddy, bent-up, year-old license plate. Then I remembered, "Oh yeah, those, well you see sir, this is my brother's bike and, uh, he didn't have current registration or something, but he's got all the papers that say he's legal."

"Well, where's he keep all these so-called documents, boy?"

"In his boot."

"And where's his boot?"

"Well, to tell you the truth, he's wearing them, but he said it was okay to ride his bike."

"He did, did he? Well that's real nice o' yo' brother, boy, but I'm afraid he didn't ask the police department if it was okay. Why don't you go sit in my police car, son."

So, giving my girlfriend a please-excuse-me-for-a-moment look, I waddled over and sat in his car while the cop got a real important-looking notebook out and wrote a bunch of stuff in it. Then he came over to his car.

"Okay, so this bike belongs to your brother, huh? What's your brother's name?"

"Dave, David Nielsen." The cop picked up his microphone and called it in. "Car nineteen to dispatch."

"Dispatch, go ahead."

"Registration for South Carolina motorcycle tag, M–Y–1–0–2."

After a pause, the dispatcher came back on: "Bike registered to Robert Marion."

"Oh my lord," I whispered.

"Sixty-seven West Fourth Street."

My brother had forgotten to change registration.

"Virginia Beach, Virginia."

I was in heap-big trouble. The cop, misunderstanding the whole problem, glared at me a minute with eyes that would knock Dracula cold, and then, very quietly, spoke: "You stole that bike, dinja, boy?"

"No sir, you can take me home and ask. . . ."

"Ain't takin' you nowhere, 'cept the police station."

By using dialog, Nielsen quickly and effectively captures both his own feelings and attitudes and those of the police officer. True to Nielsen's description of him as a "thick-skinned rhino," the officer speaks in a no-nonsense, intimidating tone. Nielsen, on the other hand, shares his confusion as he tries to avoid being taken to jail.

*Problems to avoid in dialogs* Now let's examine some problems students encounter when using dialog.

***Bravelys*** Try to let the words of the dialog show your readers what the speakers are feeling. "Bravely," "kindly," "hopefully," and "cheerfully" are descriptive overkill in this example:

"I'm all right, doctor," she said bravely.
"Of course you are, my dear," he said kindly.
"I know I'll walk again," she said hopefully.
"Without a doubt," he said cheerfully.

***Stilted English*** Try to capture the sound of real people talking about real things. No one really talks this way:

"Good evening, Mother dear; I am home for dinner!"
"How nice to see you, Lester; we are having pot roast!"

***Too Many Speech Tags*** "I said," "she retorted," and so on remind your reader constantly that a writer is present:

> "Hi," I said.
> "Hi yourself," she retorted.
> "What's new?" I inquired.
> "What's new with you?" she countered.

In good dialogs, the writer fades into the background. Use speech tags *only* to tell the reader things that aren't clear from the words of the dialog itself. Realism is the goal. In spoken English, people tend to use contractions and informal English. And if a dialog is meant to be read aloud, too many speech tags will overwhelm the speakers' words.

## ► WRITING ACTIVITY ◄

Try a dialog or a story with dialog. You can make it all up, but it will be easier just to remember and write a real dialog or one close to it. Conflict situations usually make for easy dialogs because they have built-in tension. Without tension, dialogs tend to sound like two people trying to talk to each other when they have nothing to say. Try to recall a conflict between you and your parents, you and a close friend, you and the police, you and a teacher, and so on. Put yourself in the other person's role for a moment; try out the other person's *voice*. (You can have three speakers, if you like.)

Pretend you are a reporter and go out and find an interesting dialog. Visit a supermarket, coffee shop, fast-food restaurant, a club, or a bar and eavesdrop on a conversation. You may have to eavesdrop on more than one before you find what you are looking for. Record what you hear, paying special attention to the speakers' vocabulary, phrasing, and delivery. Since it will be almost impossible to record every word of the conversation, scribble down key words, phrases, responses. You can reconstruct what is missing later when you fashion the conversation into an interesting dialog.

## ► DISCUSSION ACTIVITY ◄

Read the following two dialogs. Do they sound realistic? How do the details in each description help to develop each person's character? What various sensory details does each writer use? How does dialog deepen our understanding of the person being described?

### BORN BLACK
**Gordon Parks**

"Do all of you sleep on this one mattress?"

"That ain't nothing, brother. There's a poor fella livin' down the hall what's got six children and their place ain't no bigger'n this. There was eight of 'em till two of the young'uns got drafted in the army a month or so ago."

"Where's your toilet and bathroom?"

"Take him down the hall and show him. Lil. Show him good." Lil, his wife, nodded toward me and I followed her down a dark corridor, where she opened a door and pointed in. There was an old bathtub with most of the enamel broken off and a filthy toilet. The seat next to it had rotted and fallen apart, lying in a heap of other decaying boards and fallen plaster. The foul air was unbearable. "Would you wash your child in that mess?" she asked. I didn't answer. I knew she didn't expect me to. I just took a picture of it; and we went back to her husband and children.

"Well, how'd you like it? It's a dog, huh?" I nodded, and he went on, "Eight families use it, brother. See that baseball bat over there in the corner? Well, my boy, they don't play ball with it. We kill rats with it."

**Fred Atkins**

(A conversation between Gary and Bill and another guy at Bruno's)

Gary: What will take ink outta carpet?

Bill: Milk.

Gary: Milk??

Bill: Yea, you heard me. Don't ask me no more, cause I can't tell you.

Gary: 99 more days, 99 more shifts.

(I missed something here, but the conversation picked up something like this)

Gary: The house is all boarded up and the sign hanging on the stoop says "Touring far east."

Bill: Camel rider, eh? (Chuckles)

Gary: He took off to Bethlehem (Ohio).

Other guy: My knees ache so bad—means weather's gonna change.

Bill: What's he doing in Bethlehem? Lookin' fer a job? Ha. Like lookin' fer a star.

Gary: He's going back to his birthplace.

Other guy: They're mixin' holy water and prune juice to get a religious movement. (Laughs loudly, but others don't)

Bill: Who's bossin' late shift?

Gary: Dunno. He sold his car and everything.

Bill: What he go and do that fer?

Gary: Needs to eat. Got a wife and kids, you know.

(Beautician comes in)

Beautician: How'd ya like your wife's hair?

Gary: Great. Tanya's too. It'll take some used to for she likes it. Don't say nothin'; but Harold, he been cuttin' my hair for 20 years now and I never liked it. He's a great guy, but he just gets yappin' and you might as well have a rabbit chewin' on your hair.

## THE PERSONAL EXPERIENCE NARRATIVE

In a personal experience narrative, you are trying to recreate an event for your readers so that they will see what you saw, hear what you heard, feel what you felt. A personal experience narrative is typically an act of memory, but of selective remembering. Think of yourself not so much as a newspaper reporter but as a movie director adapting a novel for the screen. Writing for a newspaper, a reporter would objectively tell what happened, using the journalistic questions Who? What? When? Where? Why? and How? to frame the report. Movie directors, on the other hand, have a task similar to that of writers of a personal experience narrative. Suppose a movie director wanted to depict the brutality of one of the characters who, in the novel, was depicted in a dozen detailed scenes as behaving with savagery. The movie director would doubtless have to ignore ten of these incidents and concentrate on one or two, in which she would also have to collapse into a five-minute scene events that lasted two hours in the novel. The movie director has to narrow the focus and select and shape only those cinematic details that would dramatize her overall purpose—the depiction of a brutal character. She would show rather than tell.

In similar fashion, writers of personal experience narratives have to narrow their focus, shape their scenes, and select only those scenic details that will give their readers a sure sense of the point they want to make. They must include only those details that will contribute to the overall impression they want to convey, ignoring incidents that really did occur but that would distract their readers' attention.

A personal experience narrative is a story describing an important or interesting event in your life. Most successful personal experience narratives limit themselves to one or two specific incidents. If you are planning such a narrative, focus at the most on an afternoon or evening in your life, although it's usually better to limit yourself to an hour or less. Shape the events so that you can focus on one or two incidents in great detail. Although it is possible to include too many details, it's a good idea to err on the side of abundance: The more details, the better.

If you try to cover too much chronological territory, you will end up summarizing, generalizing too much, *mentioning* rather than *showing* in dramatic detail. Entertaining narratives usually begin fairly dramatically. If there are incidents that occurred earlier about which your readers should be aware, have one of your characters mention them in a dialog. Another useful "shaping" technique is to begin somewhere in the middle of the scene and use a flashback (where you switch from the present to an earlier scene and back) to bring your reader up to date. This technique—in *medias res*—is an effective method of excluding extraneous details and focusing your reader's attention on the essentials.

Although there are important differences between directing a scene in a movie and describing the same incident in a narrative—for instance, you can get into the mind of your character more readily in a story—you'll find it useful to think of your scenes from a director's viewpoint. If you are telling the story using the first person—I—you can imagine the *I* as carrying a camera with audio capability. Your character could not, for instance, know for certain what is going on in the minds of the other characters. Thinking as a movie director will help you to see the dramatic nature of the event and will encourage you to think of the viewers, your readers, and their needs.

## ► READING ACTIVITY ◄

Here is the beginning of the final draft of a personal experience narrative. What is the dominant impression Shirley wants to convey? Has she done a good job of interlacing incident and thought? Has she supplied enough details? What about her focus?

**Shirley Michaels**

We stood there alone, the pale green windowless walls ensuring our privacy. No one could see us. Still, I glanced nervously around, stunned by the request. No, stunned by the demand to remove my clothes. Nothing like this had ever happened to me—never. Now don't get the idea I'm a young naive girl. Not at all. In my thirty-odd years I've been around; I know the score. I read the newspaper daily and *Time* weekly. In fact, I had been here before. Although others had been apprehensive, maybe even frightened, when we had come here, I had never felt so. I had an easy familiarity with the place. But, this time was different.

I played for time, repeating the command: "Take off my clothes?" Maybe if I questioned I could avoid compliance. The answer was a slight but imperative nod of the head. Disbelief flooded my consciousness. I've had my share of fantasies imagining disrobing in front of others, especially at their insistence—maybe even delighting a little in showing off. This certainly wasn't playing like one of my fantasies. I joked that my fantasies had always involved men. The response was an impersonal, perfunctory "Place them on the bench behind you." Did I have an alternative? No. I awkwardly started undressing. Should I start with my blouse or with my slacks? Did I have to take all my clothes off? Could I leave my panties on ? My mother's dictum about the necessity of always wearing clean underwear in case of an emergency flashed through my mind. But one look at her face and the flippant mood and questioning died in my throat.

My breasts—my very being was shrinking, shrinking as she commanded me to sit. She seemed more concerned with separating my toes, unaware of my ashen, anemic body. Later as I stood there naked, awkwardly exposing myself to her further scrutiny—her searching, relentless examination, I thought, "What's a nice girl like you doing in a place like this! . . . For forgetting to pay a fine for doing 37 in a 25-mile-an-hour zone."

Shirley's beginning keeps readers in suspense: Why is she being asked to take off her clothes? Where is she? Shirley has consciously shaped her narrative to gain her readers' attention, to engage her readers in the experience, to make them feel as naked and vulnerable, as dehumanized, as she did.

The initial draft of this story was very different. In the exploratory draft, Shirley told her readers too much. She summarized *every* incident in her day, instead of showing her readers what was important. In the final draft, Shirley's beginning recreates the event; she dramatizes the incident so that her readers can see, hear, and feel, can relive the experience with her. She does not begin at the day's beginning. Instead, she focuses on what she is really interested in writing about—the event that started with "Take off your clothes." The initial draft was a simple act of memory. The version you read is *composed*, its incidents and details selected and shaped.

## ► Personal Experience Narratives in Action

In this section, we will be focusing on how to select an interesting incident or event from your life and shape it so that it will have an impact on your readers. Your goal is to show your readers what is significant about the event, what the event meant to you. You may say, "But I've led a dull life; I've never done anything unusual or extraordinary to write about." Few of us have anything extraordinary to write about, but you can try to show the meaning of commonplace events. The only thing new in the world is each individual. *You* are new; your perceptions, your understandings, your own experiences are new, unique to you. Almost every human being has had a love affair, or will have one sooner or later; yet writers never tire of writing about love, and people never tire of reading about love. Why? Because each story is slightly different; each writer gives the story an individual interpretation.

### ► READING ACTIVITY ◄

The next narrative's plot line could not be simpler: A woman walks up six flights of stairs, thinking to herself as she goes, and then makes an important decision. What strategies has Mary Ellen Tyus employed to give this story its power?

**Mary Ellen Tyus**

I climbed to the top floor through the murky gloom of the steep stairwell. Dust motes swirled around me, and the ancient stairs creaked ominously. After the sharp cold of the lakeside air, the building felt especially hot, dry and oppressive. Beyond the second landing my arms began to ache from the bundles which shifted precariously in my grasp. My thick coat hung heavily from my shoulders and flapped around my knees, impeding my progress up the stairs. Beneath it my clothes began to cling moistly to my body.

My face was flushed from the effort of the climb, and I could feel the tight lines along my cheeks where the tears had dried. My head throbbed slightly as a headache sought to take hold. My eyes were dry and stung. The passage was as arid as the chalk dust which lightly powdered its walls.

I reached the summit and paused, surveying the expanse of empty, dust-filled rooms opening one onto another. Once these rooms had fairly hummed with activity. For nearly one hundred years myriad feet had trod down these halls, wearing paths into the wood—deep trails, like old auto grooves in forgotten woodlands—paths now filling with the dust of the wood itself, with the dust of time.

I crossed the hall and climbed over the barricade into a wide, dusky room lighted only by the diffused Northern glow filtering through the dirty panes of a pair of French doors. The floor bowed deeply at the center, and here and there the light and shadows revealed sunken areas in the aged wood. I wondered if it would crash to the cellars beneath my feet, and I stepped in silently.

The floor did not creak as I crossed it, but there was a feeling of tentativeness in the atmosphere as though I, and the room, and the moment were caught in some delicate, timeless balance. I stopped at the windows and looked back. The dust had absorbed my foot-falls and smoothed itself as if I had not passed. I held my breath and listened. Nothing.

I turned to the windows and looked out. The stark, cold, February forenoon winds wafted no voices to my ear, no hurrying footsteps on the pavement far below. No birdsong. I turned the latch and stepped out. The rusted fire escape swayed ever so slightly from its weary moorings. Perhaps another step would send it crashing down. I peered over the rail at the small square of brickwork six flights below.

Flight. If I leapt from the balcony, would I fly? Would I plummet groundwards, veering at the last second and rising—arms spread—in a graceful soar?

The balcony shifted again under my weight and I felt the sudden rush of tears against my lashes. They would find me on those faded bricks, their worn surface new-red with the liberal glazing of my blood.

Then what? I thought of faces pale with alarm; horror. People turning away, stomachs lurching, as the blanket was spread. He'd be sorry then. The bastard. Let him look at that!

A tear fell down the six long flights, invisible as it passed the rail. I watched, unseeing, imagining its path as it spiralled earthward. Would my passing, too, be so unmarked? I turned and stepped back into the gloom.

"Hell, nobody's worth *that*!" I said, and walked swiftly through the dust and shadows, through the webs and memories, down the stairs and out to life.

Mary Ellen began her story with utter simplicity, "I climbed to the top floor through the murky gloom of the stairwell." But as she has us literally ascend the stairs along with her female protagonist, Mary Ellen transforms a simple narrative into a tale with universal appeal: courage in the face of adversity and despair, with the dust, the building itself, and a century of its occupants becoming vital atmospheric factors in this affirmation of the worth of an individual human being. The "delicate, timeless balance" is tipped in favor of life in the brief but effective conclusion as the protagonist "walked swiftly through the dust and shadows, through the webs and memories, down the stairs and out to life." We are never told why the protagonist was contemplating suicide, and the author's decision to exclude incidents explaining why the relationship was foundering gives the story a more powerful focus by making it less particular and more universal.

# THE WRITER'S MIND AT WORK

## DRAFTING AND REVISING A PERSONAL EXPERIENCE NARRATIVE

For the most part, we have been examining only the final drafts of some fine personal experience essays. Now we will be observing a student, Randy, as he works on the various stages—discovery, planning, drafting, and revising—of a personal experience narrative. (For a detailed treatment of this process, see Chapters Two and Three.) This will give us an opportunity to watch his writer's mind at work.

After producing a cluster-vignette and using the journalistic questions to generate details and a focus for a story based on an incident that occurred when he was ten years old, Randy produced the following brief exploratory draft:

**EXPLORATORY DRAFT:**
**"Finding the Door"**

When I was about ten my family and I went to my grandfather's camp in the woods–I was scared to sleep. I slept in a room with my brother–the wood noises plus the total darkness frightened me–made me uneasy–always used to the sounds of civilization–went to bed first night and had a hard time getting to sleep–finally dropped off–woke up in the middle of the night and had to go to the bathroom–no electric lights and I could not find the flashlight so I thought I'd feel my way to the door–in the pitch black I edged alongside the bed till I came to the wall–but I couldn't find the doorknob. I groped all over but I couldn't find it–immediately I panicked–I began banging on the door screaming for help—I heard my Mom's voice soon somewhere in the distance—in the dark—I told her I couldn't find the doorknob—that it must have broken off that I needed to get out—she tried to calm me down and told me to stand still—she said she'll get a flashlight—I waited for several seconds then she said she'd try to open the door. All of a sudden, I saw light behind me—I turned around to discover that I'd tried to walk through a solid wall against the adjacent bedroom and that I hadn't even been anywhere near the door.

After writing the exploratory draft, Randy did a good deal of thinking about the incident at camp. It had disturbed him then and bothered him now, years later. Here is the script of his writer's mind planning how he'll shape the narrative.

### THE WRITER'S MIND: Planning the Narrative

*I've had enough nightmares about that night, really that moment of terror. I think I should center on that moment when I panicked and mistook the wall for the door. That's what I think is the most interesting part of that whole incident—the feeling of alienation, feeling* totally *alone in the dark, jumping to an irrational conclusion. Being completely out in space, losing my bearings, having no earthly idea where I was. This I think is the most important part of this paper.*

*I think I'll begin with setting the scene—describing my age (ten years old)—where we were—why I felt so unstable at camp to begin with.*

*But I want to save the punchline—I don't want to give it away too early—that I'd mistaken the wall for the door and that would spoil the whole thing. So I'll need to be careful about describing my manner of getting out of bed and groping toward the door—so that the reader won't know that* I'd *made the mistake yet.*

*I'm not sure how to work my uncle into this—he was on the other side of the wall and he heard me pounding that night, but I didn't find out till morning that I'd woken him up—I'm not sure if I should talk about him as I pound on the wall or where? We'll see how it goes and maybe he doesn't have to be in the paper at all—see what happens.*

*I'll want to break down that feeling of panic in the dark and describe it in every way I know how—what I felt physically—what was going on through my mind.*

*The dark, my feelings of uneasiness made me mistake the wall for the door.*

*My pounding on the wall in the middle of the night woke up my uncle who was disconcerted with sleep and caused him to think irrationally.*

*Should I end with my mother that night or the next morning with my uncle and how he didn't know?*

*I think I'll try the next morning and see how it goes. I have to have closure—a conclusion. I can't let this story peter out at the end. I hope I come up with a decent ending. The middle should be fun.*

Randy then produced the working draft that follows:

**WORKING DRAFT:**
**"Finding the Door"**

My family spent two weeks of every summer of my childhood at my Grandfather's camp deep in the woods of northern Maine. It was a vacation for my parents—a chance for Mom and Dad to get away from it all in a log cabin seven miles away from the nearest town. It wasn't such a pleasurable experience for me. During the daytime I was fine—I loved to swim, fish, hike, and romp in the woods. Nighttime, however, was a different story. Like many young kids, I was petrified of the dark. All the monsters came out in the dark and without a light on you were always more vulnerable. My grandfather's camp had no electricity, which meant no hall light on during the night to ward off all the monsters. Plus, I had to sleep on a twin bed, a mere three feet from the floor. At home my brother and I shared a bunkbed. I had the top bunk, he had the bottom, an arrangement which suited me just fine because I always figured the mountain lions, witches, and dwarves couldn't get to me on the top bunk. I suppose it was callous of me to sacrifice my brother to the mountain lions so readily in my imagination but fear of the night and the unknown doesn't always bring out the best in you.

My brother and I shared a bedroom in my grandfather's camp, one across the hall from my parents' bedroom and adjacent to my uncle's. My mother would leave a flashlight on the table next to my bed so that if I woke up in the middle of the night and had to go to the bathroom I could easily find my way out the door and down the hall. This arrangement I thought was small consolation for having to try to sleep in total darkness on a twin bed no less, but it usually allowed me to sleep. Except for one memorable night.

I was ten years old and it was the first night of our annual two week's stay at camp. I was even more jittery than usual that first night. We had experienced thunderstorms that evening, beginning just as my brother and I were marched off to bed. I lay in bed terrified at the eerie green light, flashing irregularily like some crazy neon sign gone berserk. The rain pelted the roof like an army of pellets and the thunder seemed enough to collapse the roof. All this made sleeping that night for a ten-year-old kid terrified of the dark impossible.

After what seemed like hours, the thunderstorm slowly passed, leaving me lying in complete stillness and total darkness. It was then I realized that I had to go to the bathroom. I didn't want to leave the bed (outside of the covers you were even more vulnerable to monsters) but I had to, so I slowly, quietly inched my way outside of the covers, and set up on the side of the bed and groped around for the flashlight. Nothing was there. I felt all over the table which was beside my bed but I couldn't find the flashlight. I began to wave my arm wildly over the table, desperately hoping to grasp the flashlight but it was no good. It just was not there.

I slowly began to realize that if I was going to make it to the bathroom that night, it would be without the assistance of a light. I weighed the chances of being waylaid en route and decided that as long as I could grope my way along the wall, keeping one hand pressed against the sturdy logs, I'd be all right.

I slipped my feet to the floor and fighting my fear of the ocean of darkness that surrounded me I cautiously edged my way to the door, which I knew was near the foot of my bed. I made it to the end of the bed and carefully reached one arm into the darkness, the other arm clutched tightly around the wooden bedstead. Waves of panic—induced adrenaline shivered through my body when I could feel nothing. I realized that in order to make it to the wall where the door was I would have to let go my hold on the bed and for a moment abandon myself to that ocean of darkness which I dreaded so much.

I leaned forward into the darkness and regretfully released the bedstead from my grasp. For a second, I was completely and totally disoriented having no conception at all of my position in the room. I shuffled my feet slowly towards where I believed the door was, tentatively poking with my hands into the darkness, searching for a wall. Suddenly my fingers felt the welcome sensation of a log. The wall! Gathering courage at my discovery of a familiar form in the black chaos I crept slowly alongside the wall in search of the door, comforting myself with the solid feel of the rounded, cracked log, not even worrying about getting splinters.

Finally, one arm reached a surface of smooth wood. The door! Now all I need is to find the doorknob, and I've got it made. I circled one outstretched palm over the smooth wooden surface anticipating that welcome touch of smooth steel. But I couldn't find it! I slid my palm again and again over the smooth wooden surface. Nothing there! Instantly my crazed mind grasped at the worst interpretation of the situation—the doorknob had fallen off! I was trapped in this dark room with no way to escape!

This was more than I could possibly be expected to handle. I figured I needed help—and fast—that the only thing to be done was to get some help to get me out of this room. Standing there pressed against the wall, the darkness seemed to close in around me. What before was an ocean, now became a closed tomb. I had to get out!

"Mom, Mom, open the door. Help!" I shouted as I pounded frantically against the wood with my fist. "Help! The doorknob has broken off. I can't open the door! Help!"

I began to hear a stir somewhere outside my tomb of darkness, and presently heard the rattle of a doorknob and the creak of hinges. My mom had left her bedroom and had crossed the hall.

"What's the matter?" I heard her sleepily croak on the other side of my tomb.

"I can't open the door. The doorknob has broken off. Get me out of here!"

"Wait there. I'll get a flashlight."

As I heard her footsteps recede, I heaved a sigh of relief, still mingled with the shivers of my terror. I figured all I had to do was stand there against the wall and Mom would get me out. I heard her fumble with something and then her footsteps returned.

"The knob is still on out here," she said. "I'm going to open the door now. Stand back so I don't hit you."

It was difficult to tear myself away from the comfort of a solid surface, but the thought that my mom was going to rescue me gave me the mental strength to take two steps backward in the dark, anticipating seeing my mother right in front of me with the flashlight.

"Ready?" she said.

"Hurry up" I whined.

Suddenly I saw a light behind me, beaming over my shoulder. I turned my head around in bewilderment and heard a voice from the darkness.

"Are you all right?" my mother calmly asked.

I couldn't figure out what was going on. Where was she coming from? Then the beam of light zig-zagged across the wall in front of me, the one I had pounded on so frantically a few minutes earlier. It was the wall separating my bedroom from my uncle's. I was nowhere near the door of the bedroom! I had been looking for the door in the wrong wall. I had in my panic mistaken the smooth surface of the planked wall for the door.

My Mom began to chuckle softly as she walked towards me and put her arm over my shoulder. I had never before felt so foolish or so much like a baby. I guess she could tell that I was embarrassed because she knelt down and softly said to me, "We won't tell anyone about this. It'll be our little secret."

The next morning at breakfast, the table talk centered on the tremendous thunderstorm that had kept us up the early part of the night before. My uncle told us all of the strange dreams he had had. He dreamt that there was someone on the roof last night pounding and screaming to be let in. He figured that the rain drumming on the rooftop had put the idea in his mind. I, red-faced, and my mother, stifling a laugh, agreed. It had probably been his nervousness at the thunderstorm.

Randy's story has universal appeal. All of us have been terrified of something as a child. Randy has skillfully captured that feeling of blind panic. This story is humorous and serious simultaneously. He has taken a simple incident and crafted it into a fine personal experience narrative.

What advice would you give Randy about revising this working draft into a final draft? You might find the following PACES criteria questions useful.

## CRITERIA QUESTIONS: NARRATING AN EVENT

**P urpose**

Does the writer *recreate* the experience for the reader? Are there enough details, description, and action for the reader to feel, see, smell, hear, and taste the experience? Is the meaning of the experience clear to the reader? What dominant impression is the writer trying to achieve. Has the writer been successful?

**A udience**

What is the writer's attitude toward the audience? Has the writer made an effort to interest the reader? Are details and situations adequately explained for the audience? What assumptions does the writer make about the audience's knowledge of the event?

**C ode**

What strategies has the writer used to develop the story? Is the language appropriate for the subject and the audience? What words or phrases stick out? Is the tone of the paper consistent?

**E xperience**

Is it clear why the writer has written about this event? Does the paper pass the "So what" test? Has the writer shaped the personal event adequately? Is there some material that could be cut out? Some that could be added?

**S elf**

Is the writer's voice believable? Consistent? Interesting? Personable? Is the writer's point of view clear?

## ► WRITING ACTIVITY ◄

Search your experience for an incident that would appeal to your readers. Use a variety of invention techniques to explore your subject in detail. Then write an exploratory, working, and final draft of a personal experience narrative. Make sure that you limit the focus of your story to a manageable time frame. Shape the incident so that you craft an interesting introduction and conclusion. Try to use dialog as you develop your narrative. Finally, take care to show, not tell, your readers how to react to your story.

## DESCRIPTION: PLACES AND PEOPLE

Among the more challenging kinds of personal experience writing is the piece that attempts to describe a place or a person. This kind of descriptive writing concentrates less on events, although they still remain fairly important, and more on the people and places themselves. Description is the writer's attempt to freeze in time and in space an overall impression of a chosen place or person. It is the writer's attempt to embed in the reader's consciousness both the details that make the subject unique or memorable and the attitudes, the positive or negative or ambivalent feelings, the writer has toward the subject. Description is the writer's attempt to recapture for the reader the essence of the person or place being described.

### ► The Writer's Memory

Most personal experience writing involves memory. Unlike newspaper reporters who report on an event immediately after they experience it, writers who are sharing significant experiences with their readers usually write about events that occurred some time before, often many years before, in what is now the distant past.

In personal experience writing, readers are at once dependent on writers and yet suspicious of them. Is this what really happened? Did the protagonist in Mary Ellen's "Coming Up" really say, "Hell, nobody's worth *that*!" and stride out to life? Or is that what the author *wished* had happened? Mary Ellen's skill and our sense of her protagonist's integrity convince us of the truth of what she said. But we can never be certain. Eyewitness accounts are notoriously unreliable in courts of law, and yet personal experience writing is just that: an eyewitness account. The writer's memory is a crucial element in this process, and since that act of remembering is essentially subjective, the selection of concrete and specific details and images is the only way the writer can convince the reader of the truth and accuracy of the description.

### ► Describing a Place

In describing a scene, you should use the same principles as in narration: *focusing*, *shaping*, and *selecting*. You should show rather than tell. Again the analogy of the movie director is appropriate. As you use the invention techniques described in Chapter Two to stimulate your memory of a scene, think of yourself as moving through the scene using a movie camera with audio capability. The camera will pick up the sights and sounds; you can record smells, tastes, and textures. Then select only those details from your notes that will create the dominant impression you are trying to achieve. Focus in on the scene and shape it to suit your purpose. A good description is seldom an accident; it has to be consciously crafted. In describing a scene, one writer might move from right to left, another from top to bottom, another from the center outward; still another might sweep quickly across the entire scene and then zero in on visual particulars. Everything depends on the writer's intention, on the overall impression to be conveyed.

## ► READING ACTIVITY ◄

Read the following description of a place. What dominant impressions do you get from this description? How has Pam shaped her material to suit her purpose? What visual details has she used? Has she used too many descriptive details? Too few?

### WINTER ECHOES
**Pam Rothrock**

Sets up the scene through the use of detailed sights, sounds, and texture.

A few short months before, it had been the hub of sweltering summer afternoon activity. Now it lay cold and desolate, the blue-gray of the outer shell matching the steely clouds as they rushed through the sky ahead of a frigid north wind. The thin arms of the abandoned crab apple trees in front of the building clacked together in the wind, and their leaves lay piled on the yew-bordered walk that barefoot youngsters had padded carelessly up not so very long before. Cars cruised by slowly on Mill Street, but none stopped to pull into the lot any longer. The wind whined through the barbed-wire fence that herded in a lonely group of green picnic tables. I tightened the scarf that was wound around my neck and leaned down to rub a hole in the winter dust on the window and look inside. It was dusky, but a barrage of old memories came hurtling at my senses as I stopped there in the biting wind.

Flashes back to the activity of the place in the summer, using the sense of hearing.

There was the sound of a radio, blaring tinnily the unrefined lyrics of either disco or rock, depending on who was assigned to work in "The Cage," as the teenage workers called the wired-in lobby of the building. The floor was slimy with wet footprints of all sizes tracking across it. From the boys' side of the locker room came the sound of screechy adolescent voices in the midst of a war or a game of tag. Three damp teenagers were looking around at the wooden counter that was scarred with the names of past and present employees, their boyfriends, girlfriends, and acquaintances. They went boringly about their job: one deeply engrossed in a sensual romance novel; the second staring into space, trying to find a new dimension of living; and the third brandishing a homemade flyswatter, trying to beat out last week's champion in the flyswatting contest. Every so often a waterlogged lifeguard would wander in on break, whipping a towel and carrying a Diet Pepsi.

Sense of smell provides transition to description of the pool.

The way outside was through a dusty, musty-smelling locker room that was similar to a cave deep in the bowels of the earth. Outside, the pavement was hot and slightly sticky on the bottom of the feet. Kids were racing around like little daredevils in flashy bathing suits, their hair spiky, tousled, and dripping. It was almost impossible to take a step without nearly being plowed over by a swarm of six-year-olds.

The water looked clear, cool, and crisply blue. In the three-foot end, little kids splashed and screamed while their mothers looked on from the side of the pool. Little boys dolphined around close to the four-foot diving board, wiggling their bodies in pantomime of a swim and coming to the surface with a high-pitched laugh. Standing along the edge of the five-foot board was a cluster of junior-high girls, hugging their bodies with their skinny, tanned arms and giggling, not yet quite sure how to get into the cold water. Their problem was solved by the inevitable group of junior high boys, who attacked from behind and dumped them in without mercy.

The grass to the right was nearly covered by a colorful assortment of beach towels and blankets, folding chairs and umbrellas. Those mothers not inclined toward the water sat in a well-oiled semicircle and gossiped behind large tinted sunglasses. Small children lay belly-down on their towels and played game upon game of Old Maid, sloshing down endless sodas, and chewing on half-frozen Zero Bars. Teenage girls lay back for some serious tanning and talked lazily of parties, watching the boys clowning on the dives. A deeply tanned lifeguard with white sunscreen on her nose twirled her whistle on a blue-and-white macramé string and watched over her domain with an eagle eye.

Good visual description of the activity in and around the pool.

A long line of impatient youngsters clutching cold quarters and slightly soggy dollar bills extended from each of the two windows at the refreshment stand, affectionately known as "The Pit" by the teenagers who worked there. Inside the low building, teenagers screamed and swore at each other, got in each other's way, burned themselves on the ovens, and prayed that the crushed ice would give out so that they would not have to make any more of those abominable snow-cones. The person whose schedule called for work in "The Pit" usually went home that night to dream of salty soft pretzels, Charlie Chips Bar-B-Cue Potato Chips, rubbery hot dogs, and frayed nerves.

Sensory description of "The Pit."

On a hot, sticky day in the middle of August, the Quakertown swimming pool was the center of a well-timed yet chaotic ballet of confusion, splashing, screams of delight and laughter. The parking lot would inevitably be filled to the brim with cars, the bicycle racks packed with bikes of every race, color, and creed, the pool filled up with children both young and not so young. The sounds drifting through the wire fence from within were just a part of the lazy summer afternoon scenario in the middle of town. Now the sound of the wind rattling the links in that same fence brought me harshly back to the cold and the winter, the summer gone. I pulled back from the window clouded with my breath, and my eye caught the red-lettered sign that proclaimed the pool would open again on Memorial Day as it has always done, when the big red door would swing open, ushering in the heavily scented breezes of summer and scattering the dusty ghosts of a mid-November's day.

Concludes by contrasting to the present scene.

Pam contrasts the swimming pool as winter is setting in with the pool of her memory: full of the noises, sights, and smells of summer vacation. She begins by peering through the window into the lobby and then "walks" the reader from the interior of the lobby to the pavement outside, to the pool itself. She then directs the reader's eyes and ears across the pool itself to the sunbathers on the grass to the right, then to "The Pit," and finally to the sights and sounds of the parking lot. Pam uses a number of directional cues: "in 'The Cage,' " "the way outside," "Outside," "In the three-foot end," "along the edge of the five-foot board," "at the refreshment stand," "Inside the low building." These directional signals help Pam to control her reader's experiences by creating a sense of order and coherence in the scene she describes.

## ► WRITING ACTIVITY ◄

Describe some place or situation you know very well. Try to recapture the scene for your readers, carefully selecting details and giving them a shape and focus that will lead readers to see what you want them to see. Use as many of the invention techniques described in Chapter Two as you have time for to generate as many details as you can; clustering and brainstorming are especially effective for description. Then mentally explore the scene or object you are going to describe one sense at a time. First jot down everything you can see, then everything you can hear, and so on with taste, touch, and smell. After you've explored with your five physical senses, use your sixth sense. What kind of emotional vibrations do you get? Any intuitions of mood, atmosphere, or mental imagery? What analogies, similes, metaphors, or comparisons come to mind?

Decide the overall impression you want to convey and then select, from the dozens of details you have in your notes, those that will help recreate the experience for your readers. Then shape and focus these details into a coherent whole that will leave your readers with the impression you were aiming for. The following PACES criteria questions may help.

## CRITERIA QUESTIONS: DESCRIBING A PERSON OR PLACE

**[P]urpose**

Does the writing convey an overall impression of the person or place? What is the impression? Are the details and descriptions coherently related? Can the reader see, hear, feel, smell, taste—experience—the person fully?

**[A]udience**

What does the audience already know about the person or place? What can the writer assume about the reader? What can't the writer assume about the audience? Could the reader have known a similar person or place? Could the writer use the reader's experience in some way?

**C**ode

Is the writer elevating or lowering the status of the person or place with the kind of language used? How does word choice reflect the writer's interpretation of the person or place? Where is the language most memorable? Why?

**E**xperience

Does the writer convey the significance of the person or place to the reader? Is the writer's experience with the person or place fully described? What more might the reader like to know?

**S**elf

Where does the writer stand in relation to the subject? What is the distance between the writer and the subject? How are the writer's attitudes reflected in the writing?

## ► Describing a Person

Describing a person is similar to describing an event or a place. Again, memory is the key. What do you remember about all of the physical characteristics of the person? What stood out? Does she dress in a particular way? Does her voice have a particular ring to it? Many times, certain smells will trigger a memory of the individual. Is this the case with the person you're describing?

Of course your description must go beyond the purely physical. Conveying the individual's personality requires dealing with her attitudes, statements, and conduct in various situations. What was that person doing when you first met her? What experiences have you had with her? Is her behavior consistent in certain situations? What conversations have you had with her? How have these experiences and conversations shaped your attitude toward her?

Crucial to describing a person, as with describing anything else, is how judiciously you focus, shape, and select the various details, physical or otherwise. Try to show, not tell. But if you meticulously describe every detail you remember about the person, you'll bore your readers. Zero in on those particulars—certain details, bits of revealing dialog, an anecdote—that will lead your readers to see the people you describe as you see them.

### ► READING ACTIVITY ◄

Read the following description of a person. How do details in the description help to develop the character? What various sensory details does the writer use? How does dialog deepen the characterization of the person?

## THE ROOM
**Joyce Seretny**

The walls of the room were covered with faded green and gray striped paper. "Why don't they ever paint these places a bright cheerful orange?" I thought. Directly opposite the doorway were two large windows, but tightly closed venetian blinds shut out the fresh air and sunshine. The room was dim and oppressively hot. The potted red geraniums on the windowsill were wilting from the extreme heat and lack of care.

In the far corner stood a white portable commode. The attendant must have forgotten to empty it because the stench was so acrid that I had to swallow again and again to keep from vomiting.

Against the other wall, like silent partners, stood a hospital bed and night table. Strewn across the top in disarray were vitamin pills, thread, salt, camphor, brush, comb, epsom salts, and a glass with false teeth soaking in water. Within reach of her possessions an old woman rested in a wheelchair. Her fine white hair was cut too short, giving her a masculine appearance. "It used to be down to my waist," she whispered as she tugged at the uneven strands, as if the pulling would make them grow again. The skin on her face was soft and almost wrinkle-free. "Never used any of those fancy lotions, or make-up. Ain't good for the skin," she confided.

She wore a blue print cotton dress with two buttons open around the middle. "Got so fat. Nothing fits anymore. Maybe I'll get to play Santa Claus this year." She laughed at her own little joke and then repeated it several times.

With great effort she held one hand up in front of her and started rubbing it with the other. The fingers were misshapen. Dark, puffy veins covered the backs of both hands. The fingernails were long, brittle, and yellowed. "Can't cut them myself anymore," she said. She sat quietly for a moment and she inched the wheelchair even closer to the night table and slowly opened the drawer. It was crammed with greeting cards, letters, and yellowed pictures. Her hands shook as she piled them all in her lap. Her blue eyes teared. "The heat always did make my eyes water," she said. "They never forget me. Look at all these cards. Had ten children. Most of them gone now, but lots of grandchildren and great-grandchildren left. They're always sending cards . . . pretty to look at. They never forget."

# THE WRITER'S MIND AT WORK

## DRAFTING AND REVISING A DESCRIPTION

All of the previous descriptions you examined were final drafts. Now we will be observing a student, Jerry, as he works on a description called "Dream Father." In Chapter Two, we saw two examples of Jerry working at the discovery stage of planning on this same topic. Jerry first did a focused freewrite (pages 25 to 26), and then a cluster and rather sophisticated vignette (pages 30 to 33). He wrote on a different subject and then came back to "Fatherhood" and "Father," realizing that these invention notes were fertile soil for an interesting descriptive reminiscence about his father and their relationship.

The vignette, Jerry decided, would serve as his exploratory draft.

**EXPLORATORY DRAFT:**
**"Dream Father"**

My father and I have never been close. When I was a child, he was always out of town on work, and when he was home, we rarely spent much time together. By the time I went to high school, our interests were as different as could be. He loved things mechanical. I loved things artistic. With the birth of my son, we have found the one important thing of our mutual interest.

In fact, I remember only one time that my father every really talked to me about anything more important than mowing the lawn. Surely, there were other times, but I remember only one. That in itself is meaningful, I guess.

I don't remember how old-or young-I was, but

I was young enough to still be scared of the dark. It was during a neighborhood cookout on Dellwood Place, where I grew up, in Decatur, Georgia. My father took me away from the lights and the people to the other side of the house, where there were no lights, where you could barely make out the silhouette of the pine trees against the stars. Uncharacteristically, he took the time to show me how our eyes adjust to darkness, and how nothing really changes in the dark. The trees remain trees, the grass does not turn into sea nor shadows into bears. There was nothing to be afraid of in the dark, he said. This was in the time before children were stolen, before drugs and fanaticism demonized the land. This was in a time when the suburbs of Atlanta seemed safe.

On this same extraordinary evening-at least, in my memory-my father also told me the story of his experience at Pearl Harbor. He was stationed on the California. It was 7:30 A.M., Sunday, December 7, 1941. My father slept. He was awakened by a loud banging. During the week and on Saturdays, the native Hawaiian garbage collectors took great joy in waking up sailors on ships in port by pounding the metal cans as they passed. Still drowsy, my father, then a naval chief, climbed out on deck in his shorts to curse them. He saw the first bombs hit. In only his pants, he was able to escape the California after she was first struck. Many of his friends and mates were not so lucky.

How true the story is I don't know. How much such truth matters I tend to suspect more and more as I grow older. But I do know that as a child the story mesmerized me. Even today in our jaded world, to witness such events places one in league with heroes and gods. And for my father's generation, the generation I still glorified in my boyhood, before Woodstock and the shootings at Kent State, the bombing of Pearl Harbor was the event of the century. My father had almost died in the early daylight, ten years before my own birth. It explains a lot, I suspect.

For one thing, it explains why he would not fear darkness and why, even today, he does not fear it, while his son, now with a son of his own to feel protective about, fears it perhaps even more than he did as a boy.

Ever since, my father, committed much more than I to the work ethic, without exception, always took December 7 off from his job. A symbolic act, you might say, designed to forever keep the memory of the event alive. But, those days were never spent in contemplation, as I would have spent them perhaps. Instead, my father worked on our car, or fixed our television, or worked on some other mechanism. The day was always spent productively.

More puzzling than that: my father never spoke of it again. I never heard the story again. And more puzzling even than that: I never asked about it. It was too great a risk to ask. I might find out the truth and lose the memory.

Jerry then decided to produce a working draft, which he completed rather quickly. The paper seemed to write itself. The cluster and vignette had given him, in a short amount of time, an excellent frame for his description.

Jerry handed his paper to Chip and Alice, two of his classmates, who then responded to his essay by writing comments in the margins next to sections of the text where they felt he needed feedback. When Chip and Alice had completed their responding, they handed the paper back to Jerry. As you read

Jerry's working draft, note that Chip and Alice's comments occur on the page adjacent to the draft.

**WORKING DRAFT WITH PEER COMMENTS:**
**"Dream Father"**

A. My father and I have never been close. I've
learned to live with the fact after all these
years. When I was growing up, he was not at home
much. He worked out of town a lot. Apparently, my 1.
mother and he didn't get along so well that they
thought it necessary to live together all the
time. When I was in college, they separated and
B. divorced. By then, my father's interests and mine
could not have been further apart. I loved things
artistic; he loved things mechanical. I have a
lot of bad childhood memories associated with my
father. And one good one.

I don't remember how old-or young-I was, but
I was young enough to still be scared of the
dark. I remember the night my father taught me 2.
not to be scared of the dark. It was the same
night that he told me the story of how he escaped
the bombing of Pearl Harbor.

My family was still living on Dellwood
Place, in Decatur, Georgia, then. It was an idyllic period of my life in an idyllic place. It was
a time before kids ever heard about saying no to
drugs and strangers, a place where a neighbor
would never take a gun and shoot up malls or
MacDonald's restaurants. We had never heard of
acid rain or nuclear waste or Arab oil embargoes.
My memory of Dellwood Place is of one endless 3.
summer cookout at twilight.

At this cookout, my father took me away from
the lights and our neighbors and friends. We

**Reader:** *Chip*
**Author:** *Jerry*
**Date:** *December 3*
**Paper:** *#4*

A. Great Draft! You're able to create a voice which captures a complex attitude towards your father—a poignant, wistful, longing but finally accepting role. We are left with a nice sense of your resolution of your feelings toward your father.

B. I'm a little unclear on your father's divorce from your mother—did this significantly affect your feelings toward your father? Your relationship to him?

C. Great description of how kids scared of the dark can fantasize on the lurking in the dark unknown. How did your father allay your fears of the dark? What did he say?

D. The phrase "later that same evening" seems to separate the event of your father comforting you and the story father told you. You might make the relation between your father's explaining to you the realities of the dark and the story he tells you a little clearer.

**Reader:** *Alice*
**Author:** *Jerry*
**Date:** *December 3*
**Paper:** *#4*

1. I'm a bit confused by this sentence. Maybe you should rewrite it to make it less awkward.
2. I'd relate the two experiences (being scared of the dark and your father's story) more closely. So far, they seem to be loosely connected by the fact that they happen on the same day and by their role in your relationship with your father.
3. This is a great phrase.
4. You definitely need to provide some transition between these two parts of your story. The jump from one idea to another is too fast.
5. This is good. I like the way you begin to explain the significance of the story. Maybe you need to develop this a bit more. Maybe you could show us earlier how you related with your father before the story and then show here how the story changed that relationship.

walked to the other side of the house, where it was pitch dark and you could barely make out the 4. silhouette of the pine trees against the stars.
C. He took the time to show me how our eyes adjust to darkness and how nothing really changes in the dark. The trees remain trees, the grass does not turn into sea nor shadows into bears. We listened to a mockingbird sing and the traffic pass on the highway a mile away. We took the time to find the north star.

D. Later that same evening, my dad told his old war story, the one about the bombing of Pearl Harbor. He was stationed on the *California*. It was 7:30 A.M., Sunday, December 7, 1941. My father slept like most of the others on board. He was awakened by a loud banging. Groggily, he slid out of bed. Others were moaning and complaining. They
E. were all sure the garbagemen were banging metal cans to wake them up. During the week and on Saturdays, the native Hawaiian garbage collectors took great joy in waking up sailors on ships in port by pounding the metal cans as they passed. None of the men seemed to recall it was Sunday.

Still drowsy, my father, then a naval chief, climbed out on deck in his shorts to curse them. He was first out. He saw the smoke from the first bombs. In only his pants, he was able to escape the *California* after she was first struck. Most of the others didn't make it.

F. It was a sad story, but it drew me nearer to 5.
my father than I'd ever been before. It gave me a story I could tell about my father, a story, if not of heroism, of adventure, of something awfully close to heroism in a young boy's eyes. It

E. This is an especially interesting bit—it helps to add a touch of authenticity to the story since this is something a sailor would remember about life in Pearl Harbor before the attack.

F. You might add a few details here. What did your father do here that made his actions seem, in your young boy's eyes, heroic?

G. What do you think about your father's habitual acknowledgment of December 7? Has your young boy's persective of your father's experience changed? If so, how?

H. I like the way you bring the essay to a neat close in the concluding sentences, but I'm a little confused by "I never ... losing my father." Do you feel that by asking him now about that night when you were young, you will lose him?

6. This is an important detail. I learned a lot from this. I think this paragraph tells your reader a great deal about your father. I wonder if you could explain a bit how you would have dealt with such a situation in a way different from your father's. You hint at this in your last sentence, but you may want to do more with it.

7. Great ending, but I was not quite prepared for "I never learned not to be afraid of losing my father."

was communication between us. It was a memory I
could carry with me to bed when my father was not
there.

How true the story is I don't know. How real
that night of intimacy between us is I don't know
either. I do know that for as long as I can remember to this day, my father has taken December
7th off from work. That is an important piece of
evidence when you remember that my father's gen- 6.
eration is made up of workaholics and infused
with a large dose of the work ethic. Days off
were not taken lightly. It is also true, however,
that my father spent these days off like any
other: working on his car or some mechanism like
6. a radio, or just sleeping in his easy chair. I
have no evidence that any Dec. 7th was spent in
contemplation of his dead shipmates or his own
near death.

And there is one final bit of evidence: my
father has never mentioned the story to me again.

I suppose that I could ask my father. I
could ask him if it ever really happened to him
as I remember it being told to me. I could ask
him if he ever told me the story in the way that
I remember it. And I could ask him if the night
was as I remember it, if he ever really taught me
not to be afraid of the dark. But I won't. I
won't, because my father and I were never close,
because part of learning to live with the fact
that we were never and probably never will be
close was the memory of that night, and because,
while I did learn not to be afraid of the dark, I
never learned not to be afraid of losing my fa- 7.
H. ther. That was something he couldn't teach me,
even if he tried.

Jerry examined his two readers' Responding Sheets and analyzed them with care. The following script of Jerry's writer's mind shows how he ponders his readers' advice.

### THE WRITER'S MIND: Evaluating Readers' Responses

*Both respondents questioned inclusion of references to parents' divorce. So I took it out, but that made the whole thing sound trivial: My father and I had differences yeah, so what? So, I rearranged the divorce part and tried to make it more explicit that my father was not really a part of the family at all.*

*I couldn't believe one respondent suggested dialog for the scene where my father taught me not to be afraid of the dark. Dialog could ruin the whole effect. I was hinting at a kind of dreamlike effect here—a romanticism, a oneness with nature, sort of. Dialog is implied and, I thought, unnecessary. So I left as is.*

*Both respondents suggested need for more relating of two things that happened that night. I do relate them at the end, but I also added a sentence to try to relate them even more. I also discarded the "Later" and just started paragraph 5 with "That same evening."*

*One respondent wanted more explanation of how what my father did at Pearl Harbor could be described as "heroic." But rereading what I said, I realized that I didn't call it heroic. I called it "something awfully close to heroism in a young boy's eyes," something a young boy could brag about, you see, despite its not really being "brag-worthy."*

*My two respondents differed about the ending. One thought it was "great," the other didn't understand it. That respondent did get it, only wasn't sure about it. So I decided to stay with my ending. To explain it more explicitly would be to become more prosaic, and I would lose the whole dreamlike, poetic quality I was after.*

Jerry then wrote the following final draft of "Dream Father."

### FINAL DRAFT: "Dream Father"

My father and I have never been close. I've learned to live with the fact after all these years. When I was growing up, he was not at home much. He worked out of town a lot. My father's interests and mine grew significantly further apart. When he was around, he always wanted me to help him in his projects, which typically involved something mechanical-replacing the exhaust system on the car; rewiring the den for air-conditioning; etc. I always wanted to read or play baseball. Apparently, my mother and he didn't get along either. When I was in college, they separated and divorced. I have a lot of bad childhood memories associated with my father. And one good one.

I don't remember how old-or young-I was, but I was young enough to still be scared of the dark. I remember the night my father taught me not to be scared of the dark. It was the same night that he told me the story of how he escaped the bombing of Pearl Harbor.

My family was still living on Dellwood Place, in Decatur, Georgia, then. It was an idyllic period of my life in an idyllic place. It was a time before kids ever heard about saying no to drugs and strangers, a place where a neighbor would never take a gun and shoot up malls or MacDonald's restaurants. We had never heard of acid rain or nuclear waste or Arab oil embargoes. My memory of Dellwood Place is of one endless summer cookout at twilight.

At this cookout, my father took me away from the lights and our neighbors and friends. We walked to the other side of the house, where it was pitch dark and you could barely make out the silhouette of the pine trees against the stars. He took the time to show me how our eyes adjust to darkness and how nothing really changes in the dark. The trees remain trees, the grass does not turn into sea nor shadows into bears. We listened to a mockingbird sing and the traffic pass on the highway a mile away. We took the time to find the north star. It was the evening in my memory when my father was most like what a father should be.

That same evening, my dad also took the time to tell an old war story, the one about the bombing of Pearl Harbor. He was stationed on the California. It was 7:30 A.M., Sunday, December 7, 1941. My father slept like most of the others on board. He was awakened by a loud banging. Groggily, he slid out of bed. Others were moaning and complaining. They were all sure the garbagemen were banging metal cans to wake them up. During the week and on Saturdays, the native Hawaiian garbage collectors took great joy in waking up sailors on ships in port by pounding the metal cans as they passed. None of the men seemed to recall it was Sunday.

Still drowsy, my father, then a naval chief, climbed out on deck in his shorts to curse them. He was first out. He saw the smoke from the first bombs. In only his pants, he was able to escape the California after she was first struck. Most of the others didn't make it.

It was a sad story, but it drew me nearer to my father than I'd ever been before. It gave me a story I could tell about my father, a story, if not of heroism, of adventure, of something awfully close to heroism in a young boy's eyes. It was communication between us. It was a memory I could carry with me to bed when my father was not there.

How true the story is I don't know. How real that night of intimacy between us is I don't know either. I do know that for as long as I can remember to this day, my father has taken December

7th off from work. That is an important piece of evidence when you remember that my father's generation is made up of workaholics and infused with a large dose of the work ethic. Days off were not taken lightly. It is also true, however, that my father spent these days off like any other: working on his car or some mechanism like a radio, or just sleeping in his easy chair. I have no evidence that any December 7th was spent in contemplation of his dead shipmates or his own near death.

And there is one final bit of evidence: My father has never mentioned the story to me again.

I suppose that I could ask my father. I could ask him if it ever really happened to him as I remember it being told to me. I could ask him if he ever told me the story in the way that I remember it. And I could ask him if the night was as I remember it, if he ever really taught me not to be afraid of the dark. But I won't. I won't, because my father and I were never close, because part of learning to live with the fact that we were never and probably never will be close was the memory of that night, and because, while I did learn not to be afraid of the dark, I never learned not to be afraid of losing my father. That was something he couldn't teach me, even if he tried.

Did Jerry's readers give him useful advice? Jerry obviously disagreed with their advice on several points in the paper. Do you think his paper showed improvement from working draft to final draft? Has Jerry captured the essence of his relationship with his father? Does he present a consistent self to his readers? What about the integrity of Jerry's protagonist? What overall impression is Jerry trying to achieve in this description of his father and their relationship? Has Jerry focused, shaped, and selected well? Does he successfully show, not tell?

## ► WRITING ACTIVITY ◄

Write a description of someone significant in your life. Try to make the description alive and believable. Paint a word picture of the person clear and detailed enough so that an actor or actress could play that person with confidence on the stage or in a movie. Generate an abundance of details and then focus, shape, and select so that you avoid telling the reader what to think. Ideally, the reader should see this person as you see him or her. Above all, be truthful to yourself and to your subject.

# CHAPTER ▲ SIX

# *Informative Writing*

**"The only justification for our concepts and systems of concepts is that they serve to represent the complex of our experience"**

**ALBERT EINSTEIN**

We live in what has often been called the Age of Information, an age in which social scientists never tire of telling us, human knowledge is expanding at an incredible rate. Yet the twentieth century has also been characterized as an era of alienation. With the revolution in agriculture leading to a rise in the number of corporate farming combines and the demise of the small family farm, people have left closely knit rural communities where everyone knew everyone else and moved to the cities, to the "lonely crowd." Urban living has severed family and other social ties but has failed to replace them with other forms of social interaction. It is no accident that the most successful advertisement in history is AT&T's "Reach out and touch someone."

## SHARING INFORMATION THROUGH WRITING

We view the information explosion not so much as a problem, but as an opportunity for human beings to share both information and feelings. Writing to share information, to open up lines of communication, to become, as rhetorician Kenneth Burke says, "consubstantial" with other people, is, then, of vital importance to the future of the human community. How often have you heard that knowledge is power and that the truth will set you free? Informative writing attempts to free people from ignorance, from the uncertainties attached to *not* knowing. Successful informative writing builds networks, reduces alienation, increases the reader's sense of power, and binds reader and writer.

Although informative writing often involves explaining new ideas to people who know nothing about the subject, it can also provide a different perspective on a particular subject to people who feel confident and knowledgeable in that area. It can also involve interpreting or explicating or simply throwing light on a complex issue or subject, translating its complexities into understandable terms. By clarifying misunderstandings or misconceptions, informative writing can become an act of reconciliation, forming a bridge of understanding between reader and writer.

Informative writing involves *explaining* something—a process, system, issue, or entity—to your readers. For example, suppose you had worked in Washington, D.C. on a congressional campaign and wanted to share the information you had gleaned from your experiences. You might write about how to run for political office in Washington, focusing on the *process* of successful campaigning: First you do this, then you do that, and so on. You might be more interested in congressional races as *systems* and focus on how different people have conducted campaigns, successful and unsuccessful. Or you might want to focus on the nature of congressional races, on the congressional race as a unique *entity* in American life. In each case, you would examine the same experiences, but you would approach each writing task in radically different ways, born out of radically different purposes and audiences. This chapter will give you the opportunity to analyze and practice three different kinds of informative or explanatory papers: What It Is, How It Works, and How to Do It.

As you analyze samples of these three kinds of informative essays and work on drafting your own informative papers, use the following PACES criteria questions:

## CRITERIA QUESTIONS: WRITING THE INFORMATIVE PAPER

**[P]urpose**

What is the writer's overall purpose? Does the writer have other, perhaps subsidiary, purposes?

Is the thesis stated clearly?

Does the writer succeed in achieving his or her aims? How successfully?

**[A]udience**

Is the writer sensitive to the needs of the reader? Point out specific instances to back up your judgment.

Is the writer informing readers who are already expert in this area?

Is the writer too technical, talking over the reader's head?

**[C]ode**

How does the writer organize the paper? Is this plan successful?

What strategies of development does the writer use to explain the workings of the entity, system, or process? Point to specific examples of definition, analogy, metaphor, comparison, classification, simile and explain why they are effective or ineffective.

What transition devices are used with effect?

Are technical terms defined and explained satisfactorily? Is the language used to elaborate on the writer's explanations clear? Is the style appropriate to the explanation?

Is the introduction appropriate and interesting? Is the conclusion effective?

**E xperience**

Does the writer use enough examples, details, and reasons to make the explanations clear?

Has the writer depended on his or her personal experience of the entity, system, or process? Has he or she used other sources?

Has the writer discovered the essential steps or stages in the entity, system, or process or are there important elements missing?

**S elf**

Does the writer know the entity, system, or process well? Does he or she appear confident enough?

Does the writer talk down to the readers? Does the writer earn the readers' respect?

## EXPLAINING: THE "WHAT IT IS" PAPER

The informative paper that we have rather inelegantly called "What It Is" is the most common of all the types of writing you will encounter in college and in the world of commerce and industry.

In Chapters Two and Three, we examined in great detail the planning, drafting, and revising strategies of a student writer, Todd, as he developed an informative paper on cross-country skiing. This informative paper we would classify as a typical "What It Is" paper. The writer selected a subject, explored it thoroughly, developed a thesis containing the assertion he wanted to make about the subject, and then formulated a detailed plan of development. Todd was careful to select a subject that was of interest both to the reader and to himself. The "What It Is" paper is often called the "opinion" paper or the "thesis and support" paper. When you write such a paper, you present a main idea, an opinion, a guiding concept (the thesis) and then develop, explain, or substantiate it.

In this type of informative paper, the most common way to support your thesis is with examples and reasons. Todd regaled us concerning the pleasures of cross-country skiing. Of course, he had to back up his opinions with examples, reasons, and explanations. He had to earn the right to make the assertions he did. Concrete evidence is the one indispensable element in the "What It Is" paper.

There is a wide range of "What It Is" papers. In college, you may be asked to respond to a research paper or examination prompts like the following:

1. What were the major causes of the Civil War?
2. What are the seven characteristics of Romanticism?

3. Compare and contrast the contributions of Christ and Paul to the spread of Christianity.

4. Define Keynesian economics.

5. Trace the rise and fall of the theory of mercantilism.

Each of these assignments asks you to take a position, to state an opinion, to make an assertion that must be backed up with evidence.

The thesis you come up with should announce what you plan to explain to your readers and how you plan to explain it. In each of the following examples, the declarations (thesis statements) promise the reader both some kind of explanation of the thesis assertion and appropriate examples and reasons to support and enrich the explanation:

1. Its economic worth has fallen since I was a kid, but the social value of the quarter is at an all-time high.

2. The air we breathe is a sea without shores; its currents are winds. As one meteorologist has observed, "We do not live on Planet Earth, but in it."

3. Despite recent changes in styling and performance, the Corvette remains a classic American sports car.

There are trivial and nontrivial ways to approach the informative paper. Writers who look around casually and then create a thesis like "I have a number of pet peeves" or "Seven things bore me at my office" are not showing sufficient respect for their readers. At the invention and planning stage of your informative paper, consciously set up a search procedure to find a topic and a thesis that you think will interest your readers.

The intention of the informative paper is to analyze and explain the situation. Your objective is to convince your reader that the situation is as you say it is; and the way to accomplish this end is to explain without seeming either to argue with the reader or to distort the evidence. If you back up your opinions with clear, concrete evidence, your reader will not only understand the situation but will trust in your ability to present it objectively.

Finally and most important, your thesis should pass the "So what?" test. If you were to say to your readers, "I'm thinking of writing about this aspect of *X*, and I plan to defend the following thesis . . . , and they answered, "So what?" then you probably don't have a topic or thesis worth writing about. If, on the other hand, some agree and others disagree with your opinion and most seem to be interested in the topic, then you may have the makings of a worthwhile informative paper.

Let's examine some examples of "What It Is" papers to illustrate the principles we have been discussing. In Chapters Two and Three, we followed Susan, a student writer, as she selected the topic second-hand clothes and developed it through an exploratory draft. Susan then analyzed her embryonic thesis and constructed a detailed outline (see page 74) to help her produce the working draft.

## ► READING ACTIVITY ◄

In the paper that follows, does Susan have a clear sense of purpose? What is her thesis idea? Has she expressed it clearly? Does she have a clear sense of audience? Describe her audience. Does she handle her audience appropriately? What strategies does she use to develop her paper? What about her introduction? Conclusion? Has she accumulated enough evidence to convince her readers of the truth of her opinion? What about the self in this paper? Does she sound confident and convincing?

### SECOND-HAND CLASS

Most people, when they think of second-hand clothes, think of the used, "seedy" clothing found in thrift shops, where all donations regardless of condition are accepted for sale. While it's true you can find bargains in thrift shops, if you're willing to sift through some pretty unsavory items, most of the clothes found in these stores are barely one step away from the trash bin. Clothing found in resale stores, on the other hand, has been carefully selected for quality by the owner. These people are in business; they depend on steady and satisfied customers. As a result, many of the items found in resale stores have been worn only once.

A woman might buy an outfit for a social occasion and never wear it again. Rather than see a $200.00 cocktail dress take up space in her closet, she can turn it over to a resale shop for sale on consignment, and she can expect to get at least half to two-thirds of her initial investment back when the dress sells. Resale shops also often get clothing that has been outgrown (usually children's clothes) or an entire wardrobe that has become too large for the owner due to his or her weight loss. In addition to these "classy," slightly used bargains, one resale store owner reported that at least twenty-five percent of her merchandise was made up of salesmen's samples (*Columbus Dispatch*, May 3, 1987). This means the buyer has the chance to pick up an entirely new wardrobe at resale rather than retail prices. Shopping at a consignment clothing store has real advantages for anyone on a limited budget. This is especially true for students.

First of all, a student who is hard up for cash can sell items from his or her wardrobe on consignment. If it's not cash you're after but a particular item from the resale shop, you might be able to work out some kind of trade agreement with the owner. Let's say you own a suit you never wear (your mother made you buy it "just in case"). In the window of a resale shop you see a pair of "jams" with matching shirt you just can't resist (they were bought in Trinidad; there's not another pair like them in the entire midwest!), yet there's no way you can afford the twenty dollar price tag until payday. You know at any moment some spoiled rich kid is going to stroll through the door and steal that gorgeous duo. You run back to the dorm, drag your gray suit out of the closet and head for the consignment shop where you not only trade for the jams in the window, but make a deal with the store owner to take home a third of the sale-price on the suit when it sells.

Are you into name brands for your campus wardrobe? Almost every resale store has a healthy supply of Izods and Polos, Diors and Laurens. There are even shops, believe it or not, that specialize in "Yuppie" brands. If your taste runs more toward the simple life almost every resale store has a large supply of jeans—Levis, Wranglers, Guess, and Palmettos—in all sizes, shapes and states of blue. If you like patches on your pants, fringes, or strategically torn knees, you can find those in most consignment shops, too. The most I've ever paid for an almost new pair of jeans is $7.00. Compare that to the standard minimum retail price of $26.00!

If you like to dress in more esoteric threads, you might be interested in the Art Deco items found in many "vintage" resale stores. The prices run a little higher for these Thirties-style clothes than for current trend clothing, but one thing is for sure. Clothing sewn by hand, as many of these clothes were, is better made in the long run than many of the flimsey-seamed "hot" items we pay a fortune for today. Of course if you're really dated, you can buy some wild flapper beads, an English side-saddle riding habit, or a B-17 Bomber Jacket.

It's been said that clothes make the individual. If this is true, then the clothes you buy ought to express your unique personality. However, not everything on the retail clothing market today can do this—"belonging" is more important in current fashion than being yourself. Even if you are lucky enough to find a shirt or skirt that's "made just for you," if you're a student on a student's budget, the chance of being able to afford the item is pretty slim.

If you really want to make a statement about who you are by what you wear without erasing your bank statement, resale consignment stores are the answer. The next time you get the urge for new threads, don't head for the nearest shopping center. Instead, look in the yellow pages under resale clothing. You won't ever again have to spend big bucks on clothes to find the style that defines you.

"Second-Hand Class" (the change in the title was rather creative, wasn't it?) does a fine job of melding strategy and purpose to achieve its end. After an interesting first paragraph, where she contrasts the "seedy" thrift shop with the high-quality resale store, Susan gives her readers important information about the "classy" new and "slightly used bargains" in resale stores. In the last two sentences of the second paragraph, she hones in on her audience and gives them a clear statement of thesis. In the next three paragraphs she presents rich, convincing evidence to support the variety of tastes these stores will satisfy. The last two paragraphs are indeed conclusive. Susan enriches her thesis with the idea that these stores offer not just a bargain but an opportunity for students to express their individuality. The informal tone of this paper is especially effective in explaining the nature, the "what it is," of these consignment clothing stores.

# THE WRITER'S MIND AT WORK

## DRAFTING AND REVISING AN INFORMATIVE PAPER

The informative papers we have examined to this point have relied heavily on the various writers' personal experiences. We would now like to illustrate a different kind of "What It Is" paper, one in which the preponderance of the information comes from a source other than the writer. In this example, the student writer, Jamaal Jackson, focuses exclusively on one book. In terms of our PACES diagram, then, his "Writer's Experience" will be restricted to whatever information he can gather from that book and his own previous experiences with the subject. Jamaal is targeting a fairly short informative paper. If he decided to pursue this initial research further, he might find Chapters Nine and Ten, "Writing with Sources" and "Documenting Sources" of value.

Jamaal read a large section of Jan Harold Brunvard's book on urban legends and began probing his topic in the following script of his writer's mind at work:

### THE WRITER'S MIND: Planning for "Urban Legends"

*I've been reading Brunvard's book on Urban legends and thinking about folklore in general. But that isn't what I want to write about. I want to write about the legends themselves, to inform people about the legends. Because they are popular and fun. Who hasn't heard of "The Hook" or "The Vanishing Hitchhiker." I remember when I first heard about the Hitchhiker. Brunvard even mentions my Greensboro version in the book. I can take anyone there—to the place where she's supposed to appear. I remember the road dips. We go up a hill and start down, around a curve to the bridge where she'll be—on foggy, wet nights. Very believable. A girl leaves a dance angry at her boyfriend and starts walking home. It begins to rain. She takes shelter under a bridge. She decides to hitchhike. A car slides into her and kills her. She comes back—a ghost, always trying to get home. That's how it really happened, my friend Dan, told us, and then took us there one foggy night. Anyway, the legends. Many of the horror ones are interesting for psychological insight into teens. Freudian interpretations. Cultural what? Cultural restraints on kids. Girls who say no live in the Hook, The Boyfriend's Death. Like fairy tales—a way to deal with growing up. Like The Babysitter one. Babysitting is home making/mothering practice for girls. Here girl acts responsibly and gets out alive. Also acting out a fear of something gives relief. Then, there are the jokes, the comedians. The Pet in the Microwave, the Grandmother on top of the car* (Nat'l Lampoon's Vacation), *the nude in the RV story. Gotta go back to book. Interpretations. Sources. More stories. I need to take loads of notes. Remember to note page numbers and put quotes around other writers' stuff.*

The following notes were taken by Jamaal as he read Brunvard's book:

**PLANNING STRATEGY:**
**Gathering Information**

Brunvard, Jan Harold. The Vanishing Hitchhiker: American Legends and Their Meanings. NY: Norton, 1981.

"Folklore study consists of collecting, classifying, and interpreting in their full cultural context the many products of everyday human interaction that have acquired a somewhat stable underlying form and that are passed traditionally from person to person, group to group, and generation to generation. Legend study is the most revealing area of such research because the stories that people believe to be true hold an important place in their worldview" (2).

"Urban legends belong to the subclass of folk narratives, legends that--unlike fairy tales--are believed, or at least believable, and that--unlike myths--are set in the recent past and involve normal human beings rather than ancient gods or demigods" (3).

In interpreting legends, folklorists ask what these stories tell us about the culture that produced them (15). For instance, in "The Boyfriend's Death," the girl's reaction and the large role of the policeman reflect the way American society views women and authority figures (15).

Urban Legends

--"The Boyfriend's Death," collected in 1964 by Daniel R. Barnes

--usual tellers--adolescents

--normal setting for the setting--dorm rooms

--(p. 6)--1960's version

--many variants--localized settings

--some variants: body decapitated, left hanging upside down from a willow tree w/ fingernails scraping top of car

--"A developing motif . . . the character and the role of the rescuers" in 1964 they are "some people" later, they become "the police, authority figures, whose presence lends further credence to the story." May be called by missing teen's parents.

--in some versions, they tell girl to get out of car & not to look back, the role of parents lends more authority to story

--some versions--a radio warning of a lunatic killer escaping from a local asylum/prison. Girl gets upset and pleads w/ boy to take her w/him. He tells her not to get out of car for any reason.

"The Death Car" (20)

"The Philanderer's Porsche" (22)

"The Vanishing Hitchhiker" (24)

Version A (24)

B (25)

C (26)

D (27)

E (28) Korea
F (29) Moscow, Russia
G (30) London, England
H (31) Hawaii
I (Greensboro version-40)

Teenage horrors: people, esp. children, love spooky stories, a good scare.

"The ingredients of horror fiction change little through time, but the style of such stories does develop, even in oral tradition" (47).

Early teens tend to reject "the overdramatic and unbelievable" stories of their earlier youth in favor of more realistic, more plausible stories. This is the age when urban legends become popular. These legends focus on teens like themselves and involve typically teenage activities, dating & baby-sitting, for instance.

"One consistent theme in these teenage horrors is that as the adolescent moves out from home into the larger world, the world's dangers may close in on him or her" (48).

These legends play upon teenage anxieties about sex and adult responsibilities (48).

"The Hook"

--Dear Abby (1960)--(48-49)

"Part of the great appeal of 'The Hook'--one of the most popular adolescent scare stories--must lie in the tidiness of the plot. Everything fits" (50).

--interpretations: (51-52)

dread of the handicapped (Linda Deigh)

```
   Freudian fear: Hook = phallic symbol, cas-
trated (Alan Dundes)

"The Killer in the Backseat" (52)

--1st appeared in print in 1968

--variants (motifs)

"The Babysitter and Man Upstairs" (53-54)

--similar in structure to "Killer in . . ."

--interpretation (55-56)

--comic variation (56-57)

--"The Roommate's Death" (58)
   combination of "Roommate" and "Babysit-
   ter" (59-60)

"The Pet (or Baby) in the Oven"

--"Hot Dog!" (62)

--"The Hippie Baby-Sitter" (65-66)

"Nude in the RV" (132)

"Runaway Grandmother" (112)
```

When he had finished his note taking, Jamaal began to probe his topic:

### THE WRITER'S MIND: Probing the Topic

*Urban legends are stories, folklore. There are horror stories; ghost stories, comic stories; all have twists. All involve plausible plots, real people. Many (esp. horror ones) involve teenagers. Many involve death. Most set up dichotomies like Men/Women, Youth/Old Age, Adults/Teens. Many involve good guys/bad guys. Plausibility is main thing. All tend to be localized in setting & believed by teller.*

*Urban legends are like fairy tales, which Bruno Bethlehem, in his book on them, says act as catharsis for children. They have psychological effects beyond simply scaring and entertaining us. But they are different from fairy tales: no fantasy, more believable, involve more realistic settings, people, plots. Also different from myths—no gods, set in present or very recent past.*

*Makes me think of fairy tales—see above. Also, I remember when I 1st heard these tales & my own experience w/ them. In high school I heard "The Hook"—& I somehow came to believe that I had actually heard the radio announcement about his escape from Atlanta Penitentiary. I also remember when I 1st heard "The Vanishing Hitchhiker." Darwin even drove us out one foggy night to the bridge where she supposedly appears.*

*Urban legends, like all folklore, are handed down—from groups & generations & cultures. They reflect characteristics about our culture. The Boyfriend's Death, The Vanishing Hitchhiker, The Babysitter, The Roommate's Death, The Killer in the Backseat, The Hook—all show the role we traditionally place women in: Women are in these tales vulnerable, emotional. Urban legends also transmit pyschological information: the girls in The Boyfriend's Death & The Hook & some variants of The Babysitter all say no to sex and live. These tales' moral is say no to sex or else you'll get in trouble. The girl who starts out hitchhiking is going against the rules and she never makes it home.*

*Other tales also communicate themes:*

1. *The Pet in the Oven—our fear of technology*
2. *Runaway Grandmother—our fear of death*
3. *Killer in the Backseat—our fear of malls, parking lots, being alone, cars*
4. *The Death Car—our fear of cars*
5. *The Philanderer's Porsche—our sexual insecurities*

Jamaal then decided to move to some serious planning since the number of insights and the volume of information he had discovered were beginning to overwhelm him. Here are his planning notes:

**PLANNING STRATEGY:**
**Planning the Paper**

I think I'll start with my own personal experiences with urban legends.

I'm beginning to wonder if I shouldn't narrow topic to just horror tales. I'm unsure of my analysis of other types of tales. I'd have to go back and really reread Brunvard carefully if I used those.

Scratch Outline:

Possible development of (just) horror tales.

1. Intro, Brunvard, definition, comp/cont w/ fairy tales, interpretations of horror tales
2. Boyfriend's Death

3. Vanishing Hitchhiker
4. Hook
4. Babysitter
6. Roommate's Death

I am having a problem with the <u>aim</u> of this piece. What exactly am I doing? I don't want to <u>argue</u> anything. I'm not a competent folklorist. I'm just out <u>to inform</u> reader. Here is something that I'm interested in, that I find entertaining; the reader probably will too! But is that really a valid reason–I mean it is–but why do I feel uncomfortable about it? Begin a draft and discover . . . .

Jamaal examined all of his notes, organized them, and produced the following working draft. Note that his peer responders' comments appear in the page adjacent to his draft.

### WORKING DRAFT WITH PEER COMMENTS: "Urban Legends"

A. When I was in college in North Carolina, I 1.
lived in a house with four other people. Many
evenings we ended up talking around the fire-
place. On one such evening, after a particularly
rainy fall day, my friend Darwin happened to men- 2.
tion a story about a hitchhiker who turned out to
B. be a ghost. He said that she appeared to drivers
along this one stretch of road near Greensboro
every now and again, especially on rainy, foggy
nights like the one we were experiencing then. As
the story goes, she asks to be taken home and
gives explicit directions, but says very little
after that, except to express her desire to go
home. When you finally get there--some place out
in the country--and open the door for her to get
out, she has disappeared, vanished, gone. A check
with the inhabitants of the house reveals that
the description of the hitchhiker exactly matches

**Reader:** *Pauline* **Date:** *4/22/88*
**Author:** *Jamaal*
**Paper:** *Informative*

A. I like this, Jamaal. You have done a good job of explaining an interesting subject. One problem I have is that I tend to be more interested in reading the versions of the stories than in reading your explanations. You need to make me want to read the other parts as much. Maybe you could make this essay even stronger by putting more of your opinions into it. What do you think about these stories? This would help you develop those skimpy paragraphs at the bottom of page one.

B. Great introduction. You may want to just begin with the legend, rather than having your own frame story to introduce it.

C. You may want to develop these two paragraphs a bit more. Two small paragraphs like these in a row tend to make this seem choppy.

D. How does the addition of the police reflect a change in cultural attitudes?

E Why is this offset? Should it be? If it should, you

**Reader:** *Tonya* **Date:** *4/22/88*
**Author:** *Jamaal*
**Paper:** *Informative*

1. I think this is an excellent topic. Most of us have heard several of the urban legends that you describe, but probably many people aren't aware of the truly legendary quality of many of these tales. (I haven't heard about a heck of a lot of them myself.) My major suggestion would be to condense—perhaps to omit a tale.

2. Great introduction. We see here an urban legend in action. (As you begin Darwin's narration, I wasn't sure if Darwin was pretending this incident happened to him as well as to others. By the end of the paragraph, we know Darwin is passing on a story he's heard, but you might make Darwin's relation to the story clearer in the first few sentences.)

3. You might put the paragraph about the "vanishing hitchhiker" (at the end of the paper) in here since that paragraph seems to expand on ideas you introduce here.

that of their daughter, who died ten years earlier, after being run over at exactly the spot where you picked her up. No, not her, but her ghost.

It's hard to say whether Darwin actually believed the story, but certainly many others have, 3. others from all over the country, all over the world. The story of "The Vanishing Hitchhiker" is what is called an "urban legend," and has been recorded and discussed in Jan Harold Brunvand's book, *The Vanishing Hitchhiker: American Urban Legends and Their Meanings*.

Urban legends are types of folklore, defined by Brunvand as "products of everyday human interaction that have acquired a somewhat stable underlying form and that are passed traditionally from person to person, group to group, and generation to generation" (2). Brunvand claims that legends like these are important, "because the stories that people believe to be true hold an important place in their worldview" (2).

Believability is one of the distinguishing 4. characteristics of urban legends. Unlike fairy tales and myths, urban legends involve realistic settings and characters and plausible plots. And they are typically set in the present or recent past.

C. The other important aspect of urban legends, one that they share with fairy tales, is the social and psychological messages that they convey. In interpreting legends, folklorists ask what these stories tell us about the societies that produced them (Brunvand 15).

Take, for instance, the legend Brunvand 5 calls "The Boyfriend's Death." There are a vari-

need to cite where the quote comes from.

F. I think you need to explain what you mean by "the legend is a reenactment of adolescent female sexual anxiety"?

G. There seems to be a shift in the paper here. You stop giving specific examples and begin explaining the categories. I'm not sure if this is the best organizational strategy.

H. Excellent conclusion. You do a good job of getting your reader's imagination working.

4. Well, some people might claim that ghosts aren't believable.

5. Nice logical progression here. You pass from a general idea about the significance of urban legends to a specific graphic example.

6. You might expand on this. Explain how Degh's and Dundes' interpretation of the legend shows it as a "re-enactment of adolescent female sexual anxiety."

7. Is this quote from the 14-year-old Canadian boy verbatim?

8. Nice short interpretations of the legend.

9. You might bring up this idea of the different categories of urban legends earlier in the paper. Perhaps when you first define what an urban legend is.

10. You might refer to the movie <u>Vacation</u> here. The movie had a vacation in the story.

11. The short example might work better before the longer examples.

12. Great conclusion.

ety of versions, but the one that I originally heard goes like this:

> A couple went parking in a particularly lonely place, but the girl was uneasy about it. She had never done anything like that before, and she wasn't sure that she wanted to. After a few minutes, she decided that she wanted to go home, and she told her date. He got angry and flooded the car's engine when he tried to start it again. They sat there a little longer, and he tried again, but was unable to get it started. Finally, he told her that he would have to walk to the nearest gas station for help. She pleaded not to be left alone, but the guy was still angry with her. He told her to lock all the doors and lie down in the seat and not get up until he had returned. After a while, he still had not returned. Pretty soon she started hearing this scratching sound on the roof of the car. She became really scared and did not get up from the seat. Finally, when it was almost daylight, a police car arrived. The policeman helped her out of the car, saying "Please come with me, and whatever you do, don't look back." She did look back, though. And there, hanging from a tree branch above the car was her date hanging by his neck, with his shoes scraping the top of the car.

D In earlier versions of the story, the police didn't find her, but just "people." Brunvand says that the addition of the police reflects a change in cultural attitudes. The legend reveals our society's attitude toward women and sex. Women are seen as helpless and vulnerable. Teenage sex is seen as dangerous and taboo. The girl in the story survives, because she refuses to indulge in sexual activity.

These same themes appear in other teenage horror legends. One of the most popular is "The Hook." It even appeared in print, in a letter to "Dear Abby" in 1960 (Brunvand 48). I remember hearing this story when I was in junior high school, and I can testify to its power. After hearing it, I myself came to believe that it had really happened, that I recalled hearing about the escape of the dangerous criminal called "The Hook" on the radio myself. In fact, the legend seems to have originated in the late 1950s (Brunvand 49). And it has been set in a variety of places, including Utah, Maryland, Wisconsin, Kansas, Texas, Oregon, and Canada. I heard the story this way:

> As in "The Boyfriend's Death," a couple is out parking, and the girl is hesitant about going
> *E.* too far. Over the radio, they hear a report that a vicious convict has escaped from prison. He is described as having a hook instead of a right hand. The girl insists that they go home. The boy gets angry, starts the car hurriedly, and peels away. When they get to the girl's house and the boy goes to open the door for her, he discovers a hook on the door handle.

Linda Deigh interpreted the legend as "the natural dread of the handicapped" (Brunvand 51). But Alan Dundes saw a much deeper meaning in it. *6.*
He interpreted the hook as a phallic symbol, and its being torn off as castration (Brunvand 51–

52). Thus, the legend is a reenactment of adolescent female sexual anxiety.

A similar psychological meaning underlies "The Babysitter and the Man Upstairs." Brunvand quotes a "standard version" as told by a fourteen-year-old Canadian boy (Brunvand 54):

> There was this baby-sitter that was in Montreal babysitting for three children in a big house. She was watching TV when suddenly the phone rang. The children were all in bed. She picked up the phone and heard this guy on the other end laughing hysterically. She asked him what it was that he wanted, but he wouldn't answer and then hung up. She worried about it for a while, but then thought nothing more of it and went back to watching the movie.
>
> Everything was fine until about fifteen minutes later when the phone rang again. She picked it up and heard the same voice laughing hysterically at her, and then hung up. At this point she became really worried and phoned the operator to tell her what had been happening. The operator told her to calm down and that if he called again to try and keep him on the line as long as possible and she would try to trace the call.
>
> Again about fifteen minutes later the guy called back. . . . She asked him why he was doing this, but he just kept laughing at her. He hung up and about five seconds later the operator called. She told the girl to get out of the house at once because the person who was calling was calling from the upstairs extension. She slammed down the phone and just as she was

turning to leave she saw the man coming down the
stairs laughing hysterically with a bloody
butcher knife in his hand and meaning to kill
her. She ran out onto the street but he didn't
follow. She called the police and they came and
caught the man, and discovered that he had murdered all the children.

The motifs of this legend are emotionally
laden for teenage girls, according to Brunvand
and other folklorists (55-56). The telephone is a 8.
girl's "favorite means of communication," and it
is turned against her. Also, baby-sitting "is an
important socializing experience for young women,
allowing them to practice their future roles, imposed on them in a male-dominated society, as
homemakers and mothers" (Brunvand 56). In addition, the story communicates a warning to young
women to adhere to traditional values of motherhood and not to neglect their duties, by watching
TV, for instance (Brunvand 56).

Brunvand classifies these three urban legends ("The Boyfriend's Death," "The Hook," and
"The Baby-sitter and the Man Upstairs") as "teenage horrors" (47-73). They focus on adolescents
and play upon teenage anxieties, especially as
concerns sex and adult roles.

G. However, there are other categories of urban 9.
legends. One major classification involves "the
horrendous discovery theme." This category includes such legends as "The Spider in the Hairdo"
(a girl dies from having something awful living
in her hair), "The Kentucky Fried Rat" (a couple
discovers they are eating a rodent or other such
animal instead of the fast food that they or-

dered), and "Alligators in the Sewers" (strange
pets flushed down toilets survive in the sewers).
Traditional values of hair-washing, home-cooking,
and keeping non-exotic pets are typically upheld
in these stories.

Another classification involves the theme of
stolen corpses. These legends are comical and
play upon our society's uneasiness with death and
old age. In "The Dead Cat in the Package," a
thief picks up a shopper's brown bag in a store,
only to discover it contains a dead cat. In "The
Runaway Grandmother," car thieves steal vacation- 10
ers' car which has the corpse of the family matriarch tied to the roof after she had died along
the way.

A number of miscellaneous legends involve
nudity and sex. In "The Philander's Porsche," or
"The Solid Cement Cadillac," a husband pours ce- 11
ment over his boss' expensive car parked in front
of the husband's house, because the man thought
that his boss was having an affair with his wife.
Instead, the boss was helping plan a surprise
party for the husband. A man, relaxing in his
trailer, while his wife drives them home, looks
out of the door to see why they had stopped and
gets left behind in just his underwear in "The
Nude in the RV."

Finally, perhaps the most famous urban legend of them all is "The Vanishing Hitchhiker," a
version of which my friend Darwin told us that
night. There are many variants, some involving
identification of the ghost via a portrait, some
involving the hitchhiker's prophesying some fu-

ture event or events. Versions of the story have been found all over the world, from London to Moscow to Korea, and all over the U.S. Unlike most urban legends, the origins of "The Vanishing Hitchhiker" can be found in supernatural folk legends. One story from the late nineteenth century, involving a ghost who jumped on men's horses as they rode past certain woods, has been recorded. But the story has gained much of its popularity with the prevalence of automobile transportation.

The meaning of the legend depends on the motifs of the different versions. Some variants, like the one that I heard, are clearly related in theme to the teenage horror legends. The girl violates the traditional role of the young female when she sets out alone, hitchhiking home.

Urban legends are ways in which we transmit the values of, and ways in which we express the anxieties of, our culture. The popularity of certain legends over others "can be explained more simply in terms of an artistic exploration in oral tradition of the possibilities of things," Brunvand says (191). "Microwave ovens are becom-
H. ing more common in homes all the time: what if a living creature got into one . . . ? As in any age or with any subject--when a skilled storyteller begins to play with such ideas, and when members of his audience respond, repeat the stories, and begin to add their own flourishes, then legends begin to form and to circulate" (191). 12.
Even as you read this, new legends are no doubt being formed.

Jamaal carefully thought about his two respondents' reactions:

**THE WRITER'S MIND:**
**Evaluating Readers' Responses**

*My two respondents seemed to have problems with the structure of the piece. They kept wanting to rearrange some paragraphs, different ones. On looking back, I can see that instead of the original outline I'd had, which simply went through the different tales, I was making different points about urban legends and using the tales as examples. But I hadn't really alerted my reader to the fact that I was making a point. So I need to list my points and then arrange them.*

1. *I know I want to frame the whole essay with my personal experience with "The Vanishing Hitchhiker."*
2. *I know I need some brief info about what urban legends are. I want to add in here a statement about how these are tales we hear a lot, that are told as if they were really true, but that they are folklore. And I want to make more explicit the idea that urban legends transmit the values and traditions of a society.*
3. *My points:*
   (1) *Urban legends transmit values and traditions.*
   (2) *Urban legends also reveal truths about our society: These truths may be cultural attitudes toward women or psychological attitudes, or cultural warnings about morality or other miscellaneous values.*
   (3) *I'm not sure if I need to talk about the different classifications of legends—wait and see if it comes up while writing.*

Examine Jamaal's final draft. Does he have a worthwhile thesis? Has he achieved his purpose? Is he sensitive to the needs of his audience? Does he provide his readers with enough examples and illustrations to illustrate the concept of urban legends? What strategies of development does he use? Are they effective? How effective are his introduction and conclusion?

**FINAL DRAFT:**
**"Urban Legends"**

When I was in college in North Carolina, I lived in a house with four other people. Many evenings we ended up talking around the fire-place. On one such evening, after a particularly rainy fall day, my friend Darwin happened to mention a story about a hitchhiker who turned out to be a ghost. He said that she appeared to drivers along this one stretch of road near Greensboro every now and again, especially on rainy, foggy nights like the one we were experiencing then. As the story goes, she asks to be taken home and gives explicit directions, but says very little after that, except to express her desire to go home. When you finally get there--some place out in the country--and open the door for her to get out, she has disappeared, vanished, gone. A check with the inhabitants of the house reveals that the description of the hitchhiker exactly matches that of their daughter, who died ten years earlier, after being run over at exactly the spot where you picked her up. No, not her, but her ghost.

Chances are that you may have heard this same story. Except, you say, it didn't happen in North Carolina; it happened in Toronto, Canada; or Berkeley, California; or Hawaii; or Japan. And, you say, I didn't get some of the details correct. The ghost doesn't want to go home, but to a cemetery; and when she doesn't return to the car, the people in the car look for her and discover her tombstone. Or maybe the hitchhiker prophesizes about the driver's future, and her prophecy comes true. All of these are variations of an urban legend called "The Vanishing Hitchhiker," which has been recorded and discussed in Jan Harold Brunvand's book, <u>The Vanishing Hitchhiker: American Urban Legends and Their Meanings</u>.

Urban legends are types of folklore, defined by Brunvand as "products of everyday human interaction that have acquired a somewhat stable underlying form and that are passed traditionally from person to person, group to group, and generation to generation" (2). Brunvand claims that legends like these are important, "because the stories that people believe to be true hold an important place in their worldview" (2). That is, urban legends are some ways in which a society transmits its values and traditions, and so they are ways in which the folklorist and sociologist can identify those values and traditions.

Two important features of urban legends distinguish them from other types of folklore tales, such as fairy tales and myths. Believability is one of these features. Like fairy tales and myths, urban legends may involve something fantastic, like a ghost, but unlike fairy tales and myths, urban legends involve realistic settings and characters and plausible plots. And they are typically set in the present or in the recent past.

The other important aspect of urban legends, one that they share with fairy tales, is the social and psychological messages that they convey. In interpreting legends, folklorists ask what these stories tell us about the societies that produced them (Brunvand 15).

Take, for instance, the legend Brunvand calls "The Boyfriend's Death." There are a variety of versions, but the one that I originally heard goes like this:

> A couple went parking in a particularly lonely place, but the girl was uneasy about it. She had never done anything like that before, and she wasn't sure that she wanted to. After a few minutes, she decided that she wanted to go home,

> and she told her date. He got angry and flooded the car's engine when he tried to start it again. They sat there a little longer, and he tried again, but was unable to get it started. Finally, he told her that he would have to walk to the nearest gas station for help. She pleaded not to be left alone, but the guy was still angry with her. He told her to lock all the doors and lie down in the seat and not get up until he had returned. After a while, he still had not returned. Pretty soon she started hearing this scratching sound on the roof of the car. She became really scared and did not get up from the seat. Finally, when it was almost daylight, a police car arrived. The policeman helped her out of the car, saying "Please come with me, and whatever you do, don't look back." She did look back, though. And there, dangling from a tree branch above the car was her date, hanging by his neck, with his shoes scraping the top of the car.

In earlier versions of the story, the police didn't find her, but "people" did. Brunvand says that the addition of the police reflects a change in cultural attitudes. The legend reveals our society's attitude toward women and sex. Women are seen as helpless and vulnerable. Teenage sex is seen as dangerous and taboo. The girl in the story survives because she refuses to indulge in sexual activity.

These same themes appear in other teenage horror legends. One of the most popular is "The Hook." It even appeared in print, in a letter to "Dear Abby" in 1960 (Brunvand 48). I remember hearing this story when I was a teen in the late 1960s, and I can testify to its power. After hearing it, I myself came to believe that it had really happened, that I recalled hearing about the escape of the dangerous criminal called "The Hook" on the radio myself. In fact, the legend seems to have originated in the late 1950s (Brunvand 49). And it has been set in a variety of places, including Utah, Maryland, Wisconsin, Kansas, Texas, Oregon, and Canada. I heard the story this way:

> As in "The Boyfriend's Death," a couple is out parking, and the girl is hesitant about going too far. Over the radio, they hear a report that a vicious convict has escaped from prison. He is described as having a hook instead of a right hand. The girl insists that they go home. The boy gets angry, starts the car hurriedly, and peels away. When they get to the girl's house and the boy goes to open the door for her, he discovers a hook on the door handle.

Linda Deigh interpreted the legend as "the natural dread of the handicapped" (Brunvand 51). But Alan Dundes saw a much deeper meaning in it. He interpreted the hook as a phallic symbol, and its being torn off as castration (Brunvand 51-52). Thus, the legend is a reenactment of adolescent female sexual anxiety.

A similar psychological meaning underlies "The Babysitter and the Man Upstairs." Brunvand quotes a "standard version" as told by a fourteen-year-old Canadian boy (Brunvand 54):

> There was this baby-sitter that was in Montreal babysitting for three children in a big

house. She was watching TV when suddenly the phone rang. The children were all in bed. She picked up the phone and heard this guy on the other end laughing hysterically. She asked him what it was that he wanted, but he wouldn't answer and then hung up. She worried about it for a while, but then thought nothing more of it and went back to watching the movie.

Everything was fine until about fifteen minutes later when the phone rang again. She picked it up and heard the same voice laughing hysterically at her, and then hung up. At this point she became really worried and phoned the operator to tell her what had been happening. The operator told her to calm down and that if he called again to try and keep him on the line as long as possible and she would try to trace the call.

Again about fifteen minutes later the guy called back. . . . She asked him why he was doing this, but he just kept laughing at her. He hung up and about five seconds later the operator called. She told the girl to get out of the house at once because the person who was calling was calling from the upstairs extension. She slammed down the phone, and just as she was turning to leave, she saw the man coming down the stairs, laughing hysterically, with a bloody butcher knife in his hand, and meaning to kill her. She ran out onto the street but he didn't follow. She called the police and they came and caught the man, and discovered that he had murdered all the children.

The motifs of this legend are emotionally laden for teenage girls, according to Brunvand

and other folklorists (55-56). The telephone is a girl's "favorite means of communication," and it is turned against her. Also, baby-sitting "is an important socializing experience for young women, allowing them to practice their future roles, imposed on them in a male-dominated society, as homemakers and mothers" (Brunvand 56). In addition, the story communicates a warning to young women to adhere to traditional values of motherhood and not to neglect their duties, by watching TV, for instance (Brunvand 56).

Brunvand classifies these three urban legends ("The Boyfriend's Death," "The Hook," and "The Baby-sitter and the Man Upstairs") as "teenage horrors" (47-73). They focus on adolescents and play upon teenage anxieties, especially as concerns sex and adult roles.

However, there are other categories of urban legends. One major classification involves "the horrendous discovery theme." This category includes such legends as "The Spider in the Hairdo" (a girl dies from having something awful living in her hair), "The Kentucky Fried Rat" (a couple discovers they are eating a rodent or other such animal instead of the fast food that they ordered), and "Alligators in the Sewers" (strange pets flushed down toilets survive in the sewers). Traditional values of hair-washing, home-cooking, and keeping non-exotic pets are typically upheld in these stories.

Another classification involves the theme of stolen corpses. These legends are comical and play upon our society's uneasiness with death and old age. In "The Dead Cat in the Package," a thief picks up a shopper's brown bag in a store, only to discover it contains a dead cat. In "The Runaway Grandmother," car thieves steal a vacationer's car which has the corpse of the family matriarch tied to the roof after she had died along the way. You may recall that a variation of this urban legend turns up in the movie National Lampoon's Vacation.

A number of miscellaneous legends involve nudity and sex. In "The Philanderer's Porsche," or "The Solid Cement Cadillac," a husband pours cement over his boss' expensive car parked in front of the husband's house, because the man thought that his boss was having an affair with his wife. Instead, the boss was helping plan a surprise party for the husband. In "The Nude in the RV," a man, relaxing in his trailer while his wife drives them home, steps out to see why they had stopped and gets left behind in just his underwear.

Finally, perhaps the most famous urban legend of them all is "The Vanishing Hitchhiker," a version of which my friend Darwin told us that night. As I suggested above, there are many variants, and versions of the story have been found all over the world, from London to Moscow to Korea, and all over the United States. Unlike most urban legends, the origins of "The Vanishing Hitchhiker" can be found in supernatural folk legends. One similar story from the late nineteenth century, involving a ghost who jumped on men's horses as they rode past certain woods, has been recorded. But the story has gained much of its popularity with the prevalence of automobile transportation.

The meaning of the legend depends on the motifs of the different versions. Some variants, like the one that I heard, are clearly related in theme to the teenage horror legends. The girl violates the traditional role of the young female when she sets out alone, hitchhiking home. We listeners are taught a lesson when we discover the girl was killed along the way and is now a ghost, continually trying to get home.

Urban legends are ways in which we transmit the values and traditions of our culture, and ways in which we express the anxieties of that culture. The popularity of certain legends over others "can be explained more simply in terms of an artistic exploration in oral tradition of the possibilities of things," Brunvand says (191). "Microwave ovens are becoming more common in homes all the time: what if a living creature got into one . . . ? As in any age or with any subject, when a skilled storyteller begins to play with such ideas, and when members of his audience respond, repeat the stories, and begin to add their own flourishes, then legends begin to form and to circulate" (191). Even as you read this, new legends are no doubt being formed.

WORKS CITED

Jan Harold Brunvand. The Vanishing Hitchhiker: American Urban Legends and Their Meanings. New York: W. W. Norton and Company, 1981.

## ▶ WRITING ACTIVITY ◀

Write a "What It Is" informative paper, in which you explain to your readers your opinion of some concept, entity, or topic. Restrict your thesis to manageable proportions by focusing on a topic that can be dealt with in three to six pages. The key to your paper is working out a clear thesis, one you can illustrate with enough interesting examples that can be analyzed and explained in 500 to 600 words. You may want to choose a topic from the list that follows. Some of these topics can be used just as they are worded. Others can be further broken down to even more restricted statements. For example, "TV Commercials Create Distorted Views of Life" could be narrowed to "TV Commercials Create an Unnatural Concern about Body Odors."

### TOPIC SUGGESTIONS FOR THE INFORMATIVE PAPER

College is expensive
College is not barrier-free for handicapped students
Attack dogs do not make good pets
Co-ed dormitories do not promote sex
TV dramas depend on stereotypes
TV commercials use a variety of appeals to the viewer
TV commercials create distorted views of life
Film violence has become excessive
Dress reveals personality
Punk rock is junk rock
Reading fiction is a great pleasure
Discrimination is not dead in our society
Factory work is boring
Newspapers have become too commercial
Young adults do not care about politics
The dentist's office is intimidating
Superheroes act out our adolescent fantasies
Campus crime is on the rise

## EXPLAINING: HOW IT WORKS AND HOW TO DO IT

While visiting Britain, an American read in the *Daily Telegraph* the following report of a game of cricket: "Despite a slower start of 9-for-2, Davison scored a hundred before lunch. Balderstrone also batted very well, 148 until just before lunch when, against all reason, three wickets fell in six balls to Slack, who had not previously taken a first-class wicket." Obviously confused by the report, the American asked a British friend to explain cricket to him. "You have two sides, one out in the field, one in. Each man that's on the side that's in goes out. And when he's out he comes in and the next man goes in till he's out.

"When they're all out, the side that's out comes in and the side that's in goes out and tries to get those coming in out. Sometimes you get men still in and not out. When both sides have been in and out, including the not-outs, that's the end of the game."

To an American unfamiliar with the intricacies of cricket, this explanation was as confusing as the report. To someone familiar with the game, this description is accurate. But silly, too. An explanation can be both accurate and useless. If you set out to explain a process to a group of people, you must first determine what kind of information they need. The tongue-in-cheek explanation of the game of cricket was useless because it did not direct itself to solving the problem faced by people unfamiliar with cricket. Some of the group members may have wanted to know how to play cricket; others may have wanted to visit a cricket ground and watch others playing. The first group needed to know *how to do it*; the second needed to know what happens during a cricket match, *how it works*.

Each of these two basic purposes calls for its own manner of perceiving the game of cricket and thus requires its own particular approach. In this section, we will examine two different kinds of process papers: how it works and how to do it.

## ► The "How It Works" Paper

The "How It Works" paper is designed to explain to the reader how a particular system operates. The purpose of such a paper is to answer questions like the following: "What makes *X* happen?" "How does *Y* work?" "I've never understood why *Z* is so complicated. Is such a complex solution really necessary?"

The cardinal rule of the "How It Works" paper is that it should be addressed to a specific audience—people who have no idea how the system operates or people who have tried to analyze and understand the process but failed. Once you have readers who need information about the system, don't assume that they are familiar with the various stages or terms involved. After you have carefully analyzed the process and divided it into orderly stages (that is, after you have reminded *yourself* of exactly how the process works) try to get into your readers' shoes to see the process from their perspective. Anticipate where they will have problems and provide them with clear solutions. Explain *why* the system works as it does, as well as how.

## ► READING ACTIVITY ◄

The following is a passage from a chapter in Rachel Carson's book *The Sea Around Us* entitled "The Birth and Death of Islands." Carson focuses here on the origin of volcanic islands. What choices has Carson made in explaining this process? What details has she left out of the process?

> The birth of a volcanic island is an event marked by prolonged and violent travail: the forces of the earth striving to create, and all the forces of the sea opposing. The sea floor, where an island begins, is probably nowhere more than about fifty miles thick—a thin covering over the vast bulk of the earth. In it are deep cracks and fissures, the results of unequal cooling and shrinkage in past ages. Along such lines of weakness the molten lava from the earth's interior presses up and finally bursts forth into the sea. But a submarine volcano is different from a terrestrial eruption, where the lava, molten rocks, gases, and other ejecta are hurled into the air through an open crater. Here on the bottom of the ocean the volcano has resisting it all the weight of the ocean water above it. Despite the immense pressure of, it may be, two or three miles of sea water, the new volcanic cone builds upward toward the surface, in flow after flow of lava. Once within reach of the waves, its soft ash and tuff are violently attacked, and for a long period the potential island may remain a shoal, unable to emerge. But, eventually, in new eruptions, the cone is pushed up into the air and a rampart against the attacks of the waves is built of hardened lava.

In a short paragraph, Carson describes clearly and concisely a complicated process that occurs over many thousands of years by breaking the process into easily identifiable stages and taking us through the exact sequence of events as they occur. Carson relies on her readers' relative familiarity with terrestrial volcanoes when she describes the process to this point. Yet Carson emphasizes that there are significant contrasts between a submarine and a terrestrial volcanic eruption, explaining to us how the "immense pressure" of the sea serves to flatten out the lava horizontally over the sea floor. Carson succeeds by highlighting the factors distinct to the formation of volcanic islands, recognizing what her audience probably already knows, anticipating what her audience may not be familiar with, and thus allowing her readers to appreciate how this unique process works.

In the brief excerpt we examined, the writer skillfully analyzed the process and arranged it into clearly identifiable stages, carefully anticipating their readers' needs by judicious selection and focusing of details. Let's analyze a number of a "How It Works" papers produced by a student writer.

## ▶ READING ACTIVITY ◀

Read the following "How It Works" paper. How has the writer generated a topic from his personal experience? What is his focus? How does his organizational plan guide the reader through the description of this process? Who is the audience for the paper, and how does the writer keep that audience in mind throughout?

## THE BIG GULP

**Paul Christy**

The rabbit scampers nervously on the cold linoleum floor, its nose twitching, eyes searching, and ears at attention. Suddenly, the once harmless log comes alive and the rabbit realizes its fears. The rabbit is in the company of a snake, an Indian python. My pet strikes quickly, seizing the rabbit's head in its powerful jaws. The rodent hasn't a chance. The python quickly throws its thickly muscled coils around its prey; after a brief struggle, the victim suffocates. The snake may now relax its coils and begin to swallow.

The swallowing and digesting of food by a snake involves many simple but highly specialized organs. The oral cavity or mouth is comprised of the most unusual structures. The teeth of a serpent are approximately one-quarter inch long, sharp and recurved. This recurvature of the polyphyodont (replaceable) teeth prevents an organism from escaping the reptile's grasp; as the prey struggles in the snake's jaws, the teeth, like a hook in a struggling fish, sink deeper.

The jaws of a snake are unique. The mandible (lower jawbone) consists of four bones, three more than that of man. The actual mandible can be compared to that of man, except where the jaw of a man curves to form the chin, the jaw of a snake has no bone. The "chin" of a snake consists of a ligament which connects the two straight mandibles. The ligament allows the lower jawbones to separate, creating a V. This separation is one of the adaptations which allow snakes to swallow prey over three times as large as their own heads. Another swallowing adaptation of the mandible is the presence of a pair of bones called the quadrates. The mandible of a man is connected directly to the cranium; the lower jaw of snakes is connected to the quadrate bones, which are attached to the skull. The quadrate bones provide for a greater range of movement of the lower jawbones, which is very important to an animal that must feed itself without the use of limbs. The maxilla (upper jawbone) is stationary and relatively comparable to the maxilla of man.

A snake's jaws must act as hands to pull the food into the mouth. The purpose of two mandibles is to allow for unilateral movement. Unilateral movement is the movement of one mandible at a time. While one side of the jaw holds the prey, the other side releases it and, by the use of the quadrate bone, is thrust forward. This side now takes hold of the victim, while the other side of the jaw releases and thrusts forward. In this way, the snake "crawls" over its prey.

When a snake swallows an organism of any appreciable size, its nasopharynx (the tube connecting the nose to the mouth) as well as its trachea (windpipe) become blocked, thus preventing breathing. The snake gets around this otherwise fatal condition through the use of a specialized glottis. The glottis is the beginning of the trachea. Snakes, unlike any other organisms, have a convoluted glottis which can be extended from the mouth during the swallowing process. In this way, the glottis acts like a snorkel to allow the animal to breathe.

Once past the mouth, the food enters the esophagus (the tube extending from the mouth to the stomach) which has many longitudinal folds to allow for the swallowing of large prey. Muscular contractions of the tube, called peristalsis, force the food into the spindle-shaped stomach. The stomach is an extremely muscular organ which contracts forcibly to churn up the food and expose it to the digestive enzymes and hydrochloric acid. The enzymes and acid break down the protein and bones. From the stomach, the food enters the elongated small intestine, where nutrients are absorbed; it then enters the large intestine, where excess fluids are absorbed. The large intestine empties into the cloaca, an organ of storage for various wastes. *Cloaca* is the Latin word for *sewer*, which may give a better idea as to its function. Snakes do not possess a bladder, so all wastes are in the solid form. These wastes are expelled through the anal opening.

Two hundred million years ago a creature was formed with every thinkable disadvantage: no limbs, no ears, no eyelids, no fur, no ability to regulate body temperature, no voice, and a small brain. It began its history underground, with only the simple structures of an overdeveloped worm. When this animal shunned its subterranean world its organs adapted, and so today we may see the most remarkable creature on earth; the snake.

Paul has provided his readers with a dramatic introduction and an interesting conclusion. He has also made effective use of comparison ("like a hook in a struggling fish"), contrast ("three more than that of man"), and analogy ("A snake's jaw must act as hands . . . the snake 'crawls' over its prey"). Paul's paper is well organized and he is careful to define and explain any technical terms that his readers might not know.

## ► WRITING ACTIVITY ◄

Write a three- to six-page paper explaining a system or process. Focus on people who know very little about your subject. Thoroughly analyze the topic and break it into its component stages or parts. Decide where your readers will have problems in understanding your description or explanation and revise it accordingly. Anticipation is the key to success with the "How It Works" paper.

### TOPIC SUGGESTIONS FOR THE "HOW-IT-WORKS" PAPER

How a microwave oven works
How a computer works
How your school's honor system works
How a river system develops
How a nitrogen-fixing bacterial system works
How your school's financial aid system works
How a bill gets passed in Congress
How your school's athlete-recruitment system works
How a volcano comes into existence
How the lungs work
How kidney dialysis works
How the heart works
How the public ownership of a corporation works
How a car's brakes work
How clouds, tornadoes, thunderstorms develop
How a beehive functions
How a propeller plane gets and stays airborne
How atomic fusion occurs

## ► The "How to Do It" Paper

To explain in writing how to perform a certain task or activity, you should consider the specific audience you wish to address. The potential audience for the "How to Do It" paper usually falls into one or two categories: people who have never performed the task or activity before or people who have tried it before but failed. Obviously, there is no sense in explaining a process to someone who is familiar with the operation. Don't waste your time telling Jack Nicklaus how to hit a golf ball or Meryl Streep how to act. Once you have chosen readers who really need to know how to do it, don't assume that they are familiar with the various terms or stages in the process. Many recipes, directions, and instruction booklets fail because they assume that readers already know most of the process and only need to be reminded of the order of the steps. But many people today would not know what is meant by "dredge chicken parts before frying" or "prime the engine" or other explanations that do not really explain. As a general rule, a writer should assume that readers do not know even the most basic or routine information. Here, for example, is a rather standard description of how to change a flat tire, which relies on a considerable amount of assumed information on the reader's part.

> Set brakes and block wheels so that the car will not roll. Remove jack and spare tire from trunk of car. Place jack under bumper and raise car

> until flat tire clears the ground. Remove hubcap and lug nuts with jack handle. Remove flat, place spare on wheel, and replace lug nuts. Tighten lug nuts securely, using alternating pattern of opposing nuts so that tire will fit evenly on wheel. Replace hubcap. Return tire and jack to trunk.

With minor variations, most people agree that's about right—that is how to change a flat. It is basically just a matter of getting the flat off and the spare on (assuming you have a spare in working order). But this description is only a summary of the process; it is aimed at people who already know how to do it or at least have a basic understanding of the problems involved. It is not terribly helpful to someone who has never changed a tire.

It is imperative to consider the specific needs of the audience when you write the "How to Do It" paper. You must imagine the process from the readers' point of view in order to anticipate problems they may have in understanding the process. However, depending on the complexity of the process explained and on your familiarity with the process, it may be wise for you first to write an explanation of the process for yourself. When you have finished, examine this version for its accuracy and completeness, before finally revising it for an audience unfamiliar with the process. Sometimes in considering the needs of an audience, you may overlook crucial stages in the process. For instance, in the explanation of how to change a tire, it is important that the writer include *all* of the necessary information and in the proper sequence: If the writer forgets the important step of blocking the wheels (placing large wedges under the tires to keep the car from rolling) the results for the reader who tries this process based on this explanation may be catastrophic.

## ► READING ACTIVITY ◄

The following is an explanation of a process in which the writer first constructed a preliminary version for herself and then revised this version so that her anticipated audience might more readily understand her explanation. These passages are excerpted from drafts of a paper on how to prepare for a horse-riding competition. As you read the two versions, note the changes made. How has the writer's conception of her projected audience affected her decisions in revising the preliminary version?

### PRELIMINARY VERSION
**Deanna Clinger**

> The final step in preparing for competitive riding is to groom the horse. After clipping and grooming carefully, you should give him a bubble bath, usually in a shower (it's easier that way). Then wash off the horse thoroughly and dry the horse off carefully.

### REVISED VERSION

The final step in preparing for competitive riding is to give the horse a thorough grooming and bathing. Clip the long, shaggy hair on the horse's mane and legs to a uniform length. Also clip the whiskers and eyelashes. Next, brush off all the loose hair with a grooming brush. This "haircut" should give the horse a clean, professional look. After clipping and grooming the horse, you should give him a "bubble bath" in order to give his coat a shinier, healthier glow. Most stables have a horse shower—a special stall with cement floor, a rope to secure the horse, and a large shower faucet. Tie the horse carefully in the shower stall. Fill a bucket with warm soapy water, with some bubble bath, and rigorously apply the water to the horse with a sponge or a brush. You should rub the horse in a circular motion in order both to get the soap into the coat and to remove loose hair. Of course, you should be careful not to get soap in the horse's eyes. After a thorough washing, rinse the horse with lukewarm water, making sure to get all the soap out of the coat, since dried soap can easily cause dandruff. Finally, dry off the horse either with towels or a hairdryer to give the horse a sleek look that will be sure to impress judges.

In the revised version, the writer greatly expands on her instructions, explaining to the reader, for instance, what needs to be clipped on a horse and just what it means "to wash the horse thoroughly." In the revised version, she anticipates that the reader may not be familiar with the facilities for giving a horse a shower and consequently provides a brief description of this place, thus preventing the reader from conjuring ridiculous images of a horse in a shower designed for humans. She also explains *why* we should groom and wash the horse in a certain way (the circular motion in rubbing the horse is designed to get in the soap and get out the loose hair) which helps to support her authority as an "expert" on preparing for a horse-riding competition. In the preliminary version, the writer reminds herself of the exact sequence of steps in the process of cleaning a horse's coat; in the second version, the writer builds on this sequence, adapting her explanation to the anticipated needs of an uniformed audience.

## ► READING ACTIVITY ◄

In the following passage, William Wright describes what he perceives as an important part of the process the uninitiated should undertake before going to an opera for the first time. How does Wright shape his instructions for his anticipated audience?

Once you have selected the opera, you are ready for homework. The bare minimum is to learn the story. *Bel canto* singing is not the surest way of communicating hard facts. If you don't know at least the general direction of events, you might find the entire spectacle collapsing into a mishmash of sights and sounds. Even so, the world-famous tenor Pavarotti disagrees about the need to know the plots. "Even if you don't understand one word," he says, "it doesn't matter, because great singers come to you musically, vocally."

Don't count on it. If any singing can stand on its own, it is Pavarotti's; it in no way diminishes his greatness, however, to remember that Pavarotti is interpreting masterpieces that include words.

Many opera houses sell libretti for upcoming operas, and you can buy them when you buy the tickets. Or look in one of the many opera guides that synopsize plots. Failing this, get to the theater early enough to read the program summary.

Familiarity with at least some of the music is another way of assuring that the first opera will be a pleasure rather than an ordeal. An excellent investment would be a recording. Listen to it, following the words in the libretto.

Wright gears his directions to people who have never seen an opera or who have perhaps seen one but not enjoyed it. Hypothesizing that viewers who are unable to follow the story line of an opera are less likely to enjoy the performance, he wisely suggests that first-time viewers familiarize themselves with the opera's plot before they attend the production. Wright thus disagrees with Pavarotti's comment, claiming that the famous opera star has not fully anticipated the needs of an audience not already familiar with opera. In this passage Wright provides sensible, clear, practical advice that just might produce a few more fans of opera.

## ► READING ACTIVITY ◄

The following is an excerpt from an article by Carla Stephens describing a process with which everybody who ever comes near water should be familiar. How does the purpose of this passage affect how Stephens describes the procedure of drownproofing?

Developed by the late Fred Lanoue, drownproofing relies on the body's ability to float when air fills the lungs. Picture yourself bobbing restfully just under the surface of the water. With a few easy movements you come up to breathe as often as necessary. That's the basic idea of drownproofing, a technique endorsed by the Red Cross, the National Safety Council and the YMCA. It's easy to learn, even for some three-year-olds. You can teach yourself and your family.

Here's how it's done: First, take a breath through your mouth. Then, holding your breath, put your face into the water and float vertically with your arms and legs dangling. Don't try to keep your head up; it weighs fifteen pounds.

When you're ready for another breath, slowly raise your arms to shoulder height. At the same time bring one leg a little forward and the other back into a position somewhat like the scissors kick. (If injury makes it necessary, drownproofing can be done with either the arm or the leg movements.) Then gently press your arms down to your sides (not backward) and bring your legs together. Keep your eyes open and raise your head until your mouth is out of the water. Exhale through your nose, your mouth or both.

Inhale through your mouth while continuing to press your arms down. But don't press too hard, for you want to keep your chin at, not above, the surface of the water. Finally, return to the resting position with your face in the water. If you sink too far, a small kick or a slight downward push of your arms will return you to the surface.

It is important for the readers to understand the exact sequence of the drownproofing procedure, to know precisely how and when to move the limbs. Consequently, Stephens divides her explanation into neatly defined steps, describing the exact positioning and movement of the limbs at each step. Stephens' clear and straightforward manner of explaining drownproofing allows the readers to visualize this process easily, giving them the necessary information to practice it on their own.

Examine the following example using the PACES Criteria for Writing the Informative Paper on pages 178 to 179.

## ► READING ACTIVITY ◄

Read the following "How to Do It" paper. What audience is the writer addressing? How is the writer's understanding of this audience crucial in forming his purpose? What is his organizational plan? Why does the writer compare his own experience with a chainsaw against "the perfect world" of the owner's manual? Why does the writer switch to the narrative mode later in the essay? What point is he illustrating through this narrative?

### QUICK AMPUTATIONS: HOW TO AVOID THEM

**Zach Hummel**

Most people believe that operating a chain saw is a simple and easy task, requiring little experience or knowledge, except maybe how to start one. They assume that with one pull of the cord they will be instant lumberjacks—slicing through trees, logs, fence posts, and so on, quickly and easily. However, they seem to ignore the fact that it will cut through toes, fingers, arms, legs, and even torsos just as quickly. A chain saw must be handled knowledgeably and with a great deal of respect if one cares to keep his bodily symmetry intact. Remembering how to ready the saw for cutting, how to start it safely, what not to do with the saw, and precautions to take against accidents will give you a safer cutting spree, and lower medical expenses. Operating a chain saw is not as easy as it sounds; common sense, caution, and a little knowledge are required for safe usage.

One of the most important things in cutting with a chain saw is to have a saw that is ready to cut. If the saw is not prepared properly it will not cut well and may be damaged as a result. Obviously, it should have a full tank of gas. You should be sure to check the owner's manual for any special requirements, such as oil mixed in. This can sometimes be found on the saw itself, also. The oil in the saw itself should be checked and kept full at all times. The chain should also be tight. The blade on a chain saw consists of two parts—the bar and the chain. The chain, which is the real cutting edge, runs along the bar, the long flat piece of metal sticking out front. If the chain is too loose it will jam during the cutting, and this can cause it to break—which can be nasty if the pieces fly in your face. If the chains is too tight, it will not move and may ruin the saw. You also won't get much cutting done. Here, also, the owner's manual should be checked for how to adjust the tension on your particular saw. Now you are ready to begin cutting—if, that is, you can get it started.

On face value, starting a chain saw is easy; however, if you have used one before, you know better—much better. The first and one of the most important parts of starting the saw is addressing it properly. This does not mean remembering to include the zip code or its proper title (Mr., Mrs, Your Excellency, and so on) but the way you position yourself in relation to the saw—much as addressing a golf ball on the tee. The saw should be placed on a solid object below waist level (the ground, a stump, whatever) so that it has a sturdy base. Place one hand on the brace, flick on the starter switch, give a sharp pull on the starter cord, and give it a little gas with the throttle as it sputters to life, and your chain saw is now started.

It would be nice if the world were as bright and perfect as owners' manuals would have you believe. It is not, however, that simple. All saws have their eccentricities; some you have to use the choke on, others you can't or they will flood, and still others have to have a combination. Take my saw, for example. It has its own particular ritual that must be performed before it will start. First, it must be dropped on the ground from knee level; then I have to turn on the starter switch and pull on the starting cord a few times. It will not start, so I pull out the choke and yank on the cord some more—it still will not start. I then pause and utter a few choice words and threaten it with dirty oil next oil change. If, after a few more pulls, it refuses to start, I bang it up against my victim (a dead tree or whatever), hoping it will incur the saw's wrath so the saw will start just to cut it down. Now, after a few more pulls, it should start. If all this fails, I just tell my father I can't work because the saw won't start. He comes out, and it starts first pull. This *never* fails and can be applied to almost any situation—kids and parents, husband and wife, man and mother-in-law, whatever. As soon as you tell someone that you can't work because it won't start—it will start the next time it is pulled. Once the saw is running, the throttle will control the engine and, therefore, the blade speed. You are now ready to cut.

The actual cutting is the easiest, and therefore the most dangerous, part of using a chain saw. The minute the saw is started it is deadly. The ease with which it cuts is very deceiving. You should not be lulled into forgetting the power and destructive potential that the saw has. All that is required is to place the bottom of the blade on whatever you are cutting and apply light pressure. Always make sure your legs are not in the saw's path. Do not place any part of your body in the path of the blade. It is possible to slip off, especially when starting the cut, and to end up cutting what you had not intended to. Do not use the tip of the blade to gouge into an object. The saw will kick back hard, and if you aren't ready it could have disastrous results. Be very careful cutting with the top of the blade. It should only be done when absolutely necessary. You should position your body so that any kickback will not have a chance to throw the saw into you. If you remember these simple and obvious cautions, you will have a much safer time cutting.

I can best give a few tips on cutting down standing trees (the trickiest part of chain saw use) by telling how I found them out. Our house is heated by a wood furnace—not oil or electricity, but wood. This means that in winter we must have wood or no heat, and that means frozen water pipes, frozen feet, frozen hands—just plain frozen everything. I, being the oldest, was given the task of keeping the wood supply from running out. We live on a cherry farm and there is an old, dying orchard right out the back door. Convenient, huh? It would be except that all the dead ones are at the back of the orchard (you've heard of elephants going to their secret graveyard to die; well, it's much the same with cherry trees—they migrate to the back of the orchard to die), and in between are two hills that make the Matterhorn look puny.

So I slogged my way through the waist-high drifts of snow pulling my trusty toboggan (I pull all the wood I cut back in with it) and my chain saw. Just after I had scaled the first hill I spotted a small dead elm—considered the prime timber because it is much easier to cut and transport than cherry—and decided to cut that first. Amazingly, the saw started first try (the first such happening since the fall of 1970), and soon I was slicing into the trunk of the tree. About ten seconds later the chain jammed; I couldn't pull the saw out and it quit. The tree had leaned back toward where I was cutting from, and there I was with my saw stuck and no way to get it out. This illustrates two things: one, no matter how much the tree looks like it's leaning away from where you are cutting, it will most likely tilt back and trap your saw—so always cut a notch on the opposite side just below where you are cutting. This will cause the tree to fall in that direction. Two, always carry an axe, just in case. It will get you, and your saw, out of many a jam. So I waded back through the drifts, got my axe, and started off once more into the frozen North.

So now you see that operating a chain saw is not as easy as it seems. You must have some knowledge as to what the saw will do, precautions to take, and even preparations that are necessary in order to operate it safely and effectively. If you follow these basic rules you can get all the wood you want yourself—and it won't cost you (either way) an arm and a leg.

Zach's paper uses a combination of what happens and what happened to show the reader how to operate a chain saw. Thus the paper differs from the preceding one in degree of personalization; Zach primarily uses third person, but he switches to first when he brings in his own experiences as examples. Note that Zach has organized the paper so that he first presents the ideal (as stated in the owner's manual) operation and then the real, allowing him to set up a nice contrast in the paper between the way things are "supposed" to go and the way they "really" go.

## ► WRITING ACTIVITY ◄

Write a three- to six-page paper explaining to an audience how to do something. Thoroughly analyze the process, dividing it into various stages or steps. If there are preparatory stages or a necessary order to the steps, be sure to present them in the order they are needed. You must anticipate every conceivable problem and tell your readers what *not* to do before they are likely to do it correctly.

### TOPIC SUGGESTIONS FOR THE "HOW TO DO IT" PAPER

How to fry, bake, roast, or otherwise cook a chicken or other food
How to clean a rifle, carburetor, typewriter, or other machine
How to tie a fly
How to embalm a body
How to fill out the income-tax long form
How to wax skis
How to cut down a large tree
How to use the subway
How to present yourself in traffic court
How to shop in a secondhand store
How to put on makeup
How to impress a date
How to behave at a tea party
How to bathe a dog, cat, or other pet
How to conduct yourself in a job interview

# CHAPTER ▲ SEVEN

# *Evaluative Writing*

**"If people cannot write well, they cannot think well. And if they cannot think well, others will do their thinking for them."**

**GEORGE ORWELL**

Evaluating is as natural to human beings as breathing. We are constantly evaluating and making judgments as we go about our affairs. What movie or theatrical production will you go to see? What clothes will you wear for this occasion? Which of your friends will you ask to accompany you? Where will you eat? What kind of food will you eat? Where will you go after the show? All of these questions are part of a normal night out, and yet they demand of us an almost endless series of analyses, judgments, and decisions. We make these decisions easily, usually after a speedy analysis, and we base our decisions on fairly superficial reasoning: "I just don't feel like Chinese food tonight." "I'm not in the mood for a serious movie; let's go see Eddie Murphy."

In this chapter you will be dealing with a more serious and elaborate kind of judging, a *written* evaluation, and your audience will not be your friends, but members of the academic community, fellow undergraduate students, for the most part people who will listen to what you have to say but who will demand that you back up your judgments with a carefully developed, reasonable argument. To convince your readers of the soundness of your judgments, you will have to learn to analyze and describe the facts and evidence you'll use in your paper in a fair and objective manner. We will begin, then, with the skills needed to objectively summarize a written document.

## THE OBJECTIVE SUMMARY

Your objective summary presents the reader with the essential information contained in an article without stating, or hinting at, your opinion. The specific purpose of an objective summary is to condense information into a short, useful form for the reader.

Many readers want and need such a service. A supervisor might ask an employee to summarize a year's worth of memos on worker productivity as one source of information for creating a new company policy on absenteeism. A nurse may have to summarize a hospital patient's previous admission history; a day-care counselor may have to condense an article on problems of child safety for busy colleagues. There are countless important situations that arise every day which require the useful skill of objective summary.

You will discover that a good summary is often as useful as—and occasionally more useful than—an entire magazine or journal article. Two significant assets are portability and availability; you can take your own summary out of the library, and it takes much less time to review an objective summary than it does a full-length article. The objective summary should include most of what you need to know about an article, a capsulized headline version of the main points you want to remember.

To get a sense of what an objective summary might look like, we will now examine two very different kinds of articles and two objective summaries that students wrote condensing the information found in these articles. As you read the articles and the objective summaries that follow, think about other ways the articles might be effectively summarized. The following article on Bigfoot was first published in the May 14, 1985, edition of the *National Examiner*.

**"BIGFOOT"**

A foul-smelling Bigfoot left a mountain town numb with terror when he tried to kidnap an eight-year-old boy. Mothers dared not let their children out of the house and the shotgun-toting menfolk scoured the hills and hollows for the creature.

But psychic troubleshooters say that the enormous creature is actually harmless and only looking for companionship.

Parapsychologists Ed and Lorraine Warren visited the rugged area on the Tennessee-Alabama border where shaken residents report having seen the seven-foot-tall, shaggy, stinking creature.

But Lorraine discovered while in a trance that the Bigfoot had no intention of kidnapping the boy. She says it is actually sweet-natured, though smelly, and desperate for companionship.

Samuel and Clara Robertson, however, felt nothing but fear and anger when they first encountered the Bigfoot.

"I walked out on the back porch at about 8 P.M. and called for my son Jimmy," says Clara.

"I saw this gigantic creature with long brown and black hair all over its body."

"I caught this horrible odor, unlike anything I have smelled before. I called again for Jimmy, shouting from sheer panic."

"Jimmy came around the side of the house, and the creature snatched for him, missing his arm by inches."

But Lorraine says the Bigfoot explained telepathically to her that he never intended to harm anyone—and that he was a gentle vegetarian.

"This creature is more human than animal—it communicated with me psychically," she explains.

"It tried to touch the boy because the child would be less prone to violence. It just wanted companionship.

"This creature has feelings like a human. It felt alone and unwanted—all it wanted was love and affection."

Samuel Robertson's first reaction to the attempted kidnap was just as human. He wanted to kill the creature—until he thought better of it.

"I carry my rifle wherever I go," he says. "I could have shot that creature several times but I didn't want to just wound it—that would just make it angry and jeopardize the community."

Other mountaineers have seen, heard, and smelled the Bigfoot. Marvin Smith says he spotted it when he was hunting possum.

"All of a sudden I heard this high-pitched scream and saw this beast—I reckon it must have been seven or eight feet tall and weighed a good 350 pounds.

"I just stood real still and watched. It screamed again and made a funny gesture with its arm—almost as if it were telling me to get."

Longtime area resident Charles Freeman says he has known from his very first encounter with the Bigfoot that the creature meant no harm—he says he actually saw the Bigfoot giving first aid to a raccoon.

"I wouldn't have believed it myself unless I saw it with my own two eyes," he says. "I was walking when I picked up this awful smell, like nothing I've smelled in my seventy-two years.

"Then to my right, under a big tree, I saw Bigfoot stooping down over the form of a raccoon putting a mudpack on the coon's hindquarters.

"As God is my witness, he was giving that coon first aid.

"Ever since that day I knew Bigfoot was not out to hurt anyone."

Ed Warren has seen only the mammoth footprints made by the creature, but he believes in the creature's noble nature.

"It seems to me we should change its name from Bigfoot to Bigheart."

Read the following two objective summaries of the "Bigfoot" article. Note some of the similiarities and differences between them.

A.

In the rugged mountain area between Tennessee and Alabama, a foul-smelling Bigfoot allegedly tried to kidnap eight-year-old Jimmy Robertson. This near abduction caused much panic among some of the area residents, but according to parapsychologists Ed and Lorraine Warren, it was unnecessary worry. The Warrens agreed that Bigfoot was only looking for companionship. Lorraine claimed that Bigfoot telepathically communicated to her that he only wanted companionship and never intended to harm anyone. Samuel and Clara Robertson, Jimmy's parents, disagreed with the Warrens and feared Bigfoot. Longtime area resident Charles Freeman said that from the first time he saw Bigfoot he knew the creature meant no harm. He said he even saw Bigfoot giving first aid to a raccoon.

B.

The May 14, 1985 issue of *National Examiner* reported several sightings of Bigfoot. An eight-year-old boy, Jimmy Robertson, was reported to have been almost kidnapped from a mountain town, leaving some of the townfolk fearing for the safety of their children. Two different views about the reason for the attempted kidnapping have been suggested: Some townsfolk believe that Bigfoot was trying to harm the boy. Others, including parapsychologists Ed and Lorraine Warren, think that Bigfoot was only looking for companionship. Some of the people in the town who claim to have seen the seven-foot-tall, shaggy, stinking creature believe he is of a gentle nature and will bring harm to no one. Still others insist he will one day hurt someone. This small town is left wondering about the true nature of Bigfoot.

Each of the objective summaries includes some of the same essential information found in the Bigfoot article. Each mentions the attempted kidnapping of Jimmy Robertson and the claims of parapsychologist Lorraine Warren that Bigfoot is harmless. Yet there are also some dissimilarities between them. For example, *A* mentions the specific scene of the sightings, whereas *B* states that the sightings took place in a "small town." What other basic similarities and differences can you detect between these two objective summaries?

Notice that each objective summary contains only information found in the article itself; evaluation and judgment of this information are left out entirely. Either of the two summaries adequately serves the purpose of encapsulating the essential information found in the Bigfoot article.

Shortly after the death of Benny Paret, a prizefighter who was fatally injured in a boxing match, Norman Cousins wrote the following article probing the causes of his death.

### WHO KILLED BENNY PARET?
**Norman Cousins**

Sometime about 1935 or 1936 I had an interview with Mike Jacobs, the prize fight promoter. I was a fledgling reporter at that time; my beat was education but during the vacation season I found myself on varied assignments, all the way from ship news to sports reporting. In this way I found myself sitting opposite the most powerful figure in the boxing world.

There was nothing spectacular in Mr. Jacobs' manner or appearance; but when he spoke about prize fights, he was no longer a bland little man but a colossus who sounded the way Napoleon must have sounded when he reviewed a battle. You knew you were listening to Number One. His saying something made it true.

We discussed what to him was the only important element in successful promoting—how to please the crowd. So far as he was concerned, there was no mystery to it. You put killers in the ring and the people filled your arena. You hire boxing artists—men who are adroit at feinting, parrying, weaving, jabbing, and dancing, but who don't pack dynamite in their fists—and you wind up counting your empty seats. So you searched for the killers and sluggers and maulers—fellows who could hit with the force of a baseball bat.

I asked Mr. Jacobs if he was speaking literally when he said people came out to see the killer.

"They don't come out to see a tea party," he said evenly. "They come out to see the knockout. They come out to see a man hurt. If they think anything else, they're kidding themselves."

Recently, a young man by the name of Benny Paret was killed in the ring. The killing was seen by millions; it was on television. In the twelfth round, he was hit hard in the head several times, went down, was counted out, and never came out of the coma.

The Paret fight produced a flurry of investigations. Governor Rockefeller was shocked by what happened and appointed a committee to assess the responsibility. The New York State Boxing Commission decided to find out what was wrong. The District Attorney's office expressed its concern. One question that was solemnly studied in all three probes concerned the action of the referee. Did he act in time to stop the fight? Another question had to do with the role of the examining doctors who certified the physical fitness of the fighters before the bout. Still another question involved Mr. Paret's manager; did he rush his boy into the fight without adequate time to recuperate from the previous one?

In short, the investigators looked into every possible cause except the real one. Benny Paret was killed because the human fist delivers enough impact, when directed against the head, to produce a massive hemorrhage in the brain. The human brain is the most delicate and complex mechanism in all creation. It has a lacework of millions of highly fragile nerve connections. Nature attempts to protect this exquisitely intricate machinery by encasing it in a hard shell. Fortunately, the shell is thick enough to withstand a great deal of pounding. Nature, however, can protect man against everything except man himself. Not every blow to the head will kill a man—but there is always the risk of concussion and damage to the brain. A prize fighter may be able to survive even repeated brain concussions and go on fighting, but the damage to his brain may be permanent.

In any event, it is futile to investigate the referee's role and seek to determine whether he should have intervened to stop the fight earlier. That is not where the primary responsibility lies. The primary responsibility lies with the people who pay to see a man hurt. The referee who stops a fight too soon from the crowd's viewpoint can expect to be booed. The crowd wants the knockout; it wants to see a man stretched out on the canvas. This is the supreme moment in boxing. It is nonsense to talk about prize fighting as a test of boxing skills. No crowd was ever brought to its feet screaming and cheering at the sight of two men beautifully dodging and weaving out of each other's jabs. The time the crowd comes alive is when a man is hit hard over the heart or the head, when his mouthpiece flies out, when the blood squirts out of his nose or eyes, when he wobbles under the attack and his pursuer continues to smash at him with pole-axe impact.

Don't blame it on the referee. Don't even blame it on the fight managers. Put the blame where it belongs—on the prevailing mores that regard prize fighting as a perfectly proper enterprise and vehicle of entertainment. No one doubts that many people enjoy prize fighting and will miss it if it should be thrown out. And that is precisely the point.

Read the two sample objective summaries students wrote condensing the information found in Cousins' article.

A.

According to Norman Cousins, in his article "Who Killed Benny Paret?" the greatest responsibility for violence and death in boxing and, for instance, for the death of boxer Benny Paret, lies both with the fans who go to see the brutality in the ring, and with the "prevailing mores" that permit such violence to occur at what some people consider sport and entertainment. The referee, the fight manager, and the examining doctors are not directly responsible for Paret's death and other boxers' injuries. For they would not be there if the attitude of the general public would not allow two people to get into a ring and throw blows at each other that could seriously injure and even kill.

B.

Journalist Norman Cousins, in his essay "Who Killed Benny Paret?" reports of his interview with prizefight promoter Mike Jacobs on how to please a boxing crowd. Jacobs said that the crowd only comes to see two people beat up on each other. Cousins uses this insight to account for the death of prizefighter Benny Paret. Cousins examines who was primarily at fault for Paret's death: Was it the referee who didn't stop the fight, the examining doctors who certified the fitness of the fighter, or was it his manager who may not have allowed adequate time for Paret to recuperate from the previous fight? Cousins finally blames it on the mores of the prizefighting fans who think that boxing is a "perfectly proper enterprise and vehicle of entertainment."

Like the "Bigfoot" objective summaries, the two objective summaries of "Who Killed Benny Paret?" contain some of the same essential information. Each summary states Cousins' overall purpose in the essay—to ask who is primarily responsible for Paret's death—and each includes Cousins' own answer: the "prevailing mores" that accept violence and brutality as entertainment. Yet they also differ slightly in their summaries of the article. For instance, only *B* refers to Cousins' interview with Mike Jacobs. *A* begins with Cousins attributing the main responsibility of Paret's death to the spectators, while *B* states this near the end. Yet despite these fairly minor differences, each objective summary covers the most important points in Cousins' article.

In order to write a useful objective summary of an article or chapter, use most of the following questions:

## CRITERIA QUESTIONS: WRITING THE OBJECTIVE SUMMARY

**P urpose**

Have you captured the essence of the article or chapter in an objective way without commenting on or interpreting the material?

Have you reported the information as accurately and economically as possible? Have you avoided evaluating, disputing, or agreeing with the facts and ideas in the selection?

**A udience**

Have you given your readers what they need in order to understand the gist of the article or chapter you have summarized?

On the basis of your summary, will your readers have an accurate and complete idea of what the author was trying to communicate?

**C ode**

Have you used your own words in summarizing the original source? And have you clearly indicated what material, if any, is quoted directly from the original source?

Is your objective summary (or précis) short enough, about a third the length of the original piece? Have you condensed material for your summary by combining related ideas?

Have you re-created the author's ideas and arguments accurately and clearly and in the order in which she or he presented them?

**E xperience**

Have you captured all of the author's main points in order to maintain the usefulness of your objective summary?

Have you located the key sentences and words in each paragraph of the original piece and used these as the basis of your summary?

Have you avoided the urge to highlight all the supportive ideas used by the author of the article or chapter?

**S elf**

Have you maintained an informed but objective stance throughout your summary?

Have you convinced your readers that you are reliable and dependable as a reader and writer?

### ► WRITING ACTIVITY ◄

Write an objective summary of a magazine or newspaper article. Select a fairly recent article, one published within the past year. Assume that you are summarizing for an employer or other superior who has asked you to condense the material.

## THE CRITICAL SUMMARY

Every day we are all exposed to large amounts of information on a variety of subjects, but is it all equally valuable? Because something has been published does not necessarily mean that it is good. One of the most important attributes of a thinking person is the ability to look at information objectively and evaluate its worth. Writing critical summaries helps you to develop this skill because it asks you to act both as summarizer *and* as critic.

The critical summary should include both the writer's understanding of the information contained in an article and the writer's own reaction to the nature and quality of that information. The objective reading of an article is crucially important because to evaluate anything responsibly, we must first observe and try to understand it on its own terms. But since it is unwise and irresponsible to assimilate passively everything you encounter, after you have objectively read the article, you should exercise your judgment and evaluate its worth.

The following are two examples of critical summaries by students of the Bigfoot article. How does each critical summary reflect skills of both objective observation and thoughtful evaluation?

**A.**

In the May 1985, edition of *National Examiner*, there is an article about Bigfoot. Despite the observation that Bigfoot tried to grab hold of eight-year-old Jimmy Robertson, the majority of the people interviewed in the small Southern town where Bigfoot was supposedly spotted seem to think that all Bigfoot wants is companionship. In fact, parapsychologist Lorraine Warren claims that Bigfoot communicated to her through telepathy and told her that he was "a gentle vegetarian." Charles Freeman claims he saw Bigfoot giving first aid to a raccoon. The subject matter of the article is interesting; Bigfoot is a fascinating topic. However, I think that the article is somewhat slanted. The writer provides examples only of how Bigfoot is really harmless when surely there are examples of how mean he can be. The writer should have told us more about Bigfoot's trying to capture Jimmy Robertson. Also more people should have been interviewed. I wanted to hear about the history of Bigfoot sightings in the area. The examples the writer gives are only based on what a few people say.

B.

There are several flaws in the Bigfoot article's struggle for credibility. The article basically repeats several supposed sightings of Bigfoot on the Tennessee-Alabama border, with some people thinking Bigfoot is dangerous and some people, like parapsychologists Ed and Lorraine Warren, believing that he is harmless. I find it hard to believe any of this. First of all, this article was published in the *National Examiner*, a magazine on the same level of believeability as the *National Enquirer* and *Star*. Most of the stories in the magazines, like "Two year old defeats Russian army," are at least exaggerated and at most downright fabricated. Second, there are many people who don't believe in parapsychology; there is no concrete evidence that can support or any real reason to believe in things like telepathy, especially between humans and animals. And finally, the article's credibility is challenged by the reporter getting information completely from only a small number of eyewitnesses. People are not always reliable and will sometimes add their own flavor to a story.

Each of the critical summaries contains similar objective accounts of the information in the "Bigfoot" article, including many elements found in the objective summaries of the article. Yet there are greater differences between the evaluations of the article. *A* believes the article does not provide a sufficiently balanced portrait of Bigfoot, suggesting that some of Bigfoot's negative qualities should have been treated more extensively. *B* is much more skeptical about the very existence of Bigfoot; it questions whether the entire story may be entirely false. What are some of the specific differences in evaluation between the articles?

While we should expect some basic similarities between objective summaries of the same article, we need not anticipate the same degree of similarity between different critical summaries of the same article. Evaluation depends a great deal on individual experiences, which naturally differ from writer to writer. Yet while every writer may not make identical judgments, still we should expect writers to explain why they evaluated the article in the way they did. How have the writers of the "Bigfoot" critical summaries explained their evaluations of the article? Which of the summaries do you agree or disagree with? Why? What is your own evaluation of the "Bigfoot" article?

Read the following samples of student critical summaries of "Who Killed Benny Paret?" How does each summary incorporate elements of both objective observation and evaluation?

A.

In the essay "Who Killed Benny Paret?" Norman Cousins reports on his interview with Mike Jacobs, a prizefight promoter. Jacobs stated that the most important thing to keep in mind in successfully promoting a fight is to please the crowd. To please the crowd, a promoter must search to find boxers who have killer instincts because the crowd, above all, wants the knockout. This desire, Cousins believes, led to the death of a fighter named Benny Paret. Cousins claims that investigators into Paret's death looked into all possibilities except the most important one. Cousins attempts to persuade the reader that the crowd is to blame the most for the tragedy to the fighter. Cousins presents a sound, convincing case, but I can't agree that the spectators are the most to blame. If someone purposefully puts his body in front of a moving vehicle, he is more to blame than the driver if he is hit. Likewise, the fighter is the most responsible for what occurs in the ring. I think that since boxers get into the ring of their own will, knowing the risks they take, they are most responsible for what happens.

**B.**

Norman Cousins' "Who Killed Benny Paret?" is a very accurate account of what the world of boxing is like. Cousins obviously knows what he's talking about—his description of how the brain reacts to being hit is very detailed and he seems to understand all the ins and outs of the boxing industry. His in-depth interview with promoter Mike Jacobs about what people really want to see in a boxing match very effectively supports his own final contention that the crowd's demand to see blood is the primary cause of Paret's death. Cousins gives us a sense that he has thought over all the possible reasons why Paret was killed—he speculates about the referee's, the manager's, the examining doctor's role in Paret's death. This makes his final statement that the blood-thirsty crowd is the most to blame all the more powerful and convincing. I agree with Cousins when he says that "the time the crowd comes alive is when a man is hit hard over the heart or the head, when his mouthpiece flies out, when the blood squirts out of his nose or eyes . . . ."

As we saw in the critical summaries of the "Bigfoot" article, the critical summaries of "Who Killed Benny Paret?" contain much of the same objective information about the content of Cousins' article. Yet the critical summaries include differing evaluations of Cousins' major thesis. *B* agrees with Cousins' final thesis that the "prevailing mores that regard boxing as a perfectly proper enterprise" are most responsible for Paret's death. *A*, however, disagrees with Cousins, believing that a boxer assumes sole responsibility for what happens to him in the ring. How have the writers explained their individual evaluations of the article? Which critical summaries do you agree or disagree with? What is your own evaluation of Cousins' article?

There are no clear-cut, absolute rules that tell you exactly what and how to evaluate anything you read. Yet a critical summary should at least comment upon the main idea of an article. Note, for example, while the sample critical summaries of "Who Killed Benny Paret?" contain differing evaluations of the article, both address the central question of who was most responsible for Paret's death. Since Cousins' major purpose in his essay is to advance his thesis that the "prevailing mores" of society are the most to blame for Paret's death, a critical summary of "Who Killed Benny Paret?" that did not somehow respond to Cousins' main intent would seem incomplete. Similarly, a critical summary of the "Bigfoot" article which did not assess the quality of the evidence of Bigfoot's existence would seem to be missing something.

To write a useful critical summary of an article or chapter, use most of the following questions:

## CRITERIA QUESTIONS: WRITING THE CRITICAL SUMMARY

### Purpose

Did the author make the purpose of the article clear? If the author tried to prove something, did he or she fulfill your expectations? If the author intended to analyze something, did you feel he or she lived up to the commitment? Did you feel satisfied or disappointed or puzzled by the article?

### Audience

What is the author's attitude toward the reader? From the evidence in the article, what is the author's opinion of the reader? Is the author concerned about the reader's needs or is the author writing to no one in particular? Is the writing aimed at the right audience?

### Code

Is the summary readable? Are there unnecessary big words, too many long sentences, too many abstract concepts not explained in concrete terms?

Has the author chosen vocabulary that is accurate, colorful, and effective?

Is the language appropriate? Does the author treat dignified subjects lightheartedly? Are there any surprises in the language? An unusually good word or phrase? A well-crafted sentence or chunk?

Is there appropriate variety in the sentences? Or is there evidence that the writer was having a hard time writing: labored sentences, fuzzy language, humdrum words?

### Experience

Is the subject interesting? Does the material raise your curiosity about the subject? Does the subject hold your interest? Is it interesting only to you personally, or do you think it is likely to appeal to the general reader?

Is there enough information? Is this a thorough treatment or a sketchy overview? Is the author treating the subject with sufficient depth? Has the author supplied the reader with enough facts or enough details to achieve his or her overall purpose?

Is the material worthwhile? Does it treat a subject that most readers would agree is worth treating? Does the material seem trivial or light? Did the author intend it to be that way?

Are the facts accurate? Does the author distort, exaggerate, or diminish the facts?

Has the author supplied the reader with new facts, new information, or new interpretation of the facts? How newsworthy is this subject?

Can the educated general reader understand the ideas without difficulty?

**Self**

What is the author's attitude toward the subject? Does the author like the subject? Does the author think the subject is important? More important than you do?

Is the author friendly? Indifferent? Sarcastic? Patronizing? Too technical? Who does the author think he or she is? Is the author's view of self (the author's voice) appropriate for this article?

Is the author expressing a lively point of view, or does he or she sound bored? Is the author being matter-of-fact, disinterested, objective, ironic, or something else?

Did you come away feeling the author knew the subject and did a good job of presenting it to the reader?

Is the author fair? Is the overall interpretation biased, subjective, slanted, objective? Does the author present material to justify his or her stance? Does the author try to look at both sides of the issue? Do you trust this author? Can you find any faults in the author's logic?

### ► WRITING ACTIVITY ◄

Write a critical summary of a recent article from a magazine or newspaper. Although you need to summarize the contents of the article, your evaluation is the most important part of the assignment; do not devote more than one-half page to the summary.

## THE EVALUATIVE PAPER

Now that you have had some experience with written summaries and evaluations, it is time to move to the longer evaluative paper, in which you examine a subject in detail, judge its worth, and then report your evaluation to your readers. For the evaluative paper, you will have a wide range of subjects from which to choose: a performance, a television show, a movie, a political, economic, or social position or system, an object or product, a work of literature or art, an exhibition, a sporting event, a well-known personality, and so on.

## Selecting a Topic

To select a topic that will be of interest both to you and your readers, make a list of possible topics and then do a quick preliminary analysis of each. Ask yourself, Do I know enough about the topic? Do I have an opinion about this topic that will interest my readers? Do I have enough evidence to support my claims? Such an analysis is likely to reduce your list to two or three possible topics, which you should then analyze in depth, using one or two of the invention techniques treated in Chapter Two.

As you are selecting a topic for analysis, remember that some of your readers will either be or feel expert in this area, too. Therefore, you should be knowledgeable not only about the system, performance, person, or event you are judging, but also about its background, principles, traditions, and techniques. Would you feel confident having a discussion about the subject of your analysis with other people who know a good deal about the area? If the answer is no, you should abandon the topic and resume your search for a subject about which you can feel confident and knowledgeable. No one wants to listen to an analysis by someone who knows little or nothing about the topic. But you *can* be a persuasive critic without being an absolute authority on the subject. The crucial question is whether you can convince your readers of the reasonableness of your judgment.

## Identifying Evaluative Criteria

If you are writing about music, films, sports, literature, television, and so on, you need to describe for your readers what happened, assuming that most of them have not experienced the event. If you were evaluating a play, for example, you would describe how the play was performed, what techniques were used, and what actors played certain parts. You might also mention scenery, costumes, and dialog. Using these or similar *criteria* as bases for your analysis, you would also *judge* the performance. Was it good, bad, mediocre? How did this play compare with other plays by the same author, by the author's contemporaries?

To make such judgments, you need a sense of quality, and judgments about quality must be based on carefully selected criteria culled from your own experience, from study, and from cultural tradition. The evaluative criteria you use should meet with your readers' approval. They should not be trivial, whimsical, or purely subjective, based on your narrow prejudices. At times, the criteria you use will be generally accepted by most people and won't need an explanation; at others, you may have to justify or define your criteria.

## Planning Your Evaluation

You must also present your readers with a sound argument that is supported by good reasons and evidence. Using strong supportive evidence will establish your credibility with the reader. In effect it says, "Don't take my word for it; judge the evidence for yourself!" Where appropriate, try to give a balanced criticism. State both strengths and weaknesses and acknowledge counterarguments and counterevidence.

As you plan your evaluative paper, be sure to arrange your arguments and evidence in the best possible order. Consider carefully the strategies of development—comparison, contrast, analogy, definition, classification, description—you plan to use. Experiment with a variety of these techniques before settling on one or two. In the evaluative paper, comparison-contrast and description are often effective: For example, if you are evaluating a performance, you can often enrich your analysis by comparing it with similar performances Since your task is to report what you have observed and then judge it, one good way to start a review is to describe in some detail what the performance was like. Your readers are totally dependent on your descriptive skills if they are to see the play, concert, or event or hear the album or orchestra as you want them to see or hear it.

Merely describing the plot of a film or play, for example, isn't enough. Is the plot believable? Do you care about the story and the characters? Does the story have moral, social, psychological, or some other kind of value? In the same way, just describing the lines and colors of a painting isn't enough. Is the idea behind the painting clear, even if the painting is a yellow square painted on a white background? What reaction does the painting create in you? What causes the reaction: the idea, colors, lines, subject? Is there any value in the painting? In all cases, what do *you* think? How do *you* rate what you've seen, heard, felt, touched, or tasted?

The following PACES criteria questions should prove useful as you examine the evaluative papers of other writers in this chapter and as you write your own.

### CRITERIA QUESTIONS: WRITING THE EVALUATIVE PAPER

**[P]urpose**

Does this draft have a clear sense of purpose? Has the author clearly stated his or her thesis based on a firm judgment? How well does the author achieve his or her purpose?

**[A]udience**

Is the author sensitive to the needs and opinions of the readers, especially those who are unfamiliar with the topic?

**C ode**

How is the draft organized? Are the reasons and evidence organized in the best order? What strategies of development—comparison, contrast, analogy, definition, classification—have been used? Are they appropriate? Effective?

Is the introduction interesting? Does it provide the reader with necessary background information?

Is the conclusion effective? Does the draft finish with power?

Are technical, obscure, or difficult terms explained clearly? Is the draft written with an appropriate level of formality or informality? Is the style appropriate to the subject matter?

**E xperience**

What evaluative criteria has the author used? Are they important or trivial? Are they purely subjective, based only on the author's personal opinions or prejudices? Or will they be viewed as significant by the readers? Have the criteria been defined or explained well?

Has the author supplied the reader with enough information to form a judgment?

Has the author presented a strong argument backed up with good reasons and evidence?

Is the evidence believable? Authoritative? Is further evidence needed?

Has the author supported the argument with enough examples? Too many examples?

What are the author's strongest reasons? Weakest reasons? Are the reasons based on appropriate criteria? Should any of the author's reasons be edited out?

Has the author presented a balanced judgment that considers strengths and weaknesses? Advantages and disadvantages?

Does the author consider possible counterarguments? Refute them with counter evidence?

**S elf**

Does the writer project a self or persona appropriate to the topic?

Does the author have an authoritative voice, one that is confident and knowledgeable about the topic?

Does the author project a self who is objective and reasonable? Or is the author purely subjective in some or all of his or her judgments?

## ► READING ACTIVITY ◄

To use the principles of evaluative writing we have been discussing, analyze with the aid of the PACES criteria questions on pages 236 to 237, a review written by London *Observer* critic Peter Hillmore, who traveled from London to Berlin to report on the Rolling Stones in concert. What evaluative criteria does Hillmore focus on? How effective is his use of detail? Why does he choose not to criticize the Stones' musical ability? Does this choice reflect his purpose in describing the band as "The Economic Miracles"?

### THE ECONOMIC MIRACLES

*The Rolling Stones are at Wembley on 25 and 26 June—their first appearance here for five years. Peter Hillmore went to hear them in Berlin last week.*

Christopher Isherwood would surely have approved. The Rolling Stones had arrived in Berlin, and for a brief period the theatrical decadence that had made the city famous returned.

The group, and their 130-strong entourage, took the entire top floor of West Berlin's best hotel—normally so sanitized that even the fruit is wrapped in Cellophane—and for two days it became a citadel of luxurious decline. Time became meaningless, and almost confusing: vampire-like, the group seemed to avoid the daylight; the whole floor of suites and rooms was soporific and quiet during the day, but at 5 A.M., just before dawn, it was smoke-filled, echoing with the noises of music, laughter, screams, conversation, and only a few people had gone to bed early. It was the only place where you could experience the bewildering feeling of jet-lag without actually flying.

But Chancellor Schmidt, and Berlin's more staid citizens, must have approved as well. For the Rolling Stones are also examples of a post-war economic miracle. Here are five men, all born after the war ended, celebrating 20 years of profitable success in an industry where fame is often measured in months. Their tour last year of America was the largest grossing tour in the history of the world. Why, they even made £8 million profit from the sale of T-shirts alone. You don't even have to understand, let alone like, the music to appreciate that.

Ah, the music. There's really no point in reviewing a Rolling Stones concert simply by just talking about the music alone. There's no point in analysing whether Ronnie Wood's guitar-playing is lack-lustre in the quieter moments, or whether Mick Jagger's voice lacks the vibrancy and range to see him through the coloratura passages. What you have to review, because it is what people come to see and hear, is the Performance.

There were some music experts among the gaggle of people backstage who could name bands and individuals who were technically superior, and younger groups who wrote better songs—but once Jagger appeared on stage, and gave his first snarl at the audience, they readily agreed that the Rolling Stones were still the best—because they were still the best performers.

The group does not let any of their audience down, from the moment they come on before 40,000 people in an open-air stadium to the time that a firework-display finale erupts two and a half hours later. Mick Jagger taunts the crowd, whirling around, bare-chested, swirling a multi-coloured silk shawl around his shoulders, jutting and thrusting his hips at the crowd with sexual and musical arrogance.

Keith Richards, sullen-faced, not waving but frowning, plays his guitar in a half-crouch, and then duels with Ronnie Wood, as if their guitars were sabres. Bill Wyman and drummer Charlie Watts taciturnly and expressionlessly play their instruments with a relentless solidity that allows the others to gyrate—Watts as if he hates the music. They, too, know their role; they, too, perform. And perform, and perform.

Without a break, without even a pause or interval, the group play number after number. The seeming anarchy of their stage-movements is rigidly controlled (the backstage staff seem to know exactly when Jagger will spontaneously decide to leap up a catwalk), but the effect is to make it look natural. The energy is impressive, the audience is excited and even the people who have paid £60 a ticket on the black market—six times what Mick Jagger, the group's financial spokesman, decided was a fair price—feel it is worth it.

All the audience's favourite songs are played/performed in the way that the audience seem to want them to be; 20 years of accountants and tax-lawyers don't seem to have changed the cynicism in Jagger's voice, and the young don't seem to mind his age. 'One of the reasons why we have to play for so long,' Jagger tells me, 'is that even playing just our hits of 20 years takes a while, and the audiences still want our hits.'

The audience leaves the concert elated and exhausted by the energy they have expended themselves, and by the energy that has been expended on their behalf. But not the Rolling Stones—they are elated, but not exhausted.

There was one moment at the end of the concert when I think I understood why Mick Jagger had so much energy, and it wasn't because of his daily press-ups and runs. It may be another cliché—but it's the performing that gives him the energy to perform. I found myself standing behind one of the huge amplifiers, just 10 feet behind the group, gazing out at the same view of the audience as Jagger was getting. And I had a terrifying, vicarious sense of power.

There was row upon row of swaying, clapping, shouting people, all focusing their combined enthusiasm and collective will on what suddenly seemed a very small stage. It was as if a two-way intravenous drip-feed of adrenalin had been set up, with the audience feeding off the five Rolling Stones, responding to their goadings, being fuelled by their music and being charged by their energy. For their part, the Stones were being resuscitated by the urgings and enthusiasm of the audience.

Just as the audience cannot get the Stones' performance when they buy their records, and so rush to buy concert tickets (110,000 for two concerts in Gothenburg sold out in 6 hours, 32 minutes) to see the performance, so too the Stones have to give concerts—because on records they can only sing, and not perform.

And however true it may be that the Stones go on tour because they owe it to their record-buying fans to appear in public, it also became clear to me, standing behind the amplifiers, that the fans owe it to the Stones to turn up at the public appearances to fuel their energy and egos.

They are so good at it, because they never stop performing. Even in private the Stones bear out their public performances. Backstage, Keith Richards is worried that his new shoes will make him slip; suddenly, from nowhere, he pulls out not a respectable pen-knife, but a wicked looking sheath-knife, and viciously scores the soles. Afterwards, the quiet men on stage, Wyman and Watts, will be the only two members of the group not to go to a party. Wyman will be asleep, even before the others leave the hotel.

The others will sort through the 100 pieces of baggage that their personal 'bag man' has been looking after throughout the tour, select clean pairs of jeans and go on to a night club that has been specially opened for them. Just the two-day stop over in Berlin will cost the group £50,000, and I'm assured that's not at all exceptional for the way stars live these days. At the night club, the group, or at least some of them, will accept the congratulations and feed on the praise of their entourage, their hangers-on—and that of one fearless, fact-finding investigative-reporter, who will stagger out into the real world at 6 A.M.

Hillmore is an accomplished critic who goes to Berlin to report on a musical event and ends up by discounting the purely musical aspects of the Rolling Stones' concert and concentrating on "what people came to see and hear . . . the Performance." And it is the "Performance" that justifies the headline "The Economic Miracles." Hillmore's brilliant descriptions of the entourage in the hotel, their "vampirelike" behavior, the startling differences displayed by the group members in private, the moment when Hillmore had the "terrifying, vicarious sense of power" when he stood just behind Jagger—all combine to capture the tension, the terror, the mystery of a Rolling Stones performance. Peter Hillmore has won us, his readers, over by skillfully melding description and evaluation—a truly impressive *performance*.

# THE WRITER'S MIND AT WORK

## DRAFTING AND REVISING AN EVALUATIVE PAPER

Theresa, a student writer, had recently seen the movie *Turk 182* and had fairly strong feelings about it. To explore her topic, she decided to try brainstorming on her word processor.

**PLANNING STRATEGY:**
**Brainstorming for "Turk 182"**

```
clean up city
polish Big Apple
idea soon
  forgotten
idea of seeing
  spray paint
giant apple
spray paint
electronic devices
Timothy Hutton
Unbelievable
Bandwagon-jumping
  on a media blitz
Mayor claims he
  will now go on
  record as being
  behind Jimmy all
  the way.

glamour of graffiti
doesn't work
Mayor up for reelection
wants out of the paper
setup contrived
 why?
Comedy?
 Social commentary?
Robert Urich
Peter Boyle
Security Squad Leader
 Bubbling
  Bombers
 getaway car
  football game
various trash cans
banner led by airplane
Bridge celebration
```

Pleased by the rich details she had generated in her brainstorming, Theresa decided to explore her topic in more detail by using the pentad.

**PLANNING STRATEGY:**
**Pentad for "Turk 182"**

<u>Act:</u> spray painting political slogan "Zimmerman flew; Tyler knew"--adding "Turk 182" in protest--flying an airplane banner--projecting a message on a display screen during a football game--scrawling signs on trash cans

<u>Agent:</u> Jimmy what's-his-name (find out) supposedly the sole actor in the graffiti stunt, although he must have received some help--his electronics whiz kid friend helps him rig the football game stunt--but we don't see others who help Jimmy--who are they??? angry young men, out to beat the uncaring system

<u>Agency:</u> spray paint, colored lights on the bridge, some electronic device to run a program of anti mayor slogans during the mayor's political rally during the football game--some genius, technical, creative genius must have done some of the stunts--wouldn't work otherwise--the guy needs to be a technological whiz kid and we see nothing about this in his character in the movie

<u>Scene:</u> in the most public of places--the football stadium, subway car, wherever the mayor happens to be, campaigning for reelection--in subway stations, in the sky, the bridge celebration with the colored lights as the mayor makes a speech there, campaigning

<u>Purpose:</u> to protest brother Turk 182's being shafted out of his fireman's compensation (he

```
saved a little girl when he was off duty and had
a few drinks and so the department claimed he
was drunk and wouldn't honor his claim) also
part of a general political move to dash the
mayor's hopes for reelection (his treasurer had
supposedly skipped the country with some city
funds) mixed motives--I guess Jimmy just wanted
to get back at the mayor--but "Turk 182" meant
nothing to anyone but Jimmy--the slogan "Zim-
merman flew and Tyler knew" means something to
the entire city--but when the mayor jumps on the
bandwagon at the end and claims he supported
Jimmy all along, you get the feeling Jimmy has
somehow lost.
```

Theresa then decided to examine all the notes she had accumulated and formulate a tentative plan for her evaluative paper. Here is a script of her writer's mind as she worked on her planning notes:

**THE WRITER'S MIND:**
**Planning for review of "Turk 182"**

*I need to describe the main elements of the movie "Turk 182." I don't want to get too terribly detailed here, but I want to make sure that I cover all the major parts. For instance*

*—Jimmy's anger and frustration at his brother's plight, his brother's situation (he saved a girl from a burning building while he was off duty when he was a little tipsy—he gets hurt and is now ineligible for fireman's compensation or for any financial assistance with his bills because the city now claims that because he was drunk he illegally entered the scene of a fire)*

*—Jimmy's anger at the mayor, who won't listen to him when he pleads his brother's case*

*—the mayor's campaign for reelection and all the bad press he's been getting about his treasurer supposedly running off with a lot of money*

*—Jimmy's activities as a graffiti artist*

*—the conclusion in which nothing is concluded—when the mayor says he'll claim to support Jimmy, Jimmy's campaign against the mayor seems to fail*

*I don't want to take up too much space with all this stuff but I figure I can cut it later if it turns out to be too long—then I should focus on what disturbed me most about the movie—the glorification of graffiti and the contrived situation that made the graffiti "artist" seem like a hero—actually not all of what Jimmy did involved graffiti—stuff like the banner behind the airplane didn't involve vandalism or the defacement of property; it might even have been legal—but it's the idea of protesting anonymously, with the mysterious sign "Turk 182" plastered all over the city, catching people's attention by playing on their curiosity. No one except Jimmy and a few of his friends knew what "Turk 182" meant until the very end of the movie—the people only sensed it was some kind of protest against the Mayor so they joined in with the chant "Turk 182," dumbly repeating this over and over. Jimmy uses the crowd just as much as the mayor does. The crowd makes no real choice; it blindly follows its mysterious hero graffiti artist. THIS is what I object to most about the movie—maybe I could even contrast Jimmy with a picketer who brings his full complaint to the public, who tells the public the whole of his side of the story.*

*I guess I should bring up some other aspects of the movie as well—some good stuff and some bad stuff.*

> *Good stuff—acting—Timothy Hutton and Robert Urich have creditable New York accents and Robert Culp was good as the smooth politician mayor—also some good comic moments in the film—also some good special effects.*
>
> *Bad stuff—wasn't believable that one person could do all the graffiti stunts that Jimmy pulls in the movie—inconclusive, confusing ending; we're left wondering who really won, Jimmy or the mayor?*

*I'm not sure about the order of all this. Maybe I should review my minor points about the movie before my major point (that I didn't admire the way in which Jimmy protested the treatment of his brother). I'll see what happens.*

After putting her planning notes aside for a day, Theresa went back to them, read through them a couple of times, and then produced the following working draft:

**WORKING DRAFT:**
**Review of "Turk 182"**

"Turk 182, Turk 182" is the curious slogan which half the population of New York city chants in a recent movie of the same name. The mysterious words cover the city--on sidewalks, on subways, across walls, in newspapers--and are echoed in the voices of the people. The people associate the slogan with protest against the corrupt mayor, the words becoming a symbol of the power of the people against the system. It's an inspiring premise--the people united against the corrupt, irresponsible leader. Unfortunately, the protrayal of the power of the people in "Turk 182" adds a disappointing twist to this common theme: Until the end of the movie, the powerful people of New York city don't even know what "Turk 182" means.

Jimmy, played by Timothy Hutton, is the young New Yorker who plasters this slogan throughout the city. His older brother, nicknamed Turk, played by Robert Urich, was a fireman who had been injured at the scene of a fire. Turk was off duty at the time and had been relaxing in a bar with some of his friends. A little girl ran into the bar and asked Turk to save her sister from a nearby house which was on fire. Turk responded immediately, rushing into the flame-engulfed house and saving the girl, who had hidden herself in a second story room. Just as Turk is about to rush out of the building, a fireman who had just arrived, broke down the door and, unaware that anybody was in the room, sprayed water into the second story room, the force of the water throwing Turk and the little girl out of the window and onto the top of a car below. The little girl was protected from the impact by the body of Turk. Turk, however, landed on his back on top of the car and was badly hurt, spending the next six months in the hospital.

Turk had risked his life to save the little girl. Yet because he was off duty at the time and because he had had a few beers, he is considered ineligible for fireman's compensation, which he badly needs in order to pay his medical bills and to get the physical therapy he needs in order to recover fully from his fall. His brother Jimmy takes up his case and writes letter upon letter to various city offices, pleading his brother's special case, all to no avail. He even confronts the mayor face to face and is still refused help for his brother, whom the mayor labels as a drunkard.

Fed up with all the indifference he had encountered, Jimmy turns to a different medium to plead his brother's case. The mayor, who was launching his bid for reelection, was being hounded by the press because his treasurer had skipped the country, supposedly embezzling city funds. The press insinuates that Mayor Tyler knew about the corruption of his treasurer Zimmerman. At a speech in a park, in which the mayor does some campaigning by announcing his big program to "clean up the Big Apple" the mayor unveils a statue of an apple, symbolizing his new program. To his dismay, the statue of the apple had scrawled across it in huge spray-painted letters "Zimmerman flew and Tyler knew," ruining the impressive campaigning scene the mayor had set up. A light breaks across Jimmy's face and he discovers what he thinks is the most effective medium to catch the mayor's and the people's attention.

From here on out the movie becomes a type of duel between the mayor and Jimmy. Jimmy begins by plastering the slogan "Zimmerman flew and Tyler knew" all over the city, adding to this "Turk 182" (Turk was his brother's nickname; 182 was his brother's fireman badge number). Pretty soon,

Jimmy omits the first part of the slogan. The people of New York are captivated by the mysterious message and they join in rooting for the unknown graffiti artist.

Jimmy shows up at each campaign event the mayor has planned and thwarts it with his message. For instance, when the mayor christens a subway car, Jimmy manages to scrawl his message on the side of it. When the mayor campaigns at half time of a football game, Jimmy has his message flashed over the playback board. Jimmy even arranges to have a banner pulled by airplane across the New York skyline, broadcasting his slogan to the city.

The movie has an interesting premise--an angry young man gets the force of New York's populace behind him against the mayor. The acting is fairly impressive but the plot is unbelievable. It is beyond belief that one young man could pull off all the stunts that Jimmy does in the movie, especially without becoming known. Until the end of the movie, the identity of the master graffiti artist is unknown to all but the three people Jimmy confides in. With the curiosity of the entire city of New York aroused, it's impossible to believe that Jimmy could continually remain undetected in his stunts.

Yet more than the movie's plot is disturbing. The movie glorifies Jimmy's graffiti stunts, contriving the plot so as to show Jimmy in a good light. We can approve of the people's uninformed support of Jimmy because we understand the injustice done to Jimmy's brother. But Jimmy doesn't rely on his brother's story--rather, he fights the mayor with his own brand of hype, jumping on the bandwagon of opposition to the mayor already fostered by the press. To Jimmy and to the audience, the slogan "Turk 182" has a great deal of significance but to the people of New York city, the audience Jimmy tries to reach, "Turk 182" is only some ambiguous burst of protest against the system.

Theresa was pleased with this draft of her paper but she realized that it could benefit from revision. After rereading her working draft and carefully examining the PACES criteria questions for the evaluative paper (see pages 236 to 237), Theresa began to construct a scheme for her revisions. The following is a script of her writer's mind as she worked on her replanning notes.

### THE WRITER'S MIND: Replanning Review of "Turk 182"

*I like this draft, but there are a few things that could be done to make it better. I think I have covered quite a bit of what I basically wanted to say about the movie but I really do need to refine some things. My overall purpose is pretty clear—my thesis that "Turk 182" finally betrays its own theme of power to the people is stated pretty straightforwardly. Though I could perhaps stand to explain a little more about* why *I don't like the method Jimmy chooses to "plead" his brother's case. His cause is right—Turk has definitely been given the shaft by the mayor's office, but I don't like the* way *he protests against the mayor. He doesn't explain to the people about how Turk has been treated. I should probably explain this part a little more in my paper since this is so important to my overall reaction to the movie.*

*I should think a bit more about the various criteria I use for evaluating this movie. Just what have I focused on? I give the most attention to the theme, but this makes sense because the theme is most important to my overall reaction. I also comment on the plot of the movie, which is just unbelievable in parts—for instance, I just can't believe that one guy could do all the stuff that Jimmy does in the movie, like rig up a playback board at a football stadium. Plus how could he remain uncaught when the entire city of New York is asking who is the mysterious author of "Turk 182"? What other criteria should I use? What about the* acting*—that's an important part of any movie. All I've said in my draft is that the acting is "fairly impressive" but I haven't given any examples of what I mean. Actually Robert Culp was pretty good as Mayor Tyler—he was the perfect smooth, flashy politician with a big false smile. And Peter Boyle was pretty funny as his security agent who never could catch the unknown graffiti artist. I should include something about acting in my next draft—some examples of what I mean by "fairly impressive" acting.*

*How about my audience? I know I need to explain a lot about the movie's story since I can't assume that all of my readers will have seen it. But maybe I do too much of that in this draft. I think I spend too much time with the plot. I should think about condensing some of the plot summary I have here. Like the second paragraph—I don't need to say everything about how Turk got injured—it's enough to let my readers know that Turk was badly hurt while saving a girl from a burning house—in the line of duty (even though he was officially off duty)—and that he was unfairly refused fireman's compensation to cover his injuries. All that other stuff is good but it just gets in the way—it gets too much space in this draft and probably would divert my readers' attention from the most important things I want to say about this movie. I need to tell my readers only what they need to know to understand my evaluation.*

*The organization of the draft could use a little more work. The basic overall structure is all right—a general reaction, then plot summary, then a more detailed evaluation of the movie—but it could use some revising (besides those additions and deletions I came up with already). My introduction is interesting and gives my readers a pretty good sense of my overall reaction but seems a little abrupt—it's like a mini-essay in itself. I should do something with it, make it flow a little better with the rest of the paper, make it seem more like an introduction. For that matter, I think I need more of a* conclusion*—this draft just sort of ends, not a heck of a lot of power. I don't even get to the really disturbing part of the movie—the last scene in which the mayor plans to incorporate Jimmy's popularity into his own campaign. That's the worst part—we're left with a sense that the mayor will just smooth things over and that Jimmy's real cause against the uncaring and corrupt city government will just get set aside.* That *needs to be in here—right in the conclusion.*

Confident that she had devised a successful plan to help her improve her paper, Theresa produced the following final draft. How does this final draft reflect the replanning she had done?

**FINAL DRAFT:**
**"Power to the People?"**

The movie "Turk 182", directed by Bob Clarks, begins with an interesting premise but unfortunately falls short of its initial potential. The movie portrays an underdog hero fighting for a worthy cause: an angry young man whose brother is wronged by the uncaring, inhumane city government of New York "takes it to the street," enlisting the support of the populace of New York City. The adventuresome young man has the entire city mouthing his slogan, chanting "Turk 182! Turk 182!" Power to the people--the archetypal American story. The only problem is that throughout most of the movie the people of New York vigorously repeat the young man's slogan with no knowledge of what it means. The blind, unquestioning support of the people, who wholeheartedly give their assent to a cause they don't even understand, adds a disappointing, disturbing twist to the theme of power to the people, turning what could have been an inspiring film into pretty mediocre fare.

Timothy Hutton plays Jimmy, a spirited though apparently aimless young New Yorker who becomes enraged at the city government's treatment of his brother, a fireman nicknamed Turk (played by Robert Urich). Turk was severely injured while courageously saving a young child from a burning house. Yet because he was officially off-duty at the time and was a little tipsy from drinking beer with his friends, the city refuses to pay for Turk's badly needed physical therapy, claiming that since Turk was slightly intoxicated at the scene of the fire he is therefore ineligible for fireman's compensation benefits. Outraged by this injustice, Jimmy takes up his brother's cause, writing letter upon letter pleading his brother's case to various city officials, exploring every possible legal avenue to get his brother the help he needs. All to no avail--he meets nothing but indifference. When Jimmy finally confronts Mayor Tyler, his one last chance, the mayor lightly shrugs him off, dismissing Turk as an irresponsible drunkard.

Fed up with all the indifference he encounters, Jimmy turns to a different medium to "plead" his brother's case. Jimmy attends a re-election campaign speech Mayor Tyler gives in Central Park, intending to heckle him. The mayor plans to unveil a statue of a big red apple to kick off his new program to "clean up the Big Apple." Yet the mayor's clean-apple event turns sour when the unveiled apple is found to have painted all over it in large letters "Zimmerman flew and Tyler knew." (Mayor Tyler's former treasurer Zimmerman allegedly had skipped the country with embezzled city funds--"Zimmerman flew and Tyler knew" had been one newspaper's headline.) The audience, which had gathered to hear the mayor's campaign speech, breaks into laughter and begins to chant the slogan spray painted across the apple. A light breaks across Jimmy's face as he discovers what he thinks is the most powerful, effective medium by which to catch the attention of the mayor and the people of New York.

From this point on, the movie focuses on the curious duel that evolves between Jimmy and Mayor Tyler. Jimmy begins plastering the slogan "Zimmerman flew and Tyler knew" all over the city--on sidewalks, the subway walls, in newspapers--adding to this his own slogan "Turk 182" (Turk is his brother's nickname; 182 is Turk's fireman badge number). Soon Jimmy omits the first part of the slogan, the one he borrowed, and simply "publishes" the words "Turk 182" throughout the city. The people of New York are captivated by the mysterious message--even though they don't understand what it refers to, they associate it with the protest against the rumored corruption in the mayor's office, and they join in rooting for the unknown graffiti artist.

Despite all Tyler's efforts to catch Jimmy, the slogan "Turk 182" conspicuously appears at every one of the mayor's succeeding campaign events, effectively thwarting his attempts to impress the people with his "clean up the Big Apple" program. For instance, when the mayor christens a new subway car, Jimmy somehow manages to have scrawled on the side of it "Turk 182" in colorful spray-painted letters. When the mayor delivers a reelection speech at halftime of a football game, Jimmy has his message "Turk 182" flashed in huge blinking lights over the playback board. Jimmy even arranges to have a banner pulled across the New York city skyline by airplane, broadcasting his slogan to the entire city.

The movie has an interesting premise--an angry young man gets the force of New York's populace behind him against the corrupt mayor. The acting is fairly impressive--both Timothy Hutton and Robert Urich manage passable New York accents. Robert Culp, with his flashy, plastic politician's smile is very convincing as Mayor Tyler, and Peter Boyle is quite comical as Tyler's dedicated but bumbling chief security agent. Yet despite the creditable acting, the plot is unbelievable. Until the very end of the movie, the identity of the master graffiti artist remains unknown to all but three of Jimmy's close friends. That one young man could successfully pull off all the stunts Jimmy does in the movie without getting caught by the authorities, or without being unmasked by any of the inquisitive people of New York, frankly is too much to swallow. Also it is difficult to believe that Jimmy could have designed and implemented such complicated, impressive feats as tampering with the programming of a playback board at a football stadium. In the character Timothy Hutton plays, we see a driven angry young man, but we see nothing of the whiz kid, technological genius, or master of disguise Jimmy would have to be in order to believably perform what he does in the movie.

Yet more than the credibility of the movie's plot is questionable. The movie glorifies Jimmy's graffiti stunts; the plot is contrived so as to portray what essentially amounts to vandalism as acts of heroism. After he has exhausted every official avenue in pursuing his brother's claim for fireman's compensation, the frustrated young man goes "to the people." Yet instead of informing the people of the injustice done his brother, he hooks them with the mysterious slogan "Turk 182," dazzling them with his flashy, audacious stunts. We can approve of Jimmy's actions because we understand the reasons why Jimmy objects to the mayor; we know all of Turk's story. Yet the people of New York, the audience Jimmy tries to reach, are not in such a privileged position. In a way, Jimmy manipulates the people of New York almost as much, perhaps even more, than the mayor does--right up until the very end of the movie his slogan "Turk 182" means nothing to anyone but himself. Jimmy doesn't rely on his brother's story, he doesn't rely on the facts of Turk's case--rather, he fights the mayor with his own brand of hype, jumping on the bandwagon of opposition to the mayor already fostered by the press. To Jimmy and to us, the slogan "Turk 182" has a great deal of significance, but to the people of New York City "Turk 182" is only some ambiguous burst of protest against "the system."

The ending of the movie nearly defeats the movie's apparent theme of power to the people. After Jimmy ruins a new bridge dedication that the mayor includes as part of his campaign, somehow managing to twist the colored lights on the bridge's suspension wires into the omnipresent "Turk 182," the movie concludes with a lengthy sequence of shots of the crowd's reaction to Jimmy's greatest stunt. It pictures faces cheering Jimmy on and chanting "Turk 182." The mayor, dumbfounded at Jimmy's unbelievable accomplishment, turns to an aide and in the best "if you can't beat 'em, join 'em" tradition, mutters, "We'll claim in the papers tomorrow that we were always behind the kid." This throws a whole new light on Jimmy's achievement. Though we suspect that everything will somehow be smoothed out, we get no real resolution of Turk's problem. All we know is that Jimmy might become an unwitting part of the mayor's reelection campaign. So much for power to the people.

## ▶ DISCUSSION ACTIVITY ◀

Examine and discuss the following evaluative student papers, which vary both in subject matter and quality, using the PACES criteria questions for evaluative papers (pages 236 to 237).

### THE FIFTIES CONNECTION

Recently, a growing nostalgia for the music of the fifties and sixties has become noticeable. Some radio stations have changed to a completely "oldies" format. TV shows set during these decades like "Happy Days" and "Crime Story" keep cropping up. And some nightclubs and restaurants which attempt to recreate the feel of those decades have sprung up. What many of us don't realize, however, is that while there is a genuine nostalgia for the music of the fifties and sixties, there is not the same nostalgia for the culture in general. Too many nightclubs have tried to go too far in their re-creations, even to the point of making their sock-hops actual sock-hops. While such returns to the past might be nice occasionally, for a club to remain popular weekend after weekend, it will need to produce a balance between the old days and today.

Columbus, Ohio, is fortunate in having just such a nightclub/restaurant, "The Fifties Connection," located on Dublin-Granville Road, near Cleveland Ave. The outside of the building is strictly modern, without the least hint, beyond the name of the club itself, to give away its "oldies" orientation. Inside, the restaurant part may go a bit overboard in its nostalgia, but the nightclub part hits just the right balance.

"The Fifties Connection" claims to be divided into three sections: a "soda fountain" section, a restaurant, and a dancefloor. In fact, the restaurant and dancefloor are in the same large room. It is dark and hot and not conducive to a good meal. The "soda fountain" room, which you enter first, is bright and airy with large windows, white tile floors, and white tables and chairs.

Unfortunately, "The Fifties Connection" is not one of the better places to eat in Columbus, and the failure can be directly attributed to the management's attempt to recreate too well the culture of the fifties. While the soda fountain itself is really just a bar, the menu offers such staples as meat loaf and chicken pot pie. (Just what you want to eat when you go out, right?) The prices are extraordinarily low, and they should be. I had the chicken pot pie and got what I feared I might: chicken pot pie just like mom used to make—or rather just like mom used to buy frozen and stick in the oven. Friends had blue fish which was only mediocre. On the other hand, the drinks were well-mixed, and the service was fine.

The real appeal of "The Fifties Connection" is the dancing. The music is not live, but the selection is excellent. It is all from the fifties and sixties, but it is also all very good music in its own right, even without the nostalgia value attached. The music ranges from soul like "When a

Man Loves a Woman" and "I Heard It Through the Grapevine" to white soul like "Good Lovin' " to pure rock 'n roll like "Johnny B. Goode" to hard rock like "Brown Sugar" and "Honkey Tonk Woman" to soft rock like "Wouldn't It Be Nice."

There are a few problems associated with this aspect of "The Fifties Connection" that need to be noted. The disc jockey I heard on the night I was there tended to camp it up too much. He interrupted songs at times to say things like "Groovy" or to make some other outdated remark. Fortunately, such interruptions were not frequent. However, they did indicate the attitude of the management, which appears to lean a little too much on campiness. For instance, the waitresses and waiters are also entertainers. It is nice of them to get out on the dancefloor just before it is opened up to get the crowd into the mood, but it is annoying to have them all dancing on the d.j.'s platform at various times during the night—especially when you are waiting for them to bring you your order.

The other problem is directly related to that platform. The dancefloor is too small, and some extra room could be made if they would give up a little of that huge platform. The heat on the dancefloor is pretty high, too, and you are well advised to wear cool clothing. The situation is only exacerbated by the crowding due to the size of the floor.

Nevertheless, everyone who likes fifties and sixties music, dancers and nondancers alike, should enjoy his or her time at "The Fifties Connection." One of the enjoyable things about the place is the variety of people it attracts. The night that I was there I saw people of all ages, young singles, yuppie couples, and couples in their mid-thirties, and older marrieds, too. You don't have to be a great dancer to go there either. Some on the dancefloor knew all the old dances, from the twist to the shag to the boogaloo, but many others were, like me, just moving to the sound of good music.

In addition, the cost of an evening at "The Fifties Connection" is incredibly low. There is no cover charge, and as I mentioned before, the prices for food and drinks are reasonable. I saw people who appeared to be from all different income brackets, too. And no one seemed intent upon impressing anyone else. Everyone there just wanted to relax and have fun.

Although you may not want to eat at "The Fifties Connection," you will want to arrive there early. It has become very popular in a short amount of time. We had been told to arrive before seven because, typically, those who eat dinner remain to dance. When we left at eleven, a line had formed from the front door around the side of the building to the parking lot.

**1.** Why does the writer choose to begin the paper with a discussion of fifties and sixties nostalgia in general? How does this lead to the thesis?

**2.** What criteria does the writer focus on in reviewing the restaurant? What was left out? Why?

**3.** What, according to the writer, are the best and worst aspects of the restaurant? What is the writer's final recommendation?

### BREATHED AT HIS BEST

*Bloom County Babylon*: *Five Years of Basic Naughtiness* is the most recent addition to the bookshelves by cartoonist Berke Breathed. Breathed, who created the Bloom County comic strip five years ago, combines all of the strips into one large volume. This magazine of humor includes not only the daily strips but also the colored Sundays. The book, Breathed's fifth, is by far his best effort yet.

Bloom County is a small town centered around a local boarding house with a population of about one thousand people. Included in this thousand is a young editor, a child with an anxiety closet, a corrupt lawyer, a penguin, and a diseased cat. These are just a few of the characters that Berke Breathed has dreamed up for his readers.

Milo Bloom, editor of the Bloom County Beacon, is a young boy. Milo hides his young face behind wire glasses, and is constantly wearing overalls which drape his diminutive frame. Milo runs the Beacon as if it were the *National Enquirer*. He's always looking for the "story behind the story." However, Milo is not as devious as he seems. In fact, at times he can be quite nice. Take for instance the time he saved Opus, a penguin, from getting a nose job at the Betty Ford Health Clinic.

Binkley, a friend and confidant of Milo's, is often called Milo's alter ego. Binkley is a tall, lanky, and very timid boy who is continually threatened by his closet of anxieties. Binkley is a follower and definitely not the leader type. He can often get philosophical about the simplest of matters, such as Zsa Zsa Gabor's seventh wedding.

However different these two boys may seem, they do have one thing in common. They are both charter members of the American Meadow Party, and whenever a problem arises that neither can conquer they both head to the dandelion meadow to gather for a mass dandelion break.

In the blink of an eye, Breathed takes the reader from the innocence of youth to the guiltiness of adulthood. Steve Dallas, a pot-bellied, cigarette smoking, corrupt lawyer, is the strip's main adult character. Other adult characters are used, but when a scapegoat is needed, the call is usually directed Mr. Dallas' way. Steve Dallas is a man who will do anything to win a case or a babe. He is desperate not only in law but also in love. And when he sets his sights on a woman, she had better beware because she's in for a battle with a crafty old general.

Quicker than the speed of light, Breathed takes the reader from innocence to guilt to absurdity. Two of the major characters in the strip are animals. One is a penguin named Opus and the other is a cat named Bill. Opus is a short, paunchy penguin who, nine times out of ten, is the butt of the joke. He also cannot rid himself of his uncontrollable urge to buy hundreds of terrific turnip twaddlers from ads on television. His favorite food is pickled herrings in red sauce. Bill the Cat is a character who has become a druggie, an alcoholic, and a Hollywood star only to be accused of being in cahoots with a communist country and charged with espionage. Bill's favorite expression is ACK! Needless to say, Bill and Opus are roomies.

In *Bloom County Babylon* the relationships between the characters is of the utmost importance. Without the strong characters and their interaction with each other, the strips would be lacking in family feeling. However, Breathed does include interaction and develops a strong tie between characters such as Milo and Binkley, and Bill and Opus. Steve Dallas is used mainly for what he is, a corruptive figure in innocent children's lives.

However, there is much more to a comic strip than the characters, and Berke Breathed is a master of minor details. When reading *Bloom County Babylon*, one will undoubtedly notice the satire placed into the strips. Breathed is a genius with the way in which he incorporates the satire. It is not only seen through the dialog, but also in the way the characters look and act. For example, when Steve Dallas and Opus go to a money machine at a bank, Steve is told that the account is overdrawn. Immediately two thugs come from out of the machine and beat Steve to a pulp. Opus then remarks, "The real tragedy is that it was my account." This type of social satire is not uncommon in the book. But social satire is not all that Breathed deals with; he also dabbles in the political realm. He made a mockery of the 1984 election when he ran Bill and Opus for president and vice-president on the American Meadow Party ticket. Only Bill and Opus could have been used in this scenario, because absurdity was needed to carry off the clever mockery of the actual campaign. The two candidates were dubbed the "Beak and Saliva Ticket." Unfortunately, they lost by a slim margin.

None of this marvelous satire could be pulled off without well-written dialog. Dialog is essential to a comic strip. Breathed takes a relaxed approach to the way in which he writes dialog. He writes plainly so that anyone will easily be able to understand what is trying to be said. Breathed uses his dialog like an expert by changing the way each character speaks. Milo speaks very plainly, so plainly at times that it can become monotonous to read. Opus, on the other hand, speaks grandiloquently. He's always using large words and is constantly trying to impress women with his large vocabulary. Steve Dallas, however, speaks completely differently from Milo or Opus. Steve uses slang. He speaks the language of the gutter and is quite adept at it. Breathed shows with his variation of dialog that he will be in the comic business for a long time if he continues at his present quality level.

The drawing style is very important to a cartoonist. Originality is the key for an artist to find his or her own niche. Unfortunately, this is the only area in which Breathed loses points. His drawing style will remind many people of Gary Trudeau, who pens *Doonesbury*. Breathed deftly uses quick, sketchy lines to create his shading and employs thin lines for the characters' faces and expressions, both of which are Trudeau trademarks. When Breathed draws Bill the Cat, he uses scratches and quick marks of his pen to create a somewhat crazed-looking animal. However, when he draws Opus, he uses long strokes of the pen to create a more rounded-looking character. It is when he draws Opus that his drawing style resembles Trudeau's. However, even if Breathed has copied Trudeau's style, it certainly has not deterred his success in any way.

There is one more item that can be credited for Breathed's success: the energy that the strips exude. *Bloom County Babylon* is a book that has an overabundance of energy. This energy can come from the way in which Breathed uses his characters. He may continue a character, such as Binkley and his anxiety closet, for several days to get the readers hooked. And when the readers are hooked, they feel as if they are part of the story, which allows them to become immersed with the energy flowing from the strip. And if the strips are getting dull, Breathed can also throw in an occasional plot twist to get the readers excited again. For example, Breathed had been doing a lot of stuff with the *Bloom County Beacon*. It soon became dull. So to spice up the action, he reincarnated Bill the Cat from the dead. Breathed may also get this energy by drawing strips in marathon sessions. After reading a few strips, one may feel as if he/she has just come away from reading an invigorating novel or watched the ending of a scary movie. It is a blatant lack of energy that has caused other well-written and well-drawn strips to fade away. Breathed has kept his energy for five years, which has allowed him to amass a following of faithful readers.

Berke Breathed is at the peak of his profession. He has produced a fifth best-seller in five attempts and has one of the most successful comic strips in the business. So let's all take off our hats, raise our glasses, and give three cheers to the man who has created the comic strip of the decade.

**1.** Writing a review of a book of cartoons presents certain challenges. What information must this writer include as opposed to a person reviewing a novel?

**2.** What criteria for evaluation does the writer use? Does the writer focus on certain criteria more than others? Why?

**3.** How does the writer organize the review? Note the transitions each time the writer covers a different criterion.

## ► WRITING ACTIVITY ◄

Write a three-to-six-page evaluative paper on a subject like one of the following: a performance, a television show, a movie, a political, economic or social position or system, an object or product, a work of literature or art, an exhibition, a sporting event, an organization or a well-known personality.

Develop a set of appropriate criteria and come up with a firm judgment based on a strong argument supported by persuasive reasons and evidence.

# CHAPTER ▲ EIGHT

# *Persuasive Writing*

**"The most immutable barrier in nature is between one man's thoughts and another's"**

**WILLIAM JAMES**

The twentieth century has become so science oriented that most of us have been conditioned to privilege "objective fact" above all else. We are accustomed to think in terms of concrete evidence, counterevidence, data, formulas, proofs. Yet "objective, scientific fact" cannot alone solve all the problems we encounter. In most human affairs—politics, economics, and so on—science can offer information, often vitally important information, but usually not answers to our questions. For instance, scientists are alarmed at the present rate of soil erosion throughout the world, erosion that each year destroys thousands upon thousands of acres of valuable farmland. It is estimated that, by the year 2000, the demand for food in the world will have increased by fifty percent, while the amount of arable land will have *decreased* by 20 percent. People in countries like India, Nepal, Ethiopia, and China are in danger of starvation as a result of uncontrolled erosion of fertile soil. Scientists have discovered several methods of preventing soil erosion and creating new topsoil, techniques often as simple as planting trees to bind the ground against flooding. Some communities have followed the scientists' suggestions and have actually reclaimed farmland once lost to the rains. Yet soil erosion remains a devastating problem worldwide. Knowing the necessary facts or even how to solve a problem is not enough. Someone must present the ideas to those in power both to educate them and to get them, if possible, to implement changes to alleviate the problem. For it is people, not "science," who make decisions, who have the power to act. The old adage is wrong—the facts do not speak for themselves.

We are all continually faced with difficult, important decisions to make and issues to consider, decisions and issues that greatly influence our lives. Who should be our next president? Should the draft be reinstituted? What should be done about the homeless in this country? One time-honored solution to these and many other problems is to discuss them and perhaps eventually vote on them. Yet while voting may effectively settle some problems, it cannot be used to resolve every issue. Without the use of force, it is very difficult to *make* people do anything. The way you present your information will greatly determine how persuasive you are.

If facts and figures and sometimes even aggression won't affect people's attitudes and behavior, what will? Obviously something does operate on people, or we would never be able to make useful, workable decisions. The fact is that we encounter persuasion every day: Advertisers try to get us to buy products, politicians try to get other politicians to pass laws. People are often successful at convincing others to agree to their proposals and suggestions.

Persuasion is the high art of getting others to agree with you. In almost any human activity, we rely on our ability to persuade each other. Guns, bombs, armies, and other means of force may make people do certain things or act in certain ways temporarily, but they do not persuade people. True persuasion can occur only when people have a choice, when they are free to make up their own minds and exercise their own wills.

Persuading means more than just winning an argument; it means changing the opponents' minds so that they will come to agree with your position. It is important to view your opponent not as an adversary, but as someone who disagrees with you or who has not made up his or her mind about the issue at hand. If you treat your opponent as an antagonist, it will be difficult for you to arrive at a mutually agreeable solution to the problem. Persuasion means to urge, to coax, to influence, to encourage. It is much more related to psychology than to debate, because it requires you to appeal to your audience's feelings and attitudes, to their values and beliefs, as well as to their powers of reason. In a debate, you can present facts and figures, brilliant reasoning, counterarguments, and so forth, and make your opponent look foolish, and this will win the debate. In persuasion, your "opponent" is also your judge; you may argue brilliantly, but if you have failed to get your opponent at least to listen to what you have to say, you have not been truly successful.

The point to remember is that if you want to persuade, you must avoid a confrontation. Persuasion relies on some very basic human interactions, all of which can be loosely summarized by the word *reasonableness*. If you wish to persuade other people, it is not always enough to use reasonable arguments. You must also present *yourself* to them as a reasonable individual, someone who has honestly and sincerely considered their concerns and interests. Those who are most effective at persuasion understand the nature of their audiences and their particular concerns and interests. In fact, understanding the audience is the most challenging and important task in constructing a truly persuasive argument. Although the strategies you use to handle an audience will vary according to each different issue and audience you address, there are four general principles that should govern your efforts to persuade: respect for your audience, fairness, a willingness to accept compromise, and a commitment to reason and reasonableness.

## THE PRINCIPLES OF PERSUASION

### Respect Your Audience

No one knows everything, and no one knows nothing. Each of us is naturally limited in our abilities to perceive and understand the world around us. Thus you should show that you respect your readers. There is no point in trying to persuade those who do not respect you, and there is no point in trying to persuade those you do not respect. Always keep in mind that your job is not to "outargue" your reader in an attempt to impress some disinterested third party, as in a debate. Your job is to responsibly engage the thoughts and feelings of your audience, to get them to be willing to seriously consider your point of view. Any word or tone or hint that your readers are less intelligent, less well-informed, less honorable, or even less "right" than you are will most likely alienate them and thus prevent them from even hearing, let alone considering, your point of view. The way people respond to you is often greatly influenced by the attitude you project toward them. If you begin a piece of persuasion by presuming that you will not be fairly heard, if you signal to your audience the attitude "What I have to say will probably make no difference to you, but I guess I'll tell you anyway," you will most likely lose all chance of connecting with your readers. You should approach the issue with the idea that both you and those who disagree with you are capable of meaningful, constructive communication. Working together, you will both come to see the matter more clearly and understand each other better.

## ▶ Be Fair

Many people enter an argument spoiling for a confrontation. The chances for reason to prevail in such a situation are slim at best, and they will immediately disappear if you act unfairly toward your reader. Sarcasm, name calling, insults, and other attacks on an opponent violate the worthy opponent principle. Even something as hard to define as an air of superiority will set off hostile vibrations. You must be sure that your evidence is honest, your arguments fair.

Unfairness is a fatal mistake in persuasive writing. The heart of law and morality is *justice*—another word for *fairness*. The concept of fair play is so powerful that it alone may carry more weight than all your evidence. Thus it is a mistake to manufacture, exaggerate, or otherwise distort the evidence.

You cannot convince us that you have the most reasonable opinion when your evidence is dishonest and unfair. To falsify or distort evidence may make your case *appear* stronger, but by ignoring your opponents' points and exaggerating or manufacturing points that support your own position, you are actually *weakening* your argument. To present the issue as simpler than it is may greatly hinder your chances of persuading your readers, especially those who are familiar with the opposing point of view.

To be fair means to weigh the evidence, to consider all the points for and against a proposal or position you support, to examine objectively the arguments of both you and your opponents; then, if you have presented both sides well, if you have presented a convincing *and* fair case, the reader should be able to see which side has the stronger support. If you have been fair, your readers are more likely to convince themselves that you have the better position. To give your opponents' side of an issue a fair examination requires insight, diligence, and objectivity, but such an approach will ensure that your opponents will listen more carefully to what you have to say.

### Accept Compromise

Our culture is highly competitive, and most of us are conditioned to strive always to win. But you must be willing to accept less than total victory if persuasion is your goal. If your opponents are partially right and you are partially right (as will most likely be the case), then both of you must accept partial victory. Most controversial issues with which we are faced have so many different facets that it is impossible for one person always to anticipate and completely resolve all aspects of an issue. Often an effective solution may be found by combining elements of two opposing viewpoints. Sometimes the clash of two points of view on a certain problem may produce a more constructive solution than can either of the two competing viewpoints alone. Such compromise is at the heart of our democracy.

Some issues seem so loaded with emotion, so obviously one-sided, that to many people only one solution seems possible. Premeditated murder is so horrible that some people believe that nothing but the death penalty will do. Yet when you investigate these apparently one-sided questions, they often turn out to be complex and many sided. To enter into an argument at all is to acknowledge that the issue is arguable, that there are at least two sides to the question, two valid sides. Democracy is slow: We argue back and forth and eventually come up with answers, answers that may not satisfy anyone completely, but answers which the majority are willing to live with. A considered opinion is one that has been analyzed and argued and has finally been evaluated as the best answer that can be had at the moment.

You should not go into a persuasive argument to prove the opponent wrong or yourself right. Through an exchange of ideas, you advance both your and your reader's understanding of the problem at hand, not your own exclusive idea of the truth. If, after a great deal of effort, you succeed in getting a watered-down gun law passed, you are closer to your objective than you were when the debate began, when you wanted the strongest possible law. The gun law argument has at least moved off dead center. Your opponents who wanted no gun law whatsoever must accept partial change, and so must you. It is often a maddeningly slow way to proceed. But the only other alternative is violence. In a nuclear world, violence is too dangerous to use as the arbiter of human disputes.

## REASONING AND REASONABLENESS

The foundation of much formal writing is logical thinking, or more broadly, reasoning. In informal situations, especially emotional ones (such as a fight), logic may not be very effective, because once the emotions have been aroused, most people insist on settling matters at *that* level. In formal situations, especially in persuasive writing, the prevailing strategy should be logic, reasonableness, and an insistence on the facts.

## Facts and Inferences

In writing, it is important to keep clear the difference between facts and statements *about* facts, or the difference between facts and *inferences*. Facts can usually be verified by physical tests—you can count the number of people in a room, for example. An inference, on the other hand, is an unverified deduction or conclusion you come to in any of several ways, including guessing. If you can't see the people in the room, you might guess (infer) that some of them are male and some are female from the sounds of the voices. Or if you can see them through a window but can't hear them, you might infer that they were listening to a lecture from their seating arrangement and manner. Both these *inferences* can be verified, of course, if you enter the room. They are therefore low-level inferences—not very far removed from physical observation—but inferences nevertheless.

Unfortunately there is no upward limit to inferences. Suppose you happen to know that the people are listening to a political speech. Can you infer that they will vote for the speaker in an upcoming election? It would be very useful to be able to make such high-level inferences; we can't verify the facts in every situation. Even direct questioning won't always provide accurate information. If it were easy to predict election results, ours would be a different world. Beyond physical events lie abstract philosophical and legal questions that seem (so far) entirely divorced from physical tests. How shall we conduct the affairs of the nation? Since these abstract questions eventually have physical consequences, it is important for us to be able to anticipate what is likely to result from any action we take—or fail to take. No one can avoid reasoning. As long as we deal with facts and inferences, our choices are only between good reasoning and bad.

## Induction and Deduction

If we could make logic fit our world perfectly, we would work out a list of generalizations or general "laws" to cover everything. As far as possible, that is what science and education have been attempting to do. We have two sets of principles, or two methods of handling data, to help us in this work.

*Induction* The primary tool of science, induction holds that specific observations lead to general truths. (If you see enough redheads with freckles, you may conclude that, in general, redheads have freckles.) That redheads have freckles (generally) is one of our *premises*, one of the basic truths accepted by most people who have thought about the matter. Our premises are not always correct; sometimes they apply far less often than we think. But it is the business of science to keep observing and testing one incident after another, so that we become more and more confident of our premises or discard them for better ones.

*Deduction* The method of classical reasoning, deduction holds that general laws *predict* specific instances. Once you know that redheads generally have freckles, you can predict that the next redhead you meet will probably have freckles. (If your general truth is universal enough, your prediction will be true.) This is the kind of reasoning we use most often, though we usually don't realize we are doing it. Deduction, then, means "drawing out" specific cases from a general law.

Though the full development of a logical system can be complex, the basic machinery of logic is relatively simple. Logic is a system for making statements without error and as such has three components that any writer should learn: a method for making clear statements, a method for testing statements, and a list of typical errors to watch for in your own and in others' writing.

## ► Clear Statements

It is sometimes said that most of our arguments would disappear if we would just define our terms. That may not be completely true, but it is a good idea to define the terms of an argument as precisely as possible. Before you test any statement, you should reduce it to its *standard form*: the simplest statement of subject and predicate.

***Subject*** The thing being discussed; the name of someone or some other designator (of a person, usually)

***Predicate*** A statement about the subject; some characteristic or quality of the subject we can argue about

| *Subject* | *Predicate* |
|---|---|
| The government | is corrupt. |

If you choose to argue about this statement, you will soon find yourself relying on statements about how a corrupt government differs from other governments.

| *Subject* | *Predicate* |
|---|---|
| Any government that uses tax money to support vice | is corrupt. |

And this is the key to all logical statements—the distinctions made among *all*, *some*, and *none*. To test the truth of any specific statement, you need to know the possibility of truth in general. Before you can argue about any particular government, you must know what you believe about governments in general. *If* you believe that all governments are corrupt, you can assume that any given government is corrupt.

## ► Testing Statements

The syllogism is the basic formula of deductive reasoning. It is based on the assumption that whatever is true of a group of things must be true of any member of the group. The standard form of the syllogism is as follows:

*Major premise* A universal truth acknowledged by reasonable people, usually, but not necessarily, arrived at through induction.

*Minor premise* A specific instance within the general statement. If you make a general statement about *all* dogs, then any specific dog is an instance within the category of dogs.

*Conclusion* An "inescapable" result based on the formula that what is true for the group must be true for the members of the group; thus, whatever is true for all dogs ought to be true for any given dog.

| | |
|---|---|
| Major premise: | All dogs bark. |
| Minor premise: | Fido is a dog. |
| Conclusion: | Fido barks. |

*If* it is true that all dogs bark, then it *must* be true that any given dog you can find will bark. However, it so happens that some dogs do *not* bark (basenjies, for example). You can see that the syllogism would be perfectly good *if* the major premise were true. That is, if the syllogism is constructed properly. You have a major premise about all dogs and a minor premise identifying a specific dog; thus the minor premise is contained in the major premise. You could introduce a different kind of error: All dogs bark, and some squirrels bark; thus some squirrels are dogs. Here the syllogism isn't properly constructed. The minor premise does not identify a member in the major premise but instead introduces a new group entirely (squirrels).

To account for the different kinds of errors, you need different concepts. For *truth* we mean "coinciding with reality." (In reality some dogs do not bark.) For properly drawn conclusions in properly constructed syllogisms, we will use the concept *valid,* regardless of the "truth" of the premises. Thus a conclusion can be valid but not true. In fact, you can have these possibilities:

| ***Valid and True*** | ***Valid but Not True*** |
|---|---|
| All men are mortal.<br>Socrates is a man.<br>Socrates is mortal. | All men have wings.<br>Socrates is a man.<br>Socrates has wings. |
| ***Not Valid but True*** | ***Not Valid and Not True*** |
| All logicians tell lies.<br>Socrates tells lies.<br>Socrates is a logician. | All women tell lies.<br>Socrates tells lies.<br>Socrates is a woman. |

The error in the *Not Valid* syllogisms is called "affirming the predicate." In the standard syllogism, validity is achieved by affirming the subject, not the predicate. For example, in *Not Valid but True*, the fact that logicians tell lies does not preclude the possibility that others do too; the major premise does not say that *only* logicians tell lies.

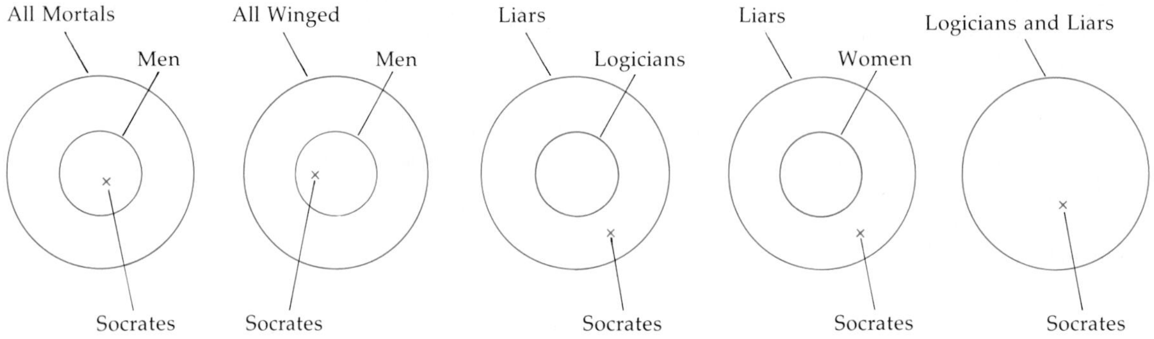


Diagrams can help you to understand syllogisms. The first diagram illustrates the *Valid and True* syllogism. Socrates is "contained" within the inner *Men* circle, and the *Men* circle is itself contained within the outer *All mortals* circle. Thus, whatever is true of the whole group of men must also be true of Socrates. Notice, though, that the diagram leaves room for mortals who are not men.

The next diagram will work for *Valid but Not True*. The circles show that all men are inside the *Winged* circle. You know this is not "true," but you may imagine such a thing anyway. Socrates, again one of the men, must be inside the *Winged* circle.

*Not Valid but True* presents a problem, as seen in the third diagram. It is clear enough that the logicians are all inside the *Liars* circle, and Socrates is inside the *Liars* circle too, because the minor premise puts him there. But there is nothing in the premises to tell you to put Socrates inside the *Logicians* circle; that is, there is no *necessity* for putting him there. The premises only tell us that he is inside the *Liars* circle . . . somewhere. Thus the conclusion is *not warranted*, and in fact, according to the diagram, is false—or at least not valid.

The same is true of the last syllogism, illustrated in the fourth diagram. You can get all the women into the *Liars* circle, and you can get Socrates in there too, but the premises do not direct you to put Socrates into the *Women* circle, and therefore the conclusion is unwarranted.

Note the difference if you change the premise to "*Only* logicians lie" demonstrated in the final diagram. In that case the *Logicians* circle and the *Liars* circle would be the same. If then you affirm the predicate ("Socrates is a liar"), Socrates will have to become a logician, since only logicians lie.

People seldom realize they are using syllogisms. They take shortcuts and leave out one of the premises, and they don't state things in syllogistic form. For example.

> Don't lend Bill money; you'll never get it back!

The implied (unspoken) syllogism is something like this:

People who don't pay me back won't pay you back.

Bill didn't pay me the $5 I loaned him.

Bill won't pay you back.

If you dig the syllogism out of its linguistic hiding place, you can determine its truth or validity. In this case, you would say that the reasoning is valid, but you would question the major premise, which seems a hasty generalization. (Bill may very well pay you back even if he hasn't paid others.) It is this same kind of questionable logic based on debatable assumptions that causes insurance companies and credit bureaus to brand customers "risky."

### Universal Negatives

Negative syllogisms are slightly more complex to work with. As with affirmative syllogisms, the negatives can be valid without being "true." For example:

| ***Valid and True*** | ***Valid but Not True*** |
|---|---|
| No dogs have wings. | No students like logic. |
| Snoopy is a dog. | Plato is a student. |
| *Snoopy has no wings.* | *Plato doesn't like logic.* |

But notice:

***Not Valid***

No good lawyer loses cases.

Katherine Hill doesn't lose cases.

*Katherine Hill is a good lawyer.*

The problem with this last syllogism is that there are too many negatives in it. It would be clearer to say that good lawyers *win* cases. (So do bad ones, occasionally.) If we were to diagram this syllogism, we would get three separate and unrelated circles: a circle for good lawyers, a separate circle for those who lose cases (containing no good lawyers), and a third circle for Katherine Hill, who also is not in the losers' circle. But there is nothing in either the major or the minor premises that allows or requires us to put Katherine Hill in the lawyers' circle. Therefore the conclusion is not warranted; it is not valid.

## LOGICAL FALLACIES: ERRORS TO AVOID

The logical fallacies discussed in this section occur often in conversation and in writing. Watch out for them in the writing of others, and avoid them when you are trying to build a reasonable case in your writing.

Logical fallacies fall into several categories: fallacies based on insufficient evidence; fallacies based on irrelevant information; fallacies based on ambiguity; and fallacies based on faulty logic. As you read the following section, it is more important to understand the flawed reasoning in insufficient evidence, irrelevancies, ambiguities, and faulty logic than to memorize the names of the logical fallacies. (But the Latin names are traditional and still used.)

## ► Fallacies Based on Insufficient Evidence

*Ad ignorantium* Appeal to ignorance, arguing on the basis of what is not known. If you can't prove something is false, must it be true? "You can't prove there *isn't* a monster in Loch Ness, so there must be one!" The same fallacy is involved whether you insist on the validity of anything not proved false or on the falseness of anything not proved true.

*Card stacking* Concealing, withholding, or ignoring the evidence; *selecting* only evidence favorable to your side. "Richard Nixon was tall, good-looking, a family man, an experienced politician, a world leader. Let's get this man back into politics!"

*Hasty generalization* Drawing conclusions from too little evidence. (This is the chief error in reasoning.) "I know several jolly fat people; therefore I conclude that all fat people are jolly!" It is unlikely that we could know enough people to draw many accurate generalizations about them. *Many* generalizations turn out to be inaccurate because they are based on insufficient evidence. In argumentation, you must learn to *back up* your generalizations with specific evidence.

*Post hoc ergo propter hoc* Literally, "after this; therefore because of this." Events that follow each other chronologically are falsely assumed to have a *cause-and-effect* relationship. "His grades started to fall after Harold met Cindy; she must have been a bad influence!"

## ► Fallacies Based on Irrelevant Information

*Ad baculum* Appeal to force. "If you insult Smith's wife, you'll get a black eye!" "If you investigate Gassone Motors, they will expose your sex life!" Force doesn't have to be physical; it can be psychological.

*Ad hominem* Literally, "to the person." *Ad hominem* attacks the person who is arguing and ignores the argument. The idea is that the person is too contemptible to have valid ideas. "What you say may be true, but aren't you a member of the Communist party?"

*Ad misericordiam* Appeal to pity. "There is no more pathetic sight than handicapped children; we must all give to the March of Dimes!" Appeals to pity are not always wrong, but most readers object to them when they seem to obscure the real question.

*Ad populum* Literally, "to the people." Appeal to popular prejudices and slogans. "Down with big government!" "Down with invasion of privacy!" A populist is someone running for office on the basis of these traditional ideas, campaigning against social change or against "newer" attitudes. Essentially populism is an appeal for a return to the good old days.

*Ad verecundiam* Inappropriate authority. "Michael Jordan says buy Nike shoes, and he should know!" When a celebrity or authority is dragged into an argument as expert witness, you have every right to challenge his or her expertise.

*Bandwagon* Appeal to peer pressure, group identity. "Join the winning side!" Bandwagon is sometimes called "snob appeal"; its opposite is "plain folks": "You can trust me, folks. I'm just a simple, unpretentious soul like you."

*Common sense* Appeal to common knowledge, practical truths. "The world cannot be round like a ball; otherwise the people on the bottom would fall off!" Appeals to common sense are not always wrong, but often they are used to oversimplify difficult issues or to assert the virtues of the commonplace over intellectual or esoteric values. Common sense is not helpful in matters requiring *uncommon* sense.

*Fallacy of opposition* Anything the opposition approves must be bad; an attack on the ideas on the grounds that those who support them are incapable of right thinking. Fallacy of opposition is different from *ad hominem* only to the degree that the idea itself is made unacceptable because of its supporters. "Sure, you favor welfare, social security, government insurance, and all the rest. But did you know that these are socialistic ideas and communistic as well?" The attack is on the ideas *because* of those who support them.

*Genetic fallacy* The source of an idea influences its worth. Similar to fallacy of opposition, but different in that the idea is attacked, regardless of who supports it, on the grounds that where the idea came from makes the argument bad. "The new tax law is ridiculous! It was written at Blah State College and everyone knows that's Mickey Mouse U!"

*Guilt by association* You are known by the company you keep. "Why are you defending the rights of criminals; do you have a criminal record?"

*Red herring* Arguing beside the point; *switching* to some side issue or entirely new issue to distract from the main argument, a favorite device of politicians when asked hard questions: "Perhaps you're right about integration and busing, but has anyone considered the *safety* of those buses?" Also favored by some students on exams: "In order to understand the causes of the Civil War, we must look at the warlike nature of human beings. The history of Europe is full of wars. . . ."

*Tu quoque* You did it too; the accusation is invalid because the accuser is guilty of the same "sin." "So what if I cheat on my taxes? So do you!"

## Fallacies Based on Ambiguity

*Amphiboly* Language ambiguity, deliberately misusing *implications*. "Three out of four doctors recommend this type of pain relief!" The implied assertion here is that three out of four means seventy-five percent of *all* doctors and also that what is true of a *type* of pain reliever is true of *this* one.

*Begging the question* Tautology, circular reasoning; the conclusion is merely a restatement of one of the premises. "The president is such a good man . . . because he is so moral!"

*Equivocation* Arguing over the meaning of a word; using the connotations of a word to disprove or distort an argument. Equivocation always involves the *meaning* of words—deliberate or accidental misuse that confuses argumentation. "Senator Gonzo claims to be a *conservative*, yet he lives lavishly!" (Two meanings for *conservative* are involved here.)

*False metaphor or false analogy* The metaphor or analogy used has more dissimilarities than similarities. "The president has seen us through a crisis of state; he has kept late hours in lonely vigil; he has brought us soothing relief; he has wasted his strength to revive our faltering nation. Let us reward him now with our gratitude!" The metaphor or analogy of the president as doctor tending a sick nation is false, however poetic it may be.

## Fallacies Based on Faulty Logic

*Complex question* Loaded questions that are not safe to answer. "If elected, will you put an end to frivolous welfare programs?" The complex question need not be put in the form of a question; it can be worded as a complex issue: "Let us examine whether the president's aggressive foreign posture is weakening our bargaining power." It is necessary to determine first whether the president's "posture" is aggressive before we can examine its influence on our bargaining power.

*False dilemma* Either/or thinking; presents only two options, both usually unattractive. "If you don't quit smoking, you'll die of lung cancer." In almost all situations, there are more than two options.

*Non sequitur* Literally, "it does not follow"; this general term is often applied to any fallacy in which the argument cannot be followed. A non sequitur argument is one in which the conclusion does not follow from the major premise. "Inflation has made our money worth less, so we might as well spend it and enjoy life."

*Rationalization* Making excuses; choosing the least threatening (or most self-serving) explanations. "I'm flunking calculus; that instructor hates me!"

*Reductio ad absurdum* Literally, "reduce to an absurdity"; disproof of an argument by showing some absurdity to which it leads if carried to its logical end. This is not always an error. It is an error if the user is merely being sarcastic, ridiculing the opposition, or erroneously leading (via hasty generalization, either/or, and so on) to an absurdity that doesn't necessarily follow. "So you would give the government the power to tax, would you? The next thing you know, they'll use that power to take away your home and property, and finally your life. We will then have the amusing consequence of the government taxing its citizens out of existence—and finally the government itself must fall with no citizens and no new taxes to support it!"

*Slippery slope* One thing leads to another. "If you eat desserts, you'll end up weighing three hundred pounds!" Of course it is possible that one thing *may* lead to another, but it is obviously not true that one thing *must* lead to another.

## THE PERSUASION PAPER

Creating a persuasion paper is perhaps the most challenging writing task you will face, since it involves getting people who disagree with you to change their behavior, to adjust their attitudes, to see the world from a different perspective. As you approach any act of persuasion, your writer's mind needs to consider a number of different dimensions of the issue. To ensure that you are approaching the task of persuasion from a thorough and comprehensive perspective, it should help to think in terms of the five components of the writing process—PACES.

### ► Purpose

In persuasion you usually have a proposal or position to which you feel committed and which you wish others to approve or adopt. Although it may be tempting to turn immediately to the larger issues that affect all of our lives, issues such as nuclear arms, when thinking of topics for the persuasion paper, these general topics may prove impossible to handle adequately in a three-to-six-page paper. The topic you choose should be narrow enough to allow you to deal with it in depth. Also make sure you choose a subject about which you feel confident and knowledgeable. Your specific purpose will be greatly influenced by your understanding and knowledge of the issue at hand.

## ▶ DISCUSSION ACTIVITY ◀

To give you practice with narrowing broad persuasion topics into more focused, more manageable subjects, examine the following statements and explore their possibilities as persuasion topics. (Note: Each statement might produce several focused topics.)

Something needs to be done about drug abuse.

We need to protect the ecology.

The system for electing presidents in the United States needs to be changed.

## ▶ Audience

All the elements of PACES continually interact with one another in any writing situation, but in persuasion, purpose and audience are even more closely linked. In many ways, audience may be said to determine purpose, since in persuasion your job is to convince readers who disagree with you about a controversial issue to adopt your point of view. You don't want to undermine the integrity of your position, but you need to carefully consider how your audience responds to the issue and use this knowledge in constructing your argument. Developing an audience profile of your opponents' backgrounds, attitudes, arguments, and feelings concerning the issue should prove useful.

### AUDIENCE PROFILE

Think about those readers whose views on the issue at hand differ from yours and ask the following questions:

1. What do they *know* about this issue?
2. What do they *feel* about it?
3. Why don't they already agree with your position?
4. What ideas or feelings do you share with them that will help to build a bridge of understanding between you?
5. What arguments and evidence might they use if they were to argue for their position?
6. How might they respond to the arguments and evidence you are planning?

If you have trouble answering these questions for yourself, find people in your college or community who are opposed to your position. Ask them why they think as they do. What do they think of your point of view? What aspects of the issue make them angry? What aspects of your position can they accept? Do they have solutions? How do they react to solutions you suggest? Try to find aspects of the issue that both you and your opponents can agree on. Answering these questions should better enable you to establish a bridge of mutual respect and understanding between you and your audience.

## ► DISCUSSION ACTIVITY ◄

Consider the following statements concerning controversial issues. How would you characterize the people who might disagree with each of these positions? If you were asked to support any of these positions, how might your understanding of the thoughts and beliefs of those opposed influence how you construct your argument?

A rating system, similar to that used for movies, should be used for record albums.

A presidential candidate's personal life should not be considered among the criteria used to judge his or her eligibility for office.

Television commercials directed toward those under the age of ten should be banned.

Cigarette advertisements should be banned from magazines and billboards.

### ► Experience

Your experience should provide you with the evidence you need to persuade your audience to consider and perhaps adopt your position. Try to remember everything you have heard, read, or seen about the issue you are addressing. In general, the bigger the subject, the more evidence you will need. If you are trying to show that capital punishment does or does not deter violent crime, you will need a great deal of evidence; the subject is so big and controversial that there might not be enough evidence to convince people one way or the other. For a short composition (three to six pages) you need to limit your subject so that you can be persuasive without having to bring in an enormous amount of evidence. If your evidence is of high quality—reliable, authoritative, and fair—you will have a better chance of persuading those who disagree with you.

As a general rule, the more evidence you have, the more convincing your argument will be. If you want to prove that the cafeteria food is not good, it is not enough to say that the vegetables are overcooked. If the vegetables are overcooked, the meat is tasteless and tough, and the potatoes are either lumpy or runny, the evidence is convincing. If you eat most of your meals in the cafeteria, the case is better yet. If your friends have the same opinion and you also observe that others return their trays with half-eaten meals, the case is highly convincing.

The quality of the evidence is also important in determining its effectiveness. Showing that the cafeteria food is tasteless and inedible is only one kind of evidence, no matter how many examples you have. Suppose, however, that the food also looks bad. Suppose, too, that it smells bad. You then have different kinds of quality evidence all supporting the same argument—that the cafeteria food is bad.

It is important to be aware, however, that there is a point of diminishing returns with evidence. To go on piling up evidence after this point can turn the tables so that you become the villain and your opponents become unfortunate underdogs. It can seem that the case is so heavily loaded against the opposing view that your reader begins to suspect you of bias.

## ► DISCUSSION ACTIVITY ◄

Consider the following arguments. What kinds of evidence might be used to either refute or support these positions? Try to think of as many different kinds of potentially useful evidence as you can. Which topics have real potential for a persuasion paper and which do not?

The university should put more pencil sharpeners in its buildings.

All hunting should be banned.

Federal taxes should be lowered.

The speed limit should be returned to 55 mph.

Contraceptives should be made more readily available to teenagers.

## ► Code

Certainly your attitude toward your reader will affect the way you write a persuasion paper. You should avoid name calling and affecting an air of superiority or condescension. Your understanding of the audience may also greatly affect the overall organization of your paper. In persuasion, remember, you are not trying to win an argument; you are trying to get your audience to change their minds. In fact, your realistic objective may not be so much to convince them to abandon their position, as to persuade them to recognize the coexistence of the two positions. It is important, therefore, to organize the arguments you plan to use in the most "psychologically" effective order.

You might describe the issue briefly in the introduction and suggest that there are reasonable ideas on both sides. You might also begin with an aspect of the issue that you and your opponents can agree on. If you can start from a position of accord, your opponents won't feel they have to respond as antagonists. Then deal with your opponents' arguments, explaining why you cannot accept these views. Finally, present your own case so that it will appeal to your audience's reason and emotions. Remember you are trying to persuade. In an ideal world, "logical" arguments (arguments based on reason) would be enough to convince your audience. But audiences are made up of people, and in people's daily lives emotions are often more powerful than reason. Avoid being melodramatic and overly sentimental, but do consider some appeal to your audience's emotions. A paper that directs itself to your audience's reason *and* emotions is likely to be more memorable and persuasive than one that depends exclusively on cold, objective facts and statistics.

A simple plan of organization is often the best. For example:

GUN CONTROL

I. Introduction: There are too many deaths by guns in the United States.

II. The opposing side: There are strong historical, sociological, and political arguments against gun control.

III. Your side: Although there are important problems associated with gun control, our legislatures must stop unnecessary carnage caused especially by "Saturday night specials."

IV. Conclusion: Gun control is a complex issue, and an effective law must be carefully drafted, but "Saturday night specials," easily concealed and with no legitimate uses, should be outlawed.

Some people favor the classical plan of organization, which reverses the second and third steps. When you organize that way, you run some risk of having the competing view remembered better than your own. Then too, people who hold the opposing view will tend to respect you and listen to your position if you deal with their arguments first, especially if you make clear that you see the merits in their position.

## Self

Throughout our discussion of persuasion, we have emphasized the importance of analyzing and adjusting to your audience. Adapting to your audience is crucial, for if you disregard their interests and concerns you stand no chance of being persuasive. They will reject both you and your arguments. But adapting to your audience, of course, does not mean abandoning your own point of view. You should be prepared to accept compromise, but it is important not only to *be* sincere but to *appear* sincere. Make sure that you truly believe in what you argue for. Perhaps the hardest task in persuasion is balancing your position with your audience's position in an attempt to build a compromise position that you both can accept. There is no easy, clear-cut way to achieve this balance, but the ability to mediate between two positions is valuable in any persuasion context. If you present yourself as a reasonable, fair-minded, flexible person, your readers will be more likely to listen to what you have to say.

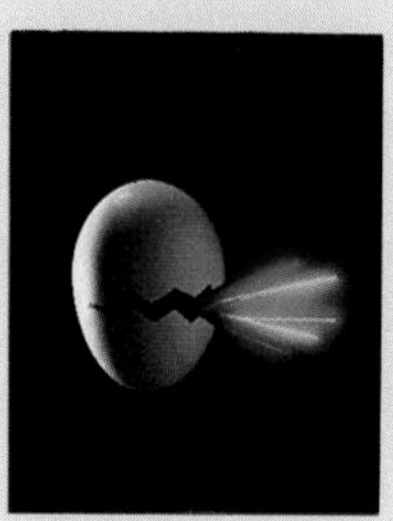

# THE WRITER'S MIND AT WORK

## DRAFTING AND REVISING THE PERSUASION PAPER

In the following pages we will observe a writer, Helen, develop a persuasion paper from the stage of selecting and refining a topic through the production of a second working draft. There is no one single right way to write any of the general types of papers we have described. Yet watching a writer in action grappling with a demanding persuasive task should give you a sense of the possibilities in persuasive writing. In her paper, Helen tries to convince us that every state should annually inspect all registered vehicles to ensure that they are in safe operating condition. The process of Helen's writing was not an automatic one in which she simply picked a topic and wrote a neat, effectively convincing argument. As you will see, her drafts are the result of a rich, complex, extended, and recursive process of thinking, planning, pausing, writing, analyzing, rereading, reflecting, and revising.

As you know, topics don't just present themselves as something that you automatically focus in on and write about. You may think you have a sound, workable topic, but until you actually start planning and writing, you cannot be fully aware of all the intricacies and complexities of your initial idea. In the following brainstorming and freewriting, Helen shows the thinking and writing that occurred before she was able to settle on a topic for a persuasion paper.

Helen had been hearing a lot on the news about car accidents. As a result of her concern for motor safety and accident prevention, she felt the need to make people more aware of the problem and to persuade them to do something to help prevent motor accidents. Not really knowing what she would say and having only a vague idea that she wanted to write a persuasion paper on highway accidents, Helen simply began brainstorming (see Chapter Two, pages 33 to 36 for a discussion of brainstorming). Jotting down whatever came into her head, probing her experience with the subject, she hoped to get down on paper some rough ideas on dealing with highway accidents.

### PLANNING STRATEGY: Brainstorming on Highway Accidents

highway accidents → potholes bad roads rain
too many cars help freezing rain more patrols
snow / drink → jail terms sleet speed = too fast
sports cars alcohol slick roads drinking age
salt old cars sand ~~graduations~~ broken horns
worn tires chains studs (cracked windshields)
loose steering sleeping drivers ← dates

Helen stopped to assess what she had generated in her brainstorming to search for potential topics. Following some of the concerns she saw emerging in her brainstorming, she began to freewrite (see pages 22 to 26 for an explanation of freewriting) on the subject of car safety.

### PLANNING STRATEGY: Freewrite on car safety

I think that something more needs to be done about car safety. I've heard that about 50,000 people die in automobile accidents each year. I know that we will probably never be able to totally eliminate this problem, but we need to do everything that we can. I hear that many states have tough drunk driving laws--that's good--we need to really clamp down on drivers under the influence of alcohol --no excuse for that--we need to really enforce these laws --the drinking age has been raised so that maybe there will be fewer teenagers under the influence of alcohol on the road--hopefully. But we need to find other ways to try to cut down on accidents. Maybe we could force everyone to take driver training lessons. Maybe we could make a law that would require all drivers to pass this education program before they could even apply for a license. At least we could be sure that people are competent. How about courses in defensive driving? Maybe we could even take licenses away from people who are known to be reckless drivers. Or drunk drivers.

There's got to be something more that we can do. What else causes accidents besides careless drivers? There's the weather. It's nearly impossible to drive safely in three feet of snow or on a sheet of ice or through a flooded road. But I guess there's not much we can do about the weather—just tell people not to go out in real bad weather. But there's also the condition of the vehicle itself. After all, you have to have something to drive. Just think of all the things that can go wrong with a car--all the things that need watching--you need decent brakes, tires--probably a lot of accidents are caused by the fault of the car itself. You hear all the time on the news that such an accident was attributed to "mechanical problems" or something like that. You need a car in decent shape in order to be safe on the road. I remember driving in the rain once and my windshield wipers weren't working right--the blades were all worn out. I could hardly see to the tip of the hood. I could have gotten in a car accident with all that rain pouring down. And I remember a cop pulling over that one driver because his taillights weren't working. In the rain he could have got into a rear ender and someone could have been badly hurt. There could have been some pretty bad damage just because of faulty upkeep on cars. Heck, I don't even know all that could go wrong with my car--I don't know how to check the brakes and all that and I bet a lot of other people are in the same situation. Most people know where to put the gas and how to check the oil and that's about it. When the car actually breaks down they take it to a garage but something could really be wrong and they might not even know it or they might not care depending on how they feel about their car. This could be taken care of. I mean, because of a wiper blade, and because of a busted taillight there could

```
have been a really bad accident--this could have been pre-
vented. I mean no one could have stopped the rain but I
could have had better wiper blades and that other driver
could have had operable taillights.
```

Initially, Helen could not anticipate whether brainstorming and freewriting would be useful to her in exploring the possibilities of a very general topic. However, Helen was able to see that these activities helped her to generate some interesting angles for a possible persuasion paper. Her strategy of generating proposals to improve car safety worked. She eventually realized, because of her own experience that we need stringent safety checks of some sort for all vehicles on the road.

Helen then decided to do some more detailed preliminary planning. In the following script of her writer's mind, Helen takes stock of what she has come up with so far, speculating as to how she might develop this material in a paper.

### THE WRITER'S MIND: Planning for "Car Safety"

*I think I have something I can work with here. I'm worried about car safety and cutting down on accidents on the highways. We need to do everything we can to prevent these accidents. I think I have a possible answer to some of the problems of car safety. We need to have all states make sure that every vehicle on the road is in adequate operating condition. This would be one way of cutting down on those accidents that are caused by mechanical failure.*

*Now of course I'll have to specify some of the hows and the whats. That is, just what would be included in those things that need to be inspected? Some states, Pennsylvania and Maine for instance, do have annual vehicle inspection, but other states, for instance Ohio, don't do anything to make sure that the cars on the roads are in good safe condition. What I should do is maybe check all those things that the states that do require vehicle inspection look at—then I'll have some ideas to use for my proposal for those states that don't have vehicle inspection. Also, I'll need to answer who will do the inspecting. I think I can prove why this needs to be done. I think this will work for a paper. It'll take a lot of work and I obviously won't be able to write up an actual bill for this proposal, but I think I'll be able to outline my plan in sufficient detail to at least get people thinking about what may be done. We'll see.*

We have followed Helen as she developed a general subject (safety on the highways) into a fairly specific topic that can be handled in a short paper. By focusing on one aspect of car safety (vehicle maintenance), Helen was able to focus her large subject into a workable topic for a persuasion paper.

After her preliminary planning, Helen then wrote an exploratory draft to test the tentative topic she had developed, to see if her topic could be adequately supported in a paper.

## EXPLORATORY DRAFT: "Car Safety"

Car safety is very important. Maintaining cars in good condition, making sure that they are in safe, operable condition, will help reduce traffic accidents, making our highways safer for everyone. A car that isn't in adequate operating condition may be dangerous--loose brakes could cause a very serious accident, worn tires could cause an otherwise careful driver to skid off the road, posing a danger to anyone near the road. A faulty horn or worn-out wiper blades, or a broken taillight could cause very serious damage if the visibility is not very good. There are many things that could go wrong with cars, things that not all owners may be aware of. Because car maintenance is so important, the state government should inspect every vehicle registered in that state once a year to make sure that it is in safe working condition. The state might do this at the time when the vehicle is registered each year to make it easier for the state to keep track of all cars on the road to be sure that they're in good general condition.

Of course, operating condition is tricky. What is meant by operating condition? You have to determine what applies to safety and what not. The only thing to be concerned about is safety--gas mileage or other concerns a person might have about the car aren't important. Certainly safety should include horns, brakes, all lights, emergency brakes. What about mufflers? It's sure a pain to have to listen to all those cars with that obnoxious roaring coming from underneath. But is this a matter of safety? Well there are other things that definitely need to be checked. Windshield wipers are especially important in rain and snow--or when a big truck goes by and splatters mud all over your windshield. And blinkers are important too. It's crucial for every driver to know where other drivers on the road are planning to go. A faulty pair of blinkers could mean a lot of trouble. It's things like these that can make a big difference to traffic safety and stopping accidents.

For these reasons, the state governments should make sure that every car on the road is in good operating condition.

After writing her exploratory draft, Helen thought that she had a topic that would work for a persuasion paper. But she knew that she had much more to do before she was ready to write a final draft. For one, she had to consider the audience, those who would disagree with her plan. Before proceeding to write the next draft of the paper, Helen decided to articulate a clear thesis statement and then speculate about how the audience might respond to this statement.

Though it is likely that you may change or refocus your thesis statement through succeeding drafts of a persuasion paper, it is a good idea to attempt stating a tentative thesis throughout your writing process. One way to deal with the thesis statement in persuasive writing is to answer the question: What do I want to persuade my reader to think, to accept, or to do? You might try to complete the statement:

I want to convince my audience that ____________________, or I want to persuade my audience to ____________________.

This strategy for identifying your thesis will also help you to focus your topic throughout the writing of your paper. The answers to these questions may help you to evaluate later drafts to see if you are sufficiently focusing on your topic. They also help you clarify just what your overall purpose is.

Helen stated her tentative thesis for the persuasion paper: *"Every state should inspect all registered vehicles once a year to make sure they are in safe operating condition."* She recognized that in order for this paper to be truly persuasive, she had to identify in detail the audience she wished to address. Here is a script of her writer's mind as she began with some questions about her potential audience (see page 274 for a set of "Audience Profile" questions).

## THE WRITER'S MIND:
## Examining the Audience

*My general audience will be all those who feel that we don't need every state to conduct an annual safety inspection of every registered vehicle.*

**1.** What does the audience know about the issue?

*Well, probably part of my audience knows a heck of a lot more about the details of car maintenance than I do; they might know exactly how to keep a vehicle in tip-top condition at all times. These people might think that the idea I'm proposing is unnecessary at least as far as they are concerned. Of course, there are also those in my audience who probably know even less than me about car maintenance; some of these people might think that there isn't much that needs to be done to keep a car safe.*

**2.** What do they *feel* about the issue?

*Those who recognize the importance of car maintenance and safety might feel insulted by my proposal—they might feel that it would be unnecessary for anyone to check their vehicles, that it might look like the state doesn't trust them. Those who don't know much about car maintenance might feel indifferent about the issue; they might not care a whole lot. I'll have to get this last group of people interested in the problem, to show that it is important.*

**3.** Why don't they already agree with your position?

*Well, the responsible, knowledgeable car owners probably feel that mandatory vehicle inspection isn't necessary. They might think that there are already too many governmental requirements, and that my plan would be just another piece of red tape. There might be others in my audience who just plain don't care about car safety, maybe because they don't realize how important maintenance is or aren't aware of the severity of the problem, maybe because they just don't care although I hope there aren't many of these.*

**4.** What ideas or feelings do you share with them that will help to build a bridge of understanding between you?

*Well, cutting down on traffic accidents and improving motor safety is something that I think virtually everyone would agree is a high priority. Those that don't care about traffic fatalities, though I can't imagine there really are any like this, are probably too far gone for me to reach, but I'll need to try. This is the key to my relationship with my audience—improving vehicle safety. I'll have to show them the link between car maintenance and safety on the highways. I'll have to show them that we need mandatory inspection to make sure that all vehicles on the road are in decent, safe operating condition.*

**5.** What arguments and evidence might they use if they were to try to persuade you to change your position on this issue?

*It's not really car safety in general that is the major issue here between my audience and me—it's making an annual automobile maintenance check* legally mandatory. *Part of my audience will be those who are all for car safety but who do not want any more laws telling them what must be done—these are people who complain about how the government or state has its fingers in too many pies. These people might think that we are turning more and more into a police state, people who are worried about corruption and abuse of the laws, because someone will have to pay and get paid for these checks—something I'll definitely have to think about—I can't answer all these questions about just* exactly *how the law will be implemented because I don't have the time or space to do that thorough a job (besides I'd need to know a heck of a lot more about law than I do now). But I'll certainly have to answer some of these major objections.*

**6.** How might they respond to the arguments and evidence you are planning?

*Some of my audience might not like my idea because they will be worried about corruption and having to pay for the inspection. Maybe they'll object to the extra fee as part of their registration charges, so I'll have to play that against the overriding benefits of my plan. Plus I'll maybe bring up the fact that other states have designated service stations to inspect cars and this opens the door for corruption in the system—because of different standards, because of mechanics that may overlook things or problems just for the repair bill. My way, the inspecting would be done by state-certified mechanics who are completely disinterested. No conflict of interests between the people inspecting and the people repairing. I'm sure this won't win over everybody, but it might help to convince those who distrust mechanics looking at their cars.*

*Also if people want to and can repair their cars themselves they don't have to bother with a mechanic. As long as they can do the necessary repairs properly. It wouldn't take much for a state-certified mechanic to just check up on those cars that are properly maintained. I can answer the charge that this would seem to show that the state distrusts people who keep up their cars. OK, I'll have to be sure to work some of this into my next draft. I need to keep in mind how my audience would react to what I have to say.*

Helen then constructed a rough outline to help guide her in writing the next draft of her paper. She had collected a number of important insights about the nature of her audience and had discovered some of the major objections that people might have to her plan. She then outlined how the next draft might be organized to accommodate the expanding argument.

### PLANNING STRATEGY: Outline for "Motor Vehicle Inspection"

I. Begin with a brief bit about my proposal: Every state should institute annual inspection of all vehicles to make sure they are in safe operating condition.

II. Then give a definition of what I mean by safe operating condition, since this might be a major point of contention between me and my audience—we both need to have a clear idea of what it is—list things that need to be inspected and explain my choice of each thing.

brakes

lights (brake, front, back)

windshield wipers
perhaps some other things

III. Explain why I suggest that the state should oversee the inspection instead of individuals themselves or others.

IV. Then tell them that not every little detail on a car needs to be brand-spanking new--to let them know that their cars won't all need costly unnecessary overhauls.

V. End with a reminder that my proposal is important to make highways safer.

Having begun to form some useful sense of the prospective audiences she needs to consider, Helen then proceeded to write a working draft, this time paying more attention to how she explained and phrased arguments. She also used her audience analysis to come up with a set of defenses to balance the objections and criticisms she suspected the audience might raise.

**WORKING DRAFT:**
**"Motor Vehicle Inspection"**

To reduce the number of motor vehicle accidents, cars need to be regularly and strictly maintained. I think that every state should have mandatory car maintenance inspection. This would ensure that all vehicles on American highways are in safe and satisfactory operating condition.

There are a few basic features of every vehicle which need to be maintained. These are important for the safety of the driver and other vehicles on the road. These features should be checked once a year by a certified mechanic. For instance, every car should have brakes which will allow them to stop or to slow down fast enough to avoid colliding with vehicles slowing down in front of them or obstacles which may roll into the road. Every car should have two working headlights and brake lights which clearly alert following vehicles that the car is slowing down. The car should have blinker lights that work, so that a driver can let other drivers know where he intends to go on the road. The treads should be deep enough to insure that the driver has adequate control of his position on the road. Also every car should have operating windshield wipers. They should adequately clear the windshield of rain, snow, or other debris. These features are all essential to a vehicle's safe operation.

Most vehicles on the road probably have all the features listed above in adequate working condition. Most drivers are responsible enough to maintain each of these safety features. But motorists don't always know or can't always tell when things are not functioning properly. The best way to do this will be to have all vehicles registered in each state inspected once a year.

Some people distrust having mechanics look over their car. They fear that the mechanic will invent or exaggerate problems so that the repair station can line its pockets with the owner's money. This might be a concern in other states which require annual vehicle inspection, such as Maine, which have designated repair stations inspect vehicles. Having repair shops as an inspection station introduces a possible conflict of interest--it might be to the mechanic's advantage to find more problems or to be more picky than he needs to be. Or perhaps if the car owner is buddies with the repair shop mechanic, the mechanic might be tempted to overlook potential problems with the owner's car.

We shouldn't expect every car or truck on the road to be in tip-top, excellent condition, every last part of the vehicle to be in brand-new shape. This would be extremely costly and unnecessary for the owner. Who cares if the back window can be rolled only half-way down, or that the trunk sticks a little when you try to open it? A vehicle doesn't need to be maintained in exactly the same shape in which it was originally purchased.

Clearly, there will be some minor problems with how to put this plan into practice. But I think they can be worked out. They need to be because traffic safety is worth it. For these reasons, you should support a plan to make a car safety check mandatory.

Helen was fairly pleased with her working draft but she was still unsure about several points. She felt she needed fresh perspectives on what she had produced, other reactions to some of the ideas she had developed and strategies she had employed. Helen gave the working draft of her paper to two of her classmates, first to Jane and then to Alex, and asked them to respond to what she had written. Alex and Jane recorded their comments about Helen's working draft with the help of the following short list of criteria.

**1.** Are the premises of the argument acceptable? How could the author improve his/her arguments?

**2.** Does the writer sufficiently understand the audience's point of view? Does he/she attempt to persuade them, or does she/he merely argue with them? Could the writer handle his/her audience more sensitively?

**3.** Is the writer fair and reasonable?

**4.** Are some of the arguments ineffective or counterproductive? In what ways could the writer's argument be strengthened? Should any of the writer's arguments be modified or deleted?

What follows is a copy of the working draft that Helen had given Jane and then Alex. Notice that Jane and Alex's comments appear alongside the draft.

## WORKING DRAFT WITH PEER COMMENTS:

1. **"Motor Vehicle Inspection"** a.

To reduce the number of motor vehicle accidents, cars need to be regularly and strictly maintained. I think that
2. every state should have mandatory car maintenance inspection. This would ensure that all vehicles on American highways are in safe and satisfactory operating condition.

There are a few basic features of every vehicle which need to be maintained. These are important for the safety of the driver and other vehicles on the road. These fea- B.
tures should be checked once a year by a certified mechanic. For instance, every car should have brakes which will allow them to stop or to slow down fast enough to

**Reader:** *Jane* **Date:** *March 2*
**Author:** *Helen*
**Paper:** *Persuasion*

1. I like your idea--but I'm sure quite a few people would have complaints. I think you should explain your plan in more detail and spend some more time telling us <u>why</u> your plan is so important.
2. Introduction could be "meatier." Why not tie your plan in with all the things we hear about safety? This might make your plan seem more relevant to concerns people already have.
3. "Treads" of what?
4. Nice description of the features of a car that need to be inspected. You explain each one clearly. This part is convincing.
5. You're right! Whenever a mechanic looks under the hood, my uncle has to stand over his back. This is a concern that many people have.
6. You might put this earlier--maybe even before you list all the things that need to be checked. That way it might not seem so much like Big Brother is making sure that everyone has perfect cars.—That way you would

**Reader:** *Alex* **Date:** *March 3*
**Author:** *Helen*
**Paper:** *Persuasion*

A. Nice draft. I never thought about this problem but you're right; it is very impotant to make sure that the car is every bit as fit as the driver.

B. How about some other things that need checking? Like horns. It's important to have a warning horn and blinkers. I hate it when somebody doesn't use signal blinkers and just turns right in front of you.

C. How would your plan to take care of this problem?

D. Nice idea. I like this part because you show people that you won't bug them about every little thing wrong with their cars. Who cares about a tear in the back seat, right?!!! This lets people know that you aren't going to be too fanatic about stuff.

E. I have a couple of questions about putting this plan in operation. I'm still not clear

avoid colliding with vehicles slowing down in front of them or obstacles which may roll into the road. Every car should have two working headlights and brake lights which clearly alert following vehicles that the car is slowing down. The car should have blinker lights that work, so
3. that a driver can let other drivers know where he intends to go on the road. The treads should be deep enough to insure that the driver has adequate control of his position on the road. Also every car should have operating windshield wipers. They should adequately clear the windshield
4. of rain, snow, or other debris. These features are all essential to a vehicle's safe operation.

Most vehicles on the road probably have all the features listed above in adequate working condition. Most drivers are responsible enough to maintain each of these safety features. But motorists don't always know or can't always tell when things are not functioning properly. The best way to do this will be to have all vehicles registered in each state inspected once a year.

Some people distrust having mechanics look over their
5. car. They fear that the mechanic will invent or exaggerate problems so that the repair station can line its pockets with the owner's money. This might be a concern in other states which require annual vehicle inspection, such as Maine, which have designated repair stations inspect vehicles. Having repair shops as an inspection station introduces a possible conflict of interest--it might be to the mechanic's advantage to find more problems or to be more picky than he needs to be. Or perhaps if the car owner is C.
buddies with the repair shop mechanic, the mechanic might be tempted to overlook potential problems with the owner's car.

We shouldn't expect every car or truck on the road to be in tip-top, excellent condition, every last part of the vehicle to be in brand-new shape. This would be extremely

be able to emphasize better that only those safety things would be inspected.

about *who* will do the inspecting and *when*. Also what happens if the inspectors do find something wrong with the car?

costly and unnecessary for the owner. Who cares if the
back window can be rolled only half-way down, or that the
6. trunk sticks a little when you try to open it? A vehicle
doesn't need to be maintained in exactly the same shape in D.
which it was originally purchased.

Clearly, there will be some minor problems with how
to put this plan into practice. But I think they can be
worked out. They need to be because traffic safety is
worth it. For these reasons, you should support a plan to E.
make a car safety check mandatory.

After reading Jane and Alex's comments about her working draft, Helen then considered how she might write the next draft. The following is a script of Helen's writer's mind as she plans this draft.

### THE WRITER'S MIND: Replanning the Working Draft

*Both of my responders liked my idea—I think it's pretty good myself. And they pointed out some things I hadn't seen before. Alex is right—I need to think more about just how this plan will be put into operation. I want to make things as convenient as possible for everybody since one of the objections of my audience will be that it is a pain to have to take their car in to be inspected. Well, since I've stated that all registered vehicles need to be inspected, why not have them inspected when they are registered? There could be state inspection stations right alongside the registration places or as near as possible. And if one of the inspectors finds something wrong with the car, the owner would have to have it fixed. But not at the inspection station—that might make people suspicious. Besides, why should the state get into the car repair business? Well the owner would have to take care of that. After all, if you own a car, you ought to be able to find some place to fix it properly. OK, that sounds all right. Now the car would have to be fixed within a certain time period—otherwise some car owners might be tempted to put things off. I'll have to think about this—what would be a good way to handle this? Also, Alex has given me some more ideas about the things that need to be inspected. I should have a larger list than I do—he's right—horns and emergency brakes are needed to make sure the car is in operating condition. How about the next draft?—how will I organize all this new stuff? How about if I open with an introduction that shows how important car safety is, as Jane suggested, so I can make my plan seem as important as I think it is. Second, define what I mean by operating conditions—including what it does* not *mean as well as what it does. Third, go over each feature of the car that needs to be checked and show why. Fourth, explain how my plan will be implemented. Fifth, explain what happens to those cars that inspectors say need some work and include something about penalties for those few car owners who refuse to fix their cars. Sixth, present my conclusion. OK, that sounds like it might work.*

Helen then wrote the second working draft of her paper. Note how the advice she was given by Jane and Alex helped Helen improve her overall argument.

### SECOND WORKING DRAFT: "Motor Vehicle Inspection"

Recently many individuals and groups have expressed much concern about making our highways safer. Stricter penalties for drunk driving have been established and ads against drunk driving fill newspapers, magazines, and television. Organizations such as SADD and MADD have exerted great efforts to ensure that every driver is sober and alert. Certainly all this attention to the driver is necessary; the driver is of crucial importance in maintaining safety on our highways. Yet the driver is only a part of highway safety. For a driver, in order to be a driver, must have a vehicle. Just as it is important that every driver be competent and responsible, so is it also important for every vehicle to be in adequate operating condition. We should direct more effort to making sure that the cars and trucks on our highways are safe. Many states have annual vehicle inspections for just such a purpose. But many states do not have this important safeguard. I propose that all states should adopt the procedure of inspecting all registered vehicles once a year to make sure they are in safe operating condition.

What is meant by safe operating condition? Clearly, we shouldn't expect every car or truck on the road to be in every way in tip-top, excellent condition. We can't expect every last part of the vehicle to be in brand-new shape. This would be extremely costly and unnecessary for the owner. Who cares if the back window can be rolled only half-way down, or that the trunk sticks a little when you try to open it? What difference does a little scratch in the paint make? A vehicle need not be maintained in exactly the same shape it was in when originally purchased. It does not have to look and perform as though it just came off the assembly line. This would be unreasonable to expect. We should all be concerned not with the cosmetic features but only with safe operating conditions of the essential features of all vehicles on the road.

There are several basic features of every vehicle which need to be maintained carefully. These are important for the safety of the driver and other vehicles on the road. These features should be checked once a year by a certified mechanic. For instance, every car should have working brakes. Their brakes will allow them to stop or to slow down fast enough to avoid colliding with vehicles slowing down in front of them or obstacles which may roll into the road. Also, every car should have a working emergency brake. This prevents a parked car from rolling into the road and possibly causing an accident. Every car should have two working headlights and brake lights. Both of these features are for clearly alerting following vehicles that the car is slowing down. The car should have blinker lights that work, so that drivers can let other drivers know where they intend to go on the road. The treads of all tires should be deep enough to insure that drivers have adequate control of their position on the road. Every car should have a windshield that is in no danger of collapsing—nor should cracks in the shield be severe enough to impair the driver's line of sight or possibly to have the windshield break through. Every car should have a working horn to alert others of its presence. Also every car should have operating windshield wipers. They should adequately clear the windshield of rain, snow, or other debris. All of these features are essential to every vehicle's safe operation.

Most vehicles on the road probably have all the features listed above in adequate working condition. Many drivers are responsible and knowledgeable enough to maintain each of these safety features. But there are also many motorists who don't always know or cannot always tell when certain features of their vehicle are not functioning properly and safely. For instance, a driver might not know that the vehicle's tires are excessively worn until the vehicle skids off the road. Or a driver might not be aware that a car's brakes need to be replaced until the car slams into another car. The best way to handle this problem will be to have all vehicles registered in each state inspected once a year.

Some people might distrust having mechanics look over their car. They may fear that a mechanic will invent or exaggerate problems so that the repair station can line its pockets with the owner's money. Having private repair shops double as inspection stations, as some states currently do, introduces a possible conflict of interests--it might be to the mechanic's advantage to find more problems with the car's essential features than there really are or to be more picky than he needs to be. Or perhaps if the car owner is buddies with the repair shop mechanic, the mechanic might be tempted to overlook potential problems with the owner's car.

To make this plan fair, inexpensive, and standardized, the check would be done by a state-certified service, perhaps specially created for the task of performing these annual checks. The owner could schedule the vehicle's inspection at the same time that it must be registered in order to make the whole process more convenient for both the owner and the state. Since the safety inspection would be state-authorized, it should be inexpensive, possibly a small charge added to the registration fee. In the event your vehicle did not pass the inspection, the owner would be given a short yet reasonable period of time, perhaps 14 days, to have the vehicle taken care of. The owner would be given a sheet by the state mechanic describing the necessary service to be performed; then it would be the owner's responsibility to find a service station to do the necessary repair work. Within the two-week period the owner would have to reschedule a follow-up inspection to see whether the vehicle had been properly serviced. If not, the owner and/or the service station would be fined, depending upon who was at fault. If the owner did not return at all, he or she would be contacted and fined. Hopefully, the punitive measures would affect only a minute percentage of drivers. Most people who get behind the wheel consider safety a high priority. Because those very few who do not care about the condition of their vehicle could pose a great danger to everyone on the road, something should be done to insure the safety of their vehicles. If these measures failed, you could be criminally charged; and your license could be revoked.

Clearly, it will be difficult for states to enact such a procedure as I've outlined. But I think the problems inherent in my plan can be worked out. And the obvious benefits of preventing accidents certainly outweigh the cost and the effort that adopting such a procedure would require.

Since Helen has been working hard on her paper, she is hoping that this second working draft is close to being a final draft. But she suspects that she can still improve the persuasive force of her argument. Following our advice, she lets this incomplete draft sit for a day or two. In the meantime, she may also get advice from friends or classmates. She then intends to do a careful analysis of this working draft, using the detailed set of PACES questions that follow:

## CRITERIA QUESTIONS: WRITING THE PERSUASION PAPER

**P urpose**

What is the writer's overall purpose? Is the thesis stated clearly?

Is the overall purpose significant? Does it satisfy the relevance question: "So what?"

Does the writer have other, perhaps subsidiary, purposes? Do they supplement or weaken the overall argument?

Does the writer succeed in achieving his or her aims? Is the argument persuasive and convincing?

**A udience**

Has the writer identified an audience that would be in opposition to his or her position?

Has the writer recognized potential counterarguments? Does the writer explicitly address the concerns of the opposing audience?

Is the writer sensitive to the needs of the reader? Does the writer understand the extent of the reader's knowledge and conduct the discussion at an appropriate level?

Does the writer try to persuade a specific reader? Does the writer seem to be arguing with a reader in mind?

**C ode**

Has the writer organized the paper according to a plan? Is this plan successful?

What strategies of development does the writer use to carry the argument? Point to specific examples of definition, analogy, metaphor, comparison, classification, and simile, and discuss why they are effective or ineffective.

Are transitional devices used effectively? Have technical terms or specialized vocabulary words been defined and explained satisfactorily? When appropriate, has the chronological development of the issue been explained?

Is the language clear? Is the style appropriate to the subject? Is it too formal? Too informal?

Is the introduction interesting? Does the conclusion effectively reinforce the argument?

**[E]xperience**

When discussing the issue, does the writer rely on personal experience, other sources, or a combination of the two?

Does the writer support the argument with enough examples, details, and reasons? Are they appropriate and effective?

Has the writer identified the major issues or are there key factors that have been overlooked?

**[S]elf**

Does the writer understand the issue? Does he or she seem to be confident with the position taken? Does the writer give the impression of being either too formal or too compromising?

Does the writer earn the reader's respect?

Does the writer respect the audience's position? Does he or she talk down to the reader?

Is the writer fair? Is there evidence of any unfair biases?

## ► WRITING ACTIVITY ◄

Respond to the second working draft of Helen's persuasion paper on vehicle maintenance. Base your response on the preceding criteria questions for the persuasion paper. First list the draft's strengths and weaknesses and then answer the following questions:

What advice would you give Helen as she works toward a final draft to make her argument even stronger?

What other concerns and interests of her audience might Helen need to address?

What other points or supporting details does Helen need to include?

In a small group, rework Helen's second working draft into a final draft. *Note that we have not supplied you with the final draft of Helen's paper for this reason.* You can then complete this activity without being influenced by Helen's final draft. Base your revision on the suggestions made by each group member for the previous writing activity. Perhaps one member of the group could concentrate on strengthening the introduction, another the conclusion; one member could concentrate on targeting the position of the opposing audience, another on providing support for the writer's argument.

## ► DISCUSSION ACTIVITY ◄

Analyze and discuss the following persuasion papers written by college students. You might supplement your analysis with the PACES "Criteria Questions for the Persuasion Paper" on pages 297 to 298.

### THE BLASPHEMY OF COLORIZATION
**Chris Warnick**

What is art? Well, to me, art is a sincere expression of someone's thoughts, ideas, and feelings. Art can be anything from music to impressionistic painting to pottery. In a sense, art is sacred. Once someone's thoughts and ideas are made visual, or are given final concrete form, they shouldn't be altered by someone else. And other people should not support these alterations either. Tampering with art occurs today under the guise of film "colorization." Colorization is a process in which a computer colors prints of black and white movies. This process may seem like a wonderful idea to some people, but it has stirred up quite a bit of controversy. Many people in the film industry abhor it, and frankly so do I. Colorization is a blasphemy to the movie industry and the movie viewer.

Even if you have never seen a colorized movie, you can easily pick one out; some of the colors are always out of place. For example, in the colorized version of *The Maltese Falcon* Humphrey Bogart's lips are taupe and his suit is pea-green. In the black and white version he looks much more dignified. Who can look dignified with dirty lips and a tacky suit? In another colorized version of a movie classic, *Yankee Doodle Dandy*, the flags aren't even red, white, and blue. They are more of an orange, cream, and aqua. In probably the most famous comedy skit ever, *The Music Box*, the colorized version has Laurel and Hardy's faces looking a yellowish-orange. They literally look sick. And the ground they walked on was so fluorescent green it looked like the grass near Chernobyl. The poor coloring done by the "colorizers" can ruin a fine movie. Colorization can take the most dignified and treasured movie and turn it into a ghastly laughing stock. When some people's first impressions of the movie are orange men with green suits, after they realize that it's not some cheap sci-fi flick but a classic movie, they're going to turn it off. And keep it off.

Yet even if computers could reproduce colors accurately, still, colorization can destroy a movie. With any movie, black and white or color, you shouldn't just look at the surface of the film. The only way to get a meaningful message out of it, the only way to enjoy it in all its fulness and richness, is to examine all aspects—including dimensions such as lighting, dialogue, and camera techniques. Just looking at the plot of a film, or any other form of discursive art, will not give you the meaning of the piece. Often when black and white movies are colorized, many of the dramatic aspects of the film are completely lost. One such aspect is shadowing. In movies such as *The Maltese Falcon* and *Citizen Kane*, shadowing serves an important dramatic function. Shadowing can make a set the size of an ordinary living room look like the Taj Mahal. In that sense, shadowing can give black and white movies that larger-than-life feeling. Shadows give a contrast with the bright white and give a feeling of conflict in a movie. When these movies are colored, the shadows and their dramatic impact are lost. In short, when a black and white movie is colored, and some of the lighting and shadows are lost, the movie has lost some of its effect.

One movie that has thankfully not been colorized yet, which many critics consider the best film ever, is *Citizen Kane*. Orson Welles is the Renaissance Man in this movie, both producing and acting in it. The use of lighting and shadows in this movie is extraordinary. The plot is, in a way, related to the life of William Randolph Hearst. It is a dark and bitter story about a rich man whose life is empty and who longs for his childhood. And to show that it is a dark and bitter movie, Orson Welles made the lighting dark. Even in the middle of the day during a snowstorm, the lighting is still very dark. Whenever Kane was in a dominant position during a conflict, he would always be in the light. Similarily, whenever he was being dominated, he was in the shadows. If this movie were to be colorized, the lighting effect, which makes the whole tone of the movie, would be lost. There would be no way to tell whether or not Kane was in the light or shadows if the movie were computer colorized. *Citizen Kane* is a movie that introduced many of the camera and lighting techniques used today. Many movie-makers refer to it almost as their form of a bible. If this movie were to be colorized, it would really stir controversy, because it is such a treasured film.

Colorizing movies is tampering with a set of ideas which affect the meaning of the film entirely. Some people argue that the colorizing of these movies will only make the movie more appealing to more people. Yet you hurt the movie when you colorize it; you don't enhance it. It is important that young people are able to see the old classics like *Casablanca*, *The Maltese Falcon*, and *Citizen Kane* in their pure original state. The movies are unique and well acted. They can give everybody a very good appreciation of fine films. I remember when I first saw Humphrey Bogart in the *Maltese Falcon*, I was amazed—he looked so dark and mysterious. The way his suits were always dark intrigued me. I really like the mysterious effect he gave off. We leave the Lone Ranger alone. Why can't we leave the works of artists like Humphrey Bogart and Orson Welles alone too?

These movies are created for the purpose of pleasing the public. In a way, they were created to be looked at for years to come. Old movies show the history of movie-making right from the beginning. It is not right to tamper with the past, with history. Filmmakers of today have learned many lessons from old movies and we should respect and preserve them intact for precisely this, if for no other, reason. Without some of these movies, the film-making industry would not be where it is today. By colorizing old classics, we are standing in the way of progress instead of helping it. And in a sense, colorization of films may stifle creativity. We should not mold these classic films to our taste, but yet have them enhance our taste in films.

Whether it's black and white or color, a movie is a form of art. It is up to us what future generations will see. We owe it to the next generation to preserve these pieces of art in the original form. Just as we preserve the Mona Lisa and the Great Pyramids in their original form, we should preserve *Citizen Kane* and *The Maltese Falcon*.

### Questions for Discussion

**1.** Why does the writer introduce a general definition of art? How does this definition lead to his thesis?

**2.** What makes a colorized movie different from a movie filmed in color? How does the writer show this difference?

**3.** How, in the author's view, does colorization detract from many of the technical and stylistic aspects of a film? What examples does the writer use? Why are these examples important in advancing his argument?

**4.** Why does the writer feel it is important that *Citizen Kane* not be colorized?

**5.** Does the author keep his audience's views in mind? What are his responses to those views?

## PROPOSITION 48
**Mark Volcheck**

Today, college athletics are very appealing to the youth of America. Its stars are glamorized in the media and are as recognizable as their counterparts in the professional ranks. High school athletes strive to better their athletic skills so that they can enjoy the same attention and success achieved by their college idols. However, these same high school athletes fail to enhance their academic skills because they focus solely on becoming athletically attractive to colleges. To encourage the student-athlete's competence in the classroom, the National Collegiate Athletic Association decided to set minimum standards on the ACT and SAT college entrance exams for those Division I athletes wanting to participate in sports during their freshman year. Even though the intentions of Proposition 48 are admirable, in fact, it actually encourages its violators to circumvent the rule, and instead of assisting them, it punishes student-athletes who desperately need help.

The NCAA rightly acknowledges the problem of student-athletes holding athletics as being more important than academics. Proposition 48 grows out of the NCAA's concern for upholding the academic integrity of Division I athletics. The NCAA is concerned about student-athletes downgrading the importance of academics in college athletics and in the schools they represent by using their full scholarships for athletic reasons only. According to the proposition, if student-athletes fail to achieve a composite score of 15 on the ACT or 700 on the SAT, they would be prohibited from participating in athletics during their freshman year. By enforcing this rule, colleges would be less likely to recruit academically-struggling athletes because they would have to sit out a year. This rule may also prompt high school stars to work harder in their studies, if they know colleges are looking for academic-minded athletes. The victims of Proposition 48, however, are warmly accepted in junior colleges.

Junior colleges do not require competence in the classroom. There have been many cases in which victims of the proposition have been told by the Division I school which recruited them to attend a junior college, so that they won't spend a year away from the sport. Then, after a year or two in junior college, the Division I school gives the players a scholarship, thus circumventing the rule. In fact, *Ballplayer*, a magazine that rates junior college players for major colleges, estimates that one-half of high school seniors who do not meet the proposition's requirements opt for junior colleges (Alexander Wolff, "The Juco Express," *Sports Illustrated*, Nov. 1987: p. 13). By attending junior colleges to bypass the rule, student-athletes forfeit all of the educational resources of a major college education that can't be matched in junior colleges. For example, Lorain Community College couldn't offer a fraction of the educational resources offered at Ohio State. The players who choose the junior college route, do so for the sole purpose of making themselves more athletically attractive to major colleges, while giving little concern to academics. Proposition 48 can't stop a university from recruiting uneducated junior college players, just as it can't stop student-athletes from over-emphasizing athletics.

Even if Proposition 48 could stop those student-athletes from entering by way of junior colleges, it would punish those students who did not meet the requirements instead of helping them. Should a slow learner or a student-athlete with a learning disability be punished? A friend of mine has a brother who is an offensive tackle at the University of Miami in Florida. His brother, Matt, has had dyslexia since he was born, but it was not diagnosed until his sophomore year of high school. Since he was diagnosed, his grades have gone up, while his reading skills have been steadily improving. However, he missed the requirement on the ACT by two points and was unable to play his first year. He was very upset, not only because of embarrassment, but because he received no extra help in his classes and was not even allowed to condition with the team. He spent his freshman year academically disgusted and out of condition. Sitting out a year is also not helping a Proposition 48 student-athlete on my floor. Because he doesn't satisfy the academic and discipline requirements of the varsity basketball team, he spends his time smoking dope and shooting hoops on the playgrounds. Student-athletes are inclined to subscribe to this behavior, because Proposition 48 doesn't require that they maintain a certain GPA during the freshman year that they sit out. Proposition 48 focuses too much of its power on punishment rather than assistance.

I propose that Proposition 48 be revised with legislation that is devoted to helping student-athletes instead of punishing them before they have taken a college course. I believe Proposition 48 violators ought to be allowed to participate in Division I sports during their first year as long as certain specifications are met. First, the NCAA must demand that these students spend at least six hours a day, five days a week, in study tables with a tutor or an aide that is provided by the college. Futhermore, the NCAA must designate officials to Division I schools to ensure that this rule is being properly enforced. Without officials, the study tables will not benefit the unmotivated student-athlete. For instance, I know of two student-athletes who do not even take a book to their study-table because the university only requires that they attend. It is very important that tutors at study tables teach student-athletes responsible study habits during their first year because student-athletes can then use these habits during their entire college career, instead of subscribing to the habits of the Proposition 48 basketball player on my floor. In addition to the above requirement, the student-athlete would also be expected to meet the academic requirements of eligibility set by the individual colleges. Only after attempting to help student-athletes make good use of their scholarships, should the university dismiss them from athletics for not making the grade.

The balance between academics and athletics is very difficult for student-athletes to maintain. Simply punishing athletes with low academic scores does not create equilibrium. However, if the NCAA creates stricter academic requirements that assist student-athletes in their studies, student-athletes will have an excellent chance to achieve academic success, and will be an asset to their universities and to college athletics.

### Questions for Discussion

**1.** What is Proposition 48? Why does the author choose to explain Proposition 48 when addressing his opponents' side?

**2.** According to the author, how does Proposition 48, a rule designed to promote academics for athletes, actually hurt the college athlete?

**3.** How do Division I schools circumvent Proposition 48? According to the author, why are junior colleges detrimental to the student-athlete's academic progress? What evidence does the author offer?

**4.** In what other ways is Proposition 48 detrimental to the student-athlete? What examples from his own experience does he offer? How effective are these examples?

**5.** What solutions to the Proposition 48 problem does the writer present? Why does he postpone these suggestions until the end of his essay?

## ► WRITING ACTIVITY ◄

Write a persuasion paper three to six pages long. Choose a topic that you can handle adequately and that you are knowledgeable about. You need a subject you have firsthand evidence on, something you have personally experienced or can fairly easily research. The length of the paper rules out most of the big, controversial subjects like inflation control and energy problems. Direct your argument to an audience who disagree with you about this issue. Remember, the goal is not to outargue your audience but to get them at least to consider and, ideally, to adopt your position.

### TOPIC SUGGESTIONS FOR THE PERSUASION PAPER

People Should Not Buy Furs.

English Should Be the Official Language of the United States.

The Trapping of Animals Should be Allowed.

Advertisements Are Sexist.

Saturday Morning Cartoons Are Too Violent.

College Athletes Should Be Paid.

Long-Play Records Are Better Than Compact Discs.

Computers Make Life Harder.

Bicycles Are Dangerous to Pedestrians.

Pop Music Is Unimaginative.

Excessive Rules Have Ruined Professional Sports.

Humanities Courses Should Not Be Required.

Television News Is Superficial.

Tips for Waiters or Waitresses Are Unnecessary.

Teachers Should Be Required to Take Regular Competency Tests.

Television Talk Shows Have Gone Too Far.

Horror Films Promote Violence.

Street Preaching Should Be Banned.

Fans Take Sports Too Seriously.

College Entrance Exams Do Not Predict Success in College.

Foreign Products Are a Better Value Than American.

People Should Be Allowed to Drive As Fast As They Want.

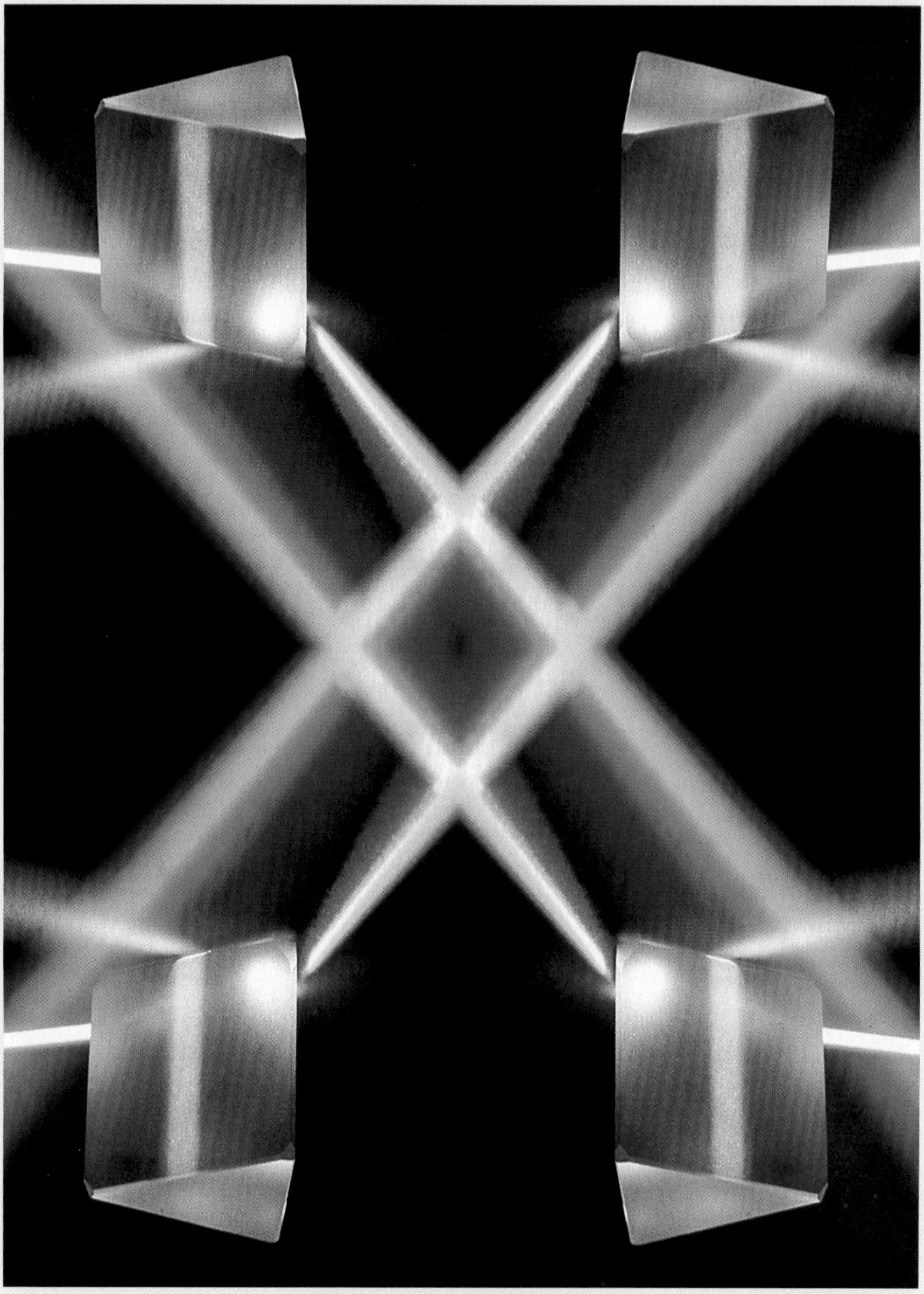

# PART ▲ THREE

# *Writing For Special Purposes*

# CHAPTER ▲ NINE

# *Writing With Sources*

**"To be conscious that you are ignorant of the facts is a great step to knowledge."**

**BENJAMIN DISRAELI**

Research writing is probably the most challenging and demanding writing you'll undertake in college. It requires the greatest attention to formal procedures and the "rules" of writing. Because formal writing is orderly and predictable, there is a danger of its becoming stuffy and boring. You have to control both style and content; the challenge is to remain lively and interesting while writing with sources. For an example of effective research writing, read the following paragraph from a respected scientific journal, reporting an experiment in which students pretended to be insane:

> The pseudopatient, very much as a true psychiatric patient, entered a hospital with no foreknowledge of when he would be discharged. Each was told that he would have to get out by his own devices, essentially by convincing the staff that he was sane. The psychological stresses associated with hospitalization were considerable, and all but one of the pseudopatients desired to be discharged almost immediately after being admitted. They were, therefore, motivated not only to behave sanely but to be paragons of cooperation. That their behavior was in no way disruptive is confirmed by nursing reports, which have been obtained on most of the patients. These reports uniformly indicate that the patients were "friendly," "cooperative," and "exhibited no abnormal indications."
>
> D. L. ROSENHAN, "On Being Sane in Insane Places," *Science*

The author of "On Being Sane in Insane Places" is a professor of psychology and law, and he is writing for psychologists and lawyers. In the experiment, no doctor ever discovered that the "pseudopatients" were only faking insanity, and this fact has serious implications for both psychology and law! The article represents very formal writing. It deals with academic subject matter, and there is little or no attempt on the author's part to "express self." The writing is clear and informative and objective. Later in the article, Rosenhan writes in the first person: "I do not, even now, understand the problem well enough to perceive solutions." He does this to avoid what many think is an awkward research point of view: "This researcher does not now understand the problem. . . ." Even with an occasional first-person reference, Rosenhan's article remains objective research writing aimed at a very special audience, and it is therefore quite formal in tone and language.

For most research writing in college, something less than extreme formality is desired. You should aim for language suitable for educated audiences; that is, you should write on the formal side but not at the extreme end of the writing continuum, where only the most specialized audiences will be able to read your work. For example, here is the beginning of a research paper written with about the right degree of formality:

> **THE NAVY'S DOOMSDAY MACHINE:**
> **PROJECT SEAFARER**
> **Mark Starbuck**
>
> The discovery of power from the atom had once accompanied a dream of a world moving on to bigger and better achievements. Atomic energy could be harnessed to do a number of things. It was soon to be discovered, however, that the power from the atom was capable of great destruction. With nations growing and becoming more powerful, with science and technology at their fingertips, the threat of a nuclear attack by an aggressive nation has been a major concern of the government's defense planners for as long as such a threat existed. The navy came up with what it believed to be the answer—a communications system capable of communicating with submerged American submarines armed with nuclear-tipped missiles.
>
> "The logic on which the U.S. retaliatory nuclear weapons system is based rests on strategies of mutual deterrence in a world where the superpowers depend upon weapons of extreme technological sophistication in order to keep their fears of each other manageable." (Morgan 276). Consider a hypothetical day in 19—. Scores of nuclear missiles advancing toward the United States suddenly show up on radar screens, early warning systems, and nearly all detection devices. The nightmares we have lived with since Hiroshima and Nagasaki begin to take place as nuclear warheads explode on their targets. There can be no doubt, our country is under a massive attack by an aggressor nation with first-strike capability (Watkins 58). To prevent such a disaster, one need possess such a strong retaliatory force to make any aggressor think twice before launching such an attack. The United States Navy has spent over seventeen years researching and developing a communications system with a proposed potential for retaliation called Project Seafarer (originally known as Project Sanguine). So far, the system has cost over $100 million (Myers 110).
>
> The construction and development of Seafarer in Michigan, has, to date, been stopped. Political and social forces have brought the controversial communications system to a halt. Nevertheless, it is still believed by the navy that Seafarer is essential to the nation's security in the event of a nuclear war, but obviously this belief is in doubt. Is Seafarer truly what the navy has envisaged or has it been an expensive miscalculation?

Mark's paper has about the right tone. The language is formal, but not too formal. We are aware of the writer's personality, though his voice is submerged under the technical talk about Seafarer. If we had to identify the writer's self, we might say, "This sounds like an intelligent, well-educated, easygoing person. He knows what he is talking about, but he isn't being stuffy or showing off." Mark offers the reader a hypothetical attack on the United States to dramatize the importance of the Seafarer question. Mark knows he has an audience that will listen to him as long as he doesn't get too technical or dull. Other than that, Mark's writing here is not drastically changed from his other writing. The subject itself has forced him to be a little technical, but that is unavoidable. Note that Mark's semiformal writing is very readable.

## SELECTING AND REFINING A RESEARCH QUESTION

Naturally we would all like to discover some important new idea or concept; we would all like to write a significant research paper. But should researchers start out with enormous questions of great significance: Is there a God? What will the future be like? How can the political structure of the world be changed? It might be rewarding to be able to answer questions like these, but they are just too big for any one researcher. A skillful researcher with endless energy, time, and financial backing must still settle for quite a small research question. For example, medical science has been trying to cure cancer for decades, but each researcher has a much smaller problem to work on, which may or may not lead to the answer to the overall question. Some researchers are in chemotherapy, others are in radiology, and still others are in immunology (the study of the body's own defense mechanisms against disease). Researching is patient, painstaking, detailed work, and it often takes years of such patient work from many researchers before the right answers are found. Generally speaking, the bigger the question, the longer the research will take.

In a classroom, then, with no more than a semester or quarter to work in, you cannot tackle a big question. You must find the smallest possible question to work on. Sexism was a popular subject throughout the 1960s and the early 1970s. Many students attempted to write research papers about it (Are men and women equal? Are girls and boys taught stereotyped sex roles?). Such questions could not be researched very well in a short time. They involved areas of research that had not been examined in depth by science or law. To answer such questions (Are girls and boys taught stereotyped sex roles?) requires elaborate *primary* research—experiments, laboratory investigations, field work. Few beginning researchers are ready for such work. For your first research paper, then you should begin with research you can do primarily in the library.

Mostly, the library contains what other researchers have said about various subjects, and it is well suited, then, to *secondary* research. Suppose we change some of those sexism questions so that they could be answered with secondary research, in the library: Do scientists believe that men and women are physically equal? Does the public believe that women and men should be paid the same wages for doing the same work? Have there been any court cases about the denial of opportunity based on sex? Questions like these could be answered through library research. The basic question for secondary research is, Who said what? Any question involving who said what or how many people said what or what kind of people said what starts research off in the right direction:

looking for things in the library. In short, the answer to the question, Does sexism exist in America? probably cannot be found in the library. What can be found is what people have said about this question, what judges, lawyers, doctors, and others have said. And this leaves the *conclusion*, the answer to the question, up to you, as it should in a worthwhile research paper.

Coming up with a good topic for research is usually the hardest job. Even after preliminary reading and thinking, you may still start off with a subject that is too big or that has some other built-in problem. You must keep reminding yourself that no matter how small the subject is, you are likely to find large amounts of research materials you will have to read, so the smaller, the better. Three guidelines—specific, limited, worthwhile—can help you develop, evaluate, and refine your research question.

*Is the question specific?* Is the wording of your research question specific enough? Is the object of investigation clear? A researcher who sets out to investigate "morality" will quickly discover that there is no single interpretation of that term, and even what people do with regard to that concept differs widely. To investigate today's morality might involve things like numbers of robberies, incidents of cheating, church attendance, any number of *subtopics* within morality. One of the subtopics may be what you should investigate.

*Is the question limited?* "Trucks," "labor unions," "World War II" all seem specific enough; at least most people will know what you are talking about. But even "trucks" is a large subject. To test the size of any subject, see how many questions you can ask about it. The more questions, the bigger the subject. (How did the truck develop? How many kinds of trucks are there? How are they made? How does a truck work? What are the political issues involving trucks? And so on.)

The *smallest* question you can ask about anything may be one that can be answered *yes* or *no*, and that is what you need for a controllable thesis. Do trucks pay sufficient taxes to pay for the damage they do to highways? (Yes or no?) Do trucks cause more pollution than cars? (Yes or no?) Are truck drivers the safest drivers on the road? (Yes or no?) You may discover through your research that these questions really cannot be answered with a *yes* or *no*; the issues may be far more complex than they seemed at the outset (they almost always are). But if you frame your question with this highly limited *yes-no* formula, your chances of having a workable research thesis will be much improved. If the answer then comes out to be "maybe" or "sometimes yes and sometimes no," so much the better; your conclusion will show the reader how to make sense out of the question. Making sense of a question is the point of research in the first place. Furthermore, stating your question in a *two-sided* manner like this avoids the problem of what to do with contrary evidence. If you start out determined to prove that trucks cause more pollution than cars, you may have to ignore evidence that contradicts your thesis.

*Is the question worthwhile?* Does the question provide information that most people would care to hear about? What seems relevant and important to the researcher may not strike the audience as worthwhile. A researcher who wants to study a rare sea creature off the shores of California will have to show why the research is worthwhile. Since almost anything will interest someone, it shouldn't be too hard to show that even very rare and unusual subjects have their value. But you should follow the formula that the more specialized and limited in interest your subject is, the fewer readers you will have. As a general rule, you should not select subjects that appeal only to a very specialized audience. Still, this is no easy decision to make. If the subject is worthwhile, even to a limited audience, perhaps it should be pursued. If you are truly interested in and excited about a subject, you should be able to show your audience why it is interesting, why it is worthwhile, why it should be researched. In college, you can assume that you have an educated audience, but your classmates all have different interests and areas of specializations. Even your professor is likely to have interests different from yours, so you cannot assume an elite audience of enthusiasts.

## ► WRITING ACTIVITY ◄

Using the criteria *specific*, *limited*, and *worthwhile*, try to decide which, if any, of these suggested topics could be turned into a workable research thesis. Which ones seem to you the most promising for research? Why would you vote against the others? The topics are given here just as they were proposed by students; some of them could be worked into good research questions; others, we decided, were not so good. What do you think?

*Honor* Is there any honor left in America? What is honor today? I plan to show how honor has declined in America.

*Hobbies* Many people have fascinating hobbies. Some surprising people have hobbies that you wouldn't think of. My paper will discuss the different kinds of hobbies different people have.

*Arabian horses* Why are these horses so much loved by everyone? What makes them wanted by kings and movie stars? I want to tell why I think the Arabian is the most beautiful and interesting horse in the world.

*Campus sex* Who is doing what on campus? I want to do a survey by interviewing students. I'll ask them about their sex lives and write up the results as a research paper.

*Republicans* What does it mean to be a Republican? I want to tell about my work as a Young Republican, what we stand for, what we are trying to do.

*Witchcraft* Are there any witches today? There have been lots of books and magazines about modern witches. I want to write about modern witchcraft.

*Lincoln* I think he was our greatest president, and I think more people should know about his real life. I want to tell about Lincoln's life.

*Euthanasia* Do we have a right to end a life? I'd like to show both sides of this issue.

*Motorcycles* The motorcycle is a fantastic device. There is more to it than most people think.

*Childless marriage* Children are no longer thought of as necessary to modern marriages. The attitude about having children has changed.

*Ecology* We have got to stop polluting our atmosphere. We will all die of suffocation if the factories don't stop.

*Horror movies* What is it about horror movies that fascinates people? Why are people drawn to terror and horrible stuff?

## USING THE LIBRARY

Most research begins in the library. You will discover that a college library can provide you with information on nearly any subject. Unfortunately, many students avoid the library or are confused and overwhelmed by it.

Good libraries are information systems, parts of which you can use on your own. Other parts of these systems you can approach through the librarians. Your librarians may set up library orientation programs; many libraries use computerized systems for storing and retrieving information, and an increasing number have computerized their catalogs. Learning how to use the library is one of the most useful steps you can take in the first months of your undergraduate career.

The next section of this chapter shows you a strategy for library research. The search strategy gives you a plan for moving from general to specific information on any subject. Keep in mind that once you get beyond the stage of gathering background information, your librarians—especially reference librarians—can help you. They know the value of different sources on a given subject. Librarians may be able to guide you to material too recent to be included in indexes, material in special collections, even local people knowledgeable about your topic.

## FOLLOWING A SEARCH STRATEGY

When you are ready to begin investigating a research subject, how can you find the information you need in the most efficient way? You need a *search strategy*, a step-by-step procedure for finding and evaluating information. A search strategy enables you to approach your topic systematically, beginning with general information and going to specific material.

You should research the smallest possible aspect of an issue, one that can be phrased as a *yes-no* question. The general-to-specific direction of the search strategy helps you to discover that sort of thesis question. You may know you want to (or have to) write about legislation or social planning. But more often than not, you won't know at the outset the exact "limited, specific, worthwhile" thesis question. The search strategy helps you to move from, for example, legislation in general to "The Freedom of Information Act: Genuine Threat to National Security?" or from social planning to "Arcosanti: Workable Model for the Future?" Through a continuous process of evaluation, you define the question *and* select the most useful materials for your needs.

The search strategy has nine steps:

Step 1: Refer to *encyclopedias*.

Step 2: Refer to *dictionaries*.

Step 3: Use the *card catalog* or the *computer catalog system*.

Step 4: Use printed indexes or computer databases for *journal and newspaper articles*.

Step 5: Locate *essay collections*.

Step 6: Consult *biographical sources*.

Step 7: Consult *book reviews*.

Step 8: Consider *statistical sources*.

Step 9: Consider *government documents*.

These nine steps are meant to be flexible. You may find yourself going back to earlier steps—to check an index for additional information, for example, or to look for more specific journal articles—as you refine your thesis and evaluate the evidence.

## ► Step 1: Refer to Encyclopedias

To get an overview of your subject and any relevant background material, begin your search with encyclopedias. For example:

***General Encyclopedias***

*The Encyclopedia Americana*: Provides excellent articles on American history, science, and technology

*New Encyclopaedia Britannica*: Emphasizes arts, literature, and the humanities; supplies excellent bibliographies

*The World Book Encyclopedia*: Includes excellent drawings, photographs, diagrams, maps, charts, and other illustrations as well as simple, clear explanations of technical topics.

***Special Encyclopedias***

*Encyclopedia of Education*: Covers educational interests, practices, philosophies, and institutions and educators

*The Encyclopedia of Philosophy*: Encompasses Eastern, Western, ancient, medieval, and modern philosophies and people important in those fields

*International Encyclopedia of the Social Sciences*: Covers economics, history, political science, psychology, sociology, and law

*McGraw-Hill Encyclopedia of Science and Technology*: Encompasses physical, natural, and applied sciences

Indeed, nearly every academic field has its own specialized encyclopedia. Check to see which ones are available in your library.

Quoting from an encyclopedia or listing one as a source may raise questions about your research, because information in encyclopedias tends to be general and cannot be completely up to date. Then why consult encyclopedias at all? First, for an overview: Articles in good encyclopedias are written by authorities in given subjects, and their coverage is broad and accurate, but not always deep. A second reason to consult encyclopedias is that many encyclopedia articles contain *bibliographies* and cite source materials that you might use in your research.

Suppose you wished to investigate the roots of contemporary political cartooning. As the following examples show, reading the articles in several encyclopedias would immediately introduce you to a considerable amount of background information.

### Selections from *The New Encyclopaedia Britannica*
### *Short Article*

**cartoon,** originally, and still, a full-size sketch or drawing used as a pattern for a tapestry, painting, mosaic, or other graphic art form, but also, since the early 1840s, a pictorial parody utilizing caricature, satire, and usually humour. Cartoons are used today primarily for conveying political commentary and editorial opinion in newspapers and for social comedy and visual wit in magazines.

A brief account of cartoons follows. For full treatment, *see* MACROPAEDIA: Caricature, Cartoon, and Comic Strip; for animated-motion-picture cartoons, *see* Motion Pictures: *Animation.*

While the caricaturist deals primarily with personal and political satire, the cartoonist treats types and groups in comedies of manners. Though William Hogarth has a few predecessors, it was his social satires and depictions of human foibles that later cartoons were judged against. Honoré Daumier anticipated the 20th-century cartoon's balloon-enclosed speech by indicating in texts accompanying his cartoons the characters' unspoken thoughts. Hogarth's engravings and Daumier's lithographs were fairly complete documentaries on the London and Paris of their times.

Thomas Rowlandson lampooned the ludicrous behavior of a whole series of social types, including "Dr. Syntax," which may well be the grandfather of the later comic strips. Rowlanson was followed by George Cruikshank, a whole dynasty of *Punch* artists who humorously commented on the passing world, Edward Lear, Thomas Nast, Charles Dana Gibson, and "Spy" (Leslie Ward) and "Ape" '(Carlo Pellegrini), the two main cartoonists of *Vanity Fair* magazine.

In the 20th century the one-line joke, or single-panel gag, and the pictorial joke without words matured and a huge diversity of drawing styles proliferated. The influence of *The New Yorker* magazine spread to other publications worldwide. The new cartoonists included James Thurber, Charles Addams, Saul Steinberg, Peter Arno, and William Hamilton of the United States and Gerard Hoffnung, Fougasse, Anton, and Emett Rowland of England.

A Pulitzer Prize for editorial cartooning was established in 1922, and a Sigma Delta Chi Award for editorial cartooning was awarded annually after 1942; such cartoonists as Edmund Burck, Herblock, Bill Mauldin, and Rube Goldberg won both. Carl Giles was honoured with the Order of the British Empire in 1959 for his achievements in editorial cartooning.

*Extended Article*

# Caricature, Cartoon, and Comic Strip

Caricature, cartoon (in the satirical sense), and comic strips (including comic books) are related forms. Historically, they arose in the order given, but they all have flourished together. All use the same artistic mediums of drawing and printmaking: caricature and the element of satire are usually present in each. This article covers their history and development. The article is divided into the following sections:



DEFINITION OF TERMS

**Caricature.** Caricature is the distorted presentation of person, type, or action. Commonly, a salient feature or characteristic of the subject is seized upon and exaggerated, or features of animals, birds, or vegetables are substituted for parts of the human being, or analogy is made to animal actions. Generally, one thinks of caricature as being a line drawing and meant for publication for

**Selection from *The World Book Encyclopedia***

Heading

Subheading

Cross-reference

CARTOON

**Editorial Cartoons** do in pictures what editorials do in words. They encourage the reader to develop an opinion about someone or something prominent in the news. Most editorial cartoons appear on the editorial pages of newspapers as single drawings with or without captions or titles. They may support a main editorial of the day, or they may deal with some event in the day's news. Many editorial cartoons, called *caricatures,* poke fun at well-known people exaggerating their physical characteristics or facial expressions (see CARICATURE).

Editorial cartoonists use a variety of symbols to help get their messages across quickly. For example, a hungry vulture identified as a large corporation might show that the company has gobbled up smaller firms. In many cartoons, a bear symbolizes Russia. A thin, bearded man in a red, white, and blue tuxedo is Uncle Sam, who stands for the United States. Thomas Nast, a famous editorial catoonist, introduced the elephant as the symbol of the Republican Party in an 1874 cartoon for *Harper's Weekly* magazine. Nast also made the donkey popular as a symbol of the Democratic Party. Examples of Nast's work appear with the WORLD BOOK articles on DEMOCRATIC PARTY and REPUBLICAN PARTY.

Look for bibliographies in *all* the sources you examine: books, handbooks, journals, biographies, and essays. Finding a bibliography in a reputable source can be invaluable. *Annotated bibliographies*—those that briefly evaluate specific works—are more useful than general bibliographies because they give you not only some clues about the content of the works cited but also the compiler's estimate of their value.

Bibliographies can also be published as separate volumes. Sheehy's *Guide to Reference Books* is a good example of a single-volume general bibliography of reference titles in all disciplines. Other bibliographies can be located by searching in the card catalog by subject; for example, "English literature—Bibliography." A very useful index to bibliographies is *Bibliographic Index: A Cumulative Bibliography of Bibliographies* (1937 to present). As you scan the bibliographies, copy the information on sources that look promising.

**Entries from Sheehy's *Guide to Reference Books***

**Social Sciences • Political Science • General Works**

*United States*

Title
Publication information

**Cyclopedia of American government**, ed. by Andrew C. McLaughlin and Albert Bushnell Hart, N.Y., Appleton, 1914. 3v. il. (Repr.: N.Y., Peter Smith, 1949) **CJ46**

Annotation

A useful work although now much out-of-date. Covers topics in theory of philosophy of political society; forms of political organization and government; international and constitutional law; history of political parties; and other American political topics. Many biographies. Arranged alphabetically by small subjects, with an analytical index. Signed articles by specialists with bibliographies. For the earlier political history of the United States, J. J. Lalor's *Cyclopaedia of political science* (N.Y., Merrill, 1888-90. 3v.) is still occasionally useful. **JK9.C9**

Library of Congress call number

**Encyclopedia of U.S. government benefits** a complete, practical, and convenient guide to United States government benefits available to the people of America. Written by a group of government experts; ed. by R. A. Grisham, Jr., in consultation with P. D. McConaughy. Union City, N.J., Wise, 1965. 1011p. **CJ47**

Entry number

Intended as a guide for the citizen; to make him aware of the variety of benefits and services available, and to tell him how and where to apply for them. Dictionary arrangement, with entries for types of benefits and administering agencies, etc.; numerous cross references. Coverage, however, is uneven, and there are inconsistencies in the arrangement. **JK424.E55**

Authors
Title

**Plano, Jack C. and Greenberg, Milton**. The American political dictionary. 3d ed. Hinsdale, Ill., Dryden Pr., [1972]. 462p. **CJ48**

Terms are grouped under 18 topics, e.g., U.S. constitution, civil liberties, the legislative process, finance and taxation, foreign policy and international affairs. Each section includes definitions and explanations (as appropriate) of terms and important agencies, cases, and statutes. The index allows the work to be used as a dictionary. Cross references within articles. **JK9.P55**

**Safire, William**. The new language of politics: an anecdotal dictionary of catchwords, slogans, and political usage. N.Y., Random, [1968]. 528p. **CJ49**

Discusses origin and development of terms and phrases relating to politics. Bibliographical references are generally too imprecise to be genuinely useful. **JK9.S2**

**Smith, Edward Conrad and Zurcher, Arnold John**. Dictionary of American politics. 2d ed. N.Y., Barnes & Noble. [1968]. 434p **CJ50**

1st ed., 1888, by Everit Brown and Albert Strauss; 2d ed., 1924, was almost completely rewritten by Edward C. Smith; 3d ed., 1944, was revised by the present editors. 1949 edition had title: *New dictionary of American Politics*. 1955 edition reverted to the earlier title and was published without edition number.

Represents a complete revision. Gives brief, concise definitions; includes slogans, political slang, nicknames, etc. **JK9.S5**

**Sperber, Hans** and **Trittschuh, Travis**. American political terms; an historical dictionary. Detroit, Mich., Wayne State Univ. Pr., 1962. 516p. **CJ51**

An alphabetical dictionary of political terms giving origins and various meanings, with references to sources, showing earliest and developing usage. Includes a bibliography of the literature searched. **JK9.S65**

## ► Step Two: Refer to Dictionaries

Dictionaries offer definitions for any unfamiliar words or terms you come across in your research and also provide information on the pronunciation, spelling, syllabication (division), usage, and etymology (origin and development) of those words. You may refer to dictionaries throughout your search.

### Entry from *Webster's Third New International Dictionary of the English Language, Unabridged*

**car·i·ca·tur·a·ble** \ |karəkə:churəbəl \ *adj* : suitable for caricature : having features easily caricatured

**car·i·ca·tur·al** \-ù (e)rel \ *adj* : like or having the characteristics of caricature

[1] **car·i·ca·ture** \ 'karēke, chū (e)r, -ūe, -rēk- *also* 'ker- *or* -,t(y) ū- *or* -keche(r) \ *n* -s [earlier *caricatura,* fr. It, affectation, caricature, lit., a loading, fr. *caricare* to load, fr. LL *carricare* — more at CHARGE] **1 a :** exaggeration by means of deliberate simplification and often ludicrous distortion of parts or characteristics <the art of ≲> **b :** an instance of such caricature <in her rambling and her idleness she might only be a ≲ of herself, but in her silence and sadness she was the very reverse of all that she had been before — Jane Austen> **2 :** a representation esp. in literature or art that has the qualities of caricature <a series of satirical ≲ *s* of the faculty of a progressive college for women —Orville Prescott> **3 :** a distortion so gross as to seem like caricature <the kangaroo court a ≲ of justice>

**syn** BURLESQUE, PARODY, TRAVESTY all indicate kinds of grotesque and exaggerated imitation. CARICATURE suggests ludicrous distortion of a peculiar feature <*caricature* is a very special kind of portraiture, permitting extravagance and enunciating the awkward and uncomplimentary —*Christian Science Monitor*> <his *caricature* of the "gentleman" . . . is a biting sarcasm of the respectable, gentle, and polite bourgeois —*Commonweal*> BURLESQUE is likely to imply humor sought or attained in imitation of the dignified, heavy, or grand <ridiculing follies with a *burlesque* as riotous as that in *The Innocents Abroad* —Carl Van Doren> <he whipped off his old slouch hat with an air of gallantry which reminded Dorinda of the *burlesque* of some royal cavalier —Ellen Glasgow> PARODY, like CARICATURE , involves the heightening of a peculiar feature and, like BURLESQUE, is likely to aim at humor. It may differ from the first in attempting less obvious and pictorial and more sustained and subtle imitation, from the second in aiming at a quieter, less boisterous effect <Dryden's method here is something very near to *parody;* he applies vocabulary, images, and ceremony which arouse epic associations of grandeur —T.S. Eliot> <played in the manner of a *parody,* an intention which . . . cannot possibly be recognized by any hearer who has not previously been warned of it —Eric Blom> TRAVESTY is perhaps the strongest word in the group. It may apply to any palpably extravagant imitation designed to mock and consistently sustained, esp. in stylistic matters <in producing *Androcles and the Lion* his motion picture executor has already managed to make a public *travesty* of his work —*New Republic*> All these terms may be used in reference to a situation that contains grotesque distortion <a *caricature* of the truth> <a *burlesque* on religious observations> <a *parody* of justice> <a *travesty* on decent marriage>

[2] **caricature** \ \ *vt* -ED -ING -S **:** to make or draw a caricature of **:** represent in caricature <he could draw an ill face or ≲ a good one —George Lyttelton>

**caricature plant** *n* [so called fr. the yellowish leaf blotches, often suggesting a human profile] **:** an East Indian ornamental foliage plant (*Graptophyllum pictum*) of the family Acanthaceae

**car·i·ca·tur·ist** \ |---| chú (e) rest *also* -| t(y)ú- \ *n* -s **:** one that makes caricatures

Word with syllable division
Part of speech
Definitions
Synonyms
Variations in form
Word as another part of speech
Pronunciation
Derivation
Example of use
Distinctions among synonyms

There are two kinds of dictionaries: general and special. General dictionaries are broad in their coverage; special dictionaries concentrate on a single subject or specific function. Dictionaries also vary in the *depth* of their coverage. An unabridged dictionary is comprehensive, containing no omissions or reductions. An abridged dictionary gives less complete information and is narrower in scope than an unabridged dictionary.

*Webster's Third New International Dictionary of the English Language, Unabridged*, and *Webster's New International Dictionary of the English Language*, 2nd edition, are the accepted general unabridged dictionaries of the English language. *The Oxford English Dictionary* (12 volumes), commonly called *OED*, is the most authoritative, scholarly, and complete English dictionary. It traces and explains the historical development and meaning of all English words in use between 1150 and 1933.

Abridged general dictionaries, also known as desk dictionaries, include only commonly used words. Since they are much smaller, abridged dictionaries are revised frequently, and they are, therefore, a good source for information on new words. Listed below are some of the better known desk dictionaries:

*The American Heritage Dictionary of the English Language*
*Random House College Dictionary*
*Webster's Ninth New Collegiate Dictionary*
*Webster's New World Dictionary of the American Language*

Special dictionaries are selective by subject or function. Subject dictionaries cover words associated with a particular subject, as you can see from the following examples:

*The American Political Dictionary*
*Black's Law Dictionary*
*Harvard Dictionary of Music*
*McGraw-Hill Dictionary of Scientific and Technical terms*
*Webster's Sports Dictionary*

Other specialized dictionaries are known by the function they perform. They cover a particular aspect of a word or group of words, such as usage, etymology, synonyms or related words, pronunciation, slang, and abbreviations. Below are some examples:

*Acronyms and Initialism Dictionary:* Abbreviations
*A Dictionary of Slang and Unconventional English:* Slang
*Roget's International Thesaurus:* Synonyms

## Step Three: Use the Card Catalog or the Computer Catalog System

The card catalog in your library—or its computerized equivalent—contains a systematic list of the books on the shelves. Many card catalogs also list magazines and other periodicals, newspapers, and, sometimes, maps, pictures, and other "nonbook" items.

Libraries use either the Library of Congress or the Dewey Decimal system of classification. If you know which system your library uses, you can quickly learn the overall scheme by which its materials have been organized and shelved.

*Library of Congress*

| | | | |
|---|---|---|---|
| *A* | General Works | *L* | Education |
| *B* | Philosophy-Religion | *M* | Music |
| *C* | History | *N* | Fine Arts |
| *D* | World History | *P* | Languages and Literature |
| *E* | U.S. History | *Q* | Science |
| *F* | Local History | *R* | Medicine |
| *G* | Geography, Anthropology | *S* | Agriculture |
| *H* | Social Sciences | *T* | Technology |
| *J* | Political Science | *U* | Military Science |
| *K* | Law | *V* | Naval Science |
| | | *Z* | Library Science, Bibliography |

*Dewey Decimal*

| | |
|---|---|
| 000–099 | General Works (bibliographies, encyclopedias, periodicals) |
| 100–199 | Philosophy, Psychology, Ethics |
| 200–299 | Religion and Mythology |
| 300–399 | Sociology (civics, economics, education, vocations) |
| 400–499 | Philology (dictionaries, grammar, language) |
| 500–599 | Science (biology, botany, chemistry, mathematics, physics, zoology) |
| 600–699 | Useful Arts (agriculture, aviation, engineering, medicine, radio) |
| 700–799 | Fine Arts (music, painting, photography, recreation) |
| 800–899 | Literature (criticism, novels, plays, poetry) |
| 900–999 | History, Geography, Biography, Travel |

Locating material by subject is a little trickier. The *Library of Congress Subject Headings* (*LCSH*) books, usually shelved near the card catalog, are the key to searching by subject in libraries that use the LC classification system. These books help you to identify both the correct subject heading and related headings for your topic. Suppose your topic is communication among animals. The card catalog has nothing under that subject heading, but when you consult *LCSH*, you discover that the subject heading used in the card catalog is *Animal communication*.

**LCSH LISTING Subject headings used in the card catalog are in boldface type. The *xx* and *sa* notations indicate related headings, ones that are similar but not identical, whereas *x* indicates terms that are not used in the card catalog.**

**Animal coloration**
*See* Color of animals
**Animal communication**
*sa* Animal sounds
Human-animal communication
Sound production by animals
*x* Animal language
Communication among animals
Language learning by animals
**Animal communication with humans**
*See* Human-animal communication
**Animal courtship**
*See* Courtship of animals
**Animal culture *(Indirect) (SF)***
*sa* Deer culture
Domestic animals
Fish-culture
Fur farming
Game bird culture
Laboratory animals
Livestock
Pets
Poultry
Radioactive tracers in animal culture
Small animal culture
*x* Animal husbandry
*xx* Animals

The first section of the *LCSH* books explains how to use them.

*Reading the information on a catalog card* Each catalog card tells a good deal about a work and its contents. Perhaps the most important information for you is the call number. Think of the call number as an address that will help you to locate material in the library. *Be sure to copy the complete call number of each item you find on your topic.*

If you were to look up in the card catalog the subject heading *Animal communication*, you would find cards like the subject-heading card shown on the next page. The card shown after the subject-heading card is the author card for the same book.

*Tracings* The author card shows an important feature of catalog cards: They list related subject headings—tracings—in the catalog. Tracings are usually given on the main entry card, which is almost always the author card.

**SUBJECT-HEADING CARD**

```
              ANIMAL COMMUNICATION.

QL 568        Lindauer, Martin
A6 L5           Communication among social bees.
1971          Cambridge, Harvard University Press
              [1971]
                x, 161 p. illus.    22 cm.   (Harvard
              books in biology, no. 2)
                Bibliography:  p. 151-156.


OU     72-3 que ns                 OSUde     75-30141
```

**AUTHOR LISTING**

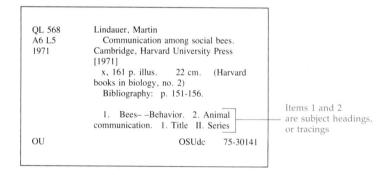

```
QL 568        Lindauer, Martin
A6 L5           Communication among social bees.
1971          Cambridge, Harvard University Press
              [1971]
                x, 161 p. illus.    22 cm.   (Harvard
              books in biology, no. 2)
                Bibliography:  p. 151-156.

                1.  Bees- -Behavior.  2. Animal
              communication.  I. Title  II. Series

OU                                 OSUdc     75-30141
```

Items 1 and 2 are subject headings, or tracings

*Searching the computer catalog* Many libraries now use computer systems to keep track of their holdings and to store information traditionally recorded on cards. Sometimes the entire card catalog is available on computer. In other cases the computer system may include all materials acquired after a certain date, thus requiring that you use the card catalog to find older materials and the computer system to find newer materials or older books recently added to the collection.

Because there are many different computer systems for keeping track of library collections, you will need to learn the particular system used in your library. Check for directions, usually very clear and easy to follow, near the terminals. If you have problems or need special advice, ask the librarian supervising that area. You might also watch for a library orientation session, designed specifically to help you become a more efficient researcher.

Whatever your library's system, you generally can hunt for a book by author, title, or subject. Sometimes a subject search will begin with one key term (such as *stress* or *college adjustment*). Other systems allow quite sophisticated searches using several key words at once to limit the search further (such as *nutrition*, *college students*, and *vitamin deficiencies* together). Of course, the more precise your key words and the more sophisticated the system, the more focused your search will be. Once the computer locates entries for you, write them down or print them, selecting all entries or those that seem most useful. If you request a printout, it will include much or all of what a catalog card does—particularly author, title, publication information, and call number.

Large research libraries often belong to groups that consolidate their members' separate data bases. For example, the OCLC (On-line Computer Library Center) Online Union Catalog consolidates millions of entries from more than 2,700 member libraries. Each entry notes library locations, and materials are available through interlibrary loan. Borrowing such materials is unnecessary and too time-consuming for most undergraduate papers but may be useful for a senior thesis or a major long-term project.

## ► Step Four: Use Printed Indexes or Computer Databases for Journals and Newspapers

*Searching print indexes* To find specific articles on your topic, examine journal and newspaper indexes. Journals (also called periodicals or magazines) and newspapers usually provide the most current information on a topic. Newspapers are especially valuable for public reactions or attitudes toward an issue or event at the time of its occurrence and are, therefore, primary sources for historical research.

Indexes are comprehensive catalogs of articles, essays, reports, and other information not published as books. Like encyclopedias and dictionaries, indexes can be categorized as general or special. A general index helps you find popular or general information on almost any topic. A special index provides information in a particular subject area, such as education, business, science, and so on. You will be able to find a specialized index for every academic discipline. In addition, many of the world's major newspapers, such as *The New York Times*, *The Wall Street Journal*, and *The Christian Science Monitor*, have their own indexes.

Most indexes list articles alphabetically by subject, but a few also index by author and by title. Many of the entries are abbreviated to save space, and most indexes contain keys to their abbreviations in the front of the book. Listed on the opposite page are examples of general and specialized journal indexes.

When you begin your search for current information, you may want to ask a reference librarian which indexes best cover the subject you're gathering information on. The right specialized index may be just what you need. Or you may want to combine both popular and more scholarly sources. You may also want to turn to a specialized index that abstracts or briefly summarizes each article listed, thus saving you time you might waste tracking down un-

***General Journal and Newspaper Indexes***

*Reader's Guide to Periodical Literature*: Indexes articles from general and popular journals; author, subject and fiction title index; 1915 to present

*The New York Times Index*: Indexes national and international news articles; primary source materials such as reports and speeches, and critical commentaries; 1851 to present

***Specialized Journal Indexes***

*Art Index*: Covers art and allied fields; subject index; 1929 to present

*Business Periodicals Index*: Covers business and industry; subject index including names of people and companies; 1958 to present

*The Education Index*: Covers elementary, secondary, and higher education; subject and author index; 1929 to present

*Humanities Index*: Covers language and literature, philosophy; author and subject index; 1974 to present (part of *Social Sciences and Humanities Index,* 1907–74)

*Social Sciences Index*: Covers history, psychology, political science; author and subject index; 1974 to present (part of *Social Sciences and Humanities Index*, 1907–74)

*Public Affairs Information Service Bulletin*: Indexes journals, books, reports and pamphlets on economics, social conditions, government; subject index; 1915 to present

related articles. The following examples illustrate how different types of indexes supply different kinds of information.

**Search for Information about Political Cartoons**

***Entries from* Reader's Guide to Periodical Literature**

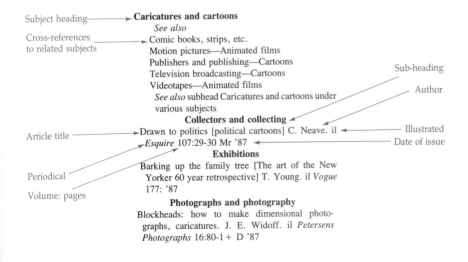

Subject heading → **Caricatures and cartoons**

*See also*

Cross-references to related subjects → Comic books, strips, etc.

Motion pictures—Animated films

Publishers and publishing—Cartoons

Television broadcasting—Cartoons

Videotapes—Animated films

*See also* subhead Caricatures and cartoons under various subjects

**Collectors and collecting** ← Sub-heading

Article title → Drawn to politics [political cartoons] C. Neave. il *Esquire* 107:29-30 Mr '87 (Author: C. Neave; Illustrated: il; Periodical: *Esquire*; Volume: pages: 107:29-30; Date of issue: Mr '87)

**Exhibitions**

Barking up the family tree [The art of the New Yorker 60 year retrospective] T. Young. il *Vogue* 177: '87

**Photographs and photography**

Blockheads: how to make dimensional photographs, caricatures. J. E. Widoff. il *Petersens Photographs* 16:80-1+ D '87

### *Entries from the more specialized* Humanities Index

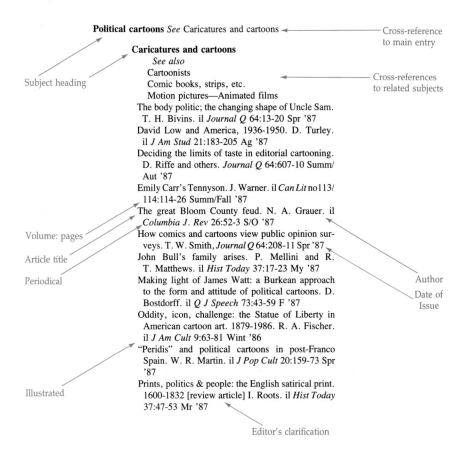

**Political cartoons** *See* Caricatures and cartoons

Cross-reference to main entry

Subject heading

**Caricatures and cartoons**
*See also*
Cartoonists
Comic books, strips, etc.
Motion pictures—Animated films

Cross-references to related subjects

The body politic; the changing shape of Uncle Sam. T. H. Bivins. il *Journal Q* 64:13-20 Spr '87

David Low and America, 1936-1950. D. Turley. il *J Am Stud* 21:183-205 Ag '87

Deciding the limits of taste in editorial cartooning. D. Riffe and others. *Journal Q* 64:607-10 Summ/Aut '87

Emily Carr's Tennyson. J. Warner. il *Can Lit* no113/114:114-26 Summ/Fall '87

The great Bloom County feud. N. A. Grauer. il *Columbia J. Rev* 26:52-3 S/O '87

How comics and cartoons view public opinion surveys. T. W. Smith, *Journal Q* 64:208-11 Spr '87

John Bull's family arises. P. Mellini and R. T. Matthews. il *Hist Today* 37:17-23 My '87

Making light of James Watt: a Burkean approach to the form and attitude of political cartoons. D. Bostdorff. il *Q J Speech* 73:43-59 F '87

Oddity, icon, challenge: the Statue of Liberty in American cartoon art. 1879-1986. R. A. Fischer. il *J Am Cult* 9:63-81 Wint '86

"Peridis" and political cartoons in post-Franco Spain. W. R. Martin. il *J Pop Cult* 20:159-73 Spr '87

Prints, politics & people: the English satirical print. 1600-1832 [review article] I. Roots. il *Hist Today* 37:47-53 Mr '87

Volume: pages

Article title

Periodical

Author

Date of Issue

Illustrated

Editor's clarification

### *Entries from* The New York Times Index 1986

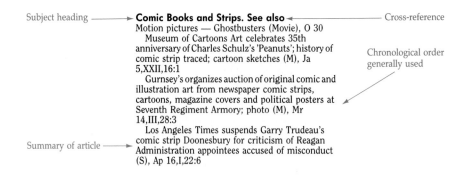

Subject heading

**Comic Books and Strips. See also**

Cross-reference

Motion pictures — Ghostbusters (Movie), O 30

Museum of Cartoons Art celebrates 35th anniversary of Charles Schulz's 'Peanuts'; history of comic strip traced; cartoon sketches (M), Ja 5,XXII,16:1

Gurnsey's organizes auction of original comic and illustration art from newspaper comic strips, cartoons, magazine covers and political posters at Seventh Regiment Armory; photo (M), Mr 14,III,28:3

Los Angeles Times suspends Garry Trudeau's comic strip Doonesbury for criticism of Reagan Administration appointees accused of misconduct (S), Ap 16,I,22:6

Chronological order generally used

Summary of article

## *Entries from* The New York Times Index 1986 (cont.)

DC Comics says it will soon present 'updated' and 'more vulnerable' version of famous comic strip character, Superman; drawing (M), Je 10,II,6:2

Editorial backs effort by DC Comics to modernize Superman/Clark Kent; suggests making him an editorial writer, Je 11,I,34:1

Op-Ed column by Rusell Baker on decision by DC Comics, publishers of Superman, to make Clark Kent a newspaper columnist; describes tips he offered Kent on becoming successful in new line of work (M), Je 17,I,27:5

Baseball card and comic book shows held every weekend at various Long Island locations draw enthusiastic young collectors; photo; several boys and their mothers comment on hobby (Our Towns column) (S) Jl 8,II,2:1

Vivien Raynor reviews exhibition at Museum of Cartoon Art, Rye Brook, NY, tracing history of Flash Gordon, Mandrake the Magician and Phantom comic strips (S), Ag 15,III,22:2

John L Byrne has been hired by DC Comics to revitalize Superman; The Man of Steel, six-issue mini-series in which Byrne retells legend of Superman, is paving way for new Superman comic strip; photo (M), O 12,XXIII,32:1

Al Smith, cartoonist who drew Mutt and Jeff comic strip for nearly 50 years, dies at age 84 (S), ← Length of article (short, medium, or long)

Date, section, page: column → N 26,II,6:6

## Search for Information about Students Adjusting to College

## *Entries from* Readers' Guide to Periodical Literature

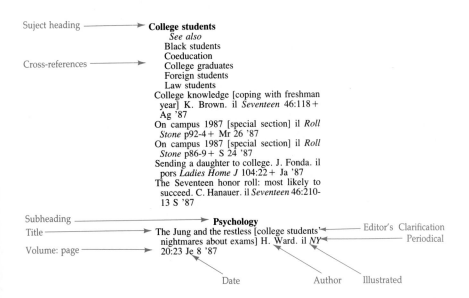

Suject heading → **College students**

*See also*

Black students

Coeducation

Cross-references → College graduates

Foreign students

Law students

College knowledge [coping with freshman year] K. Brown. il *Seventeen* 46:118+ Ag '87

On campus 1987 [special section] il *Roll Stone* p92-4+ Mr 26 '87

On campus 1987 [special section] il *Roll Stone* p86-9+ S 24 '87

Sending a daughter to college. J. Fonda. il pors *Ladies Home J* 104:22+ Ja '87

The Seventeen honor roll: most likely to succeed. C. Hanauer. il *Seventeen* 46:210-13 S '87

Subheading → **Psychology**

Title → The Jung and the restless [college students' ← Editor's Clarification

nightmares about exams] H. Ward. il *NY* ← Periodical

Volume: page → 20:23 Je 8 '87

Date — Author — Illustrated

### *Entries from the more specialized* Social Sciences Index

Labels: Subject heading; Cross-references; Subheading; Title; Bibliography included; Periodical; Authors; Volume: pages; Date of issue

**College students**
*See also*
Graduate students
Premedical students
Women college students

**Adjustment**

Family dynamics and presenting problems in college students. J. A. Hoffman and B. Weiss. bibl *J Couns Psychol* 34:157-63 Ap '87

Life tasks, self-concept ideals, and cognitive strategies in a life transition. N. Cantor and others. bibl *J Pers Soc Psychol* 53:1178-91 D '87

The stress of the transition to university: a longitudinal study of psychological disturbance, absent-mindedness and vulnerability to homesickness. S. Fisher and B. Hood. bibl *Br J Psychol* 78:425-41 N '87

**Psychology**

Affective, cognitive, and behavioral differences between high and low procrastinators. E. D. Rothblum and others. bibl *J Couns Psychol* 33:387-94 O '86

Alcoholic beverage preference as a public statement: self-concept and social image of college drinkers. J. R. Snortum and others. bibl *J Stud Alcohol* 48:243-51 My '87

Attributions and expectations: a confluence of vulnerabilities in mild depression in a college student population. J. H. Riskind and others. *J Pers Soc Psychol* 53:349-54 Ag '87

Body-image distortion and dissatisfaction in university students. H. M. Mable and others. bibl *Percept Mot Skills* 63:907-11 O '86 pt2

Causes of depression in college students: a cross-lagged panel correlational analysis. A. R. Rich and M. Scovel. bibl *Psychol Rep* 60:27-30 F '87

Concurrent validity of a stress-vulnerability model of suicidal ideation and behavior: a follow-up study. A. R. Rich and R. L. Bonner. bibl *Suicide Life-Treat Behav* 17:265-70 Wint '87

Contributions of family to men's fear of success in college. J. Balkin. bibl *Psychol Rep* 59:1071-4 D '86

Effects of cognitive information on college students' self-concept. C. A. Weinmann

**College students—**Psychology—*cont.*

*and J. M. Sifft. bibl Percept Mot Skills* 64:1159-62 Je '87 pt2

The extent and function of parental attachment among first-year college students. M. E. Kenny. bibl *J Youth Adolesc* 16:17-29 F '87

Eye-hand dominance and college major. C. J. Fry. *Precept Mot Skills* 62:918 Je '86

Facilitating growth in a personal development course. M. E. Ware and N. W. Perry. bibl *Psychol Rep* 60:491-500 Ap '87

Motivations for parenthood among young adult college students. A. V. Gormly and others. bibl *Sex Roles* 16:31-9 Ja '87

Nocturnal bruxism and Type A-B behavior in college students. R. A. Hicks and C. Chancellor. bibl *Psychol Rep* 60:1211-14 Je '87 pt2

Personal epistemology and personal experience. R. K. Unger and others. bibl *J Soc Issues* 42:67-79 Summ '86

Psychological effects on college students of raising the drinking age. J. Newman. bibl *Adolescence* 22:503-10 Fall '87

Relation between intuition and college majors. B. Fallik and J. Eliot. *Percept Mot Skills* 63:328 Ag '86

Rorschach correlates of state and trait anxiety in college students. J. D. Martin and others. bibl *Percept Mot Skills* 64:539-43 Ap '87

Sex differences in depression among selected young adults. R.J. McDermott. *Psychol Rep* 60:965-6 Je '87 pt1

Temporal personality variations among participants from a university subject pool. R. R. Holden and J. R. Reddon. bibl *Psychol Rep* 60:1247-54 Je '87 pt2

Temporality and gender: young adults' career and family plans. D. R. Maines and M. J. Hardesty. bibl *Soc Forces* 66:102-20 S '87

Toward a predictive mode of suicidal ideation and behavior: some preliminary data in college students. R. L. Bonner and A. R. Rich. bibl *Suicide Life-Threat Behav* 17:50-63 Spr '87

Type A-B status, habitual sleep duration, and perceived level of daily life stress of college students. R. A. Hicks and others. *Percept Mot Skills* 63:793-A O '86 pt2

## *Entry from* Psychological Abstracts

Authors

Entry number → 37307. **Fisher, Shirley & Hood, Bruce** (U Dundee, Scotland) **The stress of the transition to university: A longitudinal study of psychological disturbance, absent-mindedness and vulnerability to homesickness.** *British Journal of Psychology*, 1987 (Nov), Vol 78(4), 425-441. —Examined the effects of the transition to university in 66 residential and 34 home-based students. All Ss showed evidence of raised psychological disturbance and absentmindedness following the transition. Although there were no differences between resident and home-based Ss in this respect, those who reported homesickness were distinguished from the remainder in terms of higher levels of psychological disturbance and cognitive failure following the transition to university. The gain in psychological disturbance following was greater for the homesick group. The effects of stressful transitions on the psychological state and the concept of personal vulnerability are discussed.

Title

Periodical

Volume (issue), pages

Date

Abstract or summary

## *Entry from* The New York Times Index 1986

Chronological order generally

**Colleges and Universities — Cont**

Subject heading

Fred M. Hechinger comments on today's college students, and question of whether they differ from students 15 year ago; discusses highlights of study of more than 400 randomly chosen Stanford University students; study found that students fell into four general categories: careerists, intellectuals, strivers and the unconnected (M), F 4,III,1:1

Summary of article

New Jersey Gov. Kean says State Board of Higher Education should work with two-year colleges and recommended possible improvement, claiming some county colleges are not living up to their potential (M), F 11, II,2:6

Date, section page: column

Pakistani police fire tear gas at rioting right-wing students who set six buses ablaze and damage 16 others in Karachi; protest is against Government inaction in curbing lawlessness in colleges after death of student in January (S), F 13.1.12:6

Robert M. Gates, Central Intelligence Agency official, says agency has relaxed rules that barred professors from publicly acknowledging CIA's support for their research; says such arrangements could still be kept secret by scholar involved or by agency if CIA decided its formal association with topic would damage United Estates (M), F 14,I,20:1

Length of article (short, medium or long)

Here are a few hints that will help save time when searching indexes.

***How to Search Indexes***

1. Use the most precise language or terms you can think of for your topic. Unlike the card catalog, where the *LCSH* provides standardization, each index has its own subject headings and key terms, which make up the "language" of the index. Try to determine each index's language as you look through it.
2. If you don't find your topic under a specific heading, use a *broader* or *similar* term.
3. Follow the *see* and *see also* references to the correct heading or to similar headings.

*Searching computer indexes* Major periodical indexes are available in many libraries through two types of computer searches—on-line and Compact Disk and Read Only Memory (CD-ROM). Check with your library to find out what services are available and how to use them. Some computer searches must be conducted by trained staff, while others are easy for most students to carry out following the directions on a user-friendly menu.

On-line computer searches of hundreds of databases are available to libraries or to individuals who have home computers with modems. You or your library, if the service is free to students, pays a fee that varies with the database selected, generally based on the computer time used or the number of references printed. Some services offer special rates at night or during nonbusiness hours. Because an on-line search gains access to a database in its most current form, your information will reflect the latest available entries. Conducting a productive on-line search, however, may require considerable skill or even special training. Aside from learning how to use the system, you must define your search terms very carefully or risk generating—and paying for—a useless list of hundreds of items about an overly broad topic.

In contrast to an on-line search, a CD-ROM search uses a disk for which a library pays a set fee but no time or item charges. Thus, there is no need for the library to restrict you from experimenting with search terms or browsing through entries. Because a CD-ROM search usually does not require the time of a trained librarian, many libraries have acquired this technology for especially popular indexes such as the *Reader's Guide to Periodical Literature*, the *Humanities Index*, and the *Social Sciences Index*.

CD-ROMs contain fixed, but vast, amounts of data, often updated quarterly. They use simple commands and have help screens generally designed for easy use by library patrons. A CD-ROM search of the past several years of a major index might be as simple as typing in one key term, perhaps moving the cursor up or down to examine related terms, pressing a key to request the list of entries, and pressing the same key to review each entry in turn. Once you have located useful references, you can print out the entries either by requesting the entire list or by choosing what you want item by item. You may also be able to move directly from the CD-ROM to an on-line search of recent additions to the index and print these as well.

Both types of computer systems are widely available in academic libraries, and both can save you hours of work going through printed indexes. Because library technology is changing rapidly, check to see what systems are available at your library and how to use them. These computer searches, however, do have limitations. Your computer search will supply only what you request. It requires that you identify key terms thoughtfully and creatively, spell names correctly in a format the program recognizes, and so forth. Furthermore, your search can supply only what the database has stored. For example, if you are researching work spanning the last ten years and the database you are using is a five-year index, you will need to use printed volumes as well to search through the first five years.

**Sample CD-ROM Index Searches**

***Entries from* Readers' Guide to Periodical Literature**
*Search Term: College students/Psychology*

```
2 RDG
Taulbee, Pamela
Study shows stress decreases immunity (antibody
levels in saliva of college students; research by
John B. Jemmott III
and others)
Science News 124: 7 Jl 2 '83

SUBJECTS COVERED:
Stress
Antigens and antibodies
Saliva
College students/Psychology
Psychoneuroimmunology

3 RDG
Ward, Helen
The Jung and the restless (college students'
nightmares about exams)
New York 20: 23 Je 8 '87

SUBJECTS COVERED:
Nightmares
Examinations
College students/Psychology

6 RDG
Korelitz, Jean Hanff
Going-off-to-college jitters
Seventeen 43; 272 Ag '84

SUBJECT COVERED:
Anxiety
College students/Psychology
```

Annotations on the "3 RDG" entry:

- Index abbreviation → "RDG"
- Item in list called up → "3"
- Author → Ward, Helen
- Title → The Jung and the restless
- Editor's clarification → (college students' nightmares about exams)
- Periodical → New York
- Volume: page → 20: 23
- Date of issue → Je 8 '87
- Subject classifications for article → Nightmares / Examinations / College students/Psychology

## Sample CD-ROM Index Searches

### *Entries from* Social Sciences Index

*Search Term: College students/adjustment*

Item in list called up
Index abbreviation

```
4 SSI
Fisher, Shirley Hood, Bruce
The stress of the transition to university: a
longitudinal study of psychological disturbance,
absent-mindedness and vulnerability to
homesickness
The British Journal of Psychology 78: 425-41 N '87

SUBJECTS COVERED:
College students/Adjustment
Loneliness
Stress (Psychology)
Memory
```

Authors
Title
Date
Volume: pages
Periodical
Subject classifications for article

```
10 SSI
Schultz, Norman R. Moore, DeWayne
The loneliness experience of college students:
sex differences
Personality and Social Psychology Bulletin 12:
111-19 Mr '86

SUBJECTS COVERED:
College students/Adjustment
Loneliness
Sex (Psychology)


15 SSI
Marron, Jeanne A. Kayson, Wesley A.
Effects of living status, gender, and year in college
on college students' self-esteem and life-change
experiences
Psychological Reports 55: 811-14 D '84

SUBJECTS COVERED:
Self esteem
Sex (Psychology)
Life cycle
College students/Adjustment


18 SSI
Baker, Robert W. McNeil, Ogertta V. Siryk, Bohdan
Expectations and reality in freshman adjustment
to college
Journal of Counseling Psychology 32: 94-103 Ja '85

SUBJECTS COVERED:
College students/Adjustment
Expectation (Psychology)
```

## Sample CD-ROM Index Searches

***Entries from* Social Sciences Index**

***Search Term: College students/adjustment***

***On-line search for most current entries***

```
1 (SOCIAL SCIENCES INDEX)
Fisher, Shirley; Hood, Bruce
Vulnerability factors in the transition to
university: self-reported mobility history and sex
differences as factors in psychological disturbance
The British Journal of Psychology 79:309-20 Ag '88

Subjects covered
________________

College students/Adjustment
Loneliness
Sex (Psychology)
```

***CD-ROM Search Narrowed by Multiple Search Terms***

***Search Terms: College students; Psychology; Stress***

```
  1 SSI
  Fisher, Shirley Hood Bruce
  The stress of the transition to university: a
  longitudinal study of psychological disturbance,
  absent-mindedness and vulnerability to homesickness
  The British Journal of Psychology 78: 425-41 N '87

  SUBJECTS COVERED:
* College students/Adjustment
  Loneliness
* Stress (Psychology)
  Memory

  2 SSI
  Goodman, Sherryl Hope Sewell, Daniel R. Jampol, Ruth C.
  On going to the counselor: contributions of life stress
  and social supports to the decision to seek
  psychological counseling

  Journal of Counseling Psychology 31: 306-13 Jl '84

  SUBJECTS COVERED:
* Stress (Psychology)
  Help seeking
  Life cycle
* College students/Adjustment
  Social networks
```

## Step Five: Locate Essay Collections

Your next step is to look for essays, articles, and symposiums that are published in collections and are, therefore, more difficult to find. *The Essay and General Literature Index* (1900 to present) is a valuable source for locating these materials and is especially useful for criticism and biographical information.

**Entries from the *Essay and General Literature Index***

Subject heading → **Stress (Psychology)**
*See also* Life change events ← Cross-reference
Authors → Brown, G. W., and Harris, T. Establishing ← Essay title
casual links: the Bedford College studies of depression. (*In* Life events and psychiatric disor- ← Collection title
ders: controversial issues; ed. by H. Katschnig ← Editor
Pages → p107-87)
Katschnig, H. Measuring life stress—a comparison of the checklist and the panel technique. (*In* Life events and psychiatric disorders: controversial issues; ed. by H. Katschnig p74-106)
Katschnig, H. Prospects for the future. (*In* Life events and psychiatric disorders: controversial issues; ed. H. Katschnig p246-54)
Katschnig, H.; Pakesch, G., and Egger-Zeidner, E. Life stress and depressive sub-types: a review of present diagnostic criteria and recent research results. (*In* Life events and psychiatric disorders: controversial issues; ed. H. Katschnig p201-45)
**Stressful events** *See* Life change events

**Entry for collection**

Collection title → **Life events and psychiatric disorders;** controversial issues; edited by Heinz Katschnig. Cam- ← Editor
Publication information → bridge Univ. Press 1986 265p ISBN 0-521-
25596-1 LC 85-19000

## Step Six: Consult Biographical Sources

The next step is to search biographical sources for information on the education, accomplishments, and professional activities of individuals involved in your topic. These sources also help you to evaluate the credentials and reputations of the authors whose works you are examining.

To select the most appropriate biographical source, ask yourself the following specific questions and then select the index that seems appropriate.

1. Is the person living (current source) or dead (retrospective source)?
2. What is the person's nationality or place of birth?
3. What is the person's occupation or profession?

Some of the most useful indexes are listed below. Note that most of them refer to citations in books; in addition to books, *Biography Index* indexes other kinds of materials and is therefore an especially useful source.

*Biography Index*: International, retrospective and current, all occupations; indexes sources of biographical materials in books, periodicals, letters, diaries, genealogies, obituaries; 1947 to present

*Biographical Dictionaries Master Index*: Emphasis on living Americans; all occupations; indexes more than 725,000 listings in over 50 current *Who's Who* and other indexes

*Dictionary of American Biography*: Notable Americans; retrospective, all occupations; scholarly; bibliographies

*Dictionary of National Biography*: British; spans earliest historical period to the present; all occupations; scholarly; bibliographies

*Author Biographies Master Index*: Index to biographical dictionaries; international; retrospective and current

*European Authors, 1000–1900*: Brief bibliographies

*British Authors before 1800: A Biographical Dictionary*: Bibliographies of works by and about the authors; portraits

*American Authors 1600–1900: A Biographical Dictionary of American Literature*: Brief bibliographies of writings by and about the authors

*Contemporary Authors*: Long bibliographies; current and retrospective; 1962 to present

*World Authors, 1950–1970*: Long biographies; current and retrospective

*Directory of American Scholars*: U.S. and Canadian college professors and researchers; current

*American Men and Women of Science*: International; current

**Entry from *Biography Index***

Date of birth

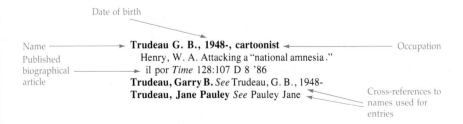

Name → **Trudeau G. B., 1948-, cartoonist** ← Occupation

Published biographical article → Henry, W. A. Attacking a "national amnesia." il por *Time* 128:107 D 8 '86

**Trudeau, Garry B.** *See* Trudeau, G. B., 1948-

**Trudeau, Jane Pauley** *See* Pauley Jane

Cross-references to names used for entries

**Entry from *Who's Who in America***

Business or job

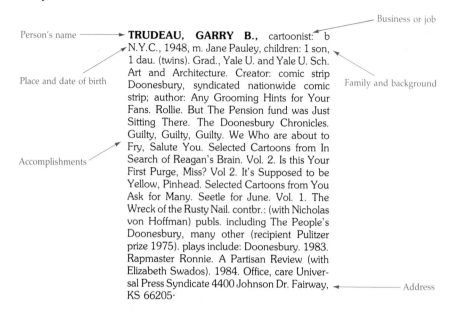

Person's name → **TRUDEAU, GARRY B.,** cartoonist: b N.Y.C., 1948, m. Jane Pauley, children: 1 son, 1 dau. (twins). Grad., Yale U. and Yale U. Sch. Art and Architecture. Creator: comic strip Doonesbury, syndicated nationwide comic strip; author: Any Grooming Hints for Your Fans. Rollie. But The Pension fund was Just Sitting There. The Doonesbury Chronicles. Guilty, Guilty, Guilty. We Who are about to Fry, Salute You. Selected Cartoons from In Search of Reagan's Brain. Vol. 2. Is this Your First Purge, Miss? Vol 2. It's Supposed to be Yellow, Pinhead. Selected Cartoons from You Ask for Many. Seetle for June. Vol. 1. The Wreck of the Rusty Nail. contbr.: (with Nicholas von Hoffman) publs. including The People's Doonesbury, many other (recipient Pulitzer prize 1975). plays include: Doonesbury. 1983. Rapmaster Ronnie. A Partisan Review (with Elizabeth Swados). 1984. Office, care Universal Press Syndicate 4400 Johnson Dr. Fairway, KS 66205·

Place and date of birth

Family and background

Accomplishments

Address

## ► Step Seven: Consult Book Reviews

Book review indexes are a vital step in your search strategy. Book reviews help you to evaluate and criticize a book and to summarize its contents. Some of the most useful book review indexes are listed below.

*Book Review Digest*: Covers reviews in popular magazines; excerpts of three or four reviews for each title; 1905 to present

*Book Review Index*: Covers humanities, social sciences, fiction, literature, and general nonfiction; citations only; 1965 to present

*Current Book Review Citations*: Fiction and nonfiction; foreign language, new editions, etc.; indexes large number of periodicals; 1976 to present

*Index to Book Reviews in the Humanities*: Covers art, drama, literature, adventure, etc.; 1960 to present

Assume that your search strategy to date has yielded several book titles that might provide useful information for your paper. Since you may not have time to read each book in its entirety, read the reviews for some idea of each book's content and quality. This process will allow you to eliminate some of the books and focus on those that seem most promising.

## Entry from *Book Review Digest*

Title

Dewey Decimal System call number

Author

**BOYER, ERNEST L.** College; the undergraduate experience in America 328p $19.95 1987 Harper & Row 378.73 1. colleges and universities—United States 2. College students ISBN 0-06-015507-8 LC 85-45182

Publication information

Subject heading for classifying book

Excerpt from book review

This work considers "strengths and suggests improvements in the undergraduate experience. . . .[It] was constructed after on-site interviews at 29 colleges and universities. Additional information was garnered from . . . questionnaires sent to faculty, chief academic officers, and undergraduates. . . . [Topics include] recruitment, curriculum, library, dormitory life, placement service, [and] campus food." (Libr J) Index

---

"[This] may be the best book to read for the student preparing to get the most out of his or her undergraduate experience. The student familiar with the range of issues raised in this book—from student housing to the artificial fragmentation of knowledge in college departments—will be better prepared to maneuver once in school. . . . The main lack this reviewer found was in Boyer's integrated core curriculum, with its paltry handling of math and science, especially physics. In a century characterized by the atom bomb and a split between science and faith, a much deeper look at the origins and principles of scientific thinking is needed—especially as that thinking relates to the liberal arts."

Source for review

*Christ Sci Monit* p23 F 23 '87. Robert Marquand (900w)

Approximate length (in words)

"A former federal commissioner of education, who now heads the Carnegie Foundation for the Advancement of Teaching, Mr. Boyer is as well informed as anyone in the education field. He provides an adequate *tour d'horizon,* but little of the discriminating intelligence that he undoubtedly possesses. He has a list of recommendations to deal with each shortcoming, large or small. Many are commonsensical, and if adopted, might result in improvements. Yet Mr. Boyer's own vision—that college, with all its faults and tensions, ought to be a model for society at large—is far from convincing."
*Economist* 303:94 My 16 '87 (450w)

"The book is replete with concrete, sometimes provocative, suggestions. Only in his examinations of campus governance and how to assess student outcomes does Boyer fall back on generalities. Sure to inspire a serious look at higher education, this landmark study belongs in the collections of all academic and large public libraries."
*Libr J* 112:73 Ap 15 '87. Patricia Smith Butcher (150w)

"There is much that is of good counsel in Mr. Boyer's report. But it is . . . a curious, contradictory and very American blend of pessimistic analysis and unsinkable optimism about the value and the possibilities of education. The American dream continues to conjure up college education as one of its key components, but with much uncertainty as to what it expects this education to accomplish. Mr. Boyer's conclusion, that the American college is 'ready for renewal,' perpetuates the ambiguities: Ready, because it needs renewal? Ready, because it's primed for renewal? One can hope that the Boyer report will be widely read, and that its diagnoses will lead to more than the remedies it proposes, perhaps even to a renewal of that discredited discipline, the philosophy of education."
*N Y Times Book Rev* p26 Mr 8 '87. Peter Brooks (1700w)

## ► Step Eight: Consider Statistical Sources

Facts and statistics can often provide credibility for your research. They reinforce the ideas you are developing. When intelligently used, they help you formulate convincing arguments.

Almanacs are published *annually* and record many kinds of facts and statistics. For this reason, almanacs are usually referred to as *books of facts*. They contain not only current and historic statistics, but all kinds of facts about government, the economy, business, sports, the arts, current events, and many institutions in our society. Listed below are two of the most important general almanacs:

*World Almanac and Book of Facts:* American; 1968 to present
*Whitaker's Almanac:* British and European; 1869 to present

Specialized statistical sources, usually published by government organizations such as the U.S. Bureau of the Census, limit themselves to publishing statistics alone. Below are two of the most useful specialized statistical sources:

*Statistical Abstract of the United States*: Covers politics, society, economics, industry, education, law, geography, and science; 1879 to present

*Statistical Yearbook: Annuaire Statistique*: Presents statistical tables about every country in the world; covers such topics as population, agriculture, mining, manufacturing, finance, trade, education, culture, housing, and social statistics; published by the United Nations

**Information from *Statistical Abstract of the United States: 1988***

## TABLE OF CONTENTS

142 Education

Table number and topic

No. **237.** College Freshmen—Summary Characteristics: 1966 to 1986

[In percent. As of fall for first-time, full-time freshmen. Based on sample survey and subject to sampling error; see source]

| CHARACTERISTIC | 1966 | 1970 | 1975 | 1980 | 1981 | 1982 | 1983 | 1984 | 1985 | 1986 |
|---|---|---|---|---|---|---|---|---|---|---|
| **Sex:** Male | 57 | 55 | 53 | 49 | 49 | 49 | 49 | 48 | 48 | 48 |
| Female | 43 | 45 | 47 | 51 | 51 | 51 | 51 | 52 | 52 | 52 |
| **Average grade in high school:** | | | | | | | | | | |
| A – to A + | 15 | 16 | 18 | 21 | 21 | 21 | 20 | 20 | 21 | 23 |
| B – to B + | 54 | 58 | 60 | 60 | 60 | 60 | 59 | 58 | 59 | 56 |
| C to C+ | 30 | 27 | 21 | 19 | 19 | 19 | 21 | 21 | 20 | 20 |
| D | 1 | 1 | 1 | 1 | 1 | 1 | 1 | 1 | 1 | 1 |
| **Political orientation:** | | | | | | | | | | |
| Liberal | (NA) | 34 | 29 | 20 | 18 | 19 | 19 | 20 | 21 | 22 |
| Middle of the road | (NA) | 45 | 54 | 60 | 60 | 60 | 60 | 58 | 57 | 56 |
| Conservative | (NA) | 17 | 15 | 17 | 20 | 18 | 18 | 19 | 19 | 19 |
| **Probable field of study:** | | | | | | | | | | |
| Arts and humanities | 17 | 16 | 11 | 9 | 7 | 8 | 8 | 8 | 8 | 9 |
| Biological sciences | 4 | 4 | 6 | 4 | 4 | 4 | 4 | 4 | 4 | 4 |
| Business | 14 | 16 | 19 | 24 | 24 | 24 | 24 | 26 | 27 | 26 |
| Education | 11 | 11 | 10 | 7 | 7 | 5 | 6 | 7 | 7 | 8 |
| Engineering | 10 | 9 | 8 | 12 | 12 | 12 | 12 | 11 | 11 | 11 |
| Social science | 15 | 14 | 10 | 7 | 6 | 6 | 6 | 7 | 8 | 8 |
| Physical science | 15 | 14 | 10 | 7 | 6 | 6 | 6 | 7 | 8 | 8 |
| Professional | (NA) | (NA) | (NA) | 15 | 13 | 13 | 14 | 14 | 13 | 12 |
| Technical | 2 | 4 | 9 | 6 | 6 | 7 | 7 | 5 | 5 | 4 |
| Data processing/computer programming | (NA) | (NA) | (NA) | 2 | 3 | 4 | 4 | 2 | 2 | 2 |
| Other[1] | (NA) | (NA) | (NA) | (NA) | 14 | 16 | 16 | 16 | 16 | 15 |
| Communications | (NA) | (NA) | (NA) | 2 | 2 | 2 | 2 | 2 | 2 | 2 |
| Computer science | (NA) | (NA) | (NA) | 1 | 1 | 2 | 5 | 3 | 2 | 2 |
| **Recipient of financial aid:** | | | | | | | | | | |
| Pell grant | (NA) | (NA) | 27 | 33 | 26 | 23 | 26 | 20 | 19 | 17 |
| Supplemental educational opportunity grant | (NA) | (NA) | 6 | 8 | 6 | 6 | 7 | 6 | 5 | 5 |
| State scholarship or grant | (NA) | (NA) | 19 | 16 | 14 | 15 | 16 | 14 | 14 | 14 |
| College grant | (NA) | (NA) | [2]9 | 13 | 11 | 12 | 13 | 17 | 19 | 18 |
| Federal guaranteed student loan | (NA) | (NA) | 10 | 21 | 17 | 11 | 15 | 23 | 23 | 25 |
| National direct student loan | (NA) | (NA) | 10 | 9 | 8 | 6 | 5 | 6 | 6 | 7 |
| College loan | (NA) | (NA) | [2]3 | 4 | 4 | 4 | 4 | 4 | 4 | 4 |
| College work-study grant | (NA) | (NA) | 12 | 15 | 12 | 12 | 14 | 9 | 10 | 10 |
| **Essential or important objectives:** | | | | | | | | | | |
| Be very well-off financially | 44 | 39 | 50 | 63 | 65 | 69 | 69 | 71 | 71 | 73 |
| Develop meaningful philosophy of life | (NA) | 76 | 64 | 50 | 49 | 47 | 44 | 45 | 43 | 41 |
| Help others who are in difficulty | 69 | 65 | 66 | 65 | 63 | 62 | 62 | 62 | 63 | 57 |
| Become involved in programs to clean environment | (NA) | [3]43 | 29 | 27 | 25 | 23 | 21 | 21 | 20 | 16 |
| **Attitudes—agree or strongly agree:** | | | | | | | | | | |
| Activities of married women are best confined to home and family | (NA) | 48 | 28 | 27 | 27 | 26 | 25 | 23 | 22 | 20 |
| Capital punishment should be abolished | (NA) | 56 | (NA) | 34 | 30 | 28 | 29 | 26 | 27 | 26 |
| Legalize marijuana | (NA) | 38 | 47 | 39 | 34 | 29 | 26 | 23 | 22 | 21 |

NA Not available. [1] Includes other fields of study, not shown separately. [2] 1976 data. [3] 1971 data.

Source of statistics

Source: The Higher Education Research Institute, University of California, Los Angeles , CA, *The American Freshman: National Norms*, annual.

## ► Step Nine: Consider Government Documents

Finally, always consider examining government documents in your search. The United States government is the largest publisher in the world and is constantly pouring out detailed census materials, vital statistics, Congressional papers and reports, presidential documents, military reports, and "impact statements" on energy, the environment, and pollution. Government publications are valuable sources of information on almost any topic in science, business, the social sciences, arts, and humanities. These materials are indexed in the *Monthly Catalog of United States Government Publications*. Published monthly, it lists books, pamphlets, maps, and serials, running from 1895 to the present.

**Entries from *Monthly Catalog of United States Government Publications***

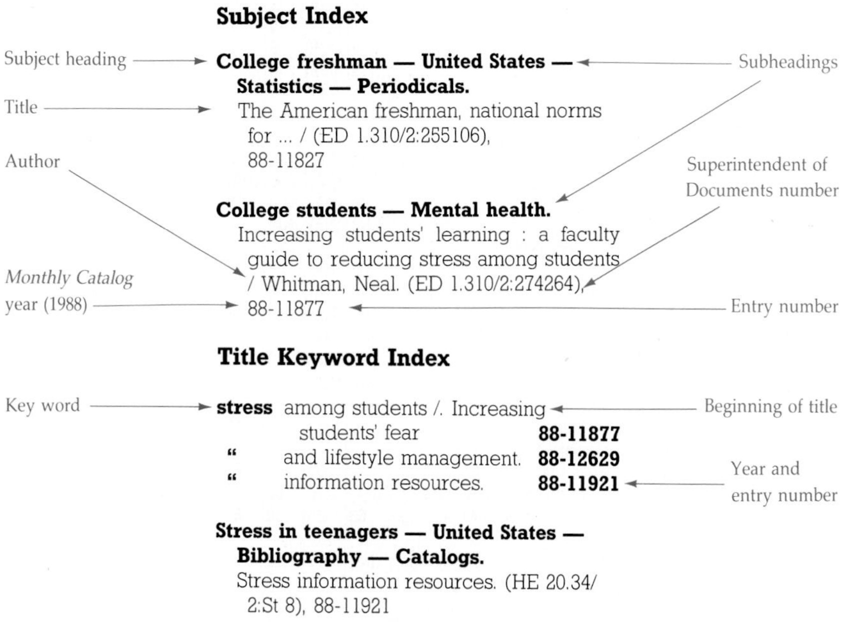

Subject Index
Subject heading
College freshman — United States — Statistics — Periodicals.
Subheadings
Title
The American freshman, national norms for ... / (ED 1.310/2:255106), 88-11827
Author
Superintendent of Documents number
College students — Mental health.
Increasing students' learning : a faculty guide to reducing stress among students / Whitman, Neal. (ED 1.310/2:274264), 88-11877
Monthly Catalog year (1988)
Entry number
Title Keyword Index
Key word
stress among students /. Increasing students' fear 88-11877
" and lifestyle management. 88-12629
" information resources. 88-11921
Beginning of title
Year and entry number
Stress in teenagers — United States — Bibliography — Catalogs.
Stress information resources. (HE 20.34/2:St 8), 88-11921


Published daily during each congressional session and consolidated at its end, the *Congressional Record* includes that body's votes, debates, and speeches. It supplies pros and cons about national issues at the present or at a given point in history. Weekly updates on congressional action also are available in *CQ Weekly Report*. The *CIS Index*, a publication of the Congressional Information Service, supplies short abstracts of documents published by Congress. Besides being a useful key to these publications, it can also identify and help you locate expert testimony and comprehensive supporting materials presented at congressional hearings. The *American Statistics Index*, published each year since 1973, is a guide to government publications with statistical information.

Because government documents are useful for research on business topics and social issues, check to see which other indexes and publications are available in your library.

## EVALUATING SOURCES

Once you have located material in the library, you next need to evaluate it. Consider both its content (whether the material addresses your research question) and its quality (whether the book or article is authoritative and reliable in itself). Here are some useful procedures for evaluating a book.

### ► How to Evaluate a Book

**1.** Open the book to its title page and study the exact title and subtitle.

**2.** Check the year of publication.

**3.** Read any information about the author's credentials, institution, or background.

**4.** Turn to the front matter (introduction, foreword, preface) and read the author's or editor's description of the book.

**5.** Turn to the table of contents and see how the author has organized the information into chapters, subsections, or other content categories.

**6.** Using the indexes of book reviews, locate and read reviews of the book if you are uncertain how to judge it or if you want other estimations of its reputation or quality.

This initial examination will tell you whether the book is current and reputable enough for your needs. In addition, any credentials listed for the writer plus his or her tone and approach can help you determine whether the book's information is likely to be reliable or idiosyncratic.

If the book seems authoritative and credible, use these next questions to help you assess how well it is likely to cover the issue that interests you. Many books are written about similar topics, but not all will be helpful in supplying information about a particular question. Your purpose, after all, is not to read every related or pertinent book, but to use only those that will best address your research question.

### ► How to Assess the Coverage of a Book

**1.** After thinking about your topic and your research question, write down three specific questions you have become curious about as a result of your preliminary evaluation of the book.

**2.** Review the first question and find in it a key word or phrase that you think might be in the book's index.

**3.** Turn to the index and look up that key word or phrase. If the word or phrase is not there, think of a synonym and see if the synonym is there. If it isn't, then see if the table of contents can lead you to the page of the book where the question can be answered.

**4.** Now turn to the part of the book that deals with your question and find the answer. If the author refers to material in other parts of the book, pursue these leads until you have all the information relevant to your question.

**5.** Follow the same procedure with your second and third questions.

Tracing several questions through a book in this way should tell you whether the book sufficiently covers the question you are working on and whether its coverage is useful at the present stage of your research. If a book is immediately helpful, go ahead and prepare note cards. If the book is not helpful at the moment, prepare a bibliography note card anyway. (See section on Preparing Bibliography and Note Cards.) Add a comment at the bottom evaluating the book and noting any points you might want to pursue later. If you encounter the book later, this card will confirm that you have already examined it. The card will also help you return to it quickly if you later decide that you need its information.

You will want to follow similar steps as you locate chapters, articles, essays, or other shorter materials. Be sure to consider the criteria of your field as you assess such materials. For example, an article written twenty or thirty years ago in the humanities might be considered a classic, while an article five years old might be viewed as outdated in the sciences. Despite such differences, the following steps will help you begin to assess a potential source.

## ► How to Evaluate an Article or Chapter

**1.** Read the complete title of the article or chapter, and consider how it fits into the context of the book, the periodical as a whole, the journal's special issue, or wherever it appears.

**2.** Check the date of the issue or collection.

**3.** Check the beginning or end of the volume or the article for a brief biography or list of the author's credentials.

**4.** Assess the authority, credibility, and possible biases of the journal or volume in which the article appears. (Books such as Farber's *Classified List of Periodicals for the College Library* and Katz's *Magazines for Libraries* evaluate a wide range of journals in these respects.)

**5.** If you are familiar with standard references in the field, check the article's notes or bibliography to see if it cites reputable sources and draws on well-regarded writers.

Your evaluation should help you decide whether the article is current and authoritative enough for your purposes. If it seems too dated, idiosyncratic, or obscure to be useful, note this on a bibliography card so that you do not forget its shortcomings and later waste time returning to it. On the other hand, if the article seems potentially useful, continue reviewing it to assess how well it will help answer your research question.

### ▶ How to Assess the Content of an Article or Chapter

**1.** Turn to the beginning of the article and read the abstract or first few paragraphs to determine its topic and approach.

**2.** Skim the headings and subheadings within the article to review what it discusses.

**3.** Turn to the end of the article and read its last few paragraphs or conclusion.

This review should clarify the exact perspective and focus of the article, helping you decide whether you need simply to summarize its approach or conclusions or to take more complete notes on its major points.

## RECORDING INFORMATION DURING YOUR SEARCH

As you conduct your library search, you need to keep two types of useful records. Of course you need to record the actual information you discover—the facts, ideas, opinions, background, interpretations, procedures, results, and other specifics that help answer your research question. All this will be absorbed into the content of your paper. In addition, you need to record bibliographic details identifying the sources you use to discover this information—the books, articles, and other materials that you review during your search. These sources will be noted briefly alongside the information in your text and in a concluding list of references.

Experienced researchers are ready, from the first library visit on, to jot down whatever seems pertinent. Most researchers use note cards—all the same size or two different sizes (often 3″ × 5″ for identifying sources and 5″ × 8″ for taking notes). Unlike sheets of paper, note cards are compact and relatively durable. Furthermore, they can be reorganized for easy reference when you are drafting your paper. After all, in your paper you will arrange the points as they fit together to answer *your* question—not as they were organized in your sources. For this reason, if you prefer using a notebook, be sure to write only on one side of each page. Then you can cut apart bits of information and avoid flipping the sheets back and forth when you need to organize and use the notes.

### ▶ Preparing Bibliography and Note Cards

Your bibliography cards should record the details necessary to identify and locate your sources. Reviewing your instructor's required format for source citations in your paper will ensure that you record every needed detail on your first visit to the library. Then you can avoid having to run back again later for a missing date or publisher. Here, using the Modern Language Association (MLA) style, are sample bibliography cards for a book and an article.

**Sample Bibliography Cards Recording Sources**

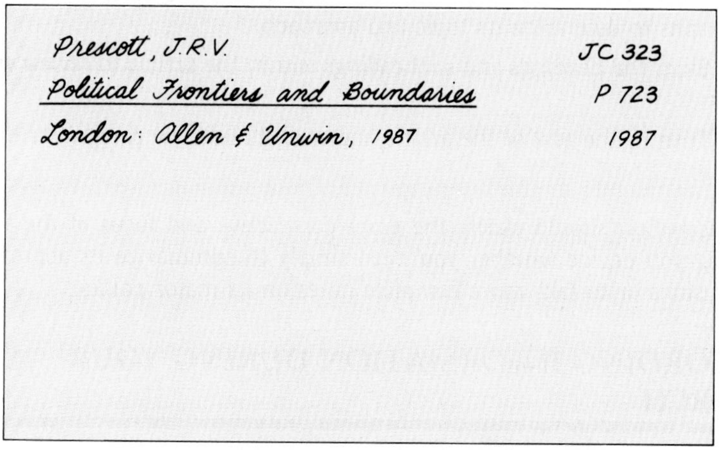
Prescott, J.R.V. JC 323
Political Frontiers and Boundaries P 723
London: Allen & Unwin, 1987 1987

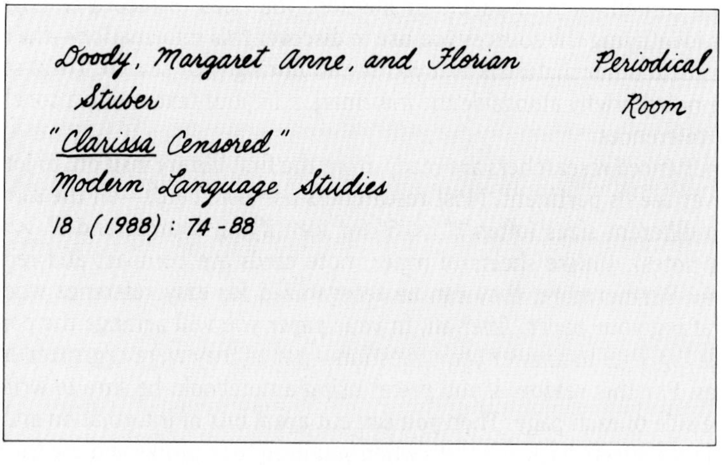
Doody, Margaret Anne, and Florian Periodical
Stuber Room
"Clarissa Censored"
Modern Language Studies
18 (1988): 74-88

Because these cards fully identify the sources you have used, you do not need to repeat the details on each card when you take notes. Instead, just begin each note card with a short source identification: the author's last name and an abbreviated title if you use several works by the same person. Then simply record whatever information you need, being sure to note the exact page where it appears. (Besides being convenient in case you need to return to the source, the page number may be needed for the source citation in your final paper.) As you take notes or as you prepare to write, you also can use the top line or the corner of the card to identify the subtopic discussed or the section of the paper where the information belongs. (Use pencil because these subtopics or divisions are likely to change as you learn more about the topic.)

Instead of packing each card with information, begin a new card for each separate point or subtopic. Even though you will use more cards, you will save time and aggravation in the long run. Later, as you group and organize your cards, you will not have to turn to one card three or four times. Instead you will have three or four separate cards, each covering a different point and each ready to go in a separate stack. Here is a sample note card.

**Sample Note Card Recording Information**

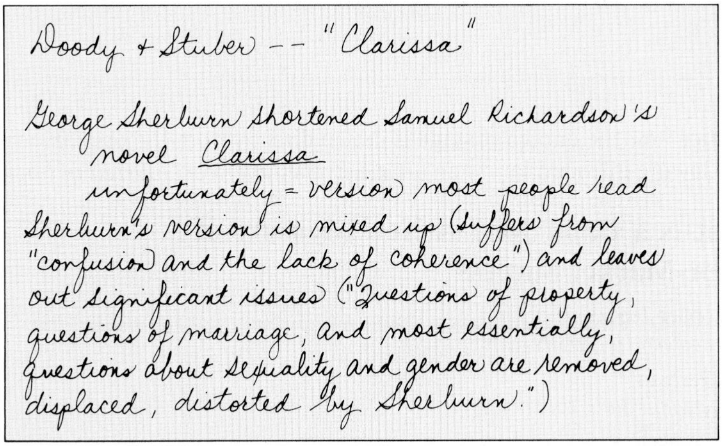

Doody + Stuber -- "Clarissa"

George Sherburn shortened Samuel Richardson's novel Clarissa
unfortunately = version most people read
Sherburn's version is mixed up (suffers from "confusion and the lack of coherence") and leaves out significant issues ("Questions of property, questions of marriage, and most essentially, questions about sexuality and gender are removed, displaced, distorted by Sherburn.")

On these cards you may record *quotations*, *paraphrases*, and *summaries* of information. Each type of note reflects a different way of recording information, and each is useful in particular circumstances.

## ▶ Quoting

A *quotation* records exactly the words used in the source. You will want to write down a quotation when a source is so precise or polished that you want to preserve its very words. When you finish copying a quotation, be sure to check the accuracy of your notes against the original. Always spell out each word, as in the original, to avoid later confusion about abbreviations or figures. Mark the passage with quotation marks so that the precise wording can be credited to the author. Also note the page on which you found it. If the quotation continues on a second page, note where the sentence splits. Then you will know which page number to use should you quote only part of the sentence in your final paper.

**Sample Quotation**

> Jencks— "Good Job"
> authors maintain "that neither occupational status nor earnings nor job satisfaction is a good measure of a job's overall desirability."
>
> p. 1323

Notice how the quoted passage is drawn directly from the original material, the following introduction to an article in the *American Journal of Sociology*.

## What Is a Good Job? A New Measure of Labor-Market Success[1]

Christopher Jencks
*Northwestern University*

Lauri Perman
*Pennsylvania State University*

Lee Rainwater
*Harvard University*

No currently available index allows investigators to estimate the overall desirability of specific jobs. With data collected in the 1980 Survey of Job Characteristics, an index of job desirability (IJD) can be constructed to fill this gap. The IJD incorporates 13 nonmonetary job characteristics along with measures of earnings and weights all job characteristics according to their effects on workers' judgements about how "good" their current jobs are compared with an average job. While earnings are the most important single determinant of a job's desirability, the 13 nonmonetary job characteristics together are twice as important as earnings. Unlike occupational status and earnings, the proposed index explains almost the entire effect of race, sex, educational attainment, and experience on


0002-9602/88/9306-0002$01.50

1322 *AJS* Volume 93 Number 6 (May 1988): 1322–57

job ratings. It also explains almost all the variation in job ratings provided by workers in different occupations. Furthermore, taking account of nonmonetary job characteristics more than doubles the estimated level of labor-market inequality. White skin, male gender, favorable social origins, high educational attainment, and extensive labor-market experience are also worth two to five times more when one considers both monetary and nonmonetary payoffs than when one considers money alone.

Some jobs are better than others. Everyone recognizes this fact, both when they discuss jobs in daily conversation and when they must actually choose among jobs. Yet social scientists have no comprehensive measure of a job's desirability. Sociologists have devised many schemes for ranking *occupations* but none for ranking the diverse jobs that fall into the same occupational category. Economists rank jobs according to their pay but have no global measure of jobs' nonmonetary benefits (or costs). Psychologists measure workers' subjective satisfaction with their jobs but have not, for the most part, tried to rank jobs on the basis of their objective characteristics.

This paper will argue that neither occupational status nor earnings nor job satisfaction is a good measure of a job's overall desirability. If follows that none of these measures provides a good measure of an individual's competitive success in the labor market. We therefore propose a new strategy for measuring labor-market success that takes account of both monetary and nonmonetary job characteristics and weights them according to their importance to the average American worker. The resulting index of job desirability differs from economists' preferred measure of jobs' desirability, namely pay, because it takes account of jobs' nonmonetary characteristics. It differs from sociologists' preferred measure because it takes account of differences among jobs in the same occupational category. It differs from psychological measures of job satisfaction because it is based on jobs' objective characteristics and ignores variation in the way different individuals evaluate jobs with similar objective characteristics. While it is not ideal for all purposes, we argue that the proposed index provides a better measure of a worker's competitive success in the labor market than any existing measure does.

The paper is divided into three parts. The first discusses the limitations of existing measures of labor-market success and proposes an alternative approach. The second describes how we selected the job charcteristics we include in the index and how we estimated their effects on a job's overall desirability. The third shows how using the index changes our picture of the determinants of both labor-market success and overall labor-market inequality in the United States.

## RANKING JOBS AND WORKERS

Our aim is to develop an index that can serve two closely related purposes. First, it should rank the jobs available in the American economy and tell us how much better

[1] An earlier version of this paper was presented at the annual meetings of the American Sociological Association, August 1985. The National Science Foundation supported the work reported here through grants SOC-7821021, SES-8024529, and SES-8121822, as did the Center for Urban Affairs and Policy Research at Northwestern University and the Institute for Advanced Study in Princeton. Susan Mayer, Faheem Sandhu, and Gary Winters helped with the computer programming. Dudley Duncan, Carol Heimer, Joseph Pleck, Albert Reiss, James Rosenbaum, Joseph Schwartz, Tom Smith, Arthur Stinchcombe, and Edward Walsh provided helpful comments on earlier drafts. Requests for reprints should be sent to Christopher Jencks, Department of Sociology, Northwestern University, Evanston, Illinois 60201.

Beware, however, of using too many quotations. When you research a difficult topic loaded with unfamiliar terms or complicated ideas, you may feel that nearly every sentence you read cannot be improved upon. And you may want to record it all, word for word. Try, instead, to master the material by putting it into your own words. You will better understand the content and more easily distinguish the complex discussion from the truly memorable statement that deserves quotation. Furthermore, you automatically will have safeguarded against a final paper that just strings together quotations from others without genuinely relating their ideas to your own research question.

## ► Paraphrasing

When you take notes in your own words, following the ideas, order, or sentence patterns of the original, you are using *paraphrase*. Again, since a paraphrase represents the thought and work of another writer, you will need to note the page number of the passage and supply this information in your paper. No quotation marks are needed, however, since the words are your own.

**Sample Paraphrase**

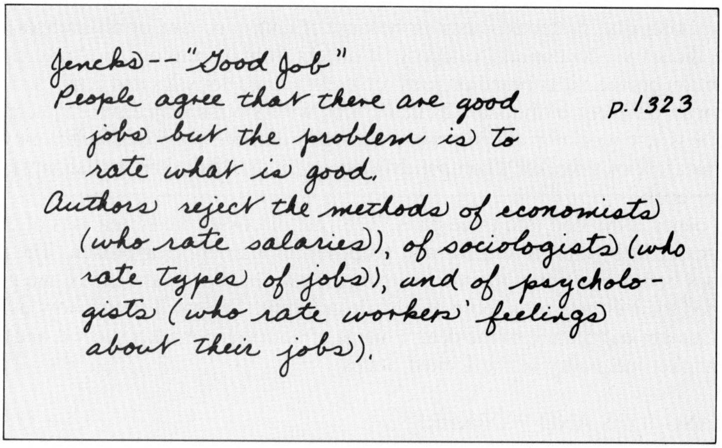
Jencks--"Good Job"
People agree that there are good jobs but the problem is to rate what is good. p. 1323
Authors reject the methods of economists (who rate salaries), of sociologists (who rate types of jobs), and of psychologists (who rate workers' feelings about their jobs).

As this example illustrates, a paraphrase is not necessarily brief. Its purpose is to convey the content and meaning of the original, not to abbreviate it.

## ► Summarizing

When you want a brief record of the point of a passage, you will write a *summary*. Like a paraphrase, a summary is in your own words. Instead of reflecting the pattern and logic of the original, however, a summary succinctly states its central points.

**Sample Summary**

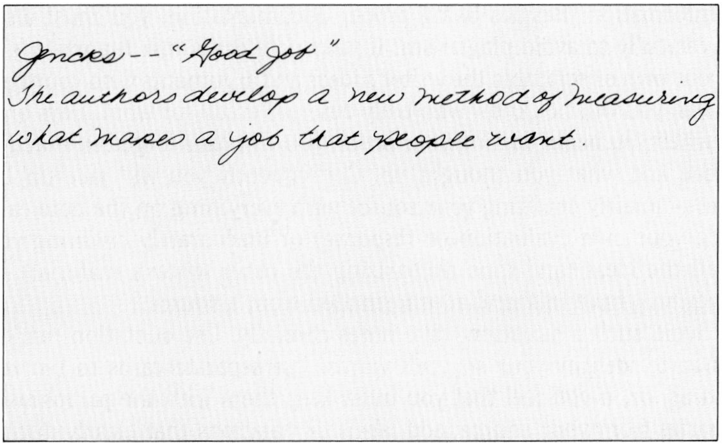
Jencks -- "Good Job"
The authors develop a new method of measuring what makes a job that people want.

Sometimes you will combine paraphrase and quotation, putting most of a passage into your own words but using a quotation for a notable section or a key definition. Other times, you will do the same with summary and quotation, summing up the whole area but quoting a particular section.

## ► Highlighting Important Information

Sometimes you will photocopy material at the library instead of taking notes. This technique is useful if your best study time is not during library hours, if you prefer to study in your own room, or if you are pressed for time but have located useful material. As you photocopy the material, be certain to duplicate the title page or carefully label the first page with all the information necessary for a source citation. Then note the author and short title on each separate page so that you will know the source if you mix up the pages. Check each page to make sure that the page numbers have been duplicated and can be read easily. Also make up a bibliography card so that you can file the entry with the other cards, order the batch, and type your list of sources directly from them.

When you review the photocopy, use a highlighter, pen, or colored pencil to mark important sections, definitions, main points or potential quotations. If you want to be able to feed the material into your stack of cards so that it is easier to incorporate in your paper, make cross-reference cards to remind you to add certain points from the duplicated article or cut out key passages and paste them on cards.

## ► Avoiding Plagiarism

However you work with your source material, you must be careful to avoid plagiarism—dishonestly repeating someone else's phrasing or thoughts without acknowledging your source. Chapter 10 explains several methods of documenting your sources—that is, of appropriately identifying where you found your information. Besides using proper documentation, you must also take notes carefully to avoid plagiarism. If your note cards mix the writer's words with your own or scramble the writer's ideas and arguments with your personal reactions, you will not know who truly deserves credit for what. Days or weeks later, when you begin writing your paper, you will have forgotten exactly what you read and what you thought up. Consequently you will face unpleasant choices—unfairly crediting your source with everything on the note card (including your own evaluation or response) or inaccurately crediting yourself with all the ideas (and thus plagiarizing the other writer's material). Either way, you will have mishandled information from a source.

To avoid such a situation, take notes carefully. Use quotation marks with precision to identify your source's words. Use separate cards to record your own ideas, or, if you feel that you must keep them with the paraphrases and summaries from your source, add labels or notations that clearly distinguish your original thoughts.

These examples of faulty and acceptable note cards illustrate how to identify and avoid common problems that may lead to unintentional plagiarism.

**Original Source**

## Computing in Public Administration: Practice and Education

**Donald F. Norris and Lyke Thompson**

The computers used in public administration before the 1980s, which tended to be large, expensive, user-hostile, and limited systems that required extensive support, have given way to user-friendly, high-speed, interactive systems. The institutionalization of the latter is bringing vast changes to public administration education and practice. *Keywords:* common practices, leading-edge practices, institutionalization, integration.

The introduction and rapid diffusion of microcomputers and user-friendly software in the 1980s have changed forever the face of computing and information management in public administration. Several studies document the rapidity with which computer technology has been embraced by public organizations. For example, Norris and Webb (1983) found that 13.2% of cities nationwide owned microcomputers in 1982, and that another 35.3% planned to buy them. In 1984, Kraemer, King, Dunkle, Lane, and George (1985) found that 77% of larger American cities had microcomputers and 74% planned to acquire at least one more in the coming year. Scoggins, Tidrick, and Auerback (1985) reported that 96% of cities with populations of 10,000 or more used central computer systems, and that 84% had microcomputers. Finally, over 160,000 microcomputers were in use in federal agencies in 1987, and that number is expected to grow to half a million by 1991 (Bergin, 1987b).

If anything, the adoption of computer technology by public organiza-

*Social Science Computer Review* 6:4, Winter 1988.  CCC 0894-4393/88/$1.50.

tions at all levels has increased since these surveys appeared. This means that today only the smallest agencies and governments find themselves without one or more computers. In addition, most government employees have either direct or indirect access to some sort of computer system. Given these developments, describing the state of the art of computer use in public administration is a difficult task, the more so because additional microcomputers are acquired daily by public agencies and uses are continually changing and expanding.

Not only have computers invaded the public work space, they are also found throughout colleges and universities in growing numbers. For example, over half of the masters of public administration and affairs programs that Bergin (1987b) surveyed had computer facilities available to their students. Moreover, 93.8% reported that the number of terminals or microcomputers for student use had increased in the previous two years. Another 82.8% indicated that they had plans to increase the number of such facilities even further.

A major problem facing graduate public administration and affairs programs is how to provide the needed education and training in computers and information management. As indicated by the report of the National Association of Schools of Public Affairs and Administration (NASPAA) (1986) and by Kiel (1987), the question of what MPA programs can and should do to graduate education in computers and information management is far from settled.

In order to understand the state of the art of computing in public administration, it is necessary to develop a clearer understanding of common and leading-edge practices in the field. To do this, we surveyed management personnel in 14 municipal governments and the directors of 12 MPA programs.[1] In the following pages we report on these practices and compare the views of public managers and MPA directors concerning what MPA programs ought to teach their students about computers and information management. We conclude by suggesting, however tentatively, which directions future developments will take both in public agencies and in the academy.

**Computing in Public Management**

The 14 public managers whom we interviewed all work in city government. Their cities range in population from 1,500 to 340,000, and the computer technology that they own ranges from the relatively modest to the relatively sophisticated. Beloit, Kansas (pop. 1,500), for example, owns an IBM and a NEC micro as well as an IBM minicomputer (with three terminals). The micros are used for word processing, budgeting, and spreadsheet analysis, and the city manager uses one with the program *AUTOCAD* to map the city's infrastructure. The minicomputer is used primarily for financial management and related activities.

Probably the most sophisticated installations are at Aurora, Colorado (pop. 235,000), Savannah, Georgia (pop. 150,000), and Pasadena, California (pop. 120,000). All three places have at least one mainframe computer and several departmental minicomputers dedicated to specific tasks like emergency dispatch, geographic information, and fleet management. They also have numerous microcomputers—Aurora over 275 micros, Pasadena over 125, and Savannah over 100—in addition to numerous terminals or other workstations connected to mainframes and minicomputers. Computerization in these cities is fairly typical of what

**Faulty Note Card**

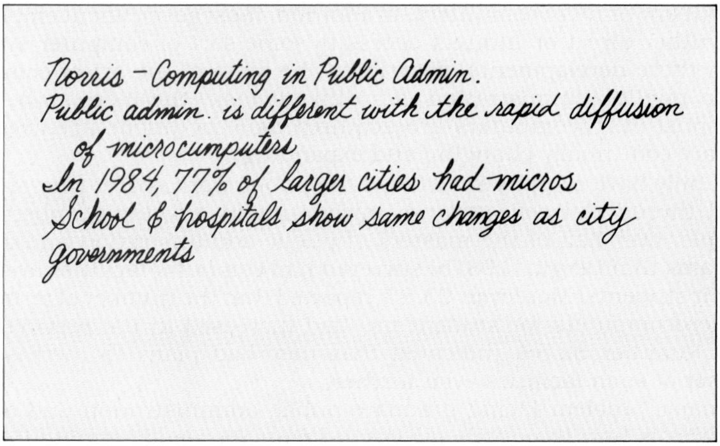
Norris – Computing in Public Admin.
Public admin. is different with the rapid diffusion of microcumputers
In 1984, 77% of larger cities had micros
School & hospitals show same changes as city governments

**Acceptable Note Card**

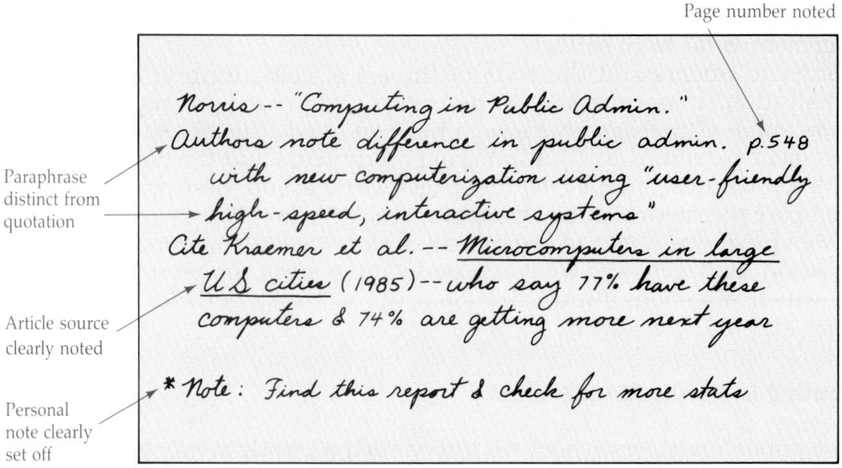

Norris -- "Computing in Public Admin."
Authors note difference in public admin. p.548
with new computerization using "user-friendly high-speed, interactive systems"
Cite Kraemer et al. -- Microcomputers in large U.S. cities (1985) -- who say 77% have these computers & 74% are getting more next year

* Note: Find this report & check for more stats

## A SAMPLE SEARCH

Imagine a student, Bill, interested in the general subject of animal communication, who hasn't yet formulated a thesis question.

### ► Step One: Encyclopedias

Bill examines the *Encyclopedia Americana*, which reveals that bees communicate by dancing, and bats through sound waves. *The McGraw-Hill Encyclopedia of Science and Technology* describes four channels of communication: acoustic, visual, chemical, and electrical. Finding the visual aspect of communication interesting, Bill begins to wonder whether animals can communicate visually with humans. The bibliography at the end of the article has one promising, although not very recent, title—*Animal Communication: Technique of Study and Results of Research*, edited by T. A. Sebeok, 1968. *Grzimek's Animal Life Encyclopedia* states that animals have the ability to speak and that "anthropoid apes are able to use words which they have learned appropriately." In the same article, B. Rensch, who raised a female chimpanzee, states that anthropoid apes "can form abstract concepts, can generalize, can recognize causal relationships and symbolic representations. . . ." The information on apes is interesting, and Bill's intuition tells him that if animals and humans *do* communicate in any complex way, apes are the most likely candidates. He decides for now to concentrate on apes—keeping his eyes open for *ape*, *gorilla*, *chimpanzee* as key words. But if another kind of animal-human communication sounds interesting, he is willing to change his focus.

### Selection from the *Encyclopedia Americana* article

#### ANIMAL BEHAVIOR

has shown that if the first moving object that the ducklings or goslings see is a human being, they tend to follow the person. Later, when the human being is placed in direct competition with the natural mother, the ducklings and goslings prefer to follow the human being. Furthermore, in adult life, animals imprinted to a person will direct social responses to people in preference to members of their own species. The universality of this phenomenon and factors affecting the critical period for its occurrence are under investigation.

***Sensory Processes, communication, and Orientation.*** Man has long speculated about the mental life of the animals that share the earth with him, and many questions concerning the existence of such processes as "consciousness" in animals have been posed. Although most of these questions may be forever unanswerable, experiments have shown conclusively that many animal species possess senses and means of communication and orientation that men do not have. Research in this area is difficult and demanding, but it can be most rewarding, since many of the most interesting problems in animal behavior are found in the areas of sensory processes, communication, and orientation. A few examples will illustrate some of the rather startling discoveries that have been made in this field.

Perhaps the earliest, and certainly the most famous, modern research in this area concerns the ability of bees to communicate a food source to the other members of the hive. They do this by means of various "dances," which they execute on the combs of the hive. The dances indicate the distance and the direction in which other bees must fly in order to locate the food source. Furthermore, it has been discovered that different species of bees have different "dialects"; that is, the pattern of the dance and the information conveyed by the dance differ from species to species. It also has been shown that bees can orientate by means of polarized light in the sky and that they are sensitive to ultraviolet light. The human eye is incapable of detecting either of these stimuli.

An active field of research has been concerned with abilities of various animals to use reflected sound waves in finding their way about in their environment and in securing food. It has been shown that bats can locate small flying insects by means of echolocation (a sonarlike process). It also has been discovered that certain species of moths have evolved a behavior pattern that affords some protection from predatory bats. Upon hearing a bat's cry, these moths power-dive into the grass. Porpoises also have an excellent sonar system, and these marvelously intelligent animals are proving of great value in behavioral research. Echolocation systems have been analyzed in detail and have been shown to depend on frequencies higher than the upper limit of hearing in man.

The abilities of animals to migrate from place to place and to "home" have interested many scientists. Certain species of fish, for example, find their way over long distances to a particular segment of a particular stream when in reproductive condition. They seem to have been imprinted to the chemical conditions of that section of the stream during their early development. The homing ability of pigeons has been investigated with the discovery that pigeons flying near the home loft find their way to the loft by means of landmarks, which they have learned of during previous flights. Pigeons released in unfamiliar territory, at some distance from the loft, however, orientate themselves in the direction of the loft by means of a little understood "navigational grid."

***Learning and Motivation.*** Learning and motivation are the experimental psychologist's favorite topics. They have been investigated intensively, and several theories about them have been formulated.

An accepted generalization in this area is that the intelligence of animals is correlated with their position on the phylogenetic scale. A chimpanzee is capable of solving more difficult problems than a rat, and a rat, on most problems, can learn better than a frog. However, behaviorists have had a great difficulty in devising experiments that would separate the learning abilities of animals in other than a very crude fashion. Modern experimentation in this area has reformulated the questions, and the results to date appear very promising. (For information on learning and motivation, see ANIMAL INTELLIGENCE; PSYCHOLOGY.)

**Selection from the *McGraw-Hill Encyclopedia of Science & Technology* article**

**Modes of communication.** Animal communication involves signal emission and reception in the visual, auditory, chemical, and electrical modalities. Some animals communicate by using just one modality, but other utilize more than one (**Fig. 2**), sometimes simultaneously. Each modality has distinct signal and ecological advantages and disadvantages, and each is studied with different tools. For the sake of simplicity, each communication channel is discussed separately below.

***Visual communication.*** Visual communication involves the use of reflected sunlight (visible spectrum, infrared, ultraviolet) or biologically produced light (bioluminescence). It may be studied by using cameras, projectors, stimulator-driven light sources, photomultipliers, two-dimensional models, and so forth. Its advantages are speed (rapid on-off, the extreme speed of light), directionality, and possibilities for signal elaboration (temporal and spatial patterning, hue). When such caracteristics of light are incorporated into the fur or feathers of the animal, metabolically inexpensive and permanent signals are produced. Disadvantages of visual signals are that, with the exception of bioluminescence, they are restricted to the daylight hours, usually occur over fairly short distances, and require that sender and receiver be in line of sight—a poor way of communicating in a vegetation-rich environment. One characteristic of visual signals (and of signals in other modalities as well) is that they can be discrete (on-off) or graded.

***Acoustical communication.*** Acoustical communication involves the use of sound pressure waves produced by vibration of a structure in air or water (for example, the avian syrinx and the cricket file and scraper). Sounds may be tape-recorded and subsequently analyzed for temporal, frequency, and intensity characteristics with a sound spectrograph. Sound can then be synthesized and their effects on behavior studied (playback experiments). Acoustical communication is rapid in air and water, although slower than light. Like light, the acoustic signal can be rapidly turned on and off, is easily locatable (depending on frequency), and can carry information in terms of temporal patterning, pitch, and timbre. It can also code for distance (loudness), go around obstacles, and be used in the dark. Its disadvantages are that it is subject to some environmental jamming by other sounds, is distorted with distance (except at very low frequencies), and requires the continuous expenditure of energy for signal production.

Singing insects, such as crickets, show stereotyped species-typical songs for specific biological purposes: advertising song, for long-distance coding of species

## ► Step Two: Dictionaries

Few words so far have given Bill any problem. He looks up *anthropoid* and *sign language* in *Webster's New Collegiate Dictionary*, *McGraw-Hill Dictionary of Scientific Terms*, and *Oxford English Dictionary*.

**Definition from the *McGraw-Hill Dictionary of Scientific and Technical Terms***

**Anthicidae**
**antiaggressin**

**anthropoid** [VERT ZOO] Pertaining to or resembling the Anthropoidea.

**Anthropoidea** [VERT ZOO] A suborder of mammals in the order Primates including New and Old World monkeys.

## ► Step Three: Card Catalog

Bill goes now to the card catalog to do a subject and author search. Using the *Library of Congress Subject Headings*, he finds that *Animal communication* is a correct subject heading; listed under the heading are three *see also* headings, one of which is *Human-animal communication*. Under "Animal communication" in the card catalog are three books that seem relevant: *Sign Language and Language Acquisition in Man and Ape*, 1978, edited by Fred C. C. Peng; *Speaking of Apes: A Critical Anthology of Two-Way Communication with Man*, 1980, edited by Thomas Sebeok and Jean Uniker-Sebeok; and *Nim*, 1979, by Herbert Terrace. The catalog cards also show that the first two books have bibliographies. Under the subject heading *Human-animal communication congresses* is a collection of conference papers, *The Clever Hans Phenomenon: Communication with Horses, Whales, Apes, and People*, 1981. The title sounds provocative, and it mentions apes, so Bill decides to include it.

At the card catalog, he also looks for information on Sebeok's book *Animal Communication*, which was listed in the encyclopedia article. For of all these sources Bill copies complete call numbers, titles, and authors from the catalog cards.

**Sample Bibliography Card**

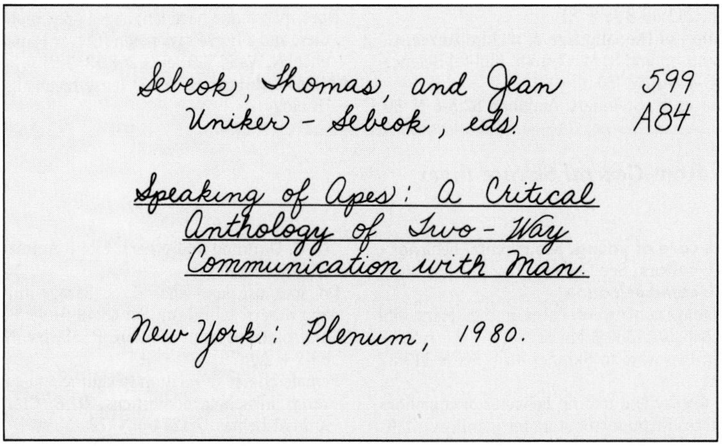
Sebeok, Thomas, and Jean Uniker-Sebeok, eds. 599 A84

Speaking of Apes: A Critical Anthology of Two-Way Communication with Man.

New York: Plenum, 1980.

## ► Step Four: Journal Articles

Now Bill goes to the *General Science Index* and *Reader's Guide to Periodical Literature*, looking up the headings *Animal communication and Human-animal communication*. Two articles are listed in *Science*: "Can an Ape Create a Sentence?" November 23, 1979, and "Ape-language Controversy Flares Up," March 21, 1980. *American Scientist* has "Do Apes Use Language?" January

1980. *Science News* has "Ape-talk Two Ways to Skinner Bird," February 9, 1980. There are three in the November 1979 issue of *Psychology Today*: "The Trouble with Ape-language Studies: An Introduction." "How Nim Chimpsky Changed My Mind," and "Performing Animals: Secrets of the Trade." Earlier volumes of the indexes note other articles, including one more in *Science News*: an untitled October, 1978 article about Koko, a talking gorilla.

### Entries from *Reader's Guide to Periodical Literature*

**ANIMAL cemeteries.** See Cemeteries. Animal
**ANIMAL communication**
*See also*
Animal sounds
Sound production by animals

Ape-language controversy flares up. J. L. Marx. bibl il Science 207:1330-3 Mr 21 '80
Ape talk: more than pigeon English? J. Greenberg. il Sci News 117:298-300 My 10 '80
Ape-talk: two ways to Skinner bird [pigeons] Sci News 117:87 F 9 '80
Are dolphins trying to say something or is it all much ado about nothing? M. Parfit. bibl (p220) il por Smithsonian 11:72-81 O '80
Are those apes really talking? il Time 115:50 + Mr 10 '80
Can an ape create a sentence? H. S. Terrace and others. bibl il Science 206:891-902 N 23 '79; Discussion. 211:86-8 Ja 2 '81
Explanation of the language of a chimpanzee. C. R. Thompson and R. M. Church. bibl f il Science 208:313-14 Ap 18 '80
Other voices. P. Steinhart. Audubon 82:5-6 N '80
Pigeon talk [research by B. F. Skinner and others] Time 115:53 F 11 '80
Reference: the linguistic essential [chimpanzees] E. S. Savage-Rumbaugh and others. bibl f il Science 210:922-5 N 21 '80
Symbolic communication between two pigeons (columbia livia domestica) R. Epstein and others. bibl f il Science 207:543-5 F 1 '80
Talking animals: spiders, fish, grasshoppers . . . even worms [excerpt from The seven mysteries of life] G. Murchie. il Sci Digest 87:49 E-51 F '80
What your cat is trying to tell you. M. W. Fox. McCalls 107:92 + S '80
What your dog is trying to tell you. M. W. Fox. il McCalls 108:62 + O '80

**Conferences**

Conference [Clever Hans Phenomenon: Communication with Horses, Whales, Apes, and People] New Yorker 56:28-30 My 26 '80
Does man alone have language? Apes reply in riddles, and a horse says neigh [Clever Hans conference] N. Wade. il Science 208:1349-51 Je 20 '80
**ANIMAL defenses.** See Defense mechanisms (Biology)

### Entries from *General Science Index*

**ANIMAL care of young.** See Parental behavior
**ANIMAL collars.** See Collars
**ANIMAL communication**
Ape-language controversy flares up. J. L. Marx. bibl il Science 207:1330-3 Mr 21 '80
Ape-talk: two ways to Skinner bird. Sci N 117:87 F 9 '80
Calling display and mating behavior of copiphora rhinoceros Pictet (orthoptera:tettigoniidae) G. K. Morris. bibl il Animal Behav 28:42-51 F '80
Chemical communication in cavia; responses of wild (C. aperea), domestic (C. porcellus) and $F_1$ males to urine. G. K. Beauchamp and others. bibl il Animal Behav 27:1066-72 N '79
Communication in Atlantic bottlenosed dolphins, M. C. Caldwell and D. K. Caldwell. il Sea Front 25:130-9 My '79
Complex courtship songs in the drosophila funebris species group; escape from an evolutionary bottleneck. A. W. Ewing. bibl il Animal Behav 27:343-9 My '79
Courtship in two species of periodical cicadas, magicicada septendecim and magicicada cassini. D. C. Dunning and others. bibl il Animal Behav 27:1073-90 N '79
Do apes use language? E. S. Savage-Rumbaugh and others. bibl il Am Sci 68:49-61 Ja '80
Early patterns of perception. P. Marier. Nat Hist 88-7 + Ag '79
Female choice in relation to calling and courtship songs in acheta domesticus. O. S. Crankshaw. Animal Behav 27:1274-5 N '79
How Nim Chimpsky changed my mind. H. S. Terrace. bibl il Psychol Today 13:65 + N '79
Monkeys cannot chatter with foreigners. il Sci 82:811 Je 7 '79
Performing animals; secrets of the trade. T. A. Sebeok and J. Umiker-Sebeok. bibl il Psychol Today 13:78-9 + N '79
Scent-marking in lone wolves and newly formed pairs. R. J. Rothman and L. D. Mech. bibl il Animal behav 27:750-60 Ag '79
**ANIMAL experimentation**
Acceptance by swine and rats of corn amended with trichothecenes. R. F. Vesonder and others. bibl il App & Environ Microbiol 38:344-6 Ag '79

Are these articles worthwhile? As one clue, Bill checks Farber, *Classified List of Periodicals for the College Library*, and Katz, *Magazines for Libraries*, for evaluations of the journals. Farber states that *Science* is the official journal of the American Association for the Advancement of Science and that its articles are excellent, and that *American Scientist* and *Science News* are reliable journals. *Psychology Today,* according to Farber, is a "scientifically accurate" journal. Bill puts an asterisk beside the titles of the *Science* articles because Farber seems to suggest that it is the most authoritative of the journals.

**Entries in Farber's *Classified List of Periodicals for the College Library***

• **SCIENCE. v. 1, 1883-**

Weekly. Washington, D.C. $20.00

Actually begun in 1880, *Science* went through two false starts — from 1880 until 1882, and from 1883 until 1894. Its editorial board as well as its contributors in these years contained some distinguished names, but it was not until James McQueen Cattell, head of Columbia's psychology department, took it over in 1895 that it began its uninterrupted publication. In 1900, the American Association for the Advancement of Science agreed to make it the official journal of the organization, and it is now sent to all members, numbering about 110,000. In 1958, *Science* absorbed the AAAS's other publication, *Scientific Monthly.*

Its "Letters" section and editorials permit airing of opinions and controversial matters. The "Reports" section contains brief research pieces (under 2000 words) of somewhat more specialized nature, in all areas of science, each preceded by an abstract; comments on previously publish reports are also in this section. "News and comment" discusses, among other things, major institutional developments and governmental activities and programs as well as announcements of grants, fellowships, awards, and new courses. A "Meetings" section describes the events and papers at some of the more important meetings, frequently in some detail, and contains a thorough listing of meetings to come during the next month. Beginning in 1963, an annual *Guide to Scientific Instruments* has appeared in November or December (from 1964 on, it has been a separate supplementary issue), containing comprehensive information on scientific instruments, equipment and their manufacturers. The signed book reviews, usually 6 to 10 an issue, vary in length, but are mostly 400-500 words. They are clear and critical, and cover as wide a range of subjects as the leading articles. There is also a listing of new books.

No library can be without it, and most libraries should have an extensive backfile.

Indexed in: R.G. 17-24346 lov.
A.S.T.I.
B.R.D.

• **SCIENCE NEWS. v. 1, 1921-**

Weekly. Washington, D.C. $7.50

Starting as *Science News Bulletin*, it became *Science New Letter* in 1922, retaining that title until 1966. Published by Science Service, a non-profit organization devoted to the popularization of science and with a board of distinguished scientists and journalists, it presents news, developments and discoveries in scientific research and technology, including news of government activities and individuals relating to them. Articles are well illustrated and usually less than 1500 words, most much shorter, though in recent years the number of longer articles has been increasing. In addition to the articles, there are now single pages devoted to brief items on the physical sciences, information sciences, life sciencies, social sciences (psychology, psychiatry, archaeology, and sociology), environmental sciences and aerospace — though not all of these in every issue. There is also a monthly page on astronomy, discussing phenomena for the coming month, with a celestial timetable. Weekly features include annotated, extensive listings of new books and films, and once a month New Products — now fairly technical items of equipment — are described.

Concise, yet providing substantial coverage interestingly and accurately, it provides an excellent way of keeping up with science, and should be in every library.

Indexed in: R.G. 37-18541

## Step Five: Essays

Bill's next step is to look for essays written on the topic. He looks in the *Essay and General Literature Index* and discovers that all the essays in the *Speaking of Apes* book are indexed there. He decides to evaluate the entire book later by looking up book reviews, but he wants to examine one specific essay that sounds especially relevant: "Language, Name, and Concept" by Bronowski and Bellugi.

**Entries from *Essay and General Literature Index***

**Human-animal communication**

Bronowski, J. and Bellugi, U. Language, name, and concept. *In* Speaking of apes, ed. by T. A. Sebeok and J. Umiker-Sebeok p103-13.

Brown, R. The first sentences of child and chimpanzee. *In* Speaking of apes, ed. by T. A. Sebeok and J. Umiker-Sebeok p85-101

Fouts, R. S. and Rigby, R. L. Man-chimpanzee communications. *In* Speaking of apes, ed. by T. A. Sebeok and J. Umiker-Sebeok p261-85

Gardner, R. A. and Gardner, B. T. Comparative psychology and language acquisition. *In* Speaking of apes, ed. by T. A. Sebeok and J. Umiker-Sebeok p287-330

Healy, A. F. Can chimpanzees learn a phonemic language? *In* Speaking of apes, ed. by T. A. Sebeok and J. Umiker-Sebeok p141-43

Hediger, H. Do you speak Yerkish? The newest colloquial language with chimpanzees. *In* Speaking of apes, ed. by T. A. Sebeok and J. Umiker-Sebeok p441-47

Hill, J. H. Apes and language. *In* Speaking of apes, ed. by T. A. Sebeok and J. Umiker-Sebeok p331-51

Kellogg, W. N. Communication and language in the home-raised chimpanzee. *In* Speaking of apes, ed. by T. A. Sebeok and J. Umiker-Sebeok p61-70

Limber, J. Language in child and chimp? *In* Speaking of apes, ed. by T. A. Sebeok and J. Umiker-Sebeok p197-220

McNeill, D. Sentence structure in chimpanzee communication. *In* Speaking of apes, ed. by T. A. Sebeok and J. Umiker-Sebeok p145-60

Marler, P. Primate vocalization: affective or symbolic? *In* Speaking of apes, ed. by T. A. Sebeok and J. Umiker-Sebeok p221-29

Mounin, G. Language, communication, chimpanzees. *In* Speaking of apes, ed. by T. A. Sebeok and J. Umiker-Sebeok p161-77

Rumbaugh, D. M. Language behavior of apes. *In* Speaking of apes, ed. by T. A. Sebeok and J. Umiker-Sebeok p231-59

Terrace, H. S. and Bever, T. G. What might be learned from studying language in the chimpanzee? The importance of symbolizing oneself. *In* Speaking of apes, ed. by T. A. Sebeok and J. Umiker-Sebeok p179-89

**Speaking** of apes; a critical anthology of two-way communications with man. Ed. by Thomas A. Sebeok and Jean Umiker-Sebeok. Plenum Press 1980 480p (Topics in contemporary semiotics) ISBN 0-306-40279-3 LC 79-17714

## Step Six: Biography

Bill is gathering many potential sources, and there seems to be a legitimate *yes-no* question about whether apes have language. With at least a tentative thesis question in mind, he wants to find out about the credentials and accomplishments of some of the researchers in the ape-language controversy. Looking up Herbert Terrace, Thomas Sebeok, and Beatrice Gardner in *American Men and Women of Science*, Bill discovers that all three researchers seem to have solid reputations. Terrace has a Ph.D. in psychology from Harvard and has received numerous grants at Columbia University, where he is a professor of psychology. Sebeok has a Ph.D. from Princeton, has an impressive list of publications, and is a professor of anthropology at Indiana University. Gardner has a Ph.D. from Oxford, is an expert in physiological psychology and verbal behavior, and has received various research awards.

**Entries from *American Men and Women of Science***

GARDNER, BEATRICE T, b Vienna, Austria, July 13, 33; nat; m 61. PSYCHOLOGY. Educ: Radcliffe Col. AB, 54; Brown, MSc, 5b, Nat Sci Found Fels, 54-55, 56-58 univ fel, 55-56; Oxford, PhD (zool), 59. Postdoctoral Fels & Grants: USPHS res career develop award, 66-71. Prof Exp: Instr psychol, Wellesley Col. 59-62; res assoc zool. Tufts, 62-63; RES ASSOC PSYCHOL & LECTR, UNIV NEV, RENO, 63- Mem: Am Psychol Asn; Psychonom Soc; Animal Behavior Soc. Res: Motivation; comparative psychology; physiological psychology; verbal behavior. Publ: Normal feeding behavior of three spined stickleback, Behavior, 60; Hunger and sequential responses in the hunting behavior of salticid spiders, J Comp Physiol Psychol, 64; co-auth, A mechanical lure that is highly maneuverable, Psychonomic Sci, 67. Add: Dept of Psychology, University of Nevada, Reno, NE 89507

SEBEOK, THOMAS ALBERT, b Budapest, Hungary, Nov 9, 20; US citizen; m 47; c 1. PSYCHOLINGUISTICS, ANTHROPOLOGY. Educ: Univ Chicago, BA, 41; Princeton Univ, MA, 43, PhD(oriental lang & civilizations), 45. Postdoctoral Fels & Grants: Guggenheim Found fel, 58-59; fel, Ctr Advan Study Behav Sci, 60-61, NFS fel, 66-67; Fulbright grants, Ger, 66 & 71, Italy, 69-71; Nat Acad Sci exchange prof. Acad Socialist Repub Romania, 67, 69 & Acad Sci USSR, 73. Prof. Exp: Mem fac, Ind Univ, Bloomington, 43-65, dir human rels area files, 65-69, PROF URALIC & ALTAIC STUDIES, IND UNIV. BLOOMINGTON, 63-, PROF ANTHROP & DISTINGUISHED PROF LING, 67-, CHMN RES CTR LANG SCI, 56- Concurrent Pos: Consult, Ford Found, Guggenheim Found, Wenner-Gren Found Anthrop Res, US Off Educ, Fel Div. Nat Acad Sci, Can Coun & NSF. Mem: Ling Soc Am (secy-treas, 69-); Am Anthrop Asn (del, 61-72); Int Asn Semiotic Studies (ed-in-chief, Semiotica, 69-). Res: Uralic linguistics; ethnology; folklore; computational linguistics; stylistics; semiotics; zoosemiotics. Publ: Auth, Spoken Hungarian, Holt, 45; co-auth, Psycholinguistics, 54 & ed & contribr, Animal communication, 69, Ind Univ; ed, Current trends in linguistics, (14 vols), 63-, ed, Biographical dictionary of linguistics (series), 71- & auth, Perspectives in zoosemiotics, 72, Mouton; plus over 100 others. Add: Research Center for the Language Sciences, Indiana University, 516 E Sixth St, Bloomington, IN 47401.

TERRACE, HERBERT S, b Brooklyn, N Y, Nov 29, 36. EXPERIMENTAL PSYCHOLOGY. Educ: Cornell, BA, 57. Josiah Macy Found fel & MA, 58; Harvard, USPHS fel, 59-61, PhD(psychol), 61, Postdoctoral Fels & Grants: NIH res grant, 62-; NSF res grant, 63-; Guggenheim fel, 69-70. Prof Exp: Instr psychol, Columbia, 61-63, asst prof. 63-66, assoc prof, 66-68, PROF PSYCHOL, COLUMBIA UNIV, 68- Concurrent Pos: Vis prof psychol, Harvard Univ, 72-73. Mem: AAAS; fel Am Psychol Asn. Res:-Acquisition of stimulus control; errorless discrimination learning; conditioned inhibition; behavioral analyses of cognitive processes. Publ: Co-auth, Introduction to statistics, Individual Learning Systs, San Rafael, Calif, 71; auth. Discrimination learning with and without errors, J Exp Anal Behav, 63; Stimulus control, In: Operant behavior: areas of research, Appleton, 66; Escape from S-, Learning & Motivation, 71; By-products of discrimination learning, In: Vol V, Learning and motivation, 72; Classical conditioning, In: Contemporary experimental psychology, Scott, 73; plus others. Add: Dept of Psychology, Columbia University, 360 Schermerhorn Hall, New York, N Y 10027

## ► Step Seven: Book Reviews

Realizing that book reviews of the four books he is considering should help him choose the most valuable ones, Bill begins with *Book Review Digest*. It guides him to the *New York Review of Books*, which has long, analytical reviews of *Nim* and *Speaking of Apes*. He also reads another review of *Nim* in the *Times Literary Supplement*. *Nim* sounds worth examining because it deals with a single case of the ape-language issue, and Bill is beginning to suspect that the only *yes-no* question he will be able to answer adequately is whether *one* ape acquired language. He then reads a review of *Sign Language and Language Acquisition* in *American Anthropologist* and decides to take all three books out of the library. The review of *Animal Communication* in *Science*, on the other hand, suggests that this book is too general for his needs.

**Entry from *Book Review Digest***

**SPEAKING of apes;** a critical anthology of two-way communication with man; ed. by Thomas A. Sebeok and Jean Umiker-Sebeok. (Topics in contemporary semiotics) 480p il $37.50 '80 Plenum Press

599.88 Chimpanzees—Psychology. Language and languages. Animal communication

ISBN 0-306-40279-3 LC 79-17714

This book "contains 23 separately authored chapters related to the theory or practice of teaching 'language' to apes. One article is a translation from the original German, and 21 others are reprinted directly from the original sources without modification except for combining the bibliographies of all into one reference section at the book's end." (Choice) Bibliography. Index of names.

---

"An introductory chapter by the editors [offers] . . . some insight into the controversies that currently swirl around this area of research. The contributions undertake a dissection of the kinds of artifacts and interpretive problems that surround animal training programs of all kinds, some straightforward, others subtle and illusory. Although the papers are recent, covering 1968-79, with most 1977-79, this arena is so thoroughly embroiled in controversy that any book seems incomplete without the inclusion of papers that have emerged these last few months. Nevertheless, [this volume] . . . will be extremely valuable for use in upper-division or graduate courses or seminars discussing these behaviors [as well as] . . . in a library that serves comparative psychologists, anthropologists, psycholinguists, cognitive ethologists, and others with similar interests."

**Choice** 18:458 n 80 180w

"[This book] gives a strong case for the view that apes do not comprehend sign sequences in any way essentially different from a dog's understanding of such commands as 'Sit up and shake hands' or 'Go get the newspaper.' . . . Consider for example, the 'Clever Hans effect.' The term comes from a classic 1907 study by Oskar Pfungst, a German psychologist, of a famous performing horse of the day who could answer difficult questions, including arithmetical problems, by pawing the ground. In most cases of such performing animals . . . a trainer tells the animal when to stop by secret cueing. . . . In the case of Hans. Pfungst was able to prove by ingenious tests that the horse has learned to respond to subliminal cueing on the part of spectators. Talking-ape researchers have tried to exclude the Clever Hans effect, but the Sebeoks show convincingly that the effect is omnipresent." Martin Gardner

**N Y Rev of Books** 27:3 Mr 20 '80 2100w

Step eight (statistical sources) and step nine (government documents) seem unlikely to yield relevant information about this particular topic, so Bill decides that his search is over, at least for now. It is time to examine and evaluate the evidence he has accumulated.

## Summary and Evaluation of the Sources

Having accumulated a substantial body of evidence for and against the question as to whether primates can use language to communicate, it is time for Bill to take stock of that evidence, to both summarize and evaluate it. Eventually, he must decide whether primates can or cannot talk; or he may decide that, given the state of scientific and linguistic thought at this time, the question cannot be answered with any certainty.

### *Evidence for*

Using American Sign Language (ASL), Beatrice and Allen Gardner of the University of Nevada taught a chimpanzee named Washoe a vocabulary of 160 signs. The Gardners reported that Washoe was able to create novel combinations, such as "water bird" for swan and "you me go out there hurry," and that her performance compared favorably with that of two-year-old children.

Rogers Fouts, a student of the Gardners, taught ASL to six chimpanzees at the University of Oklahoma. Using the same handmolding methods, Penny Patterson of the Gorilla Foundation near Stanford, California, taught a gorilla named Koko 375 hand signals. Patterson also reported that Koko was able to improvise and rhyme words (*blue, do*; *squash, wash*). According to Patterson, Koko even had a tendency to accept bribes and to lie—responses that are not a mimicry of humans but the normal workings of a mind that can predict future events.

Using plastic tiles of different shapes and colors to symbolize words, David Premack taught a chimpanzee named Sarah 130 words.

E. Sue Savage-Rumbaugh of the Yerkes Primate Research Center reported that chimpanzees Sherman and Austin were the first nonhuman primates to communicate symbolically with each other.

The Gardners, Roger Fouts, Penny Patterson, E. Sue Savage-Rumbaugh, David Premack, and others assert that, like humans, chimpanzees and gorillas can use symbols to convey information and that, since they can be taught fairly large vocabularies of symbols, nonhuman primates are capable of true language.

***Evidence Against***

Herbert Terrace, a Columbia University psychologist, taught a chimpanzee named Nim to sign by a method similar to that of the Gardners and Fouts. Like them, he raised Nim as a human child, hoping to prove that the chimpanzee would be able to form sentences. At first Terrace believed that Nim was indeed using a grammar. However, careful analysis of video tapes of Nim's training forced Terrace to conclude that Nim's sequences of words, although they looked like sentences, were in reality merely imitations of the teacher's promptings.

When Terrace examined Nim's hand signals, he discovered that they differed from the phrases spoken by children in two highly significant ways: spontaneity and length. The average length of Nim's signs was 1.5 during the last two years of his training. Children's utterances show a dramatic increase in both length and complexity over the same period. Nim's signs were essentially imitative; they lacked spontaneity and creativity, the hallmark of human language. Terrace concluded that although Nim appeared to be producing sentences, he was simply responding to his trainers' signs.

Since Terrace's conclusions were opposed to those of the Gardners, Fouts, and others, he then examined two films depicting aspects of the training of Washoe and Koko, the animals taught by the Gardners and Patterson. Viewing these films, Terrace reached the same conclusions about Washoe and Koko that he had about Nim. Washoe, Koko, and Nim's "language" production was for the most part imitative; they were merely mimicking their trainers' cues.

T. A. Pettito, R. J. Sanders, T. G. Bever, Thomas and Jean Sebeok, and Terrace grant that projects like those of the Gardners, Fouts, Patterson, and Terrace indicate that primates can learn vocabularies of visual symbols. Extending the issue beyond that of primates, Harvard behaviorist B. F. Skinner asked whether pigeons are capable of symbolic communication and concluded that they indeed are. He trained two Carneaux pigeons, Jack and Jill, to communicate symbolically. Skinner speculated that the "language" produced by primates should be viewed as nothing more than responses to conditioning.

> Pettito, Sanders, Bever, the Sebeoks, Skinner, and Terrace argue that although primates appear to be able to learn words, to use language symbolically, there is no evidence that they have grammatical competence. Primates cannot use symbols to create new meanings; they cannot combine words to produce original sentences. They are incapable of language as human beings know it.

Now that Bill has finished reviewing the evidence for and against the question as to whether primates can use language to communicate, he is aware that the issue is fairly complex. To answer this question intelligently, he'll have to decide whether sign language is a legitimate language; he'll have to think carefully about the nature of language itself. Further complicating the issue is the fact that not all linguists agree as to what constitutes human language. An additional problem is that there is no way to know what a primate, or any animal for that matter, is thinking whenever it appears to use signs symbolically. Last, and perhaps most important of all, is it reasonable to measure primate language against that of a human being?

Although the researchers who take the position that primates are capable of language have presented interesting, thought-provoking evidence, the most persuasive evidence has been presented by those who deny primates the ability to use language. Apes can use language symbolically, but so can pigeons. But neither pigeons nor apes can approach the linguistic spontaneity, dexterity, and creativity of a normal three-year-old human child. In this paper, then, Bill will present both sides as objectively and persuasively as he can. His conclusion, however, will be that although there is evidence that primates can use signs to communicate symbolically, there is no evidence that they are capable of language as human beings know and use it.

## TURNING TO SOURCES OUTSIDE THE LIBRARY

Like most researchers, you generally will begin research in the library, absorbing background information and investigating what others have done. Then, if your particular research question or your library search itself leads to other sources, you will be knowledgeable enough to use them efficiently or to design and conduct an appropriate and reliable field investigation. Although your outside research may suggest a *yes* or *no* answer to your question, it may also lead you back to additional library sources that support, qualify, or dispute the conclusions of your field study or the information supplied by people or groups with personal involvement or interest.

Depending on your research question, you may want or need to turn to different types of sources outside the library. For example, you might learn of specialized information available from businesses, organizations, or government bodies. Library materials or a helpful librarian might suggest local experts—people who could supply information about your question based on their knowledge or experience. As you become a more experienced researcher and learn the research methods of a particular field, you might need to design a research project and collect your own data from the field. Just as your search strategy helps you locate and evaluate books, articles, and other materials in the library, so similar procedures, step-by-step yet flexible, can help you gather reliable information from other sources.

## ▶ Writing Letters to Request Information

You may learn of possible sources of information through library materials prepared by an organization, books or articles or newspaper stories that quote or identify sources, or guides to organizations available in your library's reference collection. Once you come across such a lead and decide that you want to pursue it, use these steps to guide your search for additional information.

### *How to correspond with a potential source of information*

**1.** *Assess your time.* Decide whether you have time to write away for information. You need to allow time to draft and send your letter, time for mail delivery, time (probably several weeks) for the recipient to reply, time for the reply to reach you, and then time to read and incorporate the information with your other materials and notes. If your paper is due in a week or two, do not waste the good will of a source by requesting information that cannot arrive in time.

**2.** *Identify and locate your source.* Find the exact name and address of the individual or group you want to contact. Use your library's collections of out-of-town telephone directories, business and professional directories, corporation annual reports, membership lists for academic and professional organizations, guides to government agencies (local, regional, state, or federal), directories of special-interest and nonprofit groups, and so forth. Be precise and as creative as necessary in identifying and locating a contact person.

**3.** *Decide exactly what you want to request.* Before you begin writing your letter, decide precisely the information you need. You may simply want a copy of a publication available to the public. Or you may want a person with technical expertise to answer three specific questions in order to learn missing information or clarify a published account. Your request should be central to your research question and be reasonable, respecting your correspondent's time, privacy, and personal or professional loyalties. Do not expect a correspondent to supply general background information available at the library, to provide pages of personal reminiscence, or to justify an opinion you happen to dispute.

**4.** *Draft your letter.* Once you know what you need, write a clear, straightforward letter explaining what you want. Identify yourself, outline your research assignment or question, and state exactly what material you want to receive. If you have questions for your correspondent, list these clearly and succinctly. Use a friendly, businesslike tone, and be sure to thank your correspondent for helping you. Should you have any question about the clarity or tone of your letter, ask others to review this draft.

**5.** *Prepare the final version of your letter.* If possible, type or use a letter-quality printer for your final draft. Follow a standard format for a business letter, including your name, address, and, if appropriate, your telephone number in case your correspondent would prefer to call you rather than write back. Keep a copy of this letter so that you have a record of when you wrote and what you requested.

**6.** *Evaluate the information you receive.* Review the material or answer you receive just as you would other information. See how it agrees or disagrees with information from your other sources. Consider whether—and how—the special interests or vantage point of your correspondent might account for a particular point of view. Consider whether—and why—you agree or disagree with this perspective.

**7.** *Follow up on your correspondent's information.* If the information you receive from your respondent is new to you, it may suggest other material that you need to find in the library or elsewhere. Also write back to your respondent, if appropriate, with a thank-you letter or even a copy of your final paper.

**Sample Letter Requesting Information**

140 Eaton Drive, Apt. B
Cresskill, NJ 07626
February 27, 1989

Barbara Bergman
Bay View Hospital
1808 Bay View Drive
Manhattan Beach, CA 90266

Dear Ms. Bergman:

I am a student in the nursing program at Clifton College, affiliated with the Fort Lee Medical Center. While working on a paper about alternative staffing patterns for hospital nurses, I read an article in the January 1986 issue of Nursing Today about your innovations at Bay View.

I would very much appreciate the following additional information about your staffing design:

1. Is your experimental staffing design still being used?
2. How frequently and in what way has the program been evaluated?
3. What changes have been made since beginning the program in 1984?
4. What features of the design now seem most successful?

Thank you very much for taking the time to assist me with my project. Should you wish a copy of my final paper, I would be very happy to send it to you.

Sincerely,
*Jennifer Jameson*
Jennifer Jameson

## ▶ Interviewing People

You may learn of an expert on your research question who is on campus, in your home town, or in your campus community. Or you may know of ordinary people whose personal histories or experiences can supplement or illustrate your more general information. If you wish to speak with such a source personally, you will need to arrange and plan an interview.

### *How to plan an interview*

**1.** *Decide whom you want to interview.* Sometimes a single individual will emerge as an excellent prospective resource—a researcher or expert in your field, a friend of your subject, a person who lived through the events you are studying, a person typical of a type that interests you. Other times, you may need to hunt for personal, anecdotal, or authoritative information by contacting a group, looking for a representative who can talk with you. In this case, one interview may lead to others as you collect names and background information.

**2.** *Decide why you want to interview this person.* Work out your objectives as an interviewer ahead of time. If you expect just to talk and see what comes up, you will probably not be able to ask focused questions and follow up on significant points. Your interviewee may sense that your conversation has no direction and feel frustrated or aggravated at wasting valuable time. To avoid losing information and alienating your interviewee, write out your purposes and goals in advance. Consider what you want to learn, what only this person can tell you, and what kinds of information you most need to discover. If you cannot state your objectives clearly and briefly, consider more carefully why you want to talk with this person.

**3.** *Contact the person.* Write to the person you wish to interview, explaining who you are, what you are investigating, and why you hope to meet. Suggest when and where you might meet. (You might say that you would be glad to meet a local person at a convenient public place such as a local coffee shop, or to stop by the person's office or home. If the person lives at a distance, suggest that you call at a prearranged time.) Supply your address and telephone number so that the person can easily contact you. Since you are asking a favor, try to accommodate the other person's schedule or preferences. If you find that you have two hours free just on Wednesdays and can only be called after 10 P.M., trying to arrange an interview probably is not practical. Also, if time is so short that you must make your initial contact by phone, consider whether you will actually have time to schedule, plan, and conduct the interview.

**4.** *Schedule your meeting.* When the person responds to your letter, be organized and ready to arrange a meeting. Be precise about the date, time, and place where you will meet. Ask for directions if you need them. Make sure that you have specified all the details—the individual's office number, the section of the student union, or whatever. Also make sure that you and your interviewee know how to reach each other in case either of you must reschedule.

**5.** *Plan your questions.* Using your written objectives as a guide, list the key questions that you wish to ask. Try to write questions that are neither so broad that they are vague nor so detailed that they sound like a pop quiz. Try to anticipate how your interviewee may respond to certain questions so that your follow-up can be flexible yet focused. Think about different questions that you might ask after possible alternative answers. Work on phrasing so that your questions are clear and specific, so that your interviewee knows what you want to learn, and so that your questions are smooth and tactful. Once you begin writing questions, allow enough time for additional ideas to develop. Also allow enough time to do any additional library research so that your questions can go beyond the general background.

**6.** *Collect your interview materials.* When you leave for the interview, bring your questions, a notebook and pencils or pens for recording answers, and a small tape recorder if your interviewee agrees to be taped. Also bring any material that you might want to show the person or have at hand during the interview.

**7.** *Conduct the interview.* Once you and the other person have introduced yourselves, you might briefly review your project and purpose so that you both share the same expectations for the interview. Then use your list of questions to begin the conversation. Try to remain flexible if the discussion moves in an unexpected but useful or interesting direction. Return to your questions when the conversation drifts too far from your interests. Let the dialog proceed at a relaxed pace, but be careful not to take up more time than arranged. Even if you have permission to record the interview, jot down major points, any pertinent notes on themes that emerge, nonverbal reactions, and so forth. If you feel anxious about interviewing someone, try a practice interview first with a friend.

**8.** *Evaluate what you learn.* After the interview, review your notes and any tape as soon as possible. You may want to transcribe the tape word by word or take notes as you listen to it several times. The sooner you work on your records, the more accurate your recall and interpretation will be. Then you can assess how the information gained during the interview corresponds with or supplements your other material.

**9.** *Follow up on the interview.* Use the information from the interview to direct your search for additional information. You may wish to interview someone else, look for library information about points raised during the interview, or pursue a new idea suggested during your conversation. If your interviewee has offered or agreed to answer follow-up questions, perhaps by phone, begin to list and organize these as they occur to you. Wait to call until you are sure a second contact is necessary and all your additional questions are clear and orderly. Be sure also to write a short note thanking the person for talking with you.

## Sample Letter Requesting an Interview

182 Smith Hall
Jersey College
1205 So. Dresden Rd.
Jersey City, NJ 07303

Daniel Marston
37-B Paxton Avenue
Plainfield, NJ 07061

Dear Mr. Marston:

For my American history class at Jersey College, I am working on a paper about the Vietnam War. The reference librarian, Ms. Wainwright, mentioned that you were a student here and are active in a local Vietnam veterans group.

Would it be possible for me to talk with you about your experiences at that time? My special interest is the way the ordinary soldier left and returned home, including enlistment efforts, draft procedures, and the personal and public welcome back (or the lack of it).

I would be glad to come to your home or to meet you at the student union or at some other convenient place. My courses are scheduled in the morning, but I am free several afternoons and most evenings during the week. Please let me know what would best suit your schedule. I very much appreciate your assistance with my project.

Sincerely,
*Jackson Carter*
Jackson Carter
(882-7094)

## Sample First Draft of Interview Questions

1. *How did you enter military service? Were you drafted, or did you enlist?*
*What were your experiences when you entered the military?*
2. *~~What was it like at that time?~~*
*Did your experiences match your expectations?*
3. *~~Was it how you expected?~~*
4. *What happened when you came home?*
*Need to ask specific questions about draft pol-icies—how did they work out here?*
*Need to look at local newspapers from the 1960's—might have ~~been~~ incident or two to ask about.*

## ▶ Observing in the Field

Are you examining human actions and interactions, such as behavior in the cafeteria line? Are you gathering data about a recurring event, such as the regular morning traffic jam at the main entrance to the parking lot? Are you studying a situation such as company-sponsored day care about which you need more personal knowledge? In situations such as these, your research question may require data derived directly from field observations. Or your research paper may be enlivened or made more exact with details from observation. If so, you will need to follow a strategy for observation, including steps such as these.

### *How to carry out field observation*

**1.** *Decide what you need to know.* Your precise research question will determine what, when, where, and how often you need to observe. The purpose of your research also determines how carefully you must design and plan your observation. For example, if you want to visit a company day-care center so that you can describe a few activities or outline a typical schedule there, your methods might be less formal. On the other hand, if you wish to conduct a serious traffic study, you probably will need exact, quantifiable observations collected over sufficient time to be representative of actual occurrences. In many courses, your instructor will supply specific guidelines so that your observations will meet that discipline's standards for validity.

**2.** *Decide what you need to observe.* Once you know your purpose, you will be able to decide what you need to observe. For example, a study of behavior in the cafeteria line might focus on the efficiency of the workers, perhaps timing their actions, counting the number or length of their interactions with each person served, or noting the number of times they have to interrupt the routine of the line. On the other hand, another study might focus on the social relations of those in line, the number of people standing alone or in groups, the configuration by gender or class of each group, and the numbers and types of interactions within different groups while waiting. Your decisions about which variables to examine—and your hypotheses or assumptions about their effects—will help you decide what to observe.

**3.** *Figure out a system for recording your data.* Decide exactly which bits of behavior, which movements, which interactions you wish to observe. Then work out a system for recording this information, perhaps using a tally sheet, a check-off chart, a separate reporting form with notes about individual interactions, or some other appropriate method. Consider whether your method of recording data actually tests the variable you want to examine and whether the data can then be tallied or summarized in a useful way. Should you have any questions about the design of your study—or about the effects of your own presence as an observer—discuss them with your instructor or with someone knowledgeable about research in your field.

**4.** *Make any necessary arrangements for conducting your observations.* Plan exactly when and where you will observe. If you plan to visit a site such as a day care center, you obviously will need to contact the director in advance to arrange a visit. Other research situations less obviously require specific permission for your presence but may raise ethical questions about using human subjects, safeguarding individual privacy, and observing the professional standards expected of researchers in your field or institution. Turn to your instructor for advice about how to proceed in such situations.

**5.** *Test your system for recording observations.* If possible, test your method of observing and recording data to make sure that it works efficiently. Sometimes a plan for recording data sounds reasonable but turns out to be too cumbersome or too vague once it is tested in the field. For example, your test may show that you need to define categories more carefully, simplify your recording form, add categories for unexpected behaviors or events, and so forth.

**6.** *Carry out your observations.* Once you have designed and tested your research procedures, you are ready to conduct your actual study. Record as precisely as possible your observations at the established time and place. Be sure to bring all necessary equipment: recording forms, a clipboard, extra pencils or pens, measuring instruments, a watch or stopwatch, and so forth. Should the unexpected occur, make whatever notations or adaptations are necessary at the moment. Later you can decide whether you will need to repeat the entire observation.

**7.** *Analyze your data.* Whatever your method of recording observations, you probably will need to tally, computerize, or otherwise analyze your data. Your method of analysis should be appropriate for your data, your method of data collection, and your research question. Considering all this ahead of time, as you design your recording system, will ensure that your analysis will not claim too much, be too simple or too complex, or be otherwise inappropriate for your purposes. The nature of your question and the purpose of your observations will help determine how rigorously you need to analyze your data and whether you need descriptive (qualitative) or strictly numerical (quantitative) findings.

**8.** *Draw conclusions from your findings.* Once your data are analyzed, your findings will help to answer your research question or suggest the need for additional, perhaps more specific, study. Be certain that your data and your methods can support the conclusions you draw. It is one thing to use a two-week study of campus traffic congestion to support a proposal for changing the timing of a traffic signal or even turning two parallel streets into one-way routes. It is another thing entirely to generalize about commuter campuses nationwide or to complain about the driving habits of all college students. The first recommendation might be well supported; the other conclusions certainly could not be.

**Sample Recording Form for Observations**

Research Question: Does student behavior in the cafeteria line differ from meal to meal?

Circle one: Breakfast Lunch Dinner

Record number in group | Check behaviors observed

| Men | Women | Quiet talking | Loud talking | Joking | Flirting | Physical rowdiness | Other |
|---|---|---|---|---|---|---|---|

## ▶ Conducting a Survey

Certain courses or research questions may require you to tap public opinion—of students or people in general or of members of a specific group such as dorm residents, commuter students, or political science majors. A survey using a carefully designed questionnaire may help you understand the views of others or argue for a proposed change. Survey techniques are complex, so follow the specific guidelines supplied by your instructor. In general, however, use these steps to guide your survey strategy.

### *How to conduct a survey*

**1.** *Set the limits for your survey.* You will need to decide what group you want to survey, how many contacts or responses you will need for representative results, how you want to conduct the survey, and exactly what you want to investigate. You also will need to consider whether to collect demographic information (age, gender, and so forth) in order to establish that all those surveyed do indeed belong to the group under study or to establish that these other characteristics do not themselves account for a result whose cause should be assigned elsewhere. Finally, you need to consider whether your study requires any privacy safeguards or raises any ethical issues. Consult with your instructor as you work out these limits and define your responsibilities as a researcher.

**2.** *Design a questionnaire.* Once you know whom and what you want to survey, you can begin to construct appropriate questions. State your questions so that they are not ambiguous or confusing. Make sure each question focuses on one item at a time. You also need to supply directions and select a method for answering—a scale of 1 to 5, a series of choices, *yes-no* answers, comments, and so on. When you make this choice, you should consider how you plan to analyze the data later and design your form appropriately. For example, tallying up multiple-choice answers is far more manageable than analyzing open-ended comments. Adding a sample question and answer to illustrate how you want respondents to mark their answers will help ensure clear and useable responses. The method of marking answers and returning the form should be as clear as the questions themselves. Once your questionnaire is written and revised, next consider whether its physical appearance is designed as effectively as possible.

**3.** *Test your questionnaire.* Try out your questionnaire on a small group if possible. Ask your friends or classmates and your instructor to critique its content and design. Your data will be no more reliable than the instrument used for collecting them. If your test group finds the directions confusing, misreads a question, does not know how to answer, or has some other problem, you will need to rework your questionnaire.

**4.** *Make any necessary arrangements for conducting your survey.* Request permission, if needed, for distributing your questionnaire. Also make arrangements for collecting the completed questionnaires and for distributing a reminder if too few are returned initially.

**5.** *Distribute your questionnaires.* Make sure that the questionnaires go only to the group you wish to survey (sophomores, but not all students, for example), and that the method of collection (a box at back of the room or your campus address, for instance) is clear to participants.

**6.** *Analyze the responses.* Consult with your instructor for advice about how many completed questionnaires are needed for a reliable sample. (The answer depends on the nature of the survey, the method you will use to analyze the data, and the conclusions you intend to draw.) Once a reasonable period of time has passed and a reasonable number of responses has been collected, you are ready to analyze the data. Use a method appropriate for your data, your research question, and your research expertise. Whatever your statistical methods, you will need to tabulate your results so that you can present them clearly to others.

**7.** *Interpret your results.* Besides showing how respondents answered the questions on your questionnaire, you need to interpret these results, explaining what the responses may mean. Your interpretation should suggest the significance of the answers without claiming more than your survey and the quantity and quality of responses can justify. For example, a survey of ten freshmen probably is not large enough to generalize about the views of the entire class. On the other hand, a survey of ten sophomores on the swim team might be sufficient to generalize about that group.

**8.** *Follow up on your survey.* Once your survey is complete and your results are analyzed and interpreted, compare your conclusions with those of other researchers. You now can see how your study fits into a larger context, what it shows about your research question, and what it suggests might be done next.

**Sample Survey Form**

This is a survey for my Psych 100 class. Please fill out the form and return it to the box beside the library reference desk. Your participation is optional, and all responses are anonymous. Thank you for helping me with my project.

Circle your answer to each question using a scale of 1 to 5.

Sample Question and Answer

| Time spent in a typical week | Every day (7) | Many days (5-6) | Some days (3-4) | Few days (1-2) | Never (0) |
|---|---|---|---|---|---|
| How often do you eat lunch in the cafeteria? | 1 | (2) | 3 | 4 | 5 |

| Time spent in a typical week | Every day (7) | Many days (5-6) | Some days (3-4) | Few days (1-2) | Never (0) |
|---|---|---|---|---|---|
| 1. How often do you go to the library to study? | 1 | 2 | 3 | 4 | 5 |
| 2. How often do you use the reserve reading room? | 1 | 2 | 3 | 4 | 5 |
| 3. How often do you use the card catalog? | 1 | 2 | 3 | 4 | 5 |
| 4. How often do you use the search computer? | 1 | 2 | 3 | 4 | 5 |
| 5. How often do you use a magazine, jounal, or newspaper? | 1 | 2 | 3 | 4 | 5 |
| 6. How often do you go up in the stacks? | 1 | 2 | 3 | 4 | 5 |
| 7. How often do you socialize out in the hallway before studying? | 1 | 2 | 3 | 4 | 5 |
| 8. How often do you socialize outside after studying? | 1 | 2 | 3 | 4 | 5 |
| 9. How often do you go out with a group of friends? | 1 | 2 | 3 | 4 | 5 |
| 10. How often do you go out on a date? | 1 | 2 | 3 | 4 | 5 |

Class: Freshman Sophomore Junior Senior
Gender: Male Female
Age: Married: Yes No

## ORGANIZING YOUR RESEARCH PAPER

After you have read all your evidence, come to know the subject thoroughly, and given yourself time to assimilate the information, you are ready to begin structuring your paper. Since the research paper is usually longer and more formal than most of your other writing, it is almost impossible to write one without making some kind of outline. You may keep refining the outline as you work on the paper, but you will avoid headaches for yourself if you work from at least a simple version of an outline.

The overall plan of your paper and outline should follow these principles:

## ► Introducing the Research Topic or Question

Research usually needs an introduction for the same reason that everything else does—to catch reader interest. Somewhere in the introduction, you must ask your thesis question. The thesis question is preferable to the thesis statement because it does not give away at the outset what position you intend to take. Some instructors prefer to see the thesis question as the first sentence of the introduction, but it also makes good sense to have it near the end of the introduction, to finish the introduction and make an effective transition to the rest of the research paper. An introduction is most often a single paragraph, but you may write an introduction of more than one paragraph if doing so doesn't give the impression that the introduction is holding up the paper.

## ► Presenting the Opposing View

When you start to research an issue, try to be unbiased; as we said earlier in this chapter, you do not approach a research issue "knowing the answer." If you have isolated a legitimate *yes-no* issue, the question obviously has two sides. Your research, however, will help you to answer the question even if a definitive answer is not yet possible. In organizing your paper, it is wise to present the opposing view first, if there is one. Presenting the other side's position first, and presenting it well, will help you to convince the reader that you thoroughly understand the issues, that you are a fair and unbiased researcher. It also has the advantage of providing you with something to argue against.

Present the case for the other side fairly and completely with the reasons and evidence that an intelligent opponent would use. Do not offer any counterevidence or argue against the opposing view here. In this section you are trying to present the opposing side's case as well as possible. Instead of finding fault, you should end this section by showing which of the opposing arguments is the strongest. Point out to the reader what a reasonable person should concede in the opposing argument. The more positively you can treat the opposing side, the stronger you can make the opposing side look, the fairer you will seem—and, of course, the more imposing your own side will appear. Anyone can win an argument against a weak opponent; but it takes a skillful debater to win against a *strong opponent*. It is conceivable that you could concede *all* of the opposing view (the opponent is not "wrong") and still demonstrate the superiority of the other side—which may simply have newer information to offer in the argument. Keep in mind that you do not have to *prove* anything absolutely in a limited research paper; your job is only to examine both sides of the question for the reader's benefit. In the *conclusion*, you can tell the reader what a reasonable person should conclude from the data in your paper.

## ► Presenting Your View

Usually, a research writer will decide that one side of the case is superior to the other. If your research leads you to conclude that both sides are equally strong or equally weak (for lack of data, for example), then you must arbitrarily pick one side or the other to present first; but in such a case, you must also take extra precautions not to bias the arguments in favor of one side or the other.

If there is a "better view," this section can be started with counterarguments if you have some to offer. If you have discovered, for example, errors in data or reasoning in the opposing view, this is a good place to point them out. You must still try to remain the objective, dispassionate researcher; it would be a good idea to offer contradictory evidence if you are going to find fault with the opposition. But you need not go looking for flaws in the opposing view. If you have a good research question—one that is solidly two-sided and one that you feel very strongly about—you will probably find that both sides have plausible data and authorities to back them up and that the topic continues to interest and intrigue you. In a good research paper, it is to your advantage to present the opposing view in a fair and interesting way; otherwise, you will not have a worthy opponent to argue against. The better view, presented fairly and logically, will seem obvious and persuasive.

In a counterargument, an effective strategy is to concede the more reasonable points of the opposing view, especially if they have some basis in fact or are founded on believable assumptions. The challenge then is to show that the stronger side is more powerful, more persuasive, a more reasonable interpretation of the evidence.

With or without counterarguments, make the case for the better view: present examples, data, arguments. Especially if you have new arguments to offer—new meaningful ideas that apparently have not occurred to the opposition—this is the place to present them.

## ► Presenting the Conclusion

The conclusion of your paper should be the *climax* of the paper. There is still important work to do in the conclusion; so far, your paper has shown that there is a research question and that there are two opposing sides to the question. Now, you must answer the thesis question. It may be helpful to the reader if you start the conclusion with a brief summary of the arguments. But you must conclude with one of three positions: The first view is correct, your view is correct, or there is not enough evidence available for an intelligent conclusion to be drawn. If you decide after all that your view is indeed superior, you must help the reader understand why, through more substantive data, better authorities, more convincing and logical arguments, and so on.

You should save something interesting for your conclusion. The conclusion isn't just the end of the paper; it is the *point* of the paper. If you use up your most effective material in the body of the paper, the conclusion will look weak by comparison. In addition to showing the reader the outcome of the argument, you must give the reader a sense of "ending." An apt quote, some striking fact or statistic, a relevant personal note, or even an especially well-worded final sentence will round out the ending and help the reader to "get out" of the paper (similar to the problem of getting the reader into the paper in the introduction).

## ► Listing Your References

Different professors require different formats for documentation notes and other references. Before handing in or submitting documented papers, ask which format is preferred. In general, footnotes (at the bottom of the page) and endnotes (at the conclusion of the paper) are going out of style. Preferred modern practice is to include parenthetical references within the text and a complete list of "Works Cited" at the end of the text. Be sure to follow exactly whatever style sheet you use.

## ► Listing Your Bibliography

There are many different kinds of bibliographies; they serve different purposes. An annotated bibliography gives the author's evaluations of the sources cited. However, a bibliography that is nothing more than a list of the same books and articles in your references is not the best idea. A bibliography should be a useful part of your paper by itself—a list of significant books and articles on the issue, not just those you have actually cited in your paper. The bibliography lets readers see how recent your research is and also whether you are aware of important publications. Thus, the bibliography is an aid to other researchers who may come after you.

A selected bibliography is a list of resources available, not just those you actually cite in your paper. You will undoubtedly read more than the works you cite. Ideally, you should read and assimilate everything available on a research question, but practically, there is likely to be too much available for such thoroughness in anything shorter than a doctoral dissertation. You can, however, at least skim through a great deal of material to determine whether it would be useful for researchers on your topic. Research is cumulative, and as each new researcher adds to the existing bibliographies, an increasingly complete list of the works available will be compiled. You will soon get to know from a little reading which are the important works. Read as much of the available material as you have time for but never put anything into your bibliography that you haven't actually seen. You will find many things listed in indexes, for example, but you must not simply build your bibliography from the indexes without at least skimming through each item to see if it is related to the issue and likely to be useful to other researchers.

# CHAPTER ▲ TEN

# *Documenting Sources*

**"By necessity, by proclivity, and by delight, we all quote."**

**RALPH WALDO EMERSON**

The purpose of documentation is to back up what you say in a paper. It is not enough to say that current research shows that nuclear waste can be safely disposed of in deep-shaft mines; you must show the reader *who* says so and *where*. Other researchers will wish to check and verify your findings; the more thorough and accurate documentation you offer your readers, the more reliable your research becomes. Faulty documentation violates the basic concept of research.

## CHOOSING A DOCUMENTATION FORMAT

There are several different style sheets (documentation handbooks) used by modern researchers in different fields. The chief rule about documentation is to be logical and consistent in the way you write your notes; therefore, it might be a good idea to buy one or another of the available style sheets and then follow it carefully. Much of the style in this chapter is based on the *MLA Handbook for Writers of Research Papers*, 3rd edition, by Joseph Gibaldi and Walter S. Achtert (New York: Modern Language Association, 1988), a standard style sheet for work in English and the humanities. This chapter also supplies detailed examples using another widely used style sheet, the *Publication Manual of the American Psychological Association* (APA).

## DOCUMENTATION NOTES

Documentation notes (source citations) were originally, by convention, placed at the bottom, or foot of the page (hence, "footnotes") or at the end of the paper (hence, "endnotes") but modern practice eliminates them and calls instead for citation of sources within the text of the paper. If you are using the MLA style sheet, insert the author's last name and a page reference in parentheses to identify the source and specific location for all borrowed material, like this:

```
    Psychologists would agree that art therapy is pre-
ferable to art education in the prison system because
"art therapy attempts to achieve healthy individuation
```

through the use of art psychotherapy or art therapy while art education attempts to expand [a person's] consciousness by providing him or her with a wealth of new experiences and symbols" (Feder 108).

In this example, the parenthetical citation indicates that the quote was taken from page 108 of Feder's work. You further identify the source by including a "Works Cited" list at the end of the paper. The entries in the "Works Cited" list are not numbered but are instead arranged alphabetically in the following hanging indention form:

Feder, Elaine, and Bernard Feder. The Expressive Art Therapies. Englewood Cliffs: Prentice, 1981.

Similarly, when you use APA or other name-date style sheets, there are no footnotes or endnotes. Again, you use short references in the text to refer to sources fully identified in the bibliography:

The long-term effects of dumping nuclear waste in the ocean "are impossible to predict but horrifying to speculate about" (Trent, 1983, p. 89).

The full citation then appears at the end of the paper in a list headed "References."

## SUBSTANTIVE NOTES

While most of your notes will be references to source material, occasionally you may wish to include a substantive note, an actual note from you to the reader in which you give additional information relevant to your research but not entirely necessary to what you are saying at that point in the paper. There are mixed feelings about these substantive notes; many researchers believe that any relevant information ought to be included in the main text and that irrelevant information should be eliminated entirely. But because other researchers do use substantive notes, the best advice is to use them only when you cannot get the information into your text otherwise. The notes themselves should be placed at the end of the text immediately before your list of "Works Cited" in a section called "Notes." The notes should be numbered according to the order of their appearance in the paper. A corresponding note number should be inserted in the text at the point where you want the reader to note your supplemental information. The numbers should be inserted as superscripts, placed a half-line above the regular line of text.

## WHAT TO DOCUMENT: PARENTHETICAL REFERENCES

### ► Direct Quotations

Any words you copy from another source should be placed in quotes, followed by the parenthetical reference to the source.

```
     Even Holden's brutal encounters with reality are
quickly transformed into fantasy: "About halfway to the
bathroom, I sort of started pretending I had a bullet in
my guts. Old Maurice had plugged me." (Salinger 103).
```

### ► Ideas and Words from a Source

Words and concepts that you take from a source and incorporate into your own sentences should be documented:

```
     Never at a loss for words, Holden manufactures adjec-
tives from nouns and verbs to describe "vomity" taxicabs
and "hoodlumy-looking" street people (Birkfeld 73).
```

Be especially aware of the obligation to acknowledge ideas, interpretations, analyses, and concepts that represent someone else's thinking on your topic. It can sometimes be easy to incorporate ideas from your sources into your paper as though they are your own. To do so is dishonest scholarship, and it is to be rigorously avoided. People often describe plagiarism as copying words from a source and passing them off as your own. But you are plagiarizing, too, if you pass off someone else's ideas as your own. (See Chapter 9 for more advice on avoiding plagiarism.) You can document someone else's ideas the same way that you do his or her actual words:

```
     Holden can be thought of as a model of lost and con-
fused adolescence, but he is a prototype for a very small,
privileged class of modern youth (Birkfeld 75).
```

### ► Paraphrases and Restatements

When you change a source's phrases or ideas into your own words, document them as you would a quotation by mentioning the source in your text as well as listing it on the "Works Cited" page:

```
     Jefferson's notion in the Declaration of Independence
that everyone is born with the same inalienable rights and
```

privileges as everyone else simply ignores the privileges of wealth (Smith 237).

## Allusions and Incomplete References to Sources

Regardless of whether you quote them or paraphrase from them, document all allusions and incomplete references. For examples of endnote style, refer to Gibaldi and Achtert's discussion in the *MLA Handbook*.

## Source Within a Source

You may discover one author quoting another in such a way that you will want to quote the second author yourself. If at all possible, you should find the *original* source and quote from that, instead of quoting from the secondhand source (for accuracy's sake, if nothing else). Suppose you were doing a paper on the relevance of grammar to composition, and you were reading Virginia Allen's article "Teaching Standard English as a Second Dialect." In it you would find the following:

Martin Joos, who has made a special study of people's attitudes toward language, says "Long before any teacher began to correct his English, the child has learned all he needs to know, at his age, about people and their places; he has developed considerable skill in judging adults by their speech." (95).

The page number refers to Martin Joos's article "Language and the School Child." If you want to use the Joos quote, you should find and cite the article it comes from, instead of citing the page on which it appears in Virginia Allen's article. This, of course, means that you should also be sure to include the Joos article in your list of "Works Cited" as follows:

Joos, Martin. "Language and the School Child." Word Study 11.2 (1964): 92–104.

However, sometimes the original source is not available, or for some other reason the researcher must rely on the secondhand source (and you must be very certain that there is a good reason for doing so). In that case, include the secondary source in your list of "Works Cited," and cite the source as follows:

Martin Joos, who has made a special study of people's attitudes toward language, says "Long before any teacher began to correct his English, the child has learned all he needs to know, at his age, about people and their places;

```
he has developed considerable skill in judging adults by
their speech." (quoted in Allen 358).
```

When you use secondary sources, you rely on others to quote or interpret the primary source accurately. Because secondary sources are usually written by respected scholars, it is easy to assume that the quotes are accurate, but there is always the possibility of error. There is the further danger that in quoting a primary source out of context (without reading the rest of the article) you may distort the author's orginal intention or misapply his or her meaning.

## WHAT NOT TO DOCUMENT

Common knowledge need not be documented. There is no certain test for common knowledge, but in general you can consider knowledge to be "common" if it is widely known by educated people, if it is readily available in most general reference works such as encylopedias or almanacs, or if it is available through the popular communications media: television, newspapers, and popular magazines. There is no need to document, for example, who the president is or where the White House is or that Shakespeare is the author of *Hamlet*.

Uncontested knowledge also need not be documented, even if it is not "common" knowledge. Dates of historical events, for example, may or may not be considered common knowledge; but unless the date is a matter of dispute in the research, it can be considered uncontested information. A handy rule to follow is this: Anything that would damage your case if it were removed from your paper or proved wrong should be documented.

To a degree, documenting is part of the researcher's style, part of his or her view of self. Some researchers are very careful to document everything in their work. Others take a more relaxed attitude. To avoid the suspicion of plagiarism, beginning researchers should be careful to document everything taken from sources.

## HOW TO DOCUMENT IN MLA STYLE

The following examples are samples of entries you would find in a bibliographical list. The list should be placed on a separate page from the main text of the paper and titled "Works Cited." The entries should be placed in alphabetical order according to the authors' last names or the work title if no author is listed. A bibliographical list should include all works you quote from; some users of bibliographies want you to include all works you consult. In college, your instructors will generally tell you which type of list to submit.

### BOOK, ONE AUTHOR

Berry, Ralph. <u>Shakespeare and the Awareness of the Audience</u>. New York: St. Martin's, 1985.

### BOOK, ONE EDITOR

Graves, Richard, ed. Rhetoric and Composition: A Sourcebook for Teachers and Writers. 2nd ed. Upper Montclair: Boynton/Cook, 1984.

### BOOK, TWO AUTHORS OR EDITORS

Golden, James L., and Edward P. J. Corbett. The Rhetoric of Blair, Campbell, and Whately. New York: Holt, 1968.

### BOOK, MORE THAN TWO AUTHORS OR EDITORS

Britton, James, et al. The Development of Writing Abilities (11-18). London: MacMillan Education, 1975.

### CHAPTER IN AN EDITED WORK

Goren, Arthur A. "The Jewish Press." The Ethnic Press in the United States: A Historical Analysis and Handbook. Ed. Sally M. Miller. New York: Greenwood, 1987. 203-228.

### BOOK, COMMITTEE, OR GROUP AUTHOR

Commission on Obscenity and Pornography. The Report on Obscenity and Pornography. Toronto: Bantam, 1970.

### BOOK, TRANSLATION

#### *Emphasis on Comments by Translator*

Hammer, Louis, and Sara Schyfter, ed. and trans. Recent Poetry of Spain: A Bilingual Anthology. Old Chatham, NY: Sachem, 1983.

#### *Emphasis on Author*

Rilke, Rainer Maria. Sonnets to Orpheus. Trans. M. D. Herter Norton. New York: Norton, 1970.

### MAGAZINE ARTICLE, AUTHOR NAMED

Blech, Benjamin. "Don't Blame the Victim." Newsweek 19 Sept. 1988: 10–11.

### MAGAZINE ARTICLE, NO AUTHOR NAMED

"Byrd of West Virginia: Fiddler in the Senate." Time 23 Jan. 1978: 13.

### NEWSPAPER ARTICLE

Talbert, Bob. "Why Are We in Such a Downer?" Detroit Free Press. 10 Jan. 1978: A9.

### PROFESSIONAL JOURNAL, EACH ISSUE STARTS WITH PAGE 1

Rubin, David M. "Remember Swine Flu?" Columbia Journalism Review 16.2 (1977): 42–46.

### PROFESSIONAL JOURNAL, PAGES NUMBERED BY VOLUME

Fuderer, Laura Sue. "Feminist Critical Theory: A Checklist." Modern Fiction Studies 34 (1988): 501–13.

### DISSERTATION (UNPUBLISHED)

Blank, William Earl. "The Effectiveness of Creative Dramatics in Developing Voice, Vocabulary, and Personality in the Primary Grades." Diss. U of Denver, 1953.

### LECTURE OR SPEECH

Hellman, John. "Rambo: The Frontier Hero with a Cross." International Convention of the American Studies Association. New York, 22 Nov. 1987.

### FILM

Ashby, Hal, dir. Coming Home. With Jane Fonda, John Voight, and Bruce Dern. United Artists, 1978.

### PLAY

Lindsay-Hoagg, Michael, dir. Whose Life Is It Anyway? By Brian Clark. With Tom Conti and Jean Marsh. Trafalgar Theatre, New York, 19 Apr. 1979.

### RADIO OR TELEVISION PROGRAM

"TV or Not TV." Bill Moyers Journal. PBS. WNET, New York. 23 Apr. 1979.

### RECORD ALBUM OR TAPE

Taylor, Kate. Sister Kate. Cotillion Records, SD 9045, 1971.

### PERSONAL LETTER

Winterowd, W. Ross. Letter to the author. 26 July 1987.

### PERSONAL INTERVIEW

Rather, Dan. Personal Interview. 24 July 1988.

## HOW TO DOCUMENT IN APA STYLE

### BOOK, ONE AUTHOR

Brubaker, E. (1987). Working with the elderly: A social systems approach. Newbury Park, CA: Sage.

### BOOK, ONE EDITOR

Noble, H. B. (Ed.). (1988). Next: The coming era in science. Boston: Little, Brown.

BOOK, TWO AUTHORS OR EDITORS, EDITION NUMBER

Woolfolk, A. E., & McCune-Nicolich, L. (1984). Educational psychology for teachers (2nd ed.). Englewood Cliffs, NJ: Prentice Hall.

BOOK, MORE THAN TWO AUTHORS OR EDITORS

Boydston, J., Kelley, M., & Margolis, A. (1988). The limits of sisterhood: The Beecher sisters on women's rights and woman's sphere. Chapel Hill: University of North Carolina Press.

CHAPTER IN AN EDITED WORK

Warwick, P. V., & Cohen, L. J. (1985). The institutional management of cultural diversity: An analysis of the Yugoslav experience. In P. Brass (Ed.), Ethnic groups and the state (pp. 160-201). Totowa, NJ: Barnes and Noble.

BOOK, COMMITTEE OR GROUP AUTHOR

Associated Press Sports Staff. (1972). The sports immortals. Englewood Cliffs, NJ: Prentice Hall.

BOOK, NO AUTHOR

The Carnegie Council on Policy Studies in Higher Education: A summary of reports and recommendations. (1980). San Francisco: Jossey-Bass.

BOOK, TRANSLATION

Dostoyevsky, F. (1950). Crime and punishment. (C. Garnett, Trans.). New York, Modern Library.

### MAGAZINE ARTICLE, AUTHOR NAMED

Blake, P. (1988, July 4). How machines can defeat people. Time, pp. 48–49.

### MAGAZINE ARTICLE, NO AUTHOR NAMED

Medical waste just one threat to beaches. (1989, January/February). National Parks, pp. 9–10.

### NEWSPAPER ARTICLE

Cowen, R. C. (1989, January 27). Poor math skills hamper U.S., panel says. The Christian Science Monitor, p. 8.

### NEWSLETTER ARTICLE

Return of the leech. (1988, October). Harvard Medical School Health Letter, p. 3.

### PROFESSIONAL JOURNAL, EACH ISSUE STARTS WITH PAGE 1

Hahn, H. (1988). The politics of physical differences: Disability and discrimination. Journal of Social Issues, 44(1), 39–47.

### PROFESSIONAL JOURNAL, PAGES NUMBERED BY VOLUME

Massey, D. S., & Denton, N. A. (1988). Suburbanization and segregation in U.S. metropolitan areas. American Journal of Sociology, 94, 592–626.

### PROFESSIONAL JOURNAL, MORE THAN TWO AUTHORS

Johnson, M. K., Foley, M. A., Suengas, A. G., & Raye, C. L. (1988). Phenomenal characteristics of memories for perceived and imagined autobiographical events.

Journal of Experimental Psychology: General, 117, 371–376.

PROFESSIONAL JOURNAL, NO AUTHOR

New Alzheimer drug trials begun; major initiative proposed. (1987). Geriatric Nursing: American Journal of Care for the Aging, 8, 293–294.

PROFESSIONAL JOURNAL, WHOLE ISSUE

Asch, A., & Fine, M. (Eds.). (1988). Moving disability beyond stigma [Special issue]. Journal of Social Issues, 44(1).

GOVERNMENT REPORT, GROUP AUTHOR

Division of Publications, National Park Service. (1981). Clara Barton National Historical Site, Maryland (Handbook 110). Washington, DC: Department of the Interior.

OERI Japan Study Team, U.S. Study of Education in Japan. (1987). Japanese education today. Washington, DC: U.S. Government Printing Office.

## ABBREVIATIONS AND BIBLIOGRAPHIC TERMS

In general, we recommend that you avoid using abbreviations. The space they save can cost much in terms of possible misreading. However, as a researcher, you will encounter some common abbreviations and bibliographic terms used in writing and publishing and in college reading in general. If you must use an abbreviation, use the commonly accepted forms. Currently, abbreviations require neither periods after letters nor spaces between letters when the abbreviation is made up of capital letters. Most abbreviations with lowercase letters, however, do require periods. You should become familiar with the following:

| | |
|---|---|
| A.D. | *Anno Domini*, in the year of our Lord |
| anon. | anonymous; the author's name is unknown (never appropriate for an article that is merely *unsigned* as in a magazine or newspaper) |
| ante | before |
| attrib. | attributed; authorship is not positive |
| B.C. | before Christ |
| b. | born |
| bib. | biblical |
| bibliog. | bibliography |
| © | copyright |
| ca. or c. | *circa*, about; the date is approximate |
| cap. | capital, capitalized |
| cf. | confer, compare |
| ch. (chs., plural) | chapter(s) |
| col. (cols., plural) | column(s) |
| d. | died |
| diss. | dissertation |
| ed. (eds., plural) | editor(s); edition |
| e.g. | *exempli gratia*, for example |
| esp. | especially |
| est. | estimated, estimation |
| et al. | *et alii*, and others |
| etc. | *et cetera*, and so forth |
| f. (ff., plural) | and the following page(s) |
| fn. | footnote |

| | |
|---|---|
| fr. | from |
| ibid. | *ibidem*, in the same place, cited immediately above |
| i.e. | *id est*, that is |
| l. (ll., plural) | line(s) |
| loc. cit. | *loco citato*, in the place cited; in the same place mentioned earlier |
| MS. (MSS., plural) | manuscript(s) |
| n.d. | no date of publication |
| n. (nos., plural) | number(s) |
| n.p. | no place of publication; no publisher |
| obs. | obsolete |
| op. cit. | *opere citato*, in the work cited recently |
| p. (pp., plural) | page(s) |
| pl. (pls., plural) | plate(s) |
| pseud. | pseudonym |
| pt. (pts., plural) | part(s) |
| rev. | revised, revision; review, reviewer |
| rpt. | reprint; reprinted |
| sec. (secs., plural) | section(s) |
| ser. | series |
| sic. | thus it is; a mistake in the original |
| var. | variant |
| v. (vv., plural) | verse(s) |
| *vide* | see |
| vol. (vols., plural) | volume(s) |
| vs., v. | *versus*, against |

# THE WRITER'S MIND AT WORK

## DRAFTING AND REVISING THE RESEARCH PAPER

Though the research paper may be more formally planned from the start than some other, shorter papers (through the use of an outline), there is no reason to believe that revision of your ideas and structure will be any less important in this type of writing. In fact, drafting may make an even more dramatic difference in the evolution of the research paper than in shorter writing simply because there is so much more material to keep track of. It may be easier than usual to get side-tracked or to use inappropriate examples or to arrange ideas in an awkward way when you are trying to fit all the data that you've found so interesting (and worked so hard to accumulate) into your research.

Some of the planning techniques that you have learned such as clustering or freewriting or scripts of the writer's mind can be useful in helping you to generate the paper outline or to supply details throughout your writing to back up your main arguments. Scripts of your writer's mind, for instance, could help you to convert some brief notes and quotations into semideveloped paragraphs. Eva was doing some preliminary thinking about a research paper on the wolf, and she began with the following script of her writer's mind:

### THE WRITER'S MIND: Exploring a Research Topic

*As the mood of the nation changes, we become more concerned with our environment and embarrassed for what we have done to it. In an attempt to right the wrongs of the past and prepare for the future, we have made attempts in recent years to reclaim and protect our wilderness heritage. In response to this mood an idea was conceived to reintroduce an animal whose name creates an image of the wilderness: the wolf. Any good review of a subject should start with a general background of the subject. The book I found entitled* The Wolf:

The Ecology and Behavior of an Endangered Species *by David Meck will give a biological and behavioral background of the wolf plus a historical discussion of the relationship between man and the wolf. This discussion will be useful in explaining problems between man and wolf.*

*There are also numerous papers discussing the proposed plans for reintroduction and the best methods that could be taken. One work that I must really look at is the* Eastern Timber Wolf Recovery Plan. *The plan is quite complete, ranging from consideration of public response to biological feasibility. In response to a paper by Steven Fritts entitled "Can Relocated Wolves Survive?" I can discuss some ideas that may increase the success of some of the other relocation programs.*

The exploratory draft of this type of longer paper can be viewed as a sort of patchwork quilt of freewritings of initial ideas. Notice in the draft below how Eva has used the ideas she came up with in her writer's mind to begin to explain her argument to a reader.

**EXPLORATORY DRAFT:**
**Reintroduction of the Wolf: What it Means to Us and What Can Be Done**

As the mood of our nation changes, we are more and more embarrassed about our environment and concerned about what we have done to it. In an attempt to right our wrongs we have tried to preserve and reclaim our wilderness heritage. One idea was conceived to reintroduce an animal whose very name carries the image of wilderness: the wolf. However, the wolf is an animal of many images, most of them bad and reintroduction has meant the rebirth of emotions that led to the near extinction of the wolf in 48 states. Plans for reintroduction are expensive, biologically complicated and extremely controversial and as a result attract considerable attention. The public seems to sit on 3 sides of the issue, some being wolf lovers seeing the wolf as a gentle, loving parent and provider, some being wolf haters seeing the wolf as an evil monster, and some being indifferent.

Unfortunately for the wolf, the wolf-haters outnumber the wolf-lovers and any attempt at reintroduction will meet its greatest challenge not in economic feasibility or biological possibility but in social acceptability.

This paper will deal with two of these areas: biological possibility and cultural acceptability, leaving economic feasibility to the experts. It will begin with a brief introduction about why the wolf should be saved and then move to biological and cultural considerations, concluding with a look at some of the alternative plans and attempts underway.

The first question that comes to most people's minds when they are talking about why we should reintroduce the wolf is "Why are we trying to bring back an animal we have spent the last two decades trying to remove?" The answer that might come to the mind of most of those who favor wolf reintroduction is that "we learned from our mistakes." Aldo Leopold, the father of wildlife management, [who was in favor of wolf control and then changed his mind in later years] once said that "the key to intelligent thinking was to save all the parts." If you remove a piece of the puzzle the entire picture may be ruined. Aldo Leopold realized back in 1937 that nature and its workings were too complicated for man to fully understand and that extreme caution should be practiced in any attempt at wildlife management.

Caution was not used with the eradication of the wolf; biologically man has been pretty lucky. The wolf has been replaced by man as top predator in most areas and there have been only a few problems with prey population booms and the resulting habitat destruction and starvation. However, an argument can be made for the loss of the wolf as a tool in weeding out the old, sick, or injured and in the decline in the health of animals within the wildlife prey populations. Man as top predator tends to look for the "biggest and best" removing superior genes and leaving inferior genes to propagate new offspring. It should also be mentioned that the eradication of the wolf opened the door for the coyote which may represent an even larger problem for livestock growers than the wolf ever did. The reason for this is that wolves need more land and therefore their populations are less dense and fewer wolves come into contact with man. The coyote moves alone and it needs less land; therefore more coyotes come into contact with man and his livestock. Also coyotes are more at home on the grazing lands, whereas wolves tend to avoid humans more, staying to the rougher back country where there is less livestock.

These problems are important but relatively minor compared to what could have happened as a result of removing a link from the natural work of a community. But these biological problems are not the whole story. The wolf is like no other animal with the possible exception of the bald eagle. It has played an enormous role in the history of our country, not to mention the entire northern hemisphere. It has filled our thoughts and legends and literature from the beginning of our existence to the present; and filled our lives with childhood fairy tales and adult movies and books. The wolf is an image, a mirror to ourselves and our history, but more than that, it is a creature of this earth and has a right to exist just as we do. Nancy Shestak said it very well in a statement she made at a workshop for the reintroduction of wolves:

"Every living thing has an intrinsic right to live. However, the wolf is somehow more than just another animal. For man he is an important link to the animal world. He fills our mythology, our folklore, our lingo, our art, our fantasy--and as such he is esthetically important for man, . . . [the wolf knows secrets we need to know. He knows how to live in groups, how to communicate and control individuals within the pack. He is a predator, like us, and competes for the same prey population. The way we treat him says something for the way we treat other men.] Our fears, our disgust, our intensity, our thoroughness in presenting the wolf is a reflection of our perceptions of the wolf and not the wolf himself . . ." (Shestak 1979).

We have an ethical responsibility to try and return the wolf to its natural range.

Eva's plan is an ambitious one. She says that she not only wants to explain why the wolf should be reintroduced into the wildnerness, she also wants to describe how this can be achieved. Interestingly, in this early draft, Eva gives supporting details for only the first of her stated objectives: why the wolf should be reintroduced into the wildnerness. To make her paper consistent with the tentative thesis statement, Eva needs to add a second section.

She outlines the paper she intends to write, taking into account her angle on the topic. She tries to consider all aspects of PACES (purpose, audience, code, experience, and self) as she works on a second draft of "Reintroduction of the Wolf: What It Means to Us and What Can Be Done":

**PLANNING STRATEGY:**
**Outlining "Reintroduction of the Wolf"**

I "Wolf reintroduction" introduced

- A. Cultural acceptability—the many images of the wolf
    - 1. History
        - a. Ancients
            - (1) Myths
            - (2) Fairy Tales
        - b. Pioneers
        - c. Moderns
- B. Biological considerations
    - 1. Fairy tales and literature—wolf as monster
    - 2. The wolf's ruthless destruction of livestock
    - 3. The wolf as ruthless murderer

C. Evaluation of current plans for/attempts at reintroduction

In the working draft of her paper, Eva decides that her focus has been too broad. She narrows her focus dramatically by arguing for the reintroduction of the wolf into the American wilderness instead of just saying that people take different sides on the issue of wolf introduction. She opens the paper by citing the various specific responses that humans have to the wolf. Most importantly, Eva traces the history of human relationships with the wolf to demonstrate why the wolf has been erroneously viewed as a monster. In general, Eva adds detail and support from her sources to back up the claims she makes in her exploratory draft.

As Eva begins to focus attention on her audience, her language becomes more formal and more precise. The title change reflects the paper's changing focus and the new evidence that Eva has added to support her case. Eva is also more cautious about signaling to the reader the ideas she has paraphrased or restated from outside sources. Note the care with which she documents these ideas as she develops her next draft.

## WORKING DRAFT:
## Bring Back the Wolf: Biology and Culture Considered

Through the dark of a cold, crisp night a howl is heard. It drifts across the land as a shadow, touching all living things as if it had a presence, an existence of its own. Not a man can hear it without feeling some sort of emotion surging up inside him. Some men shiver in fear, some men shift their weight and look awkwardly over their shoulders into the darkness, some men burn with rage and grip their weapons tight; still others thrill with the feeling of adventure or talk quietly about the challenges they have conquered, and one might smile softly to himself and marvel at the beauty of the world in which he lives. The howl is that of a wolf and it is the wolf that gives the sound life. No other animal has inspired so many images in the minds of man, images so strong that they have existed since the first encounter between man and wolf, images so strong that they brought on the near extinction of the wolf. However it is another image of the wolf, a new image, that urges men to take up the fight to save it. These men want to bring the wolf home and bring the wilderness back to the 48 states. Their plan is wolf reintroduction and it is expensive, biologically complicated and extremely controversial (Fritts).

Unfortunately for the wolves, those that oppose reintroduction outnumber those that favor it and any attempt at reintroduction will meet its greatest challenge not in economical feasibility or biological possibility, but in cultural acceptability. In this paper I will deal with two of these areas, cultural acceptability and biological possibility, leaving economical feasibility for the money experts. In the beginning of the paper I will discuss the wolf's many images, how they were developed and why most of them are wrong. I will try to paint a truer picture of the wolf while presenting my argument for reintroduction. I will then go on to a discussion of the biological considerations of wolf reintroduction and conclude with a look at some of the plans and attempts of wolf reintroduction currently underway.

It is not difficult to imagine that public acceptance is the biggest problem to be faced in the reintroduction of the wolf when you remember that the wolf is our most infamous of predators and that we have spent over two decades trying to eradicate it from our nation. Therefore, it must be understood that the public will make or break any attempt at reintroduction. For example, 9 wolves were reintroduced several years ago, 5 in Alaska and 4 in Michigan. Most of the 5 in Alaska and all of the 4 in Michigan were killed at the hands of man, with one of the wolves killed in Michigan being dropped on the doorstep of the Michigan Department of Natural Resources (Horgan). Community sentiment can not be ignored, but in order to deal with it we must understand it and in order to understand it we must go back into the history of man's relationship with the wolf.

It may very well be that man's image of the wolf was developed in responce to the lonely, eerie howling of the wolf and a fear of the unknown, a fear of what lay beyond the borders of civilization, in the dark, forbidding wilderness. From this fear came the myths, the exaggerated stories of packs of marauding monsters numbering in the thousands, capable of running down and killing anything that crossed their path (Mech 77). Then, as most myths go, someone somewhere began to write them down and the wolf and his monster image became folklore and fairy tale in such works as "Little Red Ridinghood", "The Three Little Pigs", and "Peter and the Wolf". The Phenomenon continued until the wolf and his murderous image became so embedded in our culture that it invaded our language with slang expressions and showed up in our children's comic books and cartoons (Mech). The wolf had become evil incarnated.

Then again, to the pioneers of our country, the wolf was more than that. He was wilderness. He was a threat and a barrier, a murderer and a monster; and he was something to be conquered in the name of progress, honor, power and masculinity (Kellert). The wolf became a scape goat on which to vent their frustrations and blame all the hardships of the frontier; and in the process the wolf died. He died in such great numbers that he became extinct in most of his range. Between 1883 and 1918, 80,000 wolves were killed in Montana alone (Robbins). Even President Theodore Roosevelt, one of our countries greatest conservationist, referred to the wolf as a "beast of waste and desolation" (Kellert).

In our modern world of high technology, social improvement and environmental consciousness the negative images of the wolf remain. Part of the problem is lack of education in the true nature of wolves. Too many people still believe the myths and legends that have forever branded the wolf a monster. In a recent survey it was discovered that the least favorite attitudes towards wolves were found in children under the age of ten. The surveyors explained this by pointing out that the wolf was the 15th most depicted animal in children's stories and that it was almost always used in a negative way (Kellert). The survey went on to say that adults, on the average, view the wolf as the second most disliked creature on earth with biting and stinging insects as number one. When asked why they disliked wolves so much most responses dealt with the image of the wolf as a murderer of humans, livestock and important prey species such as deer, and as an ugly monster with black grizzly fur, red eyes and long, blood stained fangs (Kellert). These people still see the wolf through the old uninformed images of the past. They have no idea what the wolf really is. The survey went on to show that people with higher education and more familiarity or knowledge of nature seem to appreciate wolves more, and that people who live in close proximity to wolves, like Alaskans, are the most appreciative (Kellert). These people seem to have a better understanding or image of the wolf based on newer, more factual information.

The image of the wolf as a monster running in huge packs just waiting to catch a helpless child out alone is the basis for most of the negative attitudes associated with the wolf. Man has developed this image through tales like "Little Red Ridinghood" and stories like Jack London's "White Fang" in which two men fight for their lives against a pack of wolves and lose. All these stories give the murderous image of the wolf life and believability, and yet they are far from the truth. In most cases the wolf will flee from man, preferring to go unseen. In fact, there is not one documented, scientifically provable case of a healthy wolf attacking a human in North America. As for Europe and Asia, all of the recent and most of the historical cases have not stood up to scientific analysis (Mech). The wolves in question either turned out to be rabid or wolf-dog hybrids, both of which are uncharacteristic of normal wolves and highly unpredictable. One good example are the so called "beasts of Gevandan" that roamed the forests of France between 1764 and 1767 killing over 100 people before they were destroyed. They were later described as two large non-rabid wolflike animals. After reviewing the available data Dr. C. H. D. Clarke described the two infamous "monster" wolves as, "natural, first generation, dog-wolf crosses with hybrid vigor (Mech)." This means they were very big, very aggressive and not natural wolves. Another example deals with the wilderness section of the Algoguin Park. Not only does this area have the highest population of wolves in the world but it also has over 1000 children that canoe and camp in the park every year and there has never been a problem (Mech).

Another misconception of the wolf is his ruthless destruction of man's domestic livestock. The wolf does take livestock but the severity of the problem is highly exaggerated. The wolf is not the vicious marauder preying only on helpless sheep and cattle. In nature the wolf acts as a selective agent taking the more easily caught individuals such as the old, young, sick or injured and leaving the prime individuals as stock for the future generations, thus improving the overall quality of the prey population. The problem is that man's domestic livestock could not survive in the wild and therefore simulates the very prey of wolves. The wolf is only performing the function for which it was created; and besides, man brought the livestock to the wolf, the wolf did not go looking for the livestock (Mech). It should also be mentioned that the eradication of the wolf opened the door for the coyote which may represent even a larger problem for the livestock growers than the wolf ever did. The reason for this is that wolves need more land and therefore their populations are less dense and fewer wolves come into contact with man. The coyote moves alone and it needs less land, therefore, more coyotes come in contact with man and his livestock. Plus, coyotes are more at home on the grazing lands, where the wolves tend to avoid humans more, staying to the wooded back-country where there is less livestock.

In the same sense, it is just as wrong to believe that wolves are ruthless murderers of their natural prey. Here again wolves act as a selective agent, taking mostly those individuals that are predisposed or would die anyway from natural causes. Another debate centers around the fact that wolves and man share the same natural prey such as deer, elk, and moose. Most hunters feel that wolves compete with them for the large game animals and that reintroduction of the wolf would mean decreased hunting success. One example of this attitude is seen on a common bumper sticker in Minnesota that reads, "preserve our deer - shoot a wolf" (Robbins). The truth is that in the 4 counties that have wolves in Minnesota the hunting success averages out to about 51% and in the other counties the average is 41%. The Montana Wildlife Federation, a sportsmen group, welcomes the wolf because they feel the wolf will improve big game hunting by improving the overall quality of the prey population (Robbins). Scientific research tells us that the wolf is not the primary limiting factor in a prey population. The data shows that lack of food, bad weather and over hunting by man have a much greater impact on prey populations and that wolves will only have a negative effect under extreme conditions, and in specific areas (Mech). In terms of reintroduction, the target areas will be remote and will receive very little hunting pressure by man, making for fewer conflicts between the hunter and the wolf (Mech).

The wolf then, is not the ruthless, maneating monster that society has made him out to be. He is an important part of the complex workings of nature and as such has an intrinsic right to live. For this reason and this reason alone we should support the reintroduction of the wolf. However, the wolf is more than just a fellow creature. He is an image, a mirror to ourselves and our history, and how we treat him can tell us a lot about the way we treat each other. We can learn from the wolf; learn how to live in groups and how to communicate (Shestak). This is the real wolf, and we have an ethical responsibility to try and return it to the portions of its natural range where problems between man and wolf will be minimal, just as we have the ethical responsibility to use the gift of nature wisely and pass it on as we found it.

In the following final draft of her paper, Eva continues to be concerned with the structure of her essay. Has she presented her arguments in a logical order? Is her support for those arguments complete? In the final draft, Eva pays even more attention to her code, especially word choice and sentence structure, than in earlier drafts, making sure that she says what she wants to say in as concrete and compelling terms as she can. Notice how she divides her attention among concerns of the whole paper's organization, paragraph structure, and specific language choices as she writes the final draft. What is your overall assessment of this research paper?

## FINAL DRAFT:
## Bring Back the Real Wolf:
## Culture and Biology Considered

Martinez 1

If your instructor does not give you another format for identifying your papers, type your name one inch from the top of the first page, flush with the left margin. Follow this with your instructor's name, course title and/or number, and the date on separate lines, double spacing between the lines.

Eva Martinez

Professor Evelyn Gould

English 101

February 4, 1990

Double space between title and the first line of your paper. The title should be centered. Titles should not be underlined, placed in quotations, or typed in capitals.

Bring Back the Real Wolf:
Culture and Biology Considered

Through the dark of a cold, crisp night a howl can be heard. It drifts across the land as a shadow might, touching other living things as if it exists apart from them, hauntingly alien. The howl is that of the wolf. No other animal's cry inspires so many violent images in the minds of people, images that have led to the near extinction of the species. Hardly a person can hear this sound without feeling some deep emotion stirring within. Some shiver openly in fear; some shift their weight and look awkwardly over their shoulders into the darkness. Others burn with rage and grip their weapons tightly or quiver in anticipation of an adventuresome hunt. Still others talk quietly about the conquests they have already made with their guns. Only rarely since the first encounter between humans and wolves has the former smiled in recognition of the beauty and the natural value of the wolf to our environment. But recently, through the efforts of wildlife conservation specialists, people are developing new insights about the wolf, impressions that urge them to fight to save canis lupus before it is too late. Their plan for wolf reintroduction is biologically complicated and ex-

The entire research paper should be double spaced, including quotations and the Works Cited page(s).

Pages should be numbered consecutively throughout the research paper. All page numbers should be preceded by your last name. Page numbers should be placed ½ inch from the top of the page in the right hand corner.

tremely controversial (Fritts 460), but it is also necessary to bring back an essential figure in the wildness of the United States.

Unfortunately for the wolves, those who oppose reintroduction substantially outnumber those who favor it, and any attempt at reintroduction will meet its greatest challenge not in economic feasibility or biological possibility but in cultural acceptability. It is not difficult to understand why public acceptance is the wolf's biggest problem when you remember that the wolf is the most infamous of predators in the United States and that we have spent over two decades trying to eradicate it from our nation. Therefore, it must be understood that the public will make or break any attempt at reintroduction. For example, nine wolves were reintroduced into the wild several years ago, five in Alaska and four in Michigan. Most of the five in Alaska and all of the four in Michigan were killed by humans. To prove a point, one of the wolves killed in Michigan was dropped at the doorstep of the Michigan Department of Natural Resources (Horan 8). Community sentiment cannot be ignored, but in order to deal with it, we must understand it, and in order to understand it, we must examine people's past relationship with the wolf.

Use a five character identation for new paragraphs

It may very well be that our image of the wolf was developed in response to the lonely, eerie howling of the wolf and its association with a fear of the unknown, a fear of what lay beyond the borders of civilization in the dark, forbidding wilderness. From this fear came myths, exaggerated stories of packs of marauding monsters numbering in the thousands, capable of running down and killing anything that crossed their path (Mech 520). Then, as with most myths, someone somewhere began to write the stories down, and the wolf with his monster image was introduced to successive generations in folklore and fairy tales such as "Little Red Ridinghood," "The Three Little Pigs," and "Peter and the Wolf." The phenomenon continued until the wolf and his murderous image became so embedded in our culture that it invaded our language through slang expressions and even showed up in our children's comic books and cartoons (Mech 520). The wolf had become evil incarnate.

To the pioneers of America, the wolf was particularly threatening. He was a barrier in the wildnerness, a murderer and a monster; and he was something to be conquered in the name of progress, honor, power and masculinity (Kellert 169). The wolf also became a scapegoat against which pioneers could vent their frustrations and on which they could blame many of the hardships of the frontier. In the process of dealing with their "problem," the pioneers killed wolves in such great numbers that the creatures were nearly extinct in most of their natural ranges. Between 1883 and 1918, 80,000 wolves were killed in Montana alone (Robbins 12). Even President Theodore Roosevelt, one of our country's greatest conservationists, referred to the wolf as "a beast of waste and desolation" (qtd. in Kellert 172).

In the modern world of high technology, social improvement, and environmental consciousness, negative images of the wolf remain. Part of the problem is a lack of understanding of the true nature of wolves. Too many people still believe the myths and legends which have branded the wolf a monster. Citing a recent survey, Kellert explains that the least favorable attitudes toward wolves are found in children under the age of ten. The surveyors explained this by pointing out that the wolf was the fifteenth most frequently depicted animal in children's stories and was almost always presented in a negative way. The survey goes on to show that adults also view the wolf as one of the most disliked creatures on earth, second only to biting and stinging insects. Asked why they disliked wolves so much, most respondents said they thought of wolves as murderers of humans, livestock and deer and saw them as ugly monsters with black grizzly fur, red eyes, and long, blood-stained fangs (Kellert 173-79). The survey showed that people with higher education and more knowledge of nature appreciated wolves more. Further, people who lived in close proximity to wolves, like Alaskans, were most appreciative of wolves. The image of the wolf these people had seemed to be based on newer, more factual information.

Many of the negative images surrounding the wolf are simply wrong. For instance, the scenario of wolves running in huge packs just waiting for a helpless child to come along so that they can devour it is far from the real one. In most cases, a wolf will flee from people, preferring to remain unseen. In fact, there is not one documented scientifically provable case of a healthy wolf attacking a human being in North America. Even in Algoguim Park, the area with the highest population of wolves in the world and a place where over 1,000 children canoe and camp every year, there has never been a problem with wolf attacks. As for Europe and Asia, all of the recent and most of the historical cases have not stood up to scientific analysis (Mech 522). The wolves in question either turned out to be rabid wolves or wolf-dog hybrids, both of which are highly unpredictable and show behavior uncharacteristic of wolves. One good example of mistaken identity is the "beasts of Gevandan" that roamed the forests of France between 1764 and 1767, killing over 100 people before they were destroyed. First thought to be wolves, the animals were later determined by Dr. C. H. D. Clarke to be "natural, first generation dog-wolf crosses with hybrid vigor" (Mech 181).

Another misconception of the wolf is his ruthless destruction of domestic livestock. The wolf does take livestock, but the severity of the problem is highly exaggerated. The wolf is not a vicious marauder preying only on helpless sheep and cattle. In nature the wolf acts as a selective agent, taking the more easily caught individuals such as the old, young, sick, or injured and leaving the prime individuals as stock for future generations, thus improving the overall quality of the prey population. The problem is that domestic livestock resemble the natural prey of wolves. The wolf, then, is punished for performing the function for which it was created. Contrary to most people's beliefs, wolves did not go looking for livestock as prey; people brought livestock to the wolf (Mech 95).

In the same sense, it is just as wrong to believe that wolves are ruthless murderers of their natural prey. Here again, wolves are a natural selective agent, taking mostly individual animals that are most likely to die of natural causes. The real reason that wolves are disliked in the wild is that they compete with people for large game animals such as elk, deer, and moose. Most hunters feel that reintroduction of the wolf into the wilderness would mean decreased hunting success. Thus, a common bumper sticker in the game state of Minnesota reads: "preserve our deer—shoot a wolf" (Robbins 13). But research shows that lack of food, over-hunting by man and bad weather are all by far more significant contributors to the killing off of big game than is the wolf. Ironically, in the four counties in Minnesota that have wolves, hunting success averages about 51%; in the other counties hunting success averages only about 41%.

The wolf, then, is not the ruthless, man-eating, livestock-stealing monster that society has made him out to be. He is a natural part of the complex workings of nature. Moreover, the wolf actually contributes positively to both livestock growth and game population. In many places the eradication of the wolf has opened the door for an even larger predatory problem with livestock—the coyote. Because wolves need more land to roam, their populations are less dense than those of other predators. Few wolves actually come in contact with people and their livestock. But when the wolves are cleared out of the backlands, coyotes tend to move in. These predators move alone and thus have denser populations. They are also more at home on grazing land than the wolf and tend to strike livestock more frequently. In the wild, wolves also serve a positive function. The Montana Wildlife Federation, a sportsmen's group unlike most others, actually welcomes the wolf in the wild because it feels that the wolf's presence will improve big game hunting by improving the overall quality of the prey population (Robbins 14).

Even if the wolf could not help us, it is a natural part of our planet, a living thing not unlike ourselves, and as such it has an intrinsic right to live, and we have an ethical responsibility to preserve this gift of nature, to use it wisely, and to pass it on just as we found it. For that reason alone, we should support the reintroduction of the wolf.

Finally, the wolf in many ways _is_ a mirror of ourselves and our history. Like us, the wolf lives in groups, and its survival depends on communicating with others. How we treat him can tell us a lot about the ways we treat each other (Shestak qtd. in Klinghammer 153).

The problems associated with reintroduction of the wolf will not be solved easily. However, the value of restoring a useful part of our natural environment and the value of the lessons the wolf can teach us about ourselves and nature offset the labor. With an education campaign aimed at presenting the real nature of the wolf, we can make reintroduction work and reaffirm the value of this creature. The howl of the wolf must once again fill the cold, dark wilderness night, and this time hopefully more people will smile and fewer will fear.

Martinez 8

WORKS CITED

Bailey, R., ed. Recovery Plan for the Eastern Timber Wolf. Washington, D.C.: U S Department of Interior Fish and Wildlife Service, 1978.

Fritts, Steven H., et al. "Can Relocated Wolves Survive?" Wildlife Society Bulletin 13.4 (1985): 459–463.

Horan, Jack. "The Red Wolf is Coming Home." Defenders March–June 1986: 4–11.

Kellert, Stephen. "Public Perceptions of Predators." Biological Conservation 31.2 (1985): 167–189.

Klinghammer, Erich, ed. The Behavior and Ecology of Wolves. New York: Garland P, 1979.

Mech, David. The Wolf: The Ecology of Endangered Species. Minneapolis, U of Minnesota Press, 1977.

———. "Where Can the Wolf Survive?" National Geographic October 1977: 518–536.

Robbins, Jim. "Wolves Across the Border." Natural History 95.5 May: 6–15.

Double space between the title "Works Cited" and your first entry.

Arrange Works Cited entries in alphabetical order.

All entries begin flush with the left margin, and each line after the first is then indented five spaces.

Eva's thesis has now been narrowed to represent the most significant issue related to her topic, and it is supported with documentation. As she shows, there is more than one view about the problem, and all of the views are significant. Eva is investigating an argument. It is her job to present all sides of the issue and to evaluate the claims of each position.

Is Eva convincing? Can we trust her analysis of the question? She reasons logically, and her data seem compelling. She has been able to explore an issue that is of personal concern to her, something related to her major field of interest. She understands the issues because she has studied them. The writing is not an abstract exercise but a personal investigation of a problem that Eva actually believes needs to be solved.

The rearrangement of the facts from the second draft to the final draft allows Eva to make a case rather than just compile and present facts. By contrasting society's traditional conception of the wolf with scientists' recent observations, Eva is able to justify the claim that we have been harmfully prejudiced against wolves and that we need to reconsider the effects of our actions against these animals. Eva uses the popular arguments against reintroduction to illustrate society's misconceptions and then suggests how taking a new attitude toward the wolf can actually be beneficial to the very people who would oppose such a view.

And throughout the process of revising from working draft to final draft, Eva consciously eliminates potentially sexist language, replacing "mankind" with "humanity" or "people" or "us," changing "man's" to "our," and so on. Sexist language too often reflects stereotyped attitudes that assume the superiority or supremacy of one sex over the other; too often it narrows the implications of a statement, for example, "man's past," as opposed to the more general and more accurate "history of the human race." Sensitive to PACES (purpose, audience, code, experience, and self), Eva revises her code to eliminate sexist language that could affect her audience and her purpose, that could negate her self and color the reader's perception of her research.

To end the paper, Eva develops a data-related conclusion. She restates her opinion, but she also justifies her position by recalling the main points from the body of her text. If she has done a good job of her research, the reader, too, should be persuaded by the data. The list of "Works Cited" at the conclusion of the final paper directs readers to books and articles that will further support Eva's claims and help other researchers find material pertinent to their investigations of the subject.

## POSSIBLE RESEARCH TOPICS

You may find the following list helpful in determining a research issue for yourself if you are assigned a research paper for your composition course. The following are some of the topics students have researched and written about in recent years:

Is the ERA Covered by the Fourteenth Amendment?
The Resurrection: Hoax or History?
Welfare: Social Benefit or Ripoff?
National Health Insurance: Pros and Cons
Tabloids: Trash or Responsible Journalism?
Mandatory Drug Testing: Violation of Personal Rights?
Sex Education: Pros and Cons
American Nazis: A Threat?
Nuclear Waste: Safe?
Surrogate Mothers: Yes or No?
Vegetarianism: Healthful or Harmful?
John F. Kennedy's Assassination: Lone Assassin or Conspiracy?
Should Marijuana Be Legalized?
TV Evangelism: Vice or Virtue?
Modern Witches: Neurotics or Mystics?
Should Health Care Be Nationalized?
Legalized Gambling: Pros and Cons
Reincarnation: Fact or Fiction?
Malpractice: Patients' Rights versus Doctors' Rights
TV Violence: Harmful or Helpful?

If you keep in mind that a research paper is not a "report," not a mere collection of facts, you will avoid topics like "The History of the Tank," "The Advantages of Dentistry," and "The Development of Feminism."

Such one-sided topics are usually well researched in encyclopedias, history books, and elsewhere. They require you only to compile the known facts. To create a topic you can think about, one that will allow you to weigh the evidence and reach conclusions, change such topics into two-sided questions (see pages 312 to 313). For example: "Are Tanks Essential to Modern Warfare?" "What Are the Advantages and Disadvantages of Dentistry?" "Do Women Still Face Job Discrimination Today?"

# CHAPTER ▲ ELEVEN

# *Writing Responses to Essay Exam Questions*

**"Some kinds of writing must be done very quickly, like riding a bicycle on a tightrope."**

**WILLIAM FAULKNER**

Most writing assignments can be completed in the pleasant, relaxed atmosphere of the writer's own workshop. Although deadlines inevitably must be met, writers usually have a certain freedom from time and format constraints to explore their subjects by way of a somewhat leisurely travel through the writing process. As a college student, however, you will frequently be asked to complete in-class writing assignments, which impose special constraints on any fully developed process approach. Especially demanding and limiting is the essay exam, which must be written in a kind of pressurized vacuum. This type of assignment necessarily forces the writing process to become formalized and shortened; writers must rapidly compress a writing process that would normally be extended over a span of several days. They must interpret the intent of the question, determine what information is essential to a response, mentally retrieve that information from lecture notes and readings, formulate a thesis, organize a plan of attack, draft a well-written response, and edit that response—all in one brief session (perhaps one or two hours)!

We believe you can complete all of these operations effectively and write better responses to essay exam questions if you remember that "process" writing techniques are still useful, even when modified, and if you approach essay exams with these modifications in mind. The concepts of planning, drafting, and revising still apply: They merely assume varied forms. In this chapter we will outline the skills necessary for employing a process writing approach as you prepare to write and then actually compose responses to essay exam questions. Your preparation will include understanding the nature of essay exams as well as developing skills in gathering information and reviewing, while writing the response itself will include interpreting the question, using invention techniques, and developing a coherent plan.

## UNDERSTANDING THE NATURE OF THE ESSAY EXAM

The most typical advice instructors give to students about responding to an essay exam question is to "write all you know" about the given subject. Unfortunately, students often interpret this advice as meaning that writing a successful exam essay requires little more than regurgitating the information covered during the segment of the term for which they are being tested. Because students trust this kind of simplistic, linear rehashing, they seldom attempt to formulate a controlling idea (thesis statement) and synthesize relevant material into a coherent plan. As a result, their essay exam responses often take the form of a single, lengthy paragraph (the notorious ramble) or a series of loosely related paragraphs in an overall structure that lacks a sense of direction.

Despite their all-encompassing exhortations to "write all you know," most instructors do not really expect to see in your response every fact covered in class or in the readings. Instead, they tend to grade exams on how well you have assimilated the major points into a sound overview encompassing the material that has been emphasized. Consequently, you must accurately identify and address your instructor's expectations as you prepare to write your answer. You must show that you have the ability to perceive significant relationships and draw conclusions about the mass of data covered in the course. Your instructor may have merely implied concepts or assumed that you had made connections between ideas from different lessons. You will often be expected to extrapolate, to hypothesize, to consider ultimate implications—to determine the "What would happen if . . . ?" or the "What all this means is . . . ." The key here is recognizing that most essay exam questions require more than simple recall of pertinent facts; they require higher-level thinking skills—those of synthesis, analysis, and evaluation.

If you usually exclude implicit connections in your responses to essay exam questions, you may be overlooking essential words or phrases in the questions. Essay questions often indicate the specific kinds of information and organizational principles desired by the instructor. If you incorporate process writing methods as you approach an exam, you will be better prepared to perceive and organize relevant information in your responses.

Try to identify some of the problems inherent in your customary approach to interpreting and responding to essay questions by means of an analysis based on the following questions:

## PROBLEM CHECKLIST

1. Did you identify key terms in the question to guide your response? Did you determine whether the question called for simple recall or whether it required higher-level cognitive skills?
2. Did you employ any mnemonic devices (invention techniques, perhaps) to help you recall pertinent information before or during the drafting of your response?
3. Did you write a rough or scratch outline or any other organizational tool *before* writing in order to plan your essay?
4. Did you use key words from the question to direct your formulation of a controlling thesis? Did you explicitly state a thesis near the beginning of your response?

5. Did you notice whether the question implied a certain kind of structure, and did you organize your response accordingly?
6. Did each of your paragraphs relate in some way to the overall controlling thesis or guiding principle? Did you use transitional expressions within and between paragraphs to *explicitly* show connections?
7. Did you support your generalizations with specific examples drawn from lecture notes or readings? Did you *show* rather than tell? Did you cause the instructor to have to guess your intended meaning?
8. Did you use precise terms, the ones used by the instructor and text author when they discuss the subject?

If you answered *yes* to any of these questions, then you have a solid basis for developing a successful strategy for responding to essay exam questions. You will have the opportunity to refine your strategy as you work through this chapter. If you answered *no* to any of the questions, then you have begun to identify the flaws in your approach—a necessary first step in developing a successful strategy.

### ► WRITING ACTIVITY ◄

Examine a copy of an essay exam you took recently, one for which you have both the instructor's question and your written response. Using the preceding "Problem Checklist," analyze the kinds of problems you typically have in developing a successful strategy and drafting an effective response. Briefly note places where you failed to address items mentioned on the checklist. Also, note where you effectively targeted checklist priorities.

## PREPARING FOR THE EXAM: GATHERING INFORMATION

When we discussed the writer's choices, we saw that an important component of the drafting process is the proper targeting of the writer's *experience*. The experience segment of the PACES diagram contains a variety of sources for the writer's material, including lectures and books—the two primary sources of information used in a response to an essay question. Because you must rely heavily on these two sources as you draft a response, be sure that you gather information from them conscientiously; after all, what you include in your preparation becomes your sole source of information during the exam. If you approach note taking and text reading haphazardly, you may not have that solid experiential base on which to draft an effective response.

Compiling efficient, flexible notes is an important activity in preparing for essay exams because during the note-taking process you become, to an extent, the writer. You decide what is to be said, what is to be included and excluded from the wealth of information presented by the instructor.

In an earlier chapter, we discussed the distinction between what writing researcher Linda Flower calls writer-based and reader-based prose. Writer-based prose is the kind of prose that helps the writer to get the information on paper without attempting to make it understandable to another reader. Reader-based prose, on the other hand, emphasizes a responsiveness to the needs of the interpreting audience. The distinction is analogous to what happens during the transition between note taking and note reviewing. Your class notes are, in a way, writer based: They are written to yourself in an often mysterious shorthand that you understand at the time. But, remember: When you later attempt to review your notes, you become the reader; you then must be able to determine what larger body of information the statements refer to and interpret their complete meanings.

A common note-taking problem is that students who write brief, elliptical notes are unable to make sense of them later. They have taken shortcuts and left out important transitional statements that are necessary to shape the material into a coherent whole. To avoid this problem, you should make the writing of extensive notes a priority, especially when you suspect that an essay exam is forthcoming. In this way, you will have easily interpreted, reader-based statements that will help you recall more of the lecture. You won't be left wondering, "What did this mean?" or "How do these two examples relate?"

In addition to copying as much pertinent information as possible, you should include in your note-taking strategies the following:

## NOTETAKING STRATEGIES FOR ESSAY EXAMS

1. Define any key terms introduced by the instructor. If the instructor gives a specific illustration or example or undertakes a practical application of an abstract principle, copy it down. Forgetting how theoretical concepts apply to reality will result in vague, unsupported essay responses.
2. Place a question mark beside any statement about which you are uncertain. You will need to clarify these items later.
3. As you listen to the lecture, think ahead. Where might the lesson be headed? What are some of the implications of what the instructor is saying? Does it complement or contradict what you have read in the text? Challenging yourself to formulate questions will enable you to become an active listener: You will be more likely to remember what you heard and view it as a coherent whole.

4. If you do have questions, raise them at an appropriate point in the period. If you don't wish to speak out, at least write them in the margins of your notes. You can discuss them with your instructor or your classmates later.
5. Place an asterisk, a star, or some other identifying symbol beside any item that the instructor felt compelled to refer back to or explain again.
6. If the instructor mentions any secondary texts other than course textbooks, write them down. If you can review them in your spare time and bring in relevant information on the exam, you might effectively supplement the information that everyone else in the class will be relying on.

## ► DISCUSSION ACTIVITY ◄

Examine the following sets of class notes from a lecture on Sigmund Freud's distinctions among the id, the ego, and the superego. In what ways are Student 2's notes writer-based? Where do you see potential difficulties when Student 2 attempts to use these notes to prepare for an essay question? What differences in the two students' note-taking strategies can you detect? Why might Student 1's notes be more useful? Which information could be used more effectively in a response?

***Student 1: Psychology Notes***

Announcements: Answer sheets will be alphabetized today; look over right and wrong answers. New unit - Unit IV combines motivation and development

Reading Assign.: Chap. 14 - Freud's theory of development & motivation (pp 485-492)
There will be several views of motivation not in the book but covered on the next test!
Chap. 12 - focus on important aspects of childhood development
Chap 13 - from adolescence on; relevant to what we're doing now and following next test
(Next exam is 2 weeks from today!)

Freud: concerned about motivation and how development was part of that
- class used to deal with what human nature is like.
- Freud said we are not aware of the reasons behind behavior, we are not conscious of it – 90% of human behavior is caused by unconscious motives.
- Freud made unpopular statements, was doing his work about 100 yrs. ago, started as a physician, but would be called a psychiatrist now – in his own time he was known as a neurologist

example of old movie: How Freud got interested in neurology, studied in France w/someone who used hypnosis – woman in wheelchair, man w/shakes – using hypnotic suggestion he got young man to stop shaking and woman to gain feeling in her legs, then he got them to change symptoms. This doctor showed Freud that he could add and take away symptoms that were psychological; this became basis of Freud's work

slide showing id, superego, ego

id – primitive part of the mind, all have it, what we're born with

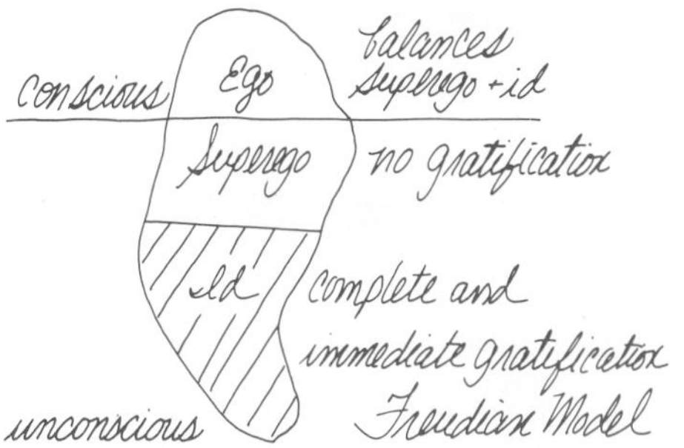

Freudian Model

– children are all id but also stays with us through life – wants it NOW
– follows the PLEASURE PRINCIPLE – maximum gratification with minimum punishment and guilt (want to reduce tension) tension reduction or gratification may be immediate and simple as blinking cinder from your eye

- we often have to dream up an image to satisfy the tension
- called PRIMARY PROCESS—dreaming up an image of a tension reducer
- id operates in SUBJECTIVE REALITY—doesn't see difference between real world and imaginary one

**Student 2: Psychology Notes**

Unit IV — Chapt. 14, Chapt. 12, Chapt. 13 — motivation & development
Chapt. 14 Sigmund Freud
Chapt. 12 childhood
Chapt. 13 adolescence on

Chapt. 14 I. Sigmund Freud, he felt we were not aware of our behavior

A. 90% of behavior caused by unconscious motives

B. example: he believes that a person was not phyoically wrong but all in the mind. the man was struck by lightning And the young lady. He showed that only you could get rid of symptoms, but you could also introduce them

C. Id, Ego, Superego he divided up along these lines

II. Division of the Mind

A. Id = is primitive

1. pleasure principle = seeks immediate gratification
2. primary process = conjures up image of tension reducer
3. operates in subjective reality = wish for something that couldn't be there

## PREPARING FOR THE EXAM: REVIEWING INFORMATION

Now that you've begun gathering information, you are ready to move toward incorporating that information into the writing of a draft or, in this case, responding to the essay exam question. Before you can use this information, however, you have to know it. In order to avoid overloading your mind by cramming right before the exam, we recommend that you review the information you are accumulating throughout the course of the term. If you do so, you will allow the material to, as we stated earlier, "percolate through your consciousness." If possible, review your information, particularly your notes, at least two or three times a week. Each time you review, you will be accommodating newly acquired material into your overall understanding as well as ensuring that important points are firmly rooted in your mind and are therefore easily accessible during the exam.

In this way, reviewing information makes up for the absence of the extended series of drafts involved in an effective process writing approach. When you challenge yourself to continually go back over material, you are more likely to achieve a deeper, more complete understanding of the subject. Most important, you will have a better chance of making a clear, valid response to the exam question—a response that is in effect a final draft in the sense that your earlier drafting was done mentally as you worked to mold the information from the instructor and the text author into your own personal body of knowledge.

Since you can seldom predict the exact emphasis of the exam question, it would be futile to compose fully developed early drafts of exam responses. It is useful, however, to do some writing in preparation for the exam itself. We suggest the following:

### PRE-EXAM WRITING STRATEGIES

1. Write a summary of the day's class notes or a précis of a section or chapter of the text maintaining the structure employed by the instructor or author.
2. Rewrite a general heading or major point in your notes or in the chapter into an arguable thesis. Briefly list the examples you would use to support the statement.
3. Try a focused freewrite or brief sketch in which you imagine yourself explaining an important concept to a friend. Or, pretend that you

must brief a classmate who missed the last lecture. Discuss what was covered and how it correlates with the overall emphasis of the course. You might want to keep a journal of these explanations.

4. A variation on no. 3 involves writing a dialogue between two people—one who is trying to explain some aspect of the material and one who is trying to understand. What questions might the listener raise? (This activity is useful in determining where your explanation and, perhaps, your understanding is unclear.)
5. An old standby is the flashcard drill with the important term or concept on one side, the definition or explanation on the other. This time *write* your answer, including an example of how this abstract term applies to a real-life situation.

Working through some of these activities will enable you to see the material in new ways, to make connections between various segments, and to move toward demonstrating your understanding on the exam.

## APPROACHING THE QUESTION: THE WRITER'S CHOICES

When you have solidified your understanding of the material, you are ready to draft a response to an essay question. As we mentioned at the beginning of the chapter, the nature of the exam situation modifies your process approach. Just as your knowledge of the subject matter is limited to information gathered from lecture notes and readings (a very small part of the writer's experience), so are the other writer's choices included in the PACES diagram limited. But in a sense, the limiting of your choices makes the task of accurately responding to the exam question much easier. How you approach the subject will largely be dictated by the question; what you will discuss in your response is, to a degree, predetermined because the question provides you with an immediate focus.

In Chapter One you learned how the writer's choices are interrelated—a decision concerning one simultaneously influences decisions about the others. (It may be useful at this point to refer to the PACES diagram on page 8.) In the writing of an essay exam response, *purpose* controls the choices that you make about *audience*, *code*, and *self* as well as *experience*. Your purpose is simple: You need to impress your instructor with your sound understanding of the problem outlined in the question by employing the knowledge gained from the course work. Properly targeting your intended audience is inherent in the assignment; you are writing directly to a single, informed reader—the college professor—whose high expectations you can identify. As a result, self will probably need to be (in terms of the diagram on page 8) academic, and certainly knowledgeable. Your code will include a tone that is semiformal, and perhaps leaning toward formal. Your decision to include as part of your code, classification, comparison-contrast, or any other strategies of development will be determined in part by the structure demanded or suggested by the question.

## APPROACHING THE QUESTION: INTERPRETATION AND TIME MANAGEMENT

Interpreting the intent of the question is the crucial first step in drafting an essay response. Before you can do anything, you must decide what the instructor *wants* you to do—what the question is asking you to do. The following suggestions may help you develop an effective strategy for tackling essay questions:

### ► Exam-room Strategies

1. Remember that instructors use varying exam formats; therefore you must apportion the time that you spend on essay questions accordingly. Some exams will include a combination of objective questions (multiple choice, true or false, and so on) and essay questions. Exams that consist solely of essay questions may require you to respond to one or several questions. You should segment your time in proportion to the point value assigned to each section. For example, if an essay question is worth twenty points on a 100-point scale, do not spend more than twenty percent of your time on it. Stick to your schedule: It is disastrous to find yourself beginning a thirty-point essay response with ten minutes left in the period.

2. No matter how much time you have allotted for each essay question, you should spend about one-third of that time planning and about two-thirds drafting the response. Allow yourself a few minutes at the end for proofreading. You won't have time for extensive revision, so polish what you have been able to get down on paper. You don't need an extensive period for the actual writing. It is better to produce a short, well-organized, well-supported essay than a long, rambling mess.

3. Read the question slowly and carefully. Underline key words that direct you to the kind of information you will need to include in your response. This strategy will make your planning more productive.

4. Make sure that you understand precisely what you are supposed to do: inform, persuade, analyze, define, classify, compare, and so on. Instructors frequently include in their questions guide words that imply a certain structure or suggest that you include certain bodies of information. In addition to the

operations listed in the first sentence of this paragraph, other commonly used guide words include the following:

***apply*** You must give concrete examples or real-life illustrations of an abstract concept or principle;

***summarize*** You should give a brief overview of the important concepts;

***trace*** You must sequentially outline changes or developments throughout the history of the subject;

***list*** You must recall pertinent information about a subject;

***illustrate*** You need to provide practical examples of a theoretical concept at work;

***explain*** You must answer the *why* or *how*;

***assess, evaluate*** You must set up a list of criteria with which to judge worth or significance;

***prove, justify, support*** You are required to demonstrate why what you say is true;

***speculate*** You should explore the topic's future implications or significance by considering "What might happen if . . . ?" or "What this means is . . . ."

5. Don't ignore highly directive instructor recommendations such as "Be sure to include" or "In your response you must . . ." It is equally dangerous to fail to respond sufficiently when the question suggests that you answer the question "Why or why not?" A brief sentence or two will not adequately complete this requirement.

## ► WRITING ACTIVITY ◄

**1.** Assume that during a two-hour essay exam, you are required to answer twenty-five multiple-choice questions worth forty points and two of three essay questions worth thirty points each. Describe the strategy you would employ to apportion your time. Include how many minutes you would spend on each stage—planning, drafting, proofreading—of the writing of each essay response.

**2.** For each sample essay question that follows, write a brief "Writer's Mind" script in which you discuss how you would interpret the intent of the question and how you would plan a response. Begin by identifying any key words that imply the kinds of information required as well as any guide words that suggest what your response must include. Be sure to include which strategies of development might be useful.

a. Develop and defend a set of ethical standards involved in the production, distribution, and broadcasting of contemporary children's television programming. Be sure to compare or contrast standards for educational programs with those for "pure entertainment" shows.

b. Trace the development of your favorite sport. What changes in regulations or style of play have come about? Why? Assess these changes and support your opinions.

## ► DISCUSSION ACTIVITY ◄

Examine the sample question and response below. How well has the student addressed the question in her response? Do you see any evidence that she has structured her answer according to directions implied by the question? Has she included details and examples appropriate to the intent of the question?

> Question: *According to Herzberg and others, what do workers want in a job? From a managerial point of view, briefly discuss the problems of providing what workers want.*

> *Response:* According to Herzberg's Two-Factor Theory, the worker wishes to maximize job satisfaction and minimize job dissatisfaction. Satisfaction is improved when motivators are employed. These include recognition, achievement, responsiblity, advancement, and personal growth in competence. Dissatisfaction can be minimized by intervening with hygiene factors such as improvements in company policies, supervisory practices, working conditions, salaries and wages, and interpersonal relationships on the job.
>
> Simply stated, the manager's dilemma is "You can't please all of the people all of the time." The theory fails to consider the point of individual differences. Not all people will respond in the same direction or degree to identical stimuli. Some jobs/tasks, especially those with an innate shortage of motivators, defy restructuring beyond the hygiene level. The satisfaction of worker needs may produce a treadmill of managerial efforts, the manager always trying to keep up with but never resolving both the employees' complaints and the organization's goals.

## WRITING THE RESPONSE: PLANNING STRATEGIES

Once you have interpreted the intent of the question and identified the kinds of supporting information necessary for a response, you need to plan how to organize it. At this point, you might employ some of the invention techniques discussed in Chapter Two. Remember, you have set aside approximately one-third of the time spent on the essay question for planning. To make your planning efficient and productive, follow this three-step method:

**1.** Concentrate on the specific knowledge demanded by the focus of the question. Try *clustering or brainstorming*; get down all you can remember from your notes and readings.

**2.** Begin to selectively shape your material according to the constraints or focus of the question. Respond to the questions using *the journalistic formula or the pentad* as a way to establish a focus and, if necessary, discover a thesis.

**3.** Do a *scratch outline*, a brief overview of your plan of attack, including structuring of paragraphs and basic kinds of examples or details to be used in each section. If you haven't done so already, formulate an explicitly stated thesis, which you will probably include in your first paragraph.

You may also find it useful to cluster or brainstorm *after* you have completed the scratch outline. You can do a quick cluster or brainstorm for each section of your proposed plan to see whether you have enough supporting information. Clustering is especially useful for both retrieving and organizing material quickly because its method of drawing lines between words and phrases helps to show relationships at the same time that it produces information. Clustering and brainstorming can also provide an efficient means of topic selection if the essay exam allows you to choose which question or questions you wish to tackle. If your invention notes produce little material for a given question, you'll save yourself the frustration of discovering halfway through your response that you have nothing to say.

When you employ the pentad, remember that you can substitute a variety of verb strings in the questions. For instance, "What is happening?" can become "What will happen?" or "What might happen if . . . ?" Similarly, "Why is it happening?" can become "Why isn't it happening?" or "Why should it be happening?" These variations on the basic format are particularly effective in developing a focus for questions that ask you to speculate or assess.

If your planning time is severely limited, try to "scribble-then-structure"—a method that simply condenses the three-step method outlined above. First, you scribble down every piece of relevant information that you can recall, then you draw arrows to connect related ideas. This is like a combined version of clustering and brainstorming. Next, you number the ideas according to some sequential plan—a quick replacement for the scratch outline. Finally, you can pencil in any additional comments about the relationships of the concepts to the focus of the question—a shorthand substitute for responding to the journalistic formula or pentad. The following is a sample scribble-then-structure outline and the resulting essay response:

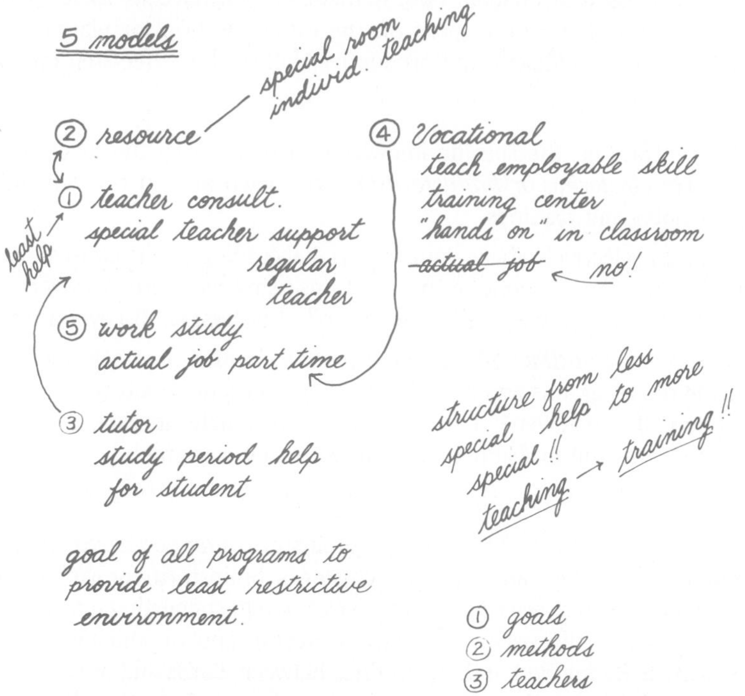


There are five possible program options available for the mildly handicapped students at the secondary level. Each of these different models has its own goals, uses various teaching methods and involves different kinds of teachers.

The teacher-consultant model is one of the least restrictive environments for students. The student remains in the regular classroom throughout the day. The special-education teacher plans with the classroom teacher, helping to modify materials and instruction techniques so that the student can remain in the mainstream classes.

The tutor model allows the student to stay in the regular classroom for the entire day also. However, the student gets help from a special-education teacher during the study period. The student is expected to cover all the regular material in the class. The special-education teacher needs to be knowledgeable about all of the subjects taught.

Students who need more special instruction may be placed in a *resource program. This model allows students to stay in the regular classroom for subjects they can handle by themselves. For subjects that are more difficult, students take instruction in the special-education room. The special classes provide individualized instruction on the students' level of functioning. The goal of this model is to provide instruction that is helpful to the student at his or her own level of learning rather than to frustrate the student with harder material or eliminate the subject from the students' program altogether.*

*Vocational training allows students to take less academic oriented subjects and provides them with classes that teach trade skills. The setting for this class may vary from a training center to an actual job site depending on the subject matter of the course.*

*The most radical adjustment in curriculum provided for special education students is the work-study model. In this program students are actually employed for part of the day and take classes in basic life skills during the course work part of the day. The goal of this program is to provide students with more experience than actual training.*

Spending some time on planning will increase the likelihood that you will know where your response is going and what needs to be said before you compose your first sentence; therefore, no time will be wasted in pausing to decide what to do next. More important, your finished product will show complexity, coherence, and focus. Since you will avoid the kind of undisciplined, tangential rambling of your less well-prepared classmates, you will be more likely to impress your instructor. After all, that's what this chapter is designed to help you do.

## WRITING THE RESPONSE: DRAFTING

You've spent several weeks gathering information and then mentally molding it into some coherent framework of understanding. Now you have one shot to get a portion of that body of knowledge down on paper. The kind of writing that you do for a response to an essay exam question should be distinctly different from the longer, out-of-class variety. Since your time is limited, you should assume an essay writing style that is straightforward (efficiency over eloquence), fact oriented (an abundance of supporting details and examples), and convincing (each statement directly and explicitly responsive to the focus of the question). You should get to the point quickly and not worry about producing elaborately developed paragraphs. The instructor will be concerned more with how well you have understood and organized the material than with the elegance of your prose style.

The first major difference between the paper and the essay exam response is the introduction. In a typical paper, you include an attention-getting introduction that compels your readers to continue by exciting their interest and, perhaps, that slowly builds toward the thesis. With an essay question response, however, your reader is already interested or, at least, predisposed to read on. State your thesis early; in fact, your opening paragraph may contain little more than a rewording of the question into a thesis or a statement of your intended focus.

Because the instructor's question asks for rather specific information and probably implies a certain approach to the problem, we suggest that, if appropriate, you order your response according to the structure of the question. For example, if the question asks you to compare and contrast and then assess, you should do so—in that order. If you are to trace historical changes and analyze the results, you should trace first and analyze second. Chances are that your instructor applies priorities to the subject in the same hierarchical structure evident in his or her question; therefore, it makes sense to match your response to those expectations.

There are few suggestions to make about the content of your response that haven't already been made in earlier chapters. Simply remember that the abbreviated length and limited focus of the essay exam demand an even greater concentration on supplying several pertinent supporting examples in each section. Avoid composing entire paragraphs that consist of vague, theoretical generalizations. For every general statement or inference, provide two or three practical illustrations or concrete details. Bring in as much relevant information from your notes and readings as you can in the time and space provided. The essay exam does test your writing abilities; but, more importantly, it tests your knowledge of the course material. Demonstrate your knowledge extensively.

Each paragraph and each explanation should explicitly relate to your thesis statement or statement of intent. In a long, out-of-class paper, you may have individual subtheses in some paragraphs; these paragraphs may contain information that is related to the subject but not directly supportive of the guiding principle. An essay exam response is too short to allow for interesting subsidiary commentary; so, again, keep to your purpose—impress your instructor with your knowledge of the facts.

## WRITING THE RESPONSE: REVISING

You won't have time for any substantial revising or rewriting, but allow a few minutes for intensive proofreading. Go back over your response, correcting any mechanical errors in spelling, punctuation, or usage. If you do discover a sentence that seems to be out of place, simply bracket it and draw an arrow to its proper position. Carefully consider your word choice: Do your words convey the proper meaning? Have you used key terms appropriately? If you wish to make word or phrase changes, cross out the previous version with a single line and write the improved version above. The following is a sample of an essay exam question and its edited response.

Question: *Weber and others have written about the concept of bureaucracy and rational models. Briefly describe some advantages and disadvantages of the use of this concept.*

~~Due to~~ The five characteristics present in a bureaucracy and the formal nature of ~~it~~ them ~~there are~~ create less chances for a confusion of role over directions. In a bureaucracy everyone should know ~~their~~ his part, scope of authority, and tasks. The expert training and high division of labor should result in people well qualified to do their jobs and to know just what exactly their job ~~is~~ are. By having formal written documents there should also be less mistakes due to lost information or unclear verbal instructions. With all of these characteristics there should also come higher productivity and reliability.

However, in some bureaucracies the paperwork may become an end rather than a means. In these cases, the bureaucracy is no longer effective.[1] Another disadvantage comes with the high division of labor. [a] I would think the division could also increase the number of both employees and managers so that people would know each kind of job because neither type of worker knows the other's job.[a] [The more specialized these positions become the harder it becomes to cover for temporary vacencies.]

[1] This seems to have happened in a number of government agencies

## ► DISCUSSION ACTIVITY ◄

Using this list of criteria, examine each of the following essay exam responses. Discuss which response is more effective and why. Make suggestions for improving each essay.

**1.** Is there evidence of an explicitly stated thesis or statement of intent? Is the statement of intent located in an effective position?

**2.** Does the thesis statement accurately address the concerns of the question? Does it target a specific body of information, or is it too broad?

**3.** Does each supporting paragraph directly relate to the overall focus established in the introduction? Is there a focus to the response?

**4.** Is the essay structured in a logical fashion? Are the transitions between sections and paragraphs smooth?

**5.** Are the details and examples appropriate? Are there enough? Are there too many unsupported generalizations?

Question: *Summarize the effects of the all-volunteer force on military professionalism.*

*Response 1*: The effects of the all-volunteer force on the military profession are both positive and negative. First, the attitude of the AVF recruits could be more positive. These people were not forced to join the armed forces by the draft. They freely chose to sign up because of their allegiance to their country.

On the other hand, the all-volunteer force employs an occupational model. Some people who come into the armed forces are looking only for job training and rapid advancement. They see being in the armed forces only as a job and not as a duty as an American citizen. Because these recruits are more interested in making money than they are in their "calling to serve," they make more demands than draftees on the military. This attitude could lead to unionization and less control over the forces.

Finally, the all-volunteer force is more costly than the draft because salaries must remain competitive with those in the civilian world for the forces to draw in the most capable recruits. Recruiting is more difficult in general because people need to be "persuaded" to join the rank and file.

*Response 2*: The all-volunteer force has increased the professional standing of the military. In the past, the draft had forced people to serve in the military (whether or not they wanted to). The result was the presence of morale problems and even lower quality job performance. With the all-volunteer force, it is the choice of the individual to be a part of the military. Therefore, a stronger internalized "sense of duty" is present. This is a part of the responsibility requirement to be a professional. Also better performance and career enhancement may result.

## ▶ WRITING ACTIVITY ◀

**1.** For each of the following two essay questions, identify the key words that target the kinds of information necessary for a successful response as well as any guide words that suggest potentially useful strategies of development. Write a brief "Writer's Mind" in which you discuss your approach to a response.

Question A: *Compare and contrast Mesopotamian religion with Egyptian religion with respect to belief, outlook, and attitudes of each. In your analysis, note development or change wherever it can be perceived. Use all appropriate materials that provide evidence for your essay.*

Question B: *Write as fully as possible on the topic "The Triumph and Tragedy of Athens in the Fifth Century." Use all appropriate materials.*

**2.** Assume that you have the choice to respond to either question A or B. If you were to base your selection on which question contains the most useful guide words and suggestions for structuring, which would you choose? Why?

**3.** Read the following sample response to Question A. Try to reconstruct the scratch outline or other methods of planning that the student may have used.

The Mesopotamian religion differed from the Egyptian in outlook. Both religions were based on human reaction to the movements in nature, but each had a very different experience of the movements in nature. The Egyptians' experience was one of harmony and accord with nature. The Nile flooded regularly, bringing life-giving water to the arid land and replenishing the minerals lost to crops by dropping mineral-rich silt. The Egyptians also experienced Re, the sun, as a giver of life. The warm, dry air and the contributions of the Nile made their crops successful. This gave the people a happy outlook in their present life. The constant cycles of sun and water also engendered a belief that life runs in cycles. What dies is resurrected. From death comes life again. This is seen clearly in the cult of Osiris. Osiris, a great teacher, is a symbol of the Nile. Evil Set comes and slays Osiris. Set cuts his body up and casts it over the earth. Isis, his faithful wife, gathers up the parts and restores Osiris to life. Here is the resurrection. Hours, the posthumus son of Osiris, arises and slays Set (conquers Evil). Osiris then becomes the judge of the netherworld. Here the people looked forward to a good life in the present and made provisions for the good life in the nether world.

The Mesopotamians, on the other hand, had a quite different experience with nature. Unlike the Nile, the Tigris and Euphrates flooded with irregularity. The floods were as likely to be harmful as helpful. The rivers were as likely to take life as give it. They often flooded into the sea without dropping mineral deposits and taking away land as well. The Mesopotamians' experience of the combination of sun and water was different from that of the Egyptians also. Their river valley was not only unpredictable but hot and humid as well. Their crops were at the mercy of "the gods." This gave the people an outlook filled with anxiety. Unlike the Egyptians, who could look with happiness at their gods, the Mesopotamians looked with fear. The Egyptians asked, "Who art Thou?" of the gods of nature without fear, only curiosity. The Mesopotamians asked "Who art Thou?" with fear and trembling. Both religions started out as animistic and in the realm of mythopoeic thought. The Egyptians moved from being polytheistic, to monotheistic, back to polytheistic. The Mesopotamians remained polytheistic and within the realm of mythopoeic thought. When the Egyptians moved into monotheism, they made the first step toward a transcendant god under Ambotep. He tried to unite the country and the gods into one. Unfortunately his plan failed. He died an untimely death and the priests from the old cults instituted the polytheism prevalent in the past. The Egyptians had moved to the edge of mythopoeic thought. They were almost ready to say "What is it?" The Mesopotamians never moved quite so far.

**4.** Assuming that the information is accurate, what are the strengths and weaknesses in the above response? Concentrate on the existence of a strong controlling thesis, the overall structure, and the use of examples.

The following is a guide to the strategies that you should keep in mind as you prepare for and take your essay exam:

## PREPARING FOR THE EXAM

### Gathering Information

Take efficient, flexible notes that can be easily interpreted

Review the information that you are accumulating, particularly your notes, a minimum of two times a week

### Pre-Exam Activities

Write summaries of your notes and/or important sections of your text

Rewrite the major point in your notes into an arguable thesis

Prepare a focussed freewrite or a dialog that explains the information to a reader or listener who is not familiar with the topic

## TAKING THE EXAM

### Interpreting the Question and Managing Your Time

Read the question slowly and carefully, underlining key words

Make sure that you understand exactly what you are supposed to do, paying close attention to highly directive statements

Divide your time in proportion to the point value of each question

Spend one third of your time on planning and two thirds of your time on drafting and revising your responses.

### Writing Your Response

Brainstorm or cluster to recall the specific information that the question calls for

Shape this material according to the focus of the question by using the journalistic formula or pentad

Prepare a scratch outline and a thesis statement

Order your response according to the structure of the question

Provide two or three specific examples for every general statement

### Revising Your Response

Correct any errors in grammar, punctuation, or mechanics

Consider your word choices

# PART ▲ FOUR

# *Composing and Revising Paragraphs and Sentences*

CHAPTER ▲ TWELVE

# *Effective Paragraphs*

**"An essay is only as good as the sum of its paragraphs."**

**BERTHA MASON**

Beginning writers are often uncertain about what paragraphs are supposed to do and how to make them effective. As the quote from Bertha Mason states, paragraphs are an integral part of the composition as a whole and therefore must develop from your overall decisions about purpose, audience, code, experience, and self. Paragraphs are the structure into which you organize your expression of purpose. Think of your essay as an organism, of its paragraphs as the living skeleton of that organism. The paragraphs that make up the skeleton will be judged to be effective or ineffective on the basis of how well each contributes to the overall framework of the essay.

Indenting to indicate the beginning of a new paragraph is a convention of writing, like punctuating or starting a new sentence with a capital letter. Hundreds of years ago, writers did not indent to signal paragraph division. Instead, they used a signal (¶) between certain sentences or in the left-hand margin; the word *paragraph*, meaning "write beside," is derived from this practice. In modern writing, however, indenting has become a firmly established convention.

## WHAT IS A PARAGRAPH?

Each writing situation and each writer are different, and no one can say that all paragraphs must be written in the same way. Paragraphs are not written by formula. They should be written in any way that serves your overall purpose. The challenge is to learn to write and rewrite paragraphs that serve your purpose and are coherent—that is, paragraphs that not only express what you want to say, but express it in ways that the reader will understand.

You might well ask: What, exactly, is a paragraph? Actually, you probably already have a good understanding of what a paragraph is. Anyone who uses language to communicate ideas is intuitively able to produce coherent discourse; otherwise sophisticated social interaction would be impossible. A paragraph is simply a way of signaling to your reader that a group of sentences is related and should be read together as a unit. Without paragraphs, readers are forced to think of all your sentences as one complete thought or to mentally group your sentences into units themselves. Paragraphing saves your readers a lot of work by helping them to concentrate on what is being said. Paragraphs also help your readers understand what is most important and what is supportive of your important points. Paragraphs possess a related psychological value, too. They give your reader hope. Paragraph divisions tell readers that they will have opportunities for rest as they read along. If you have ever tried to read a page of undivided print, you will understand how depressing such a page of reading can be, even for those of us who love to read.

## COMMON PROBLEMS TO AVOID

Modern readers expect paragraph indentions to signal breaks in units of thought or divisions in a composition's organization. Consequently, two common problems of paragraphs must be avoided: paragraphs that ramble without relief, sometimes for entire pages or more, and paragraphs that appear to be arbitrary indentions after every sentence or two. Rambling paragraphs confuse readers and often bore them. Short, single-sentence paragraphs are simply distracting. Paragraph divisions should occur regularly, but they should not be arbitrarily produced.

### PRINCIPLES OF PARAGRAPH DEVELOPMENT

1. A paragraph often has a *topic sentence.*
2. A paragraph should have a *plan of development.*
3. A paragraph should be *unified.*
4. A paragraph should be *coherent.*
5. A paragraph should have *supportive detail.*

*Coherence* (a holding together meaningfully and understandably) is the final goal of each paragraph. Coherence is enhanced by keeping a paragraph *unified* (aimed at one central idea without irrelevant sentences). Paragraph unity is achieved by stating the topic, executing a *plan of development*, and providing *supportive detail*.

Perfectly coherent paragraphs are rarely written the first time writers put pen to paper or fingers to keyboard. Typically, writers must revise their paragraphs, throwing out some sentences, adding others, moving sentences and sometimes whole paragraphs to other places in the composition. You should not only expect to make these kinds of changes, but welcome them. Revision is often necessary to produce coherent writing, and one important part of this process is the revision of paragraphs.

Most of the time, the operations that writers use to develop paragraphs are unconscious. The more you write, the easier writing becomes. If you are a beginning writer, you might want to consider going through each piece of writing that you produce, consciously looking at your paragraphs for ways to improve them independently of the overall composition.

## THE TOPIC SENTENCE

All effective paragraphs should have a controlling or central idea: what the paragraph is about, its topic. Many paragraphs clearly state this controlling idea in a topic sentence or sentences (usually no more than two). The topic or controlling idea of a paragraph is typically placed at its beginning.

Some paragraphs do not have an identifiable topic sentence; instead, the topic is implied throughout the paragraph through the use of carefully selected sentences. Also the topic sentence may not always appear at the head of the paragraph. However, these are variations of conventional practice.

We suggest that if you are uneasy with writing, you should always try to formulate a topic sentence for most of the paragraphs that you write. The topic sentence is the first sentence in the following paragraph:

> *The basic attack of the creationists falls apart on two general counts before we even reach the supposed factual details of their complaints against evolution.* First, they play upon a vernacular misunderstanding of the word "theory" to convey the false impression that we evolutionists are covering up the rotten core of our edifice. Second, they misuse a popular philosophy of science to argue that they are behaving scientifically in attacking evolution. Yet the same philosophy demonstrates that their own belief is not science, and that "scientific creationism" is therefore meaningless and self-contradictory, a superb example of what Orwell called "newspeak."
>
> STEPHEN JAY GOULD, "Evolution as Fact and Theory"

No matter where we stand on the issue of evolution, we can still see that stylistically (as opposed to thematically), this paragraph works. It is structured simply but effectively. The author intends to set forth his argument against creationism first with a generalization, his topic sentence, and then with supporting details that explain this generalization. He signals his support with the words "first" and "second." Note that in this case Gould supports his generalization with further claims that will also need support themselves in the paragraphs that follow. We can imagine that Gould might begin the next paragraph by taking up the issue raised in his first claim, and then, after supporting it, deal with the issue raised in his second supportive claim. In fact, this is exactly the plan Gould executes.

As we indicated above, however, not all paragraphs have their topic stated in one sentence. In the paragraph below, the author states his topic in the first two sentences.

> *Many people believe that reasoning and therefore science, is a different activity from imagining. But this is a fallacy, and you must root it out of your mind.* The child that discovers, sometime before the age of ten, that he or she can make images and move them around in his head has entered the same gateway to imagination and to reason. Reasoning is constructed

with movable images just as certainly as poetry is. You may have been told, you may still have the feeling, that $E = mc^2$ is not an imaginative statement. If so, you are mistaken. The symbols in that master equation of the twentieth century—the E for energy, and the m for mass, and the c for the speed of light—are images for absent things of concepts exactly the same kind as the words "tree" or "love" in a poem. The poet John Keats was not writing anything which (for him at least) was not fundamentally different from an equation when he wrote "Beauty is truth, truth beauty,—that is all/Ye need know on earth, and all ye need to know." There is no difference in the use of such words as "beauty" and "truth" in the poem, and such symbols as "energy" and "mass" in the equation.

JACOB BRONOWSKI, "The Imaginative Mind in Science"

Clearly the intention of this paragraph is to dispel the notion that there is a difference between the process of scientific reasoning and that of creative imagination. Everything that follows the topic sentences supports and enlarges that intention; in fact, the entire paragraph supports and enlarges the overall intention of the composition as stated in the title of the essay itself. Whether a writer states his or her topic idea in one sentence or two or more is unimportant, as long as it is clear to the reader.

## ► PRACTICE: Locating the Topic ◄

Analyze the following paragraph for its topic. Where is it located? How can you tell?

The effects of long-distance running are psychologically uplifting. Because many people live in a world full of suffering, cruelty, and chaos, tensions build up, causing neurosis. In such a world, running helps reinforce the view that life is good and that man can accomplish what he sets his mind to. Each hill is approached as a positive challenge, causing the runner to grow with each stride and leading him to tranquility and harmony.

PAT SVETICH, "Running for Life"

## ► Variations to Paragraph Beginnings

We have been using the term *topic* to refer to the sentence or sentences that state what the paragraph is about and also to refer to the sentence or sentences in the paragraph to which the others are related. But, as we noted earlier, some paragraphs don't have topic sentences. In fact, there are many variations on the way paragraphs begin.

***The transitional sentence*** Experienced writers sometimes start a paragraph with a sentence that relates back to the preceding paragraph. The transitional sentence does for the paragraph what the transitional signal does for the sentence: It establishes coherence. Note the following example:

**THE TRANSITIONAL SENTENCE**

(TR) At Moreton Drive peace was pouring in a bland golden flood out of the park opposite.

**TOPIC**

1. There were birds in mother's garden.

**DEVELOPMENT SENTENCES**

2. Somebody had put out seed for them, in a little terra cotta dish suspended from the branch of a tree.
3. Sparrows and finches were fluttering, flirting; a rain of seed scattered from the swaying dish.
4. From the lawn at the foot of the tree, a flight of blue pigeons took off clattering away.

PATRICK WHITE, "The Eye of the Storm"

In this paragraph, the first sentence is not the topic of the paragraph. It is a transitional sentence relating this paragraph to the preceding one. The topic sentence is sentence number 1. Notice that if you remove this sentence, the rest of the sentences have nothing to attach themselves to.

***Topic plus restriction*** Sometimes the topic idea is first stated in a general way and then restricted immediately by a more specific sentence. Often the decision to write a topic-plus-restriction beginning is simply a decision in favor of readability; the topic may be easier to read if written as two or more sentences instead of one long one.

**TOPIC**

1. The LSD state varies greatly according to the dosage, the personality of the user and the condition under which the drug was taken.

**TOPIC RESTRICTION**

1R. Basically, it causes changes in sensation.

**DEVELOPMENT SENTENCES**

2. Vision is markedly altered.
    3. Changes in depth perception and the meaning of the perceived object are most frequently described.
    3. Illusions and hallucinations can occur.

2. Thinking may become pictorial and reverie states are common.
   3. Delusions are expressed.

2. The sense of time and of self are strangely altered.

2. Strong emotions may range from bliss to horror, sometimes within a single experience.

2. Sensations may "cross over," that is, music may be seen or color heard.

2. The individual is suggestible and, especially under high doses, loses the ability to discriminate and evaluate experience.

NATIONAL CLEARINGHOUSE FOR DRUG ABUSE INFORMATION, *A Federal Source Book: Answers to the Most Frequently Asked Questions About Drug Abuse.*

The topic sentence, number 1, identifies the subject of the paragraph, the LSD state, which differs from person to person. The next sentence, number 1R, restricts the topic to the basic changes in sensation caused by LSD. All the level 2 sentences, then, refer to the topic and its restriction.

*Implied topic* Although some paragraphs have no stated topic, they have a topic that is clearly implied—that is, a topic that could have been stated, had the author felt it necessary. Here is an example:

2. The amounts and concentrations of fertilizer to be applied to your lawn depend on your lawn area.

2. The same is true for the herbicides, fungicides, and insecticides; your lawn bill is calculated on the basis of lawn area.

2. If you should die suddenly, the executor of your estate may want to know your lawn area.

TIMOTHY F. BANNON, "Lawn Order"

We have labeled all of these sentences "2," because they are all second-level examples of an implied topic: Lawn area is important. Since the examples themselves clearly make the point, there is no need for a stated topic here.

## PLAN OF DEVELOPMENT

Paragraphs don't just happen. Each one should have a plan or purpose in keeping with the overall theme of the composition. The plan or purpose of your whole composition is likely to become the plan for your paragraphs, too. For instance, if you are writing a story, you are likely to use a chronological or narrative pattern of development throughout.

As we noted earlier, writers tend to produce paragraphs often without conscious plans. However, they never produce them without conscious purposes.

For example, W. S. Merwin has written a book called *The Miner's Pale Children*, in which he describes a certain culture through brief vignettes, stories, and sketches. In "The Bar," he tries to describe bars of this particular culture. First, he introduces the sketch with a generalization: This bar is like every other bar in this country. Then, in the second paragraph, he describes the physical appearance of the bar on a typical night. In the third paragraph, he describes a certain detail about the bar that he finds especially meaningful. In the fourth paragraph, he describes what happens when someone new enters the bar. And he concludes the sketch by noting that beyond this one bar are other bars, with other barkeeps, but the same furnishings, returning to his original generalization. Each paragraph of "The Bar" has its own purpose, which supports the overall purpose of the sketch, which itself supports the overall purpose of the book.

Generally speaking, once you are clear about what you want to communicate to your reader, your paragraphs will be easier to plan. However, this is not always the case. With problem paragraphs, you must take time to consider alternative strategies of paragraph development. Here is a list of different ways to develop a paragraph:

## ► Development by Time Order

In narrative paragraphs, you may want to think of the events of your narrative in the order in which they happened. You might begin at the beginning and continue to the end—from the past to the present to the future, if need be. Or you could begin at the present and "flash back" to the past, as long as you give the reader clear signals.

## ► Development by Spatial Order

In descriptive paragraphs, you can begin where the observer (writer) is and move toward the horizon, or you can begin at a distant point and move toward the observer. Or you can select any point and move clockwise or vertically or in any other orderly fashion as long as the reader can follow the development.

## ► Development by Order of Importance

When presenting examples, explanations, arguments, begin with the least important and end with the most important. This plan fulfills your reader's expectations. Random order or diminishing order (ending with the weakest point) rarely works.

## ► Development by Order of Specificity

Many paragraphs present specific details leading up to some generalization about them (observations about specific college students, for example, may lead to some idea about college students in general). The most common plan presents the general idea first and then supplies specific examples or details to illustrate the generalization. For instance, some generalization about novels could be illustrated by citing several specific novels as examples.

## SUPPORTIVE DETAILS

Details are the heart of most effective essays. A series of paragraphs containing unsupported generalizations and unexplained abstractions soon becomes tedious to read and generally alienates your reader from you. To develop an idea or to explain a concept requires supportive details that will expand and illustrate the idea. A paragraph must do more than make an interesting assertion. Most ineffective paragraphs lack details. For example:

> There is an abundance in Nature that, if used wisely, should never outrun the earth's ability to support her inhabitants. It is mankind's greedy overreach that has caused the environmental crises of scarcity; because we have chosen to consume rather than save, we face not only a future of dwindling natural resources, but the possibility of a serious ecological imbalance as well. The time has come for a new morality towards nature.

The author of this paragraph is trying to make a point about the relationship of human beings to their environment, but despite whatever possible truth there is to the claims made, the reader gets only a general and unsubstantiated impression. The reader is justified in asking: What, specifically, has gone wrong in the relationship between human beings and nature? The paragraph implies that there is something immoral in our attitude toward the environment. What have we done wrong? How can we rectify our mistakes? All of these informative, supportive details are missing. The reader can see in a general way what the writer is trying to say, but the message does not sink in. The passage fails to convince the reader because it contains no support for its generalizations. Contrast the preceding undeveloped paragraph with the one that follows:

> The root of our problem lies deep. The real shortage with which we are afflicted is that of moral resources. Assuming that we wish to survive in dignity and not as ciphers in some ant-heap society, we are obliged to reassume our full moral responsibility. The earth is not just a banquet at which we are free to gorge. The ideal in Buddhism of compassion for all sentient beings, the concern for the harmony of man and nature so evident among American indians, and the almost forgotten ideal of stewardship in Christianity points us in the direction of a true ethics of human survival—and it is toward such an ideal that the best among the young are groping. We must realize that there is not real scarcity in nature. It is our numbers and, above all, our wants that have outrun nature's bounty. We become rich precisely in proportion to the degree in which we eliminate violence, greed, and pride from our lives. As several thousands of years of history show, this

is not something easily learned by humanity, and we seem no readier to choose the simple, virtuous life now than we have been in the past. Nevertheless, if we wish to avoid either a crash into the ecological ceiling or a tyrannical Leviathan, we must choose it. There is no other way to defeat the gathering forces of scarcity.

WILLIAM OPHULS, "The Scarcity Society"

This fully developed paragraph fleshes out the bare skeleton of ideas suggested in the first paragraph. The author provides specific details that not only convince the reader that at the very least his argument is sound, but also actually provide instructions for carrying out the paragraph's intent.

### ► PRACTICE: Revising for Details ◄

Suggest added details for the following paragraph. Type the paragraph and then mark it with a pen as if someone else were going to retype it for you. Don't just start over, writing your own paragraph—revise this one. Add extra words and sentences to help the reader feel and see and hear. Revise it so that the experience itself becomes the point of the paragraph. Then prepare a clean copy from your revised copy.

I'd been in creepy places before, but never like this. The old place was very dark, but there was a little light. It made things look strange—furniture and stuff. Some sort of weird noise was coming from upstairs. As I started up, something went past me. I was so scared. I could hardly get out of there fast enough.

## UNITY

The term *unity* comes from the Latin word *unus*, meaning "one." Typically, we want our paragraphs to develop one concept or idea, one topic, and therefore be unified. Irrelevant sentences tend to distract and confuse your reader. A good rule is to delete any sentence or detail that does not advance the topic.

Contemporary author Suzanne Langer wrote one of the following paragraphs. The other two contain irrelevant, distracting information that interferes with the development of the paragraph.

A. The momentous difference between us and our animal cousins is that they do not know they are going to die. Animals spend their lives avoiding death, until it gets them. They do not know it is going to. Neither do they know that they are part of a greater life, but pass on the torch without knowing. We have always feared death. The great poets have often alluded to the awesome finality of death, calling it "the great leveller." Death has

> been called the "ultimate joke" and religion the "opiate of the masses." The aim of animals, then, is simply to keep going, to function, to escape troubles, to live from moment to moment in an endless Now.
>
> B. The momentous difference between us and our animals is that they do not know they are going to die. Of course, plants don't know they are going to die either, but neither do they know they are alive. Animals spend their lives avoiding death, until it gets them. They do not know it is going to. Neither do they know that they are part of a greater life, but pass on the torch without knowing. Their aim, then, is simply to keep going, to function, to escape troubles, to live from moment to moment in an endless Now.
>
> C. The momentous difference between us and our animal cousins is that they do not know they are going to die. Animals spend their lives avoiding death, until it gets them. They do not know it is going to. Neither do they know that they are part of a greater life, but pass on the torch without knowing. Their aim, then, is simply to keep going, to function, to escape troubles, to live from moment to moment in an endless NOW.
>
> SUZANNE LANGER, "Man and Animal: The City and the Hive"

Paragraph A contains several extraneous sentences, as if the writer, in thinking about the difference between the way animals and people die, decided to remind the reader about the human fear of death. Having started in this direction, the sentences wander away from the subject, until they end with a statement about religion. Paragraph B contains an irrelevant sentence about plants, as if the writer had thrown in a contrastive statement about other nonhuman forms of life. Paragraph C, as written by Langer, is a unified paragraph about animal life; specifically, it describes one way that animal life differs from human life. A paragraph should not be "more or less" unified, nor "sort of" about its topic, but rather, specifically and only about that topic.

## ► PRACTICE: Revising for Unity ◄

In your rough draft, paragraphs may contain irrelevant sentences or words or phrases that are not clearly related to the central idea. Your central idea itself may not be clear, so that the whole paragraph seems like a loose collection of ideas not clearly connected to each other. Revise such paragraphs by removing the unrelated ideas and by clarifying the main point.

In the following paragraph, we have inserted two extra sentences that break the unity. Can you locate them?

> Oh it is a handsome place, green lawns and tall trees and fluted flower beds. Seasons come and go, but I think my favorite is autumn because it means an end to lawn mowing. High up on the balconies of each cottage the children stand, the girls in their red bows and white dresses, the boys

in white suits and giant red ties. As a small child, I often begged my mother to let me wear a tie, but she believed little girls should be little girls, so I had to wait until I was grown to dress the way I wanted to. The parents below shrieking up to be heard and the children shriek down to be heard, and between them the invisible wall, "Not To Be Contaminated By Parental Germs or Physical Affection."

TILLIE OLSEN, "I Stand Here Ironing"

This paragraph is about the frustration felt by both parents and children on visiting day at a sanitorium. Although the sentence about seasons may add a personal detail about the author's life, it adds nothing to the anguished tone of the moment being captured in the paragraph; nor does the comment on the propriety of wearing a tie contribute anything of importance to the purpose of the paragraph. Both were added by us and should be edited out.

## COHERENCE

Coherence, strictly speaking, means "holding together" or "being logically consistent." But when we say that a writer or speaker is coherent, we also mean that he or she can be understood. Coherence is what every writer is finally after.

Beginning writers sometimes produce incoherent paragraphs because they forget that the audience does not share their own thorough grasp of the subject. You may have a clear sense of the interrelationships between details in the paragraph, but what about your reader? Think of what you are trying to say and what you want your reader to hear.

The qualities that we have already discussed (having a topic, a plan of development, supportive detail, and unity), all function to achieve paragraph coherence. But there are additional ways we can help to make our paragraphs coherent.

### ► Repetitions

Coherent paragraphs often contain networks of repetitions—*association chains* of key words and concepts and synonyms or pronouns that substitute for these key words, as well as repetitions of grammatical structures—that is, the same kinds of sentences. The key to using such repetitions is to avoid overdoing one kind of repetition. In other words, don't simply repeat the key word of a paragraph over and over in every sentence. Note the association chains in the paragraph below.

In the seventeen-seventies **Londoners** developed a craving for **Jesse Fish oranges. These** had thin skins and were difficult to peel, but **the English** found **them** incredibly **juicy** and sweet, and **Jesse Fish oranges** were preferred before all **others** in the making of shrub, a drink that called for alcoholic

> spirits, sugar, and the juice of an acid fruit—an ancestral whiskey sour. More than sixty-five thousand Jesse Fish oranges and two casks of juice reached London in 1776, and sixteen hogsheads of juice arrived in 1778. It hardly mattered to the English who Jesse Fish was, and it didn't seem to matter to Jesse Fish who his customers were. Fish was a Yankee, a native of New York and by sympathy a revolutionary. Decades before the Revolution, he had retreated to an island off St. Augustine to get away from a miserable marriage, and he had become Florida's first orange baron.
>
> JOHN MCPHEE, "Oranges"

As you can see, McPhee—one of today's finest prose writers—has used many association chains in this paragraph. You might also want to note the repetitions of grammatical structure, especially toward the end of the paragraph.

## ► Transitional Signals

Another way that a writer can help to achieve coherence in a paragraph is by the use of words or phrases that tell the reader how one sentence relates to another. These words or phrases are called *transitions*, or *transitional signals*. Here is a list of them by function:

***For Addition***

again, also, and, and then, besides, finally, first, further, furthermore, in addition, last, moreover, next, second, too

***For Comparison***

also, as, by the same token, in comparison, likewise, similarly, then too

***For Concession***

after all, although it is true, at the same time, granted, I admit, I concede, naturally, of course, while it is true

***For Contrast***

after all, although, and yet, but, by contrast, however, nevertheless, on the contrary, on the other hand, otherwise, still, whereas, yet

***For Examples and Illustration***

by way of illustration, for example, for instance, incidentally, indeed, in fact, in other words, in particular, specifically, that is

***For Result***

accordingly, as a result, consequently, hence, in short, then, thereafter, therefore, thus, truly

***For Summary***

as I have said, in brief, in conclusion, in other words, in short, on the whole, to conclude, to summarize, to sum up

***For Time***

afterwards, at last, at length, hence, immediately, in the meantime, lately, meanwhile, of late, presently, shortly, since, soon, temporarily, thereafter, thereupon, while.

Again, the key to effective use of transitional signals, like that of repetitions, is not to overuse them.

## ► PRACTICE: Locating Transitional Signals ◄

Note the several techniques used in the following paragraph. We have italicized the transitional signals that are used there. Can you find the repetitions used for coherence?

> Two rangy shepherd dogs trotted up pleasantly, *until* they caught the scent of strangers, *and then* they backed cautiously away, watchful, their tails moving slowly and tentatively in the air, but their eyes and noses quick for animosity or danger. One of them, scratching his neck, edged forward, ready to run, and little by little he approached Tom's legs and sniffed loudly at them. *Then* he backed away and watched Pa for some kind of signal. The other pup was not so brave. He looked about for something that could honorably divert his attention, saw a red chicken go mincing by, and ran at it. There was the squawk of an outraged hen, a burst of red feathers, and the hen ran off, flapping stubby wings for speed. The pup looked proudly back at the men, *and then* flopped down in the dust and beat its tail contentedly on the ground.
>
> JOHN STEINBECK, *The Grapes of Wrath*

## ► Testing for Coherence

As we have mentioned before, most writers don't consciously plan each paragraph in detail; however, writers do test their paragraphs during revision. Frequently, changes are made, some minor, some major, a word here or there, a reworking of the whole thing; it all depends on whether the paragraph does what the writer wants it to do.

Although you could go through each paragraph of any essay you have written, looking for each of the qualities we have discussed, there is a quicker way to test for coherence in your paragraphs. If a paragraph fails the test, of course, you may want to look more closely at it to discover where you went wrong and how to improve it. This test, however, is a way to get an overall feel for the success of each paragraph.

Generally speaking, each paragraph is an answer to this question: "What am I trying to say?" That is, "What is the purpose of this paragraph?" Consider the following paragraph.

> (1) Everybody calls me "Daddy's Girl," and it's true. (2) Not only is he a great father, but he is also my best friend. (3) For his age, he is in pretty good shape. (4) He is always ready to help me with my homework as well as with whatever sport I happen to be playing at the time. (5) Dad was quite a softball player when he was in college; our family room is full of trophies. (6) Whenever I get discouraged with school, or have a fight with my boyfriend, I always go to my dad for advice. (7) He gets along really well with my boyfriend, but he always stands up for me no matter what. (8) Dad is pretty good around the house, too; he doesn't mind helping out with the housework and he is a pretty good cook. (9) Every Saturday night he makes a special dinner. (10) My favorite is spaghetti and meatballs. (11) It must be his, too, because we have it a lot.

Most of this paragraph is fairly general, but it could make a good introductory paragraph for a composition that went on to provide supportive details. If you ask, "What question does this paragraph answer?" you might say it answers the question, "What was Pamela's father like?" However, such a question is too broad and general for one paragraph. It is the kind of question that might take several paragraphs to answer.

On the other hand, perhaps sentence 2 implies the question the author really meant to answer: "Why is my father my best friend?" This question is much more specific and could be answered in a paragraph. As the editor of your own paragraphs, you will have to decide whether you need more planning to discover what you really want to say or more revision to make your paragraphs say what you intend.

To test your paragraph, change the paragraph question into a proposition and then see if all of the sentences can logically support the proposition. If we assume that Pamela wanted to write about things that made her father her "best friend," we can see that some of the sentences are clearly not about that relationship. For instance, sentence 5, concerning her father's softball career in college and his trophies, has very little to do with the topic of the paragraph. Sentence 8, about her father's willingness to do housework, is questionable, too.

## ► Revising for Coherence

Pamela is faced with several choices. She could delete sentences 5 and 8 entirely. She could put parentheses around them. (She might also want to move sentence 8 so that it follows what she says about the special dinner every Saturday night.) Placing parentheses around words, phrases, and sentences indicates to the reader that they are digressions and are less directly related to the topic than other nonparenthetical sentences. She could revise sentence 5 and keep sentence 8 as it is. (Although sentence 8 seems to be an intrusion of irrelevant information when the reader first encounters it, the information is related to relevant information in the next sentence, so that the reader would then think, "Oh, now I understand.") Again, as we have said before, a writer's decisions concerning paragraph development depend entirely upon the overall purpose the paragraph is to support. Let's begin analyzing with sentence 4 in Pamela's paragraph, having in mind her overall purpose in the essay:

> He is always ready to help me with my homework as well as with whatever sport I happen to be playing at the time.

Suppose we change the wording of this sentence in order to relate it to sentence 5, which tells us about Pamela's dad's being a softball player:

> He is always ready to help me with my homework and to coach me at whatever sport I happen to be playing at the time. Dad was quite a softball player in college; our family room is full of trophies won by both of us.

Let's turn now to sentence 8:

> Dad is pretty good around the house, too; he doesn't mind helping out with the housework and he is a pretty good cook.

Here we might add some wording to connect Pamela's father's housework and cooking abilities to the overall topic:

> Dad is pretty good around the house, too. Since Mom died, a lot of the responsibility for running things has fallen on me. Even though Dad has worked hard all day, he doesn't mind running the vacuum cleaner or doing a load of laundry, and he's a pretty good cook, too.

With these revisions, we can see that the two ideas can be made to elaborate on the special circumstances of this father-daughter relationship. The paragraph becomes more coherent. Only Pamela can tell us if the revisions correspond with the intention of the original version and if they are what she wants her reader to read.

## ► PRACTICE: Revising for Coherence ◄

What is wrong with the coherence of the following paragraph? Has the student found the question he or she wants to answer? Is it a suitable question for a paragraph? If some of the sentences do not seem clearly related, would it be better to remove them or try to revise them? Revise the paragraph for coherence.

> I believe in equality of the sexes, but I don't think women should have to serve in the army. My brother was in the army and he learned to be a computer technologist. I do think women should be granted maternity leave with pay, by their employers, but men should get maternity leave, too. Children can greatly benefit from having two parents as caretakers, and it gives men and women a chance to get to know each other better. If equality of the sexes is to work, men and women have to share the responsibility together. My parents had a traditional marriage.

## PARAGRAPH STRUCTURE

The structure of a paragraph consists of the relationship between and among the sentences in that paragraph. One useful method for analyzing a paragraph is to describe it as a sequence of structurally related sentences. Ordinarily, the topic of a paragraph is a generalization and the development of a paragraph is often made up of one or more specific instances of the generalization. In other words, a paragraph makes a general statement that is illustrated with more specific statements as the paragraph develops.

### ► Topic Plus Development

The topic-plus-development structure is produced by addition. Notice in the following example how many specifics (illustrations) have been added to the topic sentence.

#### TOPIC (GENERALIZATION)

> Dr. Steele points to a number of characteristics most abusive parents have in common.

#### DEVELOPMENT (SPECIFIC INSTANCES)

> They are immature.
> They lack self-esteem; they feel incompetent.
> They have trouble finding pleasure and satisfaction in the outside world.
> They possess a strong fear of spoiling their children and hold an equally strong belief in the efficacy of corporal punishment.
> Finally, they are markedly deficient in the ability to empathize with and respond to their children's needs.

MYRON BRENTON, "What Can Be Done About Child Abuse?"

This paragraph illustrates the basic topic-plus-development structure of many paragraphs in which the topic sentence expresses a generalization and the development is made up of specifics (illustrations) that support the generalization.

The topic sentence and the developmental sentences have a general-to-specific relationship to each other. Although all of the sentences may appear to be generalizations in the logical sense, still with reference to each other, the topic sentence is the generalization that contains all the others and to which all the others relate. The topic sentence names a category (characteristics of abusive parents), and the details of the developmental sentences are included in this category. Without the topic sentence, the others would have no explicit relationship to each other.

The paragraph also illustrates a paragraph moving from the general to the specific; but the possibilities for movement within paragraphs can be complex. Another movement is from specific to general, in which the topic sentence comes last.

DEVELOPMENT (SPECIFIC INSTANCES)

[Berger] has most of the earmarks of the workaholic: He is intense and driven; he doesn't sleep much; he works almost all of his waking hours, and vacations and time off remain firmly in the realm of fantasy. Berger's workaholic tendencies seem to fit well with his job and with his single, busy life-style.

TOPIC (GENERALIZATION)

He is what I call a fulfilled workaholic, one who gets great enjoyment from his work and who has successfully shaped the rest of his life around his central passion.

MARILYN MACHLOWITS, "Workaholics"

## Coordinate Structure

In the following example, the development sentences have all been added to the topic sentence. Each developmental sentence resembles the one above it; that is, each merely gives another example. All the developmental sentences, therefore, have the same relationship to the topic sentence; removing any of the developmental sentences would not make the paragraph incoherent, although it might leave the paragraph sounding a little underdeveloped.

This kind of relationship is called *coordinate*. All of the developmental sentences have the same kind of relationship to the topic sentence. You can number the sentences to illustrate coordinate structure.

COORDINATE STRUCTURE
TOPIC (GENERALIZATION)

1. You can buy practically anything in the supermarket today.

DEVELOPMENT (SPECIFIC INSTANCES)

2. Naturally there is food: meat, fruits and vegetables, dairy products, anything else you can think of to eat or drink.

2. But you can also buy pots and pans and mops and flyswatters, and other household goods.

2. You can also buy books and magazines and records.

2. And any large market will have a drug and medicine section where Dristan and nasal spray are sold.

2. Some stores even have a clothing section, or at least a rack full of panty hose.

IRENE SMALL, "This Little Piggy Went to Market"

## ► PRACTICE: Coordinate Structure ◄

Imagine writing a letter in which you describe a party, an athletic event, a musical performance, or some other group activity. Make the focus of your paragraph what two or three people—either performers or members of the audience—did that made the event enjoyable for you. Write your paragraph so that it has a topic plus development structure, moving either from general to specific or from specific to general.

## ► Subordinate Structure

In the subordinate structure or pattern, each developmental sentence adds only to the sentence immediately above it. If you remove any sentence but the last one in a subordinate pattern, the paragraph will probably become incoherent. To show descending order of subordinate sentences, you can give each one a different number:

TOPIC (GENERALIZATION)

1. The garlic bulb, often rejected by picky eaters as bad smelling and common, is one of nature's greatest gifts.

2. The bulb breaks into a dozen or more cloves, each shaped somewhat like a tear and covered with a paper shell.

3. Each clove releases a powerful aroma and taste of home and familiar things.

4. This wonderful garlic flavor is used by most of the people of the world to spice up the taste of bland food.

LOUISE GLEIMAN, "Garlic"

## ► PRACTICE: Analyzing Subordinate Structure ◄

Explain orally or in writing the subordinate structure of the following paragraph. How should its sentences be numbered? Why?

> The common table lamp is composed of a shade and some kind of base. The shade diffuses the light; the base contains the electrical components. The electrical components are composed of a socket and a cord running through the lamp and ending in a plug. The socket has an opening for the bulb and a switch for opening and closing contact with the cord.
>
> LOU GWAINER, "Repairing a Table Lamp"

## ► PRACTICE: Subordinate Structure ◄

Write a paragraph explaining some simple mechanism like a can opener, hair dryer, pruning shears; or some simple activity such as filling a salt shaker, sharpening a pencil, or changing a cartridge in a pen. Keep the subject simple, something you can deal with reasonably in one paragraph. Write your paragraph so that each sentence adds to the sentence immediately above. Label your paragraph like the example on the preceding page.

These examples represent two basic paragraph patterns: the sentences added directly to the topic sentence or sentences to form a coordinate pattern; and those added to each other to form a subordinate pattern. The sentences in a coordinate pattern all have the same relationship to each other; they are all of the same order and bear the relationship of addition to the topic. The sentences in a subordinate pattern are not parallel to each other, and each makes a comment on only the sentence immediately preceding it. Coordinate structure is useful for analyzing objects, events, and so on.

These examples illustrate what is meant by unity and coherence in a paragraph. Because the sentences are held together in one or the other pattern of relationship, the paragraph becomes a unit (or unified); because the sentences are related to each other, the reader is able to follow a coherent flow of information from one sentence to the next. Thus, any sentence that breaks the pattern or seems not to be clearly related to either a sentence above or the topic sentence breaks the unity of the paragraph and may cause the reader to lose the meaning.

### ► Mixed Coordinate–Subordinate Structure

The most common type of paragraph mixes coordinate and subordinate patterns, as in the following example:

TOPIC (GENERALIZATION)

1. Despite this need for public approval, football does not demand—or particularly welcome—a discriminating public.

DEVELOPMENT (SPECIFIC INSTANCES)

2. The football fan, compared to the baseball fan or the tennis fan—is an absolute oaf.

3. The baseball fan, particularly, is a man of high perceptivity and learning.

4. He can recognize each player; he knows what each batted last year, when and where each broke which clavicle, and how good the prospects are for each rookie who comes along.

2. The football fan knows nothing.

3. He can't recognize one player from another, except by the number on the uniform.

3. He can't tell a right guard from a left kidney.

3. It is all he can do to follow the ball, and often he can't even do that.

WADE THOMPSON, "My Crusade Against Football"

Wade Thompson's paragraph has several levels of generalization and several descending degrees of specification. (There is no specific limit to the number or complexity of the levels possible in a subordinate structure or mixed coordinate-subordinate structure paragraph.) All the development sentences illustrate the topic, supporting the statement that the game of football does not demand a discriminating public. But as you can see from the numbering system, there are several coordinate pattern sentences, sentences that are at the same level of specification (for example, those listing the limitations of the football fan); and the whole paragraph is built on a pattern of subordination.

Thus we have the basic patterns: coordinate, subordinate, and mixed. You can see that by relating your sentences to each other in these ways, you can generate very complex paragraphs.

## ► PRACTICE: Writing Coordinate-Subordinate Paragraphs ◄

Practice writing coordinate and subordinate sequences. Write paragraphs of your own in which the subsequent sentences are specific instances of the topics. Also write paragraphs in which each sentence comments on the one preceding it.

## ▶ PRACTICE: Revising a Paragraph ◀

Revise the following excerpt from a student's paper. As a reader-editor, help the writer express what he or she wants to say. You may delete words, add words, change words, move words around, add or delete sentences, add paragraph indentations. But *do not change the intention of the original,* as you perceive it. Copy the excerpt as it is and then mark it carefully to show how you are changing it. Assume that a typist will follow your directions to produce a clean copy. Try to reduce the excerpt to approximately 100 words or less of effective writing. Then write out the revised version.

THE MUSHROOM

The mushroom is not a type of fungus but an actual fungus which is characterized by spore-bearing gills on the underside of an umbrella-shaped or cone-shaped cap or top. The term *mushroom* is a word properly restricted to the plant's above-ground portion, an organ which also provides all the reproductive needs of the plant. Once a delicacy for the elite, mushrooms, and especially the meadow mushroom, are now grown for the purpose of providing them as a food product for everyone, regardless of income or social standing, including those who are poor. This is also true of the strawberry which is now available to the general populace. Although mushrooms are not completely lacking in minerals and vitamins, they are, for the most part, water, and their nutritive value is a limited one indeed. Inedible or poisonous species, which should be avoided at all costs, are commonly referred to as toadstools; one of the best known of these "stools of the toad" is the notorious and sometimes even lethal death angel (*genus Amanita*).

## INTRODUCTORY PARAGRAPHS

The first paragraph is often the most important. You may win or lose your reader at the beginning of your composition; therefore, the extra time it takes to write an effective beginning is time well spent. Since it is usually the hardest part to write, some writers postpone serious work on the introductory paragraph until after they have completed a rough draft of the entire paper. Other writers find that work on the introduction helps them to define their purpose and set the tone for the rest of the essay. If you have not established a routine way of writing, then we suggest that you try the first method first. Remember: You must have a clear purpose already in mind. With a clear sense of the overall scope of your paper—its details, its method of development, its conclusion—you will be in a better position to shape an effective introduction.

The introduction should convince the reader that you offer an original approach to an interesting topic. A well-crafted introduction must be accurate; it is confusing and disappointing for the reader to discover that the subject of a composition is something other than what was promised by the writer in the introduction. In fact, that is a good way of thinking about the introduction to an essay: as a promise to the reader. Finally, the introduction should lead the reader smoothly into the body of the paper.

## Problems to Avoid

*The one-sentence introduction* Formal writing seldom uses the one-sentence introduction. Usually, one-sentence paragraphs are empty statements, and they must be edited out. The true introduction is likely to be found in your next paragraph. Remove these one-liners entirely, connect them to the next paragraph, or develop them into substantive introductions.

*The empty introduction* Essays sometimes begin with several sentences that wander around without really saying anything. These sentences are often simply variations of the title of the paper.

> Skiing is a very exciting sport. There are many people who take it up for the excitement. The rewards of skiing can be great. There is nothing like the excitement of skiing down a snowy hill.

Do you get the idea that the writer finds skiing exciting? The writer is hitting the reader over the head with that idea. The writer is skiing around trying to find a subject or an entrance into a subject. Most readers would anticipate that the rest of the essay is likely to be as empty as the introduction and would simply stop reading.

*The assumption-of-knowledge introduction* The writer assumes that the reader knows the subject and consequently fails to include important information. Your introduction must stand on its own, informing, as well as interesting and leading the reader. Avoid references to this assignment, such as "This is a very difficult subject," and "I am not an expert on this subject." Avoid starting off with pronouns whose antecedents are assumed: "It is a very sad play," referring to whatever play is the subject. Avoid references to the title of your essay: "Yes, he certainly was!" (title: "Was Hamlet Crazy?"). Though every paper should have a title, the title is not part of the introduction.

## Effective Introductory Paragraphs

The following introductory paragraphs come from works of fiction and nonfiction by writers with widely different styles. As you read them, decide what is effective about these introductions, using the following criteria:

**1.** Who is the likely audience? Young people? General readers? Sports enthusiasts? The academic community? Do you think the introduction will appeal to its audience?

**2.** What personality does the writer project? Does the author sound intelligent, bland, humorous, superior, knowledgeable, sarcastic? Is the author's tone suitable for the subject and audience?

**3.** Is the introduction interesting? Informative? Does it lead smoothly into the paper?

### *Start with a dramatic incident*

It was all very hush-hush. In the winter of 1973 a top official of the National Cancer Institute flew from Washington, D.C., to Oakland, California, carrying in his briefcase five plastic flasks. Growing in a milky film at the bottom of each flask were live tumor cells. The cells came from cancer patients in five different medical centers in the Soviet Union. In the spirit of detente Russia had given the cells to American scientists, who hoped they might contain new clues to the cause of cancer.

MICHAEL GOLD, "The Cells That Would Not Die"

### *Start by telling a story*

I have long looked for an opportunity to pay a certain debt which I have owed since I was seven years old. Debts are usually burdens, but this is no ordinary debt, and it is no burden, except as the feeling of warm gratitude may ache in one until it is expressed. My debt is to an Englishman, who long ago in China rendered an inestimable service to a small American child. That child was myself and that Englishman was Charles Dickens. I know no better way to meet my obligation than to write down what Charles Dickens did in China for an American child.

PEARL BUCK, "A Debt to Dickens"

### *Start with a contrast*

City people are more supple than country people, and the sanest city people, being more tested and more broadly based in the world of men, are the sanest people on earth. As to honesty, though, or good sense, no clear-cut distinction exists either way.

EDWARD HOAGLAND, "Thoughts on Returning to the City After Five Months on a Mountain Where Wolves Howled"

### *Start by setting the scene*

The last inch of space was filled, yet people continued to wedge themselves along the walls of the store. Uncle Willie had turned the radio up to its last notch so that youngsters on the porch wouldn't miss a word. Women sat on kitchen chairs, dining-room chairs, stools, and upturned wooden boxes. Small children and babies perched in every lap available and men leaned on the shelves or on each other.

MAYA ANGELOU, "Hope"

### *Start with a question*

How many of you have ever wondered where certain slang expressions come from? Like "She's the cat's pajamas," or to "Take it on the lam." Neither have I. And yet for those who are interested in this sort of thing I have provided a brief guide to a few of the more interesting origins.

WOODY ALLEN, "Slang Origins"

### *Start with a description*

Niagara Falls is a city of unmatched natural beauty; it is also a tired industrial workhorse, beaten often and with a hard hand. A magnificent river—a strait really—connecting Lake Erie to Lake Ontario flows hurriedly north, at a pace of a half-million tons a minute, widening into a smooth expanse near the city before breaking into whitecaps and taking its famous 186-foot plunge. Then it cascades through a gorge of overhung shale and limestone to rapids higher and swifter than anywhere else on the continent.

MICHAEL BROWN, "Love Canal and the Poisoning of America"

### *Start by explaining the thesis*

Steven Spielberg's E.T., the *Extra-Terrestrial* is one of the most beautiful fantasy-adventure movies ever made—a sublimely witty and inventive fable that goes so deep into the special alertness, loyalty, and ardor of children that it makes you see things you had forgotten or blotted out and feel things you were embarrassed to feel. Watching it, children will be in heaven; adults, I think, will be moved by how funny, even hip, innocence can be. You may wonder how so commercial a work can be innocent, but Spielberg has pulled it off. He's used his fabulous technique and boundless savvy to create the ecstasy of first responses, when friendship, danger, the physical world itself strike the child as awesome, revelatory. It's a Wordsworthian science-fiction movie.

DAVID DENBY, "The Visionary Gleam"

### *Start with a brief historical background*

Early in the morning of August 6, 1945, the United States dropped on the Japanese city of Hiroshima, the first atomic bomb ever used on a human population. The destruction and chaos wrought by that bomb were so immense that it has never been possible to make a precise count of the number of people killed. Most estimates are in the range of 100,000 to 200,000 people. Even for the hundreds of thousands who experienced the bombing but remained alive, the vision and taint of nuclear holocaust left lifelong scars.

ROBERT JAY LIFTON AND ERIC OLSON, "The Nuclear Age"

### *Start with unusual facts and figures*

There are 435 members of the House of Representatives and 417 are white males. Ten of the others are women and nine are black. I belong to both of these minorities, which makes it add up right. That makes me a celebrity, a kind of side show attraction. I was the first American citizen to be elected to Congress in spite of the double drawbacks of being female and having skin darkened by melanin.

SHIRLEY CHISHOLM, *Unbought and Unbossed*

### *Start with a definition*

I regard gifted children as those who possess some quality or innate ability which has been recognized and identified by any number of testing and observation devices and who manifest interest and success in either physical, intellectual, or artistic pursuits.

KENNETH MOTT, *Group the Gifted*

### *Start with an idea to be refuted*

An argument often advanced on behalf of special classes for gifted children is that in regular classrooms these children are held back and possibly thwarted in their intellectual growth by learning situations that are designed for the average child. There can be little doubt that special classes for the gifted can help them to graduate earlier and take their place in life sooner. On the other hand, to take these students out of the regular classroom may create serious problems for them and for society.

BRUNO BETTLEHEIM, "Grouping the Gifted: Pro and Con"

## CONCLUDING PARAGRAPHS

It is important to keep in mind that the function of the conclusion is to bring the paper to an end. Papers should not arbitrarily stop. Especially in nonfiction, the reader expects the writer to give a clear signal that the final point has been made.

A summary is the most common but not always the most effective technique that beginning writers use to conclude their essays. Everything depends on your purpose. In a report, the summary may be a good ending; in other writing situations, the summary ending may insult your readers' intelligence and thus alienate them at a crucial stage in your essay. Since the conclusion is the last thing your readers encounter, it tends to have a disproportionate impact on them. A weak conclusion can too easily spoil an otherwise competent essay.

The conclusion is your last chance to establish the significance of what you have to say; therefore, it should be one of the high points of your essay. End on a strong note, leaving the reader something to remember, satisfied that you have delivered what you promised in the introduction.

## ► Problems to Avoid

*The one-sentence ending* "Winning the lottery was one of the most exciting moments of my life." Like the one-sentence introduction, this kind of ending is weak. It suggests that you couldn't think of a better way to conclude. Sometimes, these one-liners can be simply deleted; sometimes, however, you have to rethink and revise the ending you have.

*The tacked-on moral or lesson* Especially in personal experience essays, readers should know what the moral is from what has been said in the body of the paper. An ending like "I'll never take Dead Man's Curve at ninety miles an hour again in my father's station wagon" can ruin a strongly written paper. Trust your readers to get the point of your narrative for themselves.

*Contrived endings* "I awoke as the light flooded my room; thank goodness, it had only been a dream!" The inexperienced writer may have been impressed with these kinds of surprise endings, like those written by O. Henry. Or he or she may have resorted to such an ending out of desperation at being unable to think of a stronger one. But such artificial endings are rarely appropriate.

*Trite concluding phrases* In your conclusion, try to avoid mechanical expressions such as "In conclusion," "To sum up," and so on. It is sometimes better to be trite than to be misunderstood. But trite, obvious conclusions can also seem condescending or boring. Know your audience!

*Self-conscious endings* Drawing attention to yourself is usually not a good idea, even in personal experience writing. It is one thing to write about an event that happened to you some time ago, even if you write it in the present tense. It is quite another thing to draw attention to yourself as a writer with phrases like "I will now conclude by . . . ," "Now that I have reached the end of this paper . . . ," "The time has come for me to end this . . . ," and so on. Such phrases call attention away from what you are saying.

*Introducing new problems or subjects* "Yes, sky diving is really an adventure, although there are some problems to avoid if you've never tried it before."

For obvious reasons, you don't want to get your reader started thinking about subjects other than the one you are writing about.

*The weak ending* Don't use up all your material in the body of the paper; save something interesting for the conclusion: a final example; a relevant quotation; a well-worded analysis of the point of the paper. The conclusion must have some substance; it cannot be mere ornament. In most papers the conclusion is not just the end of the composition: It is the *point* of the composition.

## ▶ Effective Concluding Paragraphs

The following passages are concluding paragraphs from articles, essays, books, and chapters in books, written by a variety of authors. First, note the specific techniques used to develop each paragraph; then decide what is effective about each paragraph.

*End with a call for action*

It is up to you, then, and up to everyone, to support science and, where possible, to keep abreast of it, for today's science is tomorrow's solution—and tomorrow's problems, too—and most of all, mankind's greatest adventure, now and forever.

ISAAC ASIMOV, "Of What Use"

*End with a prediction*

Punk rock is a movement which has become popular in the United States and will no doubt last through the 1980's. However, knowing the change of styles and tastes in the past, I believe the next decade is bound to bring an entirely new wave of rock music to the world.

ALEXANDRA WITT, "Punk Rock"

*End by drawing a deduction from the facts*

It is too soon to say where the questions and the new quests will lead. It is clear that a civil war may be developing between two philosophies of life, two value systems. And in the chaos that is bound to result from this clash we might best be guided by the words, but not the example, of Freud. It may help us to remember that in his prescription of love and work—lieben und arbeiten—he designed love as the first among equals.

SAM KEEN, "Lovers Versus Workers"

### *End with a question*

It might seem to even out. If school has become an active experience, then why shouldn't the child spend a few passive hours watching television? The answer is that no matter how child-centered, "free" a school situation may be, it is still organized and goal-centered. The child hasn't the freedom of choice and freedom to control his own time that he has after school, when he can play a game or not, throw stones or not, daydream or not. Though the hours in a modern classroom may be more active, more amusing, less punitive and repressive than in the old-fashioned classroom, the child is still being manipulated in certain directions, by the teacher, by the equipment in the classroom, by the time organization of the day. If he spends his nonschool time watching television, that time is also being effectively organized and programmed for him. When, then, is he going to live his *real life*?

**MARIE WINN**, "Television and Free Time"

### *End with a quotation that illustrates your point*

Poverty—grim, degrading and ineluctable—is not remarkable in India. For few, the fate is otherwise. But in the United States, the survival of poverty is remarkable. We ignore it because we share with all societies at all times the capacity for not seeing what we do not wish to see. Anciently this has enabled the nobleman to enjoy his dinner while remaining oblivious to the beggars around his door. In our own day, it enables us to travel in comfort by Harlem and into the lush precincts of midtown Manhattan. But while our failure to notice can be explained, it cannot be excused. "Poverty," Pitt exclaimed, "is no disgrace but it is damned annoying." In the contemporary United States, it is not annoying but it is a disgrace.

**JOHN KENNETH GALBRAITH**, "The Position of Poverty"

### *End with a strong contrast*

Ross, Tom and I grew up to the same music, worshipping the same idols, suffering from the same inhibitions. It was remarkably easy for me to slip into their adolescent skins. As an adult and a writer, I could recognize in those highs of self-certainty, in those plunging lows of self-doubt, my own emotional weather. Finally, in each of their natures—one black, reckless; the other a marching band of virtues—I saw two halves of my own.

**JOHN LEGGETT**, "Ross and Tom"

### *End by dismissing an opposing idea*

The androgynous man is not your opponent but your teammate. He does not seduce: he invites. Sensuality is a pleasure for him. He's not quite so goal-oriented. And to conclude, I think I need only remind you here of his greater imagination, his wit and empathy, his unpredictability, and his receptivity to new impressions and connections.

AMY GROSS, "The Appeal of the Androgynous Man"

*End with a final illustration*

But Lebanon's agony was far from over. The country was still a tinderbox. Syria has more than doubled the number of its troops in Lebanon since the fight began, and Sharon estimated that the Palestinians could still count on 15,000 to 20,000 combatants. The "Peace in Galilee" that Prime Minister Begin had proclaimed as his goal when the shooting started was still far out of the Israelis' reach—and may have been moved even farther away by the assault.

ED MAGNUSON, ET AL., "Israel Strikes at the P.L.O"

## ► WRITING ACTIVITY ◄

Before starting the paragraph-writing activities here, reread Chapter 1. The considerations that inform effective paragraph writing are the same as those that govern the whole composition: purpose, audience, code, experience, and self.

**1.** Write a response of two paragraphs or less to a recent editorial published in your school newspaper.

**2.** A television survey requests your view of television programs and advertisements that insult viewer intelligence. Write a paragraph illustrating the "insult" of just one program or ad.

**3.** Your political science exam asks for a summary of a current political event. Write a one-paragraph summary based on a newspaper or magazine article about some domestic or international happening.

**4.** The physical education department is doing a survey on violence in sports. In a one-paragraph summary, point out the violent aspects of a recent sporting event you attended or watched on television.

**5.** Write a paragraph to be put up on the public memo board, advertising a room for rent. Describe the room for prospective renters.

**6.** You're thinking about transferring to another school. Write a one-page letter to your advisor explaining your reasons for transferring.

**7.** An application form for a job asks you to describe either the one aspect of your previous work (including chores at home) you liked best or the one aspect you liked least. Illustrate in detail for an employer who wants to see how you handle a writing assignment.

**8.** You're in a psychology class that emphasizes the study and discussion of dreams. In a one-page summary, describe your worst nightmare.

**9.** You must return to your high school to deliver a short speech on the question, Do Americans admire conformity and obedience more than individuality and creativity? Illustrate one incidence of conformity or obedience you have observed or experienced.

**10.** Your animal husbandry exam asks you to speculate about why Americans spend so much money on the care and feeding of their pets. Illustrate one aspect of the appeal pets have for people.

**11.** Write a paragraph to be added to your lawyer's directions, in case of accident or illness, concerning euthanasia for yourself. From a personal point of view, describe any situation in which you would or would not want the doctors to "pull the plug."

**12.** You are a caseworker for the Office of Student Affairs. You must write a paragraph for the files, reporting the facts in an incident in which a student was disorderly at a party you attended. Write a second paragraph describing the same incident to a friend back home.

**13.** You have failed your earth sciences final exam; write a paragraph to the dean of students explaining why that happened. (Do you, for example, need a tutor, or a reduced workload?) Write another letter explaining the failure to a friend at a distant school.

**14.** A future employer asks for a biographical sketch that will show your personality. Describe just one event from your life that might be part of the biography.

**15.** Write a letter to your representative or senators urging them to support or speak against some issue currently before Congress.

**16.** Assume that you have lost something: write a paragraph for the "Lost-and-Found" section of your local newspaper, describing your lost item, any reward, and so on.

**17.** A national newspaper is offering space to students who need a job and would like to advertise in the "Positions Wanted" section of the paper. Write a paragraph in which you try to sell yourself (Limit: 100 words).

**18.** An instructor is using a text that you think is ineffective. Write a one-paragraph summary of the problems with the text to submit to your instructor.

**19.** Your testimony is needed for a trial in a distant state concerning a traffic accident you witnessed. Since it would be a hardship for you to travel a great distance, you are asked to submit a written deposition. Write a paragraph describing in detail what you witnessed.

**20.** Your history professor has asked you to speculate about what the world would be like if any event in history had been different: If you could change anything in the world now to alter future history, what would you change? Write a paragraph in which you explain in detail what you would change and why.

# CHAPTER ▲ THIRTEEN

# *Revision Using Sentence Combining*

**"There is the satisfaction of arranging it on a bit of paper; after many many false tries, false moves, finally you have the sentence you recognize as the one you are looking for."**

VLADIMIR NABOKOV

As we saw in Chapter 1, you may approach an essay from a number of perspectives (purpose, audience, code, experience, and self). One area of writer's choice that will be important for every type of paper you write is *code*. Code includes four different types of choices: organizational, paragraph level, sentence level, or mechanical. Where you are in the composing process determines which of these aspects of code will be most important when you revise a draft. Obviously, you need to concern yourself with the larger issues of organization, strategies of development, or paragraphing before dealing with anything smaller. But sooner or later, regardless of the quality of your ideas, the amount of evidence you have to back up your claims, or the organization you have decided upon, you need to work on making sure you are presenting your ideas in the best possible way. Your writing appears on the page one sentence at a time, and the sentences you write can draw your readers into your essay or turn them away.

For example, student writer Joseph had just finished writing a working draft of a paper in which he was explaining why he liked a particular local band. In looking over his draft, he came across a paragraph describing the lead singer of the band:

> David, the leader of the band, is the lead singer. He came out singing at the top of his lungs with his mouth engulfed around the mike. His curly, red hair was hanging over his eyes at about shoulder length. He resembled a sheep dog. Wearing a red flannel shirt, with the sleeves rolled up, and a pair of jeans with holes in the knees, he carried the stick, the infamous stick, which on top of it contained a shrunken head and he kept time by constantly pounding it on the stage. He sings to the fast and vigorous beat of his musicians. Pounding his stick, David was the heart of the band.

Joseph noticed that, while the paragraph contained all the information he wanted to convey concerning the singer, he had not done a very good job of presenting that information. When he read the paragraph aloud to himself, it sounded choppy in places. He also noticed that the sentence beginning with "Wearing a red flannel shirt" seemed to ramble on. Joseph decided he needed to make some changes to his paragraph on the sentence level by combining some of his short, choppy sentences into longer ones and by dividing that long sentence into more manageable pieces. After working on the revision of this paragraph, Joseph produced the following:

> David, the lead singer and leader of the band, came out singing at the top of his lungs, his mouth pressed close to the mike. With his curly, shoulder-length, red hair hanging over his eyes, he resembled a sheep dog. He wore a red flannel shirt with the sleeves rolled up to his elbows and a tattered pair of jeans with holes in the knees. He carried the stick, his infamous stick, which had a shrunken head on top. Pounding his stick to the fast and vigorous beat as he sang, David was the heart of the band.

Joseph's new paragraph is an improvement on his previous attempt. He is far from finished with his essay—even this paragraph could use some more work—but he has made a step in the right direction.

Joseph's experience with revising his paragraph is a typical one. Writers must develop good revision skills on the sentence level before they may feel confident writing and revising their work. For most writers, sentence skills come through years of experience and practice in revising their sentences to make them more effective. While there really is no substitute for sentence revision experience, there are methods that may speed up the process of acquiring this kind of language-manipulation skill. One of these is *sentence combining*. Sentence combining focuses the reader's attention on the connective devices of language that let experienced writers generate good sentences. Though a writer of English has millions of possible ways to combine words into phrases, clauses, and sentences, there are surprisingly few ways to connect those phrases, clauses, and sentences with each other. It is this connecting, or *sentence-combining*, skill that experienced writers have mastered and beginning writers need to practice. Research shows that if you practice these sentence-combining skills, you can quickly learn to write mature, effective sentences.

You can see this for yourself. Read the following two passages. Passage *B* was written by a professional writer, Sinclair Lewis. How does it differ from passage *A*?

> ***A.*** He dipped his hands in the bichloride solution. He shook them. The shake was quick. His fingers were down. His fingers were like the fingers of a pianist. The fingers of the pianist were above the keys.
>
> ***B.*** He dipped his hands in the bichloride solution and shook them, a quick shake—fingers down, like the fingers of a pianist above the keys.

Sinclair Lewis's sentence sounds smoother; he uses fewer words, is less repetitive, and builds a more consistent image. Passage *A*, on the other hand, sounds choppy, wordy, repetitious; it lacks flow. The immature sentences are harder to read, and in fact, reading many such sentences could become an unpleasant chore.

Both passages contain the same information. The chief difference between them is in the way Lewis has combined that information. Here's how the first passage can be revised:

and a quick

He dipped his hands in the bichloride solution/ He shook them/, The shake was quick/, His fingers were down/, His fingers were like the fingers of a pianist/, The fingers of the pianist were above the keys.

Lewis has gained rhythm, emphasis, and power by deleting redundant expressions (*he, his, his fingers were*) and by using simple connecting devices (*and* plus commas). With practice, you can learn to use these sentence-combining devices to revise your own sentences.

Suppose you were asked to revise the following three sentences into one, more mature sentence:

The officer took out his pistol.

The officer calmly pointed it at the prisoner's head.

He then pulled the trigger.

You might come up with the following revision:

The officer took out his pistol, calmly pointed it at the prisoner's head, and then pulled the trigger.

Revising these three sentences involves three easy operations: First, you delete redundant phrases, *the officer* and *he*; then you add a comma between *pistol* and *calmly*; and last you put, *and* between *head* and *then*.

Different writers would probably combine the three sentences in different ways. For example:

The officer took out his pistol, calmly pointed it at the prisoner's head, and then pulled the trigger.

The officer took out his pistol and calmly pointed it at the prisoner's head before pulling the trigger.

The officer took out his pistol and calmly pointed it at the prisoner's head, then pulled the trigger.

After taking out his pistol and calmly pointing it at the prisoner's head, the officer pulled the trigger.

And there are still other possible combinations. It is obvious, then, that three short sentences can be revised into a number of different sentences, each with its own emphasis and rhythm. A writer can, with relative ease, convey essentially the same information in a variety of ways.

In this chapter you will work with many of the language-manipulation devices experienced writers use, and you will exploit the language ability you already have. As you practice revising sentences, you will begin to produce better-sounding sentences in your compositions. Remember, though, that because writing is a physical as well as a mental act, you must go beyond merely solving the sentence problems in your head. You must practice putting sentences on paper, one word at a time.

## WORKING THE PROBLEMS

To help you with sentence combining, we will begin by using a series of *signals*. These signals show you how you can revise your writing by combining several sentences into one. Generally, signals to the right of a sentence direct you to move whatever is inside the parentheses to the beginning of the sentence.

***Example***

The armies of Alexander the Great swept through Baktria and Scythia.
~~The~~ ~~armies~~ invaded India. (,)
Then ~~they~~ returned to Persia. (, AND)

The *slash* signal (/), a diagonal line through a word, means to delete that word. In the example, the slash signals direct you to delete *the*, *armies*, and *they*.

The *comma* signal (,) means to add a comma at the beginning of the line on which the comma signal appears. Since you have deleted *the* and *armies* in the example, you would be left with, *invaded India* after inserting the comma signal.

The *comma-and* signal (, AND) means to put a comma and *and* at the beginning of the line on which the signal appears. In the example, put, *and* in front of *Then* to complete the solution. You must, of course, change the capital letters and remove periods to fit the new sentence.

In general, work the problems in your head and then write out the one-sentence answer. In particular:

***Step 1: Read the Whole Problem***

The students read everything their professors assigned.
~~They~~ spent long hours studying their notes. (,)
Then ~~they~~ took their final exams. (, AND)

***Step 2: Solve Each Line of the Problem Before You Try to Solve the Whole Problem***

The students read everything their professors assigned.

~~They~~ spent long hours studying their notes (,)

Then ~~they~~ took their final exams. (, AND)

It is usually possible to do step 2 in your head, but write it out if you feel it will help.

***Step 3: Write Out the New Sentence***

The students read everything their professors assigned, spent long hours studying their notes, and then took their final exams.

## ► PRACTICE: Sentence Combining ◄

Write out each of the following problems as a single sentence. You have been given all the necessary signals in the first two and limited assistance with the third. In the last two, combine the sentences in any way you choose.

1. The snowmobile roared through the trees.
   ~~The~~ snow~~mobile~~ plowed through the brush. (,)
   ~~The~~ snow~~mobile~~ disappeared into the wilderness. (, AND)
2. Set your government's affairs in order.
   The opposing party will do it for you. (, OR)
3. The drought hung over Oklahoma.
   ~~The~~ dro~~ught~~ ~~was~~ drying up rivers. (,)
   It was emptying ponds and lakes.
   It was parching the land.
   It was threatening the region with another Dust Bowl.
4. Genghis Khan spent his nights in revelry.
   Genghis Khan spent his days in butchery.
5. The alien creature was lost.
   It was alone on earth.
   It was afraid of humans.
   It was lonely.
   It was looking for its companions.

What is gained by revising these ideas into one sentence? Think of someone learning to ice skate. At first the movements are short, jerky, and uncertain. With practice, these separate, disconnected movements will blend together into the smooth and gracefully flowing motions of the mature skater. So, too, with sentence combining. With practice, you will develop the ability to make the disconnected elements of your thoughts flow together. As you work the sentence problems, concentrate on creating a better sentence and not merely on getting the problem "right." Soon, when you can see several possibilities for a sentence, you will be well on your way to writing mature sentences. Eventually, mastery over your sentences will help you to achieve the effects you desire in your writing.

The remainder of this chapter is divided into seven parts. In the first five of these, you will learn five basic techniques for revising on the sentence level: adding, deleting, embedding, transforming, and punctuating. Then, because writers seldom work with sentences in isolation, we will discuss revising sentences in a slightly larger context, the chunk. Finally, we will look at sentence-level revision within the context of an entire essay.

## REVISING BY ADDITION

One of the easiest devices for revising sentences is to connect one idea to another, without changing either one. You can do this with certain marks of punctuation (comma, semicolon) or with one of the many connecting words in the language (*and, but, when, because, or, so, while, though*, and so on). For example:

*A.* At 9 A.M. he assembles his own staff.
Each in turn talks about where difficulties may lie for the president.
(, AND)

At 9 A.M. he assembles his own staff, and each in turn talks about where difficulties may lie for the president.

TIME, "Hannibal Astride the Potomac,"

*B.* My cells are no longer the pure line entities I was raised with.
They are ecosystems more complex than Jamaica Bay. (;)

My cells are no longer the pure line entities I was raised with; they are ecosystems more complex than Jamaica Bay.

LEWIS THOMAS, *The Lives of a Cell: Notes of a Biology Watcher*

*C.* The writer intends to cut out a piece of his thought.

He must cut a piece that his reader can perceive as having a kind of wholeness. (, BUT)

The writer intends to cut out a piece of his thought, but he must cut a piece that his reader can perceive as having a kind of wholeness.

JOHN E. JORDAN, *Using Rhetoric*

*D.* Inflation since 1960 is also taken into account. (WHEN)

The retooling costs due to style changes are conservatively estimated to average one billion dollars annually. (,)

When inflation since 1960 is also taken into account, the retooling costs due to style changes are conservatively estimated to average one billion dollars annually.

RALPH NADER STUDY GROUP ON AIR POLLUTION, *Vanishing Air*

In these examples, the signal at the end of the sentence moved to the front of that sentence before it was combined.

This practice was designed to demonstrate that ideas can be effectively connected together, unchanged. However, the fact that you can revise sentences by connecting ideas to each other does not necessarily mean that you always should. Arbitrarily running sentences together is not the idea; such a practice will often produce baby talk: "I have a dog, and his name is Spot, and he is cute, and he follows me, and I play with him." You need not limit yourself to simple concepts that can be expressed in the language of children. Where two ideas cover a single, broader concept, you can express that completeness by connecting the ideas in a single sentence. Remember, the point of revising your paper on the sentence level is to help you get your ideas across to your reader more effectively; always revise with that goal in mind. Never simply connect two sentences for the sake of connecting them. How effective you are as a reviser depends a great deal upon how judicious you are in using the addition skill.

## ► PRACTICE: Revising with Signals ◄

Write out each of the following sentences as a single sentence, using the signals to help you create a sentence that better communicates the author's ideas to the readers.

1. The fragility of her loveliness was emphasized by the inevitable comparisons with the rose.
   She was urged to employ her beauty in love-making before it withered on the stem. (, AND)

   GERMAINE GREER, *The Female Eunuch*

2. The President was not a stupid man.
   The intricacies of government bored him. (, BUT)
   The dirty work of politics repelled him. (, AND)

   DREW PEARSON, *The Senator*

3. This poem can help explain Keats' life.
   His life cannot explain the poem. (;)

   HAROLD BLOOM, *The Visionary Company: A Reading of English Romantic Poetry*

4. You are at the heart of this city. (WHEN)
   You are at the heart of Nature. (,)

   JEAN-PAUL SARTRE, "New York, the Colonial City," *Literary and Philosophical Essays*

## ► PRACTICE: Revising without Signals ◄

Revise the following sentences in any way you please. Although you could revise each example into one sentence, occasionally you may choose to create answers that consist of more than one sentence. Take the sentences in each example in any order at all, and try to produce as many different answers as you can. Then decide which answers work better and for what reasons. The important thing to remember is that there are no right answers in this exercise; there are many possible answers, and each has its own merits. A large part of revising on the sentence level involves learning to decide which of a multitude of possible sentence configurations does the best job of helping you get your message across.

1. In the end we shall make thoughtcrime literally impossible. There will be no words in which to express it.

   GEORGE ORWELL, *1984*

2. I'll go in for my chest x-ray. I have finished my tenth cigarette.
3. It will spread out into space. After four or five years it will reach the next star.

   ARTHUR C. CLARKE, "The Star of the Magi," *Report on Planet Three*

4. Albert smashed into the police chief's car. He was taking his driving test. Needless to say, he didn't pass the test.
5. The self-educated genius is therefore becoming rarer. He still has not vanished.

   ISAAC ASIMOV, *Fact and Fancy*

## REVISING BY DELETING

There is more to revising on the sentence level than just connecting ideas. Many times, the best revisions you can make at this level involve eliminating repetitious words or phrases and combining the remaining ideas. For example:

*A.* Darling trotted back.
He was smiling. (,)
He was breathing deeply. (,)
He was breathing easily. (BUT)
He was feeling wonderful. (,)
He was not tired. (,)
This was the tail end of practice. (, THOUGH)
He'd run eighty yards. (AND)

Darling trotted back, smiling, breathing deeply but easily, feeling wonderful, not tired, though this was the tail end of practice and he'd run eighty yards.

IRWIN SHAW, "The Eighty Yard Run"

The slashes direct you to delete repetitious words. Another way to signal deletion is to underline the words to be retained and connected. Italics direct you to keep the italicized words and delete the words not italicized in that sentence. In example *B*, for instance, you would delete *He* and *is*, move the comma to the front of that sentence, and then combine the remaining idea, *bruised and aching*, with the sentence above.

*B.* Picture poor old Alfy coming home from football practice every day.
He is *bruised*. (,)
He is *aching*. (AND)
He is *agonizingly tired*. (,)
He is *scarcely able to shovel the mashed potatoes into his mouth*. (,)

Picture poor old Alfy coming home from football practice every day, bruised and aching, agonizingly tired, scarcely able to shovel the mashed potatoes into his mouth.

PAUL ROBERTS, "How to Say Nothing in Five Hundred Words," *Understanding English*

Writers often revise their sentences by deleting a repetitious word or phrase and substituting words like *who*, *which*, *that*, *whom*, and *whose* for the repeated element. In example *C*, the (*WHO*) signal directs you to delete the repeated phrase *The witnesses* and substitute *who*. The (*WHICH*) signal directs you to delete the repeated element *the facts* and substitute *which*. You would then move the phrase *upon which* to the front of its sentence.

*C.* In court cases, considerable trouble is sometimes caused by witnesses.
The witnesses cannot distinguish their judgments from the facts. (WHO)
Those judgments are based upon the facts. (UPON WHICH)

In court cases, considerable trouble is sometimes caused by witnesses who cannot distinguish their judgments from the facts upon which those judgments are based.

S. I. HAYAKAWA, "Reports, Inferences, Judgments," *Language in Thought and Action*

In addition to achieving unity and economy of expression, Shaw, Roberts, and Hayakawa have succeeded in creating unified images or ideas, always a difficult task because English is a linear language (it is produced "straight line," one word after another), and reality is seldom linear. In the sentence by Irwin Shaw there are many separate items, but if we had seen Christian Darling on the football field, we would have perceived these details simultaneously. By deleting repetitious words and using commas to "blend" sentences, Shaw has fused these disparate elements into a single sentence and, more important, into a single image. Deleting and connecting, then, are important creative skills that will enable you to effectively revise your sentences to make your writing more accurately reflect your perception of reality.

## ► PRACTICE: Revising with Signals ◄

Write out each of the following sentences as a single sentence, using the signals to help you create a sentence that better communicates the author's ideas to the readers.

1. The hurricane smashed into the village.
   The hurricane killed most of the people. (AND)
2. On top of the craft's triangular surface, a 30-inch antenna dish unfolds.
   The antenna dish searches the star-sprinkled sky for homing signals from earth. (AND)
   It finds them. (,)
   It locks on. (AND)

   K. E. KRISTOFFERSON, "Message From the Surface of Mars"
3. The mortally wounded King Kong beat his chest in defiance.
   King Kong stumbled to the edge of the skyscraper. (,)
   He plunged to the street below. (, AND)
4. Religion and other ways of knowing lost their power to enrich thought for many. (WHILE)
   Science became the truth of truths. (,)
   Technique became the holy principle. (, AND)

   T. GEORGE HARRIS, "The Religious War Over Truth and Tools"

## ► PRACTICE: Revising Without Signals ◄

Revise the following sentences in any way you please. Although you could revise each example into one sentence, occasionally you may choose to create answers that consist of more than one sentence. Take the sentences in each example in any order at all, and try to produce as many different answers as you can. Then decide which answers work better and for what reasons. The important thing to remember is that there is no one right answer in this exercise; there are many possible answers, and each has its own merits. A large part of revising on the sentence level involves learning to decide which of a multitude of possible sentence configurations does the best job of helping you get your message across.

1. Bruce Springsteen sauntered onto the stage. Bruce Springsteen picked up his guitar. Bruce Springsteen played a few casual bars. He paused. He launched into a song that had his audience groaning their approval. The song had the audience gasping their approval. The song then had the audience thundering their approval of the Boss.

2. Patriotism can be an asset for any society. The asset is great. The society is organized. It can also be a tool. The tool is manipulated by leaders and elites. They are unscrupulous. They are cowardly.

RALPH NADER, "We Need a New Kind of Patriotism"

3. The bull charges. The banderillero rises to his toes. He bends in a curve forward. Just as the bull is about to hit him he drops the darts into the bull's hump just back of his horns.

ERNEST HEMINGWAY, "Killing a Bull," *By-Line Ernest Hemingway*

4. Iron is strong. Iron is heavy. It is clamorous. It is struck. It is avid of oxygen. It is capable of corruption.

DONALD CULROSS PEATTIE, "Chlorophyll: The Sun Trap," *Flowering Earth*

5. The Oak Grove Warriors trained hard during spring practice. The Warriors swept their conference. The Warriors were edged out in the playoffs.

## REVISING BY EMBEDDING

To achieve economy and clarity in their writing, experienced writers often revise by embedding all or part of one sentence into another sentence. Embedding allows them to show that two ideas are not merely related to each other, but that one is actually part of the other.

### ▶ The (THAT) and (THE FACT THAT) Signals

When you work on the embedding skill, think of one sentence as having a slot (which we will label SOMETHING) in it. The SOMETHING signal is simply directing you to put a clause or phrase into that slot. For example:

*A.* She knew SOMETHING.
He was going to leave her. (THAT)

She knew that he was going to leave her.

JAMES BALDWIN, "Come Out the Wilderness," *Fifty Years of the American Short Story*

In example *A,* THAT moved to the front of its sentence and the clause *that he was going to leave her* was then inserted into the SOMETHING slot.

*B.* The great thing about human language is SOMETHING.
It prevents us from sticking to the matter at hand. (THAT)

The great thing about human language is that it prevents us from sticking to the matter at hand.

LEWIS THOMAS, *The Lives of a Cell: Notes of a Biology Watcher*

*C.* This is due largely to SOMETHING.
Many writers think, not before, but
as they write. (THE FACT THAT)

This is due largely to the fact that many writers think, not before, but as they write.

W. SOMERSET MAUGHAM, *The Summing Up*

*D.* She wants me to believe SOMETHING.
The body is a spiritual fact. (T̸HAT)
The body is *the instrument of the soul.* (,)

She wants to believe the body is a spiritual fact, the instrument of the soul.

SAUL BELLOW, *Herzog*

The word *that* is often optional in English. In example *D,* Saul Bellow chose to delete *that* and simply embed *the body is a spiritual fact* into the SOMETHING slot in the first sentence. We have signaled the deleted *that* by putting a slash mark through the signal: (T̸HAT).

*E.* Freud continued his studies. (BUT)
F̸reud denounced religion as an illusion. (,)
F̸reud accumulated additional clinical
evidence showing SOMETHING. (, AND)
His patients' immature concepts of God were contributing to their mental illness. (HOW)

But Freud continued his studies, denounced religion as an illusion, and accumulated additional clinical evidence showing how his patients' immature concepts of God were contributing to their mental illness.

GEORGE CHRISTIAN ANDERSON, *Man's Right to be Human*

Variations on the (THAT) signal are (HOW), (WHEN), (WHERE), (WHY), (IF), (WHO), (WHAT). In example *E,* (HOW) moved to the front of its sentence and the clause *how his patients' immature concepts of God were contributing to their mental illness* was then inserted into the SOMETHING slot.

## ► The (IT . . . THAT) Signal

When you encounter the IT . . . THAT signal, remember the following rule: The IT substitutes for the SOMETHING slot above; the THAT goes to the front of its own sentence. For example:

*A.* SOMETHING is incomprehensible.
Such drugs could be dispensed without
competent medical advice. (IT . . . THAT)

It is incomprehensible that such drugs could be dispensed without competent medical advice.

NORMAN COUSINS, "The Toxified Society"

*B.* Throughout this book, SOMETHING is important to remember.
We are not considering language as
an isolated phenomenon. (IT . . . THAT)

Throughout this book, it is important to remember that we are not considering language as an isolated phenomenon.

S. I. HAYAKAWA, "The Language of Reports," *Language in Thought and Action*

*C.* SOMETHING was lucky.
We were both of us only fourteen. (IT . . . ~~THAT~~)

It was lucky we were both of us only fourteen.

WILLIAM GOLDING, "Thinking as a Hobby"

It is obvious that embedding and the other sentence-level revision skills often produce longer sentences. Thus, you may feel that revising on the sentence level is merely a matter of writing longer sentences. Although there is some truth to that idea, it is not true that long sentences are better than short ones. Short sentences are often as effective as long sentences. Variety in sentence length is just as important as variety in sentence style. But if you compare them, you will discover that the sentences of experienced writers are, on the average, substantially longer than those of beginning writers, and—more important—that beginning writers use more words to express an idea. Experienced writers are more economical with their words; they manage to say more with less. They achieve this economy of expression through deletions, embeddings, and the other revision skills.

## ► PRACTICE: Revising with Signals ◄

Write out each of the following sentences as a single sentence, using the signals to help you create a sentence that better communicates the author's ideas to the readers.

**1.** The transactional analyst believes SOMETHING.
Psychiatric symptoms result from some form of self-deception. (THAT)

ERIC BERNE, *What Do You Say After You Say Hello?*

**2.** SOMETHING should tell you SOMETHING.
We are at the conference table.
(THE FACT THAT)
We are genuinely interested in a settlement. (THAT)
The settlement is *negotiated*.

3. SOMETHING would put him in an awful spot.
   Lois Farrow somehow found out SOMETHING. (IT . . . IF)
   He had let her daughter go to sleep with her legs across Duane's.
   (T~~H~~AT)

LARRY MCMURTRY, *The Last Picture Show*

4. Some psychiatrists claim SOMETHING.
   The psychiatrists are *well-known.*
   Murders shown on television cause unstable people to believe SOMETHING. (THAT)
   Killing is normal in our society. (THAT)

## ► PRACTICE: Revising without Signals ◄

Revise the following sentences in any way you please. Although you could revise each example into one sentence, occasionally you may choose to create answers that consist of more than one sentence. Take the sentences in each example in any order at all and try to produce as many different answers as you can. Then decide which answers work better and for what reasons. The important thing to remember is that there is no one right answer in this exercise; there are many possible answers, and each has its own merits. A large part of revising on the sentence level involves learning to decide which of a multitude of possible sentence configurations does the best job of helping you get your message across.

1. I took a course in tap dancing. I found something. My coordination left much to be desired. My sense of rhythm was nonexistent.
2. I have been assured by an American of my acquaintance in London of something. The American is very knowing. A young healthy child if well nursed is at a year old a food, whether it is stewed. It is roasted. It is baked. It is boiled. The food is most delicious. The food is nourishing. The food is wholesome. I make no doubt of something. It will equally serve in a fricassee, or a ragout.

JONATHAN SWIFT, "A Modest Proposal"

3. Joe went red in the face with anger. He discovered something. The exercise gym consisted of a three-foot piece of plastic. He had paid thirty dollars for the gym. The gym consisted of two pages of instructions. The gym consisted of a card. The card told him something. He should say to himself every day before breakfast something. "Every day I'm getting stronger and stronger."
4. I knew something. I could never win that way. There were whites. They were many. There were blacks. They were but few.

RICHARD WRIGHT, *Black Boy*

5. Woody Allen joked something. His psychiatrist thinks something. He is perfectly balanced. He now has a chip on both shoulders.

## REVISING BY TRANSFORMING

Up to this point, you have been practicing sentence-level revision skills that focused on how to connect and embed ideas by deleting single words or phrases from a sentence and inserting the remainder into the preceding sentence. In this section, you will expand your repertoire of sentence-level revision operations by developing expertise with a variety of sentence-transforming skills. Transforming involves rearranging or changing the insert sentence before connecting it to the preceding sentence.

### ► The (-ING) and (WITH) Signals

Two of the more effective techniques used by experienced writers are *-ing* and *with* phrases. In example *A*, the (-ING) signal directs you to change *kept* to *keeping*; *she* is then unnecessary in the first sentence, so you delete it:

*A.* She kept a firm hand on her committee.
(-ING)
She issued precise instructions. (,)

Keeping a firm hand on her committee, she issued precise instructions.

CECIL WOODHAM-SMITH, *Florence Nightingale*

*B.* The trackers scuttled along.
They stopped. (,-ING)
They looked. (,-ING)
They hurried on. (, AND + -ING)

The trackers scuttled along, stopping, looking, and hurrying on.

JOHN STEINBECK, *The Pearl*

*C.* The children catapulted this way and that across green lawns.
They shouted at each other. (,-ING)
They held hands. (,-ING)
They flew in circles. (,-ING)
They climbed trees. (,-ING)
They laughed. (,-ING)

The children catapulted this way and that across green lawns, shouting at each other, holding hands, flying in circles, climbing trees, laughing.

RAY BRADBURY, *The Illustrated Man*

*D.* The social scientists, especially the economists, are moving deeply into ecology and the environment these days.
The results are disquieting. (, WITH)

The social scientists, especially the economists, are moving deeply into ecology and the environment these days, with disquieting results.

LEWIS THOMAS, *The Lives of a Cell: Notes of a Biology Watcher*

*E.* Monterey sits on the slope of a hill.
It has a blue bay below it. (, WITH)
It has a forest of tall dark pine trees at its back. (AND WITH)

Monterey sits on the slope of a hill, with a blue bay below it and with a forest of tall dark pine trees at its back.

JOHN STEINBECK, *Tortilla Flat*

*F.* The room was just as Jake had left it.
The fan was turned on and the pitcher of ice water was beside the table. (, WITH)

The room was just as Jake had left it, with the fan turned on and the pitcher of ice water beside the table.

CARSON MCCULLERS, *The Heart Is a Lonely Hunter*

## The ('S), (OF), and (LY) Signals

*A* SOMETHING enchanted the audience.
Nureyev danced. ('S + -ING)
Nureyev's dancing enchanted the audience.

The sentence is derived like this:

Nureyev + ('s) = Nureyev's
danced + (-ING) = dancing

You then insert "Nureyev's dancing" into the SOMETHING slot.

*B.* Alfred Lord Tennyson recalled SOMETHING.
The innumerable bees murmured in immemorial elms. (-ING + OF)

Alfred Lord Tennyson recalled the murmuring of innumerable bees in immemorial elms.

*C.* The television audience was delighted by SOMETHING.
Nadia Comanechi won a gold medal at the 1976 Olympics.
('S + -ING + OF)

The television audience was delighted by Nadia Comanechi's winning of a gold medal at the 1976 Olympics.

*D.* SOMETHING put the class to sleep.
The professor lectured endlessly. (-~~LY~~ + -ING + OF)
The endless lecturing of the professor put the class to sleep.

Note that the signals (-~~LY~~ + -ING + OF) tell you not only what to do (delete *-ly,* add *-ing,* insert *of*) but how to change the order of the words: the deleted *-ly* word comes first (*endless*), then the *-ing* word (*lecturing*), and finally the *of* insertion (*of the professor*).

*E.* SOMETHING was morally outrageous.
He butchered political opponents mercilessly. ('S + -~~LY~~ + -ING + OF)

His merciless butchering of political opponents was morally outrageous.

In example *E*,

He + ('s) = His

People obtain such drugs. (IT . . . FOR . . . TO)

Similarly, when you add *'s, I* should be changed to *my, we* to *our, she* to *her, they* to *their*, and *it* to *its*. (Note the spelling of *its*.)

## ► The (FOR . . . TO), (IT . . . TO), and (IT . . . FOR . . . TO) Signals

The (FOR . . . TO) signal directs you to change a sentence like *John runs* to *for John to run* . . . . The (IT . . . TO) and (IT . . . FOR . . . TO) signals function like the (IT . . . THAT) signal. The *it* replaces the appropriate SOMETHING signal and *to* or *for . . . to* operate on their own sentences. For example:

*A* SOMETHING is easier than SOMETHING.
A camel goes through the eye of a needle. (IT . . . FOR . . . TO)
A rich man enters into the kingdom of God. (FOR . . . TO)

It is easier for a camel to go through the eye of a needle than for a rich man to enter the kingdom of God.

MATTHEW, 19:24

*B* SOMETHING won't be easy.
We send him into any of the three phases. (IT . . . TO)

It won't be easy to send him into any of the three phases.

THOMAS PYNCHON, *Gravity's Rainbow*

## ► The Discover→Discovery Signal

Certain transformations involve changing the form of a word; thus *discover* can be changed to *discovery*, *fail* to *failure*, *investigate* to *investigation*, and so on. Rather than supply a signal for these changes, we will simply give you the word you need. For example:

*A* Winston Churchill denounced SOMETHING.
Hitler seized Czechoslovakia. ('S + SEIZURE + OF)

Winston Churchill denounced Hitler's seizure of Czechoslovakia.

*B* The nation finally insisted on SOMETHING.
Richard Nixon immediately resigned as President.
('S + -LY + RESIGNATION)

The nation finally insisted on Richard Nixon's immediate resignation as President.

## ► PRACTICE: Revising with Signals ◄

Write out each of the following sentences as a single sentence, using the signals to help you create a sentence that better communicates the author's ideas to the readers.

**1.** The only thing necessary for the triumph of evil is SOMETHING.
Good men do nothing. (FOR . . . TO)

EDMUND BURKE, "Letter to William Smith"

**2.** SOMETHING made Angela shiver.
The owl hooted. (THE + -ING + OF)

**3.** Samuel Clemens often wrote.
Samuel Clemens is *better known as Mark Twain*. (, . . . ,)
He was *lying in bed*. (WHILE)
He was *propped up on pillows*. (,)
He was *smoking a cigar*. (AND)

**4.** SOMETHING was announced. (AFTER)
Barbiturates are involved in 5,000 deaths annually. (IT . . . THAT)
Several members of Congress began drafting bills. (,)
The bills would make SOMETHING more difficult. (WHICH)
People obtain such drugs. (IT . . . FOR . . . TO)

### ▶ PRACTICE: Revising Without Signals ◀

Revise the following sentences and sentence fragments in any way you please. Although you could revise each example into one sentence, occasionally you may choose to create answers that consist of more than one sentence. Take the sentences in each example in any order at all, and try to produce as many different answers as you can. Then decide which answers work better and for what reasons. The important thing to remember is that there is no one right answer in this exercise; there are many possible answers, and each has its own merits. A large part of revising on the sentence level involves learning to decide which of a multitude of possible sentence configurations does the best job of helping you get your message across.

1. I went upstairs. I felt like a criminal.

   RICHARD WRIGHT, *Black Boy*

2. Something kept the cowhands awake until dawn. The cowhands were exhausted. The steers bellowed noisily.
3. We were all fanatics about our hair. We worked on it in the school restrooms. Our arms grew weak.

   WILLIAM ALLEN, "Haircut," *Starkweather*

4. It was a day. The day was in springtime. The day was lovely. The sun glistened on the lake. The sun lifted everyone's spirits.
5. They were maddened. They were angry. They leaped and howled round the trunks. They cursed the dwarves in their horrible language. Their tongues hung out. Their eyes shone as red and fierce as flames.

   J. R. R. TOLKIEN, *The Hobbit*

## REVISING BY PUNCTUATING

You have already had extensive practice with the comma, semicolon, and period. Two other punctuation marks favored by many modern writers are the colon and the dash; they allow writers to express their ideas with economy and clarity. Mastery of the colon and dash will provide you with two more revision tools that indicate connections and relationships between ideas in your text.

### ▶ The Colon (:) and Dash (—) Signals

Note the use of the colon and dash signals in the following examples:

*A* In sum, there are at least two types of faith.
There are *possibly many more.* (, THOUGH)

There is *the faith of the true believer.* (:)
There is *the faith of a heretic.* (AND)

In sum, there are at least two types of faith, though possibly many more: the faith of the true believer and the faith of a heretic.

*B* The pipeline workers were *masked.*
The pipeline workers were *insulated by down clothing.* (AND)
These pipeline workers know well the same enemy as Jack London. (,)
The enemy is *killing cold.* (:)

Masked and insulated by down clothing, these pipelines workers know well the same enemy as Jack London: killing cold.

EDWARD J. FORTIER, "Jack London's Far North"

*C* Fifty years have expired since this adventure.
The fear of punishment is no more. (—)

Fifty years have expired since this adventure—the fear of punishment is no more.

JEAN JACQUES ROUSSEAU, *Confessions*

*D* The hour of Yellow Sky was approaching. (BUT)
It was the *hour of daylight.* (— . . . —)

But the hour of Yellow Sky—the hour of daylight—was approaching.

STEPHEN CRANE, "The Bride Comes to Yellow Sky"

The double-dash signal (— . . . —) in example *D* indicates an interrupter set off on both sides by dashes. The interrupter *the hour of daylight* was inserted into the sentence above, not just attached to the end of it.

*E* There is, after all, another side to the human spirit, too.
It is a *dark side.* (— . . . —)

There is, after all, another side—a dark side—to the human spirit, too.

ERIC SEVARIED, "The Dark of the Moon"

*F* Nevertheless, character is the source.
Character is the willingness to accept responsibility for one's own life. (— . . . —)
Self-respect springs from the source. (FROM WHICH)

Nevertheless, character—the willingness to accept responsibility for one's own life—is the source from which self-respect springs.

**Joan Didion**, "On Self-Respect," *Slouching Towards Bethlehem*

*G* The crimes have changed in rapid succession.
The Jews have been charged with the crimes in the course of history. (WITH WHICH)
They were crimes. (—)
The crimes were to justify the atrocities. (WHICH)
The atrocities were perpetrated against them. (. . . —)

The crimes with which the Jews have been charged in the course of history—crimes which were to justify the atrocities perpetrated against them—have changed in rapid succession.

**Albert Einstein**, "Why Do They Hate the Jews?"

The signal (. . . —) instructed you to put a dash at the end of its sentence, immediately after *perpetrated against them* and, of course, immediately in front of *have changed*.

## ► PRACTICE: Revising with Signals ◄

Write out each of the following sentences as a single sentence, using the signals to help you create a sentence that better communicates the author's ideas to the readers.

**1.** Sitka, Alaska, has a nickname.
The nickname is *the Paris of the Pacific*. (—)
That might be an exaggeration. (;)
Sitka is certainly one of the loveliest towns in North America. (, BUT)
It sits below mountains on a bay across from Mount Edgecumbe. (SINCE)
The mountains are ***spruce-covered***.
Mount Edgecumbe is a volcano. (,)
The volcano is ***cone-shaped***.
The volcano is ***snow-capped***. (,)

**2.** At the age of three the average child moves into a phase.
The phase is new.
The phase is graphic.
It starts to simplify its scribbling. (:)
Its scribbling is confused.

**Desmond Morris**, *The Naked Ape*

3. Meryl Streep has talent.
   The talent is ***enormous***.
   Meryl Streep is ***one of Hollywood's most popular actresses***.
   (— . . . —)

4. This revolution has resulted in a growing understanding of the forces.
   This revolution is *as profound as the revolution in astronomy 500 years ago*. (—)
   Copernicus displaced the Earth from its position at the Center of the Universe. (WHEN + . . . —)
   The forces shape the continents. (WHICH)
   The forces *set them drifting about the world*. (AND)

   JOHN R. GRIBBIN AND STEPHEN H. PLAGEMANN, *The Jupiter Effect*

## ► PRACTICE: Revising without Signals ◄

Revise the following sentences and sentence fragments in any way you please. Although you could revise each example into one sentence, occasionally you may choose to create answers that consist of more than one sentence. Take the sentences in each example in any order at all, and try to produce as many different answers as you can. Then try to decide which answers work better and for what reasons. The important thing to remember is that there is no one right answer in this exercise; there are many possible answers, and each has its own merits. A large part of revising on the sentence level involves learning to decide which of a multitude of possible sentence configurations does the best job of helping you get your message across.

1. Here man attains the ultimate in fear. He fears himself.

   NORMAN COUSINS, "Where Hell Begins," *Present Tense: An American Odyssey*

2. Alice was his woman. The woman was ideal. She was charming. She was sensitive. She was intelligent.

3. There are two types of connotation. One is personal. One is general.

   RICHARD D. ALTICK, *Preface to Critical Reading*

4. The students came out of school. They were rushing. They were yelling at the top of their lungs. The last class of the year was over.

5. The classic mode, by contrast, proceeds by reason. It proceeds by laws. The laws are themselves forms of thought and behavior. The forms are underlying.

   ROBERT M. PIRSIG, *Zen and the Art of Motorcycle Maintenance*

6. Picasso was a rarity. He was a genius. The genius was serious. The genius was brilliant. The genius was creative. He had a love for life. He had a real sense of humor.

7. Something is often said. Stoicism was un-Greek. It suited Romans far better. Something is true. It had won its most distinguished and con-

spicuous success in Rome. It won over two men of genius. They were the slave and the emperor.

EDITH HAMILTON, *The Echo of Greece*

8. He felt his opponent weaken. The boxer moved in for the kill. His eyes were narrowing. His shoulder muscles were bunching ominously. Every sinew was ready to explode into action.
9. So in recent times we have seen a split develop between a culture and a counterculture. The split was huge. The culture was classic. The counterculture was romantic. The two worlds were growingly alienated. They were hateful toward each other. Everyone wondered something. It will always be this way. It is a house divided against itself.

ROBERT M. PIRSIG, *Zen and the Art of Motorcycle Maintenance*

10. *Jaws II* has everything to make it popular. It has an excellent cast. It has tremendous advance publicity. It has an already successful plot. The plot has gallons of blood.

## BEYOND THE SENTENCE

Revising sentences is good practice. In each of the problems so far your goal was to produce, for the most part, a single sentence. However, few compositions are made of one sentence alone; furthermore, the revision of any sentence frequently depends on relations with sentences preceding or following. Effective writing depends on a series of sentences working together smoothly.

### ► Sentence Chunks

The following exercises are composed of multisentence structures we have named *chunks*. They are groups of two or more sentences from a paragraph; that is, a chunk can be any group of coherent sentences lifted out of a paragraph. You can think of a chunk as a unit between the sentence and paragraph—longer than one sentence, but shorter than a whole paragraph. This is of course a theoretical distinction, because sometimes a paragraph might be a single sentence—Chapter 12. But for our purposes here, you can say that a chunk is any group of sentences less than a full paragraph that hang together syntactically and/or semantically.

Sentences can surprise you. Looked at in isolation, a single sentence may be uninteresting, even boring. Used with other sentences, that same sentence can come alive. It can gain much of its meaning and effect from the surrounding sentences. For example, a short sentence can have a strong impact if you place it either after or between longer sentences. A long sentence can attract and hold the reader's attention if you contrast it with a short sentence. Rhythm, variety, meaning, and structure all contribute to cohesive discourse, not merely within a single sentence, but within longer units of writing.

Look, for example, at the following sentence:

> It happens in an instant.

If you were asked whether you find that sentence interesting or well written, you might reply that the sentence isn't especially interesting and you have no idea what *It* refers to. But if you were provided with a limited context for the sentence—if you were given the sentence immediately preceding *It happens in an instant*—and then asked to comment, your reaction would probably be very different:

> Most people tend to think of going to sleep as a slow slippage into oblivion, but the onset of sleep is not gradual at all. It happens in an instant.

In this context, "It happens in an instant" is a very effective piece of writing because it plays off the first, longer sentence. It is short, sharp, and to the point in this context. The first sentence provides *going to sleep* and *the onset of sleep* as referents for *"It"* in the second sentence. The first sentence (twenty-five words) sets up a sharp contrast with the second sentence (five words). *It happens in an instant* gains most of its meaning and effect *from the other sentence*.

A third sentence locks into the unit:

> Most people tend to think of going to sleep as a slow slippage into oblivion, but the onset of sleep is not gradual at all. It happens in an instant. One moment the individual is awake, the next moment not.

The last sentence clearly relates to the second sentence by emphasizing how fast "happens in an instant" is. You can find less obvious examples of the interplay between this sentence and the two that precede it. (Look at *moment* and *instant*, for example.)

You may wonder why this set of sentences is not a paragraph. Indeed, if a short paragraph suited the writer's purpose in a specific composition, these three sentences might make an effective one. But, in this case, the writer uses the paragraph to say more about the onset of sleep. Notice how smoothly the chunk we have been discussing coheres with the rest of the paragraph:

> A number of curious experiences occur at the onset of sleep. A person just about to go to sleep may experience an electric shock, a flash of light, or a crash of thunder—but the most common sensation is that of floating or falling, which is why "falling asleep" is a scientifically valid description. A nearly universal occurrence at the beginning of sleep (although not everyone recalls it) is a sudden uncoordinated jerk of the head, the limbs, or even the entire body. Most people tend to think of going to sleep as a slow

slippage into oblivion, but the onset of sleep is not gradual at all. It happens in an instant. One moment the individual is awake, the next moment not.

PETER FARB, "The Levels of Sleep," *Humankind*

Working with chunks can help you to extend your writing proficiency beyond the sentence. As sentence-combining practice improves the maturity of your own sentences, practice with sentence chunks will translate into a noticeable improvement in longer stretches of your writing. Revising groups of concepts and strings of words into more than one sentence will give you useful practice in playing one sentence off another, as you would in your own writing.

## Revising Chunks

The groups of sentences you will be working with in this section have been taken from the paragraphs of experienced writers. When revised, these strings of ideas will form chunks—groups of two, three, or more sentences that go together in some way; they form a subset within a paragraph. Think of these strings of information as a hurriedly written first draft of a composition, an invitation to revise. For example:

There are no books. There are no newspapers. There are no magazines. There are no pictures on the wall. There is a television set. He watches the television set all day long. He drinks beer. He smokes cigarettes. I am sufficiently familiar with the literature. It is on schizophrenia. I realize something. This room is a statement. He is making a statement about himself.

There are any number of ways this information might be revised, depending on the writing situation.

***The original author's version***

There are no books, no newspapers, no magazines, no pictures on the wall. There is a television set, which he watches all day long while drinking beer and smoking cigarettes. I am sufficiently familiar with the literature on schizophrenia to realize that this room is a statement he is making about himself.

JOHN LEONARD, "An Only Child"

***Another version***

There are no pictures on the walls. There is a television set, and he spends his whole day watching it, drinking beer and smoking cigarettes. There are no newspapers; no magazines; not even a book. I am familiar enough with the literature on schizophrenia to perceive that the room is a reflection of what he thinks of himself.

## ► PRACTICE: Revising Chunks ◄

Revise these strings of sentences into an effective chunk. You are free to add or delete words and information, to revise in any way that seems effective to you. In some cases you may feel the information could be expressed in a single sentence; feel free to do so. However, the original authors of these chunks used more than a single sentence. The important thing to remember is that there is no one right answer in this exercise; there are many possible answers, and each has its own merits. A large part of revising on the sentence or chunk level involves learning to decide which of a multitude of possible sentence configurations does the best job of helping you get your message across.

1. It is on Ellis Island. They pile into the hall. The hall is massive. It occupies the entire width of the building. They break into dozens of lines. The lines are divided by railings. The railings are metal. There they file past the first doctor.

   IRVING HOWE, *World of Our Fathers*

2. The doctor seemed disconcerted by this. The doctor drew back in his chair. The doctor rested a hand on either knee. The hands were fat. The hands were white. The smile faded from his face. The smile faded slowly.

3. Many recounted their own experiences. The experiences were bitter. They were at the hands of funeral directors. Hundreds asked for advice on something. It was to establish a consumer organization in communities. None exists in the communities. Others sought information about pre-need plans. The membership of the funeral societies skyrocketed.

   JESSICA MITFORD, *The American Way of Death*

4. She shut the door. She leaned against it. She felt the wood. The wood was hard against her shoulder blades. Her head was throbbing from too much noise. Her mouth was dry. All she planned was to get between the sheets of her bed. The sheets were flannel.

5. Mental retardation occurs in some parts of your city. It occurs at a rate. The rate is five times higher than it is in the remainder of your city. Twenty-five per cent of some prison populations are mentally retarded. Mental retardation does not just happen. It is caused.

   RAMSEY CLARK, *Crime in America*

6. The lifeguard kept looking at me for a long time. He was unable to speak. He put the gray sack down on the sand. Water whispered wet up around it. The water went back.

7. A commencement orator advises students. They enrich themselves culturally. Chances are something. He is more interested in money than he is in poetry. A university president says something. His institution

turned out 1,432 B.A.'s last year. He tells us something. He thinks something. He is running General Motors. The style is the man.

DONALD HALL, "An Ethic of Clarity," *Modern Stylists*

**8.** The man reached over. The man was old. The man grasped the boy by the collar of his jacket. The jacket was leather. The man gave him a shake. The shake was gentle. The shake was little. His eyes gazed down. His eyes were green. His eyes were unblinking. His eyes were grave.

**9.** He [Richard Wagner] had the emotional stability of a six-year-old child. He felt out of sorts. He would rave. He would stamp. He would sink into gloom. The gloom was suicidal. He would talk darkly of going to the East to end his days as a Buddhist monk. Then it was minutes later. Something pleased him. He would rush out of doors. He would run around the garden. He would jump up and down on the sofa. He would stand on his head.

DEEMS TAYLOR, "The Monster," *Of Men and Music*

**10.** In its collection, the Computer Museum has calculators. The Computer Museum is in Marlborough, Mass. The calculators are not-so-old. The Computer Museum has murals. The murals are computer-designed. The Computer Museum even has a computer made of Tinkertoys. The computer plays ticktacktoe. Everything is tucked in the lobby of a building. The building has six stories. The building is made of glass. The glass is bronze-tinted.

**11.** Velva has no organized charity. A farmer falls ill. His neighbors get in his crop. A townsman has a catastrophe. The catastrophe is financial. His personal friends raise a fund. It is to help him out. Bill's wife, Ethel, lay dying. She lay so long in the Minot hospital. Nurses were not available. Helen and others took their turns. They drove up there just to sit with her. She would know in her gathering dark something. Friends were at hand.

ERIC SEVAREID, "Velva, North Dakota," *This Is Eric Sevareid*

**12.** Your legs contain some of the most powerful muscles in your body. As a result, kicking is one of a female's best weapons against a variety of attacks. The weapons are defensive. Your legs are longer than your arms. A kick keeps more distance between you and an attacker than a punch or chop.

**13.** Once, I entered a mansion. I blew the safe. I removed six thousand dollars. A couple slept in the same room. The husband woke up. The dynamite went off. I assured him. The entire proceeds would go to the Boys' Club of America. He went back to sleep. Cleverly, I left behind some fingerprints of Franklin D. Roosevelt. He was President then.

WOODY ALLEN, "Confessions of a Burglar," *The New Yorker,* October 18, 1976

**14.** She awoke. It seemed as if many hours had passed. The room was still pitch-black. Her body was on fire. The sweat poured off her body. Her head throbbed horribly. She had a pain under her right ribs. The pain was excruciating.

**15.** The dog backed up. It did not yield. A rumbling began to rise in his chest. The rumbling was low. The rumbling was steady. It was something out of a midnight. The midnight was long gone. There was nothing in that bone to taste. Shapes were moving in his mind. The shapes were ancient. They were determining his utterance.

LOREN EISELEY, "The Angry Winter," *The Unexpected Universe*

**16.** Researchers have found something. The rhythm of drowsiness persists even in the absence of sleep. The rhythm of drowsiness is normal. The rhythm of drowsiness is daily. People are most tired in the early morning. People perk up during the day. People revive again in the evening. People revive again after an afternoon lull. We research volunteers had gone without sleep for seven days. We research volunteers spent a reasonably normal Saturday. It was because of this cycle.

**17.** I can think back over more than a hundred nights. I've slept a hundred nights in the truck. I sat in it. A lamp burned. I was bundled up in a parka. I was reading a book. It was always comfortable. It was a good place to wait out a storm. It was like sleeping inside a buffalo.

BARRY LOPEZ, "My Horse," *North American Review*

**18.** Students complete a first draft. They consider something. The job of writing is done. Their teachers too often agree. Professional writers complete a first draft. They usually feel something. They are at the start of the writing process. A draft is completed. The job of writing can begin.

DONALD M. MURRAY, "The Maker's Eye: Revising Your Own Manuscripts," *The Writer,* October 1973

**19.** Just then the hyena stopped whimpering in the night. The hyena started to make a crying sound. The sound was strange. The sound was almost human. The woman heard it. The woman stirred uneasily. The woman did not wake.

**20.** The lifeguard tried to persuade Tally to come out. She did not. He came back with only bits of waterweed in his fingers. His fingers were big-knuckled. Tally was gone. She would not sit across from me at school any longer. She would not chase balls on the streets on summer night. The streets were brick.

## SENTENCE REVISION IN ACTION: A WRITER REVISING

As you have been completing the language-manipulation exercises in this chapter, you should also have been practicing on your own essays the techniques you have learned. Sometimes making the transition from using language-manipulation techniques in exercises from the book to using them in your own essays can be difficult. To get a better idea of what it means to revise a paragraph in the context of a whole essay, it may be helpful to go back to the revisions Joseph made in his essay. Joseph, you will remember, was working on a paragraph describing the lead singer of a local band:

> David, the leader of the band, is the lead singer. He came out singing at the top of his lungs with his mouth engulfed around the mike. His curly, red hair was hanging over his eyes at about shoulder length. He resembled a sheep dog. Wearing a red flannel shirt, with the sleeves rolled up, and a pair of jeans with holes in the knees, he carried the stick, the infamous stick, which on top of it contained a shrunken head and he kept time by constantly pounding it on the stage. He sings to the fast and vigorous beat of his musicians. Pounding his stick, David was the heart of the band.

Joseph then revised this paragraph, coming up with a new version:

> David, the lead singer and leader of the band, came out singing at the top of his lungs, his mouth pressed close to the mike. With his curly, shoulder-length, red hair hanging over his eyes, he resembled a sheep dog. He wore a red flannel shirt with the sleeves rolled up to his elbows and a pair of tattered jeans with holes in the knees. He carried the stick—his infamous stick—which had a shrunken head on the top of it. Pounding his stick to the fast and vigorous beat as he sang, David was the heart of the band.

In revising his paragraph, Joseph tried to keep in mind the choices he had already made in terms of PACES. He knew that he wanted his code to match his subject matter and audience. Because he had a fairly informal topic, and his audience, college students who might be interested in seeing the band, was fairly informal, too, Joseph decided to avoid overly complex sentence constructions. On the other hand, his audience was educated and would expect something more than a string of simple sentences. Joseph attempted to create sentences that eliminated the choppiness of the early draft while retaining the informal feel of the essay. He combined the first two sentences of the paragraph by embedding the first sentence in the second:

***Original***

David, the leader of the band, is the lead singer.

He came out singing at the top of his lungs with his mouth engulfed around the mike.

***Revised***

David, the lead singer and leader of the band, came out singing at the top of his lungs, his mouth pressed close to the mike.

Next, Joseph transformed the following two sentences into one, using the *with* transformation technique:

***Original***

His curly, red hair was hanging over his eyes at about shoulder length. He resembled a sheep dog.

***Revised***

With his curly, shoulder-length, red hair hanging over his eyes, he resembled a sheep dog.

Joseph then noticed that the next sentence rambled and was a little awkward. He seemed to be trying to do too much in the one sentence. To solve this problem, he decided to make this long sentence into two shorter ones:

***Original***

Wearing a red flannel shirt, with the sleeves rolled up, and a pair of jeans with holes in the knees, he carried the stick, the infamous stick, which on top of it contained a shrunken head and he kept time by constantly pounding it on the stage.

***Revised***

He wore a red flannel shirt with the sleeves rolled up to his elbows and a pair of tattered jeans with holes in the knees. He carried the stick, his infamous stick, which had a shrunken head on the top of it.

Finally, Joseph transformed the last two sentences in his paragraph into one, using the -ing transformation technique and embedding the second-to-last sentence within the last sentence:

***Original***

He sings to the fast and vigorous beat of his musicians. As he pounded his stick, David was the heart of the band.

***Revised***

Pounding his stick to the fast and vigorous beat as he sang, David was the heart of the band.

Look over Joseph's new paragraph. How have the revisions he made altered the flow of the writing? Do the sentences communicate his message better? Worse? How would you revise this paragraph? What things would you change or leave the same? What sentences would you leave alone? What changes would you make that Joseph did not?

## ▶ PRACTICE: Revising Paragraphs ◀

The following two paragraphs were taken from drafts of students' papers. For each paragraph, read over the description of the situation the writer faces and then revise the paragraph as if you were the author, keeping in mind the overall aim of the paragraph and its place within the context of the entire essay.

Carla is working on a paper in which she is trying to persuade college students like herself that dieting and concern over weight loss are not as important as they may think. In this paragraph, Carla wants to tell her readers about her own personal experience with fad dieting. Given Carla's purpose and audience, what changes would you suggest she make to improve her paragraph?

> When I was in Junior High School, I wanted to look thin. I decided to go on a diet. I cut down on eating meals and bought some Nature Diet Pills. I bought the pills—they looked like brown horse pills—from a discount store. I did not know it at the time, but I was killing myself. I took the pills for a week or two, but then the skin under my nails turned yellow and I started feeling sick. I went to the doctor, and he told me that I had anemia from not eating right. I lost a little weight after getting sick, but my mother and my doctor made me quit my diet. I slowly started gaining my weight back. My goal in dieting was to look like a cover girl, but I discovered that it was not worth dying for, and my case is one of many that occur. Many individuals want to change their appearance. Sometimes individuals even suffer and die to become more attractive.

Bill has been working on a paper explaining why he likes the movie, *Nightmare on Elmstreet: Part 3*. Bill has found that the students who looked over his draft had trouble following his first paragraph. Since Bill knows that his first paragraph may make or break his paper, he decides to concentrate on revising it before working on the rest of the essay. What kinds of changes should Bill make to clarify the point of his paper and make his introduction interesting for his reader?

> The movie "Nightmare on Elmstreet part 3" is a very different movie from the first two Nightmare films but is entertaining. The difference between the third film and the other two was the third film had very little gory scenes in the picture. The first two were full of these scenes. Freddy

Kruger killed a lot of people in the first two films, but not in the third movie. Kruger ripped open the bellies of innocent teenagers. The third movie made up for not having a lot of violence. There was a lot of special effects and humorous lines for Freddy. This was bad, because the third movie was not scary. I thought that it was entertaining, though. The first two pictures kept me on the edge of my seat and my hands sweating. The third film was humorous, in a way, when he killed the teenagers. I was entertained by the third movie and scared by the first two.

## ► PRACTICE: Revising an Essay ◄

Frank is writing an essay in which he is trying to persuade the athletic director at Ohio State University to revise his policy on steroids. Revise the following essay, keeping Frank's purpose and audience in mind. You may want to review the chapter on paragraphs, because one of Frank's problems with his draft is deciding where to make paragraph breaks.

### STEROIDS

I am writing you concerning the growing problem of steroid use by Ohio State athletes. I feel that some changes should be made in the testing of athletes and penalties for this should be changed. It is unfair for the non-steroid user to have to compete against a steroid user. I also am concerned about the health of the steroid user because of the serious side effects of steroid use.

As an athelete I work hard to improve my performance. It discourages me that there are other athletes who perform better than I, but use artificial means to achieve this. I understand that besides taking steroids. They still have to work out, so it isn't as if they don't have to work at all. What steroids do is promote muscle growth, and speed up the process of repairing muscle tissue broken down from working out. The steroid user doesn't have to work any harder than the non-user to get a lot more out of his training. The way I feel, is if you can't train honestly with hard work and sweat then you shouldn't be given the right to participate. The problem lies with the athlete who comes up here and tries to compete at the collegiate level. The athletes are big and strong here. The only way the average athlete can survive is to get bigger and stronger themselves. Some can do this with steroids. Its a big decision and they don't take the time to weigh the advantages and disadvantages.

I, myself, will be trying out for the Ohio State Cross-Country team. I know I am not as good as most of the guys on the team. At this point I really want to work hard and improve to get up to their level. This will be very difficult but I have to try and give it my all. That's what I'm doing but so many athletes see steroids as an easy way to get up to the level of competition here at Ohio State.

I am also concerned about the health and welfare of the steroid user. Steroids are great for growth and development, and they have grave side effects. Many users overlook the side effects. The real sad part of this is that they don't realize what these drugs do to their bodies. Steroids can cause infertility, liver damage and problems with gender identity especially with females. When females take steroids they develop male characteristics.

I think serious steps should be taken to get steroids out of sports here at O.S.U. First of all there should be mandatory drug testing for all varsity athletes. Not just testing for a small percentage of the athletes who are randomly picked, These tests should be conducted four times a year, at the University Hospitals. The only setback will be the cost I suggest OSU takes the money out of the athletic department's annual budget. This is a set back, I know, but you have to draw the line somewhere. There is no reason why these athletes should go on competing while using steroids unfortunately this is where most programs stop the funding. To keep the tradition of a great university sports programs steriods need to be cut out. You may think that these tests if they do bring out some steroid users will hurt the University's great sports tradition. I feel the opposite, bring it out in the open will make people say *"Hey this University is cleaning up its program we should do the same,"*. Other Universities will look up to us for this. After you get funding and testing then comes the enforcing of rules. I think anybody coming up positive on steroid use should be suspended from competition for that season. This will only mean the athlete will not be able to compete against other teams. Keeping them on the team is a must. If you kick them off the team you defeat the whole purpose. OSU should also let the athlete go on practicing with the team. OSU should give a program to teach all incoming athletes the rules and regulations concerning drug use. Inform them about the serious side effects involved with steroid use. The best way to avoid misuse is to educate the athletes before they consider use of steroids. The problems are clear and are very serious. They involve health and unfairness to other athletes. I just hope you can take what I have said and get some thing out of this to try to better your athletic program.

# CHAPTER ▲ FOURTEEN

# *Effective Sentences*

**"By being so long in the lowest form (at Harrow) I gained an immense advantage over the cleverer boys . . . I got into my bones the essential structure of the ordinary British sentence—which is a noble thing."**

**SIR WINSTON CHURCHILL,** ***Roving Commission*: *My Early Life***

In Chapter 13, you learned to combine and rewrite sentences to make your writing more effective. Chapter 14 describes other challenges you may face in producing well-crafted sentences: how to avoid common sentence flaws and how to create particular effects. Both of these skills will be especially useful when you revise and polish. To write effective sentences you must present ideas clearly and accurately, without wasted words. To make your ideas stand out for the reader, focus on clarity, economy, emphasis, and variety.

## CLARITY

Clear writing is a fulfilled transaction between you and your reader. The sentence faults discussed in this section tend to obscure your ideas from the reader. At the writing and rewriting stages in each draft of a composition, edit and revise so that each sentence is clear in itself and in the way it reflects your overall purpose.

### ▶ Illogical Sentences

Sometimes, beginning writers will write one sentence while thinking of another, putting parts of both of them on the paper. The result usually doesn't quite make sense. For example, imagine a writer thinking, "The story contains many good details. I admire the outcome of the story." But instead of writing two sentences, the author writes, "The details of the story admire the outcome." This is an illogical sentence (*details*, inanimate, can't *admire*), the result of faulty combining of ideas.

#### ▶ PRACTICE: Analyzing Illogical Sentences ◀

In the following pairs, why is sentence *B* illogical?

*A.* From the basement, the sounds of pounding and grinding broke the silence of the August night.
*B.* From the basement, the sounds of pounding and grinding examined the darkness of the August night.

*A.* Few, if any, of my classmates had the personal or social maturity to admit that they were wrong to tease Juanita.
*B.* The personal or social maturity to admit that they were wrong to tease Juanita included few, if any, of my classmates.

*A.* After sitting on the front step for five minutes trying to clear my head, I slowly rose and opened the front door of my parents' house.
*B.* After sitting on the front step on which I was sitting for five minutes by trying to get my head together, I slowly rose and opened the front door of my parents' house.

### ► Rambling Sentences

It is possible to get carried away with sentences. Sentences that ramble on and on, especially when they cause the reader to lose the main idea, should be broken up into shorter units and revised.

#### ► PRACTICE: Analyzing Rambling Sentences ◄

What is the effect of writing the sentences of *A* as one long sentence in *B*?

*A.* I went to the drug store yesterday to get my prescription filled, but the man behind the counter said he couldn't fill it. When I asked him why, he just looked at me in amazement. He held out the prescription form and pointed to the date: September 5, 1988. Boy, was I embarrassed!
*B.* When I went to the drug store yesterday to get my prescription filled, the man behind the counter said he couldn't fill it, and when I asked him why he just looked at me in amazement, holding out the prescription form and pointing to the date, which was September 5, 1988, a fact that made me embarrassed.

## ECONOMY

Economical writing wastes neither words nor the reader's time. Whether an idea is simple or complex, it should be expressed in economical sentences.

### ► Wordiness

A good rule of thumb for any writer is *don't waste words*. The idea is not simply to use as few words as possible, but to use only as many words as necessary to express what you mean. If any words *can* be removed without changing the meaning of your sentences, they *should be*.

## ▶ PRACTICE: Analyzing Wordiness ◀

What is the effect of adding words to the original versions of the following sentences?

*A.* President Bush announced today he favors a total ban on nuclear weapons.
*B.* President Bush, who has a dog named "Lucky," announced today he favors a total ban on nuclear weapons.

*A.* With an incredible second effort, Hershel Walker lunged through the wall of defenders and into the end zone.
*B.* With an incredible second effort, Hershel Walker lunged through the wall of defenders (that is, they looked like a wall) and into the end zone.

*A.* There are four stages in a successful highjump attempt: the approach, the plant, the arch, and the kick.
*B.* Although there is a great deal of room for doubt and controversy concerning many areas of the sport of high jumping, no one could possibly deny my thesis that there exist, in effect, four distinct stages, or phases, in any high jump attempt which has any hope of success: the first being the approach, the second being the plant, the third being the arch, and, of course, the fourth and final being the kick.

## ▶ Redundancy

Redundant expressions are phrases like *repeat again*, *completely unique*, and *hurry quickly*.

## ▶ PRACTICE: Analyzing Redundancy ◀

Explain the redundancy in sentence *B* in the following:

*A.* For four years I sat behind the same girl in home room every day.
*B.* For four years I sat behind the same identical girl in home room every day.

*A.* As the airplane passed between Bob and the sun, it vanished in the glare.
*B.* As the airplane passed between Bob and the sun, it vanished from view in the glare.

## ▶ Excessive *Who, Which, That*

The use of *who*, *which*, or *that* is often optional. Where such words are necessary to make the meaning of the sentence clear, they should be used. But when the sense is clear without them, they can be removed. In most cases, the result will be a more economical, more natural-sounding sentence. "Jane is a girl who likes cigars" is more economically expressed as "Jane likes cigars." "Lucas knows exercise is good for him" is equivalent to "Lucas knows that exercise is good for him."

### ► PRACTICE: Analyzing Excessive *Who, Which, That* ◄

What is the effect of adding *who, which,* or *that* in sentence *B*?

*A.* Mr. Kessler defined sentence diagramming as mindless busy work.
*B.* Mr. Kessler defined sentence diagramming as that of mindless busy work.

*A.* Billy scraped a small circle of frost from the windowpane and gazed out on the new snow, glistening in the morning light.
*B.* Billy scraped a small circle of frost from the windowpane and gazed out on the new snow, which was glistening in the morning light.

## EMPHASIS

As you begin to write longer, more sophisticated sentences, you must craft them consciously to give the right emphasis to your ideas. Even in short sentences a writer must make clear for the reader which ideas are to be emphasized.

### ► Effective Repetition

Deliberate repetition of words or phrases is one way to achieve emphasis within a sentence.

### ► PRACTICE: Analyzing Effective Repetition ◄

What would be the effect of substituting *B* for *A* in the following?

*A.* In the morning, in the evening, in the middle of the night, Dr. Schmidt was ready to jump into his car to call upon sick chickens.
*B.* In the morning, evening, and the middle of the night, Dr. Schmidt was ready to jump into his car to call upon sick chickens.

*A.* Once again, Eric's roommate had made his infamous meatloaf—meatloaf from hell.
*B.* Once again, Eric's roommate had made his infamous meatloaf, which came from hell.

## ▶ Parallelism

Parallelism is a basic concept in writing, much like consistency, to which it is related. It is a convention that similar concepts should be written in similar forms; that is, they should be parallel. Parallelism is a form of repetition. Thus, "I like fishing and skiing," not "I like fishing and to ski."

### ▶ PRACTICE: Analyzing Parallelism ◀

Discuss the use of parallelism in the following examples. What would be the effect of substituting sentence *B* for sentence *A*?

*A*. Maria was popular because she spent most of her time fighting, spitting, and swearing.
*B*. Maria was popular because she spent most of her time fighting, spitting, and she swore.

*A*. John hit the ground, bounced once, and rolled off the edge of the cliff.
*B*. John hit the ground, bounces once, and rolls off the edge of the cliff.

## ▶ Inverted Sentences

One way of achieving emphasis is to invert your sentences. (Inverting your sentences is one way to achieve emphasis.) However, one kind of inversion is not much admired: the *backward* sentence, a sentence whose inverted structure sounds unnatural or obscures meaning (for example, "Learning English are the students").

### ▶ PRACTICE: Analyzing Inverted Sentences ◀

How does the inverted sentence change the emphasis in the following?

*A*. AIDS is frightening a growing number of educators.
*B*. Frightening a growing number of educators is AIDS.

*A*. My home is where the buffalo roam.
*B*. Where the buffalo roam is my home.

## ▶ Passive Sentences

A passive sentence is one in which the doer of the action is invisible ("The bear was shot"), or the doer is hidden behind the word *by* ("The bear was shot by the hunter"). Whether there is any real need for the passive depends on whether the doer or the receiver of the action is being emphasized. The most direct statement is, of course, "The hunter shot the bear"; but if we ask what happened to that bear, the correct answer may be, "The bear was shot by the hunter." Even so, some passives are more awkward than others, and many sound pointlessly indirect by comparison with the active voice: "The paper was received by him" as opposed to "He received the paper."

### ▶ PRACTICE: Analyzing Passive Sentences ◀

In the following sentences, why does the passive seem less effective than the active?

*A.* Much to Tank's surprise, Leonard, the scrawny kid he'd tormented in gym class for twelve years, turned and cracked him in the face with a field-hockey stick.
*B.* Much to Tank's surprise, he was cracked in the face by the field-hockey stick of Leonard, the scrawny kid he'd tormented in gym class for twelve years.

*A.* Racing down the icy slope, his broken ski poles no help to him, Todd slammed into the pine tree.
*B.* The pine tree was slammed into by Todd, who was racing down the icy slope, his broken ski poles no help to him.

## ▶ Sentence Rhythm

Just as you have learned to recognize the flat intonation of a recorded telephone message, and just as you know when someone is reading "without expression," you can learn to tell when there is something wrong with the rhythm of a sentence. It is very difficult to describe poor sentence rhythm; teachers usually just mark such sentences "awkward." But you can probably already tell when a sentence doesn't sound right. Something halting, unnatural, or awkward announces that the rhythm is off beat. Or the rhythm may be so homogenized, without variation or motion or emphasis, that it sounds flat, dead—a robot sentence.

### ▶ PRACTICE: Analyzing Sentence Rhythm ◀

What is the matter with the rhythm in sentence *B* of the following? What do the *A* sentences achieve that the *B* sentences do not?

*A.* Wilbur set his derby upon his head and strode into the night.
*B.* Upon his head, Wilbur set his derby and into the night strode.

*A.* The students were feeding among the trays and the long tables, with old ultraviolet lights twinkling in the ceiling panels above.

***B.*** Where there were trays the students were feeding where the long tables were below the ceiling panels above which were twinkling old ultraviolet lights.

## ▶ Other Options

Inexperienced writers sometimes use exclamation points, underlining, and quotation marks to show emphasis (This *is* important!), but there are other options.

*Emphasis through structure*

She reacted *sarcastically* to his proposal. (Single word)

She reacted *with sarcasm* to his proposal. (Phrase, more emphatic)

As she reacted to his proposal, *her sarcasm was evident.* (Clause, most emphatic)

*Emphasis through position* Moving things around usually causes a change in emphasis. There is no hard rule about position except that ideas gain emphasis when they show up in unexpected places. Modifiers tend to be most emphatic at the beginning of the sentence; independent clauses tend to be most emphatic at the end.

She reacted to his proposal sarcastically.

She sarcastically reacted to his proposal.

Sarcastically she reacted to his proposal.

While he was making his proposal, she reacted sarcastically.

## ▶ PRACTICE: Analyzing Emphasis ◀

How does the *B* sentence change the emphasis in the following?

***A.*** Just as Sir Edmund Hillary reached the peak of Everest, he realized he'd left the oven on in his flat back in London.
***B.*** Sir Edmund Hillary realized he'd left the oven on in his flat back in London just as he reached the peak of Everest.

***A.*** If you blame yourself for not liking lima beans, stop.
***B.*** For not liking lima beans, stop blaming yourself.

## ▶ Emphasis Through Contrast

It is not always sufficient to say what a thing is; it is sometimes necessary to say what a thing is *not*. Furthermore, contrast is an excellent way of achieving emphasis.

### ► PRACTICE: Analyzing Emphasis ◄

What do the contrastive sentences below accomplish that the others do not?

*A.* Jane kicked Spot, not a nudge with the foot, but a full followed-through boot.
*B.* Jane kicked Spot with a full followed-through boot.

*A.* John finished his entire sales pitch, though he could plainly see the woman would buy none of his band candy.
*B.* John finished his entire sales pitch, and he could plainly see the woman would buy none of his band candy.

## VARIETY

Avoid monotony in your writing. The normal order for an English sentence is *subject—verb—object*, but if every sentence in your paper runs in normal order, you will put your reader to sleep. To achieve variety, use the techniques described in this section.

### ► Varied Beginnings

***Begin with a prepositional phrase.***

*In his rearview mirror*, Jeff watched as the policeman slowly emerged from the cruiser.

***Begin with more than one prepositional phrase***

*On this shirt*, as *on all his shirts*, Fred wore the monogrammed insignia of the Secret Order of Waterbuffaloes.

***Begin with a simile***

*Like a slug*, Calvin oozed out of bed Monday morning.

***Begin with an adjective or several adjectives***

*Terrified*, Tasha eased open the door of her boss's office.

***Begin with an appositive***

*A girl from down the street*, Maggie won a gold medal in the hurdles at the U.S. Track and Field Championships.

***Begin with an infinitive***

*To be an effective complainer*, you must be both persistent and loud.

***Begin with a modifying clause***

*Whenever I make chocolate chip cookies*, I end up eating half the chips before they make it into the dough.

***Begin with a noun clause***

*Whoever gets there first* gets the most to eat.

***Begin with a participle***

*Popping a Certs into his mouth*, Tony hesitated before ringing the doorbell.

***Begin with a suspended transition***

*Scientists, however*, have recently developed new superconductors that may someday make commercial fusion reactors a reality.

## Varied Types of Sentences

***The cumulative sentence*** The cumulative sentence is built by addition; it adds details either before or after the main idea has been established. For example:

He strode into the bowling alley carrying his new shoes, brand new, two-tone bowling shoes, the ultimate in sophisticated bowling apparel.

Set up as a problem in sentence combining, the sentence looks like this:

He strode into the bowling alley carrying his new shoes.
They were brand new, two-tone bowling shoes. (,)
They were the ultimate in sophisticated bowling apparel. (,)

The two modifying sentences are reduced to descriptive phrases and added to the main clause. Since these cumulative modifers are nonrestrictive (they can be removed without changing the main idea of the sentence), they must be set off with commas. Notice too that the modifiers add not only descriptive details, they also add specificity.

Note the same additive process in the following sentence, in which we get a specific detail about a woman's appearance added to the main clause:

Mary ran across the front lawn, her arms outstretched, her hair loose, flowing.

The cumulative sentence permits you to add more and more specific details, building highly descriptive pictures for the reader. The more specific details you add, the more highly textured your sentence will become, as in the following:

He watched, fascinated, as the workmen pounded at the wall, their heavy hammers rhythmically swinging, first down and then, in a low, flat curve, up past shoulder height and into the wall, its cinder blocks refusing, then yielding, then tumbling, shattered, to the ground.

***The balanced sentence*** The balanced sentence is very formal and elegant and is often used in public oratory. It is crafted by balancing two similar ideas in similar words and structures. For example:

And so my fellow Americans, ask not what your country can do for you; ask what you can do for your country.

JOHN F. KENNEDY, Inaugural Address

## ► PRACTICE: Analyzing Balanced Sentences ◄

What does the balanced sentence achieve that the other sentences do not in the following pairs?

*A.* Extremism in the defense of Liberty is no vice; and . . . moderation in the pursuit of Justice is no virtue.

BARRY GOLDWATER, Acceptance Speech, Republican National Convention

*B.* It is no vice to be extreme in defending liberty; and . . . to pursue justice only moderately lacks virtue.

*A.* Winners never quit; quitters never win.
*B.* The only way to win is through perseverance; however, if you quit, you obviously cannot win.

*A.* When the going gets tough, the tough get going.
*B.* Those who are successful are at their best when they are faced with adversity.

***The periodic sentence*** The periodic sentence builds to a climax: readers must wait for the end of the sentence before they can get the meaning. The periodic sentence is created by suspending part of the sentence, frequently the verb, until the end. Technically, even a short sentence could be called *periodic* if it were properly constructed, but the term usually applies to long sentences in which there is a clear sense of ***waiting*** for the end. For example:

> If Beethoven had been restricted to a less enlightened court circle, had not known the Breunings, had not been exposed to the repercussions of the French Revolution, he might have remained a talented and serious musician but not much more.
>
> FRIDA KNIGHT, *Beethoven and the Age of Revolution*

## ► PRACTICE: Analyzing Periodic Sentences ◄

What do the periodic sentences achieve in the following pairs? What would be the effect of substituting sentence *B* for *A*?

***A.*** In that instant, in too short a time, one would have thought, even for a bullet to get there, a mysterious, terrible change had come over the elephant.

GEORGE ORWELL, "Shooting an Elephant"

***B.*** A mysterious and terrible change had come over the elephant in that instant, which was too short a time, one would have thought, even for a bullet to get there.

***A.*** From this dream and its associations with a number of rather ordinary childhood memories and several fairy tales familiar to the patient during his early years, some remarkable conclusions are derived.

C. H. THIGPEN AND HERVEY CLECKLEY, *The Three Faces of Eve*

***B.*** Some remarkable conclusions are derived from this dream and its associations with a number of rather ordinary childhood memories and several fairy tales familiar to the patient during his early years.

***Long and short sentences*** There is no rule about length of sentences in English. Long sentences are not better than short sentences; short sentences are not better than long. This book teaches beginning writers to combine short sentences because new writers tend to write many more short than long ones. A paper made up of too many short sentences may sound immature, and a paper made up of too many lengthy sentences is likely to sound boring. Note the variety and emphasis gained by juxtaposing long sentences and short in the following examples:

> To raise morale and get rid of the troublemakers, he now planned a second reconnaissance under Hojeda, consisting of four hundred men with orders to march to Santo Thomás, relieve Margarit's garrison, and then explore

the country and live off the natives. This was one of Columbus's worst decisions.

SAMUEL ELIOT MORISON, *Christopher Columbus, Mariner*

There was absolutely no end to that awful song with its eternal "I will kiss thee!" and at last neither I nor Sir Henry, whom I had summoned to enjoy the sight, could stand it any longer; so, remembering the dear old story, I put my head to the window opening and shouted, "For Heaven's sake, Good, don't go on talking about it, but *kiss* her and let's all go to sleep!" That choked him off, and we had no more serenading.

H. RIDER HAGGARD, *Alan Quatermain*

## ► PRACTICE: Evaluating Sentence Effectiveness ◄

In each of the following pairs, one sentence is thought to be better than the other in one or more aspects of sentence effectiveness. Which is the better sentence?

**1**[1] *A.* My wife was overwhelmed by the number of things she had to do that seemed to have nothing to do with teaching when she first taught.
*B.* When my wife first taught, she was overwhelmed by the number of things she had to do that seemed to have nothing to do with teaching.

**2** *A.* Sitting in the dentist's office, I waited for what seemed to be an eternity that lasted forever.
*B.* Sitting in the dentist's office, I waited for what seemed to be an eternity.

**3**[2] *A.* ORU exists to serve the whole body of Christ, worldwide.
*B.* To serve the whole body of Christ, worldwide, exists ORU.

**4**[3] *A.* The boys were a more rowdy lot, and no teacher in her right mind would have turned her class over to them.
*B.* They were boys who were such a rowdy lot that no teacher who was in her right mind would have turned her class over to them.

**5**[4] *A.* Leroy was the best athlete, the best whistler, the best horseshoe player, the best marble shooter, the best mumblety-pegger, and the best shoplifter in our neighborhood.
*B.* Leroy was the best athlete, whistler, horseshoe player, marble shooter, mumblety-pegger and shoplifter in our neighborhood.

**6**[5] *A.* The medulla is laid just inside the skull, just above the large hole at the bottom of it.

*B.* The medulla lies just inside the skull, just above the large hole at the bottom of it.

**7**[6] *A.* Edison developed a 100-watt carbon-filament lamp having an efficiency of 1.61 p.w. and a life of 600 hours.

*B.* A 100-watt carbon-filament lamp having an efficiency of 1.61 p.w. and a life of 600 hours was developed by Edison.

**8** *A.* The personnel here at Engineering Technologies can handle the planning, producing, and the financial aspects of all your business ventures.

*B.* The personnel here at Engineering Technologies can handle the planning, producing, and financing of all your business ventures.

**9**[7] *A.* A curious choice for a starring role in Disney's bright, upbeat world Mickey Mouse may have seemed at first.

*B.* At first glance Mickey Mouse may have seemed a curious choice for a starring role in Disney's bright, upbeat world.

**10**[8] *A.* Teachers accept the concept of the whole child; this concept includes the child's social immaturities, her feelings of inadequacy, her anger, her joy and her exuberance, which must be dealt with.

*B.* Teachers accept the concept of the whole child, but they are not ready to deal with the child's social immaturities, her feelings of inadequacy, her anger, her joy and her exuberance.

**11**[9] *A.* When Father Cassidy drew back the shutter of the confessional, he surprised the appearance of the girl at the other side of the grille.

*B.* When Father Cassidy drew back the shutter of the confessional, he was a little surprised at the appearance of the girl at the other side of the grille.

**12**[10] *A.* Before the rich man was a fish casserole, baked in a cream sauce and garnished with parsley.

*B.* There was a casserole in front of the man who was rich; it was a fish casserole, baked in a sauce of cream, and garnished with parsley.

**13**[11] *A.* A star crept out from among the overhanging grasses as the time passed.

*B.* As the time passed, a star crept out from among the overhanging grasses.

**14**[12] *A.* He had come to avoid a scandal, to make plain the danger, and to offer the truth.

*B.* He had come not to make a scandal but to avoid it; not to raise a danger but to make one plain; not to oppose a truth but to offer it.

**15**[13] *A.* Sex can be an exaggeration to a point where it becomes dull.
*B.* Sex can be exaggerated to a point where it becomes dull.

**16**[14] *A.* You should report any lost keys at once to the head resident.
*B.* Any lost keys should be reported by you at once to the head resident.

**17**[15] *A.* Of the four, Peanuts, who was the quiet one, was living in a land of silence.
*B.* Of the four, Peanuts was the quiet one, living in a land of silence.

**18** *A.* When Kip paid for the car, he pulled a wad of $100 bills from his pocket which immediately drew a suspicious glance from the car dealer.
*B.* When Kip paid for the car, he pulled a wad of $100 bills from his pocket, immediately drawing a suspicious glance from the car dealer.

**19**[16] *A.* Denied political freedom and economic capability, people accomplish little in their homes or communities.
*B.* People can accomplish little in their homes or their communities denied political freedom and economic capability.

**20** *A.* Floyd, who had never known love before, had finally met the woman of his dreams, a woman with no past and no future.
*B.* Floyd, who had never known love before, had finally met the woman of his dreams with no past or future.

**21**[17] *A.* More than the traditionally enumerated five senses are the way human beings know their world.
*B.* Human beings know their world through more senses than the five that are traditionally enumerated.

**22**[18] *A.* A dog is an animal of much greater intelligence than a chick, and in Pavlov's laboratory, dogs require long series of repeated experiences for learning to relate certain perceptual signals to the imminence of food.
*B.* A dog is an animal of much greater intelligence than a chick, and yet in Pavlov's laboratory, dogs require long series of repeated experiences for learning to relate certain perceptual signals to the imminence of food.

**23**[19] *A.* With her marriage, Tehani seemed to take on a new dignity and seriousness, though in the privacy of our home, which had a thatched roof, she showed at times that she was still the same wild tomboy who had beaten me at swimming at Matavai.
*B.* With her marriage, Tehani seemed to take on a new dignity and seriousness, though in the privacy of our home she showed me at times that she was still the same wild tomboy who had beaten me at swimming in Matavai.

**24** *A.* The final touchdown, an eighty-yard run, was scored by Ickey, but the ball was not spiked by anyone in the end zone.

*B.* Ickey scored the final touchdown, an eighty-yard run, but no one spiked the ball in the end zone.

**25**[20] *A.* The course of the *Mayflower* was now in mid-Atlantic and making steady headway.

*B.* The *Mayflower* was now in mid-Atlantic and making steady headway.

[1] HERBERT R. KOHL, *The Open Classroom*

[2] ORAL ROBERTS, *ORU Catalogue*, 1973–1974

[3] JAMES MICHENER, *Hawaii*

[4] ED LUDWIG and JAMES SONTIBANE, *The Chicanos*

[5] GUSTAV ECKSTEIN, *The Body Has a Head*

[6] "Lighting," *Encyclopaedia Britannica*

[7] ANTHONY LUCAS, *"The Alternative Life-Style of Playboys and Playmates"*

[8] DON DINKMEYER, *Understanding Self and Others*

[9] FRANK O'CONNOR, *"News for the Church"*

[10] CARSON MCCULLERS, *"The Jockey"*

[11] RICHARD ADAMS, *Watership Down*

[12] GIORGIO DE SANTILLANA, *The Crime of Galileo*

[13] EDWARD FORD, *Why Marriage?*

[14] *CMU Residence Hall Handbook*

[15] THOMAS THOMPSON, *Richie*

[16] JOSEPH R. BRANDT, *Why Black Power?*

[17] ROBERT WHITMAN, *Understanding the Behavior of Organisms*

[18] ARTHUR KOESTLER, *The Act of Creation*

[19] CHARLES NORDHOFF and JAMES NORMAN HALL, *Mutiny on the Bounty*

[20] GEORGE F. WILLISON, *Saints and Strangers*

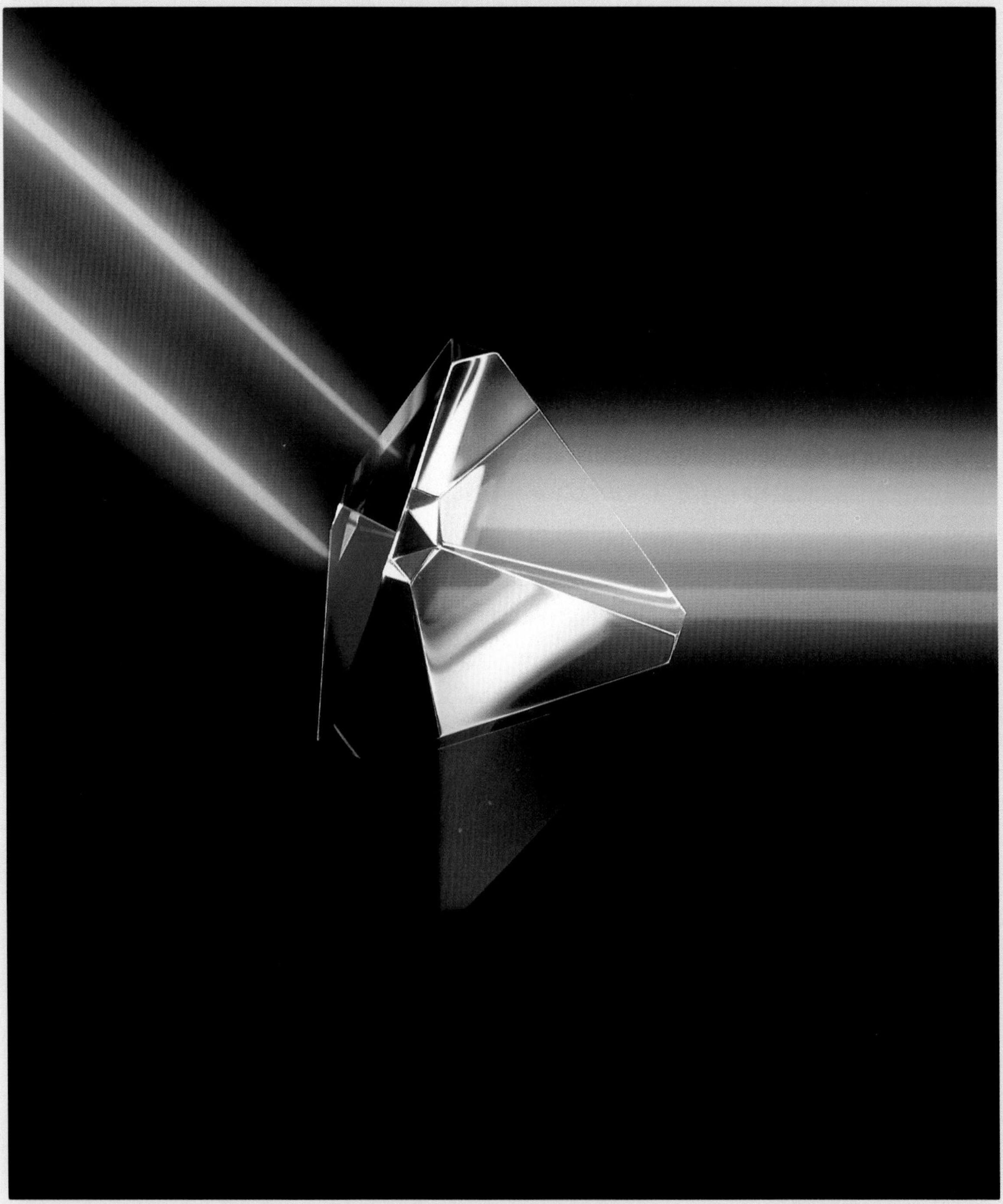

# PART ▲ FIVE

# *Handbook of the Writer's Conventions*

# CHAPTER ▲ FIFTEEN

# *Effective Diction*

**"The difference between the almost right word and the right word, is really a large matter—'tis the difference between the lightning bug—and the lightning."**

**MARK TWAIN,** ***The Art of Authorship***

No two words in English have exactly the same meaning, nor do they carry exactly the same attitudes or values. For the writer this means choosing exactly the right word for any situation; and choosing words means considering your audience, knowing the effect you want to make, understanding the words you might use. In short, word choice is directly related to your purpose. In this chapter, you will learn to consider all the shades of meaning and subtleties of context our language has to offer.

## CONNOTATION AND DENOTATION

Words do not automatically "mean" what the dictionary says. There are two kinds of meaning: connotation and denotation. When people ask for the "definition" of a word, they are usually asking for the denotation of the word, its generally accepted meaning. The dictionary maker must do what you and I would do upon encountering a new word—see how people use it and then *deduce* its meaning. Thus the denotation of a word becomes the general definition of the word. The denotation of *sear*, for example, is "to cause to wither or dry," or in some cases "to burn or scorch," as when we sear meat to trap the juices inside. It is this general definition that we all more or less agree to when we say the word *sear* denotes (means) to dry, parch, or burn.

However, words change over the course of time. They pick up "extra" meanings or they acquire particular associations. Very often words acquire emotional or attitudinal labels (some words are "bad" and some are "good"). These additional associations, connotations, can cause problems for writers. For example, we can accept "sear the meat," "sear the cloth with the iron," "the sun will sear the flowers," and even "her kisses will sear his lips!" But most native speakers of English will not accept "sear the wood in the fireplace," "sear the garbage," nor "fell and seared my knee," though in every case the meaning "to burn" is intended. Historically, the word has come to be used in some contexts but not in others, so we say that the word *denotes* burning and scorching perhaps, but it *connotes* the effect of heat on moisture. (When we speak of a "searing pain," we have in mind the kind of pain caused by touching a hot stove: scorched flesh.)

Thus, knowing the denotation of a word is usually not enough; you need to be aware of its connotations, too, in order to avoid the kind of language error involved in an old story about the first translating computer, which when translating the English "Out of sight, out of mind" into Chinese, came up with "Absent idiot." Although the dictionary will not solve all your problems when revising for effective diction, it is a good place to begin.

## USING THE DICTIONARY

To make effective word choices, you need a thorough understanding of at least one good dictionary. Since dictionaries vary considerably, it may be worth your while to become familiar with several. A little investigation will reveal that the dictionary can provide an astonishing amount of information if you know how to use it. For example, *Webster's New Collegiate Dictionary*, in addition to the definitions of words, contains a detailed explanatory chart to show what all the parts of the definitions mean; additional notes that explain each element of the entries (pronunciation, spelling, usage, and so on); a brief essay on the English language and its history by W. Nelson Francis; a list of abbreviations and pronunciation symbols used in the dictionary; a long list of famous and important people; an equally long list of geographical names; an exhaustive list of the names and addresses of colleges and universities in English-speaking North America; a list of signs and symbols; and even a handbook of style. Thus the writer can have a small encyclopedia of useful information in a good dictionary.

### Reading the Entries

The entry for *choreography* shows a number of features of the dictionary:

Guide to pronunciation — Part of speech and plural

Word listed → **cho·re·og·ra·phy** (kôr′ē äg′ra fē) *n* -ES [F *chorégraphie*, fr. *choré-* choreo- + *-graphie* -graphy] ← Etymology

Meanings → **1 :** the art of representing dancing by signs as music is represented by notes **2 :** DANCING; *esp* : stage dancing as distinguished from social or ballroom dancing **3 :** the composition and arrangement of dance movements and patterns (as for ballet) created usu. to accompany a particular piece of music or to develop a theme or a pantomime; *also* : a composition created by this art

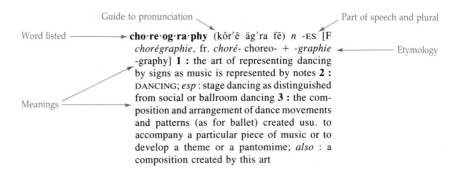

Note that the word is given with dots between the syllables (for the purpose of word division). It is followed by a guide to pronunciation with a secondary accent on the first syllable and a primary accent on the third. The vowel chart at the bottom of the dictionary page (not shown here) explains the pronunciations indicated by the umlaut (ä) and the schwa (ə). Note that the first syllable is pronounced with either a long *o* (kōr) or an *aw* sound (kȯr). In this dictionary, variant pronunciations are equally valid unless specifically marked otherwise. Note that the syllabication, marked with dots, does not exactly correspond to the divisions of pronunciation, marked with hyphens (see "Word Division" in Chapter 17).

Following the pronunciation guide is the part of speech *n* (noun) and the spelling of the plural. In this dictionary, plural forms are not usually given unless the plural requires some change in the root word: In *choreography*, *y* changes to *i*, as **-phies** shows.

The etymology of the word (history of its development) is given in reverse order. The immediate ancestor of *choreography* is the French word *chorégraphie*, which is itself formed from the Greek word *choreia* (dance) and the French *-graphie* (write). The word has its origin, then, in the two concepts, dancing and writing.

The dictionary shows three meanings for this word. They are given in order of development; that is, the oldest meaning is given first. And you can see from this that *choreography* originally referred to pictures or diagrams of dances. The third meaning has two submeanings, marked *a* and *b*, relating to either the art of composing or the composition of a dance.

Last, the dictionary gives an adjective and an adverb form for this word, and the pronunciations of each of them.

Other entries show various other kinds of information about words. For example:

Context Aids

**civ·il** \ 'sivel, *esp Brit sometimes* -(ˌ)vil\ *adj* [ME, fr. MF, fr. L *civilis*, fr. *civis* citizen — more at CITY] **1 a :** relating to, growing out of, or involving the relations of citizens one with another or with the body politic or organized state or its divisions and departments <~ institutions> <interested in ~ affairs> <a contribution to ~ philosophy> **b :** concerned with or pertinent to internal affairs of a state or its citizenry in contrast to external affairs <~ strife between two political groups> <~ embargo> **2 a :** composed of or shared by individuals living and participating in a community <the oldest form of ~ society were the early city-states of oriental antiquity —H.E. Barnes> **b :** given to or marked by group activity or organization < man is a ~ creature> **3 :** concerning, befitting, or applying to the collective citizenry or the individual citizen < a ~ duty> <the individual's ~ right of free speech> — see CIVIL LIBERTY, CIVIL RIGHTS **4 a :** living in or exhibiting a condition of social advancement marked by organization and stability of community life or government **:** not uncivilized or primitive <tribal anarchy giving way to ~ order> **b :** marked by public order **:** quiet and peaceable in behavior <areas still ~ in the turbulent country> **c :** educated, cultured, or sophisticated **:** not rustic and unlettered <a ~ philosophy > <~ jests > **5 a :** based on or skilled in the roman civil law <a ~ doctor —Shak.> **b :** relating to private rights and to legal proceedings in connection learned in the war just ended, should be put into ~ use —Henry Wallace> <the old conflict between the ~ and the sacerdotal powers —Edward Clodd> **b :** representing or serving the general public in the sphere of political rule or administration; *esp* **:** belonging to or sanctioned by an executive department of a nation, state, or municipality < officials of a ~ board> <prohibiting a member of Congress from being appointed to any ~ office> <rates and hours set by ~ regulations> **9** *obs* **:** virtuous by nature but not regenerate **:** moral as distinguished from religious <~ righteousness>

Discussion of synonyms

Syn POLITE, COURTEOUS, COURTLY, GALLANT, CHIVALROUS: CIVIL now implies adequate consideration of others and forbearance from rudeness or unpleasantness <remember, then, that the *civil* . . . is the only way to be beloved and well received in company, that to be ill-bred . . . is intolerable —Earl of Chesterfield> <I mean to return his visit tomorrow. It will be only *civil* in return for his politeness, to ask to see him, —Sheridan Le Fanu> POLITE may imply cold, formal, perfunctory deference to etiquette <let's be *polite*, but act as though she didn't exist —Sherwood Anderson> Often it differs from CIVIL in suggesting somewhat warmer or more sincere consideration of others <the bishop seldom questioned Jacinto about his thoughts or beliefs. He didn't think it *polite* —Willa Cather> <under ordinary circumstances he would have tried to be

with them **:** relating to rights and remedies sought by action or suit distinct from criminal proceedings — distinguished from *criminal* and *political* <a ≲ liability> <≲ jurisdiction> <a ≲ suit> <a ≲ remedy>; see CIVIL LAW **c :** as defined by law **:** having to do with legal rights or status <≲| disabilities> — compare NATURAL 5; see CIVIL DEATH **6 a** *sometimes* -ER/-EST **:** adequate in courtesy and politness **:** marked by satisfactory adherence to social usage and sufficient but not noteworthy consideration for others **:** MANNERLY <even if he didn't like them he sould have been ≲ —W.S. Maugham> <it was all he could do to be ≲ to her —Mary Austin> <I asked a ≲ question, and I expect a ≲ answer —D.H. Lawrence> **b** *sometimes* -ER/ -EST **:** showing goodwill, humaneness, or clemency **:** not savage or fierce <the *civilest* and most friendly people that we met with —Daniel Defoe> **c** *obs* **:** SOBER, STAID **:** not showy or audacious **:** QUIET **d :** seemly in aspect **:** compatible with human sensibilities **:** PRESENTABLE, SHIPSHAPE **e** *dial, of weather* **:** not inclement **:** FAVORABLE **7** *of time* **:** based on the mean sun and legally recognized for use by the general public in ordinary affairs — distinguished from *sidereal* <the ≲ calendar> <a ≲ day begins at mean midnight> **8 a :** belonging or relating to the general public, the pursuits, experiences, ways, and interests of the citizenry, or to civic or temporal affairs as distinguished from military, naval, ecclesiastical, or like specialized membership or affairs **:** CIVILIAN <new educational techniques, *polite*. As it was, he could hardly bring himself to give them a *civil* word of welcome —Norman Douglas> COURTEOUS may suggest a certain polish and delicacy of action; it may connote either mere formal deference, however perfect, to custom, or a genuine sincere consideration and regard <the baronet peeped at his grandson with the *courteous* indifference of one who merely wishes to compliment that mother of anybody's child —George Meredith> <M. Laval owns a fine old historical painting in Chateldon, and he was *courteous* enough to permit me to view it —Upton Sinclair> COURTLY suggests the stately or ceremonious <Pitt Crawley treated her to a profound *courtly* bow, such as he had used to H. H. the Dutchess of Pumpernickel, when he was attaché at that court —W.M. Thackeray> GALLANT and CHIVALROUS, in this sense, indicate esp. courtesy and attention to women, the former often suggesting either the spirited and dashing or the elaborate and over-attentive <the qualities . . .of surface chivalry and *gallant* attentiveness in her brilliant American friend had for a moment seemed to reveal a lack in me —Havelock Ellis> CHIVALROUS in this sense often connotes high-mindedness and disinterested attention <ladies were supposed to be without sexual desire . . . gracious beings they were, without a sordid thought, according to the *chivalrous* notions of the time —W.E. Woodward> <she had fainted from weakness, and he had felt strangely *chivalrous* and paternal —Ellen Glasgow>

Connotative explanations

Note the context aids for this word <~institutions> and <~affairs>. Note too the presentation and discussion of synonyms. Here all the synonyms more or less "denote" the shared meaning element: "adequate consideration of others." But notice too the connotative explanations provided for each of them. The context aid < let's be *polite*, but act as though she didn't exist—Sherwood Anderson > indicates a quote from the author Anderson.

If you have a good college dictionary and understand how to use it, you can improve the quality of your diction. This does not mean finding "fancier" words but rather the words best suited to what you are trying to say. As a general rule, it is a mistake to ransack the dictionary for new words; a writer needs to be thoroughly familiar with a word before using it in a composition.

## USING WORDS

Most readers agree that clear, concise, and accurate language is the preferred style for formal or semiformal writing, but even these simple guidelines must be interpreted in the light of an author's purpose. A letter to a United States senator should not be written in street slang. On the other hand, there may be times when street slang is the most effective language to use. The best language is whatever is most appropriate and effective for an author's purpose.

In the following sections, which have been alphabetized for convenient reference, we discuss some stylistic problems good writers avoid and some options you may wish to incorporate into your writing. By comparing sentences revised for effective diction with less effective ones, you will begin to develop a sense of the kinds of choices skilled writers make.

## ABSTRACTIONS

*Abstract* means removed from physical reality; it refers to qualities and ideas. Abstractions are necessary and worthwhile aspects of language; they help to carry our intellectual concepts. Few writers can do without them entirely; but too many abstractions, without tying ideas to concrete reality now and then, may bore and frustrate your readers. Abstractions can also contribute to blurring reality, as for example when a salesperson claims to want to discuss your "insurance needs" but actually wants to sell you a policy.

***Abstract Sentence***

That a governmental agency should exercise regulatory influence over private transportation is analogous to the same extension of power over private possession of weaponry.

***Revised for Concrete Diction***

Just as people are licensed to drive cars, they should be licensed to possess firearms.

## CLICHÉS

A cliché is a worn-out word or phrase, an expression so familiar that it no longer has any force: "She's as pretty as a picture, as smart as a whip, as cute as a button," and so on. These tired old expressions are poor substitutes for more forceful, direct ways of saying things.

***Cliché***

It's not whether you win or lose, it's how you play the game that matters.

***Revised for Effective Diction***

I'd rather win than lose, but I love the game.

## CONFUSING NEGATIVES

Avoid the double negative ("I don't have none.") Any time a sentence contains more than one negative, there is likely to be confusion: "It is by no means not shameful not to stand up to a bully." "They didn't realize that they were not the ones who wouldn't be going." For clarity, these should be revised into positive statements, if possible.

***Confusing Negatives***

He was not an unattractive man.

***Revised for Clarity***

He was an attractive man.

## EFFECTIVE MODIFIERS

Not every sentence requires modifiers, but when you do use modifiers, you will gain clarity and accuracy by choosing carefully. It is not just more "interesting," it is more accurate to use specific modifiers in your descriptions.

***Imprecise***

The fish turned evenly and followed the sound that was fading.

***Revised with Specific Modifiers***

The fish turned, banking as smoothly as an airplane, and followed the receding sound.

PETER BENCHLEY, *Jaws*

## EFFECTIVE NOUNS

Nouns can powerfully influence your writing. Searching for the right word, the one that is most specific for your meaning, is one mark of a skilled writer. Given the context of why you are writing, who you are writing to, and what you are writing about, any word ought to be selected because it is the clearest, most concise, most accurate word. Students sometimes hunt through dictionaries to come up with a *new* word for a familiar concept, but this can be dangerous if the word has subtle connotations.

***Imprecise***

It was like a heat pump outside, with the illumination splintering into bright spots on the surface and water.

***Revised with Specific Nouns***

It was like a furnace outside, with the sunlight splintering into flakes of fire on the sand and sea.

ALBERT CAMUS, *The Stranger*

***Imprecise***

The Russians were on the verge of Hungary.

***Revised with Specific Nouns***

The Russians were on the edge of Hungary.

WINSTON CHURCHILL, *Triumph and Tragedy*

## EFFECTIVE VERBS

While some textbooks advise beginning writers to select "colorful" or "vivid" verbs, keep in mind that *accuracy* is the best guideline. "She passed out" may be more vivid than "She fainted," but the difference between the verbs in those phrases isn't just a matter of degree. The danger of overstatement often accompanies efforts to be colorful. Thus a paper on hunting may speak of "blasting to bits" when, in fact, the less vivid "shooting" may be more accurate.

***Imprecise***

Inside the plane, the handful of boys who were able took a shot at getting up the seats which held so many of the wounded.

***Revised with Specific Verbs***

Inside the plane, the handful of boys who were able tried to prize away the seats which trapped so many of the wounded.

PIERS PAUL READ, *Alive*

***Imprecise***

William now instructed his archers to make the arrows go to substantial altitudes, such that these arrows would end up on the far side of the shield wall, and one of these arrows entered Harold's right eye and wounded him unto death.

***Revised with Specific Verbs***

William now directed his archers to shoot high into the air, so that the arrows would fall behind the shield wall, and one of these pierced Harold in the right eye, inflicting a mortal wound.

WINSTON CHURCHILL, *A History of the English Speaking Peoples: The Birth of Britain*

Note: The forms of *to be* (*am*, *is*, *are*, *was*, *were*, *be*, *being*, *been*) are often the weakest of all.

## EMOTIONAL LANGUAGE

Emotional language means that instead of calm and objective reporting, the reader finds name calling, exaggeration, and unfair and unreasonable language abuse: "loaded language." Such emotionalism may be intentional in humorous writing, but for most nonfiction writing, more objective language is preferred.

***Emotional Language***

The market place will continue to pay women criminally less than men as long as wives kowtow to the jobs of their breadwinning husbands.

***Revised with More Objective Diction***

The market place will tend to pay women less than men as long as wives give priority to their husbands' jobs.

GEORGE E. GILDER, *Sexual Suicide*

## EUPHEMISM

Using pleasant words, or inoffensive ones, to cover hard truths is generally considered evasive writing. There are legitimate uses for euphemisms (when trying to spare someone's feelings perhaps), but in general, authors avoid them. Common euphemisms, such as "pass on" for "die," are easy to spot because they have obvious plain English equivalents.

***Euphemism***

You see, sir, we spent those two hours telling tales of questionable taste.

***Revised with Plain English***

You see, sir, we spent those two hours telling dirty jokes.

MURRAY LEINSTER, "First Contact," *Science Fiction Hall of Fame*

## FIGURES OF SPEECH

A figure of speech should be fresh and clear and should make an image for the reader. The purpose of the figure of speech is to create a picture, to make an idea clear and forceful through comparison. An effective figure pleases the reader, brings the "Well said" reaction. Writers must judge whether their images will work for the reader. "She's as graceful as a squirrel," for example, would probably fail. The squirrel may be graceful to some, but to most people it is a symbol of quickness; using it to evoke gracefulness may not work very well. Does the following figure work for you? "The sun came up in the morning like a huge grapefruit."

## ► Metaphor

A metaphor makes an implied comparison, as in this description of Nabisco's Mallomar cookies:

> The result is a cultural icon—the cookie equivalent, surely, of the Coke bottle.
>
> PAUL GOLDBERGER, "Quick! Before It Crumbles: An Architecture Critic Looks at Cookie Architecture."

## ► Simile

An expressed comparison, a simile uses the words *like* or *as*.

> The train was curving the mountain, the engine loping like a great black hound, parallel with its last careening cars, panting forth its pale white vapor as it hurled us ever higher.
>
> RALPH ELLISON, *The Invisible Man*

## ► Personification

In this form of comparison, some object or animal is given human qualities.

> The ground seemed to welcome me, embracing me as I lay down.

## ► Mixed Metaphors

These metaphoric comparisons are illogical or inconsistent; the writer mixes more than one idea into an image.

> He thought he had the bull by the horns, but then the rug was pulled out from under him.

## ► Dead Metaphors

These metaphors have become part of the language and are no longer considered figures of speech. Too many of them make your writing trite. They can sometimes create accidental humor.

> You have to wear heavy shoes on the foot of the mountain.
>
> Mr. Blaine dropped his false teeth into the mouth of the river.

***Mixed Metaphor***

Then the lids opened, revealing pale pools of blue vagueness that finally cleared into clouds that hung over the vet, who looked down unsmilingly.

***Revised for Consistent Image***

Then the lids opened, revealing pale pools of blue vagueness that finally solidified into points that froze upon the vet, who looked down unsmilingly.

RALPH ELLISON, *The Invisible Man*

***Literal Language***

She would search his character for any signs of weakness and, upon finding any, would exploit them without considering his discomfort.

***Revised with Metaphor***

She would look for dark spots in his character and drill away at them as relentlessly as a dentist at a cavity.

MARY MCCARTHY, *Cruel and Barbarous Treatment*

***Ineffective Figure***

She wore her hair in two braids wound tight around her head like pale silk strings.

***Revised for More Effective Image***

She wore her hair in two braids wound tight around her head like pale silk ropes.

PAUL DARCY BOLES, "The House Guest"

## JARGON

Jargon covers all specialized vocabulary and terminology, but it often means unnecessarily technical language. Most readers would call the following *necessary* jargon; it is very difficult to express this idea in simpler words.

***Necessary Technical Language***

The photons which strike a crystal on the stage of a light microscope do not alter the crystal's position.

A. TRUMAN SCHWARTZ, *Chemistry: Imagination and Implication*

*Unnecessary Jargon*

By two months of age, a child of typical development will express facial pleasure at the face of his maternal parent.

*Revised for Plain English*

By two months of age, the average child will smile at the sight of his mother's face.

ATKINSON AND HILGARD, *Introduction to Psychology*

## NEOLOGISMS

Inventing new words is one of the privileges of writers, but there is no point to creating new words when old ones will serve as well. In general, readers expect a new word to achieve something that old words do not. In this example—"The team's attackage strength was low"—*attackage* isn't an improvement over an existing word such as *offensive*.

*Neologism*

She held out her hands to him and he lipped her.

*Revised for Plain English*

She held out her hands to him and he kissed her.

PAT FRANK, *Alas Babylon*

*Neologism*

The character provides comic relief in the play because she often malaprops.

*Revised for Plain English*

The character provides comic relief in the play through her frequent malapropisms.

## OVERSTATEMENT

Using unnecessary intensifiers, exaggerating, or overdramatizing with language strikes most readers as amateurish. For example: "The *worst* day of my life was the day Buffy Allen discovered I had been using her tennis shoes! I was just *devastated* when she found out!" The writer is trying to make a relatively insignificant event sound more important than it could possibly be.

***Some Intensifiers to Use with Restraint***

absolutely, basically, certainly, completely, definitely, incredibly, intensely, passionately, perfectly, positively, quite, really, simply, totally, unbearably, very

***Some Dramatic Modifiers to Use with Caution***

awful, fabulous, fantastic, gigantic, horrible, horrid, incredible, sensational, stupendous, terrible, terrific, unbearable, unbelievable

***Overstatement***

The adorable little plane zipped over the perfectly square fields, all of them containing far too much water—it had rained here very recently indeed.

***Revised for Simplicity***

The small plane flew over square fields, all of them flooded—it had been raining here recently.

SVETLANA ALLILUYEVA, *Only One Year*

***Overstatement***

When we look at the stars, we see them without a doubt arranged in precise geometrical figures—lines, semicircles, triangles, squares.

***Revised for Simplicity***

When we look at the stars, we see them arranged in the form of geometrical figures—lines, semicircles, triangles, squares.

ROBERT S. RICHARDSON, *The Fascinating World of Astronomy*

## SEXIST LANGUAGE

People have rightly begun to question the use of *he* as a generic singular or common-sex pronoun referring to both women and men. Consider how the following sentence is problematic.

If you think you have experienced whiplash, see your lawyer. *He* will explain your legal options.

Whether intended or not, the use of *he* shows a sexist assumption on the part of the writer since, of course, not all lawyers are men.

Do not use masculine pronouns when referring to both men and women. Using *he, his,* or *him* when referring to people of both sexes will probably create unnecessary conflicts with your audience. You can eliminate sexist language in sentences in a number of ways:

**1.** Recast into the plural.

***Sexist***

Give each actor *his* lines before rehearsal.

***Revised***

Give the actors *their* lines before rehearsal.

**2.** Reword to eliminate the potentially sexist pronoun.

***Sexist***

The typical researcher is concerned about *his* results.

***Revised***

The typical researcher is concerned about results.

**3.** Replace the masculine pronoun with *one, you,* or *he or she* (do not overuse them, however).

***Sexist***

If a patient needs a second opinion, *he* can feel free to see another doctor.

***Revised***

If a patient needs a second opinion, *he or she* can feel free to see another doctor.

Besides pronouns, gender-free equivalents should be used when speaking of people in general or when making certain words and titles:

| ***For*** | ***Use*** |
|---|---|
| man | the human race |
| mankind | humanity, people, human beings |
| manpower | workers, personnel |
| manmade | synthetic, machine-made |
| chairman | chair, presiding officer, head |
| businessman | business executive or manager |
| policeman | police officer |
| mailman | mail carrier |

Use *Miss* or *Mrs.* only when you are sure a person desires that form of address. Otherwise, use *Ms.*

## SWITCHING TENSE

You may write in any tense that fits your purpose; the rule is to be consistent. Write in the present tense or in the past, but not both. Present tense is difficult to manage (you must somehow account for the fact that words appear on the page while, for example, "I am running for my life"). For formal and semiformal writing, the past tense is usually easiest to use as well as most logical.

***Tense Switch***

He lives in a home which, although cheap and unfashionable, possessed its picturesque distinction.

***Revised for Consistent Tense***

He lived then in a home, which, though cheap and unfashionable, possessed its picturesque distinction

REBECCA WEST, *The New Meaning of Treason*

## SWITCHING VOICE

### ► Switching from Personal to Impersonal

The rule is to be consistent. Switching from personal *I* to impersonal *one*, for no apparent reason, sounds as though the writer has forgotten who he or she is.

***Voice Switch***

When I came back, she had the pillow off her head all right—one could have predicted that she would—but she still wouldn't look at me, even though she was lying on her back.

***Revised for Consistent Voice***

When I came back, she had the pillow off her head all right—I knew she would—but she wouldn't look at me, even though she was laying on her back.

J. D. SALINGER, *The Catcher in the Rye*

The same fault sounds equally inconsistent the other way around—switching from impersonal *one* to personal *I*; some readers feel *one* is too impersonal and vague to be used at all. To avoid the choice between *I* and *one*, writers sometimes substitute the editorial *we* or the all-purpose *you*:

The changes, we may notice, had to be made by the state.

C. B. MACPHERSON, *The Real World of Democracy*

If you find yourself in difficulties, call us.

Other voices include the *invisible* writer: "The experiment was conducted under difficult conditions" (by a phantom? See "Passive Sentence" in Chapter 14); and the *masked writer*: "This researcher believes the evidence will show . . ."; "This reporter was present when . . ."; "The present writer is of the opinion . . .".

Each of these voices has its uses as long as the writer is consistent in presenting that voice. What voice you use depends on what, to whom, and why you are writing. The question of voice is closely related to the degree of formality of your writing.

## ► Switching from Formal to Informal

In the following pairs, consider the effect of the switch from formal to informal or from informal to formal:

***Voice Switch***

The prospect of being alone with the young man seemed all of a sudden like a total downer.

***Revised for Consistent Voice***

The prospect of being left alone with the young man seemed suddenly unendurable.

MARY MCCARTHY, *Cruel and Barbarous Treatment*

## ► Choosing a Stance

*Stance* refers to the author's point of view, a complex of attitudes toward self, experience, code and audience. The author may be serious, humorous, sarcastic; personal or impersonal; formal or informal. The range of stances in English is very broad, covering everything from the hip, cool, half-secret lingo of the streets to the difficult, technical jargon of scholarly writing. For most writers, the best stance is somewhere in the midddle between very personal and very impersonal, very formal and very informal. Whatever stance you choose, your reader will expect you to stick with it. Switching back and forth is a fault except when done for humor or irony.

Why might a writer choose one stance over another? You will be able to answer that question for yourself if you can determine what each of the following writers achieves with stance:

***A Writer Choosing the Most Formal Stance***

The basis of the family is, of course, the fact that people feel a special kind of affection toward their own children, different from that which they feel towards each other or towards other children.

BERTRAND RUSSELL

***A Writer Choosing Informal English***

The boomerang is a neat weapon for streetfighting and is as easy to master as a Frisbee.

ABBIE HOFFMAN, *Steal This Book*

***A Writer Choosing a Middle Level, on the Formal Side***

I belong to that classification of people known as wives.

JUDY SYFERS, "Why I Want a Wife."

***A Writer Choosing a Middle Level, on the Informal Side***

Absolutely anyone can set a world record.

WILLIAM ALLEN, "How to Set a World's Record"

***A Writer Deliberately Mixing Diction***

If the other parts of the books aren't so great, here's where the real value lies—every picture tells a story, don't it?

## UNCONSCIOUS ECHOES

People who "read with their ears" often pick up things that others miss, such as the jingle-jangle noise of unconscious rhymes and alliterations and other echoes.

***Unconscious Echoes***

The payroll plans are prepared on punched cards each pay period for each person.

***Revised for More Effective Diction***

The payroll data are prepared on punched cards each week for each employee.

DONALD H. SANDERS, *Computers in Society*

## UNDERSTATEMENT

Understatement is the fine art of restraint in language. The good writer knows when to restrain the impulse to hammer home a point. The more the point seems worthy of heavy emphasis, the more it achieves by understatement.

A famous example is attributed to Mark Twain: "The reports of my death have been much exaggerated."

What does the understated sentence achieve in each of the following pairs?

***Weak***

She had been trying to read, though she was really too anxious to concentrate, and when she heard Paula's car rattle to a stop out back, she closed the book and darted joyfully toward the door.

***Revised for Understatement***

When she heard Paula's car rattle and pop out back, she closed the book she hadn't really been reading and darted joyfully toward the door.

ARTHUR LAURENTS, *The Way We Were*

## WORD PLAY

In informal essays and personal experience stories, you may have the opportunity to play with words. A cleverly turned phrase can be highly effective—as the world of advertising has discovered.

***Weak***

Try the light, smooth whiskey that's becoming America's favorite import from Canada.

***Revised with Word Play***

Try the light, smooth whiskey that's becoming America's favorite Canadian.

Advertisement, *Time*

## ► PRACTICE: Evaluating Diction ◄

In each of the following pairs, one sentence is better than the other in some aspect of diction. Which is the better sentence?

**1.** *A.* The hoses were attached at water pipes that stood out of the brick bases of the houses.
*B.* The hoses were attached at spigots that stood out of the brick foundations of the houses.

**2.** *A.* She was locked away in a cellar from which she is never heard of again.

*B.* She was locked away in a cellar from which she was never heard of again.

**3**[2]**.** *A.* A district's sports programs may be ripe for a penalty call from the courts if those programs deny participation to an individual because of dress or hair styles, marital status, or sex.
*B.* It is possible that judicial intercession may be required where there is a conflict between the requirements of athletic activities and the civil liberties of participants.

**4**[3]**.** *A.* I don't suppose anybody ever deliberately attunes a watch or a clock.
*B.* I don't suppose anybody ever deliberately listens to a watch or a clock.

**5**[4]**.** *A.* It's really happening, Serpico thought, and identified himself as a police officer.
*B.* It's really happening, Serpico thought, and named himself as a police officer.

**6**[5]**.** *A.* That spring when I had a great deal of potential and no money at all, I took a job as a janitor.
*B.* That spring when I had a great deal of potential and was living from hand to mouth, I took a job as a janitor.

**7**[6]**.** *A.* Those who own the land shall govern it.
*B.* Government is the prerogative of ownership.

**8**[7]**.** *A.* She pulled on her overshoes, wrapped a large tartan shawl around her, put on a man's felt hat, and ventured out along the causeways of the first yard.
*B.* She put on her overshoes, put a large tartan shawl around her, put on a man's felt hat, and went out along the causeways of the first yard.

**9**[8]**.** *A.* As soon as the seat-belt sign goes off and people began to move about the cabin, I glanced around nervously to see who's on board.
*B.* As soon as the seat-belt sign goes off and people begin to move about the cabin, I glance around nervously to see who's on board.

**10.** *A.* I was sitting at my desk when I suddenly think of a good example.
*B.* I was sitting at my desk when I suddenly thought of a good example.

**11.** *A.* The moment I saw him, one knew he was in love.
*B.* The moment I saw him, I knew he was in love.

**12**[9]**.** *A.* There's not much better you can call the color of an orange than orange.
*B.* It is likely that the best description available for the color of the orange fruit is simply that which is customarily given it, namely, and simply, orange.

**13**[10]**.** *A.* He had sort of reddish hair and a kind of cute face and I couldn't help but keep looking at him.

*B.* He had deep dark red hair falling in waves into a face that was pure elf, and I couldn't do anything but stare love-struck at him.

**14**[11]**.** *A.* As the P.M. walked very slowly to the aircraft, there was a grey look on his face that I did not like, and when he came at last to this house, he collapsed wearily into the first chair.

*B.* As the P.M. dragged himself to the aircraft, there was a grey look on his face that terrified me, and when he came at last to this house, he keeled over with exhaustion into the first chair.

[1] JAMES AGEE, *A Death in the Family*

[2] DAVID L. MARTIN, "Schoolboy Sports a Bone-Crushing Financial Problem"

[3] WILLIAM FAULKNER, *The Sound and the Fury*

[4] PETER MAAS, *Serpico*

[5] JAMES ALAN McPHERSON, "Gold Coast"

[6] JOHN JAY, in Michael Parenti, *Democracy for the Few*

[7] D. H. LAWRENCE, "The Blind Man"

[8] ERICA JONG, *Fear of Flying*

[9] TONY HARMON

[10] JULIE MASTERSON

[11] LORD MORAN, "Churchill," from *The Diaries of Lord Moran*

# CHAPTER ▲ SIXTEEN

# *Usage*

**"A problem well-stated**
**is a problem half-solved."**

**CHARLES F. KETTERING**

The rules of English are not actually rules at all; they are customs and conventions. They grew out of the history of the English-speaking peoples, and throughout history these conventions have changed as writers have changed with the times.

Very few people worry about "mistakes" in slang or informal English. But most educated readers are concerned when they find mistakes in formal writing. Therefore, this chapter on usage will help you review those problems that sometimes come up in formal writing.

Formal English is, in general, the language used in printed works: newspapers, magazines, books, and other writing aimed at the educated public. It is the language of schools, businesses, sciences, and the professions. Formal English does not mean "fancy" or pretentious language; it means having a standard *form*. It is the language you yourself use when you are conscious of *how* you are writing as well as *what*. If you scribble a telephone message for a roommate, you probably don't care whether your words are precise. But if you take a message for your employer, you may be very conscious of *how* your writing looks. For example, here is a telephone message written in three different styles:

***Informal***

Nita dropt by—get in touch riteaway—she's at jaimes

***Formal***

Juanita dropped by. Get in touch with her immediately. She is at Jaime's apartment.

***Pretentious***

Ms. Juanita Velasquez attempted to contact you while you were otherwise engaged. She intimated that you should communicate with her by telephone at your earliest convenience. At the present time she is paying a social call at the residence of Mr. Jaime Rodriguez.

Your roommate would accept either the formal or the informal message without question. But the pretentious message might cause him or her to assume that you were joking or being stuffy. The pretentious message attempts to sound more important than the situation warrants.

The rule of thumb for the usage guidelines in this chapter is not what is "right" according to some arbitrary authority, but what educated readers are accustomed to. Not every authority agrees on just what those expressions are, but this chapter presents the majority solutions to most of the common problems in formal writing. The following items of usage have been arranged in alphabetical order for ease of reference.

## AGREEMENT

Educated readers expect things to *agree*. Mixing singulars and plurals distracts the reader. In most cases, you just have to remember how many things you are writing about, but you must handle a few cases in agreement with special care.

### ► Group Words

Words like the following are considered *singular* in form.

| | |
|---|---|
| the army | the faculty |
| the band | the generation |
| the body (of students) | the group |
| the class | the majority |
| the company | the minority |
| the crowd | the part (of the group) |
| the enemy | the portion |

*Conventional usage* Group words like these take *singular* verbs and *singular* pronouns:

The company *has its* work to do.

The band *is* playing *its* introduction.

*Optional usage* Group words *may* be given plural verbs and pronouns to emphasize the actions of all of the members of the group. (Although this usage is customary in British English, many Americans think it sounds strange.)

The orchestra *are* tuning *their* instruments.

The class *are* studying *their* books.

### ► Confusing Singulars

| | |
|---|---|
| anyone, everyone, no one, one | none (of these students) |
| a box of, a cup of, a trainload of | the number of (students) |
| each (student), each of (the students) | physics |

everybody, nobody, somebody
either Jack or Jill, neither Jack nor Jill, either person
fifteen miles
five minus three
ham and eggs
mathematics
that she likes milk and pickles
two plus six
Jack as well as Jill
Jack together with Jill
this kind (of apples)
that kind (of apple)

***Conventional usage*** These expressions are confusing because they often sound plural—they are frequently followed by a plural phrase (one *of the boys*)—but they are all *singular* and take *singular* verbs and *singular* pronouns.

Each of them *has* her book.

Every male student *has* his dictionary.

Electronics *is* a good major.

Five cents *doesn't* buy as much as *it* used to.

Special Note—Gender-specific References: The use of masculine pronouns when *both* sexes are referred to or implied is totally unacceptable in modern writing. For example, when a group of students contains both men and women, "Each student should have *his* work finished on time" can be revised to "Each student should have *his or her work* finished on time" or "Students should have *their* work finished on time."

## ► PRACTICE: Understanding Agreement ◄

Select suitable forms from the choices in parentheses.

1. Neither of the cars (have/has) good enough mileage for you to buy (it/them).
2. Neither of these novels (have/has) enough adventure in (them/it) to keep your interest up.
3. One of the greatest ideas of twentieth century psychology (was/were) Freud's concept of the subconscious mind.
4. They had come thither, not as friends nor partners in the enterprise, but each, save one youthful pair, impelled by (his/their) own selfish and solitary longing for this wondrous gem.

   NATHANIEL HAWTHORNE, "The Great Carbuncle"
5. Every student in the class (have/has) (his/their/his or her) strengths and weaknesses, and each specialty (is/are) of interest.

## Confusing Plurals

Words and phrases like the following are considered *plural* in form:

both the girls and the boy
both (men), both of (the men)
the boys as well as the girls
either the boy or the girls
eleven assignments
girls and boys
Jack and Jill
women who, men and women who, people who, those who
neither the girl nor the boys
a number of (students)
one of those who (study), one of those girls who (study)
these kinds (of apples)
those kinds (of apples)
those days, those years, the years
two sixes ($2 \times 6$)

Expressions like these are all *plural* and take *plural* verbs and *plural* pronouns.

Neither the girls nor the boys *are* ready.

These kinds of apples *are* good.

Note: Clauses starting with *who*, *which*, or *that* often function as modifiers. In the second example below, *have* is plural because its subject, *who*, refers to the plural *girls*.

An odd number of girls *have their* books.

She is one of those girls who *have their* books.

### PRACTICE: Understanding Agreement

Select suitable forms from the choices in parentheses.

1. The months I spent working (was/were) profitable.
2. His tunic and breeches (was/were) so thickly soaked through with Italian blood that they thought at first he had been shot through the chest.

   CARLOS BAKER, *Ernest Hemingway*
3. My uncle, however, was one of those men who (is/are) always prepared with expedients.

   JULES VERNE, *A Journey to the Center of the Earth*
4. Gardenias and the peerage (was/were) his only weaknesses.

   OSCAR WILDE, "The Canterville Ghost"
5. Eight articles to discuss in one hour (is/are) too many.

Because they have been borrowed from different languages, many nouns have a plural form that is irregular.

## ► Irregular Plurals

| *Singular* | *Plural* |
|---|---|
| alumna | alumnae (f) |
| alumnus | alumni (m) |
| analysis | analyses |
| bacterium | bacteria |
| cactus | cactuses, cacti |
| crisis | crises |
| criterion | criteria |
| curriculum | curriculums, curricula |
| datum | data |
| formula | formulas, formulae |
| index | indexes, indices |
| medium | media |
| nucleus | nuclei |
| octopus | octopuses, octopi |
| parenthesis | parentheses |
| stimulus | stimuli |
| stratum | strata |
| thesis | theses |
| die | dice |

As a matter of fact when data are [not *is*] of this type, all of the usual mathematical and statistical implications may be made.

N. M. DOWNIE AND R. W. HEATH, *Basic Statistical Methods*

## ► Special Problems in Agreement

*Mixed compound subject* It is possible to write a compound subject that is part singular and part plural. The rule is, the verb agrees with the part closest to it.

Neither his sisters, his parents, nor Jack *has* the answer.

Neither the space nor the things in it *were* in the room before.

SUSANNE K. LANGER, *Problems in Art*

*Some* The word *some* is either singular or plural depending on context.

We thought *some* of the *books were* too mature for children.

*Some* of the oil *was* used for fuel.

*Separated subject and verb* In a long or complicated sentence, words may get between the subject and the verb, causing you to "lose" the subject. Figure out who is doing what in a sentence before you decide whether the verb should be singular or plural.

The *superiority* of stockades built by the Union Troops over those built by the Confederates *was* striking.

OTTO EISENSCHIML AND RALPH NEWMAN, *Eyewitness: The Civil War As We Lived It*

*Atypical word order* Usually, the subject comes first in the sentence, before the verb:

***1 2***
***Subject Verb***
*The dog was* young and healthy.

But writers sometimes change the order of their sentences:

***2 1***
***Verb Subject***
Young and healthy *was the dog.*

Put the sentence in normal order (mentally) before deciding whether the verb should be singular or plural. Why is the verb singular in each of these examples?

There *is*, so far as I know, no good *reason* for these excuses.

For the many, there *is* a hardly concealed discontent.

STUDS TERKEL, *Working*

*Does each* of the boys *belong* to the club?

*Agreement and logic* Because educated readers expect things to *agree* in formal writing, certain expressions sound illogical:

The sophomores are clever as foxes [not a *fox*].

The frat brothers made up their minds [not *mind*] in a hurry.

The verb agrees with its subject, not with what comes after the verb:

The best *bargain* for lunch *is* sandwiches and a cup of soup.

*Sandwiches and a cup of soup are* the best bargain for lunch.

## ▶ PRACTICE: Understanding Agreement ◀

Select suitable forms from the choices in parentheses

1. As I walked along, it occurred to me that the two children's behavior (was/were) a true reflection of all mankind.

   THEODOR REIK, *Of Love and Lust*

2. A number of shoppers (is/are) being surveyed about the product.
3. The number of days left till Christmas (is/are) twelve.
4. Each kind of bacterium (produce/produces) a juice that creates the kind of fermentation that is necessary to do the work.

   ALAN L. BENSON, *The Story of Geology*

5. Every generation (has/have)(its/their) styles of living.

   SUSANNE K. LANGER, *Problems of Art*

6. There (was/were) usually several reasons for his behavior.
7. It is Steve's roommates who (cause/causes) the problems.
8. Neither the atomic bomb nor its effect (is/are) very well understood by most people.
9. The implications of this argument (has/have) been examined.
10. Those (sort/sorts) of places are being patrolled by the police.

## COMPARISONS

### ▶ Illogical

"She is taller than any girl in the class" is illogical since it seems to imply either that she is taller than herself, or that she is not part of the class. "She is the tallest girl in the class" or "She is taller than any other girl in the class" both solve this problem.

| *Illogical* | *Revised for Clarity* |
|---|---|
| Corky was faster than anyone on the team. | Corky was the fastest runner on the team. |

### ▶ Incomplete

A comparison is meaningful only if its terms are fully expressed. For example, in "She is young, if not younger, than you are," the parenthetic phrase "if not younger," not only interrupts, but disconnects the first part of the sentence from the rest ("She is young . . . than you are"). The full comparison requires "She is *as young as*, if not younger than, you are."

| ***Incomplete*** | ***Revised*** |
|---|---|
| You need math more than Jim. | You need math more than Jim does.<br>You need math more than you need Jim. |

## DANGLING AND MISPLACED PARTS

### ► Dangling Parts

Some modifiers seem to "dangle" when they do not modify anything in the sentence. Often these modifiers produce humor by accidentally attaching to something unintended: "Riding my bike through the woods, the bear suddenly appeared in front of me." The modifier attaches to the *nearest* noun, and therefore *the bear* is *riding my bike*. To avoid the problem, move modifiers next to what you intend them to modify or supply an appropriate subject: "Riding my bike through the woods, *I* suddenly saw the bear in front of me."

### ► PRACTICE: Evaluating Usage ◄

Which is the better sentence in the following pairs?

**1**[1]. *A.* Reading carefully through the text, several concepts appeared.
*B.* As I read carefully through the text, several concepts began to appear.

**2.** *A.* Approaching the lunch counter, the smell of cheeseburgers was strong.
*B.* Approaching the lunch counter, she noticed the strong smell of cheeseburgers.

**3**[2]. *A.* Having departed from my friend, some remote spot in Scotland was selected where I could finish my work in solitude.
*B.* Having departed from my friend, I determined to visit some remote spot in Scotland and finish my work in solitude.

**4.** *A.* Looking up, I noticed I was late.
*B.* Looking up, the clock informed me I had little time to spare.

**5**[3]. *A.* Long and tangled and hanging down, his eyes were shining through his hair like he was behind vines.
*B.* His hair was long and tangled and hung down, and you could see his eyes shining through like he was behind vines.

## Misplaced Parts

*Movable modifiers* Movable modifiers (*only, just, almost*) usually come before the verb. But in some cases an ambiguity can arise. For example, "I only lost the money" can be interpreted "I only lost the money [I didn't steal it]" or "I lost only the money [I still have the receipts]." Avoid ambiguity by placing the modifier next to the word it modifies and, when necessary, giving the reader additional information to make your meaning clear:

| ***Ambiguous*** | ***Revised for Clarity*** |
|---|---|
| I just earned three dollars. | I earned just three dollars [not four or five dollars.] |
| | I earned three dollars just now. |
| I only looked at the shirt. | I only looked at the shirt; I didn't buy it. |
| | I looked at only the shirt [not at slacks, shoes, or socks]. |
| School begins after the summer vacation in September. | School begins again in September, after the summer vacation. |

*Negatives* Informally, many people accept the movable *not*, as in "Everyone can't [cannot] be rich." But formally, you gain greater precision by placing the *not* next to the word it negates. "*Not everyone* can be rich."

| ***Informal*** | ***Revised for Formal English*** |
|---|---|
| Everyone doesn't have to hold the same opinion. | Not everyone has to hold the same opinion. |
| Everybody doesn't own a Cadillac | Not everybody owns a Cadillac. |

*Squinting modifiers* "Squinting" modifiers seem to modify in two directions at once, modifying two words at once. To clear up any doubts in the reader's mind, move the squinting modifier next to the word you intend it to modify.

| ***Ambiguous*** | ***Revised for Clarity*** |
|---|---|
| The coach told them often to jog. | The coach told them to jog often. |
| | The coach often told them to jog. |

*Awkward split infinitives* An infinitive is the word *to* plus a verb (to run, to go, to think). Putting a word or words between *to* and its verb is called "splitting the infinitive" (to quickly run, to slowly go, to really think). Often the split infinitive sounds perfectly natural, but sometimes it can sound unnecessarily awkward.

| ***Awkward*** | ***Revised*** |
|---|---|
| You have to usually read with care in his class. | You usually have to read with care in his class. |

| | |
|---|---|
| They liked to seldom dance together at parties. | They seldom liked to dance together at parties. |

## ► PRACTICE: Evaluating Usage ◄

Which is the better sentence?

**1.** *A.* Teachers should understand history who teach it.
*B.* Teachers who teach history should understand it.

**2**[9]**.** *A.* And now there are gas water heaters with double-density insulation and improved utilization that save gas.
*B.* And now there are gas water heaters that save gas with double density insulation and improved utilization.

**3.** *A.* They like to while they jogged compete with each other.
*B.* They liked to compete with each other while they jogged.

**4**[10]**.** *A.* At the end of the corridor a door stood open, down which M. Chasle made his way on stumbling feet.
*B.* A door stood open at the end of the corridor, down which M. Chasle made his way on stumbling feet.

**5**[11]**.** *A.* Apart from "Super Fly" midi-coats and the like, there is little tangible evidence so far that life on the street has begin to imitate art.
*B.* There is little tangible evidence so far that life has begun to imitate art on the street apart from "Super Fly" midi-coats and the like.

## -LY WORDS

Much informal writing, especially in advertising, dispenses with the *-ly* on modifiers, and thus it is easy to drop the *-ly* from your own writing: "His trouble is that he can't think logical." Most verbs, however, express action (*drive* slowly) and require *-ly* modifiers:

Think *carefully* [not *careful*] before you answer.

The grand major domo, white plumes on his head, knocked *loudly* [not *loud*], but there was no response.

TROUP AND GREENE, *The Patient, Death and the Family*

## ▶ PRACTICE: Evaluating Usage ◀

Select the formal English alternative in the following sentences.

**1**[15]**.** Everyone wants to surround (himself/theirself) and (his/their) family with objects of lasting beauty, meaning and value—objects to be owned now with pride and passed on as valuable heirlooms to future generations.

**2**[16]**.** Rushed by ambulance to Harlem Hospital, I (lay/laid) in bed for hours while preparations were made to remove the keen-edged knife from my body.

**3**[17]**.** *A.* "The Alteration" starts out far better than it ends.
*B.* "The Alteration" starts out well, if not better than, it ends.

**4**[18]**.** I am being (make/made) witness to matters no human being may see.

**5**[19]**.** You're one of those charming women with (who/whom) it's nice to talk, and nice to be silent.

**6**[20]**.** American blacks had (become/became) recognized as a species of human being by amendments to the Constitution shortly after the Civil War.

**7.** You have to aim very (careful/carefully) in order to hit the target.

**8.** If everyone (was/were) to agree with you, the situation would deteriorate.

**9**[21]**.** They find so often that instead of having (laid/lain) an egg, they have (laid/lain) a vote, or an empty ink-bottle, or some other absolutely unhatchable object, which means nothing to them.

**10**[22]**.** A modern poet has characterized the personality of art and the impersonality of science as follows: Art is (I/me); Science is (we/us).

**11**[23]**.** Hail, Emperor, we (who/whom) are about to die salute you.

**12.** It is one of those situations which (is/are) impossible to remedy in a week or two.

**13**[24]**.** *A.* Coming down the slope, my skis suddenly started to ripple.
*B.* As I was coming down the slope, my skis suddenly started to ripple.

**14.** Each of the members (was/were) supposed to bring a friend.

**15**[25]**.** The fact is that the number of officials and the quantity of the work (is/are) not related to each other at all.

## PRONOUN REFERENCE

### Ambiguous

A pronoun must not appear to refer to two words simultaneously: "The President told the vice-president *he* couldn't make the speech." What does *he* refer to? Clear up such confusing references when you revise:

| *Ambiguous* | *Revised* |
|---|---|
| Don't touch the dishes with your hands when *they* are dirty. | Don't touch the dishes when your hands are dirty.<br>When the dishes are dirty, don't touch them. |

### Vague

It should always be *completely* clear to the reader what your pronouns refer to. The farther away the pronoun gets from its referent, the greater the possiblity that the reader and perhaps the writer too will "lose" the referent:

*Vague*

Helen is giving a party, *which* is a good idea.

What is good: the fact that it is Helen who is giving the party or the fact that she is giving a party instead of a speech? Often, you'll find that the best solution for vague pronoun reference is to revise the thought, getting rid of the pronoun completely:

*Revised*

Helen has decided to give a party, since we've all been studying too hard for exams.

### Illogical

In this situation, a pronoun refers to something missing from the sentence—an implied idea that must be expressed for the sentence to be understood.

*Illogical*

Although my school gave much attention to reading, *they* didn't do me any good.

The reading exercises didn't do any good? The teachers didn't do any good? There is no reason for *they* in this sentence; the reader has to guess at your meaning. The best course is to revise the sentence so that you convey a precise idea to the reader.

***Revised***

Although my school gave much attention to reading, even remedial classes didn't prepare me for college reading assignments.

## ► Excessive

A proliferation of pronouns usually creates childish-sounding sentences:

***Excessive***

Science has always been my worst subject and *it* is hard to study when *it* isn't taught very well and when *it* comes so early in the day and especially when *it* is so hard to understand *it* anyway!

Using the skills you learned in Chapter 14, rewrite such sentences for better clarity and emphasis:

***Revised***

Science—scheduled at 8 in the morning before I'm really awake, hard to understand if not taught well, and almost impossible for me to comprehend in any case—continues to be my worst subject.

## ► PRACTICE: Evaluating Pronoun Reference ◄

Which is the better sentence? Why?

**1**[38]. *A.* Cunegonde fainted; as soon as she recovered, she slapped her face; and everything was confusion in the most beautiful and agreeable of all possible castles.

*B.* Cunegonde fainted; as soon as she recovered, the Baroness slapped her face; and everything was confusion in the most beautiful and agreeable of all possible castles.

**2.** *A.* The new desk was Ed's delight, which he dusted every weekend.

*B.* The new desk, which Ed dusted every weekend, was his delight.

**3**[39]. *A.* Its front foot caught a piece of quartz and little by little the shell pulled over and flopped upright.

*B.* Its front foot caught a piece of quartz and little by little it pulled over and flopped upright.

**4**[40]. *A.* Her thin musical voice died away over the water; Leon could hear the wind-blown trills pass him by like a fluttering of wings.

*B.* Her thin musical voice died away over the water; Leon could hear it pass by him like a fluttering of wings.

5[41]. *A.* Now Gregor's sister had to cook too, helping her mother; true, it didn't amount to much, for they ate scarcely anything.

*B.* Now Gregor's sister had to cook too, helping her mother; true, the cooking didn't amount to much, for they scarcely ate anything.

## PRONOUNS AS SUBJECTS AND OBJECTS

Subjects and objects can cause problems for writers using pronouns. The typical order of the English sentence is:

| 1 | 2 | 3 |
|---|---|---|
| ***Subject*** | ***Verb*** | ***Object*** |
| The man | shot | the bear. |

The subject does the acting, the verb names the action, and the object receives the action.

However, sentences are not always in normal order. You must turn the sentence around in your mind before deciding which word is the subject and which is the object (see "Passive Sentence" in Chapter 14):

Jazz I love, but opera I hate.

***Sub Ob Sub Ob***

I love jazz, but I hate opera.

| ***Subject Pronouns*** | ***Object Pronouns*** |
|---|---|
| I, you, we, he, she, it, they, who | me, you, us, him, her, it, them, whom |

Why are the object pronouns required in the following?

They have known *her* for years.

*Him* we have known only for a short time.

***Objects with prepositions*** Prepositions are followed by objects: *for* him, *to* us, *with* us, *by* her, *between* them, *between* you and me, *after* him, *near* whom. Most prepositions are words of position that tell the reader where something is. Though not position words, *but, except, since, until,* and a few others sometimes function as prepositions and can thus take objects. When these words join with a noun or pronoun to make a modifying phrase (*in the winter,* *for him, to the store*), they are called prepositions, and the noun or pronoun after them is considered an object. But note a different use for these words: "She stepped onto the ice and fell *through*." Here *through* has no noun or pronoun after it; it acts as an independent modifier. Some of the other words function as conjunctions: "She laughed, *but* I didn't see the joke."

***The* to be *exception to the subject-object rule*** Forms of *to be* (*am, is, are, was, were, be, being, been*) do not take objects in formal writing.

It is *I* [not *me*].

The girl who said it was *she* [not *her*].

It was *who*?

## ▶ PRACTICE: Understanding Subject-Object Agreement ◀

Select suitable forms from the choices in parentheses.

1. My wife and (I/me), on our later study of chimpanzees right inside the forest, found the same thing: noisy, mobile males and quiet, slow mothers.

   VERNON REYNOLDS, *The Apes*

2. The deficit is a problem that (we/us) Americans must face.
3. Then, as he thought, he realized that if there was any such thing as ever meeting, both (he/him) and his grandfather would be acutely embarrassed by the presence of his father.

   ERNEST HEMINGWAY, *For Whom the Bell Tolls*

4. There followed a weighty correspondence between (he/him) and the King, and the King at last relented to the change in the plan, thanking his minister for his advice. . . .

   CHARLES W. FERGUSON, *Naked to Mine Enemies: The Life of Cardinal Woolsey*

5. She looked up from her notes and said that if any student wanted to try something else (he or she/they) should say so immediately.

## ▶ Who and Whom

The difference between *who* and *whom* causes more trouble than it is worth. *Whom* has almost completely disappeared from informal English. (No one asks "Whom did you see?" except those who habitually speak formal English.) But the distinction between the two forms is still important in formal writing. *Who* is the subject form (it can be the subject). *Whom* is the object form (it can be the object).

It is necessary to figure out who is doing what in the sentence in order to know which word is the subject and which is the object. Why is the object form required in the following?

*Whom* are you discussing?

*Whom* are you looking for?

*Whom* did you see?

*Whom* does he want to marry?

With *whom* were you dancing?

Sometimes words get between the subject and the verb, changing the appearance of the sentence but not the grammar. Break the sentences down into basic sentences to see what goes where:

| ***Who/Whom Problem Sentence*** | ***Solution with Sentence Combining*** |
|---|---|
| The girl (who/whom) they think was in the car has escaped. | The girl has escaped. They think *she* was in the car.<br>She = *who*<br>The girl *who* they think was in the car has escaped. |
| Laura pointed out a boy (who/whom) she said was the team captain. | Laura pointed out a boy. She said [that] *he* was the team captain.<br>*He* = *who*<br>Laura pointed out a boy *who* she said was the team captain. |
| He is the thief (who/whom) the police agree is the most clever. | He is the thief. The police agree [that] *he* is the most clever.<br>*He* = *who*<br>He is the thief *who* the police agree is the most clever. |

A related substitution trick can help you figure out *who* or *whom* problems. Substitute some other pronoun (*he, she, they, him, her, them*) into the sentence. Remember, if *he, she,* or *they* fits, use *who,* and if *him, her,* or *them* fits, use *whom.*

I know (who/whom) phoned this morning.

I know *he* phoned this morning.

*He* = *who*

I know *who* phoned this morning.

## ► PRACTICE: Understanding Subject-Object Agreement ◄

Which is the right word? How do you know?

1. She is a leader (who/whom) everyone supports.
2. (Who/Whom) does he think he is?
3. To (who/whom) was it addressed?
4. Anyone (who/whom) you pick will have to work hard.
5. She is one athlete (who/whom) should not be ignored.
6. (Who/Whom) are you?
7. He might not be the one (who/whom) you think he is.
8. List the ones (who/whom) you think should come.
9. She is the kind of leader (who/whom) we want for president.
10. (Who/Whom) do you think is best qualified?
11. (Who/Whom) shall I say called?
12. We have the man (who/whom) we were looking for.
13. I wonder (who/whom) is in there.
14. You should see (who/whom) is standing outside.
15. For (who/whom) is this intended?

## VERBS

Every verb has four forms: *write, wrote, written, writing*; a few have alternative forms; a few have repeated forms. Check the dictionary if you have any doubts about the form of a verb. A few of the more troublesome ones are listed for you here:

| *Present* | *Past* | *Perfect** | *Progressive** |
|---|---|---|---|
| awake | awoke, awaked | awaked, awoke, awakened | awaking |
| awaken | awakened | awakened | awakening |
| begin | began | begun | beginning |
| break | broke | broken | breaking |
| bring | brought | brought | bringing |
| buy | bought | bought | buying |
| dive | dived, dove | dived | diving |
| draw | drew | drawn | drawing |

| | | | |
|---|---|---|---|
| drink | drank | drunk | drinking |
| freeze | froze | frozen | freezing |
| get | got | got, gotten | getting |
| go | went | gone | going |
| know | knew | known | knowing |
| lay | laid | laid | laying |
| lie (recline) | lay | lain | lying |
| lie (tell a lie) | lied | lied | lying |
| make | made | made | making |
| set | set | set | setting |
| sing | sang | sung | singing |
| sink | sank | sunk | sinking |
| sit | sat | sat | sitting |
| take | took | taken | taking |
| wake | woke, waked, wakened | waked, woken, wakened | waking |
| wear | wore | worn | wearing |

* The perfect and progressive forms are used with forms of *to be* (*am, is, are, was, were, be, being, been*) and with forms of *to have* (*have, has, had*): *am writing, was beginning, has begun, had known, have been singing,* and so on.

## ► Slang Verbs

In informal writing and personal experience stories, slang may be both appropriate and desirable, but in formal writing, slang verbs should be avoided:

> We was busted by the fuzz last night. We was just sittin' around rappin', ya know, like it was so cold I nearly frosted my butt. My old lady's all busted up about it.

## ► Unconventional Verb Forms

Within formal English, inexperienced writers sometimes have trouble with the verb form:

> It was so cold that we were *frozen* [not *froze*] by noon.
>
> I have *woken* [not *woke*] up at eight o'clock every morning since the semester started.
>
> The ship *sank* [not *sunk*] in minutes.
>
> They have *gone* [not *went*] to the library together for months.

Equally unconventional, and unacceptable in semiformal or formal writing, is the creation of new forms by mixing parts of verbs:

> I have *tooken* this course twice now, and I still don't get it.
>
> He has *drunken* so many beers he can't stand up.

## ▶ Lie and Lay

The difference between *lie* and *lay*—like the difference between *who* and *whom*—often causes trouble. The words are different in *meaning*. *To lie* (*lie, lay, lain, lying*) means to be at rest; this word tells you *where* something is. *To lay* (*lay, laid, laid, laying*) means to put something somewhere.

The words are different in *grammar*. *Lie* never takes an object; it is usually followed by a *place* expression (lie *down*, lie *on the bed*). *Lay* always takes an object: lay *the book* down; lay *it* on the bed.

The problem is in the past tense of *lie*.

> Today I lie down; yesterday I *lay* down [not *laid*].

To decide which verb is needed, you must either be certain of the meaning you intend, or you must check to see whether the verb has an object (lay) or not (lie). But remember that writers don't always use normal order in their sentences: subject—verb—object.

> He—laid—*the book* down.
>
> *The book* was laid down by him.

Remember, in a passive sentence, the object appears in the subject slot (see Chapter 14). Figure out who is doing what before you decide whether the sentence has an object in it.

## ▶ PRACTICE: Understanding Verb Forms ◀

Select suitable forms from the choices in parentheses.

1. Teachers should not (lay/lie) hands on students.
2. The report has been (laying/lying) there all day.
3. (Lay/Lie) the carpeting straight.
4. They (lay/laid) in bed until noon yesterday.
5. The cat has (lay/lain) there since noon.
6. If you're ill, you ought to (lie/lay) down and rest.
7. The book is (lying/laying) there where you left it.
8. They have (laid/lain) tracks right across our field.

**9.** I (lay/lie) here daydreaming all through yesterday's test.
**10.** Better let sleeping dogs (lie/lay).
**11.** The treasure (lies/lays) buried six feet under.
**12.** He (lay/laid) his checkbook down while he checked his pockets.
**13.** The leaves were (lying/laying) all over the yard.
**14.** She (lay/laid) awake all night worrying.
**15.** You need to (lie/lay) aside your fears.

## ► Double Past Tense

Much prose is written in the past tense, and this sometimes makes a problem for writers. How do you refer to a past or prior event when you are already writing in the past? Use the past perfect:

> He *said* that he *had seen* her.

"He said that he *saw* her" and "He said that he *seen* her" are both unacceptable in this case.

> He knew that he *had passed* [not *passed*] the test when he saw his mark.

Putting both verbs in simple past is sometimes acceptable in informal spoken English, but doing so is unacceptable in formal writing situations.

## ► Conditional Statements

People sometimes use a redundant conditional ("If you *would* do it, you *would* be sorry"). Use the *will* (*would*) verb forms to express only the consequences, not the condition. (The *if* statement is the condition.) Formal writing requires the following:

> If you *do* it, you *will be* penalized.
> If you *did* it, you *would be* penalized.
> If you *hadn't done* it, you *wouldn't have been* penalized.

## ► Statements of Doubts, Wishes, Probability, Conditions Contrary to Fact

The rule on *was* and *were* for statements of doubt, probability, and so on, is changing. It is disregarded by many modern writers; but the distinction is still important to many educated readers.

> I wish I *were* [not *was*] dead.
> It it *were* [*was*] true, I could forgive her.

Would you do it if it *were* [not *was*] possible?

*Were* [not *If he was*] he a foot taller, he might make the team.

### ► PRACTICE: Understanding Verb Forms ◄

Select suitable forms from the choices in parentheses.

1. The house (set/sat) at the end of a long lane.
2. The jailers fed us in the morning, and it tasted good because some of us hadn't (ate/eaten) in twenty-four hours.

   DICK GREGORY, WITH ROBERT LIPSTYE, *Nigger: An Autobiography*
3. We all (lay/lie) there, my mother, my father, my uncle, my aunt, and I too am (laying/lying) there.

   JAMES AGEE, *A Death in the Family*
4. If it (was/were) possible that he had actually done it, I'd congratulate him myself.
5. At daylight, Rainsford (lying/laying) near the camp, was awakened by a sound that made him know that he had new things to learn about fear.

   RICHARD CONNELL, "The Most Dangerous Game"
6. Gurov (lay/laid) awake all night, raging, and went about the whole of the next day with a headache.

   ANTON CHEKOV, "The Lady with the Dog"
7. If he (would break/broke) into a run, they'd chase him.

   JOHN DOS PASSOS, *Forty-Second Parallel*
8. Unless there is a remarkable biological breakthrough in geriatrics, we have (gone/went) just about as far as we can go in raising life expectancy.

   ISAAC ASIMOV, *Of Time and Space and Other Things*
9. The cries of the dying were (drownded/drowned) in the martial music of trumpets and drums.

   WILL DURANT, *The Reformation*
10. And even if it (was/were) possible to devise a method for maintaining an innocent vacuity of mind, the wisdom of such a policy is surely questionable.

    LUCIUS GARVIN, *A Modern Introduction to Ethics*

## DICTIONARY OF USAGE PROBLEMS

a, an    Use *a* before words beginning with a consonant sound (*a cat, a union, a historical novel*). Use *an* before words beginning with a vowel sound or silent *h* (*an experiment, an onion, an hour, an honor*).

abbreviations In general, avoid abbreviations in formal writing. Except for some scientific papers, in which abbreviations are common, avoid abbreviations other than for names and titles (*Mrs.*, *Mr.*, *Dr.*, and so on); do not abbreviate words like pound [*lb.*], ounce [*oz.*], inch [*in.*] in an essay or term paper, for example. See Capitalization in Chapter 17.

accept, except *Accept* means "to receive" or "to take." "I accept the responsibility." *Except* means "to exclude" or "but." "Everyone left except Bill."

A.D. A.D. means *Anno Domini*, "in the year of the Lord," and therefore it is redundant to write "in the year A.D. 750." Note that A.D. usually precedes the number. Write it without underlining or spaces between the letters.

advice, advise *Advice* is a suggestion, a recommendation. "They give us good advice." *Advise* means "to make a recommendation; to give a suggestion." "They advise us to take the shorter road."

affect, effect *Affect* means "to influence." "Your health affects your personality." It also means "to pretend or take on airs." "She affects indifference to her critics." As a noun, *an affect* is a nonphysical aspect of emotion (pronounced with the emphasis on first syllable). *Effect* means "to bring about directly, make happen." "We will effect the changes in your directions as soon as they arrive." To *put into effect* is to make happen. "The changes will be put into effect as soon as the plans arrive." As a noun *an effect* is a result or outcome: "One effect of not studying is poor grades."

allude, refer *Refer* is the more direct word; *allude* means "to make indirect reference." "She alluded to the president when she spoke of 'whoever is responsible for the mistake,' but she did not refer to him by name."

all of a sudden *Suddenly* is more concise. *All of a sudden* is oral English.

allusion, illusion *Allusion* means "a reference to something." "Your allusion to Shakespeare should be documented." *Illusion* means "ghost, imaginary vision, false appearance." "He created the illusion of prosperity by living on credit."

alot Not recognized in formal writing as a spelling of *a lot*. Compare with *a little*.

already, all ready *Already* means "previously." "You have already explained the answer." *All ready* means "everything is ready." "They are all ready for the exam."

alright Not recognized in formal writing as a spelling of *all right*. Compare with *all wrong*.

A.M., P.M. *Ante meridiem, post meridiem*. Do not add redundant *morning*, *evening*, or *o'clock* with these designators of time. "It was 9:00 A.M. [*9:00 A.M. in the morning*] when she arrived." Do not use them as synonyms of *morning* or *night*. "We finished at four in the morning [*in the A.M.*]." By tradition, midnight is 12:00 P.M. and noon is 12:00 A.M. Publishers use small capital letters, but on your typewriter use lowercase: *a.m., p.m.*

among, between  Use *among* when you are writing about more than two things. "We note minute differences among several plants." Use *between* for two items. "We found no differences between pre- and posttest results."

amount, number  *Number* is used for things that can be counted (number of trees). *Amount* is used for things that are measured by volume (amount of corn, amount of noise). Formal usage suggests "amount of money" and "number of dollars," but some writers use "amount of dollars," particularly where large sums of money are involved. "When the amount of dollars held in foreign banks exceeds foreign imports, we have an exchange imbalance."

and which, and who  Use only to connect with a preceding *who* or *which* clause. "This is an experiment which interests us and which we would like to try." [Unacceptable: *This is an interesting experiment, and which we would like to try*.]"

anymore  Not recognized in formal writing as a spelling of *any more*.

anyplace  Not recognized as a spelling of *any place*.

anyways  Oral English, not used in formal writing.

anywheres  Oral English, not used in formal writing.

as good as, as much as  Oral English for *virtually*. "They virtually [*as good as*] admitted their calculations were wrong."

authored  Informal for *wrote*.

at this point in time  Pretentious for *now* or *at this time*. Such wordy phrases are falsely legalistic and are distracting to many readers.

a while, awhile  *While* is a noun. "We sat for a while to think about our plans." *Awhile* is an adverb. "We sat awhile and then left."

bad, badly  Use *bad* to describe emotions and state of health. "She felt bad about the tests." "The child looked bad." Use *badly* as an adverb to describe actions. "He typed badly, but he got the work done."

B.C.  B.C. means "before Christ." It is unnecessary to use *in the year* or *in the year of* with B.C. dates. "Britain was invaded in 55 B.C." Note that B.C., unlike A.D., customarily follows the date. It is typed in capital letters without a space between the letters and without underlining.

being, being as, being that  Oral English for *since* or *because*. "Since [*Being as*] I knew the way, I drove."

between you and I  Oral English for *between you and me*.

bias  Oral English for *biased*. "They were biased [*bias*] in favor of their own interests."

bored of    Oral English for *bored by, bored with, tired of.* "She was bored by [*bored of*] long hours of reading statistical abstracts."

both . . . and    Use *both . . . and* to emphasize a pair, not *both . . . as well as*. "Both the government and [*as well as*] private industry have projects involving environmental protection."

can, may    Not considered interchangeable. "You can pass the test" is not the same as "You may pass the test." But in making requests, the distinction between *can* and *may* is often ignored; you can use either, depending on how polite you want to sound. "Can I visit you soon?" "May I visit you soon?"

capital, capitol    When used as an adjective, *capital* means "large or major." As a noun, it means "wealth, supply of money, or the government center of a state or country." The noun *capitol* indicates "a building or group of buildings where a state or national government meets."

cause is due to    Redundant. "The cause of the long lines was [*was due to*] a gasoline shortage."

censor, censure    To *censor* means "to deny permission to publish or broadcast." To *censure* means "to express disapproval of an action."

cite, site    *Cite* means "to refer to." "Your paper cites Hemingway." *Site* means "place." "We applied a local anesthetic to the site of the wound."

complected    Oral English for *complexioned.* Not used in formal writing. "They were a light-complexioned [*complected*] people."

compliment, complement    To *compliment* is to praise. "I won't compliment him for that terrible pun." To *complement* is to balance or complete. "The professor's handouts complement her textbook."

consensus of opinion    Redundant. "The consensus is that smoking is bad for you."

continuous, continual    *Continuous* means "without interruption." "A continuous supply of electricity is essential to industry." *Continual* means "happening frequently, but not without interruption." "The continual ringing of the phone kept me from studying."

contractions    Usually not found in the most formal writing (legal documents, doctoral dissertations), but otherwise acceptable if they serve the writing purpose—if they help to alleviate a too-formal tone: *I'll, haven't, don't, isn't, it's,* and so on.

contrast from, contrast to    Informal for *contrast with*. "The red end of the spectrum contrasts with [*to*] the blue end." "In contrast with [*from*] more advanced nations, the developing countries lack technology."

could of    Oral English. Not recognized in formal writing as a spelling for *could have*.

credible, credulous *Credible* means "that which sounds believable, such as a witness or testimony." *Credulous* means "believing too easily, gullible." "I am so credulous I'll believe anything you tell me."

data *Data* is a collective noun that takes either a singular or a plural verb. Most people prefer the plural in formal situations.

desert, dessert *Dessert* is the last course in a meal. *Desert* means "arid land," and *to desert* means "to abandon." "She deserted him in the desert after dessert."

differ from, different from Formal writing requires *differ from* and *different from*. "One thing differs from another." "She is different from other girls." But *different than* is widely used in less formal writing.

disasterous Not accepted as a spelling of *disastrous*.

disinterested, uninterested Disinterested means "impartial, unbiased." "A referee must be disinterested in the outcome." *Uninterested* means "having no interest." "She appeared uninterested in his proposal."

double negative Oral English, not accepted in formal writing. The double negative is produced by two negatives or two words whose sense is negative, in the same sentence—*can't hardly, don't scarcely, haven't got none, can't get no*, and so forth.

emigrate, immigrate To *emigrate* is to leave your country. To *immigrate* is to enter a foreign country.

eminent, imminent *Eminent* means "well-known, outstanding" (*eminent physician*). *Imminent* means "approaching, soon to arrive" (*imminent danger*).

enthuse, enthused, enthusing Informal derivatives of *enthusiasm*.

etc. Do not use the abbreviation *etc*. Instead, use *and so on* or *and so forth*. It is often better to list the additional items. Note that *and etc*. is redundant; *and* is already contained in *et cetera*.

farther, further In formal writing, *farther* is used for progress in space, physical distance. "Her room is farther down the hall." *Further* is used for degree or progress in time. "We were able to get further with these procedures than any other." Less formally, the words are interchangeable, except when you mean *additional*. "No further applications can be accepted."

few, less *Few* should be used with countable items: *few people*. *Less* should be used with items measured by volume or degree: *less milk, less noise*.

figuratively, literally To use words or phrases *figuratively* means to use them metaphorically, or in an exaggerated sense. *Literally* means "in accordance with the real meaning." Do not use *literally* in statements that are clearly not to be taken literally, as in this sentence: "His eyes were literally glued to the tempting dessert."

flunk Oral English for *fail.*

former, latter In referring to two items, the first is the *former*, and the second is the *latter*. "Oak and pine—the former is strong, and the latter is soft." Use *former* and *latter* instead of *first* and *last*.

fun Not accepted as a modifier in formal writing. "Waterskiing is a thrilling [*fun*] sport." "She is an enjoyable [*fun*] person to be with."

good, well *Good* is an adjective. The adverb form of *good* is *well*. *Good* is used to explain what something is. "The cake tastes good." Use *well* to explain how something occurs. "Kyle plays football well."

hanged, hung *Hanged* means "executed by hanging." "He was hanged by a mob of racists." For any other kind of hanging, use *hung*. "The stockings were hung by the chimney with care. . . ."

hopefully Weak substitute for *maybe* or *I hope*. "I hope [*Hopefully*] this report will get done on time. *Hopefully* is correct when used to mean "with hope." "Despite her problems, she faced the future hopefully."

how Oral English for *that* or *the fact that*. "This book shows that [*how*] crime does not pay." "We were impressed by the fact that [*how*] they had the reports done quickly."

if, whether, whether or not Use *whether* to discuss doubt. "She wondered whether [*if*] she should go." *Or not* is redundant in such cases.

in back of *Behind* is less wordy and more formal.

in, into Most educated readers believe "He fell *in* the closet" means he fell while in the closet. "He fell *into* the closet" means he fell while outside the closet. The distinction is often ignored in less formal writing.

in the area of Vague, wordy, and imprecise. "We are working in chemical reactions [*in the area of chemical reactions*]."

in this day and age Wordy for *now* or *today*.

infer, imply *Imply* means "to suggest." *Infer* means "to deduce." "We infer that you are implying our statistics are faulty."

inside of *Inside* is less wordy and more formal. "She is inside [*inside of*] the house."

incidence, incidents An *incident* is a happening, an event. "Several incidents of unrest have been reported." *Incidence* means "rate of occurrence." "The incidence of these disturbances is rising."

irregardless Not recognized in formal writing. "Regardless [*irregardless*] of the criticism, we intend to proceed." "The project looks unpromising but we intend to proceed regardless [*irregardless*]."

its, it's *It's* is a contraction of *it is*, not to be confused with the possessive form of *it*: *its*. "It's time to give the dog its annual bath."

leave, let *Leave* means "depart" or "abandon." *Let* means "allow or permit." "The officer let us go, but we could not leave the city."

like, as Formal usage avoids using *like* in place of *as*. "They did things as [*like*] their ancestors had done them." Less formally, the two words are interchangeable.

loan, lend There is no difference in the meaning of the two words. Many writers prefer to use *lend*.

lots of Informal for *many, much*. "There are many [*lots of*] reasons for going to high school."

mad Not recognized in formal writing as a substitute for *angry*. Less formally, *mad* and *angry* are interchangeable.

might of Oral English for *might have*.

monsterous, monsterosity Not recognized as spellings of *monstrous, monstrosity*.

most every Oral English for *almost* or *nearly*. "Nearly everyone [*most everyone*] approves of charity." "She hits the ball almost [*most*] every time."

must of Oral English for *must have*.

not too distant future Wordy for *soon*.

nowheres Oral English for *nowhere, anywhere*.

numbers In general, any number that can be expressed in one or two words should be written out (*ninety-nine, two thousand, five million*), especially in literary essays. But in technical reports, informal writing, and any other writing in which numbers are a significant component, numerals are usually preferred (*99; 2,000; 5 million*). Avoid starting a sentence with a numeral; revise so that the numeral does not come first.

off of, off from Redundant. "Send whatever you can take off [*off of*] the shelves."

ourself Not recognized in formal writing, except for royalty. "We voted ourselves [*ourself*] a pay raise."

OK, O.K., okay All are accepted spellings, but the word itself should be restricted to informal writing. "Everything seemed ready [*okay*] for the next day's tryout."

particular Redundant in the presence of *this, that, these*, or *those*. "This type [*this particular type*] of chemical reaction is very common."

persecute, prosecute *Persecute* means "to bother, often cruelly or brutally." *Prosecute* means to charge with a crime.

predominate, predominant *Predominant* is an adjective; *predominate* is a verb. "The predominant [*predominate*] rule was economy." "Southern accents predominate in New Orleans."

prejudice Oral English for *prejudiced*. "We are prejudiced [*prejudice*] in favor of our own interpretations of the data."

pretty Oral English for *somewhat* or *rather*. "The serum produced from the roots made them rather [*pretty*] sick."

principal, principle The principal is the head of the school. The word can be used to designate any main or chief thing. "The principal cause of poverty is unemployment." In economics, *principal* is the sum of money on which interest is earned. *Principle* refers to ethics, theories, guidelines, moral quality. "His actions seem good, but his principles are suspect."

proceed Pretentious when the context requires *go*. "After dinner we should go [*proceed*] to the library."

prophecy, prophesy A *prophecy* is a prediction. *To prophesy* is to make a prediction.

rarely ever Redundant. "I rarely [*rarely ever*] go out at night."

real Oral English for *very*. "The results were very [*real*] good."

reason is because Redundant. "The reason for the fire was that [*because*] the wiring was faulty."

reason why Redundant. "They wanted to know the reason [*reason why*] the engines overheated."

repeat again Redundant.

said A pretentious legalism [*the said property*; *the said individual*].

shall, will The distinction between these words is seldom observed today. Some writers still use *shall* when they want to be especially formal or emphatic: "We shall surely die." But generally *shall* is no longer used except for formal requests: "Shall we do it?"

should of Oral English for *should have*.

somewheres Oral English for *somewhere*.

stationary, stationery *Stationary* means "unmoving." *Stationery* means "sheets of paper for writing."

suppose Oral English for *supposed*. "We were supposed [*suppose*] to receive new supplies in a week."

that, which, who Use *who* to refer to human beings. *Which* never refers to human beings. "The woman who bought the bike was deaf." "The record which George bought was old." "Sue, who likes dogs, recently purchased a terrier." *That* is sometimes used informally to refer to people.

theirself, theirselves, themself None of these is recognized in formal writing. Use *themselves*.

there, their, they're *There* means "in that place." "There is my house." *Their* is a plural possessive pronoun. "The girls lost their books." *They're* is a contraction for "They are." "The boys said they're taking the bus."

today's modern world, today's modern society, modern world of today Wordy and redundant for *now* and *today*.

use to Oral English for *used to*. "We used to [*use to*] give public demonstrations."

ways Oral English for *way*. "We have a long way [*ways*] to go yet on this project."

when Informal for *in which*, particularly in definitions. "Inflation is a condition in which [*when*] there is too much money for too few goods." But note: "Inflation *occurs when* there is too much money and too few goods."

where Informal for *in which*. "This is a book in which [*where*] crime does pay, at least temporarily."

where . . . to, where . . . at Redundant. "Where are you going [*going to*]?" " Where is my pencil [*pencil at*]?"

would of Oral English for *would have*.

## ▶ PRACTICE: Using Formal English ◀

Select the formal English alternative in the following sentences.

1. The reason is (that/because) they are overladen with ideas.

   ALFRED NORTH WHITEHEAD, *The Aims of Education*

2. The old idea that the hen deliberately selects the male she thinks the most beautiful is putting the matter in human terms which certainly do not apply to a bird's mind; but it seems certain that the brilliant and exciting display does have an (affect/effect) on the hen bird, stimulating her to greater readiness to mate.

   JULIAN HUXLEY, *On Living in a Revolution*

3. It is only with science that the (allusion/illusion) exists; the (allusion/illusion) of a neutral, inhuman activity separate from the world of "telegrams and anger."

   JOHN H. STEELE, "The Fiction of Science," *The Listener*

4. The (amount/number) of college bulletins and adult-education come-ons that keep turning up in my mailbox convinces me that I must be on a special mailing list for dropouts.

   WOODY ALLEN, *Getting Even*

5. (Suddenly/All of a sudden) the superintendent made up his mind.

GEORGE ORWELL, "A Hanging," *Shooting an Elephant and Other Essays*

## ► PRACTICE: Revising Usage Problems ◄

Revise any of the following sentences that contain a problem in usage. Some of the sentences may not require revision.

1. In our modern world of today, drugs have become quite a problem.
2. Adrienne stepped into her closet.
3. They didn't know whether they shouldn't ask for permission.
4. The one who always understands is he.
5. Their racing shell sunk in six feet of water.
6. You can't lay around all the time.
7. I knew he was guilty when I seen him look away.
8. It is all ready hard to find him when you need him.
9. I felt so badly about missing the test that I went back to sleep.
10. Irregardless of the time it takes, you must keep hunting data.
11. I wonder whether or not it will snow by Christmas.
12. I was just walking through the park when suddenly I find a four-leaf clover.
13. It's easy to guess whom you mean.
14. At this point in time, I'm not prepared to answer the question.
15. No one understands why this data is so unusual; its totally unique.
16. This is one of those schools which provide financial aid to students.
17. The reason grammar is so hard is because it seems so arbitrary.
18. The test was quite a surprise to him and me.
19. She wore a outfit of lavender and cream.
20. In her last letter, Bernice had written that she hoped she would be excepted into the sorority.

[1] HOWARD ADAMS

[2] MARY WOLSTENCRAFT, *Frankenstein*

[3] MARK TWAIN, *Huckleberry Finn*

[4] ROBERT MURPHY, *A Certain Island*

[5] DAN THOMPSON

[6] BRAM STOKER, *Dracula*

[7] AYN RAND, *Atlas Shrugged*

[8] EMILY BRONTË, *Wuthering Heights*

[9] Advertisement, American Gas Association

[10] ROGER MARTIN DU GARD, *The Thibaults*

[11] CHARLES MICHENER, "Black Movies: Renaissance or Ripoff?"

[12] BONNIE SULLIVAN

[13] CHARLES DICKENS, *The Old Curiosity Shop*

[14] ROBERT LOUIS STEVENSON, *Travels with a Donkey*

[15] Advertisement, *Saturday Evening Post*

[16] MARTIN LUTHER KING, Jr., *Why We Can't Wait*

[17] "Now and Forever," *Newsweek*

[18] JAMES AGEE AND WALKER EVANS, *Let Us Now Praise Famous Men*

[19] LEO TOLSTOY, *Anna Karenina*

[20] VINE DELORIA, JR., *Custer Died for Your Sins: An Indian Manifesto*

[21] D. H. LAWRENCE, *Cocksure Women and Hensure Men*

[22] CLAUDE BERNARD, *Bulletin of the New York Academy of Medicine, IV, 1928*

[23] SUETONIUS, *Life of Claudius*

[24] DEANNA CROSS

[25] C. NORTHCOTE PARKINSON, *Parkinson's Law and Other Studies in Administration*

[26] FELICIA STRAUSS

[27] RICHARD D. ALTICK, *The Scholar Adventurer*

[28] ARTHUR C. CLARKE, *Profiles of the Future*

[29] HENRY SLOANE COFFIN, *The Meaning of the Cross*

[30] GRETCHEN FUNNEL

[31] VIRGINIA WOOLF, "How Should One Read a Book?"

[32] OLIVER GOLDSMITH, *The Citizen of the World*

[33] WILLIAM FAULKNER, *The Hamlet*

[34] DEE BROWN, *Bury My Heart at Wounded Knee*

[35] WILLA CATHER, *Willa Cather on Writing*

[36] MARJORIE KINNAN RAWLINGS, *Cross Creek*

[37] ADLAI STEVENSON, *Looking Outward*

[38] FRANCOISE-MARIE DE VOLTAIRE, *Candide*

[39] JOHN STEINBECK, *The Grapes of Wrath*

[40] GUSTAVE FLAUBERT, *Madame Bovary*

[41] FRANZ KAFKA, *The Metamorphosis*

# CHAPTER ▲ SEVENTEEN

# *Mechanics and Punctuation*

**"You have to really work at it to write. I guess there has to be talent first; but even with talent you still have to *work* at it to write."**

**JAMES JONES, *Writers at Work*, George Plimpton, ed.**

In comparison to large matters of purpose, ideas, and organization, punctuation, spelling, and capitalization may seem trivial. But the mechanics of writing are tools the writer uses to signal meaning for the reader, signposts to guide the reader, much like street signs signal the automobile driver. You can occasionally get away with driving through a stop sign; you may not even get a traffic ticket. But continually breaking the law is bound to catch up with you. The same is true with regard to breaking the conventions of formal writing. At the least, mechanical errors may distract the reader and interrupt the train of thought; at worst, they can distort your meaning or lose you the respect of your reader.

The mechanics of writing are simply formal conventions of our culture, and these aspects of the writers' code have changed over the years. They are not static rules. In fact, even within our culture there are variations in mechanical details. Some publishers require more commas than others, for instance. And poets and fiction writers sometimes deliberately break with these conventions. The poet e. e. cummings' interesting and creative "misuse" of capitalization is an example. Whether to adhere to certain writing conventions depends, like every other decision you make while composing, upon the impression you want to make on your reader.

These conventions, while in some ways arbitrary, can be important devices that eliminate confusion. To show possession for the word *it* by simply adding an "s" rather than an *'s* may be simply a convention, but this convention also clarifies the difference between *Its time* (time belonging to it) and *It's time* (It is time).

Knowledge of writing mechanics will give you greater facility and maturity of expression. Beginning writers frequently avoid words they cannot spell readily. Such avoidance has the effect of limiting the means of expression available to the writer. You need to experiment. Try using less familiar punctuation marks or more sophisticated sentence structures. In short, don't worry about making mistakes. Even the best writers sometimes make mechanical errors. As you work on these aspects of code while revising your drafts, you will find you can expand your options as a writer and your skills as well.

## PUNCTUATION

Punctuation is a signal system that helps the reader interpret your sentences. Formal punctuation used in academic, business, and scientific writing differs from that used in more popular writing such as journalism. In college and university courses you will be asked to use the conventions of formal composition more often than those of popular writing, and so *The Writer's Work* uses punctuation guidelines that are considered standard for formal writing. Listed below are the marks most commonly used for punctuation.

| | | | |
|---|---|---|---|
| apostrophe | ' | parentheses | ( ) |
| brackets | [ ] | period | . |
| colon | : | question mark | ? |
| comma | , | quotation marks | " " |
| dash | -- | semicolon | ; |
| exclamation mark | ! | slash | / |
| hyphen | - | italics/underlining | ___ |

### ► Apostrophe '

The apostrophe has three main uses: (1) to show ownership or possession, (2) to indicate abstract or inanimate possessives, and (3) to form contractions.

*Possessives* To show a singular possessive, add *'s*—unless the word already ends in *s*.

girl's purse, bird's beak, boy's hair.

If the word already ends in *s*, add only the apostrophe.

Charles' house, Keats' poetry, a bass' color.

To show a plural possessive, add *'s* to the plural form of the word. If the plural ends in *s*, add only the apostrophe.

women's shoes, men's socks, birds' beaks

Option: If you wish to indicate that the possessive is to be pronounced as a separate syllable, you have the option of adding an extra *s* to a word ending in *s*.

Charles's house, Keats's poetry.

To indicate abstract or inanimate possessives, follow the rules for indicating possession given above.

sidewalk's cracks, trees' leaves, life's gifts, investigation's conclusion, countries' economies.

*Contractions* To form contractions, use the apostrophe to replace a letter or letters in the contracted word.

*I'm* (I am), *they*'re (they are), *it's* (it is), *Diane's a pretty girl* (Diane is a pretty girl).

Using contractions gives your writing a more informal sound, but they are acceptable in most college writing today.

***The Problem with It's/Its***

*It's* is used only to indicate a contraction of the phrase *it is*. *Never* use *it's* to show possession. To indicate possession for the word *it*, use the form *its* (*it* + *s*, without the apostrophe).

***The Problem with Plural Formation***

Avoid using apostrophes to form plurals: *the 1990s*, *the ins and outs*, *the three Cs of management*. The difference between plurals and possessives can be seen in the following examples:

***Plural***

The economy of the 1940s was more expansive than that of the 1970s.

***Possessive***

Car buffs are always on the lookout for 1957's Chevrolets and Fords, but no one wants 1967's vans.

The 1990s' job-seekers will be better prepared.

## ► Brackets [ ]

Brackets are used to insert information into quoted material. If your typewriter or word processor doesn't have brackets, draw them in with a pen. Use brackets for the following situations:

To insert clarifying information into quotations

"Egyptians had no literature as we know it . . . . This [*temples and monuments*] is their writing."

OSCAR G. BROCKETT, "The Origins of the Theatre," *History of the Theatre*, 4th ed.

To insert editorial comments into quotations

> According to Nancy Reagan, "The concept of the family is coming back [*many of us hope so*!], just as the whole feeling in the country has changed over the last few years."
>
> *Family Circle*

To indicate errors in source material

When quoting material containing an error, insert *sic* in brackets immediately after the error. This signals the reader that the error appears in the original material and that the writer is quoting it accurately. *The report said, "The child died of miningitis* [sic]." In this case, *meningitis* is misspelled in a report that the writer is quoting. Perhaps the writer of the report actually thought the word was spelled that way or it is a misprint (commonly referred to as a "typo"). Whatever the reason, the writer does not want to repeat the error, and yet she must quote the report exactly as it is written (that's what a quotation is). Therefore, the use of [*sic*] helps to clarify the situation for the reader.

To indicate parentheses within parentheses

> Some business writers rarely revise memos. (See p. 15 [*bibliography*] for further documentation.)

## ► Colon :

Uses of the colon include the following:

To introduce a series of three or more items

> They told the travel agent they wanted to visit the following places: China, Japan, Australia, Denmark, and Sweden.

To indicate an example, illustration, complement

> The strike could be solved in one of two ways: Either management could make some major concessions, or the union could persuade their workers to return to their jobs.

To introduce a formal quotation

> The remark was attributed to the Queen: "Let them eat cake."

A quotation given as an illustration or example should be introduced with a colon.

They were given to excessively dramatic statements: "We will surely all die quickly if we continue this policy." (Smith 65)

To follow the salutation in a formal letter

Dear Katy:
Dear Dr. Fishback:
To Whom It May Concern:

## ► Comma

Uses of the comma include the following:

To separate sentences joined by *and, but, or, nor, so, for*

The women who do the most work get the least money, and the women who have the most money do the least work.

CHARLOTTE PERKINS GILMAN, *Women and Economics*

The lion and the calf shall lie down together, but the calf won't get much help.

WOODY ALLEN

Note: Two sentences can be joined either by commas alone or by conjunctions alone if the sentences are very short, closely related, and structured alike:

I work in a bakery, I work alone.
My mother is 53 and she is a college student.

Long sentences joined by a comma produce what is called a comma splice (also referred to as a run-on sentence):

Albino squirrels behave just like normal, gray squirrels, it's just that they are more easily seen in the trees.

Separate such spliced sentences with a period or semicolon:

Albino squirrels behave just like normal, gray squirrels. It's just that they are more easily seen in the trees.

or

Albino squirrels behave just like normal, gray squirrels; it's just that they are more easily seen in the trees.

To separate introductory words from the rest of the sentence

> When you are finished typing your paper, meet me at Bernie's.
>
> Of course, my family comes first.
>
> First, finish your homework.

The comma signals a pause to the reader. Sometimes writers omit this comma to deemphasize the introductory expression:

> In minutes the fire had spread to the roof.
>
> For Americans freedom is too often taken for granted.

When in doubt, however, use the comma.

To separate three or more items in a series

> They had pepperoni, sausage, green peppers, onions, mushrooms, and cheese on their pizza.

Do not put a comma after the final item when the series comes first in a sentence; do not separate the series from its verb. No commas follow "Sue" or "lettuce" in the sentences below:

> Sherry, Tamita, Phil, Olivia, Maria, Bruce, and Sue were chosen as cheerleaders.
>
> Hamburgers, ketchup, mustard, onions, and lettuce were on my grocery list.

The writer has the choice of whether or not to use a comma before the final item in a series. In order to be clear, though, we advise you to use it rather than run the risk of being misinterpreted.

Items in a series can also be joined with conjunctions instead of commas:

> Today she bought gothic romances and mysteries and fairy tales at the bookstore.

To set off explanatory and parenthetical elements

> The workers at Myer Packing, like most workers, are interested in retirement benefits.
>
> Mrs. Campbell, according to published reports, is only sixty-two.

To set off appositives

An appositive is a word that identifies or renames a following or preceding noun or pronoun:

President Gorbachev, the Russian leader, set the tone for the meeting.

Both women, Dolores and Nancy, were competing for the leading role in the play.

The purpose of the appositive is to help identify the noun or pronoun preceding it. But sometimes you may omit commas from appositives if the identification is unnecessary, as in the phrase *My boyfriend Dan* or *My wife Marilyn*. You may also want to omit commas in cases where they would cause confusion. But some appositives are necessary in order to identify which one is meant.

She had three dogs, but only the poodle Fifi was pure bred.

Note the trouble that the writer of the following sentence got into by not using the necessary commas with the appositive:

My husband, Wally, and Jeff went bowling.

In fact, the writer's husband's name was Ed. She would have clarified the sentence if she had inserted an appositive without commas:

My husband Ed, Wally, and Jeff went bowling.

Titles after names should be treated like appositives—set off with commas

Andrew, president-elect, chaired the meeting.

To set off elements of dates and addresses

She began writing the book on August 18, 1986, at Myrtle Beach.

Apply at the main office on High Street, Glasgow, Scotland.

Military style requires no commas for dates:

The book was begun on 16 August 1986 at Myrtle Beach.

To set off speaker tags

Speaker tags are identifiers in dialog: *she said, he said, they claimed*, and so on.

"Now, get my horse," she said, addressing her unknown kinsman as she would one of the stable boys at the Grange.

EMILY BRONTE, *Wuthering Heights*

The church says, "If you sin, you shall be punished hereafter."

A. S. NEILL, *Summerhill*

If the quoted material ends with a question mark or exclamation point, no separating comma is necessary:

> "Oh, good grief!" she shouted. "You made me spill my coffee."

To set off contrastive elements

> "I've been on a calendar, but never on time."
>
> MARILYN MONROE

> Some children will pay attention, while others will not.

To set off nonessential modifiers.

Nonessential modifiers, those modifiers that you can edit out of a sentence without changing the main idea, should be set off with commas. These modifiers often begin with *who*, *which*, or *that*:

> My mother-in-law, who grew up in Florida, hated long, hot summers.
>
> The rain in Spain fell mainly on the plain, a great part of which is still rural farmland.

Cumulative modifiers, those modifers added after the main clause of a sentence, are usually nonessential and should be set off with commas:

> She cried softly, her voice weakly whimpering, her body shaking uncontrollably.

Essential modifiers are restrictive and do not require the use of commas. They tell the reader how many or what kind or which one is being discussed.

> The robber was a convict who had escaped from the state prison.
>
> The same committee that lobbied to put the school bill on the ballot is trying to build up support again.

To take the place of *and* between movable adjectives

If all the adjectives describe the same word, so that you could rearrange them in some other order, separate them with commas:

> The singer they hired was a pale, thin, sultry blond.
>
> The child snuggled in his mother's big, warm, comfortable lap.

If one or more adjectives describe the idea formed by an adjective and the noun, no comma should be used:

She put a lampshade on her head and started singing a bawdy Irish ballad.

To indicate clarity

Commas can help the reader avoid possible misreadings:

While he shaved, his wife made breakfast.

Without the comma in this sentence, the reader could easily stumble, thinking as he or she progressed through the sentence that *he shaved his wife*.

To introduce the salutation of an informal letter

Dear Isabelle,
My dear Roslyn,
Frank,

To indicate the close of a letter

Most sincerely,
Yours truly,
Love,

To indicate direct address

Hi, Harold
Good night, Rosa, my sweet
Happy Birthday, Kimberly

## ▶ Dash --

In typing or word processing, you make a dash with two hyphens (--), leaving no space before, between, or after them. Dashes are used in the following ways:

To indicate a speaker's words ending abruptly or falteringly

Get this straight, buddy. The boss says that you had better--well, you'd better find the money somehow.

To embed questions, exclamations, declarations

We stood there freezing our you-know-whats off--they'd even taken our underwear!--hoping and not hoping someone would come along and help us.

My professor gets up every day at four in the morning--can you believe it?--and expects her eight o'clock class to be on time no matter what.

To follow an introductory series

Julia Child, James Beard, The Frugal Gourmet--they are my favorite cooks.

A series that is the subject of the sentence does not use the dash. Typically, the writer has the choice of using the series as the subject or as an introductory series:

Snips, snails, and puppy dog tails are what little boys are made of.

Snips, snails, and puppy dog tails--these are what little boys are made of.

To indicate a sudden break in the thought of a sentence

She visited him in the nursing home--she didn't want to--because of her guilty conscience.

To add emphasis or to indicate a dramatic pause

Only two of the players--the two I had hoped wouldn't--failed to show up for practice.

To emphasize explanatory or clarifying information

Senior citizens often find that retirement requires--more than a typical nest egg--a substantial investment of time and energy.

## ► Ellipsis . . .

Ellipsis marks (three spaced periods, or points) indicate omission of material from a quotation. Use ellipsis marks in the following ways:

To indicate that part of the quotation has been omitted

***Original Quote***

Unity of aim, by ordinary vigor of character, will generally insure perseverance, a quality not ranked among the cardinal virtues, but as essential as any of them to the proper conduct of life.

***Quote with Ellipsis***

Unity of aim . . . will generally insure perseverance, a quality not ranked among the cardinal virtues . . . .

When creating an ellipsis, leave a space before and after each period. Note that if the ellipsis comes at the end of the sentence, you use four periods.

## ► Exclamation Point !

The exclamation point indicates strong emotion or surprise and should be used sparingly. Never use two or more in a row [!!] in formal writing. Use the exclamation point in the following ways:

To emphasize

> He once said of a little, half-starved wayside community that had no subsistence except what they could get by preying upon chance passengers who stopped over with them a day when traveling by the overland stage, that in their Church service they had altered the Lord's Prayer to read. "Give us this day our daily stranger!"
>
> MARK TWAIN, *Roughing It*

> I'll never let you go!

## ► Hyphen -

Use the hyphen in the following ways:

To divide a word at the end of a line

> When you ask me for an expression of opinion on the matter of sexual enlightenment for children, I assume that what you want is the independent opinion of an individual physician whose professional work offers him special opportunities for studying the subject, and not a regular conventional treatise dealing with all the mass of literature that has grown up around it.
>
> SIGMUND FREUD, "The Sexual Enlightenment of Children"

To indicate a compound word

> a well-acted play
> the vice-chairperson of our department
> twentieth-century technology

To indicate a common root for two or more prefixes

> The school is having trouble getting the parents of the fourth- and fifth-grade children to go on field trips.

## ► Parentheses ( )

Parentheses are used to insert nonessential information into the sentence and to deemphasize the material they enclose. Use parentheses in the following ways:

To insert additional nonessential information

> These men, you understand, now say (at least in private to younger working women in their office) that they are bored with women who "don't do anything."
>
> ELLEN GOODMAN, "The Just-Right Wife"

> There is nothing so unnerving to a teacher engaged in trying to explain something, or a student engaged in trying to understand something, as the crackle of the loudspeaker prepared to issue an announcement, and the harsh and gravelly voice (the systems are not obviously of the highest grade) of the announcement itself.
>
> NATHAN GLAZER, "Some Very Modest Proposals for the Improvement of American Education"

Note that even if parenthetical material should be a full sentence, as in the second example above, you do not need a capital letter to begin it or a period to end it. Also, do not use a comma in front of the beginning or after the closing parentheses. A period is necessary after parentheses that end the sentence, as in the following example:

> Most how-to-do-it essays analyze processes, as do most accounts of how something works (a typewriter, a city transit system, gravity).

However, sometimes writers insert parenthetical material as separate sentences, in which case end-of-sentence punctuation falls within the parentheses:

> His face was coated with mud, the eyes wide open, the teeth bared and grinning with an expression of unendurable agony. (Never tell me, by the way, that the dead look peaceful. Most of the corpses I have seen look devilish.)
>
> GEORGE ORWELL, "Shooting an Elephant"

To number items in a series

> You have three choices: you can (1) marry him immediately, (2) marry him when he gets a job, or (3) forget him altogether.
>
> When you go on vacation, you should (a) cancel the newspaper, (b) have a neighbor take in the mail, and (c) leave a light on inside your house.

### *Other punctuation marks with parentheses*

A colon, comma, or semicolon always goes outside a closing parenthesis:

> I successfully completed a number of courses (while holding down a full-time job, too, by the way): math, biology, English, and Italian.
>
> A recent report on American schools (it was aired on national television, you may recall) claimed that students are not properly motivated.
>
> More physicians are studying nutrition nowadays (unlike in the past); by doing so, they can help their patients tremendously.

A question mark or exclamation point goes inside a closing parenthesis if the parenthetical material is a question or exclamation but goes outside a closing parenthesis if the sentence is a question or exclamation but the parenthetical material is not. Note the different punctuations of the two parenthetical insertions below:

> I was shaking like a leaf (who wouldn't be?) when I opened the letter and found the check my parents had sent without explanation or recrimination (I was down to my last dollar).

## ► Period .

To complete a sentence

> Spit frequently. Spit at all crucial moments. Spit correctly. Spit should be blown, not ptuied weakly with the lips, which often results in dribble. Spitting should convey forcefulness of purpose, concentration, pride.
>
> GARRISON KEILLOR, "Attitude"

To end an indirect question

> Now what I want to know is why I shouldn't have to wait until age forty-three to get an education somewhat worse than that which any sophomore ought to have.
>
> ROBERT HUTCHINS, "Education for Freedom"

To indicate abbreviations and initials

> M.D., Ms., B.A., U.S., Mr., Dr., Inc.,

When an abbreviation ends a sentence, use only one period.

> They worked on the plans until 3 A.M.

After the name of a well-known organization has been given in full once, you may use initials without periods.

Columbia Broadcasting System (CBS)
North Atlantic Treaty Organization (NATO)
American Medical Association (AMA)

To mark decimal numbers

.01 .001 .10 1.0

*Period faults (errors)*

*Fragments*: A fragment occurs when part of a sentence is punctuated as a complete sentence. Sometimes, however, a fragment can work intentionally and effectively as a way of emphasizing material:

> If a player's wife or girlfriend wants to play, we give her a glove and send her out to right field, no questions asked, and if she lets a pop fly drop six feet in front of her, nobody agonizes over it.
>
> Except me. This year. For the first time in my life . . . , I find myself taking the game seriously.
>
> GARRISON KEILLOR, "Attitude"

However, anything that slows, or interferes with, the reader's comprehension should be considered a flaw in writing. In academic writing and other formal writing, many readers always count the fragment as an error. The best rule for college students is this: The more formal writing becomes, the less acceptable fragments become.

*Fused or Run-On Sentence*: A fused or run-on sentence occurs when two independent clauses are joined together without correct punctuation.

The nuclear plant malfunctioned radiation levels were high.

Revise such sentences by separating them with a period, semicolon, or other appropriate punctuation.

The nuclear plant malfunctioned. Radiation levels were high.
The nuclear plant malfunctioned; radiation levels were high.
The nuclear plant malfunctioned, and radiation levels were high.

Writers often punctuate sentences incorrectly because they have not fully analyzed the relationship of one idea to another. If in doubt, rewrite the sentence to make the relationship clear.

Because the nuclear plant malfunctioned, radiation levels were high.

## ▶ Question Mark ?

The question mark may be used in the following ways:

To indicate direct questions

Was physical beauty the most important attribute a person could have?

To indicate a question after an item in a series

Who should have the responsibility of caring for aging parents? The daughter? The son? The government?

To express doubt or uncertainty

If you are uncertain about information, use a parenthetical question mark to indicate your doubt.

The value of the picture (painted by Renoir?) exceeded our estimate.

Note that a question inserted into a statement retains its question mark.

Thus the question which you put to me—what is to be done to rid mankind of the war menace?—took me by surprise.

SIGMUND FREUD, Letter to Einstein"

## ▶ Quotation Marks " "

Use quotation marks in the following ways:

To indicate exactly repeated words (direct quotes)

I recognize it from Zora Neale Hurston's description in *Mules and Men* "the city of five lakes, three croquet courts, three hundred brown skins, three hundred good swimmers, plenty of guavas, two schools and no jailhouse."

To indicate a quote within a quote, use single quotation marks:

"I missed the touchdown," Rob lamented. "The coach specifically said to me, 'Miss one more and you're off the team!' So now what do I do?"

Note: Quotation marks are not used for indirect quotes. *She said Rachel was her best friend in the world.*

To indicate dialogue

Indent for each new speaker in dialogue.

"What time is it?" he asks.
"Three o'clock."
"Morning or afternoon?"
"Afternoon."
He is silent. There is nothing else he wants to know.
"How are you?" I say.
"Who is it?" he asks.
"It's the doctor. How do you feel?"
He does not answer right away.
"Feel?" he says.
"I hope you feel better," I say.
I press the button at the side of the bed.
"Down you go," I say.
"Yes, down," he says.

RICHARD SELZER, "The Discus Thrower"

To indicate titles of short works

Use quotation marks for titles of short poems, short stories, articles, book chapters, songs, television episodes, essays, and one-act plays.

"Because I Could Not Stop for Death" is a poem by Emily Dickinson.

"My Man Bovanne" is a well-known short story by Toni Cade Bambera.

Dolly Parton wrote a song about her childhood called "My Coat of Many Colors."

To indicate odd or invented words or words used with special meaning

I began playing a game in which I had to choose between jobs with imaginary titles like "torpist" and "varisator."

MARVIN GROSSWIRTH, "Let This Computer Plan Your Future"

Instead, applicants for teacher in New York City spend months or years learning a peculiar "correct" pronunciation that is heard nowhere on land or sea.

PAUL GOODMAN, *People or Personnel*

To indicate words referred to as words

Your pronunciation of "nudnik," by the way, is appalling. It's "nudnik," not "noodnik."

S. J. PERELMAN, *Writers at Work*, ed. George Plimpton

The following rules apply when using quotation marks with other punctuation:

**1.** Always place commas and periods inside the quotation marks.

"I want you to finish this project," he said.

**2.** Always place colons and semicolons outside the quotation marks.

The author argued that his book most reflected modern society's "spiritual descent"; his assertion, to me, was totally unconvincing.

**3.** Always place a question mark or an exclamation point inside a closing quotation mark if the quotation is a question or an exclamation.

The question that he kept asking me was "Will you take the job or not?"

After she opened the unlocked door she screamed, "We've been robbed!"

**4.** Always place a question mark or an exclamation point outside a closing quotation mark if the sentence is a question or exclamation but the quotation is not.

Which one said, "I have no intention of repaying my loan"?
She was foolish to say, "I'll never have to worry about money"!

***Longer quotations*** If you quote more than three typewritten lines, indent all lines of the quotation five spaces from the left margin, and as in the rest of your paper, double-space the quote. Triple space above and below indented quotes. Do not use quotation marks if you indent your quotation in this manner. Also, typically, longer quotations are introduced with information about the source of the quote.

In <u>The Resisting Reader: A Feminist Approach to American Fiction</u>, Judith Fetterly asserts:

> American literature is male. To read the canon of what is currently considered classic American literature is perforce to identify it as male. Though exception to the generalization can be found here and there--a Dickinson poem, a Wharton novel--these exceptions usually function to obscure the argument and confuse the issue: American literature is male.

If quoting four or more lines of poetry, indent each line five spaces and single-space the lines. Type each line exactly as it appears in the poem. Do not use quotation marks. Examine the following excerpt from a student's paper:

> Although Percy Bysshe Shelley did not know John Keats intimately, the first nine lines of the poem "Adonais" suggest that Shelley suffered intense personal grief at Keats's death.

```
I weep for Adonais—he is dead!
Oh, weep for Adonais! though our tears
Thaw not the frost which binds so dear a head!
And thou sad Hour, selected from all years
To mourn our loss, rouse they obscure compeers,
And teach them thine own sorrow! Say: "With me
Died Adonais" till the Future dares
  Forget the Past, his fate and fame shall be
  An echo and a light unto eternity.
```

Note that the last line of each stanza of this poem appears two spaces to the left; therefore, the quote will also.

## ▶ Semicolon ;

Use the semicolon in the following ways:

To separate two sentences joined by a conjunctive adverb

> I had a long list of excuses for being late; however, my teacher was impressed.

To connect two closely related sentences

> Youth is something very new; twenty years ago no one mentioned it.
>
> COCO CHANEL

> Today's children read few books; they watch television instead.

To separate items in a series containing commas

> She listed several residences including London, England; Zurich, Switzerland; Kingstown, Jamaica; and Louisville, Kentucky.

## ▶ Slash /

Use the slash in the following ways:

To separate lines of poetry in running discourse

Walt Whitman, in *Song of Myself*, writes, "I celebrate myself, and sing myself/And what I assume you shall assume/For every atom belonging to me as good as belongs to you."

To indicate fractions and inclusive dates.

1/3  7/10  (June/Sept., 1987)

To indicate grammatical choices

and/or  neither/nor

Note: Use such constructions sparingly in your formal writing.

## Underlining and *Italics*

Printers use italics in a printed text to highlight certain words. Underlining, in a hand- or typewritten paper, serves the same function. It makes the material stand out. Use underlining in the following instances:

To indicate titles of long works

Underline titles of books, magazines, newspapers, long poems, plays, operas, movies, radio and television series, albums, and musical compositions.

*The Scarlet Letter* was written by Nathaniel Hawthorne.

*I Love Lucy*, starring Lucille Ball, was one of the first comedy series on television.

Jefferson Starship's *Kneedeep in the Hoopla* is reminiscent of albums by the Jefferson Airplane of the 1960s.

To indicate names of ships, planes, and trains.

The *Queen Mary* is now a tourist attraction in California.

One of my greatest dreams is to fly on the *Concorde* to London.

Folksinger and songwriter Arlo Guthrie wrote a song about the gradual demise of trains in the United States, based on the story of the old train *The City of New Orleans*.

To emphasize a word

I wouldn't even *think* of doing such a thing!

You just *have* to see that movie.

Mistress, in teaching me the alphabet, had given me the *inch*, and no precaution could prevent me from taking the *mile*."

FREDERICK DOUGLAS, "Learning to Read and Write,"
*Narrative of the Life of Frederick Douglas: An American Slave*

Note that most writers are very careful about not overusing this option. Too much underlining tends to weaken your writing.

To indicate uncommon foreign words and phrases

> The whole Gandhian concept of *satyagraha* . . . was profoundly significant to me.
>
> MARTIN LUTHER KING, "Pilgrimage to Nonviolence"

> He had been among the first to be invited to the institute, and was offered *carte blanche* as to salary.
>
> BANESH HOFFMAN, "My Friend, Albert Einstein"

> The child was adopted by her aunt *in loco parentis*.

To introduce special or technical terms

> Jean Piaget defined the concept of using the environment to learn a new behavior as *assimilation*.
>
> The first part of an argument, according to Cicero, is the *exordium*.

## ► PRACTICE: Working with Punctuation ◄

Punctuate the following sentences. If a sentence is correct as it stands, place a check mark next to the number.

1. Ask not what your country can do for you ask what you can do for your country said President Kennedy.
2. The factory closed its doors and hundreds of workers had to look elsewhere for a job.
3. Some parents think its strictly the schools responsibility to educate their children.
4. In my first year at college, I took the following courses English 101 American Civilization Theatre 111 and Power-Walking
5. Leningrad has many English speaking schools, the students learn to read Jack London novels in the elementary grades.
6. "Why shouldn't he be promoted?", asked the personnel manager.
7. Robert Frosts poem, Stopping By Woods on a Snowy Evening is widely anthologized.
8. You are a capable student nevertheless you dont apply yourself to the task.
9. To analyze literature successfully you must be familiar with terms such as plot theme characterization and point of view.

10. Although smallpox has been eliminated in the United States it still occurs in many parts of the world.
11. About ten days elapsed before we were able to identify the winner of the contest Martha Miller.
12. Looking annoyed she the salesperson said We don't have it in any color but blue.
13. When he was with his buddies he Joe was always in the best of moods.
14. The star of the play said, "Are you going to allow him to upstage me?"
15. People continue to criticize the president, but he doesn't change his policies.
16. He said, "Mrs. Brown please take my seat.
17. The chairman of the board Herman Hill refused to recognize the woman in the back row.
18. June 14 1993 is my projected date of graduation.
19. Petty theft, insubordination, resisting an officer, those were the charges he faced.
20. My mother in law refuses to visit for less than a week.
21. The Wall Street Journal is necessary reading for the astute business owner.
22. Youve been a big help she said gratefully.
23. To recount the entire days receipts would be too much of a bother.
24. This gift the donation of three million dollars is the largest the foundation has ever received, however more money is needed.
25. The Santa Maria was one of the three ships used by Columbus.

## SPELLING

At best, misspelled words distract your reader; at worst, they can undermine your authority and make your reader think you are not intelligent enough to be listened to. In fact, spelling has little, if any, relation to intelligence. Many gifted writers are bad spellers. However, they make sure that their readers never discover their secret. They have friends and editors check their spelling, and they work hard at improving it, too.

If spelling presents a problem for you, the following steps can help you master this trouble spot in your writing.

**1.** Make a habit of memorizing the words you continually misspell. Sometimes little tricks can help, like remembering the *science* in *conscience* or the *pal* in *principal*.

**2.** Keep a notebook and record the words that give you trouble. Try to arrange these words in alphabetical order so that you can refer to them as you need to. As you notice that you have conquered the spelling of certain words in your notebook, check them off or mark them out. Always remember, however, that you could relapse into misspelling the words without practice.

**3.** You might also find a spelling dictionary useful. These small dictionaries don't define words, but they can quickly tell you whether *store* or *stoar* is the correct spelling of the word you need.

**4.** Learn to proofread carefully. Generally, poor spellers are poor proofreaders as well. Carefully scrutinize your final drafts for misspelled words, slowly reading each line, character by character.

**5.** Ask a friend, roommate, or classmate to check for errors you may have missed. Sometimes another person can easily spot errors that are invisible to the writer. This double-checking is not a bad idea, even if you are not worried about your spelling.

**6.** If you can, let your manuscript rest twenty-four hours before you give it that final proofreading. In this way, you can be more objective about your writing, and you can zero in on your mistakes more readily.

**7.** Identify trouble spots. Get in the habit of checking out the correct spelling of words that continually trouble you. Practice reviewing combinations such as *ei* and *ie* or *able* and *ible*. As you progress, you will find yourself remembering more and more of the correct spellings of these words.

Remember: Like anything else, the more you work at spelling, the more you will improve.

## TROUBLE SPOTS IN SPELLING

English, like every other language, has its spelling quirks. Here are some of them:

***-able, -ible*** *-Able* is the more common spelling of these two endings (suffixes), which are pronounced alike; *-ible* often follows an *s* sound (as in *defensible* and *producible*). Since there are no useful rules about these endings, it is best to look up the words and memorize them.

***-ant, -ance and -ent, -ence*** These endings are generally pronounced alike (as in *abundant, existent,* or *abundance, existence*). Look up any word you are unsure of.

***-ceed, -cede, -sede*** Check any words with the *-eed* sound. *Supersede* is the only word ending in *-sede*. *Exceed, proceed,* and *succeed* are the only words ending in *-ceed*. All of the rest of the *-eed*-sounding words are spelled with *-cede*: *precede, secede*.

***double consonants*** Many words double the final consonant before adding a suffix: *The rabbits are hopping*. But "long-vowel" words do not:

*We are hoping for a cool summer*. There are exceptions to the rule: *benefited*. To say it another way, doubling the last consonant generally has the effect of changing long vowels to short ones, so *hopping* would not be pronounced as the *-ing* form of *hope*.

***-ei, -ie*** "Use *i* before *e* except after *c* or when sounded as *a*, as in *neighbor* and *weigh*." You probably remember this little rhyme from elementary school. It is fairly accurate, but there are exceptions, such as *leisure* and *seize*. Memorize any *-ei* or *-ie* combinations that trouble you.

***final -e*** The final *e* is usually dropped to avoid doubling vowels: *hop[e]ing, scrap[e]ing*. However, some words keep the final *e*: *changeable, peaceable*. It is always kept when the suffix begins with a consonant: *hopeful, boredom*. Many words today are spelled either way: *livable, liveable*. Check any word you are not certain about.

***-ery, -ary*** The more common ending, by far, is *-ary*, but a few words end with *-ery*: *cemetery, stationery* (sheets of paper).

***-or, -er, -ar*** All these endings sound alike: *author, painter, grammar*. The safest practice is to check a spelling dictionary.

***plurals of -y words*** Most words that end in *-y* change the *-y* to *-ie* for the plural: *babies, families*. When the *y* follows a vowel as in *monkey*, the plural is formed by adding *s* only: *monkeys*.

***pre-, per-, pro-*** Check words with these beginnings (prefixes): *perspiration, performance, prepare, protect*. Don't spell them by the way that you hear them spoken. Many people pronounce them all alike; a few incorrectly interchange them: *prespiration, pertect*.

***suffixes with -y words*** Change *-y* to *-i* before all suffixes (endings) except *-ing*: *beauty, beautiful; noisy, noisily; buy, buying*.

***look-alikes and sound-alikes*** Homonyms and near-homonyms account for a large number of spelling mistakes. Writers who "spell with their ears" are likely to mistake words like *board* and *bored*, or *stare* and *stair*, and so on. In many cases readers feel these errors are worse than spelling errors because the writer appears to have used a wrong word, instead of having misspelled the right word. Be sure you have the right form with very common words like *there, their*, and *they're* and *your, you're and yore*.

## ► Hyphens in Compound Words

Check your dictionary for the spelling of any compound word. Many are spelled as two words: *high school*. Others are spelled as one word: *coffeepot*. And still others are spelled as hyphenated words: *half-dollar*.

## Compound-Word Modifiers Before a Noun

These compounds should generally be hyphenated: *high-school graduate, left-wing politics, round-trip ticket*. This guideline does not apply to *-ly* words, which are never hyphenated.

| *-y compound* | *Hyphenated compound* |
|---|---|
| roughly cut diamonds | rough-cut diamonds |
| softly spoken man | soft-spoken man |

## Compound-Word Modifiers After a Noun

Modifiers that are hyphenated when they precede the noun do not need hyphens when they come after the noun.

She is a graduate of high school.

Their politics are left wing.

His ticket was round trip.

## Prefixes and Suffixes.

Prefixes *all-*, *half-*, and *self-* and the suffix *-elect* are usually hyphenated: *all-encompassing, ex-officio, self-sacrifice, president-elect*. When *self* is the root of the word, however, it is not hyphenated: *selfhood, selfish*.

The prefixes and suffixes listed below form words spelled as one word (*overworked, substandard, underfed, counterpoint*):

| | | | |
|---|---|---|---|
| anti- | intra- | pro- | super- |
| co- | -like | pseudo- | supra- |
| counter- | non- | re- | ultra- |
| extra- | over- | semi- | un- |
| -fold | post- | sub- | under- |
| infra- | pre- | | |

## Guidelines for Word Division

**1.** Words containing double letters usually divide between the double letters: *com-mit, es-sence, lit-tle*.

**2.** Prefixes usually form syllables and can be divided: *ob-serve, pre-vail un-kind, re-spect*.

**3.** Suffixes starting with consonants always form syllables: *-ful* (*delightful*), *-ness* (*randomness*), *-ship* (*friendship*), *-tion* (*mention*), *-wise* (*crosswise*).

**4.** One-syllable words or words that are pronounced as one syllable are never divided: *rhythm, school, width, through.*

**5.** Single letters, even if they form a syllable, should never end a line or carry over to the next line. For example, never split words such as *a-bove, e-rect, tack-y,* and *man-y.*

**6.** Hyphenated words must be divided only at the hyphen: *hand-wash, all-star.*

**7.** Proper names should not be divided: *Jessica, Johnson, Reagan.*

**8.** The verb ending *-ing* is a separate syllable when it is merely added to a word: *cook-ing, lay-ing, read-ing.* When *-ing* causes a doubling of consonants in the root word, the rule for double letters applies; *run-ning, step-ping, hop-ping.*

**9.** The suffixes *-able* and *-ible* should *not* be divided: *a-ble, i-ble.* Put the entire suffix on the next line.

**10.** The last word of a paragraph or the last word of a page should not be divided.

**11.** Divided words should not occur at the end of more than two lines in succession.

## ► PRACTICE: Word Division ◄

Divide the following words:

| | | | |
|---|---|---|---|
| 1. affliction | 7. dispossessed | 13. immaterial | 19. population |
| 2. anthology | 8. disappoint | 14. jealousy | 20. puritanical |
| 3. brilliancy | 9. double-talk | 15. knowledge | 21. quantify |
| 4. brokerage | 10. exclamation | 16. litterbug | 22. restorable |
| 5. corruption | 11. guttural | 17. monthly | 23. sensible |
| 6. curriculum | 12. hypodermic | 18. nonverbal | 24. strength |

## FREQUENTLY MISSPELLED WORDS

Below is a list of fifty words frequently misspelled by college students. Look for the ones that give you trouble and copy those words into an alphabetized spelling notebook. Periodically practice spelling them correctly.

| | | | |
|---|---|---|---|
| absence | disappoint | paralyze | recommend |
| accommodate | embarrassment | pastime | separate |
| achieve | forty | possesses | sergeant |
| assistant | grammar | principal | succeed |
| benefited | incidentally | privilege | supersede |
| category | irrelevant | proceed | surprise |
| committee | irritable | pursue | truly |
| conscience | judgment | quantity | vacuum |
| conscious | leisure | realize | vicious |
| definitely | library | recede | vigilant |
| description | license | receipt | whole |
| despair | necessary | receive | wholly |
| development | occurrence | | |

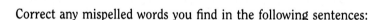

## ► PRACTICE: Correcting Mispelled Words ◄

Correct any mispelled words you find in the following sentences:

1. Periodically, she stopped at the bakeery on her way to the office.
2. We had to order more food to acommodate all the wedding guests.
3. The principle of the school gave the opening addres.
4. If you want to recieve a high grade on you examinnation, make sure that you've studied the material thoroughly.
5. My conscious was bothering me because I hadn't visited my aunt regularly.
6. My roomates often yell at the top of there voices, and I am unable to study effectively.
7. Some people are unable to complete the necessary job application forms.
8. The professer had no idea she had lectured past the time limit.
9. All I wanted to do was streach out on the beach.
10. The results of the election were disasterous for the Democrats.
11. I was conscience of the fact that no one in the room was wearing a formal evening gown.
12. John was dissapointed that the football game was not broadcast on the local television station.
13. Having to take a speling test at the beginning of the quarter often makes students nervus.
14. One of the happiest days of my life occured when I was able to get my driver's license.
15. A firm comitment is required if you expect to acheive your goal.

## CAPITALIZATION

**Capitalize the first word of a sentence:**

Weather is often a subject of conversation.

**Capitalize the first word of a direct quote:**

President Truman said, "The buck stops here."

**Capitalize the first word in each line of poetry (some modern poets may choose not to do so):**

Horses carry back
The silence of grass.

A bell rings in the distance,
And the day disappears
Into a blanket of stars.
(Anonymous)

**Capitalize the names of awards, grants, or scholarships:**

Nobel Peace Prize, Fulbright scholarship, Pulitzer Prize, National Merit scholarship

**Capitalize the names of bodies of water:**

Lake Erie, the Atlantic Ocean, the Dead Sea, the Mississippi River, Mirror Lake

**Capitalize names of buildings, structures, monuments:**

the Brooklyn Bridge, Shea Stadium, the Ford Museum, the Empire State Building, the Bolshoi Ballet, the Smithsonian, Boone County High School

**Capitalize names of geographic features:**

the Canary Islands, the Smokey Mountains, the San Andreas Fault

**Capitalize names of holidays and religious observances:**

Hannukah, Memorial Day, Easter, Martin Luther King Day

**Capitalize names, nicknames, and descriptive names of people:**

Maria, Kevin, Cookie, Ethan Fromme, Linda R. Smyth, Richard the Lion-Hearted, Fats Domino

Capitalize names of military groups, engagements, awards:

the Royal Air Force, the Korean War, the Purple Heart

Do not capitalize an informal reference to a branch of the armed services:

My sister was honorably discharged from the air force.

Capitalize the names of places:

Santa Barbara, Walla Walla, West Milton, Walker Avenue, Hong Kong, Liverpool, the West Indies, the South, Yellowstone Park, College Drive

Do not capitalize general terms like *city*, *county* or *state* when presented without a name when the general term precedes:

My family still lives in that state.

Capitalize the names of ships, planes, and trains:

the Titanic, the Orient Express, the Concorde, the Challenger

Capitalize titles of address (and abbreviations) with names:

Ms. Ratcliffe, Mr. and Mrs. Weems, Miss Williams

Note: *Ms.* is appropriate for either single or married women.

Do not capitalize general forms of address:

gentlemen, madam

Capitalize titles of family members with names or (optional) used as names:

Dad, Grandfather Ginter, Uncle Howard, Aunt Ruby, Cuz

Do not capitalize family titles used without a name:

sister-in-law, his nephew, your mother

Capitalize titles of high honor, even without names:

Mr. President, her Majesty, Your Highness, Your Reverence, My Lady

Capitalize titles of position and rank with names:

Father Greeley, Chairman Mao, Archbishop Tutu, Mother Theresa, Dr. Hatala, Sergeant York, Professor Straub

Titles without names are usually not capitalized:

> the corporal, a nurse, the president, the doctor, the congresswoman from New York, the bishop of our congregation.
>
> The campaign was launched by the mayor: Tom Bradley of Los Angeles

Capitalize words formed from proper nouns:

> Elizabethan, Miltonic, Slavic, Spanish

Do not capitalize words that no longer connote their original meanings:

> english muffin, irish whiskey, swiss cheese, russian roulette

Do not capitalize school subjects, except languages:

> sociology, biology, chemistry, economics, French, English

Capitalize the title of a specific school course:

> Sociology 112, Economics 350, History 200

Do not capitalize school years:

> freshman, sophomore, junior, senior

Do not capitalize academic degrees:

> master of business administration, bachelor's degree, doctorate

Capitalize the initials of academic degrees:

> B.A., B.S., M.A., Ph.D.

Capitalize brand names but not products:

> Whoppers, Jordache jeans

Capitalize titles for heads of state:

> the King, the Archbishop, the President

Capitalize the names of organizations, institutions, and companies:

> the University of Maryland, Merrill Lynch and Co., K-Mart and Co., United States Senate, the Department of Labor

Capitalize the names of political parties and organizations:

> the Socialist party, the Gray Panthers, the Democratic party

Capitalize periods of history:

The Age of Johnson, the Dark Ages, the Enlightenment, the Bronze Age

References to historical or cultural periods usually are not capitalized:

the twentieth century, the colonial period, ancient Rome

Capitalize historical events:

the Alamo, Custer's Last Stand, Black Tuesday

Capitalize formal documents:

the Declaration of Independence, the Magna Carta

Capitalize names of months and days of the week:

September, November, Tuesday, Sunday

Do not capitalize the names of seasons:

winter, spring, summer, fall, autumn

Capitalize the names of gods, deities, and revered figures:

Yaweh, Neptune, Aphrodite, Thor, Jesus, St. Augustine, Krishna, the Apostle Paul, the Virgin Mary, Buddha, Rä

Capitalize the names of biblical and religious events:

the Transfiguration, the Creation, the Crucifixion, Passover, the Diaspora

Do not capitalize names of religious objects except for books:

rosary, altar, minaret, the Bible, mitre, icon, the Koran, the Torah

Capitalize the scientific names of plants and animals.

Scientific names are underlined. Capitalize the genus but not the species.

<u>Ursus horribilis</u>, <u>Geranium pelargonium</u>

Do not capitalize the common names of most plants and animals:

robin, zinnia, maple tree, killer whale

But some names have achieved official status:

Tennessee Walker, Golden Bantam

Capitalize the names of heavenly bodies:

the Milky Way, the Northern Lights, Uranus

*Earth* often appears with a capital letter, especially in scientific works. But do not capitalize *sun*, *moon*, *star*, *galaxy*, and other generic terms.

Do not capitalize the names of diseases or medical conditions:

multiple sclerosis, polio, chicken pox, tuberculosis

Note: Some diseases have a proper noun as part of the name: Hodgkins disease

Capitalize the significant words in the salutation of a letter:

Dear Frank,  My dear Ms. Catto,  Dear Personnel Manager:

Capitalize only the first word in the complimentary close of a letter:

Yours truly,  Most sincerely,  Sincerely yours,

Capitalize the pronoun *I* and the exclamation *O*:

"O, Lord, help me," I cried.

Capitalize the titles of publications

Exclude articles (*a*, *an*, *the*); coordinate conjunctions (*and*, *but*, *or*, *nor*, *so*, *for*); and prepositions (*at*, *by*, *below*, *from*, *in*, *on*, *to*, *up*, *with*, and so on)

Capitalize the first word of a subtitle following a colon:

Composition Research: The State of the Art

Do not capitalize *the* as part of a newspaper title in your paper:

the *Des Moines Register*, the *Christian Science Monitor*

Note that *the* is usually dropped from footnote and bibliographic references to newspapers and journals, even when it appears as part of the title on the periodical itself.

Capitalize hyphenated words in titles:

It is customary to capitalize both elements of a hyphenated word in a title except when the second element is clearly less important or when together the elements form a single word.

An End to the H-Bomb, "New Sino-Soviet Accords," Modern Anti-Inflammatory Drugs, The Low-key Lawyer

## ► PRACTICE: Proofreading for Capitalization ◄

Supply the appropriate capitalization in the following sentences:

1. Did you fish in the olentangy river when you visited columbus?
2. I visited mrs. locker when she was a patient at bethesda hospital.
3. The next convention of the national council of teachers of english will be held at the sheraton grande.
4. When we vacationed in the caribbean, we were passengers on the the queen elizabeth.
5. The governor will take the oath of office on Saturday morning.
6. I hope that dr. long, the new president, will have some ideas for the organization.
7. Please, professor, try to get the exams graded by next Monday.
8. All of the auto companies, including ford, are experiencing a slump.
9. Last year nearly one million people attended the franklin county fair.
10. Have you tried the new recipe for irish soda bread that I gave you?

## ► PRACTICE: Proofreading for Capitalization ◄

Supply the appropriate capitalization in the following sentences:

1. chippewa hills superintendent lavern alward has said the 20 mill request on monday's ballot is necessary.

   PAM KLEIN, "It's Decision Time at the Polls Monday"

2. for instance, kikkoman's soy sauce has a very strong flavor while la choy's is more mellow.

   NANCY SELIGMAN, *Homesteading in the City*

3. and on a january morning in 1945, in fifteen-inch snow in the vosges mountains, by order of the man who is now president of the united states, private slovik was marched out and bound to a post.

   WILLIAM BRADFORD HUIE, *The Execution of Private Slovik*

4. Starting point of the international quasar hunt is the molonglo observatory in new south wales.

   SIMON MITTON, "Mysteries of Quasar Redshifts," 1975 *Yearbok of Astronomy*

5. there were not nearly enough life boats, and for reasons never explained, several of those that got away were barely filled, and passengers who were left on board when the ship sank were frozen in the icy water before captain rostrum of the *s. s. carpathia* could come to their rescue.

   PEGGY GUGGENHEIM, *Confessions of an Art Addict*

**6.** the city university of new york, the country's third largest university system, sits these days like a giant battered orphan amid the financial ruins of new york city.

LARRY VAN DYNE, "City University of New York"

**7.** either the thread has snapped, or the muscle wall has broken through, but the moment the tube was extracted there appeared an open hole and, out of it, a spurt of blood a meter high!

NIKOLAI AMOSOV, *The Open Heart*

**8.** as dr. winnicott has put it: "at origin, aggressiveness is almost synonymous with activity."

ANTHONY STORR, *Human Aggression*

**9.** about thirty years ago, miss maria ward, of huntington, with only seven thousand pounds, had the good luck to captivate sir thomas bertram, of mansfield park, in the county of Northampton, and to be thereby raised to the rank of a baronet's lady, with all the comforts and consequences of a handsome house and large income.

JANE AUSTEN, *Mansfield Park*

**10.** greek wisdom, she declares in her great essay on the *iliad*, has been taken from us because the twin roman and hebrew world views supplanted it.

EDWARD GROSSMAN, "Simone Weil: A Life"

# Acknowledgements

P. 107 Excerpt from "Four Kinds of Reading" by Donald Hall. Copyright © 1969 by The New York Times Company. Reprinted by permission.

115 Kirkpatrick Sale, "The Miracle of Technofix," from *Newsweek*, June 23, 1980, published by *Newsweek*, Inc. © 1980 by *Newsweek*. Reprinted by permission.

121 James Jeans, "Why the Sky Looks Blue," from *The Stars in Their Courses*, published by Cambridge University Press. Copyright 1931 by Cambridge University Press. Reprinted by permission.

122 Frank Trippet, "Air Conditioning" from *The Great American Cooling Machine* in *Time*. Copyright 1979 Time Inc. Reprinted by permission.

125 From *Pornography and Obscenity* by D. H. Lawrence. Copyright 1930 by Alfred A. Knopf, Inc. Reprinted by permission of the publisher.

224 "Bigfoot" from National Examiner, published by National Examiner. May 14, 1985 by Globe International, Inc. Reprinted by permission.

226 Norman Cousins, "Who Killed Benny Paret?" from *Saturday Review*, published by Saturday Review, Inc. Copyright © 1962 by Saturday Review, Inc.

238 Peter Hillmore, "The Economic Miracles" from *The Observer*. Copyright © The Observer. Used by permission.

316 and 317 (top) Reprinted with permission from *Encyclopaedia Britannica*, 15th edition, 1986 by Encyclopedia Britannica, Inc.

317 (bottom) From *The World Book Encyclopedia*. 1989 World Book, Inc. Reprinted with permission.

318 Reprinted with permission of the American Library Association, excerpt taken from *Guide to Reference Books*, 9th edition, edited by Eugene Sheehy; copyright © 1976 by ALA.

319 By permission. From *Webster's Third New International Dictionary* 1986 by Merriam-Webster Inc., publisher ® the Merriam-Webster dictionaries.

325 From the *Readers' Guide to Periodical Literature*, 1987, edited by Jean M. Marra. Used by permission.

326 (top) From the *Humanities Index*, 1987–1988, edited by Joanna Greenspan. Used by permission.

326 (bottom) Copyright © 1986 by The New York Times Company. Reprinted by permission.

327 (bottom) From the *Readers' Guide to Periodical Literature*, 1987, edited by Jean M. Marra. Used by permission.

328 From the *Social Sciences Index*, 1987–1988, edited by Joseph Bloomfield. Used by permission.

329 (top) From *Psychological Abstracts*, 1988, edited by Lois Granick. Used by permission.

329 (bottom) Copyright © 1986 by The New York Times Company. Reprinted by permission.

331 From the *Readers' Guide to Periodical Literature*, 1987, edited by Jean M. Marra. Used by permission.

332 and 333 From the *Social Sciences Index*, 1987–1988, edited by Joseph Bloomfield. Used by permission.

334 From the *Essay and General Literature Index*, 1980–1984, edited by John Greenfieldt. Used by permission.

335 From the *Biography Index*, 1986–1988, edited by Charles L. Cornell. Used by permission.

336 Copyright © 1986–7, Marquis Who's Who Inc. Reprinted by permission from *Who's Who in America*, 44th edition, 1986–7.

337 From the *Book Review Digest*, 1981–1982, edited by Martha T. Mooney. Used by permission.

346 From the *American Journal of Sociology*. 1988 by the University of Chicago. All rights reserved.

350 Reprinted with the permission of the publisher from *Social Science Computer Review*, vol. 6:4 (Winter 1988), pp. 548–549. Copyright 1988 by Duke University Press.

353 Reprinted with permission from *The Encyclopaedia Americana*, International Edition, copyright 1987, Grolier Inc.

354 (top) From the *McGraw-Hill Encyclopedia of Science and Technology*, 16th edition. Used by permission.

354 (bottom) From the *McGraw-Hill Dictionary of Scientific and Technical Terms*, 1974, edited by Daniel N. Lapedes. Used by permission.

356 (top) From the *Readers' Guide to Periodical Literature*, 1987, edited by Jean M. Marra. Used by permission.

356 (bottom) From the *General Science Index*, 1979–1980, edited by Joyce M. Howard. Used by permission.

356 From the *Classified List of Periodicals for the College Library*, 5th edition, 1972, edited by Evan Ira Farber. Used by permission.

358 From the *Essay and General Literature Index*, 1980–1984, edited by John Greenfieldt. Used by permission.

359 From *American Men and Women of Science*, 12th edition, edited by the Jaques Cattell Press. Reprinted with permission from R. R. Bowker.

360 From the *Book Review Digest*, 1987–1988, edited by Martha T. Mooney. Used by permission.

444 Excerpt from "The Scarcity Society" by William Opuls. Copyright © 1974 by *Harper's Magazine*. All rights reserved. Reprinted from the April issue by special permission.

459 Excerpt from "The Cells That Would Not Die" by Michael Gold in *Science '81*. Copyright 1981 by the American Association for the Advancement of Science.

460 Excerpt from "The Visionary Gleam" by David Denby. Reprinted with the permission of New Yorker Magazine. Copyright 1989 News America Publishing, Inc.

465 Excerpt from "Israel Strikes at the PLO" by Ed Magnuson et al. in *Time*. Copyright 1982 Time Inc. Reprinted by permission.

493 Excerpt from "Private Lives" by John Leonard. Copyright © 1977 by The New York Times Company. Reprinted by permission.

# Index

## T